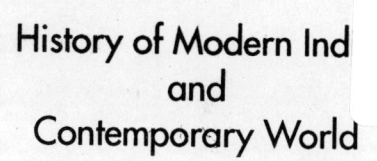

History of Modern India and Contemporary World

History of Modern India and Contemporary World

[In accordance with the syllabus prescribed by the Central Board of Secondary Education, Delhi for Class XII]

A. BISWAS
J.C. AGGARWAL

VIKAS PUBLISHING HOUSE PVT LTD

VIKAS PUBLISHING HOUSE PVT LTD
576 Masjid Road, Jangpura, New Delhi 110 014 Ph. 4314605, 4315313
Email: chawlap@giasdl01.vsnl.net.in   Fax: 91-11-327 6593
http://www.ubspd.com

First Floor, N.S. Bhawan, 4th Cross, 4th Main,
Gandhi Nagar, Bangalore 560009 Ph. 2204639

Distributors:
UBS PUBLISHERS' DISTRIBUTORS LTD
- 5, Ansari Road, **New Delhi**-110002 Ph. 3273601, 3266646
- Apeejay Chambers, 5 Wallace St., **Mumbai**-400001 Ph. 2070827, 2076971
- 10, First Main Road, Gandhi Nagar, **Bangalore**-560009 Ph. 2263901
- 6, Sivaganga Road, Nungambakkam, **Chennai**-600034 Ph. 8276355
- 8/1-B, Chowringhee Lane, **Calcutta**-700016 Ph. 2441821, 2442910
- 5-A, Rajendra Nagar, **Patna**- 800016 Ph. 652856, 656169
- 80, Noronha Road, Cantonment, **Kanpur**-208004 Ph. 369124, 362665

Copyright © A. BISWAS, J.C. AGGARWAL, 1998

All rights reserved. No part of this publication may be reproduced in any form without the prior written permission of the author and publisher.

Printed at Modern Printers, Delhi-32

History Syllabus for Class XII
Prescribed by the
Central Board of Secondary Education, Delhi

One Paper	3 hours	100 marks

Unitwise Weightage

Units		Marks
MODERN INDIA		**60 marks**
1.	Indian States and Society in the 18th century	
2.	Beginning of European Settlements	
3.	British Conquest of India	(Units 1-6)
4.	Structure of Government and Administrative Organisation of the British Empire in India	
5.	Economic, Social and Cultural Policy of the British Empire in India (1757-1877)	15
6.	Social and Cultural Awakening in the first half of the 19th Century	
7.	The Revolt of 1857	
8.	Growth of New India : Religious and Social Reforms	(Units 7-11)
9.	Administrative Changes after 1858	20
10.	India and her Neighbours	
11.	Economic Impact of the British Rule	
12.	Growth of New India : Nationalist Movement	
13.	Nationalist Movement (1905-1918)	(Units 12-14)
14.	Struggle for Swaraj	20
15.	Map Work on Modern India	5
CONTEMPORARY WORLD		**40 Marks**
16.	Introduction.	(Units 16-17)
17.	The world from about the end of the 19th century to the end of the First World War	7
18.	The World form 1919 to 1939	
19.	The Second World War	9
20.	The World after the Second World War	(Units 19-20)
21.	Main features of Development in Economy, Society and Polity	13
22.	Developments in Science, Technology and Culture	(Units 21-23)
23.	The Future Outlook	6
24.	Map Work on Contemporary World	05

MODERN INDIA

Unit 1	:	**Indian States and Society in the 18th century**	10 Pds.

Hyderabad and Carnatic, Bengal, Avadh, Mysore, Kerala; Areas around Delhi—Bangash Pathans and Rohelas; The Sikhs; The Rise and fall of the Maratha Power; Social and Economic Condition of the People; Education; Social and Cultural life.

Unit 2	:	**Beginning of European Settlements**	6 Pds.

New Trade Routes; European Companies and Settlements in India; The Growth of the East India Company's Trade and Influence (1600-1744); The Internal Organisation of the Company-Organisation of the Company's Factories in India; The Anglo-French Struggle in South India.

Unit 3	:	**British Conquest of India**	10 Pds.

Foundation and Expansion of the British empire (1756-1818); British Occupation of Bengal; Dual System of Administration in Bengal; Expansion under Lord Hastings; The Consolidation of British Power (1818-1857); The Conquest of Sindh; The Conquest of the Punjab; Dalhousie and the Policy of Annexation.

Unit 4	:	**Structure of Government and Administrative Organisation of the British Empire in India (1757-1857)**	6 Pds.

Structure of Government; Civil Service; Army Police; Judicial Organisation; The Rule of Law; Equality before law.

Unit 5	:	**Economic, Social and Cultural Policy of the British Empire in India (1757-1857)**	8 Pds.

British Economic Policies in India; The Drain of Wealth; Means of Transport and Communication; Land Revenue Policy; Permanent Settlement; Ryotwari System; Mahalwari System; Social Legislation.

Unit 6	:	**Social and Cultural Awakening in the First Half of the 19th Century**	8 Pds.

Ram Mohan Roy; Young Bengal Movement; The Brahmo Samaj; Ishwar Chandra Vidyasagar; Social and Cultural Awakening in Western India.

Unit 7	:	**The Revolt of 1857**	8 Pds.

Causes of Discontent Against British Rule; Early Revolts; Immediate Causes of the Revolt of 1857; Spread of the Revolt; Causes of Defeat; Nature and results.

Unit 8	:	**Growth of New India: Religious and Social Reforms after 1858**	16 Pds.

Brahmo Samaj; Religious Reform Movement in Maharashtra; Jotiba Phule; Ramakrishna and Vivekananda; Dayananda and Arya Samaj; Narayana Guru; Veeresalingam; Theosophical Society; Syed Ahmed Khan and the Aligarh School; Muhammad Iqbal; Religious Reforms Among the Sikhs; Social reforms; Emancipation of Women; Struggle Against the Caste System.

Unit 9	:	**Administrative Changes after 1858**	12 Pds.

Administration; Provincial Administration; Local Bodies; Changes in the Army; Public Services; Relations with Princely States; Administrative Polices; Hostility to Educated Indians; Attitude Towards the Zamindars; Attitude Towards Social Reforms; Backwardness of Social Services; Labour Legislation; Restrictions on the Press; Racial Arrogance.

Unit 10	:	**India and her Neighbours**	4 Pds.

War with Nepal; Conquest of Burma; Relations with Afghanistan.

Unit 11	:	**Economic Impact of the British Rule**	6 Pds.

Disruption of the Traditional Economy; Ruin of Artisans and Craftsmen; Impoverishment of the Peasantry; Ruin of Old Zamindars and Rise of New Landlordism; Stagnation of Agriculture; Development of Modern Industries;

History of Modern India and Contemporary World vii

Unit 12 : **Growth of New India: Nationalist Movement (1858-1905)** — 8 Pds.
Consequence of Foreign Domination; Administrative and Economic Unification of the Country; Western Thought and Education; Role of the Press and Literature-Rediscovery of India's Past; Racial Arrogance of the Rulers; Immediate Factors; Predecessors of the Indian National Congress; The Indian National Congress; Congress During its Early Phase (1885-1905); Constitutional Reforms; Economic Reforms; Administrative Reforms; Defence of Civil Rights; Methods of Congress Political Work; British Government's Attitude.

Unit 13 : **National Movement (1905-1918)** — 16 Pds.
Growth of Militant Nationalism; Recognition of the True Nature of British Rule; Growth of Self-respect and Self-confidence; Growth of Education; Unemployment; International Influences; Militant Nationalist School of Thought; Partition of Bengal; The Anti-Partition Movement; Swadeshi and Boycott; All India Aspect of the Movement; Growth of Militancy; Growth of Revolutionary Terrorism; The Indian National Congress (1905-1914); The Muslim League; Growth of Communalism; Nationalist Movement and the First World War; The Home Rule League; Lucknow Session of the Congress (1916).

Unit 14 : **Struggle for Swaraj** — 16 Pds.
Nationalist Movement after the First World War; Montagu; Chelmsford Reform; Rowlatt Act-Emergence of Mahatma Gandhi; Gandhiji's Ideas; Champaran Satyagraha; Movement Against the Rowlatt Act; Jallianwala Bagh Massacre; Khilafat and Non-Cooperation Movement; The Swarajists Constructive Programme; Revolutionaries; Simon Commission; Lahore Session of the Congress and the slogan of Purna Swaraj; Civil Disobedience Movement; Government of India Act of 1935; Formation of the Congress Ministries; Movements of Peasants and Workers; Growth of Socialist Ideas; Congress and International Developments; Movements of the States' People; Growth of Communalism; Nationalist Movement During the Second World War; Quit India; INA; Nationalist Movement After the Second World War; Achievement of Independence; Immediate Problems.

Unit 15 : **Map Work on Modern India** — 8 Pds.

CONTEMPORARY WORLD

Unit 16 : **Introduction** — 4 Pds.
Contemporary Period in World History; Distinction Between Contemporary History and Modern History; Characteristic Features of Contemporary History; A broad Survey of the Historical Background of Contemporary World.

Unit 17 : **The World From About the End of the 19th Century to the End of the First World War** — 12 Pds.

(i) Developments upto 1914 : Imperialism and the Hegemony of Europe; Rise of the United States of America; Developments in Asia, Africa and Latin America; Imperialist Rivalries and Conflicts.

(ii) The First World War: The Underlying Causes; Course of the War; U.S. Entry; End of the War; Immediate consequences.

(iii) The Russian Revolution: Political, Economic and Social Conditions in Tsarist Russia-Russian Empire; Revolutionary Movement in Russia; 1905 Revolution; Russia and the First World War; February Revolution; October Revolution; Significance of the October Revolution.

Unit 18 — The World from 1919 to 1939 — 18 Pds.

Political consequences of the First World War for Europe, Asia and Africa; The Peace Settlement; The League of Nations.

Developments in Europe and North America: Failure of revolutions in Germany and Hungary; Fascism in Italy; Economic Depression, Its Economic, Social and Political Consequences-Nazism in Germany-Developemnts in U.S.A.-The New Deal-Growing importance of U.S.A. in the world-Developments in Britain and France.

Emergence of USSR Major Developments in USSR; Role of USSR in World Affairs. Developments in Asia, Africa and Latin America (1919-1939); Rising Strength of Nationalist Movements in Asia; Developments in Africa; Militarism in Japan; Aggression and Appeasement; Japanese Invasion of China; Italian Invasion of Ethiopia; Civil War in Spain; Nazi Germany's Role in World Affairs; Munich Pact.

Unit 19 — The Second World War — 6 Pds.

(i) Underlying Causes of the Second World War.

(ii) German Invasion of Poland and Outbreak of Hostilities; Fall of France.

(iii) The War Becomes a Global War; Invasion of USSR; U.S. Entry into the War-Course of the War.

(iv) End of the War; Destruction Caused by the War; The Atom Bomb; Plans of the Post; War Reconstruction of the World; United Nations.

Unit 20 : The World after the Second World War — 27 Pds.

General Features; Political Composition of the World After the Second World War; Disintegration of the Colonial Imperialist System; Neocolonialism; Emergence of U.S.A. and USSR as World Powers; Formation of NATO and the other U.S. and Western Sponsored Military Alliances; Warsaw Pact; Cold War; Nuclear Weapons; Trend Towards International Cooperation; End of the Cold War.

Developments in Asia, Africa and Latin America with special reference to National Liberation Movement; Their Role in World Affairs.

Panchsheel; The Non-Aligned Movement; Problems of Development.

Developments in Europe: Political Map of the Post-War Europe; Main Features of Political, Economic and Social Developments in Europe; Main Features of Developments in USSR from 1945 to 1991; Break-up of USSR. Main Features of Developments in USA. Recent Developments.

Unit 21 : Main Features of Developments in Economy, Society and Polity — 6 Pds.

Main Features of Changes in the World Economy, Particularly After the Second War; Globalization; Problems of Development.

Patterns of Social Changes; Population; Urbanization; Changes in Occupational Structure; Social Divisioins; Role and Position of Women; Minorities

Growth of Political Democracy; Mass Politics; Changes in the Role and Fuctions of the State; Human Rights.

Unit 22	:	**Developments in Science, Technology and Culture**	8 Pds.

Revolutionary Developments in Science; Application of Basic Science to Technology; The Second Industrial Revolution; New Sources of Energy; Industrial Production; Transport and Communications; Means of Destruction; Impact of Developments in Biological Sciences; Information Technology.

Literature and Art in the Contemporary World.

Impact of the Revolution in Communications; The Mass Media; Newspapers, Radio, Cinema, Television-Impact on Culture.

Unit 23	:	**The Future Outlook**	10 Pds.

Major Issues, Problems and Trends; Problem of Survival; Awareness of Common Concerns; Interdependence; Indivisibility of the World; The Imperative of International Cooperation.

Unit 24	:	**Map Work on Contemporary World History**	7 Pds.

Contents

FOREWORD xv

MODERN INDIA

1. **The Political Conditions in India During the 18th Century** 1
   Significant Characteristics of the 18th Century in India; Mughal Rulers after Aurangzeb; Mughal Disintegration.

2. **Indian Society in the 18th Century (Social and Economic Conditions)** 21
   Dark Period of Socio-Economic life; Main Features.

3. **The Beginning of European Settlements in India** 27
   Gold, Glory and God: Discovery of Trade Routes: From Traders to Colonisers. The Portuguese, The Dutch, The British, The French; Wars of Domination: Anglo French struggle in South India, Carnatic Wars.

4. **The British Conquest of India** 36
   Battles: From Plassey to Buxar; Dual Government in West Bengal; Warren Hastings; Lord Cornwallis; Sir John Shore; Lord Wellesely; Sir George Barlaw; Lord Minto; Marques Hastings; John Adams; Lord Amherst; Lord William Bentinck; Sir Charles Metcalfe; Lord Auckland; Lord Hardings; Lord Dalhousie; The Maratha Wars; Conquest of Burma.

5. **Maharaja Ranjit Singh: Conquest of Punjab** 54
   Lion of the Punjab: Ranjit Singh; Annexation of the Punjab.

6. **The Structure of Government and Administrative Organisation of the British Empire in India (1757-1857)** 59
   The Objectives of the system: Development of the Administrative Structure and Control; Administrative Organisation; Justic.

7. **The Economic, Social and Culture Policy of the British in India (1757-1857)** 66
   Exploitation of India; East India Company - A Trading Organisation; Revolutionary Changes in the Economic Policy after the Industrial Revolution in England; Land Revenue Policy of the British Rulers; Cultural Policy of the British in India; Culture and Education Policy of the British; Means of Transport and Communication.

8. **Social and Cultural Awakening in the First Half of the 19th Century** 74
   Raja Ram Mohan Roy: Founder of Modern India; Ishwar Chandra Vidyasagar; Henry Vivian Derozio; David Hare; The Young Bengal Movement; Brahma Samraj; Social and Religious Reformers and Modern India.

9. **The Revolt of 1857** 80
Early Revolts; Early Sepoy Revolts; Revolt of 1857: Main Leaders of the 1857 Revolt, Main Events and Suppression of the Revolt, Nature of the Revolt, Causes of the Failure of the Revolt, Results of the 1857 Revolt.

10. **The Administrative Changes After 1858** 92
Far Reaching Changes; Local Self Government; Reorganisation of the Army; Public Services; Relations with Princely states; Policy of Divide and Rule; Hostilities of the British Ruler Towards Educated Indians; Attitude of the British Towards the Zamindars; Attitude Towards Social Reform; Backwardness of Social Service; Labour Legislation; Press in India; Policy of Racial Discrimination.

11. **India and Her Neighbours (India's Foreign Policy)** 101
Indias Relations with Nepal; Relations with Burma (Myanmar); Relations with Afghanistan; Relations with Tibet; Relations with Sikkim; Relations with Bhutan.

12. **The Economic Impact of the British Rule on India** 107
Overview of the Economic Condition of the People; Disruption of Traditional Economy of India; Ruin of Artisans and Craftsmen; Impoverished Peasantry; Ruin of old Zamindars and Rise of New Landlordism; Stagnation and Deterioration of Indian Agriculture; Development of Modern Industries; De-Industrialisation of India; Poverty and Famines.

13. **Social and Religious Reforms after 1858—Growth of New India** 117
Period of Reflection on Social and Religious Issues; Important Ideas that Led to Religious and Social Reforms; Significant Aspects of Religious and Social Reform Movements; Contribution of Reform Movement; Methods Adopted by Religious and Social Reformers; Limitations of these Movement; Striking Balance between Religious and Social Reforms.

14. **The Growth of New India** 127
The Nationalist Movement (1858-1905) National Awakening; Indian National Congress; The Moderates or the Moderate Nationalists.

15. **The Nationalist Movement (1905-1918)** 139
Background of the Rise of Militant of Extremist Nationalist Movement; The Partition of Bengal -1905, Differences between the Extremists and the Moderates; Prominent Extremist Leaders; Growth of Revolutionary Terrorism; The Indian National Congress (1905-1914); The All India Muslim League; National Movement and the First World War.

16. **The National Movement (1919-1928)** 157
Impact of the First World War; Emergence of Gandhiji on the Political Scene of India; Movement and Reforms 1919-22; Constructive Programme; The Simon Commission (1927-28); The Revolutionaries or the Revolutionary Terrorist Movement.

Foreword

Dr. R.C. Majumdar, the renowned historian, while editing the volumes of the *History and Culture of the Indian People* kept in view the scope of history as defined by Dr. K.M. Munshi, the inaugurator of this historical project, as :

"To be a history in the true sense of the word, the work must be the story of the people. It must be a record of their life from age to age presented through ..... political changes....... through characteristic social institutions, beliefs; through literary and artistic achievements; through the movement of thought...."

The stress was laid on people and culture and it is quite a happy coincidence that the curriculum of History for Classes XI and XII of Central Board of Secondary Education has laid a similar emphasis on people and their culture. This textbook also highlights along with the rulers and their reigns the conditon of the people in each period, their new ideas and beliefs, their new feelings and realizations and a new reawakening. This new awakening is found expressed in their cultural achievements in the form of literature, architecture, painting, music and the like. This is required by the syllabus and is needed for the basic awareness about India's rich cultural heritage.

All that happened in the past cannot be covered in the limited space between two covers of a textbook. The prescribed syllabus has to be selective at places. This book has preserved the sense of continuity by suitable notes.

The descriptive and narrative level of the subject matter has been raised to a thought provoking analytical plane, with interactive play of cause and effect and with a wider elbow room for discussion, so as to suit the mature level of learners at this last school stage.

One thing need not escape us. A textbook has to be examination oriented for the dual purpose of securing wider knowledge and scoring higher marks. This brings us to the new prescribed pattern of questions to be set for the examinations. It has been found that students are facing many difficulties especially in answering the questions requiring short answers within 20 to 30 words. To extend help in this area, the topics have been presented in simple units or sub-units according to important points needing emphasis. These units are logically, psychologically or chronologically linked up with one another like threading pearls so that the total effect remains quite impressive.

Views of renowned historians pertaining to important rulers or periods are quoted to widen the student's mental horizon.

This textbook does not claim any special superiority over others in use. All that has been done is to depend on authentic facts, free from any bias, to lay emphasis on the people and their culture, to use simple language and style supported by illustrations and maps for easy comprehension, to secure a sense of continuity, to place clear and direct pointers to all the important points and to provide a comprehensive coverage of the syllabus within easy reach of the average students and without missing challenging encouragement for the brighter ones. This is all what need be said about the new approach followed in this book. Moreover what really prompted us to write this detailed account of the prescribed syllabus was a statement in the Quarterly Bulletin CENBOSEC, Oct.—Dec. '97. The CBSE has stated, "It has been brought to our notice by many school teachers that the 2nd volume of the NCERT History Textbook 'Contemporary World History' for Class XII... does not cover full topics prescribed in the history syllabus for units 21, 22 and 23."

Only this book fully covers all the topics of the syllabus, particularly all the 35 topics of units 21, 22, 23 of Contemporary World. Thus it removes the present, difficulty of the students in procuring proper textbook material.

We owe a deep debt of gratitude to all the great historians whose books based on lifelong research have lighted our path and guided our steps. We are also very thankful to Shri Ashok Verma, Siddhart and Jayant Biswas for helping in drawing illustratious and maps.

We also express our thanks to Shri Dev Raj Khosla for procurring rare books on history for our work.

Modern India

CHAPTER 1

The Political Conditions in India During the 18th Century

SIGNIFICANT CHARACTERISTICS OF 18TH CENTURY IN INDIA

Eighteenth century was marked by three major political developments in India. The first was the decline and disintegration of the Mughal empire. The second was the emergence of a number of independent and semi-independent kingdoms and powers. The third was the greed of several European powers to have their foothold on India. All this resulted in fierce struggles, conspiracies, battles and wars.

Some historians view the eighteenth century in India as one of the darkest periods of Indian history. India became a slave country of the British for about two hundred years. The people of India had to fight a long and arduous battle for the liberation of the country from foreign domination.

The history of India during the eighteenth century was the history of decline - decline in almost all walks of national life.

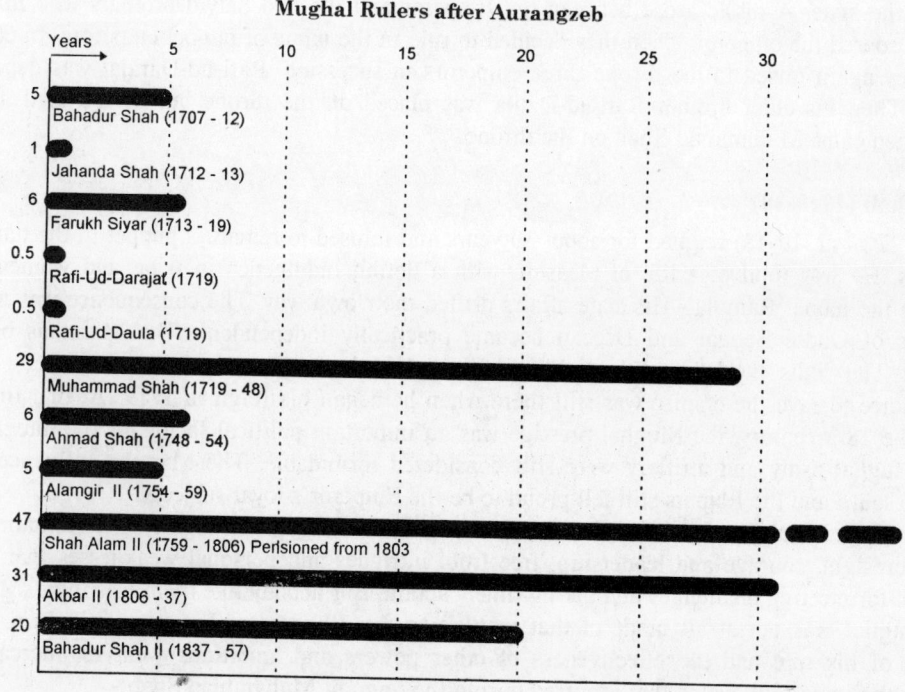

Chart 1: **Mughal Rulers after Aurangzeb**

The chart above indicates that most of the rulers after Aurangzeb occupied the Mughal throne for very short periods. Several of them were very weak puppets in the hands of others. They were mostly devoted to the pleasures of wine and women neglecting the affairs of the state. They were thoroughly unfit to rule India or to represent the glorious dynasty of Babur. Most of them were victims of intrigues and faced unnatural death. These facts alone were sufficient indicators for the speedy decline of the Mughal empire under their unworthy ruling hands, though other major factors provided a catalystic support for the quick final drop of the curtains.

Bahadur Shah I (1707-12)

Bahadur Shah I (1707-12), the eldest son of Aurangzeb, ascended the throne after wading through a pool of blood of the war of succession that ended the life of two of his brothers. He was too weak to say 'no' to his nobles. Thus, intrigues and conspiracies ruled his court. He was incapable of suppressing the forces of disintegration which threatened imperial unity. Rajasthan rebelled, the Sikhs rose in Punjab under Banda and a civil war broke out among the Marathas.

Jahandar Shah (1712-1713)

Jahandar Shah (1712-13), Son of Bahadur Shah, was dominated by a dancing girl Lal Kunwar and his minister Zulfiqar Khan. He was unfit to rule. Within a year he was murdered by his nephew Farrukh-Siyar who ascended the throne by the help of two Saiyid brothers, Abdullah Khan and Husain Ali Khan, the Deputy Governors of Allahabad and Bihar respectively.

Farrukh-Siyar (1713-19)

Farrukh-Siyar (1713-19), was feeble, false, cowardly and contemptible. The two Saiyid brothers acquired full control of the state. A tussle arose between the Emperor and the two Saiyid brothers who imprisoned, blinded and murdered the emperor. Then they decided to rule in the name of puppet emperors. In course of a few months they again raised to the throne three emperors in sucession. Rafi-ud-Darajat was deposed after three months. Then his elder brother Rafi-ud-Daula was placed on the throne but he too died after three months. And then came Muhammad Shah on the throne.

Muhammad Shah (1719-48)

Muhammad Shah (1719-48) reigned for about 30 years and refused to remain a puppet in the hands of the Saiyid brothers. He was fond of a life of pleasure with a doting indulgence in wine and women. He was therefore given the name 'Rangila'. His state affairs drifted their own way. The consequence was most fatal. The Governors of Oudh, Bengal and Deccan became practically independent. The Marathas became an imperial power. The Sikhs, the Jats and the Rohilla Afghans laid the foundation of their powers.

The last chance to save the empire was still there when he began his reign in 1719. At that time, in the beginning of the 18th century, the Mughal prestige was an important political factor for the integrity of the empire. The Mughal army and artillery were still considered formidable. The Maratha influence was still confined to the south and the Rajputs still felt proud to be the Emperor's loyal subjects.

The empire needed someone nearer to the stature of the Great Mughals in dignity, determination, power, imagination, foresight, courage and leadership, free from intrigues and personal weaknesses that dilute the energy and will for meeting challenges and taking timely action. But nobody like them was there. Muhammad Shah, the 'Rangila' was not at all made of that mettle. As the 30 years of his reign rolled on, the sheer ineffectiveness of his rule and the effectiveness of other powers and ambitions went on increasing. The following were the important events that occurred during the reign of Muhammad Shah:-

The Political Conditions in India During the 18th Century

(1) The liquidation of the Saiyid brothers. The Saiyid brothers- Abdullah Khan and Husain Ali- known as 'king makers' wielded the administrative powers of the state from 1713 to 1720 and made an effort to stem further deterioration of the empire by reconciling the Hindus and the Marathas. But their liberal religious policy, the jealousy of a powerful group of nobles, a wave of public revulsion against them for drenching their hands with the blood of the Emperor Farrukh Siyar and the hostility of the Emperor ultimately caused the murder of one, and the overthrow of the other brother from the corridors of power.

(2) Rampant corruption flourished in his court and made him share the bribes collected by his corrupt officers. Such corruption, besides court intrigues, demoralised the administration.

(3) Several powerful rulers carved out semi-independent or fully independent states like Oudh, Hyderabad and others.

The Invasion of Nadir Shah (1739)

Nadir Shah, the Persian ruler, was greatly attracted by the fabulous wealth of India and the chaotic conditions prevailing in the country due to the intrigues, corruption and disunity among the nobles and rulers. As Nadir Shah embarked on his ambitious expedition, he conquered country after country- Ghazni, Kabul, Peshawar and Lahore - and then defeated the Mughal army at Karnal. Next, he entered Delhi in 1739, imprisoned the emperor Muhammad Shah and plundered the whole city. As a few of his soldiers were murdered on a false rumour that Nadir Shah was dead, he ordered a general massacre in Delhi. Innocent people were butchered mercilessly. Besides the two centuries of accumulated wealth of the Mughals, he carried away the famous Kohinoor diamond and the jewel studded peacock throne of Shah-Jahan to Persia. He departed after 57 days leaving the Mughal empire politicially crippled and financially bankrupt. In addition to the loss of prestige, power and self, the invasion exposed the hidden weakness of the Mughal empire to several powers that had their eyes glued to the throne of Delhi.

Invasions of Ahmad Shah Abdali (1743-1766)

It so happened that Ahmad Shah Abdali, one of the ablest generals of Nadir Shah, became emperor after his master's murder and followed his master's footsteps in conquering country after country before his first invasion of India in 1743 during the reign of Muhammad Shah.

Abdali, also known as Durrani, invaded India seven times - 1743, 1751, 1756, 1759, 1761, and 1766. Every invasion was a repeat performance of plundering the Northern India right down to Delhi and Mathura. In 1761, he defeated the Marathas, the most supreme powers in India, in a famous battle, in the famous field of Panipat, that is, the Third Battle of Panipat. Abdali won the support of the Rohillas and the Oudh but the Marathas failed to get the help of the Jats and the Rajputs. This defeat crushed the high ambitions of the Marathas to be the master of the entire North and made the Mughal empire to exist in name only ruling Delhi and a small territory around it.

Ahmad Shah (1748-54):

Ahmad Shah, the son of Muhammad Shah, proved to be a puppet emperor who allowed his chief eunuch to look after the affairs of his state. He made peace with dishonourable conditions with Abdali, who invaded India twice, in 1749 and 1752, during his reign. At that time, for the lack of prestige, power and control of the puppet emperors, quarrels among the nobles grew so intense that riots became an everyday occurrence on the open streets of Delhi. His powerful *wazir* (prime minister) blinded and imprisoned him before installing another puppet emperor, Alamgir II, on the throne.

Alamgir II (1754-59):

When he fell from the grace of the *wazir*, Ghazi-ud-din Imad-u-mulk, he was murdered. The *wazir* took upon himself the role of kingmaker like the Saiyid brothers.

Shah Alam II (1759-1806):

When Alamgir was murdered, his son was in Bihar. He declared himself the emperor and took the title Shah Alam II. For the fear of the *wazir* who murdered his father, he remained away from Delhi for 12 years. During his stay in Bihar he joined Mir Qasim of Bengal and Shuja-ud-Daula of Oudh in declaring a war against the East India Company. The joint forces were defeated in the Battle of Buxar fought in 1764. The East India company recognised him as an emperor and gave him a pension. He gifted the *Diwani* (power of collection and administration of revenue) of Bengal, Bihar and Orissa to the East India Company in 1765. In 1772, after staying for sometime in Allahabad, he returned to Delhi under the protection of the Marathas, who at that time dominated Delhi. In 1803 when General Lake captured Delhi, he lost Delhi but continued to be on the British role of pensioners.

Akbar II (1806-37):

He succeeded his father and lived on the British pension.

Bahadur Shah II (1837-57):

He was the last Mughal Emperor, though in name, and a British pensioner. During the rebellion of 1857, the sepoys declared him as their emperor and leader to overthrow the British. He was tried by the British and was deported to Rangoon where he died in 1862. Thus, the tottering Mughal dynasty totally came to an end.

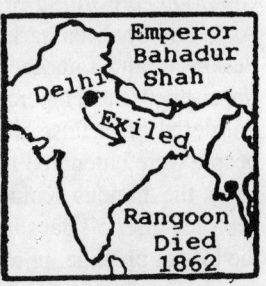

Map 1: **Bahadur Shah Exiled in Rangoon**

The Third Battle of Panipat (1761)

Causes :

The Maratha's penetration into Delhi and the Punjab was a challenge to Ahmad Shah Abdali as he considered the north-west India as his own sphere of influence due to his earlier invasions. Secondly, he was financially deprived as the earlier Mughal tributes were now diverted into the hands of the Marathas. Thirdly, he was encouraged by the Rohillas who had greatly suffered by the Maratha raids. Finally, clashes and conflicts between the two aspirants for the complete domination of North India were inevitable.

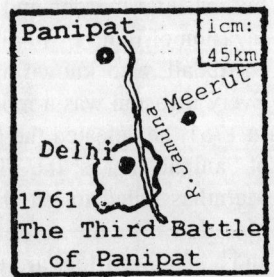

Map 2: **The Third Battle of Panipat 1761**

Effects :

1. The defeat of the Marathas entirely changed the course of Indian history. It proved very disastrous to them. They lost the cream of their army. It is said, "There was not a single home in Maharashtra that was not mourning the death of a young man."
2. The East India Compay made the best use of the defeat of the Marathas. It was now in a very advantageous position to consolidate its hold in different parts of India. In fact, the English benefited more as compared to Ahmad Shah Abdali.
3. The Mughal power received a severe blow with the victory of Ahmad Shah.
4. Ahmad Shah plundered without any check on him.
5. Ahmad Shah did not attempt to found a new Afghan Kingdom in India.

The Political Conditions in India During the 18th Century

Reasons of the Defeat of the Marathas:
1. Abdali's forces outnumbered the Maratha forces.
2. The Afghans proved to be great military strategists. They cut the communication line to Delhi. As a result, the Maratha army could not get the essential supplies and virtually faced near famine conditions.
3. The mutual jealousies among Maratha Sardars stood in the way of providing a unified Maratha command.
4. The Marathas failed to win the support of Indian rulers, rather the Rohillas and the Oudh aided Abdali.
5. Ahmad Shah Abdali won over a few important Indian rulers.
6. The Maratha forces were not well trained in fighting on the plains, as they were adept in waging guerilla wars.

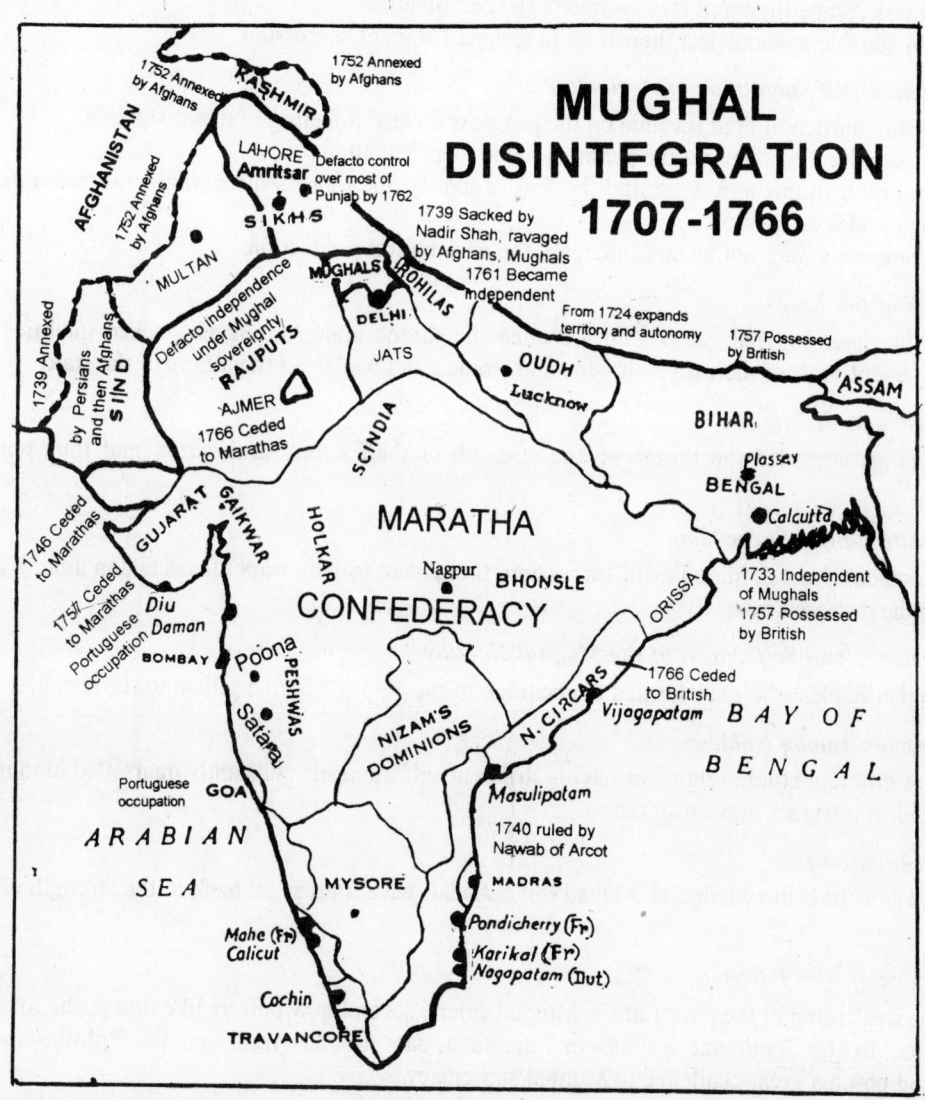

Map 3: **Mughal Disintegration 1707-1766**

Causes of the Downfall of the Mughal Empire in the Eighteenth Century

1. Weaknesses of the Mughal Army:
(i) In due course it became indisciplined.
(ii) It lost its fighting morale.
(iii) For want of money, the strength of the Mughal army was considerably reduced.
(iv) It was not modernised and thus failed to match the European armies.
(v) In several cases, Mughal commanders and nobles began to take along with them family members and indulged in pleasure-seeking as if a battle field was a picnic spot.
(vi) There was competition and rivalry among the commanders.
(vii) Several capable generals lost their lives in frequent wars of succession.

2. Deterioration and Stagnation of Agriculture:
(a) Increasing burden of land revenue on the peasants created a feeling of dissatisfaction.
(b) Oppression by the nobles on the peasants made them rebellious.
(c) Deterioration in law and order and the fear of loot by the robbers discouraged the peasants to increase the area under cultivation.
(d) Adequate steps were not taken to increase the agricultural production.

3. Weakness of the Kings:
Most of the later Mughal rulers who ascended the throne after Aurangzeb, lacked qualities of efficient rulers. They spent most of their time on wine and women and neglected the affairs of the state.

4. Dependence on Nobles:
Several kings ascended the throne on the strength of their nobles and *wazirs* and thus remained their puppets.

5. No Definite Law of Succession:
In the absence of any definite law of succession, there were usually wars of succession among the sons and relatives of the deceased ruler.

6. Incompetency and Selfishness of the Mughal Nobility:
The Mughal nobles who once formed the bedrock of the empire became selfish to the backbone.

7. Conspiracies Among Nobles:
Nobles of different ethnic origins or having different self interests, constantly quarrelled among themselves and indulged in intrigues and conspiracies.

8. Foreign Invasions:
The invasions of Nadir Shah and Ahmad Shah Abdali gave a great set back to the strength of the Mughal empire.

9. Emergence of New Powers:
With the weakening of the power of the Mughal rulers, several new powers like that of the Sikhs in Punjab, the Marathas in the South, the Rajputs in Rajputana, Jats around Agra, and the Rohillas in Rohilkhand emerged and posed a great challenge to Mughal supremacy.

10. Coming of the Europeans:
Many European nations appeared on the scene, first as traders and then as rulers. They took an active part in the political affairs of the country and sided with one or the other Indian ruler.

11. Neglect of Sea-Power:

The Mughal rulers failed to appreciate the importance of naval power.

12. Fanatic Religious Policy:

Most of the Mughal rulers who followed Aurangzeb, were intolerant towards Non-Muslims.

13. Intellectual bankruptcy:

The sons of the Mughal nobility received neither good education nor any practical training.

14. Financial Bankruptcy:

The Mughal empire faced all the more bankruptcy after the death of Aurangzeb. In the 1750s, the financial bankruptcy reached its height. Sir J.N. Sarkar, an authority on Mughal rule, has described the pathetic state of the Mughal ruler Alamgir, how once no fire was kindled in his harem and kitchen for three days and how the princes had to bear the torture of starvation.

Alamgir II once had no coveyance to take him to Idgah and he had to walk the long distance on foot.

15. Evoking Little Emotional Sentiments:

The Mughal Emperors did not evoke as much emotional sentiments from their subjects as the Maratha, the Rajput and the Sikh rulers.

16. Wide-spread Corruption:

Corruption in administration became almost universal — from the higher nobility to the lowest clerk.

HYDERABAD

Founder of the Asaf Jahi Dynasty

As the Mughal Empire of Aurangzeb started disintegrating and shrinking, vassals, feudatories chiefs and governors started carving out or consolidating their territories at different places or founding their dynasties. Nizam-ul-Malik Asaf Jahz, a *wazir* of Mughal emperor Muhammad Shah founded the state of Hyderabad in 1724. The dynasty that ruled the state of Hyderabad came to be known as the Asafjahi dynasty after his name. Nizam-ul-Malik was very helpful to Muhammad Shah in his efforts to get rid of the Saiyid Brothers. In 1722, he was made the Viceroy of the Deccan, where he worked for about two years. He proved his administrative skills in the Deccan, and consolidated his position. He was recalled to Delhi in 1722 and made the *wazir* of the empire. He attempted to bring about administrative reforms but failed to do so as the emperor was very lukewarm to reforms. So he went back to the Deccan and founded the Hyderabad state and ruled with a strong hand till his death in 1748. Thereafter, the State of Hyderabad lost its supremacy.

Diplomatic Skills and Achievements of Nizam-ul-Malik:

1. He was a great diplomat. He never openly declared his independence from the Mughal ruler although in practice he acted like an independent ruler. He waged wars, concluded peace with some powers, conferred titles, gave jagirs and appointed officers without seeking permission from the Mughal ruler.
2. He established an orderly system of administration.
3. He followed a policy of tolerance towards the Hindus.
4. He kept the powerful Marathas out of his dominions.
5. He forced the big and powerful zamindars to respect his authority.
6. He attempted to reform the revenue system.

CARNATIC

Carnatic was one of the *subahs* of the Deccan and therefore it fell under the authority of the ruler of Hyderabad.

Saadatullah Khan, the Deputy Governor of Carnatic, known as the Nawab of Carnatic, became practically independent of Hyderabad's authority, just as Hyderabad had become independent of the Mughal authority. He made his nephew, Dost Ali, his successor without the approval of any authority, either of the ruler of Hyderabad or of Delhi. After 1740, the affairs of Carnatic deteriorated because of the repeated conflicts for its Nawabship. The European trading companies began to interfere in the internal affairs of Carnatic.

OUDH

A Prosperous Province and Lucknavi Culture

The prolonged period of comparative peace and economic prosperity under Sadat Khan (1722-39) and Safdar Jang (1739-54) resulted in the growth of a distinct Lucknow or *Lucknavi* culture around the Oudh or Awadh court. Lucknow remained for a number of years the capital city of Oudh or Awadh and became an important centre of arts and literature, crafts and culture under the patronage of the Nawabs, chieftains and zamindars.

Saadat Khan Burhan-ul-Malik (1722-39)

Saadat Khan, the founder of the state of Oudh was earlier a *wazir* of the Mughal emperor Muhammad. He rendered valuable help to the emperor in getting rid of the Saiyid Brothers. For his services, he was made the Governor of the Oudh province in 1722. He was very adventurous, brave and courageous. He made the most of the declining power of the Mughal emperor and established an independent State of Oudh. He hardly maintained any link with the Mughal ruler.

Chief Achievements of Saadat Khan:

1. He suppressed lawlessness in the state and brought about law and order.
2. He disciplined the zamindars.
3. He won over nobles by giving several concessions.
4. He organised an efficient system of administration.
5. He introduced several reforms in the land revenue system which proved very beneficial to the farmers.
6. He took many steps to organise a well-trained, disciplined and well-equipped army. He also raised the salaries in the army.
7. He did not discriminate between the Hindus and the Muslims and gave many high offices to the Hindus.

Safdar Jang (1739-54)

After the death of Saadat Khan, his nephew and son-in-law Safdar Jang, became the ruler. His rule witnessed a period of peace and prosperity, and of cultural development. He led an austere and simple life. He was a man of high morals in his personal life.

Safdar Jang Tomb at New Delhi is a great monument in his memory. He served as *wazir* of the Mughal emperor.

Main Events and Achievements of Safdar Jang:

(i) Like Saadat Khan, he was quite liberal in his outlook and gave responsible positions to the Hindus.
(ii) He suppressed the rebellious zamindars.

(iii) He entered into an alliance with the Maratha Sardars.
(iv) He won over the loyalty of the Rajputs.
(v) He also won over the support of the Rajputs.
(vi) He carried on warfare against the Rohillas and Bangash Pathans, who rose to rebellion.
(vii) He organised an equitable system of justice.
(viii) His most important contribution was in the patronage of the development of *Lucknavi* culture—a great landmark. Lucknow became a famous centre of art and literature.

Shujah-ud-Daula (1754-75)

After the death of Safdar Jang, his son Shujah-ud-Daula became the Nawab of Oudh. During this period, the English were making serious efforts to bring under their domination several parts of India. They began to interfere in the internal administration of Indian rulers. The three Indian rulers, namely Nawab Mir Qasim of Bengal, Mughal Emperor Shah Alam II and Nawab Shujah-ud-Daula of Oudh organised a Confederacy to check the growing power of the East India Company. The combined armies of these powers numbering between 40,000 and 60,000 met the British army of the East India Company, made up of only 7000 soldiers, at Buxar in 1764. It was a very unevenly balanced fight but victory came to the British army. With this victory over the Confederacy, the British power in India became unchallengeable. The Battle of Buxar almost sealed the fate of the Indian rulers.

In 1775, the Treaty of Allahabad was signed between the East India Company and the Nawab of Oudh. The Nawab agreed to pay Rs. 50 lakh to the Company as compensation for the Battle of Buxar. The Nawab also agreed to render military help to the company in time of need. He also had to surrender two districts—Kara and Allahabad. The Nawab remained loyal to the English up to his death in 1775.

MYSORE

In the later half of the 18th century, Mysore produced two great rulers, namely Hyder Ali and his son Tipu Sultan. It is usually believed that these were among the first to realize the danger posed by the English in India. Both of them were hostile towards the British but friendly towards the French.

Both realized that for having a stable government, three things were very essential—a strong economy, an efficient army and religious tolerance.

Hyder Ali (1766-82)

Rise to Power:

Hyder Ali started his career as a petty officer in the Mysore army when it was ruled by a king, Chikka Krishna Raj. The king had been reduced to the position of a mere puppet by two ministers, Nanjaraj and Devraj. Hyder Ali, on account of his military skill and qualities of leadership, became the chief of Mysore army and overshadowed the two ministers. When he was the Faujdar of Dindigal, he managed to raise an independent army for himself.

In 1766, Hyder Ali became an independent ruler after the death of the king. He made Seringapatam as the capital of Mysore state. He captured several territories and extended his kingdom.

Wars Fought :

Hyder Ali had to fight many battles with the Marathas, the Nizam of Hyderabad and the English. In the First Mysore War (1767-69) with the British, Hyder Ali managed to win over the Nizam of Hyderabad. The English forces proved no match with the forces of Hyder Ali and they had to beg for peace. Hyder Ali virtually dictated the terms in the treaty of 1769.

Peace between the two parties was short-lived but there was no war for about eleven years. In 1780, the Second Mysore War (1780-84) started and in the early phases of the war, Hyder Ali had an upper hand over the British. He defeated the English army a number of times and went upto Madras after capturing Carnatic. Hyder Ali was supported by the French in this war. He was suffering from cancer. The battles, one after the other, had fully sapped his energies. Madras settlement of the English was almost on the verge of collapse when Hyder Ali suddenly died. After his death, his son Tipu Sultan continued to fight with the British.

Achievements of Hyder Ali:

Though an illiterate, Hyder Ali proved to be an able administrator and an efficient commander. Some of his achievements were as under.
(1) He established an independent kingdom of Mysore.
(2) He established control over the rebellious section of the population.
(3) He raised a well-equipped and efficient army.
(4) He set up a modern arsenal with the help of French experts.
(5) He introduced several revenue and administrative reforms.
(6) He was tolerant towards all communities and religions. His first Diwan and many senior officers were Hindus.

Tipu Sultan (1782-99)

'Tiger of Mysore':

On account of his daring courage and strength, Tipu Sultan is usually called the 'Tiger of Mysore'. He fought three wars with the British.

After the passing away of his father, Tipu Sultan continued the Second Mysore War. In 1784, a treaty was signed according to which both the parties agreed to the position that existed before the start of the war. The conquered territories were returned to each other.

Map 4: **Mysore Wars—The Partition**

In the Third Mysore War (1789-92), Tipu had to face defeat and made to sign the Treaty of Seringapatam in 1792. He had to pay a huge amount to the British, besides surrendering some parts of his territories.

The Treaty of Seringapatam was short-lived and the Fourth Mysore War took place in 1799. Tipu died in the battlefield. Some parts of Mysore Kingdom were annexed by the British and some were given to the Nizam of Hyderabad as a reward for his help given to the British in defeating his neighbouring Indian ruler. A child of a Hindu family was placed on the throne of Mysore.

Achievements of Tipu Sultan:

A Far-Sighted Statesman: Tipu Sultan realized fully the design of the British, and attempted to check their influence. He sent his missions to countries lke Afghanistan, Arabia, France and Turkey to seek help against the British.

An Efficient Military Organiser: (i) Tipu made attempts to build a strong navy on modern lines and set up dockyards for this purpose (ii) He maintained a modern arsenal with the help of the French (iii) He trained his army on European lines (iv) The army was equipped with guns and ammunitions (v) He disciplined his army.

An Enlightened Economist Devoted to Progress in Agriculture Trade and Industry

Tipu took several steps to improve the financial position of the state. For this, he fully realised the importance of the development of agriculture, trade and industry. Tipu tried to eliminate the inter-mediaries between the state and the cultivators. He checked the collection of illegal cesses and granted liberal remissions whenever needed. Peasants in Mysore became more prosperous as compared with other states. Several British observers and government officials spoke very highly of the conditions of the peasantry in Mysore under Tipu Sultan. The labour of the peasants was encouraged and well rewarded. About the general economic condition, it was observed that people were prosperous and well cultivated as well.

For the development of trade, Tipu Sultan took the following measures:

(i) He used scales for weights and measures.
(ii) He introduced a new system of coinage.
(iii) He sent emissaries to France, Turkey, Iran and Pegu (Burma) to develop foreign trade.
(iv) He attempted to establish a trading company on the model of European companies to help the Indian traders.
(v) He encouraged trade with China.
(vi) He tried to promote trade with Arabia and Russia by setting up state trading institutions in the port towns.
(vii) He paid stress on the indigenous industries and encouraged the export of goods produced by these industries.
(viii) He imported foreign workmen also to modernise industries in India.

A Good Administrator: Tipu tried to reform every branch of administration.

Encouragement of Art, Literature and Education: He set up a vast library containing books on mathematics, medical science, military science, history and literature.

Religious Toleration: According to some British historians, he was a religious fanatic. But the facts seem to be otherwise. It is true that he was a devoted Muslim but was tolerant towards other faiths. He gave money for the construction of the image of goddess Sharda in the Shringeri Temple. He gave regular gifts to this temple as well as other temples.

Summing up: He was an able administrator, efficient military organiser, great innovator, far-sighted statesman and liberal religious ruler, and yet he failed to protect the kingdom established by his father. Fortune did not favour him.

BENGAL

Bengal remained independent between 1717 and 1765.

Murshid Quli Khan (1717-27)

In 1705, Murshid Quli Khan was appointed the Governor of Bengal by Aurangzeb. Soon he was also made Subedar of Orissa. He transferred his capital from Dacca to Murshidabad and during the rule of the weak successor of Aurangzeb, he founded an independent kingdom of Nawabs of Bengal. He, however, regularly sent large tribute to the Mughal emperor. His important achievements were as under:

(i) He was successful in crushing all the three revolts that took place during his rule.
(ii) He confiscated the jagirs of all those who opposed him and distributed these among his favourites.
(iii) He tried to improve his financial position by reducing the expenditure.
(iv) He made the foreign companies pay the octroi duty like other traders.
(v) He collected the revenue in a strict way.
(vi) He gave *taccavi* loans to the farmers to clear their dues.
(vii) He gave equal opportunities for employment both to the Hindus and the Muslims.
(viii) He appointed Bengalis, mostly Hindus, on various civil and army posts.

Shuja-ud-Din (1727-39)

After the death of Nawab Murshid Quli Khan, his son-in-law Shuja-ud-Din succeeded him in governing Bengal and Orissa. Bihar was also added to his territory and he appointed Ali-vardi Khan as its Deputy Governor. He continued to follow the policies of his father-in-law and maintained peace in the state.

Ali-vardi Khan (1739-56)

After the death of Shuja-ud-Din, his son Sarfaraj Khan became the Nawab but soon Ali-vardi Khan deposed him and he himself became the ruler. He legalised his usurped position by securing an imperial *farman* from Delhi. Like his predecessors, he also took several steps to strengthen the state. He made all possible efforts to keep the foreign companies and officials under his control. He treated the Hindus on equal basis.

Siraj-ud-Daula (1756-57)

He was the grandson of Ali-vardi Khan. He became the Nawab at the age of 23 in 1756 after the death of his grandfather. But peaceful succession is rare in Muslim period. His cousin, the Governor of Purnea and his aunt Ghasiti Begum opposed his accession to the throne and were looking to the British for help. He knew the game the British played in Carnatic and was aware of their design on Bengal. He first crushed the designs of his home rivals. On the other side, the British had become too ambitious and they gave offence to Siraj by abusing their trade privileges and adding to their fortification without Nawab's permission. His orders to dismantle were treated with contempt. This roused Siraj to fury. Acting with great energy and haste but with inadequate preparation, Siraj-ud-Daula seized the English factory and occupied the Fort William at Calcutta. The British officials took refuge at Fulta near the Sea, waited for a large military aid from British Council of Madras and meanwhile organized a web of treachery with Mir Jafar, the commander-in-chief of Nawab's army. Mir Jafar was promised the throne of Bengal. From Madras came a strong naval and military force under Admiral Watson and Colonel Clive.

Calcutta was taken back by the British. The British wanted to remove the Nawab. So they put forward certain demands which the Nawab did not accept. As a result, the fateful battle of Plassey was fought on June 23, 1757. The Nawab's army was defeated due to the treachery of Mir Jafar. The victory of the British paved the way for their mastery of Bengal. Nawab was captured and killed.

The Political Conditions in India During the 18th Century

Mir Jafar (1757-60) and (1763-65)

Mir Jafar was merely a figurehead and the real power was in the hands of Clive with whose help he became the Nawab after deceiving his master, Siraj-ud-Daula. He was unable to fulfil his commitments. He had no money to pay to his soldiers. He also lacked the qualities of a strong and efficient ruler. He was hostile to Hindu officers. In the meanwhile, Mir Qasim, son-in-law of Mir Jafar, began to conspire to be the Nawab of Bengal. He entered into an agreement with the English and promised to pay the money which Mir Jafar was unable to pay. He also agreed to surrender three districts of Burdwan, Midnapore and Chittagong to the Company. In return, Mir Qasim was made the Nawab and Mir Jafar was deposed off. Mir Jafar deserved this fate. He himself had betrayed his master in 1757 to become the Nawab.

Mir Qasim (1763-65)

Mir Qasim had to pay a heavy price to the British to become the Nawab of Bengal. However, he did not like the British interference in the administration of his state. He wanted to pursue an independent policy which led him to clash with the British. He shifted his capital from Murshidabad to Monghyr which was quite away from Culcutta but was in possession of the British. He abolished all the duties on trade, a measure also not liked by the British. He was therefore asked to reintroduce the duties. On his refusal to do so, he was removed from the throne and Mir Jafar was again made the Nawab in 1763. Now Mir Qasim became a dead enemy of the British. He left Bengal and went to Oudh where he formed a Confederacy with Nawab of Oudh, Shuja-ud-Daula, and the Mughal emperor Shah Alam to fight against the British. A battle was fought at Buxar in 1764. Mir Qasim and his other allies were defeated. Mir Qasim died in wilderness.

THE SIKHS

The Sikh Religion: Transformation of a Religious Faith to a Military and Political Power

The Sikh religion was founded by Guru Nanak Dev (1469-1538). The followers of Guru Nanak Dev began to be called Sikhs. The Sikhs were guided in their religious and spiritual matters by the Gurus. There were ten Gurus—Guru Nanak Dev being the first and Guru Gobind Singh (1675-1708) the last. Thereafter, the *Granth Sahib*, the most sacred book of the Sikhs was accepted as their Guru. Under the leadership and inspiration of Guru Gobind Singh, the Sikhs became a political and military force. He waged constant wars against the armies of the Mughal Emperor Aurangzeb.

Banda Bahadur (1670-1715 or 16)

Banda Bahadur's original name was Lachman Dass and he became a 'Bairagi' (renouncer of worldly life). Guru Gobind Singh happened to meet him and prevailed upon him to fight for the cause of the Sikhs and asked his followers to rally under him. Banda Bahadur carried on a vigorous struggle against the Mughals for about eight years. His first important victory was in 1710 over the Mughal Governor of Sirhind. It was a bloody battle. He abolished zamindari and struck coins in the name of Guru. Banda Bahadur captured a vast territory between Lahore and Delhi. But his strength could not match the strength of the Mughal Emperor of Delhi. He was arrested and he along with several Sikh soldiers was excuted.

The Sikhs After the Death of Banda Bahadur:

For about half a century after the death of Banda Bahadur, the Sikhs lost their glory. They had to undergo severe atrocities at the hands of the Mughal governors of the Punjab. The invasions of Ahmad Shah Abdali paved the way for the rise of the Sikhs in Punjab.

The Sikh Misls

There was complete anarchy in Punjab after the invasions of Ahmad Shah Abdali and his departure from India. The Sikhs began to be organised into groups and in due course, twelve strong groups emerged. These groups came to be known as Misls. Ordinarily reference is made to twelve Misls, viz. (i) Srigapuria or Faizalpuria (ii) Ahluwalia (iii) Ramgarhia (iv) Bhangi (v) Kanheyia (vi) Sukarchakya. (vii) Pulkian (viii) Dallewalia (ix) Karorsinghia or Panjgarhia (x) Nishanwalia (xi) Nakkai and (xii) Shahid. These Misls were associations of warriors united by ties of Sikh faith.

The term Misl is an Arabic word, meaning equal or alike. A Misl was democratic in nature because every soldier or member of the Misl enjoyed political and social equality. Each Misl had a Sardar or Misldar at its head. He, however, did not interfere in the day-to-day affairs of his followers. Every village under a Misl was a small republic. There was a panchayat in every village. It is estimated that the combined fighting strength of all the Misls was about one lakh. Sometimes the Misls fought among themselves. At the end of the 18th century, Maharaja Ranjit Singh, Chief of the Sukarchakya Misl of Gujranwala (in West Punjab), succeeded in annexing most of the Misls and established a strong Sikh kingdom in the Punjab.

When only 19 years old, he had helped Zaman Shah, the Afghan ruler of Kabul, in invading the Punjab, and was appointed by him, the Governor of Lahore with the title of Raja (1799). In 1802, Ranjit Singh made himself master of Amritsar and gradually brought all the Sikh misls west of the Sutlej under his control. By degrees he increased his power till he made himself master of the Punjab and Kashmir. He sought to extend his authority over the territory of the Sikh Chieftains east of the Sutlej and occupied Ludhiana. The Sikh chiefs took alarm and appealed to the English for protection. A treaty was signed between the English and Ranjit Singh. A born ruler of men, Ranjit Singh's fame rests on his success in effecting a marvellous transformation of the warring Sikh states into a compact national monarchy.

THE JATS

Suraj Mal

The most glorious period for the Jats was the rule of Suraj Mal (1756-63). The Jats were agriculturists who lived around Delhi, Baghpat and Tilpat, Meerut, Mathura, Agra and Bharatpur etc. Mughal persecution drove them into revolts during the time of Aurangzeb. The Jat state of Bharatpur was founded by Churaman and Badan Singh. The Jat power reached its highest glory under Suraj Mal. Suraj Mal was a far-sighted statesman, an able administrator and a successful commander. He extended his kingdom to the areas covering Agra, Mathura, Hathras, Aligarh, Etawah, Meerut, Rohtak, Rewari, Gurgoan and Mewar. Bharatpur became the centre of his kingdom. After his death in 1763, the Jat kingdom was split up among petty zamindars.

THE RAJPUT STATES

Raja Sawai Jai Singh of Amber (1699 to 1743)

After the death of Aurangzeb, several Rajput states emerged as independent states. Among the most outstanding ruler was Jai Singh, who ruled for about 44 years. He was a great astronomer, builder, engineer, jurist, social reformer and a wise statesman.

Jai Singh erected observatories at Delhi, Jaipur, Mathura, Ujjain and Varanasi. Some of the instruments were of his own invention. His astronomical observations were remarkably accurate. He designed a set of tables called Zij Muhammad Shahi to enable people to make astronomical observations. These observatories are known as 'Jantar Mantars'.

He founded the modern Jaipur, commonly known as the 'Pink City' and made it a great centre of art and

The Political Conditions in India During the 18th Century 17

science. The city was well-planned and built on sound scientific lines. Its wide roads crossing each other at right angles are a testimony of his engineering skill.

Jai Singh was a great literary figure. He got several important works of science and mathematics translated into Sanskrit. Among the important ones, mention may be made of Euclid's *Elements of Geometry* and Napier's work on the construction and use of logarithms.

As a social reformer, Jai Singh tried to enforce a law to reduce the extravagant expenditure which the Rajputs used to incur on their daughter's marriage. He also put a check on the killing of girls at birth by Rajputs.

THE MARATHAS, THEIR RISE AND FALL

Period of Disunity

After Shivaji's death in 1680, the kingdom established by him could not be kept intact by his successors. His son Sambhaji (1680-89) succeeded him but he was not a competent ruler. He was defeated by Aurangzeb in 1689 and tortured to death. He was succeeded by Raja Ram (1689-1700), another son of Shivaji. He also lacked the qualities of his father. He had constant warfare with the Mughals. He died in 1700. After his death, his widow Tara Bai (1700-07), managed the affairs of the state in the name of her son Shivaji II. She was a vigorous lady and possessed a lot of knowledge of civil and military affairs. She was the very soul of Maratha resistance against the Mughals who were successful in dividing the Marathas. Sahu, the grandson of Shivaji and son of Sambhaji, was released after more than 18 years in Mughal captivity. Sahu put forward his claim to the throne, but Tara Bai declared Sahu, an impostor. As planned by the Mughals, a tussle for the throne began between Sahu and Tara Bai. Sahu emerged victorious with the help of Balaji, a Maratha Sardar. Internal discords continued. Tarabai was still powerful at Kolhapur, although she had lost Satara to Sahu. Sambhaji II, the son of another widow of Raja Ram was also a constant nuisance. The two wives of Sahu indulged in intrigues.

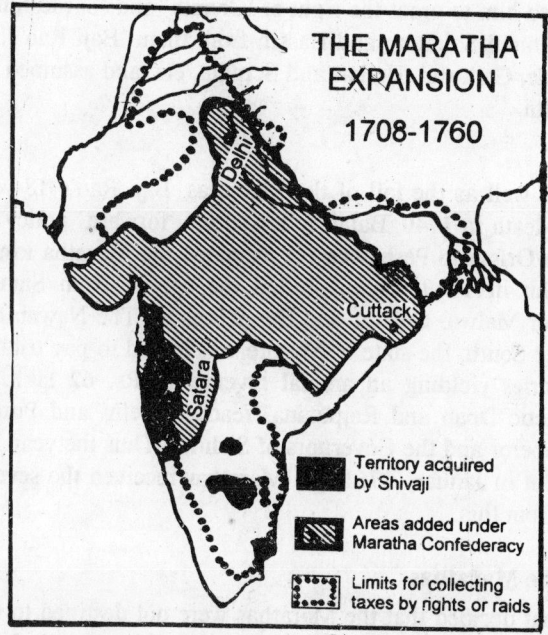

Map 5: **The Maratha Expansion 1708-1760**

The Rule of the Peshwas

Sahu was successful in his struggle against Tara Bai with the help of Balaji Vishwanath, who was his loyal minister. In appreciation of his services, Sahu made him a Peshwa (Chief Minister). Since Sahu was a weak ruler, Balaji was able to concentrate all power of the state in his office. With this started the rule of the 'Peshwas'. The office of the 'Peshwa', in due course became hereditary. The subsequent 'Peshwas' became the real rulers of the kingdom and the king was reduced to a figurehead and ruled in name only. The regime of the Peshwas continued during the period 1713 to 1760.

Balaji Vishwanath (1714-20):

He excelled in diplomacy. He was able to unite a large number of Maratha Sardars under one banner. He made friendship with the Saiyid Brothers, dethroned Mughal emperor Farrukh Siyar and put Muhammad Shah (Rangila) on the Mughal throne. Balaji got three concessions from the Mughal ruler which proved to be very helpful in stregthening the Maratha power. These were as under:

(a) The Marathas got the right to collect 'chauth' (one fourth share) of the revenues of the Deccan and Southern India, including Hyderabad, Carnatic and Mysore.
(b) The Marathas got the right of 'Sardeshmukhi' (one-tenth) of the revenue over and above the 'Chauth'.
(c) The Marathas's right of control over all the territories earlier held by Shivaji was accepted by the Mughal ruler.

Baji Rao I (1720-40):

After Balaji's death in 1720, his 20-year old son Baji Rao became the Peshwa. Next to Shivaji, he is considered to be the bravest and the most shrewd Maratha Chief. He was a master in the 'guerilla' warfare. He died in 1740 and with him faded the glory of the Maratha power. The Marathas never regained the prestige and power which they enjoyed under him. Under his leadership, the Marathas led many successful campaigns against the Mughal empire. They won over Malwa, Gujarat and some parts of Bundelkhand, defeated the Nizam of Hyderabad and forced him to grant the right of 'Chauth' and 'Sardeshmukhi'. They also invaded the Portuguese territories and captured Salesette and Bassin from them. Baji Rao I formed a confederacy of the Marathas consisting of Bhonsle, Gaikwad, Holkar and Scindia, etc. and assumed its leadership. The Marathas plundered the outskirts of Delhi.

Balaji Baji Rao (1740-61):

The period saw the rise as well as the fall of the Marathas. Baji Rao's 18-year old son, Balaji Baji Rao, became the Peshwa after his death in 1740. Balaji followed the 'forward' policy of his father. His slogan was "Cuttack to Attock" i.e. from Orissa to Peshawar. He extended the Maratha kingdom in different directions. After the death of king Sahu in 1749, Balaji shifted the capital from Satara to Poona. The Marathas consolidated their control over Malwa, Gujarat and Bundelkhand. The Nawab of Bengal was forced to cede Orissa to the Marathas. In the South, the state of Mysore was forced to pay tribute. The Nizam of Hyderabad had to part with vast territories yielding an annual revenue of Rs. 62 lakh. In the north, the Marathas marching through the Gangetic Doab and Rajputana, reached Delhi and Punjab. The Marathas collected tributes from the Mughal Emperor and the Governors of Sirhind. Thus the year 1760 marked the phenomenal rise of the Maratha power. But in January 1761, the Marathas received the severest blow from Ahmad Shah Abdali and never recovered from this.

Causes of the Downfall of the Marathas

The Third Battle of Panipat decided that the Marathas were not destined to rule India after the decline of the Mughal power. Only for a while, after their defeat at the hands of Abdali, they could get some of their lost power, but the English proved to be very strong and they annexed most of the territories which were once

under the Marathas. Following were the main reasons of their downfall:
(i) Weak successors of Shivaji
(ii) Mutual distrust and jealousy of the Maratha Sardars
(iii) Poor economy and bad financial position
(iv) Policy of aggression, loot and plunder
(v) Traditional methods of warfare
(vi) Outmoded war weapons
(vii) Lack of organisation and discipline in the army
(viii) High handedness of the Maratha Sardars
(ix) Lack of diplomacy
(x) Neglect of seapower
(xi) Crushing blow by Ahmad Shah Abdali in the Third Battle of Panipat
(xii) British power and diplomacy.

KERALA

In the beginning of the 18th Century, there were several petty chiefs and nobles having small territories. By 1763, three feudal states emerged in Kerala. These were: Calicut, Cochin and Travancore. In 1766 Hyder Ali of Mysore annexed Kerala upto Cochin, including the territories of Calicut.

Travancore

There were two important Kings of Kerala during the 18th century—King Martanda Varma and his successor Rama Varma.

King Martanda:

He was one of the leading statesmen of the 18th century who ruled in the first half of the century. He possessed a rare foresight, strong determination and courage.

His chief achievements were:

(i) Organisation of a strong army (ii) Establishment of foundries to make new weapons (iii) Subjugation of the feudal elements through relentless military action (iv) Building roads (v) Constructing canals (vi) Encouraging foreign trade (vii) Extending boudaries of his state from Kanyakumari to Cochin.

Rama Varma:

He was known for the following.
(i) He himself was a famous actor, musician, poet and fluent speaker in English and was keenly interested in European affairs.
(ii) Promotion of the Malayalam literature.
(iii) Trivandrum, the capital of Travancore became a great centre of Sanskrit learning.

BANGASH PATHANS AND ROHILLAS

The Rohillas were ethnically, Pathans. They nursed amibition to carve out independent kingdom of their own in the Gangetic Valley, in the early 18th Century. Khan Bangash was their leader who probably was a Jat by origin but was brought up by an Afghan Officer named Daud. During the rule of the Mughal emperor Farukh-Siyar (1713-19), he established his control over the territory around Farrukhabad, between Aligarh and Kanpur. Following Nadir Shah's invasion, Ali Muhammad Khan established a separate principality, known as Rohilkhand at the foothills of the Himalayas between the Ganga in the south and the Kumaon hills in the north. He first established his capital at Aolan in Bareilly and later shifted it to Rampur. The Rohillas clashed constantly with Awadh and Delhi, and with the Jats and the Marathas. In 1774, the Nawab of Awadh, with the help of the East India Company, annexed Oudh and Hafiz Rahmat Khan, the leader of Rohillas was killed.

EXERCISES

A. Very Short Answer Type Questions (Answer in 20 to 30 Words)

1. Why is the 18th Century in India called the darkest period in its history?
2. Mention any two important characteristics of political conditions in India.
3. "None of the Mughal rulers of the eighteenth century died a natural death". Point out four names and indicate how their lives ended.
4. Why was Muhammad Shah nicknamed as 'Rangila'?
5. Why is Jahandar Shah called utterly degenerate?
6. Why were the Saiyid Brothers called the 'King Makers'?
7. What is 'Guerilla Warfare'?
8. Mention two significant contributions of Tipu Sultan in administration.
9. How was an independent state established in Carnatic in the 18th century?
10. Give the two main achievements of the Nawabs of Bengal in the 18th century.

B. Short Answer Type Questions

1. Why did the Battle of Buxar take place? State its impact.
2. What were the causes of the Battle of Plassey? What was its impact on the British power in India?
3. Assess the character and achievements of Hyder Ali of Mysore.
4. How did the Peshwas come to power? What was their main contribution to the state?
5. Explain the word 'Misl'. How did the Misls come into being?

C. Essay Type Questions

1. What were the causes leading to the invasions of Nadir Shah? Give a brief account of his invasion. What was its impact on the Mughal rule?
2. Why did Ahmad Shah Abdali invade India? State the reason of his suceess against the Marathas. What were the effects of the Third Battle of Panipat?
3. "The Third Battle of Panipat sealed the fate of the Maratha power". Explain this statement.
4. What were the chief causes of the failure of the Marathas to establish their supremacy in India?
5. Write notes on the following:-
    (a) Banda Bahadur
    (b) Maharaja Suraj Mal
    (c) Sawai Raja Jai Singh
6. Who is called the 'Tiger of Mysore'? State his chief reforms in administration, military, agriculture, trade and industry.

D. Map Work

1. On an outline map of India, show the extent of the Maratha power in 1760.
2. On an outline map of India, indicate the areas under various political powers in India in 1765 or 1766.

CHAPTER 2

Indian Society in the 18th Century
(Social and Economic Conditions)

DARK PERIOD OF SOCIO-ECONOMIC LIFE

In general it may be observed that India during the 18th century failed to make progress in any area of national life - cultural, economic, educational, political and social. Rather, conditions deteriorated in all these fields. Following were the important factors that led to this sorry state of affairs:

(i) Very little of law and order was left, almost nearing political anarchy (ii) Increasing revenue demands of the state on the people (iii) Oppression of the Indian officials (iv) The greed of the nobles (v) The marches and countermarches of the rival armies (vi) Loot and plunder of the foreign invaders (vii) Trade routes infested with robbers (viii) Growing interference of the European powers in the affairs of India (ix) Extortion of money by the officials of the East India Company.

MAIN FEATURES

Firstly, the *Stagnating Society* had lost all vigour, creativity and resourcefulness. There was stagnation and dependence on the traditional past. Secondly, *the society was sharply* divided on the basis of religion, region, caste, tribe and language, etc. Thirdly, the *caste system* divided both the Hindus and the Muslims. Apart from the traditional four varnas, Hindus were divided into numerous castes (jatis) which differed in nature from place to place. Caste rules were extremely rigid with caste regulations regarding interdining and intermarriage among members of different castes. Untouchability was practised widely. Caste system was a great barrier in emotional and national integration of the society.

Although, Islam enjoins social equality, there were divisions in the Muslim society. The Shias and the Sunnis-two important religious sects of the Muslims were sometimes at loggerheads on account of their religious differences. Often the Afghani, the Hindustani, the Irani and the Turani Muslim nobles and officials stood apart from one another.

Fourthly, *the family system* was basically patriarchal i.e. the family was dominated by the senior male member. In Kerala, however, the family was matriarchal. Fifthly, the *position of women* was vulnerable. Following were the chief features:
(i) Women in general possessed little individuality of their own.
(ii) Women of upper classes were not supposed to work outside their homes. However, there were exceptions. Tara Bai of Kolhapur and Ahilya Bai of Indore ruled in their regions. Women of the lower classes usually worked outside, in the fields and at other places.
(iii) Purdah was a common practice among the upper class women in the North.
(iv) Polygamy was a common feature.

(v) Widow remarriage, especially among the higher classes and castes was uncommon. The life of a widow was very miserable.
(vi) The custom of *sati* was prevalent in Rajputana, Bengal and other parts in North India. It was mostly practised by the upper classes.
(vii) The custom of early marriage of girls was common in several parts of India.
(viii) Boys and girls were not permitted to mix with each other.
(ix) Education of girls and women was rare phenomenon.

Sixthly, the *marriage system* was encumbered with dowry demands bringing misery to the helpless parents with limited means. It also encouraged heavy expenses for massive and dazzling displays on a competitive spirit among the wealthy classes.

Seventhly, *moral degeneration* was evident on account of enormous wealth among the nobles. Most of them had scant regard for virtues like faithfulness, gratitude and loyalty. The dominant feature of life was single-minded pursuit for power and wealth. The common people were comparatively free from these declining morals.

Finally there was great disparity in living standards. The rich lived in plenty and luxury and the poor who formed three-fourth of the population lived in poverty and misery.

Economic Condition

Chief characteristics of the economic conditions of the people during the eighteenth century were the following:

(1) India was a land of contrasts. Extreme poverty existed side by side with extreme riches and luxury. (2) Agriculture was backward and stagnant. (3) There was decline in internal trade and commerce. (4) Foreign trading companies were making huge profits. (5) Indian indigenous industries received a set-back. (6) The village economy was more or less self-dependent and self-sufficient.

Worsening Indian Agriculture:

Indian agriculture was in a bad shape. The condition of Indian peasants was very poor. They were faced with increasing burden of the land revenue and were oppressed by the nobles and big zamindars. No attempts were made to increase production per acre. The methods of production remained outmoded. There was lack of technology. The soil was gradually losing its fertility. The peasants were poor and were not in a position to invest anything in agriculture to improve it. They lived at the subsistence level. They were exploited by several sections of the society—the state, the nobles, the jagirdars, the zamindars and the revenue officials.

Decline in Internal Trade:

Some of the important reasons for the decline of internal trade were:

(i) The means of communication were backward (ii) Trade routes were infested with bands of robbers and thugs which made trade unsafe (iii) The rise of independent local chiefs and small kingdoms led to an increase in the number of custom houses and octroi chowkies. Heavy duties were imposed on various items of trade (iv) The impoverishment of the nobles, who were the largest consumers of luxurious articles also adversely affected the trade (v) Trading centres were looted by the invaders (vi) There were no patrons to promote trade and commerce (vii) Nadir Shah attacked Lahore and Delhi. Agra was affected by the rebellious Jats. Surat was repeatedly plundered by the Marathas. Sirhind was plundered by the Sikhs. Besides, the mutual rivalry of warring camps created such political instability which disrupted and discouraged trade and commerce.

Trade with the West :

Foreign trade of India continued to flourish in the 18th century. Following were its chief characteristics.
(i) India's most important article of export was cotton textile. It had a wide market all over the world for its excellent quality.

Indian Society in the 18th Century 23

(ii) Apart from cotton textile, other items of export were: raw silk and silk fabrics, hardware, indigo, saltpetre, opium, rice, wheat, sugar, pepper and other spices, drugs and precious stones.
(iii) India imported dates, dry fruits, pearls, raw silk, rose water and wool from the Persian Gulf region.
(iv) India imported coffee, drugs, gold and honey from Arabia.
(v) Porcelain, silk, sugar and tea from China were imported.
(vi) India imported gold, musk and woollen cloth from Tibet.
(vii) India's imports from Indonesian Islands included arrack, perfumes, spices and sugar.
(viii) Tin was the chief item of import from Singapore.
(ix) From Africa, India imported drugs and ivory.
(x) India's items of import from European countries were metals such as copper, iron and lead, paper and woollen cloth.
(xi) The main centres for European trade in India included Ahmedabad, Broach, Cambay, Surat, Masulipatnam, Nagapatnam, Visakapatnam, Calicut, Cochin, Madras, Bombay, Goa and Daman.

Important industries and industrial centres in India

In spite of the adverse political situation in India, several industries and industrial centres came up during the 18th century on account of the close interaction between India and the European trading companies.

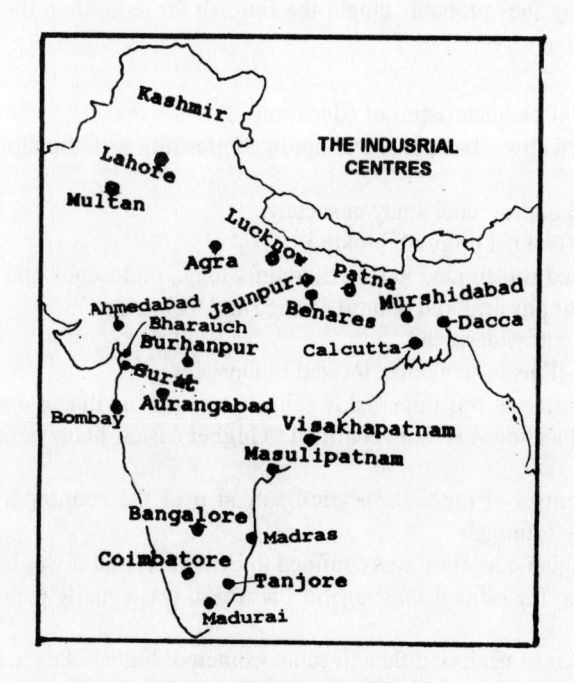

Map 6: **Industrial Centres**

Emergence of local nobility and zamindars led to the coming up of new cities such as Faizabad, Lucknow, Varanasi and Patna.

Indian artisans still enjoyed reputation all over the world for their skill and fine qualities of work.

India remained a large scale manufacturer of cotton and silk fabrics, dyestuffs, jute, minerals, sugar and metal products like arms, metawares, saltpetre and oils.

Following chart lists the important industries and centres.

Industry	Industrial Centre/Centres
1. Textile industry especially sarees	Dacca and Murshidabad (Bengal), Patna (Bihar), Surat, Ahmedabad and Broach (Gujarat), Aurangabad (Maharashtra), Burhanpur (Madhya Pradesh), Jampur, Benaras, Lucknow and Agra (U.P.). Masulipatnam, Chicacole and Visakhapatnam (Andhra). Bangalore (Karnataka). Coimbatore (Tanjore) and Madurai (Tamil Nadu). Multan and Lahore (Punjab).
2. Woollen Industry	Kashmir
3. Ship building	Maharashtra

Indian ship building industry was very popular in European countries. Ships made in India were of such a high quality that European companies bought several Indian made ships. In this regard, an English observer remarked, "In ship-building they probably taught the English far more than they learnt from them".

Education

Following were the chief characteristics of education:
1. On the whole it was defective, traditional and not in comformity with the rapid developments taking place in the west at that time.
2. It neglected the factual and rational study of society.
3. It emphasised memory and not original thinking.
4. The knowledge imparted was limited to law, literature, logic, philosophy and religion.
5. It neglected the study of physical and natural science and technology.
6. Elementary education was widespread.
7. The Maulvi taught Muslims in 'maktabs' located in mosques.
8. Among the Hindus, education was imparted in schools situated in villages and towns.
9. Though elementary education was more confined to higher castes, many persons from the lower classes also received it.
10. There were several centres of higher education spread over the country which were usually financed by Nawabs, Rajas and big Zamindars.
11. Among the Hindus, higher education was confined to Brahmans and it was based on Sanskrit.
12. Persian language being the official language of the times, was equally popular among the Hindus and the Muslims.
13. Girls education was almost neglected though some women of higher classes received education.
14. The teachers enjoyed high prestige in society.

Culture

Culture on the whole remained traditional. It was rather monotonous and ritualistic. In the past, cultural activities were patronised by nobles, Nawabs and the Zamindars. The rulers in the past also played an important role in the cultural development. In the eighteenth century, there was little political stability and the patrons of culture were also faced with financial difficulties. These two factors led to stagnation in cultural development.

Indian Society in the 18th Century

Following were the main developments.

Architecture:

Architecture in general declined. However, the Imambara of Lucknow presented some new ventures in architecture. The Rajput style seemed to have reached its peak. The city of Jaipur and its buildings were the hallmarks of Rajput architecture.

Music:

Music which had gone to background during the reign of Aurangzeb made significant progress under the rule of Mohammad Shah.

Painting:

Several of the renowed painters of the Mughal court migrated to provincial courts and flourished at Hyderabad, Patna, Lucknow and Kashmir. At the same time, new schools of painting emerged and achieved distinction. The Himachal or Pahari and the Rajasthani schools of painting exhibited new creativity and vitality in style.

Urdu and Urdu Literature:

Urdu gradually became the medium of communication especially among the upper classes of North India. There was growth of Urdu literature. Urdu poetry produced brilliant and illustrious poets like Mir, Sauda and Nazir. Mirza Ghalib, the great genius among the literary figures, flourished in the 19th century.

Literature in Languages other than Urdu:

The Travancore rulers gave great encouragement to Malyalam literature. Kuncham Nambiar, one of the great poets of Kerala, lived at that time. *Kalhakali* literature also developed.

Tayaumanakar (1706-44) was one of the best exponents of 'sittar' poetry in Tamil.

The Tanjore rulers gave great encouragement to dance, music and poetry.

Ahom kings of Assam gave great patronage to Assamese literature.

In Gujrat, Dayaram was known for his lyrics.

Warris Shah composed his famous romantic epic 'Heer Ranjha' in Punjabi.

Sindhi literature also witnessed enormous growth. Shah Abdul Latif composed 'Risalo' — the famous collection of poems.

Hindu Muslim Relations

Political Life Free from Religious Fanatacism:

The post Aurangzeb period saw little fanatacism in the political life of the country. The entire country was almost free from religious complexes and consideration. Several Mughal rulers like Bahadur Shah and Farrukh Siyar abolished the pilgrimage tax and 'Jazia' in deference to the Hindu sentiments. Nizam-ul-Mulk of Hyderabad, Saadat Khan of Awadh (Oudh), Ali Vardi Khan of Bengal, Hyder Ali and Tipu Sultan of Mysore were above religious considerations. Likewise, Shivaji of Maharashtra, Jai Singh of Amber, Suraj Mal of Bharatpur and Ranjit Singh of the Punjab were broadminded and free from narrow religious feelings. In the Third Battle of Panipat, the chief of the Maratha artillery was a Muslim.

Sufi Cult and Bhakti Movement:

The Sufi saints and the Bhakti saints influenced the religious environment which was conducive to amicable contacts, mutual understanding and religious toleration.

Cultural Impact:

Several Hindu writers wrote in Persian and many Muslim writers wrote in Hindi, Bengali and other Vernacular languages. This cultural integration had a soothing effect on religious feelings.

Celebration of Festivals:

The Muslim rulers and nobles took great interest and participated in the Hindu festivals of Holi, Diwali and Durga Pooja. Similarly the Hindus participated in the Muharram processions and other festivals of the Muslims.

Donation to Places of Worship:

The Marathas gave financial support to the shrine of Shaikh Muinuddin Chisti in Ajmer and the Raja of Tanjore supported the Shrine of Shaikh Shahul. Tipu Sultan gave support to various Hindu temples.

EXERCISES

A. Very Short Answer Type Questions

1. Give any two reasons for the deterioration of the economic condition in India during the 18th century.
2. Give two reasons for the decline of agriculture in India during the 18th century.
3. Give two reasons for the decline of internal trade in India in the 18th century.
4. Give four items of import into India.
5. Give four items of export from India.

B. Short Answer Type Questions

1. Give the main features of education in India in the 18th century.
2. Describe the chief characteristics of religious relations among the Hindus and the Muslims.
3. Give four features of the cultural life of the people of India in the 18th century.
4. "Education in India in the 18th century was defective." State any three reasons.
5. "Hindu Muslim relations were cordial in the 18th century." Explain.
6. State the political factors which contributed to the decline of trade and industry in the later Mughal period.
7. Name the important industries and the industrial centres in India during the 18th century.
8. Explain how the caste rules were becoming rigid.
9. Give examples to show how various rulers showed due respect to other religions.
10. "The cultural life in India degenerated in the 18th century". Elucidate.

CHAPTER 3

The Beginning of European Settlements in India

GOLD, GLORY AND GOD: DISCOVERY OF TRADE ROUTES

The discovery of trade routes in the 15th century was the outcome of three motives of the European nations. Of course, in the beginning, the main motives were acquiring of gold and glory. The third motive of promoting Christianity (in the name of spreading the glory of God) was a by-product. The Renaissance and the Reformation movements had led to the development of the spirit of inquiry and discovery.

Portugal was the first European country to embark upon 'Voyages of Discovery' for earning profits through trade. Even before Vasco-Da-Gama, several other Portuguese adventurers had attempted to sail round several countries. In 1498, an epoch making event took place in the history of the world when Vasco-Da-Gama of Portugal, discovered a new sea-route from Europe to India. He sailed round Africa via the cape of Good Hope and reached Calicut. Vasco-Da-Gama found that the price of pepper in Calicut was one-twenty-sixth of the price prevailing in Venice (Portugal). With the discovery of the trade route to the East, the Portugese were able to establish a big trade with India, Java, Sumatra, East India and Ceylon. He returned with a cargo which sold for sixty times the cost of his voyage. When he returned to Portugal, the king of Portugal received him with great honour. In 1501, Vasco-Da-Gama came to India for the second time and established a factory at Cannanore and returned to Portugal in 1503.

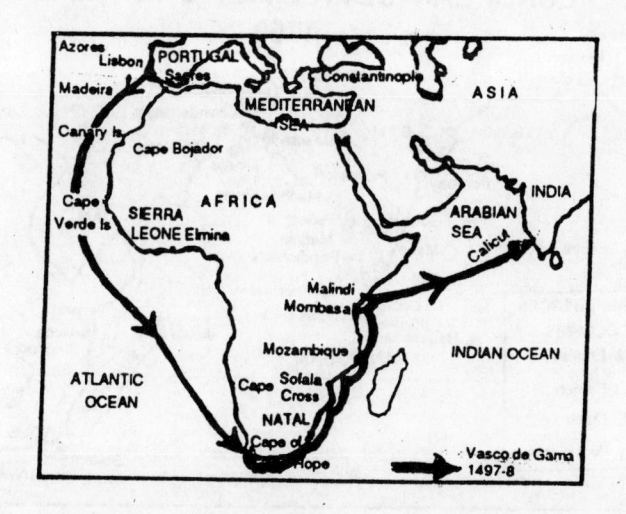

Map 7: **Route of Vasco-Da-Gama (1497)**

Most Immediate Cause that Led to the Discovery of the New Sea-Route to India

In the 15th century, the Turks took possession of the city of Constantinople which cut off Europe from Asian trade.

All land and sea routes were practically blocked for the Christian countries of Europe. The Turks and the Europeans were on the warpath. It, therefore, became necessary for the European nations to find new sea-routes to trade with India. There were two compelling reasons for this. One was that Europe needed spices from India and other Asian countries for preserving meat—the main diet of the Europeans. Another reason was that a number of traders in the cities of Europe depended on Asian trade.

The traders were followed by the missionaries. In due course, the traders formed trading companies which became so powerful that they began to interfere in the political affairs of India and succeeded in establishing their settlements.

FROM TRADERS TO COLONISERS

Portugal was joined by Holland, England, France and Denmark in the race for trade with India. The trading companies of Europe brought goods from India at cheap rates and sold them in the European markets at very high prices. Saltpetre was bought, as it was needed in the manufacture of gunpowder. Indigo was needed for dying cloth. Cotton textiles prepared on Indian handlooms were very popular in European circles.

In the coastal areas, many factories came to be established. These factories produced goods that were readily purchased by the European traders. The respective governments of the trading companies gave help and support to them. In due course of time, some of these European trading companies came into direct competition and conflict with each other. They tried to establish their empires.

The British succeeded in ousting the French, the Dutch, the Spanish, and the Portuguese. One by one they annexed the Indian states and ultimately became the masters of the country in which they had once come to seek permission to trade. For about 200 years, the British ruled over the territories that now comprise India, Bangladesh, Pakistan, Myanmar (Burma) and Sri Lanka (Ceylon).

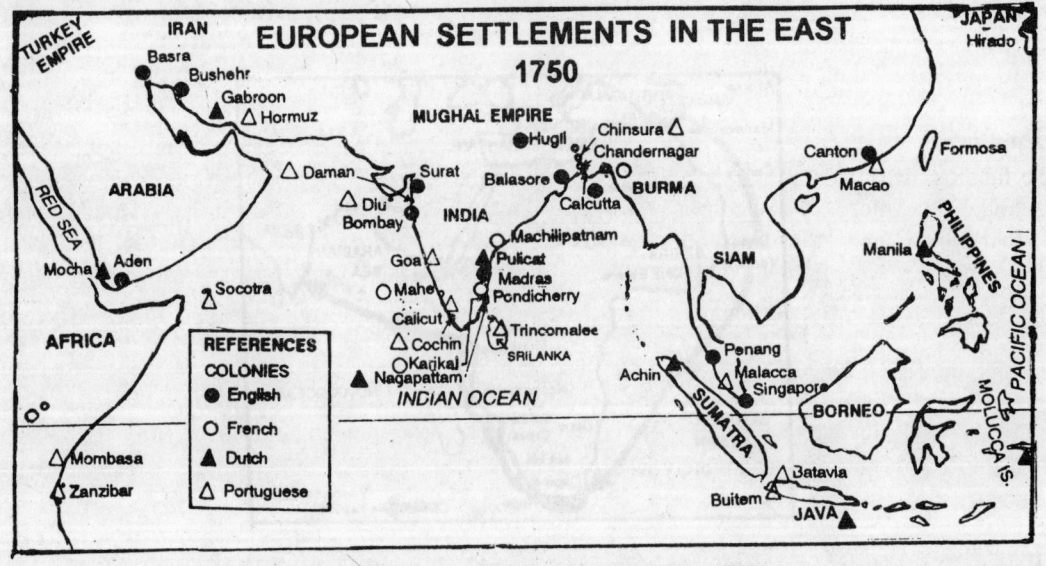

Map 8: **European Settlements in the East 1750**

The Portuguese in India

The First to Come:

The Portuguese, who were the first to establish themselves in the field of eastern trade, enjoyed the monopoly of trade for about a century. It was shattered by the British in 158 by defeating the Spanish Armada. Spain captured Portugal. Thus the Portuguese failed to establish themselves in India. They were left with a small territory of Goa, Daman and Diu. These territories, however, remained under the Portuguese even after India's independence. In 1961, Goa, along with Daman and Diu was made an integral part of India. Goa was conferred statehood on May 30, 1987 and Daman and Diu combined made a separate Union Territory.

De Almeida (1505-09) and Albuquerque (1509-15):

De Almeida, the first viceroy of the Portuguese could remain the ruler for about four years only. He and his son were defeated and killed in 1509 by the Egyptians. Albuquerque is usually called the founder of the Portuguese empire in India. He was a great conqueror and efficient administrator and possessed a commanding character. On account of his sterling qualities he was called 'Albuquerque, the Great' by his countrymen. He conquered Goa in 1510 from the Sultan of Bijapur and made it the capital of Portuguese possessions in India. The Portuguese empire in India extended to over 150 km along the West Coast of India. It included Diu, Daman, Bassein, Salesette and Goa. The Portuguese also established their colonies at Chittagong and Hoogly in Bengal.

Downfall:

From the beginning of the 17th century, the power of the Portuguese began to decline. Ultimately they were uprooted from India. The following causes were responsible for their failure in India.

(i) After the death of Albuquerque, no strong officer was sent to India by the Government of Portugal.
(ii) Corruption was rampant in the Portuguese administration in India.
(iii) The Portuguese missionaries adopted coercive measures to convert people of India to Christianity.
(iv) The resources of the Portuguese were divided between their possessions in India and Brazil. After sometime the Portuguese began to take more interest in Brazil than in India.
(v) The defeat of Spanish Armada in 1588 enabled England and Holland to use the Cape of Good Hope route. Portugal had already become a Spanish dependency in 1580. In this way, the Dutch replaced the Portuguese in Indonesia, whereas the English did the same in India and Ceylon.

The Dutch in India

The fabulous wealth of India and the huge profits made by the Portuguese traders in India tempted the Dutch traders to explore trade opportunities in India. In 1592, a few merchants formed the Dutch Company. In 1595, four Dutch ships sailed to India and returned with large cargo. The success was so great that many trading companies were started. In 1602, all the Dutch Companies were amalgamated into the Dutch East India Company. The Dutch ships were better designed and faster than those of the Portuguese. They soon managed to capture all Portuguese settlements in the East Indies and the entire trade came in their hands.

In India, the Dutch established their trading centres at Surat, Baroach, Cambay and Ahmedabad in Gujarat, Cochin in Kerala, Nagapatnam in Madras, Masultipatnam in Andhra, Chinsura in Bengal, Patna in Bihar and Agra in Uttar Pradesh. They exported indigo, silk, cotton textiles, saltpetre and opium from India. The Dutch power in India was, however, completely wiped out by the British in the 18th century. They concentrated their entire attention on the East Indies.

The British in India

The year 1588 A.D. and the year 1600 A.D. are among the important days in the history of England. In the year 1588, England gave a crushing defeat to the 'invincible' Spanish Armada and established its naval supremacy. This victory made England the foremost power in the World. The British merchants had been greatly attracted by the highly profitable trade of the Portuguese with India but they were not very sure of the strength of their naval power. Now this naval victory encouraged them to embark upon trade adventures with the east. They also thought of establishing their colonies. In 1600, the British East India Company was set up It ultimately paved the way for the British to establish their rule over the vast territories of the world. In the subsequent 17th and 18th centuries, they began to occupy so many countries that it was said that the 'sun never sets in the British empire'. A small group of merchants of London combined to form the British East India Company in 1600 and got permission of their government to carry on trade with India and East Indies and several countries of Africa and Asia. Queen Elizabeth I became a shareholder of the Company.

Trade Concession and Establishment of Factories:

In 1608, Captain Hawkins came to the court of Mughal emperor Jahangir and was successful in getting certain concessions for the British. In 1608, the British set up their first factory at Surat and in 1611 at Masulipatnam. In 1615, James I, King of England sent Sir Thomas Roe as his ambassador at Jahangir's court. The British were permitted to set up factories in various parts of India.

The Portuguese were greatly upset with the success of the British Company. Fierce naval battles were fought between them. However, the British won and subsequently established their factories at Baroach, Ahmedabad and Agra.

From Factory to Forts:

In 1639 A.D., the factory set up at Masulipatnam was shifted to Madras. At that time, Madras was a small fishing village. The British Company purchased this village from a local Raja and built its first fort at Madras and named it Fort St. George.

It may be remembered that from the very beginning the British tried to combine trade with diplomacy.

In 1651, the Company set up a factory at Hugli.

In 1688, the British Company acquired Bombay from king Charles II of England at an annual rent of £10. Charles II who married Queen Catherine Braganza, sister of the king of Portugal, got Bombay as part of his dowry.

In 1690, the British Company purchased the villages of Sutanuti, Govindpur and Kalicuta. With the passage of time, a big town grew up around these villages and the town came to be known as Calcutta.

In 1717, the Mughal Emperor Farrukh Siyar allowed the British to trade freely in Bengal, Bihar and Orissa in lieu of only Rs.3,000 per annum. Now the Company concentrated in capturing territories in India. In doing so they had to face confrontation with the French in India. Ultimately, the British were successful. They also had to wage several wars with various powerful Indian rulers. By following the policy of 'Divide and Rule', they were able to extend their control over the whole of India. Their rule in India lasted for about two centuries.

Internal Organisation of the Company:

The East India Company was floated by merchants but it had the great support of the British Government. The Charter of 1657 provided that anyone could become a member of the Company by paying an entrance fee of £5 and by subscribing at least £100 to the stock of the Company. The member could vote in the general meeting only if he had stock worth £500.

In 1661, the Company was authorised to send ships of war with men, women and ammunition, for the security of their factories. They could also erect forts. The Charter Act of 1683 gave the Company full power to declare war and peace with any power. The Charter Act of 1686 authorised the Company to issue coins.

The Beginning of European Settlements in India

Organistion of Company's Factories in India:

Immediately after establishing their trade on a sound basis in India, the Company began to establish factories at prominent places. On the premises of the factory itself, godowns, offices and residential houses were generally built. In due course, the factory premises assumed the shape of some sort of a fort. These premises were called factories although goods were not manufactured in these factories. In fact, these places stored merchandise.

The employees of these factories fell under three categories—clerks, workers and traders.

A Governor was the overall administrator of all these factories. He was advised and guided by a Council. His powers were not unlimited. Besides the Council, a separate Minister in England looked after its affairs.

The Company's servants were paid very low salaries. To supplement their income, they were permitted to carry on private trade within the country and from this they made huge profits. Often in India, they indulged in malpractices to increase their personal gains.

Lord Clive: The Founder of the British Empire In India:

Lord Clive, the founder of the British empire in India, started his career as a clerk in the East India Company and bored with his routine in the office, he twice tried to commit suicide. Later on he left this job and joined the British army, where he made astonishing progress. Ultimately, twice he was appointed as the Governor of the East India Company. His achievements may be categorised under three heads namely (i) Military achievements (ii) Revenue Achievements and (iii) Administrative achievements.

(i) *Military Achievements:* These include (a) The seige of Arcot in 1751 A.D. with just a few hundred soldiers and giving a severe blow to the French power (b) Victory in the Battle of Plassey in 1757 and establishing supremacy in Bengal.

(ii) *Revenue Achievements:* With the Treaty of Allahabad in 1765, the English obtained the 'Diwani' revenue rights from the Mughal ruler in Bengal which strengthened the financial position of the company.

(iii) *Administrative Achievements:* Clive reorganised the adminstrative set up of the company and increased its profits. He checked corruption.

The French in India

Following the example of the Portuguese, the Dutch and the English, the French also formed the French East India Company in 1664. The French Government took a keen interest in the establishment of this Company. The first French factory was established at Surat in 1667. Francis Carton was nominated as its Director-General. Another French factory was established at Masulipatnam in 1669. The King of Golkunda freed the Company from import and export duty. After Carton, Mastin became the Director General of the Company. Under his leadership, the Company founded the settlement of Pondicherry. Another important settlement was Chandernagar, near Calcutta. In due course, the Company established several colonies and among the important ones were the colonies at Mahe and Karaikal where the French Company posed a serious challenge to the British Company. Ultimately after a fierce struggle for supremacy, the English won. The French territories of Pondicherry, Karaikal, Mahe, yanas (South India) and Chandernagar in Bengal became free from French control on November 1, 1954 and became an integral part of India.

Dupleix (1742-1754):

Dupleix was the French Governor of Pondicherry in India. He wanted to establish the supremacy of the French in India over the British. Initially in the Carnatic Wars, he won some success but later on, his diplomacy and military skill could not match the British. He was recalled by the French Government and he died in poverty and despair. Dupleix remained in India for about 12 years.

WARS OF DOMINATION

The Anglo-French Struggle in South India

The English and the French fought fierce wars for about 20 years between 1746 and 1763 to obtain India - 'the jewel of the east' as booty. These wars, known as Carnatic Wars, sealed the fate of the French and paved the way for the British domination over India.

The main trading centres of the British East India Company in the 18th century were Bombay, Karwal, Cananore, Madras and Calcutta while the French had Chandernagar, Masulipatnam, Pondicherry, Karaikal and Surat.

Important Causes of the Conflict:

The conflict between the English and the French took place on account of the following reasons:-

1. *Trade Rivalry:* The English and the French trading companies were constantly trying to outdo each other in trade. Both were trading almost in similar commodities and same areas. Rivalry, therefore, was inevitable in trade.

2. *Traditional Rivalry:* England and France were both neighbours in Europe. They had a long-standing political rivalry. This rivalry was carried over to the colonies established by them.

3. *Unstable Political Situation in India:* The 18th century is regarded as the 'Dark-Age' in the history of India. The Mughal power had almost disappeared in India and there was no power to replace it. There were four important powers in South India - the Marathas, the Nizam of Hyderabad, the Nawab of Carnatic and the Sultan of Mysore. They posed threat to each other to establish supremacy. This provided a good opportunity to the English and the French to increase their power.

4. *Struggle for Succession to the Throne of Different States:* There were three important cases of succession to the throne of Tanjore, Carnatic and Hyderabad. The English and the French sided with the opposite claimants to the throne.

5. *War in the Continent of Europe:* Whenever there was a war between England and France in Europe, it had its repurcussions on their counterpart trading companies in India. Thus, when the Seven Years War and the Austrian War of succession were fought in Europe, there were wars in India between the British and the French.

6. *Close Proximity of the English and the French Territories in India:* Both the Companies had established their factories and settlements quite close to each other. This also became one of the factors of conflict.

Carnatic Wars

The First Carnatic War (1746-48):

Causes:

War known as the Austrian War of Succession broke out in Europe, in 1746. The English and the French joined the war on opposite sides. The British supported the claim of Prussia and the French of Austria. The war had its effect on the relationship of the two powers in India also.

Events:

From the very beginning the French had an upper hand. The British tried to capture Pondicherry, a settlement of the French but failed. The French retaliated and captured Madras—a settlement of the British. The British appealed for help to the Nawab of Carnatic in whose territory Madras was located. The Nawab sent an army of about 10,000 soldiers to drive away the French from Madras. The French, under the leadership of Dupleix, who was the French Governor of Pondicherry, defeated the Nawab's army with a very small force of just 230 French and 700 Indian soldiers. In 1748, as the Austrian War of Succession came to an end, the hostilities also ceased in India.

Results:

As a result of the Treaty of Aix-la-Chapell in Europe between the parties, confrontation in India also ended. The French returned Madras to the British. The French prestige increased and Dupleix also got popularity.

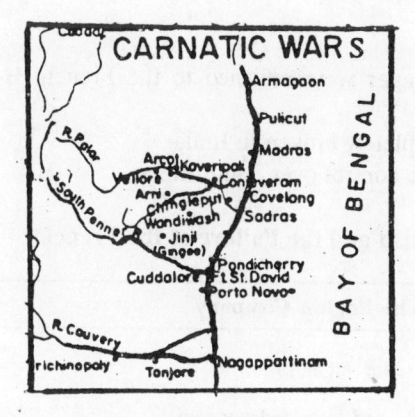

Map 9: **Carnatic Wars**

The Second Carnatic War (1749-54):

Causes:

There was confusion and disorder in Carnatic and Hyderabad on account of the war of succession to the throne. In Carnatic, dispute arose between Chanda Sahib and Anwar-ud-Din because of their claims and counter claims over the throne. In Hyderabad, Nasir Jang and Muzaffar Jang claimed the throne. The British and the French supported the opposite parties. Consequently both the powers i.e. the British and the French were on the warpath once again.

Events:

Chanda Sahib, with the help of the French defeated and killed Anwar-ud-Din. After the death of Anwar-ud-Din, his son Muhammad Ali put forward his claim. Chanda Sahib gave a very fertile area to the French. Muhammad Ali took shelter in the Fort of Trichinopoly. Fortunately for the British, at this juncture, a British soldier, Clive, acted very bravely, diplomatically and wisely. His plan entirely changed the course of the war. Chanda Sahib at that time was away from his capital and had surrounded Muhammad Ali at Trchinopoly. Clive, with the help of only 500 soldiers took Arcot, the capital of Carnatic. Clive received timely help from other British forces and proceeded further and defeated the French and Chanda Sahib. Muhammad Ali was appointed the new Nawab of Carnatic.

In Hyderabad, the French were successful in making Muzaffar Jang the Nawab of Hyderabad. While the war was on, Dupleix, the Governor of the French Company was called back. The successor of Dupleix signed the Treaty with the British on humiliating terms.

Results:

(1) The treaty enhanced the prestige of the British.
(2) The British got ample opportunity to consolidate their influence in Bengal also.

The Third Carnatic War (1757-63)

Causes:

In 1757, the Seven-Year War broke out in Europe. The French and the English took opposite sides. In

India, this led to the final phase of the Carnatic Wars. The French were finally defeated in the Battle of Wandiwash in 1760. In 1761, the French lost Pondicherry and Chandernagar. The Seven-Year War in Europe came to an end with the signing of the Treaty of Paris. In India also, the war between the English and the French came to an end.

Results:

(1) Pondicherry and Chandernagar were returned to the French. However, they were not permitted to fortify these places.
(2) The French power was completely broken in India.
(3) The British gained complete control over South India.

Causes of the Success of the English and the Failure of the French

S.No.		The English Company	The French Company
1.	*Organisation*	Better organisation.	Poor organisation.
2.	*Nature of organisation*	By and large independent.	Very dependent on the French Government.
3.	*Shareholders*	Shareholders more interested in the efficient running of the Company.	Shareholders not very much interested.
4.	*Financial position*	Very Sound.	Very weak.
5.	*Cooperation*	Team spirit among the workers of the Company.	Lack of cooperation and team spirit.
6.	*Stability of the Government*	The British Government was more stable.	Comparatively less stable French Government.
7.	*Interest of the Government in the Company*	British Government took a keen interest.	The French Government was lukewarm.
8.	*Political leadership*	Very sound.	Very weak.
9.	*Military leadership*	Clive's military tactics and strategies of a very high order.	Dupleix's weak command and arrogance.
10.	*Naval power*	Very superior.	Very weak.
11.	*Trading centres*	Calcutta's better position than Chandernagar.	Pondicherry's weak trading position than Madras.
12.	*Diplomacy*	Very superior.	Recall of Dupleix by the French Government at a very crucial hour.
13.	*European politics*	England comparatively free from wars and conflicts in Europe.	French very actively involved.
14.	*Rich resources of Bengal*	Conquest of Bengal provided rich resources.	Lack of such a fertile region.

The Beginning of European Settlements in India

EXERCISES

A. Very Short Answer Type Questions
1. Give two factors which led to the beginning of European settlements in India.
2. Explain the significance of the terms 'Gold, Glory and God' in the context of European settlements in India.
3. State any two reasons for the downfall of the Portuguese empire in India.
4. List any two weaknesses of the French Company.
5. List any two strong points of the East India Company.

B. Short Answer Type Questions
1. Explain from 'traders to colonisers' in the context of European colonisation of India.
2. State any three reasons for the success of the English and the failure of the French in the Carnatic Wars.
3. Write any three effects of the Carnatic Wars.
4. "Clive is sometimes considered as the founder of the British empire in India". Why?

C. Map Work
On an outline map of India, show the European settlements in the East.

CHAPTER 4

The British Conquest of India

BATTLES: FROM PLASSEY (1757) TO BUXAR (1764)

The conquest of India by the British was greatly facilitated by their supremacy in Bengal. The British from the very beginning were interested in Bengal on account of the following reasons:
(i) Bengal was the most fertile and the richest province in India at that time.
(ii) Its industries and commerce were well-developed.
(iii) In 1717, the East India Company had secured the 'firman' (permission/order) from the Mughal emperor Farrukh Siyar to import and export articles from Bengal without payment of custom duties.
(iv) The East India Company and its servants had highly profitable trading interests in the province.
(v) All the European Companies had established most of their settlements in the south.
(vi) The English had learnt several important lessons about the nature of the Indians during their struggle in the earlier two Anglo-French wars which helped them to acquire control over Bengal and subsequently over the entire country. These lessons were:
(a) The British noticed that the Indians lacked the nationalist spirit.
(b) There were rivalries everywhere among various political powers and their courts were marked by intrigues.
(c) Indian armies depended mostly on old types of weapons and strategies.
(d) The Indian soldiers trained and armed in the European manner proved as good as their European counterparts. Therefore, by employing Indian soldiers with suitable training, the English raised a powerful and strong army suitable for their territorial expansion in Bengal and, thereafter, over the whole India.

The victories of the English in the Battles of Plassey and the Battle of Buxar paved the way for them to conquer India.

The Battle of Plassey (1757)

Parties:

The Battle of Plassey was fought between Siraj-ud-Daulah, the Nawab of Bengal, and the East India Company.

Reasons:

1. Misuse of the 'firman' of 1757:

The 'firman' had permitted the East India Company only to trade without any duties. However, in violation of this agreement, the employees of the company indulged in personal trade also and evaded the payment of taxes.

The British Conquest of India

2. Fortification of Trade Centres by the East India Company:

The East India Company began to fortify its trade centres in anticipation of future conflicts and wars with the French. When Nawab Siraj-ud-Daula forbade them to do so, they refused to obey the orders.

3. Instigating the Hindu Subjects:

The East India Company began to instigate the Hindu subjects of the Muslim Nawabs and even gave shelter to the son of a rich Hindu businessman, Rajballabh who had earned the wrath of the Nawab, as there were serious charges of embezzlement against him.

4. Violation of the Treaty of January, 1757:

The various acts of omission and commission on the part of the East India Company enraged the Nawab Siraj-ud-Daula of Bengal, and he captured the city of Calcutta which the East India Company had earlier founded. When this news reached Madras, Clive and Watson were sent to recapture Calcutta. They were successful in their attempt to do so. Both the parties i.e. the East India Company and the Nawab entered into an agreement in January, 1757. The hostilities ceased for a while. The East India Company did not follow the agreement.

5. Capture of Chandernagar:

With a view to strengthen his power, Clive captured Chandernagar in Bengal from the French. This was in violation of the 1757 agreement.

6. Conspiracy Against the Nawab:

Clive was bent upon waging war against the Nawab. He, therefore, entered into a conspiracy with Mir Jafar (the commander of the Nawab), Rai Durlabh (a commander), Manik Chand (the officer-in-charge of Calcutta), Ami Chand (a rich merchant), Jagat Seth (the biggest banker of Bengal) and Khadim Khan (another commander of troops).

7. Clive's Charge Against Siraj-ud-Daula:

Having entered into conspiracy, Clive who was determined to fight a war, falsely charged the Nawab Siraj-ud-Daula of entering into a conspiracy with the French and the Dutch. The Nawab refuted this allegation. Nevertheless, Clive marched against the Nawab.

Events:

The battle was fought at Plassey between the East India Company and the Nawab on June 23, 1757. The battle was in name only. Clive who had earlier in the Anglo-French struggle captured Arcot, again followed a war strategy which proved quite successful. As a matter of fact, he had won the battle even before its start by entering into a conspiracy. With a force of just 3,000 soldiers, Clive was able to defeat Siraj-ud-Daula's 50,000 soliders.

The parties met for the battle on the field of Plassey, 32 km from Murshidabad (65 km from Calcutta) on 23 June, 1757. The English army under Clive took position in front of the mango grove, on the left was the Bhagirathi river and on the right was the large army of the Nawab in a semi-circular formation commanded by Mir Jafar, the commander-in-chief and Rai Durlabh (see map). Only a small force of the Nawab under Mohanlal and Mir Madan loyally fought the English forces. After half an hour's fighting Clive had to withdraw his forces behind the trees for protection. At this moment a stray shot killed Mir Madan and Mir Jafar advised the Nawab treacherously to recall the troops under Mohanlal which were fighting and advancing with great courage and determination. Mohanlal repeatedly informed, "This was not a time to retreat." But Nawab's pressing messages made Mohanlal to retreat. This demoralized the whole troop which deserted the field one by one. The height of treachery is noteworthy that the major armed forces in a semi-circular formation having the capacity of swallowing or sweeping away Clives army did not waste a single shot as per order of their commanders Mir

Jafar and Rai Durlabh. It was a battle only in name. Clive with an army less than one-sixteenth of the Nawab's, won. Infact, it was the treachery that won. "It was a night of eternal gloom for India." The Nawab was forced to flee but was captured and put to death by Mir Jafar's son Miran, Mir Jafar was proclaimed as the next Nawab of Bengal. Mir Jafar paid a sum of Rs. 17 crore as compensation to the East India Company for Siraj's attack on Calcutta, and also distributed large sums as gifts or bribes to the high officials of the company.

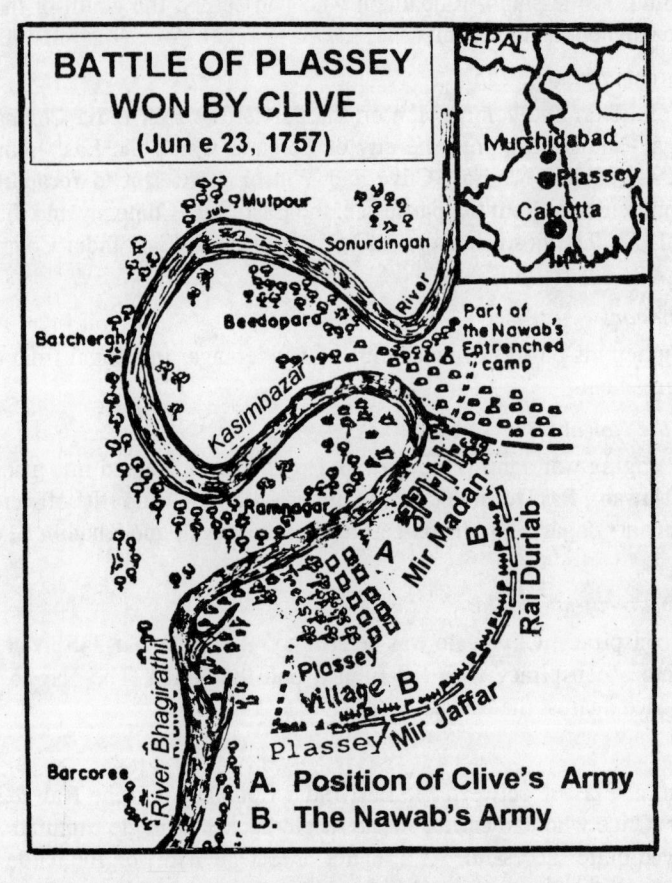

Map 10: **Battle of Plassey won by Clive 1757**

Results :
1. The victory of the East India Company opened the doors to its subsequent victories in India.
2. The English observed that there could be numerous Mir Jafars and Seths who could be easily bought.
3. The victory of Clive convinced him that he could easily defeat the Indian rulers with his small army.
4. The Company got control of the fertile and rich province of Bengal.
5. *New Nawab as a Puppet:*
   Nawab Siraj-ud-Daula was put to death and the new Nawab became a puppet in the hands of the East India Company.
6. *Huge Financial Gains to the Company:*
   The Company received about Rs. 2 crore from the new Nawab. The Company acquired zamindars of 24

The British Conquest of India

Parganas near Calcutta and got concession for carrying on tax-free trade in Bengal. The Company's officials also received huge bribes. Clive himself is said to have received Rs. 30 lakh as bribe.

7. *From a Trading Company to a Ruling Power:*
   The East India Company which was started as a trading company became a ruling power in India.
8. *Upper Hand of the East India Company Over the French Company:*
   The Battle of Plassey enhanced the prestige of the East India Company. It obtained enormous wealth and resources which proved to be of great use in the struggle for supremacy in the South.
9. *Rapid Changes in Bengal:*
   The British were able to destabilise the power of the Nawab of Bengal by deposing and installing rulers one after the other.

Causes of Siraj-ud-Daula's Defeat and the Victory of the East India Company:

1. The struggle of succession to the throne of Bengal led to disunity among nobles who took sides.
2. The English got an opportunity to make use of this rivalry to their advantage.
3. The English entered into conspiracy with several influential persons in the court of Nawab Siraj-ud-Da of Bengal.
4. The Nawab of Bengal, after capturing Calcutta, put it in the charge of a weak officer who was won over by the English.
5. Because of the treachery of Mir Jafar, the commander-in-chief of Nawab, his soldiers did not show resistance worth the name.
6. Clive was a great military strategist.
7. Neither the Nawab, nor the French came to each other's help aganist their common enemy, the East India Company.
8. The East India Company had a strong naval power.
9. Siraj-ud-Daula was so indifferent that he failed to have any clue of conspiracy against him.

The Battle of Buxar (1764)

Parties in the Battle:

The battle was fought between Mir Qasim, the Nawab of Bengal, Shuja-ud-Daula, the Nawab of Oudh, Shah Alam II, and the Mughal emperor on one side and the British on the other.

Causes of the Battle:

(i) Mir Jafar had become the Nawab of Bengal with the help of the British. So, soon they started asking for more and more concessions.
(ii) Mir Jafar was asked to pay expenses of their settlements at Bombay and Madras.
(iii) The officials of the East India Company began to interfere in the day-to-day affairs of the state.
(iv) Mir Jafar was not happy with this state of affairs. The British were quick to notice a change in his attitude.
(v) The British deposed him and made Mir Qasim, his son-in-law, the Nawab of Bengal.
(vi) Mir Qasim also did not come upto the expectations of the British. He clashed with the company over the issue of inland duties. The Nawab objected to their unfair trade practices.
(vii) The abuse of inland trade adversely affected the revenue of Bengal.
(viii) The Company adopted a rigid attitude. The Nawab challenged the Company.

Map 11: **Battle of Buxar 1764**

Events:

The armed conflict started between the Nawab and the Company in 1763. The Nawab was defeated and fled to Oudh. He organised a confederacy of Nawab Shuja-ud-Daula of Oudh, the Mughal Emperor, Shah Alam II and himself. The combined armies of these powers numbering between 50,000 to 60,000 met the British army of only 7,000 soldiers at Buxar. It was a very unevenly balanced fight and yet the British army won on October 22, 1764.

Results:

1. With the victory at Buxar, the British power became unchallengeable in India.
2. The victory at Buxar firmly established the British as the masters of Bengal, Bihar and Orissa.
3. The victory of the British over the combined powers of Bengal, Oudh and the Mughal armies demonstrated the superiority of the British.
4. After the outbreak of war with Mir Qasim, the British once more made Mir Jafar the Nawab. But after his early death in 1765, his son Nizam-ud-Daulah was made the Nawab on specific conditions as per a treaty.

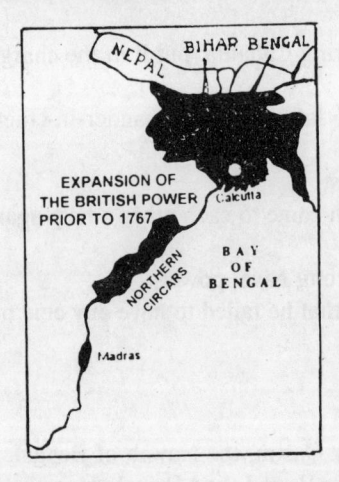

Map 12: **Expansion of British Power Under Clive 1767**

The Treaty was signed between Nizam-ud-Daula and the British at Allahabad on February 20, 1765. According to the Treaty of Allahabad:
(i) The Nawab of Bengal was to disband most of his army.
(ii) The Nawab of Bengal was required to leave the administration of the state in the hands of a Deputy Subedar who would be appointed by the British and could not be dismissed without their consent.
(iii) The Nawab of Bengal was to pay the Bengal Council of the British a sum of Rs. 15 lakh.
(iv) The Mughal Emperor was to grant the *Diwani* to the East India Company, that is, the right to collect revenue.
(v) The Mughal Emperor was to remain under British protection for six years at Allahabad.
(vi) The Nawab of Oudh was to cede Allahabad and Kora. These were handed over to the Mughal Emperor for maintaining his dignity.
(vii) The Nawab of Oudh was to provide the British a war indemnity of Rs. 5 million in return for restoring Oudh to the Nawab.
(viii) The East India company was to support the Nawab of Oudh against any outside attack and he was to pay for the services of the troops sent to his assistance.

The British Conquest of India 41

Importance of the Battle of Buxar (1764):

It has been remarked that Buxar deserves far more than Plassey to be considered as the real origin of the British power in India. The remark is true: Plassey was a mere skirmish and British victory was due more to treachery than to the superiority of British arms. But Buxar was a straight fight in which the British defeated Mir Qasim, a veteran statesman not inferior in capacity to an average Indian ruler, who had equipped his army and husbanded his resources as best as he could and was supported by the greater power of Oudh. Besides, there were many advantages that the British gained following the victory at Buxar:

(1) Mir Jafar died in 1765. With great haste the Calcutta Council installed son of Mir Jafar, Nizam-ud-Daula, on the condition laid down by a treaty that the entire management of administration should be left in the hands of a Deputy Subedar to be nominated by the British and not to be dismissed without their consent. Thus the supreme control over the administration passed into the hands of the British.

(2) Clive returned as Governor of Bengal for the second time in 1765. He restored Oudh to its Nawab on payment of Rs. 50 lakhs. Only Allahabad and the surrounding tracts were detached from Oudh and handed over to Emperor Shah Alam for his financial support.

(3) The Emperor, in return of these concessions, formally granted the *Diwani* of Bengal, Bihar and Orissa to the company in 1765. The *Diwani* made the company the supreme authority over the territories. It was the first great step towards real territorial domination.

DUAL GOVERNMENT IN BENGAL (1765-1772)

Origin and Meaning of Dual Government

The word dual means double. Thus, the dual government implies administration of two powers. The dual system of government or administration was introduced in Bengal by Lord Clive in 1765 and was abolished by Lord Warren Hastings in 1772. According to this system, the entire administration was divided broadly into two categories. One category of administration relating to the military defence of the country and revenue came under the East India Company, and the other, i.e. internal administration, law and order and police, came under the purview of the Nawab of Bengal. The control of entire finances of the state was to rest with the East India Company and the Nawab was to get Rs. 53 lakhs per year from the company to carry on the allotted administration.

The establishment of the dual system of administration was a diplomatic move of Clive who wanted to have a complete control over Bengal without any direct involvement. There were two strong reasons for it. It was impossible for the Company to take over the full administration of Bengal owing to the limited number of Company's servants. Secondly, the Company wanted to hide the fact that it had the full control of Bengal from rival European powers.

Demerits of the Dual Government

(1) Since the Nawab depended on the East India Company for finances, he became powerless to run the administration efficiently and smoothly.
(2) Law and order situation in the state began to deteriorate speedily.
(3) The Nawab could not undertake any welfare measures for the people.
(4) Bribe and corruption became rampant.
(5) There were frequent conflicts between the officials of the Nawab and the Company.
(6) The peasants were fleeced and virtually reduced to paupers.
(7) The terrible famine of 1769-70 claimed one-third population of Bengal.
(8) Trade also suffered.

WARREN HASTINGS (1772-1785)

After the retirement of Lord Clive, Warren Hastings was appointed the Governor of Bengal in the year 1772 and two years later, he was made the first Governor-General of India. He used all means - fair and foul to promote British interests in India. In this process, he made a huge fortune for himself too. On his return to Britain, he was impeached in the British Parliament. He was accused of accepting bribes and committing atrocities on Indian rulers. However, he was acquitted as it was felt that he had done all that with a view to expand British influence in India.

Expansion of Empire under Warren Hastings

1. Relationship with Oudh:

Warren Hastings was determined to have good relations with the Nawab on account of the danger from the Marathas. He wanted Oudh to serve as a strong buffer state between the British territories and the Maratha territories. He feared that if it was not done, the Nawab might join the Marathas. Accordingly, Benaras Treaty was concluded with the Nawab of Oudh in 1773. According to the treaty, the districts of Kora and Allahabad which were given to the Mughal Emperor by Clive were taken from the Emperor and were sold to the Nawab of Oudh for rupees fifty lakhs. The Nawab agreed to increase the subsidy of the Company's troops from Rs. 30,000 to Rs. 2 lakh a month for military service to the Nawab. It was also agreed that in case the Nawab asked for more troops from the Company, he would pay a sum of Rs. 40 lakhs to the Company.

2. The Rohilla War:

The Rohillas, a peace loving people lived in the north of Oudh in the area known as Rohilkhand. They wanted protection from the frequent raids and plunder of the Marathas and entered into a treaty in 1772 with the Nawab of Oudh who would be receiving 40 lakhs for repulsing the Maratha invaders when such help was needed. The treaty was very short-lived. The Nawab wanted to annex Rohilkhand to his territory. He requested Warren Hastings for help. In return for military service to the Nawab, the Company was to get Rs. 40 lakhs in addition to all the expenses of the war. British troops were sent to crush the Rohillas. Rohilkhand was conqered. Hafiz Rahmat Khan, the Rohilla leader was killed. Atrocities were committed by the troops on the innocent people of Rohilkhand and the territory was annexed to Oudh. This was one of the main charges on which Hastings was later impeached in England.

3. Trial of Raja Chet Singh:

Chet Singh was the Raja of Benaras. Benaras had been transferred to the company by the Nawab of Oudh in 1775. The Raja used to pay an annual tribute of Rs. 23½ lakhs to the Company. Warren Hastings began to extract more and more tribute from Raja Chet Singh on one pretext or the other. The Raja obliged him for some time but refused to do so indefinitely. This angered Warren Hastings and he was fined Rs. 50 lakhs for some delay in making the last payment. On his refusal to pay the fine, he was arrested. Thereupon Raja's troops massacred a number of English sepoys. Chet Singh was removed from the throne. His nephew was installed in his place and made to pay the tribute at double the rate. Such a conduct of Hastings was unjust, improper and tyrannous.

4. Trial of Nand Kumar:

Nand Kumar was a very influential person in Bengal. He also indulged in politics. He accused Warren Hastings of having received among other bribes, a large sum of money from Muni Begum. As the new Council of four members made by the Regulating Act wanted to try Hastings, he dissolved the Council. Hastings retorted by bringing a charge of conspiracy and forgery against Nand Kumar who was tried by the Supreme Court and was sentenced to death. It is generally believed by historians that this punishment was given by the Chief

The British Conquest of India

Justice of the Supreme Court after being influenced by his close friend, Warren Hastings. Moreover, according to the prevailing penal code, death sentence was not permissible in case of forgery.

5. Case of the Begums of Oudh:

The Nawab of Oudh owed huge amounts to the East India Company to maintain British troops. But on account of several financial constraints, he was unable to make payment. When Hastings pressed him for payment, the Nawab told him that the Begums of Oudh i.e. his mother and grandmother had lots of jewels and money with them. Warren Hastings tortured the Begums and extracted huge amounts from them.

Warren Hastings has been severely criticised for his high handness in all the four cases mentioned above, i.e. Rohilla war, case of Raja Chet Singh, trial of Nand Kumar and Begums of Oudh.

6. Mysore Wars:

After the first Mysore War (1767-1769), the second Mysore War took place during 1780-84 when Warren Hastings was the Governor-General. Hyder Ali and his son Tipu Sultan fought the war with great determination. As neither the British nor the Sultan of Mysore could hope to win, they concluded a treaty in 1784. Warren Hastings was, however, able to save the prestige of the Company with the honourable terms of the treaty.

7. The First Anglo-Maratha War (1776-82):

After recovering from the blow of Panipat in 1771, Maratha's soon recovered some of their lost prestige. However, the struggle for succession on the death of Peshwa Madhav Rao I, weakened them and broke their unity. One of the claimants, Raghunath Rao or Raghoba was appointed as the new Peshwa but he was opposed by another powerful lobby led by Nana Phadnavis. Raghoba concluded a treaty with the British in Bombay and agreed to give Salsette and Bassein to the British as the price of their help. This was not liked by most of the Maratha chiefs and they fought under the leadership of Nana Phadnavis - a great Maratha statesman and strategist. The war between the Marathas and the British lasted for seven years, yet neither side could win. Finally a peace treaty was signed at Salbai in 1782. The Marathas agreed to remain neutral if Salsette and neighbouring islands around Bombay already given to the British by Raghoba, were allowed to remain with the British. Raghunath Rao was given a pension. Madhav Rao II, posthumous son of Narayan Rao, was recognised as the Peshwa. The Treaty of Salbai gave the British twenty years of peace with the Marathas. They used this period in consolidating their rule over the Bengal Presidency. The treaty also prevented any major alliance between the Indian powers.

Reforms of Warren Hastings

(i) He abolished the Dual system of government in Bengal and the Company assumed all administrative powers.
(ii) The company began to collect 'Diwani' revenue through its own supervisors who were helped by the native revenue officials.
(iii) He checked several malpractices of the officers of the company in trade transactions and thus added to the revenues of the Company.
(iv) He made several improvements in the procedures followed in the courts to decide cases. Different types of courts dealing with different types of cases were established.
(v) Warren Hastings effected economy in several fields. He reduced the pension of Nawab of Bengal and the Mughal Emperor.
(vi) He extorted large sums of money from the Begums of Oudh and Raja Chet Singh of Benaras.

Summing up, Clive is regarded as the 'founder' of the British empire in India and Warren Hastings as its 'saviour'.

LORD CORNWALLIS (1786-93)

Lord Cornwallis is famous for his several reforms which are briefly mentioned below:

Administrative Reforms

He introduced two important reforms relating to administration (i) He increased the salaries of the employees of the East India Company with a view to checking large scale bribes on their part as they received very meagre salaries (ii) He made stringent rules to check private trade by them.

Judicial Reform

Four separate provincial courts were set up. He separated the function of collection of revenue and administration of justice. The collectors were made responsible for the collection of revenue and the district judges for the administration of justice.

Police Reforms

A police department was set up and the zamindars were deprived of their police powers. A district was divided into several 'thanas'.

Commercial Reforms

Cornwallis ended the practice of buying goods by the Company through intermediaries and introduced a new system of making direct purchases from the merchants.

Land Reform and the Permanent Settlement of Bengal

Cornwallis abolished the old system of giving land to the highest bidder and in 1789, he introduced a new system according to which, settlement was made permanent. The zamindars became the permanent owners of the land. They became staunch supporters of the British rule in India (Discussed in detail in a subsequent chapter).

SIR JOHN SHORE (1793-98)

Sir John Shore succeeded Lord Cornwallis as the Governor-General. He, by and large, followed the policy of 'Non-interference' in the affairs of Indian states. The only exception was the state of Oudh. After the death of the Nawab of Oudh, Sir John Shore interfered in the succession issue. He also entered into a treaty with the new Nawab. The Nawab was to pay an annual subsidy to the English Company, a sum of Rs. 76 lakhs for the defence of Oudh.

LORD WELLESELY (1798-1805)

Policy of 'Expansion and Intervention'

Lord Wellesely, who remained the Governor-General for seven years, followed the policy of expansion of the British power in India. For following this policy, he was guided by the following factors.
(a) By 1798, the power of Indian rulers had been considerably weakened.
(b) There was no strong power in India which could challenge the British.
(c) The British industrialists, merchants and traders favoured the policy of expanding British influence in several parts as it suited their interests.
(d) There was no competing European power in India. The field for the British expansion was wide-open.
(e) The expansionist policy was favoured to forestall any invasion of British India from the north-western side.

Methods used by Lord Wellesely to Expand the British Power in India

Wellesely adopted the following methods for this purpose:
(i) Subsidiary System of Alliances
(ii) Waging Wars
(iii) Lame excuses for annexation.

Subsidiary System of Alliances:

Lord Wellesely entered into alliances with the various Indian rulers. The ruler accepting the alliance had to agree to the following conditions.
1. The ruler must recognise the East India Company as the paramount power in India.
2. British troops must be maintained by the ruler in his state. The expenses of the troops were to be borne by the ruler in alliance. In case, the ruler was unable to bear their expenses, he should agree to surrender a part of his territory.
3. The ruler must keep a British Resident in his court to watch the interests of the Company.
4. The ruler should not enter into any political agreement with any party without the permission of the British Company.
5. The ruler would not employ any non-British European in his service.
6. In case of any conflict with any other power, the ruler would abide by the decision of the English.
7. In return for accepting these conditions, the Company would protect the ruler from any internal disorder or external danger.

States Accepting the Subsidiary System:

These were the states (i) The Nizam of Hyderabad (ii) The Nawab of Oudh (iii) Peshwa Baji Rao II (iv) The Gaekwad of Baroda (v) The ruler of Travancore (vi) Several Rajput states.

Impact/Results of the Subsidiary System:

(i) The system proved as a boon to the British as it strengthened their hold on several Indian states.
(ii) The Indian rulers lost their right of self-defence, to maintain diplomatic relations and to employ foreign experts.
(iii) The Indian rulers lost their sovereignty.
(iv) The system brought decay to the internal administration in the states.
(v) The subsidiary to be paid to the British put heavy burden of taxes on the common people.

Waging Wars:

Lord Wellesley fought three wars and thereby increased the British power in India.

(i) He won the Fourth Mysore War (1799). Tipu Sultan, the ruler of Mysore was killed in the war. After his death, territories of Canara, Coimbatore and Seringapatnam were annexed to the British empire. The kingdom of Mysore was restored to a descendent of the old Hindu royal family. The new ruler accepted the Subsidiary Alliance.

(ii) In the Second Maratha War (1802-1815), Bhonsle and Scindia, two powerful Maratha Sardars were defeated. Both of them surrendered several territories to the British and also accepted the Subsidiary Alliance.

Annexation by Excuses:

Wellesley annexed the states of Tanjore, Surat and Carnatic on one pretext or the other. He took full advantage of the issue of succession and granted pension to the heirs.

LORD CORNWALLIS (1805)

He spent only a few months in India.

SIR GEORGE BARLOW (1805-1807)

Sir George Barlow followed the policy of 'Non-intervention' in the affairs of the Indian rulers. He gave back some territories to the Maratha Sardar, Scindia of Gwalior. He also won over Holkar of Indore by offering favourable terms to him.

LORD MINTO (1807-1813)

Lord Minto helped the ruler of Berar when his territory was invaded by a Pathan Chief, Amir Khan, who had with him 40,000 horsemen and more than 20,000 Pindaris (usually associated with raids and plunder). Amir Khan was defeated and peace was restored in Berrar.

In 1809, Lord Minto entered into the Treaty of Amritsar with Maharaja Ranjit Singh of the Punjab. The Sikh territory was to be on the other side of the river Sutlej. The British agreed not to interfere in the affairs of Maharaja Ranjit Singh. This treaty was observed by both the parties for 30 years.

MARQUESS HASTINGS (1814-1823)

Marquess followed the policy of active interference in the affairs of the Indian states.

War with Nepal (1814-1818)

Hastings waged a war with the Gorkhas of Nepal. After initial heavy casualties, the British were able to strengthen their position. With the Treaty of Sanguli, the British gained three famous hill stations—Simla, Mussori and Nainital. The ruler of Nepal remained independent as ever. A large number of Gorkhas were given jobs in the British army in India.

War with the Pindaris (1816-1818)

Pindaris were a gang of plunderers who carried out their raids in different parts of the country. Hastings crushed their power. (See map about the expansion of powers.)

JOHN ADAMS (1823)

John Adams' rule lasted for seven months only. He is known for his censorship of the press.

LORD AMHERST (1823-28)

First Burmese War (1824-26)

The Burmese war proved to be very expensive for the British but they were able to defeat the Burmese. The Burmese King agreed to part with two provinces and also to pay war indemnity.

Capture of Bharatpur

After the death of the ruler, there was a dispute of succession. The English took advantage of the situation and captured Bharatpur.

LORD WILLIAM BENTINCK (1828-1835)

Lord William Bentinck introduced several reforms.

(1) Social Reforms:

(i) He abolished the practice of 'Sati' (ii) He banned the practice of female infanticide - killing of new born daughters among several Rajput tribes (iii) Banned human sacrifice which was prevalent among some tribes of Orissa (iv) Changed the Hindu law of inheritance and allowed full rights in ancestral property after the change of religion (v) Abolished 'Thugee' i.e. robbing, deceiving etc.

(2) Educational Reforms:

(i) Introduced English as the medium of instruction (ii) Introduced the system of education as recommended by Lord Macaulay, the Law Member. The system was intended to produce an educated class that was Indian in blood and colour but English in manners and tastes. Besides, the educated class was expected to take up petty administrative jobs under the company.

(3) Public Works:

(i) He got the Grand-Trunk Road constructed between Delhi and Calcutta (ii) Another road between Bombay and Delhi was also constructed (iii) He got many canals dug for irrigation purposes.

(4) Financial Reforms:

(i) Reduction in the salary of civil servants and in allowances for effecting economy (ii) Licensing the opium trade to earn profits (iii) Reforms in the revenue settlements in North West province.

(5) Administrative Reforms:

(i) Employment of Indians at suitable posts for reducing expenditure as the Indian employees could be engaged at lower salaries as compared with the English officers (ii) Appointment of Indians as judges

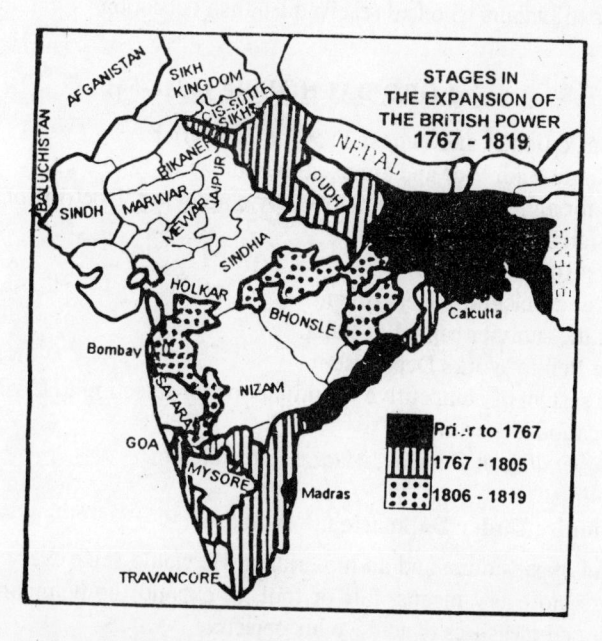

Map 13: **Expansion of British Power 1767-1818**

(iii) Replacement of Persian by vernaculars as the court language (iv) Codification of laws (v) Introduction of the Jury system of justice in Bengal which provided for associating respectable Indians to sit with European judges while deciding cases.

SIR CHARLES METCALFE (1835-36)

(i) Allowed freedom of press to the Indians.
(ii) Negotiated the Treaty of Amritsar with Maharaja Ranjit Singh.

LORD AUCKLAND (1836-42)

1. He waged war with Afghanistan without any success.
2. He instituted large number of scholarships.
3. He announced that the medium of instruction at the primary stage should be the vernacular language of the area.
4. He deposed the Raja of Satara when he refused to be loyal to the English.

LORD ELLENBOROUGH (1842-1844)

1. He won the First Afghan war.
2. He conquered and annexed Sindh in 1843.

LORD HARDINGS (1844-1848)

1. Won the First Anglo-Sikh War.
2. Gave appointments to Indians who had received English education.

LORD DALHOUSIE (1848-56)

1. He was a great annexationist and annexed several territories.
2. Won the second Anglo-Sikh War and annexed the Punjab in 1849.
3. He is very famous for annexing many territories by employing 'Doctrine of Lapse'.
4. He abolished pensions of several rulers.
5. He founded the first Indian Railway.
6. He set up the Post and Telegraph Department.
7. He made Simla as the summer capital of India.
8. He established the Public Works Department.
9. He introduced the system of competitive examinations for selection to Civil Services.
10. He set up the Education Department.
11. He established Universities at Bombay, Madras and Calcutta.

Expansion of British Empire Under Dalhousie (1848-1856)

Lord Dalhousie was an expansionist and an imperialist. He would seize every opportunity to grab territories in India. He took recourse to every means, fair or foul, to expand the boundaries of the British empire. He followed the undermentioned measures to achieve his objective.

(i) Policy of Doctrine of Lapse

The British Conquest of India 49

   (ii) Expansion by conquests
   (iii) Expansion on ground of maladministration
   (iv) Expansion on account of default in payment
   (v) Expansion by abolishing titles and pensions

The Doctrine of Lapse or the Law of Succession:

The Doctrine of Lapse states, "If the ruler of a dependent state should die without any heir (i.e. son), his adopted son would not succeed him but the state would lapse or go back to the British Company".

Lord Dalhousie applied this principle in these states: Satara in Maharashtra (1848), Jaitpur and Sambalpur in Orissa (1849), Baghat near Simla (1850), Udaipur in Rajputana (1852), Jhansi in Bundelkand (1853) and Nagpur in Maharashtra (1854).

Expansion by Conquests:

Lord Dalhousie annexed the Punjab (1849), Lower Burma (1850), and Sikkim (1850) through waging wars.

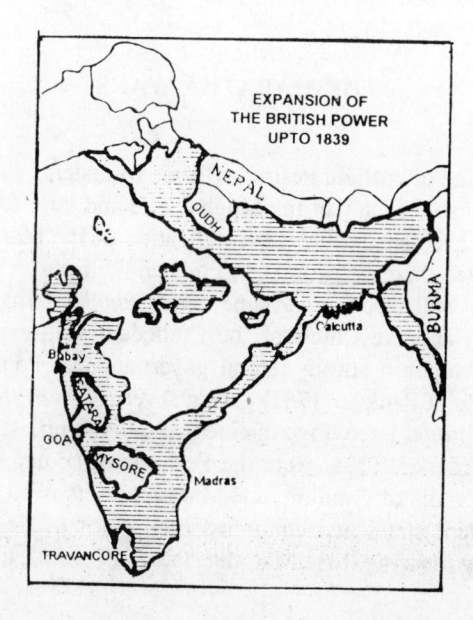

Map 14: **Expansion of British Power up to 1839**

Expansion on Ground of Maladministration:

Oudh was the only state annexed by Dalhousie on account of maladministration. At that time Oudh was ruled by Nawab Wajid Ali Shah, known for being surrounded by women. He wrote his 'Ishqnama', a diary. He was surrounded by gay persons. His officials were corrupt, inefficient and indulged in intrigues. Lord Dalhousie asked him to sign a treaty. On his refusal to do so, Oudh was annexed to the British empire. This was a seizure by mere threat on the plea of misrule.

Expansion on Account of Default in Payment:

The Nizam of Hyderabad who owed a lot of money to the British Company on account of the payment of stationing troops, sold Berar to the Company. Berar was earlier held as a security for the regular payment of the British soldiers stationed in Hyderabad.

Expansion on Account of Abolishing Pension and Titles:

After the death of the ruler of Poona, Dhondu Pant or Nana Sahib was denied pension. Similarly, he abolished the title and pension in the case of Nawab of Carnatic and Raja of Tanjore.

Several historians attribute the 1857 events to the acts of omission and commision of Lord Dalhousie. The application of Doctrine of Lapse and his policy of annexation created a large number of discontented elements who were ready to avail of any opportunity to hit back at the East India Company.

No other single Governor-General of India added even half the extent of territories which were snatched and incorporated into the British territory of India during the administration of Lord Dalhousie. His acquisitions were nearly twice the area of England and Wales. During his rule he expanded the area of the British territory a third and a half larger than what he himself received, from his predecessor. The heavy burden of responsibility and enormous amount of work carried during eight years, amid domestic sorrows, broke down his health. He left India in 1856, and the controversies aroused in Britian regarding his policy of annexation, which were widely and justly criticized, as contributary factors to the rebellion of 1857, overshadowed his achievements in modernization. It added vexation and sorrow. He died within four years in 1860, at the age of 48 years.

THE MARATHA WARS

Six Maratha Groups

Under the able guidance of a line of brilliant Peshwas (Prime Ministers), the Marathas embarked on a policy of expansion and proved a formidable enemy of the Mughal rule and later of the British ascendancy in India. The struggle against Aurangzeb necessitated the decentralization of the Maratha power by granting *jagirs* to the Maratha Chiefs. Many enlarged their jagirs and consolidated their positions as independent Maratha rulers at different places. Later, they collected *chauth* and *sardeshmukhi* which were distributed among the *chatrapati* (ruler of Maharastra) and the Chiefs of the Confederacy. It served to unite and strengthen the Maratha state. But all depended upon a strong central government at Poona. Peshwa was the head of the Confederacy. But the Third Battle of Panipat (1761) gave a severe blow to the mighty power of the Marathas. The Marathas were no longer a united force. Five distinct Maratha families, besides the ruler of Maharashtra (in name only), came into prominence. These were the Peshwas of Poona, Gaekward of Baroda, Bhonsle of Nagpur, Holkar of Indore and Scindia of Gwalior. The Maratha rulers lived at Satara. Some of these families were able to establish independent states and continued their rules till India became independent and the Indian states were reorganised by merging these Maratha states.

First Anglo-Maratha War (1776-1782)

The war lasted for seven years, yet, neither side could win. The British succeeded in dividing the Maratha Sardars.

Second Anglo-Maratha War (1801-1804)

Nana Phadnavis (1742-1800) was a great Maratha statesman. He was able to unite several Maratha chiefs. But after his death, Maratha unity could not remain intact. Situation in Maharashtra deteriorated very fast. There were constant conflicts among Maratha chiefs. Each Maratha chief wanted to control the weak Peshwa. The Peshwa sought the protection of the British and entered into the Subsidiary Alliance through the Treaty of Bassien in 1803. The British succeeded in defeating the three prominent chiefs- Holkar, Scindia and Bhonsle.

Another Maratha War or conflict (1805)

Holkar was defeated in several conflicts. Sometimes this war is not treated as Maratha War.

Third Maratha War (1817-18)

The Peshwa was not happy with the terms of the Subsidiary Alliance. Bhonsle, Holkar and the Peshwa formed a Confederacy to fight with the English at different places. The members of the Maratha Confederacy were soon defeated primarily because their forces did not jointly fight with the British. The Peshwa was defeated at Kirkee, Ashti and Koregaon, Bhonsle at Sitabaldi and Holkar at Mahidpur.

Following were the results of this war:

(1) The Maratha power was completely broken, the power of the Maratha chiefs was crushed forever and the British became the paramount powers.

(2) The office of the Peshwa as the nominal head of Maratha Confederacy was abolished and all his territories annexed to the British empire.

(3) The Bhonsle ruler was deposed and the Narbada territories of the Bhonsle were annexed to the British empire.

(4) Half of Holkar's state was also annexed. He renounced all his claims over the Rajput states.

(5) Although Scindia had not taken part in this war, he was deprived of Ajmer.

The causes of the Fall of the Marathas

1) The Third Battle of Panipat (1761) against Abdali shattered the Maratha Confederacy as a single power. Disintegration set in because of the individual ambition of the Maratha chiefs. This gave the British the opportunity to dabble in their affairs. Raghoba sought the British help regarding his succession to the Peshwa's throne. The rivalry between Scindia and Holkar made Baji Rao II to enter into a Subsidiary Alliance with the British.

2) It was the mistaken policy of the Marathas to abandon their guerilla tactics, a training ill-suited to the genius of their people.

3) Treatment of the Marathas of conquered provinces was oppressive. Their rule did not strike root into the soil. It gradually degenerated into a system of plunder, pressing hard upon the people.

Conquest of Sindh (1843)

A number of chiefs or Amirs were the several rulers of Sindh. The Amir of Khairpur region claimed surzerainty over other Amirs of Hyderabad and Mirpur. Both, Maharaja Ranjit Singh and the British, wanted to have their control over Sindh. By controlling Sindh, Ranjit Singh wanted to have access to the sea trade. The British had a twin design (i) to check the entry of French (ii) to have access of easy passage to capture Afghanistan.

In 1832, the English entered into a treaty with the Amirs on the following terms.
(i) The British could carry on their trading activities through Sindh
(ii) The British merchants would not settle in Sindh
(iii) The British would not use the passage for transporting military personnel and military stores
(iv) The British would protect the Amirs from any external aggression.

When the First Anglo-Afghan War broke out, Maharaja Ranjit Singh refused to allow the British forces to pass through his territory in the Punjab. The British in utter disregard to the Treaty with the Amirs, sent their troops through Sindh. The British also extracted huge sums from the Amirs on one or the other pretext. During the Afghan War, Sindh was made the base of operations. The British began to interfere in the affairs of the Amirs. After two important battles at Miani and Dabo, Sindh was conquered and annexed to the British empire.

Conquest of Punjab

[For details see next chapter].

CONQUEST OF BURMA (1856)

Two Burmese Wars were fought in 1824-26 and 1852. Burma was annexed in due course and it remained a part of India till 1937 when it became a separate country. Its new name is Mynamar.

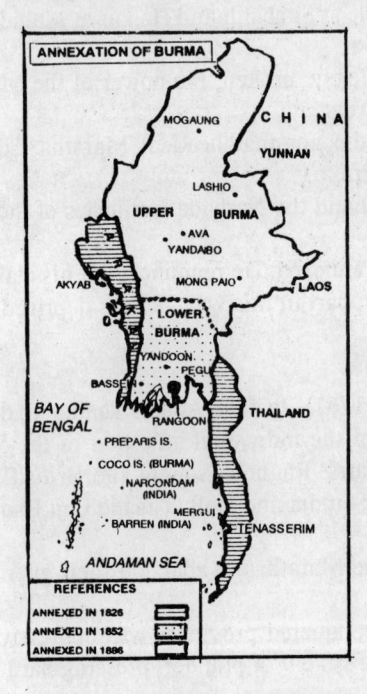

Map 15: **Annexation of Burma**

First Burmese War (1824-26)

The First Burmese War was fought on the pretext that the Burmese ruler had occupied various territories in the eastern region of India including Assam and Manipur. So, Burma was invaded. By the Treaty of Yandeboo in 1826, Burma gave up its claim over Assam. Manipur became independent. A British Resident was stationed at the Burmese court. The British got many territories that contained valuable forest resources.

Second Burmese War (1852)

Several British merchants were carrying on trade in Burma. They complained that the attitude of the Burmese officers was insulting and they asked for help from the East India Company. Lord Dalhousie sent forces and occupied Rangoon. Many more territories in Burma were also annexed and infact the entire Burma came under British domination.

EXERCISES

A. Very Short Answer Type Questions
1. State any two chief results of the Battle of Plassey.
2. Mention any two reforms introduced by Warren Hastings.
3. Name any four Maratha Sardars with their areas of influence.
4. What was the effect of the Burmese Wars?
5. State any two reasons of conflict between the Nawab and the East India Company.
6. Mention any two major provisions of the Treaty of Allahabad (1765).

B. Short Anwser Type Questions
1. Why were the British interested in the conquest of Bengal from the very beginning?
2. State any four reforms introduced by William Bentinck.
3. "The Third Anglo-Maratha War completely broke the Maratha power." Elucidate this statement.
4. Why were the British interested in Sindh? How did they conquer it?
5. Explain the 'Doctrine of Lapse.'
6. What was the Subsidiary System of Alliances? How did it help the English to strengthen their position?

C. Long Answer Type Questions
1. Why were the Battles of Plassey and Buxar fought? State their effects.
2. Explain the meaning of Dual Government. What were its demerits?
3. "Clive is regarded as the founder of the British empire in India and Warren Hastings its saviour". Explain.
4. Explain the policy of expansion and intervention followed by Lord Wellesly.
5. "Lord Dalhousie has been called an imperialist and an expansionist." Give any two examples to prove this?

D. Map Work
1. On an outline map of India show the major political powers in India in 1823.
2. On an outline map of India, show the British territories and Indian states in 1846.

CHAPTER 5

Maharaja Ranjit Singh: Conquest of Punjab

LION OF THE PUNJAB

Popularly known as the 'Lion of the Punjab', Maharaja Ranjit Singh is regarded as the last independent Indian ruler. The people of Northern India especially of the Punjab, Haryana, Himachal Pradesh and Delhi still cherish the memory of this great Maharaja. He has left behind a tradition of strength, combined with religious tolerance. He rose to power not only on account of wars but also through diplomacy. He was the only Indian ruler who could not be subdued by the British. He was also shrewd enough, not to come into clash with them on minor matters. Each feared the other. Both the parties maintained good relations. The Punjab was annexed by the British ten years after the death of Maharaja Ranjit Singh.

Early Life and Conquests of Ranjit Singh

Ranjit Singh, the founder of the Sikh state in the Punjab was born in 1780 at Gujranwala (now in Pakistan) in the Shukarchakia Misl. He was hardly twelve years old when he assumed the leadership of the Misl after his father's death. His marriage in the Kanahiya Misl of Kangra strengthened his position. The Sikh Misls were in a state of disintegration at that time and Ranjit Singh brought the Sikh Misls west of the river Sutlej under his control. First, he conquered Lahore, and then Amritsar. Thereafter he turned his attention to the cis-sutlej States (Sikh states to the eastern side of the river Sutlej). However, he entered into a treaty at Amritsar in 1809 according to which he was not to annexe any state on the eastern side of Sutlej. He, therefore, turned his attention to the west. He conquered Multan, Kangra, Attock, Kashmir, Hazara, Derajat, Peshawar, Jamrud, Ladakh and other cities.

Ranjit Singh took full advantage of the internal political struggle in Afghanistan and helped Shah Shuja, one of the claimants to the throne. Ranjit Singh took the famous diamond 'Kohinoor' from Shah Shuja.

The Sikhs under Hari Singh Nalwa, the Marshal of the Sikh forces of Ranjit Singh, defeated the Afghans and captured many important places.

Ranjit Singh left behind a large empire that extended from the river Sutlej to the Khyber Pass and the Sulaiman mountains.

Ranjit Singh's Army:

Ranjit Singh gave special importance to the maintenance of a strong and well-disciplined army. He employed foreign officers to train his army on modern strategies and techniques. He provided modern equipment. He adopted the system of monthly payment of salaries to his army—earlier it was seldom done by most of the Indian rulers in the 18th century. His forces consisted of artillery, cavalry and infantry.

Administrative Set-up:

He divided his kingdom into four provinces (Subas), namely, Lahore, Multan, Peshawar (now all three in Pakistan) and Kashmir. Each was further divided into districts (Parganas), tehsils (Taluqas) and finally villages (Mouzas). Nazim or governor was the head of a province.

Personal Attention:

Maharaja had deputed special officers to tour his kingdom and listen to people's grievances and do justice. He made himself available to his subjects and decided cases personally. This made him very popular among his subjects.

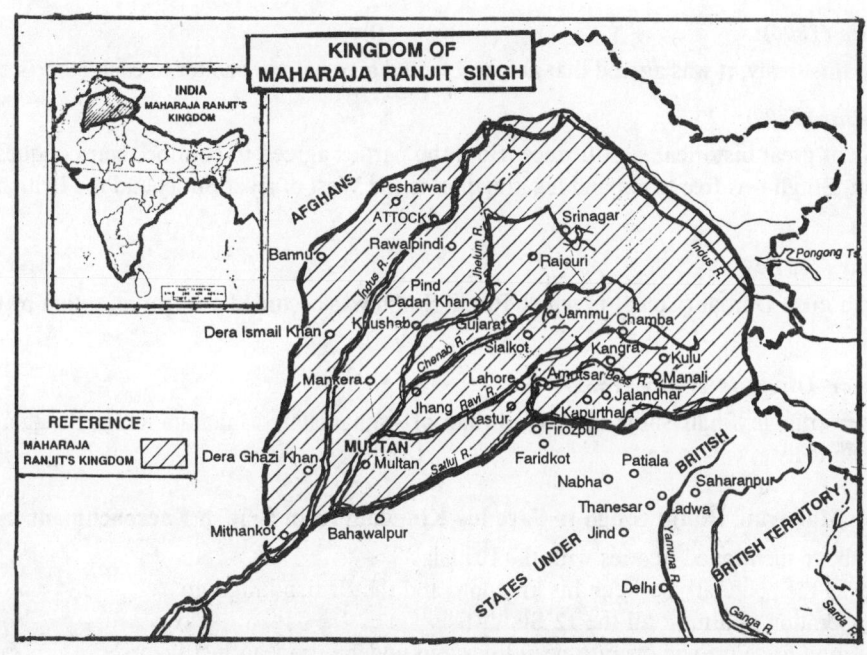

Map 16: **Kingdom of Maharaja Ranjit Singh**

Religious Toleration:

Ranjit Singh was a devout Sikh. He ruled in the name of the Khalsa and issued coins in the name of the Sikh Gurus. He visited the Golden Temple and covered its inside and outside with gold plates.

Ranjit Singh was very tolerant to the people of other faiths. Many Muslims were employed to key posts in the army and administration. Mian Ghaus Khan and General Illahi Baksh were incharge of 'Topkhanas' (artillery). Faqir Azizuddin was his foreign minister.

Love for Knowledge:

Ranjit Singh did not have much formal schooling but he kept himself fully informed with the latest developments in many fields in Europe and other neighbouring countries. He patronised scholars, and got several English, French and Sanskrit books translated into Persian and Punjabi.

Though deprived of his left eye, he was well-versed in hunting, riding and swimming.

Maharaja Ranjit Singh's Relations with the East India Company

The two powers, i.e. Maharaja Ranjit Singh and the East India Company, had cordial relations, lived at peace and made progress side by side. Both the parties had realized the importance of mutual goodwill. Both had realized their assets and limitations. Maharaja was free to expand his territories to the west of Sutlej and the British to the East of Sutlej. Both did not interfere in this arrangement. Although from time to time, small matters presented some temporary problems, but they were solved mutually. Following were the important events regarding the relationship of Ranjit Singh and the British.

The British Mission 1800:

The British and the French were not on friendly terms in Europe. British feared that the French might invade India with the help of the ruler of Afgahnistan. They, therefore, sent a goodwill mission to Ranjit Singh.

Treaty of Lahore (1806):

According to this treaty, it was agreed that no party would give help or shelter to each other's enemy.

Treaty of Amritsar (1809):

This treaty is of great historical significance. Both the parties agreed to confine their conquests to separate directions. Ranjit Singh was free to expand his kingdom to the West of river Sutlej and the British to the east of river Sutlej.

Durbar at Rupar (1831):

English held a great Durbar (Court) in which Ranjit Singh was accorded a warm reception by the Governor-General himself.

Triple Alliance or Tripartite Treaty (1839):

In the Afghan struggle, Shah Shuja, the exiled ruler of Afghanistan, Maharaja Ranjit Singh and the British agreed to work unitedly.

Steps Taken by Maharaja Ranjit Singh to Save his Kingdom from British Encroachment

(1) Signed the above mentioned treaties with the British
(2) Fixed Sutlej as the boundary between his kingdom and the British kingdom
(3) Enlisted cooperation of almost all the 12 Sikh Misls
(4) Built up a strong force trained on European lines and under European instructors
(5) Fostered Hindu Muslim unity and thus presented a united front
(6) Used diplomatic realism and did not side with Indian rulers.

ANNEXATION OF THE PUNJAB (1849)

Political Instability

Maharaja Ranjit Singh and the British had cordial relations. After Ranjit's death in 1839, there was chaos and confusion in the Punjab. His successors were very weak. There were court rivalries. Three of his sons were killed in this struggle. Finally his youngest son Dalip Singh was put on the throne with Rani Jhindan, his mother, as his regent. This political instability in the Punjab offered an ideal opportunity to the British to conquer the Punjab.

After two Anglo-Sikh Wars, the Punjab was annexed in 1849.

First Anglo-Sikh War (1845-1846)

Causes:

(1) The English had set their eyes on the Punjab. However they dared not attack the Punjab during the rule of Ranjit Singh who was equally powerful. After his death, the English, regardless of their treaty with Ranjit Singh, became very arrogant and began to provoke the Sikhs.

(2) The Sikhs and especially the Khalsa army that had assumed more powers, began to look upon the British with suspicion after their caputure of Sindh.

(3) The British stationed a large number of troops on the borders of the territories under the Sikhs.

Maharaja Ranjit Singh: Conquest of Punjab 57

Events:

Four fierce battles took place at Mudki, Ferozepur, Aliwal and Sobran, betwen the British and the Sikhs. The treachery of two of the most important military commanders of the Sikhs led to the ultimate defeat of the Sikh army.

Results:

Treaty of Lahore (1846): Following were the main provisions:
(i) The British got the fertile lands of Doab between the rivers Beas and Sutlej.
(ii) The strength of the Sikh army was greatly reduced.
(iii) A war indemnity of Rs. one and a half crores was imposed on the Sikh ruler of the Punjab.
(iv) A British Resident and a strong British force came to be stationed at Lahore.
(v) Dalip Singh, the youngest son of Ranjit Singh was recognised as the ruler of the Punjab.
(vi) Lal Singh, one of the commanders of the Sikh army, who had played into the hands of the British, was made the Chief Minister of Maharaja Dalip Singh.
(vii) Gulab Singh, another commander, who had also sided with the British got the state of Jammu and Kashmir. Since the Sikh ruler was not able to pay the war indemnity, Gulab Singh paid a sum of Rs. 50 lakhs and purchased the state of Jammu and Kashmir.

Second Anglo-Sikh War (1849-49)

Causes:

(1) The Treaty of Lahore was short-lived. The British had an eye on the remaining part of the Punjab.
(2) The British Resident at Lahore ill treated the Sikh Sardars.
(3) Several Sikh forts were destroyed and they could no longer maintain their troops at various places.
(4) The British Resident at Lahore encouraged several revolts.
(5) Rani Jhindan was deposed on charges of conspiracy.

Events of the War:

It was the most dreadful and fierce war that the British had to fight in India. Two battles were fought at Chilianwala and Gujarat. In the first battle, the British suffered heavy losses. The second battle was won by the British. The Gujarat battle is called the 'Battle of Guns'. It was mainly due to the use of guns that the British forces were able to defeat the Sikh army.

Results:

(1) The Punjab was annexed by Lord Dalhousie on 29th March, 1849.
(2) Maharaja Dalip Singh was given a pension and sent to England.
(3) The British took away the famous 'Kohinoor'.

EXERCISES

A. Very Short Answer Type Questions

1. Give any two examples to show that Maharaja Ranjit Singh was a tolerant ruler in religious matters.
2. How did Maharaja Ranjit singh acquire the 'Kohi-Noor'?
3. What steps did Maharaja Ranjit Singh take to train his army on modern lines?
4. What was the result of the Anglo-Sikh wars?
5. Why was Kashmir given to Gulab Singh?

B. Short Answer Type Questions

1. Explain the significance of the Treaty of Amritsar.
2. Why did Maharaja Ranjit Singh and the British maintain good relations?
3. Why do we call Maharaja Ranjit Singh as the 'Lion of the Punjab'?
4. Why is it said that Maharaja Ranjit Singh was the last independent Indian ruler?
5. What were the causes that led to the defeat of the Sikhs in the Anglo-Sikh wars?

C. Long Answer Type Questions

1. Give an estimate of the achievements of Maharaja Ranjit Singh.
2. Give an account of civil and military administration of Maharaja Ranjit Singh.
3. Describe Anglo-Sikh relations during the rule of Maharaja Ranjit Singh.
4. Describe the events leading to the conquest of the Punjab by the British.

D. Map Work

On an outline map of India, show the extent of Ranjit Singh's empire.

CHAPTER 6

The Structure of Government and Administration Organisation of the British Empire in India (1757-1857)

THE OBJECTIVES OF THE SYSTEM

The East India Company was basically a trading organisation. Its controlling authority was situated in Britain. In due course, apart from trading, it acquired several territories. Thus, it combined two major functions i.e. earning profits and administering territories. As a matter of fact, when slowly and gradually it brought in its control, a vast territory in India, the administration of the conquered territories became a major function. With a view to have a firm control, the administrative practices began to be modified in light of the experience gained. Broadly speaking, the administration had the following objectives:
1. Increasing the profits of the Company
2. Maintaining the hold of the British on India
3. Maintaining law and order in the areas under control
4. Increasing the efficiency of the working of the Company
5. Exercising adequate check on the Board of Governors of the Company and its employees.

DEVELOPMENT OF THE ADMINISTRATIVE STRUCTURE AND CONTROL

The period between 1757 to 1857 may be divided broadly into two categories.
(i) Period upto 1772, of relative independence of the Company.
(ii) Period between 1773 to 1857, of control by the British Parliament.

Period upto 1772

The East India Company was comparatively free to pursue its commercial and administrative policies in India. By 1765, the Company had established its hold over Bengal. In Bengal, it followed the Dual System of Administration. It excersied control over the collection of revenue but the law and order situation remained with the 'Nawab of Bengal'. The period was one of plunder by the East India Company resulting in a famine in Bengal in 1769-70. The officials of the East India Company were making huge personal profits in India whereas the Company itself was running into losses and in fact was in debt. The Directors of the Company returned to Britain after amassing huge wealth from their stay in India. Other sections of the British society became jealous of the officials of the Company. For example, Clive returned from India with crores of rupees earned illegally. On the contrary, the Company requested for a loan of one million pounds from the British Government. Two Parliamentary Committees were set up by the Parliament which were highly critical of the Company. It was remarked, "Such a scene of tyranny and plunder has been opened up as makes one shudder."

Period of Regulation and Control

Issues before the British Government:

Following were the important issues relating to control:
(1) How could a commercial organisation like the East India Company be allowed to exercise political power in India?
(2) What kind of relationship was best when the central authority was located in Britain far away from India?
(3) What could be done to check the Company's officials, servants and officers from indulging in bribery and corruption?
(4) How could the Company increase its profits?
(5) How could the British Government hold its control over their colonies in India when they had lost their colonies in America?

Acts Passed by the British Government:

With a view to find a proper solution to above mentioned issues, the British Parliament passed the following Acts:
1. The Regulating Act 1773
2. Pitt's India Act 1784
3. Charter Act of 1813
4. Charter Act of 1833.

Regulating Act 1773:

Circumstances Leading to this Act
(1) The dual administration of the Company led to maladministration.
(2) The officials of the Company indulged in malpractices.
(3) The Company was in huge debt and appealed to the British Government for help.
(4) There was a lot of criticism of the working of the Company in the British Paliament.

Importance of the Act: This was the beginning of the control of the British Government on the affairs of the Company.

Main Provisions of the Act: (i) The Directors of the Company were required to place before the Ministry all correspondence regarding civil revenue and military matters relating to India (ii) The Government in India was to be carried on by the Governor of Bengal who was designated as the Governor-General (iii) The Governor-General was assisted by a Council of four members (iv) The Governors of Bombay and Madras were required to work under the Governor-General (v) The Governor-General was bound to take decisions with the majority vote of the members (vi) The Act provided for the establishment of a Supreme Court at Calcutta (vii) Every employee of the Company was required to submit a list of his properties and the sources of acquiring these.

Working of the Act and its Shortcomings: The Act failed to achieve the desired results on account of its following shortcomings:
(a) The Governor-General was at the mercy of the Council as three members could combine and outvote the Governor-General.
(b) The members themselves quarrelled occasionally.
(c) The Governor-General's control over Governors of Bombay and Madras proved inadequate.
(d) The jurisdiction of the Supreme Court was not clear.
(e) The Supreme Court had little knowledge about Indian customs and rites.

The Pitt's India Act, 1784:

Need for this Act: This Act was passed with a view to remove some of the shortcomings of the Regulating

Act of 1773. It took into consideration various issues involved in the efficient implementation of the Regulating Act.

The Act is named after William Pitt, the Prime Minister of Britain at that time.

Main Provisions:
(i) The Company's political work was separated from its commercial work.
(ii) For political purposes, the Company was placed in complete subordination to the British Government.
(iii) A Board of Directors including two Cabinet Ministers of the British Government was to look after the affairs of the Company.
(iv) The Governors of Bombay and Madras were made fully subordinate to the Governor-General.
(v) A special court was set up in England to decide the cases of corruption against the officials of the Company.

Significance:

The Act laid down the framework in which the work of the Company was to be carried on in India. In fact, the functioning of the Company came under the complete purview of the British Parliament. The Board of Control was to be constituted by the British Government. Arrangements provided for in the Act, remained the basis of administration upto 1857. However, the monopoly of trade with India remained with the East India Company.

The Charter Act of 1813

The Charter Act of 1813 abolished the Company's monopoly of trade with India. The Indian trade was thrown open to all British merchants.

The Charter Act of 1833

The Act was largely influenced by a wave of liberalism that had been passing over the British people and resulted in Britain's, Reform Bill (1832), the Abolition of Slavery (1833), the Factory Act (1833) and other liberal measures. The Directors of the East India Company took note of the changing mind, and the liberal measures of Governor-General Bentinck as well as of Munro and Elphinston were probably due to this policy. Besides this, another idea consciously or unconsciously was influencing the British mind regarding the ultimate take over of the Indian government by the crown. The Charter Acts of 1833 and 1853 and the discussion in Parliament amply illustrate it. The Charter Act of 1833 sought to give effect to three principles as indicated below (1) Gradual strengthening of control of the British crown over East India Company. (2) Elimination of mercantile interests of the Company. (3) Abolition of partronage in making appointments by substituting competitive examinations.

ADMINISTRATIVE ORGANISATION

Early Administrative Organisation

Initially, the Company's officials combined two functions i.e. trading as well as performing administrative duties. With the acquiring of several territories in India, it was not possible to combine these two functions. Besides performing these functions, the employees of the Company indulged in private trade also and earned huge profits. They resorted to all sorts of unfair means to amass wealth. They were tempted to do so as they received very meagre salaries. The situation continued during the period of Clive and Warren Hastings.

Beginning of Administrative Reforms

Lord cornwallis (1786-93) was the first Governor-General to introduce administrative reforms. Important

reforms made by him were the following:
(i) He raised the salaries of the employees with a view to motivating them to perform their duties honestly and efficiently
(ii) He demanded whole time service from the servants of the Company
(iii) He abolished private trade completely
(iv) He made all appointments on merit
(v) He gave the best jobs only to the Europeans in general and the Britishers in particular
(vi) According to the promotion policy, all promotions were to be made on the basis of seniority.

Civil Service

Company's Civil Servants became the highest paid in the World. The Collector of a District was to be paid Rs. 1500 a month and one percent commission on the revenue collection of the district. In the context of the modern times, the salary would run into several lakhs.

Training of Civil Servants:

The second stage in the administrative organisation was marked by the training of the civil servants of the Company. The employees of the Company who came to India from Britain were very young, with little experience and without any knowledge of Indian languages. So Lord Wellesely set up a training college known as Fort William College, Calcutta. Later on, the college was replaced by the East Indian Hailebury College in England.

Appointment of the Civil Servants:

The Charter Act of 1813 provided that no person could be appointed in India unless he had studied four terms at the Hailebury College. This college functioned till 1858.

Till 1853, the appointments were made by the Directors of the Company. Some nominations were also made by the members of the Board of Control.

The Charter Act of 1853 put an end to this system of appointments and these were to be made by open competition.

Discrimination against the Indians:

Indians were excluded from higher posts. Even at lower posts they were not given the same salary as given to the British and the European civil servants.

Army

Important Functions:

The second most important pillar of the administration was the army. It fulfilled three important functions (i) It was the chief instrument through which the English established their empire in India (ii) It defended the British empire in India from foreign rivals (iii) It helped in the maintenance of internal law and order by checking rebellions from different sections of population (iv) Indian army was very helpful in extending the British empire in other parts of Asia and Africa.

Composition of the Indian Army:

The bulk of the Company's army consisted of Indian soldiers recruited chiefly from U.P. and Bihar.

Discrimination in the Army:

The highest Indian officer was in the rank of a 'Subedar'. All the posts above this rank were held by the British officials. Besides, Indian soldiers were not paid adequate salaries.

Training:

Suitable equipments and training were provided to the army. Regular payment of salary was made to the soldiers. These two factors made the Company's army much more disciplined and efficient in comparison to those maintained by the Indian rulers. It is not, therefore, surprising that Clive was able to win the Battle of Plassey with just a force of 900 Eurupean and 1500 Indian soldiers against about 50,000 soldiers of the Indian rulers.

How Could a Handful of Foreigners Conquer and Control India?

There were four important factors that led to the success of a handful of British army. One was that there was an absence of nationalism among the rulers, the people, as well as the soldiers. A soldier from Bihar or Oudh or South did not ever think or feel that by helping the Company to defeat the army of another Indian ruler, he in fact was crushing down his own country men.

Secondly, the Indian soldier had a long tradition of loyalty to the 'salt he ate' i.e. loyalty to those who provided food or means of livelihood. As he was paid by the Company, he was loyal to it.

Thirdly, the Company gave regular salary.

Lastly, the Company provided suitable training and equipment to its army and thus it was more disciplined.

The Police

Traditionally a Disappointing Image of the Police:

The police was the third pillar of the British administration in India. It was organised for the following purposes (i) To crush anti-British sentiments (ii) To check rebellions (iii) To maintain law and order (iv) To apprehend thieves, dacoits and to curb crimes (v) To organise a secret service to nullify any conspiracy against the Government.

All the above functions of the police relate to repression and coercion. Obviously, its task was very unpleasant and therefore made it unpopular among the people.

Police Set-up:

Before Cornwallis, the functions of the police were performed by the Zamindars. Cornwallis relieved the zamindars of their police duties and transferred them to the District Magistrates. He brought about the following reforms (i) A separate police department was created (ii) A system of circles or *Thanas* each headed by a *Daroga*, who was an Indian, was established (iii) A post of District Superintendent of Police was created to head the police organisation in a district (iv) Indians were excluded from all superior posts in the police department (v) In the villages, the village watchmen continued to perform the duties of the police. This system, however, proved to be an "expensive failure". The crimes increased everywhere. In 1814, the Board of Directors, after enquiring into the state of police administration, condemned the establishment of darogas and recommended for the establishment of the village police. Many times, many changes were introduced, but corruption and inefficiency in police adminstration increased. The Lt. Governor of Bengal, in 1855, recorded that "the corruption and extortion of the police causes it to be popularly said that dacoity is bad enough, but the subsequent police enquiry very much worse".

Three Pillars of British Administration in India

The Civil Service, the army and the police are regarded as the three pillars of British administration in India. The British, being the foreigners, could not hope to earn the affection of the Indian people. They, therefore, relied on the strength of their administrative machinery, army and the police, rather than on public support, to maintain their control over India. Civil service was needed to perform the day-to-day work of administration, including supervision of trade. Army was needed to conquer territories and the police helped in the maintenance of law and order, without which the British merchants and manufacturers could not hope to sell their goods in India.

JUSTICE

Equality Before Law

The Indian legal system under the British, as it applied to Indian citizens, was based on the concept of equality before law which implied that, in the eyes of law, all persons, irrespective of status or caste etc. were equal. The law made no distinction between persons. According to the customary laws prevailing at that time in India, the laws differentiated between the so called high born and low born. For the same crime, punishments were different in different cases depending upon one's religion and status. The British law removed this distinction as far as its application to the Indians was concerned.

Inequality Before Law

This principle of equality before law did not apply in cases where Europeans were involved with Indians or vice versa. The Europeans and their descendants had separate courts and even laws.

Judicial Organisation

Justice was enforced through a series of courts at the district level, provincial level and at the centre. Accordingly, there were District Courts, Provincial Courts and there upon the Supreme Court.

In each district, there were two types of courts i.e. civil (diwani) and the criminal (faujdari-involving murder, physical violence and conspiracy etc.). The courts were usually presided over by the British judges assisted by Hindu Pandits well-versed in Hindu law and Muslim Maulvis well versed in Muslim law.

Codification of Laws

The British gradually evolved a new system of laws. They codified and systematised the existing laws. In 1833, the British Government appointed a Law Commission under Lord Macaulay to codify the Indian laws. It resulted in the formation of an Indian Penal Code and it paved the way for a uniform system of courts all over the British territories in India.

Defects in the System of Justice

(a) Justice was expensive. Court fees, lawyers' fees and distances to be travelled to reach the courts - all increased the cost of justice. By and large, the justice is still expensive. (b) The law suits dragged on for years. (c) The peasants and the common people, who were mostly illiterate had to face hardships. (d) Cases of injustice with the Indians were frequent when British citizens were the other parties. The judges did not punish the British subjects when they were charged with crimes against the Indians. (e) Corruption became rampant. (f) The rich could exercise their influence.

The picture of administering justice is a rude reminder that the security of life and property and an efficient system of administration based on the rule of law, regarded as the chief blessings of British rule, had been largely absent at the end of the first century of British rule in India. The Law Member, Macaulay pointed out, "The expenses of litigation in England are so heavy that people sit down quietly under wrongs, but the people of India are poor and expenses of litigation in the Supreme Court are five times as great as the expenses at Westminister". And a Britisher would, with impunity, dare to loot or break a native's head without the fear of being caught or punished by a magistrate or a judge, for a 'white' sees a 'white' spotlessly clean, a racial privilege no court could change or challenge.

EXERCISES

A. Very Short Type Questions
1. State the concept of 'Equality before law'.
2. List any three objectives of British administration in India.
3. Why does the police not have a good image among the people?
4. Why was it felt necessary to change the administrative set up of the East India Company?

B. Short Answer Type Questions
1. State the three pillars of British administration in India and their significance.
2. Mention the measures undertaken by the British to introduce changes in Indian legal system.
3. State the circumstances that led to the creation of civil services.
4. Why did the British follow the policy of excluding Indians from higher posts?
5. Mention the important functions performed by the British army in India.

C. Long Answer Type Questions
1. Explain the important features of judicial administration under the East India Company.
2. Why was the Regulating Act passed? State any three of its provisions.
3. State any four provisions of the Pitt's India Act.
4. "In spite of a small army, the British were successful in defeating large armies of the Indian rulers". Explain.

CHAPTER 7

The Economic, Social and Cultural Policy of the British in India (1757-1857)

EXPLOITATION OF INDIA

The British domination brought about several fundamental changes in the economic life of the people of India. New forms of production and consumption emerged during the period. The British derived enormous economic benefits in several ways from their Indian empire. Starting by making profits from trade with India, the British made India a major market for goods manufactured in Britain and a source of raw materials for their British factories.

The British factories in India did not manufacture goods. These were just trading offices. The term 'British factory' was thus a misnomer.

EAST INDIA COMPANY-A TRADING ORGANISATION (1600-1757)

During the period 1600-1757 A.D., the Company remained a trading organisation, and its profits were primarily from the sale of Indian goods abroad. The Company constantly made vigorous efforts to open new markets for export of Indian goods.

REVOLUTIONARY CHANGES IN THE ECONOMIC POLICY AFTER THE INDUSTRIAL REVOLUTION IN ENGLAND

Even before the Industrial Revolution in England which took place in the second half of the 18th century, the British manufacturers had become jealous of the popularity of Indian goods in the European markets, including Britain. During the first quarter of the 18th century, laws had been passed in Britain which forbade the wear and use of printed or dyed cotton cloth. In 1760, in Britain, a lady had to pay a fine of £200 for possessing an imported handicraft.

The British Government levied such high duties on several categories of Indian goods that their import to Britain virtually ceased. For example, in 1824, a duty of 67½ per cent was levied on Indian calico and a duty of 37½ per cent on Indian muslins. Indian sugar had to pay an import duty in England that came to be over three times its cost price. In some cases, duties in England went up as high as 400 per cent.

After their victory in the Battle of Plassey in 1757, the British could use their political control over Indian trade and production to push their trade.

The Industrial Revolution in Britain completely changed its economy after second half of the 18th century. The British industry developed and expanded rapidly on the strength of their modern machinery and other technological advances. A powerful group of manufacturers came up in Britain. They were in a position to influence the economic and commercial policy of the Company. They also found support from the British Government. They prevailed upon the Company to follow such a policy that encouraged the import of raw material in Britain from India and export of manufactured goods from Britain to India.

The two-fold strategy followed in the economic matters was as under:

(1) Duties on Goods

The British Government was determined to protect its growing machine-based industries. Heavy import duties on the Indian made goods in Britain were imposed. As a result, Indian imports to England declined. India was forced to export only raw material like cotton and silk.

(2) Monopoly of Raw Materials

East India Company monopolised the sales of raw material in Bengal. On the one hand, they did not offer reasonable rates for the raw materials produced in India, and on the other, they forced the weavers and highly skilled artisans to sell their products to them at very cheap rates. Thus the Indian artisans lost both ways—by buyers as well as sellers.

Impact of British Economic Policy on Indian Economy

The above mentioned policy adversely affected the Indian economy in a number of ways.

Drain of Wealth from India:

There is no parallel of the English exploitation of India. The English used all means—fair and foul, to collect wealth from India, spend it on the improvement of English economy and to enjoy a comfortable life. The various methods of exporting wealth from India were as under:
(1) Heavy tributes levied on Indian rulers on different pretexts
(2) Heavy dividends to the shareholders of the Company
(3) Pay of civil servants of the Company
(4) Enormous profits by the Company and British merchants from trade
(5) Maintenance of armies at the cost of Indian rulers and thereby saving a lot of money
(6) Bribes and gifts extorted from several sections of population in India
(7) Heavy tribute paid by the Company to the British Government in lieu of their permission to trade and exercise control over India.

Decline of Indigenous Indian Industry:

The British led to the near destruction of Indian handicrafts. Prior to the coming of the British, India exported large quantities of cotton textiles, silks and muslins, metalwares, ivory, glass, jewellery, sandalwood, etc. Large quantities of the goods were also used by wealthy Nawabs, Rajas, Nobles, etc. But the British government, with a view to discouraging the use of Indian goods by the British people, banned the import of Dacca muslin in 1720. Indian handicrafts were starved as there were not enough Indian buyers, since the place of nobles, who loved to patronize industries, was taken over by the British civil servants, indifferent to Indian interests. With the Industrial Revolution in England, large quantities of British machine-made goods flooded the Indian markets and the local manufacturers could not compete with them either in price or in durability of the goods.

Slow Growth of Modern Industries:

It was not in the interest of the British economy to develop industries in India because of their desire to keep India as a flourishing market for their manufactured goods. It was only in 1833 that the first cotton mill was set up in India by a Parsee businessman.

Disruption of Village Economy:

For centuries, Indian villages had remained self-sufficient. They produced most of the goods and services that were consumed by them. They had very few necessities. With the establishment of the British hold over India, the villages lost their self-sufficiency. They became dependent on machine-made goods. The barter system, the chief characteristic of village economy, was gradually replaced by transaction through money. The village economy became more and more dependent on the cities and the towns.

Deterioration of Agriculture:

Indian agriculture stagnated and deteriorated on account of factors like overcrowding on agricultural land, excessive land revenue, growing indebtedness and the apathy of the zamindars. Overcrowding land led to fragmentation of land into small holdings (fields) which could hardly meet the minimum needs of the cultivators and on which modern techniques of cultivation could not be applied.

Impoverishment of the Peasantry:

The chief factor of the impoverishment of the peasants was heavy land revenue charged from them. The new Zamindari system put the peasants on the mercy of the zamindars, who extracted illegal dues, forced them to free labour or 'begar' and oppressed them in numerous ways. The cultivators had to pay the land revenue even if crops failed on account of drought or were destroyed by floods. With the fear of losing land on account of non-payment of land revenue, the peasants borrowed money at exorbitant rates of interest from the moneylenders. The moneylenders, taking advantage of the helpless and illiterate cultivators, adopted several deceitful measures like false accouting and forged signatures. Often the cultivators were forced to sell a part of their land to the moneylenders to repay their debts.

Poverty and Famines:

The major factors responsible for the poverty of the common people were their economic exploitation by the British, high taxes, decay of handicrafts, deterioration of agriculture and exploitation of the helpless peasants and workers by the moneylenders, zamindars, merchants and the government officials. The poverty of the people culminated in famines.

LAND REVENUE POLICY OF THE BRITISH RULERS

Main Objective of the Land Revenue Policy

The main objective of the land revenue policy of the British in India was to collect as much revenue as possible from the land. As a matter of fact it became the major source of income. And the income went on increasing as the British went on acquiring control of more and more territories in India. The British needed money for several purposes (i) To pay for the army needed to expand and consolidate their conquered territories (ii) To pay for the thousands of Englishmen in superior administrative and military positions (iii) To pay for the purchase of Indian handicrafts and other goods for exports (iv) To pay tribute to the British Government in England and (v) To pay to the shareholders of the Company. An unofficial charge was to get bribes from different sections of the population. The burden of revenue fell on land revenue to be charged from the peasants.

Systems of Land Revenue

The British did not follow a uniform system of land revenue in the entire country. There were three major systems of land revenue.

Permanent Settlement of Bengal:

After the victory in the Battle of Buxar in 1765, the *Diwani* i.e., collection and retention of land revenue in

Bengal, Bihar and Orissa came into the hands of the Company.

Lord Clive did not introduce any change in the method of collection of revenue. The old practice continued. The revenue officials and the zamindars collected land revenue from the cultivators. They kept a part of the revenue with them as their commission and deposited the balance in the treasury. Warren Hastings wanted to collect more revenue for meeting the growing administrative and other changes. He, therefore, introduced the system of bids. The land was given to the highest bidders who were called the collectors. This system proved to be very defective. The highest bidders began to extract more and more revenue from the cultivators which resulted in severe hardships to them. Cornwallis therefore, changed this system and introduced in 1793 a new system known as Permanent Settlement.

Main Features of the Permanent Settlement:
1. The revenue Collectors or the Zamindars who collected the land revenue were made the owners of the land.
2. They were to act as agents of the Government in collecting land revenue from the cultivators.
3. They were to retain a part of the land revenue collected from the cultivators.
4. The rights of ownership of land were given to the Zamindars and were made hereditary.
5. The share of the land revenue to be paid was fixed permanently.

Merits:
1. The income from land revenue to the Company became certain
2. A class of zamindars emerged which became very loyal to the Company.

Demerits:
1. The land revenue was fixed, but the day-to-day expenditure of the company began to increase
2. The zamindars began to extract more and more money from the cultivators and their condition became very miserable.

The Ryotwari System:

This system was introduced in parts of Madras and Bombay Presidency. The system derives its name from the word 'Ryot' which means 'cultivator peasant'. This system had the following features:
1. The cultivators became the land owners
2. The land revenue was raised after every 20 to 30 years
3. The cultivators themselves deposited the land revenue.

Merits:
1. The Company gained financially as it could increase the land revenue
2. The peasants had the satisfaction that they had become the owners of the land
3. The peasants were free from the tyranny of the zamindars.

Demerits:
1. The Company had to deal with lakhs of cultivators directly instead of a few zamindars
2. In most cases, the land revenue fixed was very exorbitant. In Madras, the revenue was fixed as high as 45 to 55 per cent of the gross production from the land. The situation was no better in Bombay
3. The 'ryot' had to pay revenue even when his produce was partially or wholly destroyed by flood or drought etc.
4. The Government retained the right to enhance the land revenue.

Mahalwari System:

This system derives its meaning from the word *Mahal* which means a village or an estate. Under this system the land revenue was charged on the village or the estate. An estate was held by a group of families. The land revenue was collected from the village as one unit. It could be collected through the representative of the village.

The amount of revenue was revised periodically.

The system was prevalent in parts of Central India, Gangetic Valley, North-West Province and the Punjab.

CULTURAL POLICY OF THE BRITISH IN INDIA

Meaning of Culture

Before taking up the cultural policy in India, we may briefly give the meaning of the word culture. In simple language, culture may be defined as a way of life of a group of people or society. It is inherent in thinking, feeling and doing, which are interrelated. One thinks, feels and does or one does what one thinks and feels. One feels something, thinks about it and does it. Thinking is associated with knowledge, ideas, beliefs, philosophy and so on. Feeling develops attitudes, morals, values, likes and dislikes about things, persons and ideas. Doing refers to how the community or the society or the individuals respond to their physical, political, religious and social environment, how they spend their life, how they earn their living, what they eat and wear, what they make, how they sing and dance. In fact culture is concerned with the entire living style of the individuals, the groups and the society as a whole.

Chief Characteristics of Culture

Culture of a group, or society, or individual is never static. It changes. The changes may be partially good or partially bad. Culture is influenced by a number of factors: economic, geographical, legislative, political and religious. It is influenced by a continuous and cumulative process but not always a progressive process.

Modernisation of a culture may sometimes be seen as a derogatory step.

Major Influences on Indian Culture

Indian culture was influenced by a number of factors. Among the important ones were the following:
1. Industrial Revolution influencing several cultural areas.
2. Ferment of new ideas, new attitudes of mind, manners and morals, as a result of French Revolution in 1789. The Three Characteristics of the new thought were rationalism or faith in reason and science, humanism or love of man and confidence in the capacity of man to progress.
3. Critical attitude about Indian society and culture. Indian culture was condemned as static and irrational, full of outmoded, unscientific and superstitious ideas.
4. Imitation of the foreign ruler's language, dress, food, manners and life styles and adopting their ideas and beliefs.
5. Work of Christian missionaries.
6. Spread of education.
7. Social and religious reformers-Indian as well as foreign.
8. Publication of literature in different disciplines.
9. Legislative measures or laws.
10. Mixed marriages.
11. Means of communications.
12. Changes in Indian agriculture—emergence of a new class of zamindars and their changed lifestyle in the light of new official and social requirements necessitated by the British civil servants and other officials.

Cultural Change through Social Legislation

The British rulers passed the following laws to bring about cultural changes in the Indian society.
1. Abolition of Sati in 1829 by William Bentinck
2. Suppression of human sacrifice through various efforts in 1795, 1802 and 1804
3. Prohibition of female infanticide by William Bentinck in 1802
4. Widow remarriage 1856
5. Prohibiting slavery in 1849.

Among the important social reform movements, and social reformers, who played an important role in cultural awakening and supporting legislation, mention may be made of the following:
(a) Atmiya Sabha 1815
(b) Brahma Samaj in 1828
(c) Tatlvabodhini Sabha in 1843
(d) Raja Rammohan Roy (1772-1833)
(e) Iswar Chandra Vidyasagar (1820-1891)

CULTURE AND EDUCATIONAL POLICY OF THE BRITISH

There is a constant interaction betwen culture and education. Culture is the key which unlocks the creative potential of a society and education is the tool which could shape and guide the development of the potential. Education is an important means of transmitting culture from one generation to another. It is therefore natural that the English, who wanted to transmit Western Culture, should have made education as the vehicle.

Macaulay as the Architect of the English System of Education in India

Lord Macaulay was the Law Member of the Council of William Bentinck, the Governor General of India. He was also appointed as the Chairman of the Society of Public Instruction. He was a great protagonist of English culture and education. He favoured the introduction of European literature through the medium of English. His views are recorded in a document popularly known as Lord Macaulay's Minutes. He outlined the following three main objectives of the English education in India.
1. He wanted to create "a class of persons, Indian in blood and colour, but British in taste, opinion, morals and intellect". In other words, he was for the Europeanisation of the culture of India.
2. He wanted to form a class of interpreters between the Indian rulers and the millions whom they governed.
3. The third objective was to obtain a cheap supply of Indian clerks for holding subordinate posts in administration and British commercial concerns.

Macaulay argued that English culture was far superior to Indian culture. He wrote, "A single shelf of good European library, was worth the whole native literature of India and Arabia". He further condemned everything in Indian culture "false history, false astronomy, false medicine and false religion". Most Indian historians have pardoned his remarks, biased by an overt sense of racial superiority, prejudiced by an overbearing arrogonce of a ruling class, and aberrated by sheer lack of knowledge about the wisdom of Indians treasured in Vedas, Upanishads and other ancient Indian literature, produced at a time when Europe had not yet seen the dawn of civilization.

A section of India's social reformers also supported the views of Macaulay as regards his view on promoting European literature and sciences through the medium of English language. The Government of India accepted the recommendations of Macaulay in 1835. The Government's declaration in 1844, that English knowing Indians would be given preference in public employment made English very popular.

About the cultural effect of education on the Indians, Macaulay, in a letter, wrote to his father in 1836, "Hindus are much influenced with education. There is no Hindu who may keep faith in his religion after studying English".

The English system of education exercised positive as well as negative effects. While on the one hand, the system of education created a wide gulf between the educated class and the masses, on the other hand, it led to the opening of doors of the western thought and culture, science and technology.

MEANS OF TRANSPORT AND COMMUNICATION

Objectives

Means of transport and communication play a major role in the development of trade and commerce, in extending territories by the swift movement of troops, in bringing under control, officers and officials carrying on administrative work in distant parts, on sending speedy government instructions, in intermingling of cultures and above all, in the national and emotional integration of the people of a vast country like India. (This last objective was not in the minds of the British when they thought of developing rapid means of communication in India.)

Roads

The first step in the development of roads was taken in the construction of the Grand Trunk Road from Sonargaon near Calcutta to Delhi in 1839, and it was completed in the 1850's. It was extended up to Peshawar and now touches the border of Afghanistan. Efforts were also made to link the major cities, ports and markets of the country by road. Calcutta had the first metalled road is 1825. The first motor bus was introduced in Bombay in 1826.

Railways

The first railway line running from Bombay to Thana was opened in 1853. Lord Dalhousie took a keen interest in the rapid construction of railways.

Post and Telegraph

The first post office was established by the East India Company in Calcutta in 1727.
The first Telegraph line from Calcutta to Agra was opened in 1853.

EXERCISES

A. Very Short Answer Type Questions

1. List some economic changes brought about by the British domination of India.
2. List any two economic benefits derived by the British from India.
3. List any two measures adopted by the British to discourage the import of goods from India.
4. List any two objectives of the land revenue policy of the British in India.
5. List any social laws passed by the British Government.
6. Mention any two main objectives of the English system of education in India.

B. Short Answer Type Questions

1. Why did the British Government impose heavy import duties on Indian goods?
2. In what ways did the Industrial Revolution in England affect Indian economy?
3. State the main features of the Ryotwari System.

4. Explain the role of education in the promotion of culture.
5. List any two positive and any two negative effects of the English system of education in India.

C. Long Answer Type Questions

1. Explain the impact of the British economic policy on Indian economy.
2. Explain the meaning, main provisions, merits and demerits of the Permanent Settlement of Bengal.
3. Give the meaning of 'culture'. How was Indian culture influenced by the Western culture?
4. Why did Lord Macaulay suggest the promotion of European art, literature and science? Also state how he tried to influence Indian culture through education.

CHAPTER 8

Social and Cultural Awakening in the First Half of the 19th Century

With the interaction of the Europeans and the Indians, there was a lot of social and cultural awakening in India. On the one hand there was a good deal of deep study and reflection on ancient Indian culture and thought and on the other, the impact of western science and technology on the rapid progress made by the European nations. The thinkers of India realized in general that there was great scope for social and cultural reforms to lift India from its degraded position.

RAJA RAMMOHAN ROY (1772-1833): FOUNDER OF MODERN INDIA

Raja Rammohan Roy is regarded as the founder of modern India as there was hardly any aspect of nation-building which he left untouched. He laid the foundations for the reform of Indian society through his crusades against social evils, illiteracy and religious orthodoxy. He raised his voice against the economic and political exploitation of the Indians. He promoted national consciousness among the Indian people.

Synthesiser of the East and the West

Rammohan Roy represented a synthesis of the East and the West. He had a great love and respect for the traditional cultural and philosophical thought of the East, but, at the same time he believed that modern culture and thought, which emphasises rational and scientific approach, would help in the regeneraion of Indian society and the principles of human dignity and social equality of all men and women.

He knew over a dozen languages of the East and West. He was a scholar of Arabic, Persian and Sanskrit languages of the East and also a scholar of English, French, Greek, Hebrew and Latin languages of the West. He had studied Hindu philosophy at Varanasi and the Muslim philosophy at Patna. He was well acquainted with the philosophic thought of Jainism and other sects of India. Later on, he made an intensive study of Western thought and culture.

Brief Life Sketch

Rammohan Roy was given the title of 'Raja' by the Mughal Emperor Akbar II when he sent him as his envoy to the king of England in 1830.

In 1815, he started the 'Atmiya Sabha' a spiritual society. In 1818, he launched a crusade against 'Sati'. In 1820, he wrote *The Precepts of Jesus*. In 1821, he started the Persian journal *Mirat-ul-Akhbar*. He started the Bengali paper *Sambad Kamudi* in 1821-22. He protested against the Press Act of 1823. In 1829, he founded the Brahma Samaj which later came to be known as Brahmo Samaj. He spent about three years (1931-33) in England where he breathed his last.

Raja as a Religious Reformer

The religious views of the Raja were greatly influenced by a number of factors: unacceptability of the staunch orthodoxy of his family religion, deep study of the Hindu philosophy enshrined in the Vedas and the Upanishads, study of the holy Quran and Arabic and Persian literature, study of the Bible and his association with English friends.

Rammohan's contribution to religious reforms may be summed up as under:-

1. He insisted upon applying rationalism to religious beliefs. He regarded reason as the touchstone of the truth of any doctrine
2. He tried to separate the moral and philosophical messages of religion
3. He believed in an 'omnipotent' god and opposed the worship of several gods
4. He condemned idol worship
5. He opposed the caste system
6. He opposed meaningless religous rituals and the ways of the priestly classes
7. He started the Atmiya Sabha - a spiritual movement
8. He published the following religious literature:
   (a) He wrote in Persian, his famous work *Gift to Monotheists* in defending the worship of one god against belief in and worship of many gods.
   (b) He published the Bengali traslation of the Vedas and five of the Principal Upanishads.
   (c) He published his *Precepts of Jesus* bringing the moral message of Jesus.
9. He found the Brahma Samaj, later known as Brahmo Samaj.

Rammohan as a Social Reformer

1. He denounced the nasty custom of *Sati* which compelled a Hindu widow to burn herself alive on the pyre of her husband. On several occasions, he went round the burning ghats, to stop this evil practice. He even organised groups of men to persuade the mourners to save the widow's life.
   He rendered all possible cooperation to Lord William Bentinck to pass a law declaring *Sati* as an illegal act.
2. He favoured widow remarriage.
3. He wanted to secure a place of honour for women.
4. He pleaded for women, the right of inheritance to property.
5. He condemned the practice of polygamy.

Rammohan as a Promoter of Education

Rammohan Roy was one of the earliest propagators of modern education as he was convinced that education was a major instrument for the awakening of the people of India. His major contributions to the spread of education may be summarised as under:

1. He exhorted Indians to abandon the medieval classic system of education and seek education in the methods, spirit and ideas of modern science and technology.
2. He was opposed to the establishment of Persian or Sanskrit institutions.
3. He wanted to promote a moral, liberal and enlightened system of education, embracing Anatomy, Chemistry, Mathematics, Natural Philosophy and other useful sciences.
4. He wanted the promotion of Indian vernaculars.
5. He maintained at his own cost, an Enlish school in Calcutta.
6. He established a Vedanta college in which courses in Indian learning as well as Western, social and physical sciences were provided.
7. He encouraged education of women.

As a Multifarious Reformer

1. As a political reformer, Rammohan showed passionate attachment to the concept of political liberty.
2. As a judicial reformer, he suggested the extension of the jurisdiction of the Indian Courts over Europeans.
3. As a press reformer, he believed in the freedom of the press.
4. As an internationalist, he considered mankind as one family.
5. As an economic reformer, he wanted the Board of Control to save the cultivator from the clutches of the landlord.

To sum up, Rammohan Roy was a fine and unyielding reformer, fighter against orthodoxy, champion of women's rights, pioneering journalist, humanist and rationalist and above all he was a precursor of enlightened approaches and modernising influences. Undoubtedly, he is the founder of modern India and a synthesiser of the Eastern and Western thought.

ISWARA CHANDRA VIDYASAGAR (1820-91)

A helpless poor student, who had to study standing under a street lamp, turned out to be a scholarship holder, award winner, and topper, in his student life. Later, he became an Inspector of Schools, founder of more than three dozen schools, Head Pandit of the Fort William College, Principal, educational consultant to successive Governors of Bengal, crusader of women education and their emancipator and Honorary Member of the Royal Asiatic Society of England.

Personification of the Ideal 'Example is better than precept'

Iswar Chandra Vidyasagar practised what he preached: He married his son to a widow. He worked for the poor. His generosity was unrivalled. He would often take off his coat to leave it on the shivering shoulders of a beggar in the way. He believed in the dignity of labour. He was a man of simple habits.

A Great Scholar

Iswara Chandra was a profound Sanskrit scholar. He wrote a series of primers in Sanskrit and also a primer in Bengali that is still popular. He wrote histories, grammars and commentaries on epics. He was directly concerned with the running of such well-known papers as the 'Somprakash' and the 'Hindu Patriot'. On account of his scholarship, he earned the title of 'Vidya-Sagar' (Ocean of Knowledge) from the authorities of the Sanskrit College, Calcutta.

Contribution in the Field of Education

(i) He established several educational institutions (ii) He developed a new method of teaching Sanskrit (iii) He threw open the doors of his Sanskrit College to even the Non-Brahmans (iv) He developed a new script for the Bengali language (v) Through his writings, he helped in the evolution of a prose style in Bengali (vi) He introduced the study of Western thought in the Sanskrit College.

His Contribution to Social Reform's and Women's uplift

(i) He carried a crusade for widow remarriage. In 1855, a large number of petitions from Bengal, Madras, Bombay and Nagpur and other cities of India were presented to the government, asking to legalize widow remarriage. Ignoring the threat of furious orthodox people to burn him, he performed the marriages of 25 widows during the period from 1855 to 1860 (ii) He gave financial help to the couple where required in the widow remarriage (iii) He opposed polygamy throughout his life (iv) He established several educational institutions for girls with a view to bring an awakening among women (v) He protested against child marriage.

Social and Cultural Awakening in the First Half of the 19th Century

The Bethune School

Iswar Chandra founded this school in Calcutta in 1849. The school spearheaded a powerful movement for women's education. The orthodox Hindus fiercely opposed the school, tooth and nail. In the beginning it became very difficult to find girl students for this school. However, Iswar Chandra stood like a rock and at last through his steadfast efforts, this school became an important centre of women's education.

HENRY VIVIAN DEROZIO (1809-1831)

Henry Vivian was a fiery poet-patriot of Bengal. He was the son of a Portuguese father and an English mother. He regarded India as his motherland and wrote poems on its past glory. These were published in the *'India Gazette'* of Calcutta. Derozio, while a teacher at the Hindu College, inspired his students for the love of the motherland. His house became the centre of debates and discussions on patriotism, social evils, idolatory and priesthood. He tried to develop in his pupils, a new awareness based on enquiry, free thinking and truth.

Derozio helped his students to bring out a weekly journal *Parthenon*. He published articles on the importance of female education, eradication of social evils and evils of European colonisation of India.

The authorities stopped the publication of the journal and blamed Derozio for instigating students. He was forced to resign from the Hindu College.

Derozio brought out an evening daily *The East Indian* in 1831. The same year he died of cholera at the very young age of 22.

Derozio founded the Young Bengal Movement, to inspire young people, for the love of motherland. He is remembered as a teacher of a new awakening, a new learning and a friend, philosopher and guide to his students whom he inspired to symbolise the Renaissance in Bengal.

DAVID HARE

A Scottish, he adopted India as his motherland. He was an active associate of the Young Bengal Movement. He spent about 40 years in the service of the people of Bengal. He gifted his house to the Hindu College, Calcutta. He was a free thinker and devoted to the cause of new education and Renaissance in Bengal. He opposed the Press Regulations of 1835. He was secular and liberal in his outlook.

THE YOUNG BENGAL MOVEMENT

The Young Bengal Movement was founded by Henry Derozio, a young lecturer of Hindu College, Calcutta. The followers of this movement were also called *Derozians*. Surendranath Banerjee (1848-1925), a great national leader, was so impressed by this movement, which of course was short lived, called Derozians as 'the pioneers of the modern civilization of Bengal'.

The Young Bengal Movement was inspired by the ideas of liberty, equality and fraternity.

The movement worked for the removal of several superstitions. According to the followers of the movement, truth must conform reason. The members of the movement emphasised female education and supported the rights of women. They worked for the protection of peasants from the tyranny of the zamindars.

BRAHMA (BRAHMO) SAMAJ

Origin. The Brahma Samaj was founded in Bengal in 1828 by the great social and religious reformer, Raja Rammohan Roy. Its main objective was to reform the Hindu Society.

Main Principles of the Brahma Samaj: (1) It believed in one God (2) It repudiated the doctrine of polytheism (several gods) (3) It condemned image worship (4) It believed in the eternity of soul (5) It preached that the true worship of God lies in the service of humanity, love and devotion (6) It opposed useless customs and costly sacrifices (7) It believed in social equality (8) It condemned superstitions.

Prominent leaders of the Brahma Samaj: Raja Rammohan Roy (1772-1833), Debendranath Tagore (1818-1905) and Keshav Chandra Sen (1838-1884) were the most important leaders of the Brahma Samaj. Most of the leaders of the Samaj had received their education through the English medium. So they wanted to give due place to the liberal ideas of the West.

SOCIAL AND RELIGIOUS REFORMERS IN WESTERN INDIA

Gujarat

1. Bal Shastri Jambekar was one of the first reformers in Bombay (Earlier Bombay was a part of Gujarat State). He attacked orthodoxy of Brahmans. In 1832, he founded a weekly of Brahmans called *Darpan* with the objective of removing superstitions from the minds of the people and shedding new light on social and religious issues.
2. Karsondas Mulji started the *'Satya Prakash'* in Gujarati in 1852, to advocate widow remarriage.
3. Dadabhai Naoroji (1825-1917), a Parsi, devoted himself to several reforms. He championed the cause of female education. He was instrumental in establishing prominent societies like the Students Literary and Scientific Society, the Bombay Association and the Widow Remarriage Association etc.

Maharashtra

In 1849, the Paramahansa Mandali was founded in Maharashtra. Branches of the Mandali were formed in several towns like Poona and Satara in Maharashtra. The Chief objectives of the Mandali were (i) Breaking caste system (ii) Education of women (iii) Widow remarriage.

In 1851, Jotiba Phule and his wife started a girls' school at Poona and soon many educational institutions came up. Jotiba Phule, born in a low caste Mali family, carried a campaign against the domination of upper classes and Brahmanical supremacy.

Gopal Hari Deshmukh (1823-1892), popularly called Lokhitwadi, advocated widow remarriage. He vehemently criticised social evils like child marriage, shaving of the heads of the widows, caste distinctions etc. He started a 'Punar-Vivaha Mandal' (Widow Remarriage Institute). He contributed funds for educational institutions, orphanages, public wells etc. He wrote several books and started newspapers to promote his views.

EXERCISES

A. Very Short Answer Type Questions

1. Mention any four achievements of Raja Rammohan Roy in the social field.
2. Why was Rammohan called the 'Raja'?
3. List any four disabilities from which women suffered in the 19th century.
4. List any four evils that had crept up in the Hindu society.
5. List the aims and objectives of the Young Bengal Movement.
6. List the two objectives of the Paramahansa Mandali.
7. Mention the work done by Jotiba Phule.
8. Explain the contribution made by Gopal Deshmukh in the field of social and educational reform.
9. In what ways Henry Vivian Derozio influenced the young men of Bengal?

B. Short Answer Type Questions

1. Why is Raja Rammohan Roy hailed as the founder of modern India?
2. "Raja Rammohan Roy tried to bring out a synthesis between the East and the West." Explain the statement with examples.
3. Explain the main principles of the Brahma Samaj.
4. Why did Rammohan Roy oppose caste system?
5. "Iswar Chandra Vidyasagar's contibution to the making of modern India is many-sided." Explain.
6. Name any two social reformers of Western India and their contribution.

CHAPTER 9

The Revolt of 1857

How does a revolt occur? The signs of an approaching revolt are not very distinctive. It sometimes so happens that unbearable load of grievances, insults and injustices, humiliations and harassments keep on building intense discontent among groups or masses of people against unsympathetic or oppressive authorities. Suddenly, somewhere the bounds of toleration give way and the discontent erupts like a volcano in the form of corrosive anger, bitter hatred and revengeful fury. Like red molten lava of a volcano, these gush forth on all sides in fiery streams. Other groups join. The fury expands and spreads. It burns, destroys and kills everything and everyone that comes in its way. Then reason departs and the fear of consequences is flung aside. Indiscriminate destruction and pillage become the rule. The authorities are caught unawares in a shocking surprise, as they have been used to bask under the absolute confidence that their conquered subjects, with supple backbones and submissive nature, will never dare to lift their heads. This is how the 1857 revolt of the Indian sepoys took place.

EARLY REVOLTS

Different sections of people by and large resisted the British rule in India from its very start in 1757, after the defeat of Siraj-ud-Daula by the treachery of Mir Qasim at the battle field of Plassey. Hardly a year passed till 1857, which did not witness some sort of revolt in one or other part of India. Between 1763 and 1856, there were 40 major outbreaks.

After the British conquest of Bengal, one of the earliest revolt was lead by *sanyasis* (ascetics, fakirs) organizing a 50 thousand strong mass of displeased peasants and farmers. The British took 30 long years to suppress it. The tribals of different regions—the Santhals, the Khasis, the Kols, the Bhils, the Gonds, the Kolis revolted at different times.

There wer revolts against the British rule in Gujarat, Maharashtra, South India and several centres of Northern India.

EARLY SEPOY REVOLTS

There were a number of sepoy revolts on account of low pay, distant postings, hurt of religious sentiments, bad food, insults and discrimination between the European and the Indian sepoys. There was a revolt at Vellore in 1806 by the Hindu soldiers. Native infantry, stationed at Barrackpur, revolted in 1824 when asked to proceed to fight the First Burmese War. In 1838, there were sepoy revolts at Sholapur, Secundrabad, Milligaon and Hyderabad. Madras cavalry revolted in 1843 at Jabalpur. All these revolts were crushed.

REVOLT OF 1857

The Revolt of 1857 was distinctive as compared to the aforesaid revolts. It was not confined to one group

The Revolt of 1857

or one regiment or one place. The revolt began at Meerut, 58 km from Delhi on 10th May 1857, and then gathering force it rapidly embraced a vast area from the Punjab in the north to the Narmada in the south, and from Bihar in the east to Rajputana in the west. But the ruthless repression of the British, with heap over heap of atrocities ended the chapter of the revolt by hanging Tantia Tope on 18th April 1859.

The causes were various that fermented the first blast and its fury spread like fire under the patriotic blaze and heroic valour of great leaders at different places which were soaked by the blood and sanctified by the sacrifice of thousands of martyrs. Thus, thousands of mothers lost their beloved sons, thousands of children mourned their father's loss, and thousands of young widows sobbed in shocked silence and, with their shattered life and broken bangles, paid the price for India's first great fight to break the chains of slavery of their motherland. But the British might with bayonets, bullets, bombs and the hangman's noose, suppressed the fire and upturned the boiling cauldron of freedom. But it brought in great changes. The Chart below jots the points.

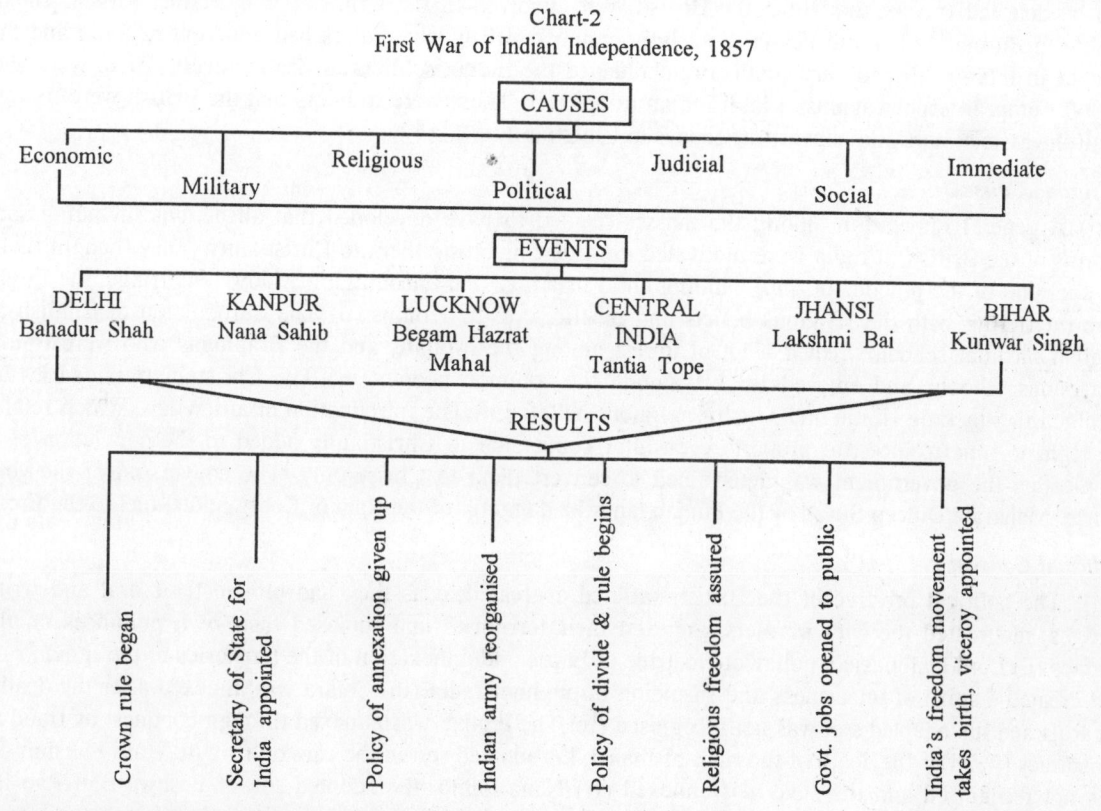

Chart-2
First War of Indian Independence, 1857

CAUSES

Economic | Military | Religious | Political | Judicial | Social | Immediate

EVENTS

DELHI	KANPUR	LUCKNOW	CENTRAL INDIA	JHANSI	BIHAR
Bahadur Shah	Nana Sahib	Begam Hazrat Mahal	Tantia Tope	Lakshmi Bai	Kunwar Singh

RESULTS

- Crown rule began
- Secretary of State for India appointed
- Policy of annexation given up
- Indian army reorganised
- Policy of divide & rule begins
- Religious freedom assured
- Govt. jobs opened to public
- India's freedom movement takes birth, viceroy appointed

Factors/Causes Responsible for 1857 Events

The events of 1857 were the culmination of people's mistrust of the British and of their discontent and disaffection, hardships and the sufferings caused under the oppressive British rule. However, for the sake of convenience, the causes may be grouped under six heads namely economic, military, political, religious, social and immediate.

Economic Causes:

The peasants which constituted the vast majority of the people had to face several famines on account of poverty, insecurity of essential commodities, and hunger. Agriculture was in a very bad shape. The artisans had lost their means of livelihood. The wealth of India was drained to England. The Company and its employees made huge profits. Almost all trade and commerce had gone into foreign hands. Indian industries suffered on account of the industrial policy followed by the Company for selling British manufactured goods in India.

Military Causes:

(i) There was a general feeling among the Indian sepoys that they were discriminated in several matters and their foreign counterparts were given several privileges (ii) There were few opportunities for promotion of the Indian sepoys (iii) The Indian sepoys could be sent to foreign lands to fight. They considered it against their religion to go overseas (iv) A major part of the British army was composed of the sepoys of Oudh and with the annexation of Oudh, there was resentment among them (v) The humiliating defeat suffered by the British army in the First Afghan War (1839-42) developed a belief in the Indian sepoys that the British army could also be defeated (vi) At that time, the British were involved in the Crimean War against Russia, and the trouble in Burma, China and Persia. So a large number of English soldiers had gone out of India and their number in India remained very small. It emboldened the Indian soldiers to rise in revolt. There were about 40,000 European sepoys against 3 lakh Indian troops (vii) There were rumours that the British were trying to break the caste system and convert the sepoys to Christianity.

Religious Causes:

(i) A general impression among the masses seemed to have developed that all actions including social reforms of the British in India were motivated towards converting them to Christianity. They thought that by the abolition of the practice of *Sati*, banning child marriage and encouraging widow remarriage, the English were interfering with the religious beliefs and practices of the Hindus (ii) The introduction of English and English medium schools created a lot of unrest among the Mullahs and the Brahmans who were running indigenous schools, and enjoyed respect among the common people (iii) The Christian missionaries also indulged in attacking Hindu and Muslim religious beliefs (iv) The introduction of a new law, which retained the right to inherit ancestral property even after conversion to Christianity added to the conviction of the people that the government was determined to convert them to Christianity. The conversion of the young prince, Maharaja Duleep Singh of the Punjab, and the daughter of the Raja of Coorg added fuel to the fire.

Political Causes:

(i) The political prestige of the British suffered a great deal as they had broken their oral and written pledges, maltreated the Indian rulers, annexed their territories and imposed their own nominees on their thrones (ii) Lord Dalhousie's policy of Doctrine of Lapse and annexation of the territories of the Indian rulers had created a spirit of uneasiness and suspicion throughout India (iii) Satara was annexed after the death of the Raja and his adopted son was not recognised (iv) The Punjab was annexed through conquest by fraud and conspiracy (v) After the death of the ruler of Jhansi, his adopted son in the care of his wife, Rani Lakshmi Bai, was not recognised and the state was annexed (vi) Nana Sahib, the adopted son of Peshwa Baji Rao II of Poona, was refused recognition as a ruler (vii) The state of Oudh was annexed on the plea that it was not governed properly (viii) It was announced in 1849, that the successor of the Mughal Emperor Bahadur Shah would have to move out of the Red Fort.

Judicial:

The complex judicial system had made justice beyond the reach of the common man. There was a good deal of corruption at the courts. The rich could easily get justice decided in their favour. Besides, law discriminated between the Indians and the Europeans.

The Revolt of 1857

Social Causes:

Unlike other foreign conquerors who settled in India, the British did not settle in India and always considered themselves socially very superior. They seldom mixed with the upper classes of India. They had a strong feeling of racial superiority and treated Indians with arrogance and contempt. The British remained perpetual foreigners in India with hardly any social link with Indians. The middle and upper classes found themselves excluded from the well-paid and higher posts.

Immediate Cause:

The Greased Cartridges:

By 1857, the ground for a mass upheaval was ready and only a spark was needed to set it to fire. This spark came in the form of greased cartridges to be used in the new rifles issued to the sepoys. The tip of the cartridges had to be bitten off before loading. The soldiers believed that the grease used on the cartridges was composed of fat derived from beef and pork. The Hindu and the Muslim soldiers found it offending to their religious beliefs. So, they refused to use the greased cartridges and considered it a concealed strategy to crush their religious faith.

Mangal Pandey:

Usually, the beginning of the revolt is attributed to the third Native Cavalry, whose sepoys on May 10, 1857 revolted and killed some British officers. In fact, Mangal Pandey, a young soldier of 34th Native Infantry at Barrackpur (Bengal), became the first martyr who openly mutinied, single handed. The rumour that the fat of the cow and the pig was deliberately used in the cartridges to convert the sepoys into Christianity, made the 19th N.I. very restless and at midnight on Feburary 26, they loaded their muskets and shouted violently. But the next morning the excitement subsided. But it hurt the conscience of the religiously bent Mangal Pandey at the 34th N.I.O. On March 29, Mangal Pandey fired at sergeant-major but missed. Hearing the news, Lt. Baugh, adjutant, galloped down to the military station. But as he entered, Mangal Pandey fired a shot and his horse fell under him. Baugh and the sergeant-major rushed towards Mangal who severely wounded both with his sword. But another sepoy came to their rescue, held Mangal and the two British officers escaped. During all this time no other sepoy came to save the officers or arrest Mangal who was calling upon his comrades "to join him, to defend and die for their religion." Mangal Pandey was later arrested, tried and hanged. The 19th and the 34th Infantries were disbanded and the sepoys of the two regiments returned to their distant homes in Oudh to spread the story of greased cartridges and the martyrdom of Mangal Pandey.

Map 17: **Mangal Pande the First Martyr**

Beginning of the Revolt, Meerut

The main revolt began from Meerut which was a military cantonment containing several Indian and British regiments, forming the strongest British force in the north-west of India. Here, as elsewhere, the sepoys were excited about the greased cartridges. The matter came to a head when on April 2, 1857, 85 sepoys out of 90, of the Third Cavalry, refused to touch the cartridges. They were court martialled and sentenced to 10 years imprisonment. The sentence itself was a heavy one, but the way it was done by heaping a mountain of disgrace on the head of these helpless sepoys outraged every

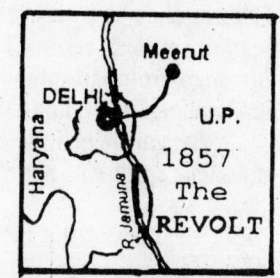

Map 18: **Meerut, Delhi The Revolt 1857**

sense of decency. They were brought to the open parade ground, surrounded by the public and all the troops of the station. The sentence was read aloud and their uniforms were stripped out or torn out from their backs. Then came the blacksmiths with their shackles and tools and fastened their wrists and ankles with iron rings joined by chains. It was a piteous spectacle and every Indian sepoy was moved with great compassion, some with tears in their eyes. Then the prisoners, lifting up their hands and voices, implored the General for mercy. But seeing no hope they turned to their comrades for shamelessly witnessing and silently suffering this disgrace to descend on them. But in the presence of loaded guns, grooved rifles and glittering swords in the white hands, there could not be any thought of striking the whites or jumping into the parade ground to save the browns—their own men from their own native land.

As the prisoners, their comrades, were marched off to their cells and the sepoys returned to their barracks, the tragic spectacle of the parade ground haunted their conscience and they felt ashamed of their manhood. Outraged at the pitiable condition, and disgraced helplessness of their comrades, they at once prepared for a revolt. On May 10, Sunday, at about sunset, several hundreds of the 3rd cavalry galloped to the jail and released not only their 85 comrades but also other inmates. Meanwhile the infantry regiments had also grown restive. Suddenly a sepoy galloped past and shouted out that British troops were coming to disarm them. At this point, Col. Finnis was shot dead by a sepoy and all joined the revolt. Then followed a scene of indescribable horror and confusion. The released convicts and other soldiers joined them to slay the Britishers and burn and plunder their houses. They killed indiscriminately. Meerut set an example which was too closely imitated, quite soon, in numerous localities over a wide area.

The sepoys marched towards Delhi almost immediately and reached there soon after daybreak. When the British could shake away the shock and get ready to quell the disturbances, the sepoys were nowhere to be seen in Meerut. The old Bahadur Shah was proclaimed emperor and the massaacre of Britishers began in full fury. There was no means of resistance as the authorities were taken completely unawares. Then the mutineers proceeded to the cantonment. The Britishers, both civil and military, fled from Delhi. The sepoys became the undisputed masters of Delhi under the nominal authority of the Emperor.

Spread of the Revolt

The Mughal Emperor had been the traditional symbol of unity. It just happened that Meerut was so near Delhi, that the sepoys of Meerut rushed to Delhi and proclaimed Bahadur Shah, the Emperor of India. The very act transformed the revolt into a legitimate war; many Indian chiefs jumped into the battle and proclaimed their loyalty to the Mughal Emperor; all turned their victorious steps toward Delhi. In many cases revolts of sepoys were followed by the revolts of civil population. The next to rise were the sepoys at Aligarh (May 20). This was followed by mutinies at Naushera (Punjab-May 21), Lucknow (May 30), Bareilly and Shahjahanpur (May 31), Moradabad and Budaon (June 1), Azamgarh and Sitapur (June 3), Varanasi and Kanpur (June 4), Jhansi and Allahabad (June 6), Fyzabad (June 7), Fatehpur (June 9), Fategarh (June 18), Hathras (July 1) and several other localities. In general, these mutinies of Oudh and Rohilakhand followed the pattern set by Meerut. The sepoys killed the officers on whom they could lay their hands. They released the prisoners from jail, plundered the treasury, burnt government offices. Troops in Central India also mintinied at Gwalior, Indore and Dhar. In Rajasthan, troops mutinied at Nasirabad (May 28) and Nimach (June 3).

In Bengal there were two sporadic outbursts at Dacca (November 8) and Chittagong (November 22). The mutinous spirit was not alltogether lacking in the Deccan as the sepoys of Kolhapur mutinied on July 31.

Main Leaders of the 1857 Revolt

Bahadur Shah:

Abu Zafar Mohammad Sarajuddin Bahadur Shah Ghazi, popularly known as Bahadur Shah Zafar, the las word was his poetic title, was the last and the thirty-second ruler of the Mughal dynasty. In fact, he was a rule

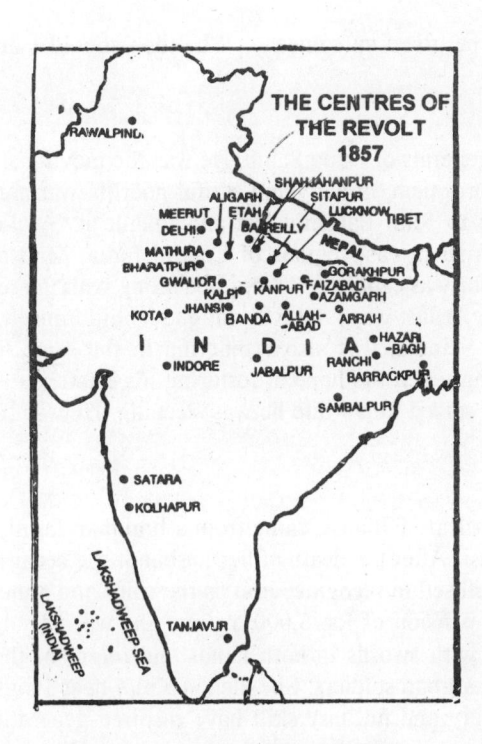

Map 19: **Centres of Revolt 1857**

in name only and his jurisdiction was confined to the walls of Red Fort. He was a pensioner who got a monthly stipend of Rupees one lakh from the British. He was 82 years old when the sepoys from Meerut captured Delhi and declared him the Emperor of Hindustan.

When the fall of Delhi became imminent, Bahadur Shah, with his family, took shelter in the tomb of Humayun, about 9 km. from the Red Fort. Hudson captured him with his family. He along with his Begum Zinnat Mahal and one son was taken to the Red Fort. Next day Hudson arrested the two sons of the Emperor and one of his grandsons and sent them in a bullock cart to the Red Fort. On the way, Hudson found the cart surrounded by a huge crowd. Thinking that the people might rescue them, he ordered the three princes to strip off their upper garments and seizing a carbine from one of his soldiers, shot them all dead. Even British historians criticized this brutal conduct as outrage against humanity. Bahadur Shah was tried, found guilty and exiled along with his queen to Rangoon where he died in 1862. His last verse reflected the agony of his heart that "Zafar was indeed so unfortunate for he was not granted even a six feet grave in the streets of his beloved Motherland."

Nana Sahib:

The leader of the uprising at Kanpur was Nana Sahib. He was the adopted son of Baji Rao, the last Peshwa of Poona. His pension had been stopped after the death of his father. He accepted Bahadur Shah as the Emperor of India and declared himself to be a Subedar (Governor) of Bahadur Shah. He was assisted by his two very capable officers Tantia Tope and Azim Ullah.

In Kanpur the British population, civil and military, took their shelter in an entrenchment which could not be captured by several assaults made by the rebels. Then a regular treaty was signed between the rebels and the British contingency, according to a letter from Nana, ordering a safe passage to Allahabad to every member of the British garrison. After his defeat and Queen's proclamation, Nana refused to surrender and with his last words to the British, "Life must be given up someday. Why then should I die dishonoured?", he escaped to Nepal.

Tantia Tope:

He was one of the most loyal generals of Nana Sahib. He was the moving spirit behind Nana Sahib's army. He achieved great fame for his patriotism, bravery and skilful guerilla warfare. He defeated the British forces at Kalpi. He rendered great help to Rani Lakshmi Bai and fought at Gwalior on the side of the Rani. He carried on his fight with the British in vast regions of Central India, Malwa, Bundlekhand, Rajputana and Khandesh. After the fort of Gwalior was captured, Tantia fled along with the rebels. Throughout one month he was pursued by the British forces. At last worn out with fatigue he hid himself in the jungles of Saronge. Man Singh, deprived of his estate by Scindia, was also wandering in the same forest. Both met by chance and became friendly. Man Singh, being given the hope of restoring his estate, surrendered and showed the hiding place of Tantia Tope. The sepoys seized him while he was sleeping. He was tried and hanged in the presence of a large crowd.

Lakshmi Bai:

Popularly called Rani Lakshmi Bai of Jhansi, came from a brahman family of Satara. She was married to Maharaja Gangadhar Rao of Jhansi. After the death of her husband, she became the Regent of her adopted son aged five. However, the British refused to recognise him as the ruler and annexed Jhansi. She had to quit the fort-palace and live on a meagre pension of Rs. 6,000 a year. She was very brave, highly energetic, fearless and resolute. She fought stoutly, with swords in both hands and reigns of the horse in her mouth. She was helped by Tantia Tope and brave Afghan soldiers. She died at Kalpi near Jhansi fighting on the battle field on June 17, 1858. Tales of her bravery and military skill have inspired generations of Indians ever since then. Rani of Jhansi had said, "To fight against the English has become my Dharma."

Begam Hazrat Mahal:

In Oudh, the former Nawab was in exile at Calcutta after the Nawab's family was displaced by Dalhousie in 1856. But Nawab's cause was taken up by his Begam, Hazrat Mahal. She was the leading spirit behind the uprising in Lucknow. The mutinous sepoys besieged the residency at Lucknow on June 30. Sir Henry Lawrence, the Resident fell in July while defending the residency, sheltering all British military and civil population. When Havelock failed to relieve the besieged Britishers, he was replaced by Outram, who under the guidance of the new C-in-C of the British forces, vacated the residency in November. Begam Hazrat Mahal was given an offer of amnesty by the Queen, but she did not believe the Britishers and therefore escaped to Nepal.

Kunwar Singh:

A Rajput zamindar, he was the leader of the revolt in Arrah. He also tried to organise the rebel forces in Uttar Pradesh and Central India. He died of a wound received in an engagement with the British forces.

Main Events and Suppression of the Revolt

The rebels received a severe blow when the British captured Delhi on September 20, 1857, after bitter and prolonged fighting. Bahadur Shah was captured and exiled to Rangoon. One by one all the great leaders of the revolt fell. Nana Sahib was defeated at Kanpur. Tantia Tope escaped into the jungles of Central India. The Rani of Jhansi died on the battle field on June 17, 1858.

The revolt lasted one and a half years in one or the other form. By the end of 1859, the British authority over India was fully established.

John Lawrence, Outram, Havelock, Neill, Campbell and Hugh Rose were some of the British commanders who earned military credit by Britain in the course of the revolt of 1857.

The Revolt of 1857

Atrocities:

An important feature of the Revolt is that horrible deeds of cruelty were committed on both sides—Indian and British. But the cruelties of the British have no parallel. General Neill who proceeded from Calcutta in May 1857 with a regiment towards Banaras and Allahabad, gave written instructions "to attack and destroy all places on the route close to the road occupied by the enemy." As the British army marched onwards it left everywhere behind them, desolated villages turned into ashes and corpses stenching and dangling from the branches of trees. On June 9, Martial Law was proclaimed in Varanasi and Allahabad. Kaye, the compiler of the Official History of the Mutiny, described how natives were slain and butchered regardless of the sex or age. Englishmen boasted that they spared no one. 'Peppering (shooting) away the niggers (blackmen) was very pleasant pastime.' For three months eight dead-carts throughout the day were busy taking down the hanging corpses and carrying them away from the city of Allahabad. 6000 bodies were thus disposed off. After the fall of Delhi, almost every house and shop was looted after its inmates were killed. There was no question whether one was guilty or innocent. The ruthless repression became so hideous that many husbands slashed the throats of their wives and then committed suicide for fear they should fall into British hands. British Officers used to sit and puff at their cigars and look on at the convulsive struggles of the rebels officially hanged. In Jhansi, 5000 persons were slaughtered or hanged. The people of Kanpur had to bear a heavy toll of vengeance for what the rebels did under the orders of Nana Sahib.

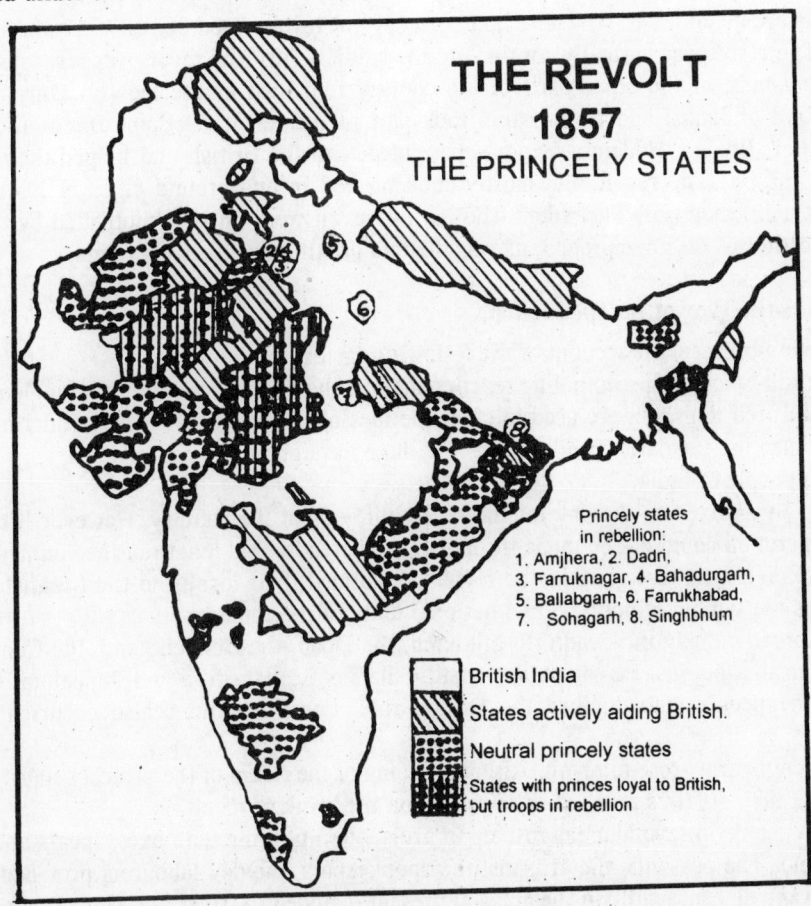

Map 20: **Revolt of 1857, The Princely States**

The record of these cruelties makes painful reading. Dr. R.C. Majumdar, the great historian writes, "But they form an essential part of the story and cannot be ignored. ...why we would refuse to face realities. They have a great lesson for humanity. They prove that the much-valued culture of the progressive world is only skin-deep, whether that skin is black or white...Mankind would do well to ponder over this that only a very thin line demarcates human being from an animal. There may be some hope for the future if the naked realities of the grim tragedy touch our conscience, and make us strive for a radical change in our outlook.'

Nature of the Revolt

Several divergent views have been expressed by historians. The European historians in general call it a 'mutiny' or 'revolt' of Sepoys (Soldiers). Vir Savarkar, a great nationalist revolutionary, in his book *War of Indian Independence* described the events of 1857 as a War of Indian Independence. Asoka Mehta, another national leader, tried to bring out the national character of the events of that year in his book *1857; The Great Rebellion*. Dr. Tara Chand in his *History of Freedom Movement in India* comes to the conclusion that certainly it would be inappropriate to call it 'mutiny', but it is also historically not sound to title it as the 'National War of Independence'.

Why is it Called a Military Revolt?

Several reasons are given for it. (i) There had been several revolts even before 1857 and it was just one of such revolts (ii) The revolt was basically confined to the soldiers (iii) The revolt was restricted to a small area in North India and most of the other parts of the country remained unaffected (iv) Only a few rulers like Bahadur Shah, Rani of Jhansi and Nana Sahib took part in the revolt (v) Some rulers as those of Patiala, Kapurthala, Gwalior, Bhopal, Hyderabad and Nepal sided with the British and helped them to suppress the revolt of the Indians (vi) The revolt was mostly concentrated in and around cities of North India and the villages remained unaffected (vii) The rulers who led the revolt were initially motivated by the fear that they might lose their territories on some pretext, as was the fate of other dispossessed rulers.

Why is it Called as the War of Independence?

It was a people's movement on account of the following factors.

(1) It was the result of a widespread public reaction against the British rule as secret emblems in the form of 'chapatis' and 'red lotuses' were used to carry the message of freedom by the wandering 'sanyasis' and 'faqirs' and also the 'madaris' from village to village throughout the country. These groups represented the common people of India.

(2) May 31, 1857 was fixed as the day for the revolt throughout the country. However it broke out earlier and full preparation could not be made throughout the breadth and length of the country.

(3) The Indian Chiefs who took part in the revolt proclaimed their loyalty to the Mughal King, who was considered as the symbol of political and national unity of the country.

(4) The revolt spread quickly in Awadh, Rohilkhand, the Doab, the Bundelkhand, the Central India, large parts of Bihar and the East Punjab. Many small Chiefs of Maharashtra and Rajasthan revolted with the support of the people who disliked the British rule. Local rebellions also occurred in Bengal and Hyderabad.

(5) The entire Bengal army rose to revolt. Although many of the rulers of the princely states remained loyal to the British, their soldiers revolted or remained on the brink of revolt.

(6) The common people in several areas rose up in arms, often fighting with axes, spears and arrows, lathis and sickles etc. The peasants, the artisans, the shopkeepers, the day labourers provided strength to the freedom movement, espcecially in the areas at present included in Bihar and Uttar Pradesh. It is of some

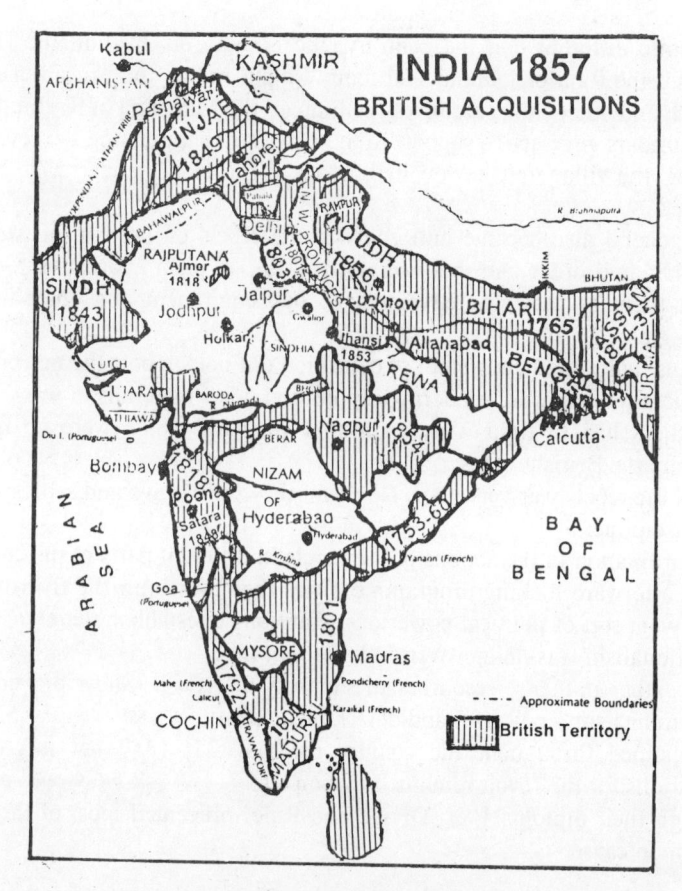

Map 21: **British Acquisitions, 1857**

importance to note that in many of the battles with the British armies, commoners even outnumbered the sepoys who participated in the revolt. It is estimated that in Awadh alone, over one lakh people died fighting. An Indian boatman refused to ferry General Havelock and his troops across the river.

(7) The commoners at various places who did not actively participate in the revolt, showed great sympathy for the rebels. They rejoiced at the victory of the rebels. They even boycotted those sepoys who remained loyal to the British.

(8) There was remarkable Hindu-Muslim Unity to face the Britishers during this struggle. Hindus and Muslims were well represented at all levels of leadership.

(9) This revolt would not have spread so swiftly had there been no popular support behind it.

(10) The movement was so popular that even women put on men's attire to take part in it.

Causes of the Failure of the Revolt

(1) Although the revolt was widespread among the people, yet it cannot be denied that it did not embrace the entire country. It did not spread to south India and most of the Western India because these regions had revolted earlier.

(2) A large number of rulers of the Indian states and the big zamindars did not join the movement.

(3) Had the rulers of the Indian states, who did not support the movement, remained neutral, the situation

might have been quite different. On the contrary, the Scindia of Gwalior, the Holkar of Indore, the Nizam of Hyderabad, the Raja of Jodhpur and many Rajput rulers, the Nawab of Bhopal, the rulers of Patiala, Nabha, Jind, and other Sikh sardars of the Punjab, the Maharaja of Kashmir, the Ranas of Nepal and several big zamindars gave active support to the British in suppressing the revolt.

(4) In most of the cases, the villagers who revolted, attacked the moneylenders who became hostile to the movement.
(5) The merchants in general also became unfriendly to the rebels on account of two reasons: First, they wanted peace and law and order and this was not possible in such a situation. Second, the rebels put heavy demands on them as they wanted money to buy equipment and other things needed for the conduct of the struggle.
(6) The educated Indians under the new system of education did not support the movement in general.
(7) The rebellious soldiers were short of modern weapons and other materials of war.
(8) The rebellious soldiers had to fight with traditional weapons which were no match to the modern weapons possessed by the British forces.
(9) The organisation of the rebels was very poor. No doubt they were brave and selfless but they lacked unity of command and discipline.
(10) There was little coordination in the actions of the rebels in different parts of the country.
(11) The leaders lacked a forward looking programme. Once they overthrew the British power from an area, they did not know what sort of political power or institutions to establish there.
(12) Modern type of nationalism was unknown in India at that time.
(13) The British could gather immense resources to suppress the revolt. Sheer bravery and courage of the sepoys could not win agaisnt a powerful and determined enemy.
(14) The revolt was planned throughout the country on May 31, 1857 but it broke out prematurely. Obviously, preparations for the revolt remained incomplete.
(15) The British, through their diplomacy of 'Divide and Rule' prevented most of the Indian rulers to join together for a common cause.

Results of the 1857 Revolt

1. The Mughal rule came to an end.
2. The rule of the East India Company in India came to an end.
3. The entire administration of India came into the hands of the British crown and the British Parliament.
4. The Indian princes were assured that the policy of annexation would not be followed.
5. It was ensured to the Indian rulers that all the agreements and treaties that they had entered with the East India Company would be fully honoured.
6. The right of the Indian rulers to adopt sons was accepted.
7. Indian people were assured of full religious freedom.
8. The people of India were assured that they would be given opportunity to hold higher posts of responsibility under the government.
9. The strength of the European army stationed in India was increased and the artillery was put under their exclusive charge.
10. A number of Indian communities were debarred from joining the armed forces.
11. The Governor-General of India now came to be known as the Viceroy.
12. The heroes of the revolt soon became household names in the country and they even now inspire bravery and patriotism.
13. The struggle of 1857 sowed the seeds of Indian nationalism and freedom which led to a continuous struggle and culminated in the freedom of the country from the British rule in 1947.

EXERCISES

A. Very Short Answer Type Questions

1. Why did Delhi become the focal point of the Revolt of 1857?
2. State the role of Kunwar Singh in the Revolt of 1857.
3. Mention any two political reasons for the Revolt of 1857.
4. Mention any two economic reasons for the Revolt of 1857.
5. List any two military reasons for the Revolt of 1857.
6. What was the impact of the social reforms introduced by the British in India?
7. State any two reasons for the failure of the Revolt of 1857.
8. Mention any two major effects of the Revolt of 1857.
9. Mention any two names assigned to the Revolt of 1857.
10. Name any two Indian rulers who supported the British in the suppression of the Revolt.

B. Short Answer Type Questions

1. Describe the role of any three leaders of the Revolt.
2. Why did Rani Lakshmi Bai join the Revolt? What was her contribution to it?
3. State any five causes that led to the failure of the Revolt of 1857.
4. Analyse the nature of the Revolt of 1857.
5. Why did the Hindus and the Muslims join in the Revolt?
6. What were the main symbols of the Revolt of 1857? How did it spread so wide?

C. Long Answer Type Questions

1. "The uprising of 1857 was the outburst of popular discontent with the economic, social and political policies of the British in India." Explain.
2. "The Revolt of 1857 came as a culmination of popular discontent with the British policies and exploitation." In the light of this statement explain the reasons of discontent of Indian people before 1857.
3. "The uprising of 1857 is sometimes called as the "First War of Indian Independence". Explain.

CHAPTER 10

The Administrative Changes After 1858

FAR REACHING CHANGES

After the suppression of the 1857 Revolt, several important changes were introduced in the administrative set-up of India. The most significant change was in the very nature of the constitutional set-up. Now India was no longer under the rule of a trading company i.e. the East India Company. India came under the direct control of the British Sovereign and the British Parliament.

Following were the important Acts and other Proclamations which introduced changes:
1. Government of India Act, 1858
2. Queen Victoria's Proclamation of 1858
3. Indian Councils Act, 1861
4. Indian Councils Act, 1892
5. Minto-Morley Reforms, 1909 and Act of 1909
6. Montagu-Chelmsford Reforms, 1919.

Proclamation of Queen Victoria of Britain

The policy changes incorporated in the Act of 1858 which were to govern India, were announced through a proclamation of Queen Victoria, at a 'Durbar' held at Allahabad in 1858. The Queen's proclamation included the following points (i) It assured the Indian princes that their territories will not be annexed by the British Government (ii) The Indian princes shall be given the right to adoption (iii) The servants of the British Government in India will not interfere in the religious affairs of India (iv) In framing and administering laws in India, due regard would be shown to the customs and ancient traditions of the Indians (v) Equal rights and opportunities would be given to the Indians along with the British subjects (vi) Pardon and amnesty would be given to all those Indians who revolted against the British Government but were not guilty of murder of British subjects (vii) Treaties already entered with the East India Company would remain in force.

The Queen's proclamation remained the basis of Indian administration upto 1917 when a new declaration was made by the British Government with regard to India.

Central Administration

Following changes were made under the Government of India Act 1858:
1. India came under the direct control of the British crown and British Parliament.
2. The rule of the East India company came to an end.
3. The Secretary of State for India, member of the British Cabinet (a Minister of the British Cabinet) was appointed to run the Government of India.
4. The Secretary of State for India corresponded with the Government of India. In relation to the Government of India, the Secretary of State for India exercised almost unlimited authority.

5. A council of 15 members was set up to give expert advice to the Secretary of State for India. However, he was responsible to the British Parliament and not to the Council.
6. The Governor-General was given the additional title of Viceroy which no doubt added dignity of a personal representative of the crown, but it did not make any difference in his position.
7. An Executive Council of five members was set up to assist the Viceroy, but it was not binding upon him to accept its advice or suggestions.
8. Up to 1909, all members of the Viceroy's Executive Council were Europeans.

The Indian Council's Act, 1861

It made the following changes:

(1) The Executive Council of the Viceroy was to be strengthened by having not less than 6 and not more than 12 members.

(2) At least half of the members were to be non-officials who could be Indian or British.

(3) The Council, known as the Imperial Legislative Council, possessed no real powers.

(4) The Imperial Legislative Council can be seen as a sort of weak Parliament. The Viceroy's approval was necessary for the passing of any law. It had no financial powers. The Indian members were not elected by the people of India. They were nominated by the Viceroy and usually belonged to princely classes or were big zamindars, big merchants or retired senior government officials.

Provincial Administration

Its chief features were:

(1) For administrative convenience, India was divided into a number of provinces. However, three provinces of Bengal, Bombay and Madras were designated as Presidencies.

(2) Each Presidency was administered by a Governor and his Executive Council of three members who were appointed by the crown. The Governors of the Presidencies had more powers than the Lt. Governors/Chief Commissioners of other provinces.

The Indian Council's Act, 1892

It made the following important changes in the functioning of councils:

(i) The councils could now discuss the annual financial statements under certain conditions.

(ii) The number of members in the council was increased.

Powers of the Centre and of the Provinces: Decentralisation of Financial Powers

A good deal of autonomy was enjoyed by the provincial governments before 1833, when they were deprived by their powers to pass laws. Their financial powers also came under strict control. Now the revenues from all the provinces were gathered at the centre and then distributed by it to the provincial governments. As a matter of fact, this issue of financial powers between the Centre and the States, even after independence at times becames a bone of contention between the Centre and the States. The system of central control was followed during the period between 1833 and 1870, when steps were taken to separate central and provincial finances. Fixed sums were granted to the provinces for the administration of certain subjects/services like Education, Medical services, Jail, Police and Roads. They were allowed a lot of freedom in the administration of these departments. In 1877, certain other departments like Excise, Land Revenue, Law, Justice etc. were also transferred to the provinces. The provincial governments were given a fixed share of the income derived from sources like Income Tax, Excise Tax and Stamps to be spent on the running of these new departments by the provinces. In 1882, further changes were made in the distribution of finances. All sources of revenue were divided into three categories: Central, Provincial and Common, to be divided between the Centre and the Provinces.

The most important objective of financial administration was to keep down expenditure and increase income.

For all practical purposes, in spite of the three fold division of revenue resources, the Central Government remained supreme and exercised effective control over the provinces. In fact this continues to be so even today. This is very essential for the stability and strength of the country.

LOCAL SELF GOVERNMENT

From times immemorial, local bodies such as village panchayats had functioned quite successfully in India. With the decline of the Mughal empire, it almost disappeared in the towns and became very weak in the villages.

Local self-government in India was revived to a considerable extent by Lord Ripon, the Viceroy of India (1880-84). He has been called the father of local self government in India. His Resolution of 1882 is a great landmark in its growth. About this Resolution, he observed, "It is chiefly desirable as an instrument of political and popular education." He emphasised the necessity of putting more faith in the non-official members of the local bodies.

Following were the main features of the Resolution:
(1) The area of jurisdiction of every Local Board was to be so small that both—local knowledge and local interest—on the part of the people could be secured.
(2) The number of non-official members was to be very large.
(3) Wherever possible, the system of election was to be introduced for the members of the Local Bodies.
(4) It was expected that the government would 'check' and not 'dictate' the Local Bodies.
(5) Emphasis was on control from 'within' and not from 'without'.
(6) The Local Bodies were given powers to levy charges on some items.
(7) Non-official members could become chairmen of the Local Bodies.

Notwithstanding these provisions, the progress in the efficient working of Local Bodies was not very encouraging on account of certain limitations. First, a majority of the non-official members were nominated. Second, as the right to vote was very restricted, so the elected members were elected by a very few voters. Third, the government had the right to supersede the local bodies on certain grounds. Fourth, the local institution lacked initiative and in general worked like a government department.

Although, during the course of time, several changes have been made to make them very effective but in reality and in practical terms, even now their work falls short of expectation of the common man. At several places, members indulge in intrigues.

REORGANISATION OF THE ARMY

Policy Consideration

The reorganisation of the army received special attention of the British rulers after the events of 1857, as the Indian sepoys started and spread the revolt and the British forces suppressed it. Following were the main policy considerations in the reorganisation of the army in 1858.
(1) Minimising the capacity of the Indian soldiers to revolt.
(2) Policy of 'divide and rule' i.e. division of army into 'martial' and 'non-martial' classes.
(3) Policy of discrimination on the basis of caste, region and religion.
(4) Increasing the proportion of European soldiers.

(5) Excluding Indians from high ranks in the army.
(6) Utilising Indian soldiers for expanding British domination in India as well as abroad.

Significant Measures Adopted

1. The domination of the army by its European officers was carefully guaranteed in several ways.
2. The European troops were stationed at key places.
3. The crucial branches of the army, like artillery was exclusively put under the Europeans.
4. Indians were excluded from higher posts. Till 1914, no Indian could rise higher than the rank of a subedar.
5. The Bengal army which initiated the 1857 events was completely reorganised. The ratio of European and Indian troops in the Bengal army was fixed at one to two and in the Bombay and Madras armies at two to five.
6. The proportion of Brahamans in the army was drastically reduced and their place was taken by Gorkhas.
7. Gradually, the northern element was increased by the recruitment of the Punjabis and the Pathans in the army and the Southern element reduced.
8. The policy of balance and counter-balance was followed in the army. Various groups were so arranged in the units that there should remain no sentiment of national unity. Indian regiments were made a mixture of various castes and groups. Communal, caste, regional and tribal loyalties were encouraged among the soldiers.
9. Every effort was made to keep the army isolated from the rest of the population. Newspapers, journals and nationalist publications were kept outside the reach of the soldiers.
10. The Indian army began to be used for expanding the British empire in several countries of the world.
11. The maintenance of the huge army needed large funds which naturally put a heavy burden on the people of India.

PUBLIC SERVICES

Europeanisation of the Higher Services

Europeanisation of the higher services in India was the watchword of the British rulers. In 1899, in the Civil Departments of the government of India, only 55 Indians out of 1200 officers drew an annual salary of Rs. 12,000 or above. In the army, out of a total of 855 such officers, there was just one Indian.

The Indian Civil Service (I.C.S.)

The I.C.S. was the most coveted and the prestigious civil service in India. All higher administrative posts were filled by I.C.S officers.

Some of the important reasons for the low rate of success of Indians in the ICS examination were as under:

(i) This competition was held in England i.e. far away from India. It entailed enormous expenses of voyage and stay.
(ii) Several talented Indians did not go to London for they had to cross seas and orthodox Indians would declare them as outcastes.
(iii) The examination was conducted through the medium of English which was a foreign language and a difficult one for the Indians.
(iv) The examination included Greek or Latin as one of the compulsory subjects, the mastery of which could be acquired only after a prolonged study for which no facility existed in India.
(v) The drastic reduction in the minimum age limit for I.C.S. examination from 21 to 19 handicapped the Indians.

(vi) Efforts were made to edge out Indians from the I.C.S. S.N. Bannerjee and Aurobindo Ghose were disqualified on flimsy grounds, like failure in riding test.

For these disadvantages, very few Indians could afford to compete. The first Indian to successfully compete in the I.C.S. examination was Surendra Nath Tagore, elder brother of Rabindranath Tagore. In 1869, three Indians were successful. They were Surendrenath Banerji, Biharilal Gupta and Romesh Chander Dutt. In 1870 out of 332 candidates, only seven were Indians and only one of them succeeeded. In 1880, out of 182, only two were Indians but without any success.

RELATIONS WITH PRINCELY STATES

Creating a Loyal Class of Princes

The policy of the British rulers towards the princely states underwent a drastic change after the revolt of 1857. There were three important guiding factors (1) The British rulers realised that only those Indian princes sympathised with the revolt who were adversely affected by the policies of annexation followed by Dalhousie. Therefore, they did not want to repeat such acts. (2) The British rulers wanted to create in India, a section of the society that should always support them in India. They had already realised that a majority of the Indian rulers had not participated in the Revolt of 1857. (3) They believed in the policy of 'Divide and Rule'. By allowing freedom within certain limits to the princely states, they wanted to have two types of subjects: one totally under the British rule and the other partially under them but totally under British paramountcy.

The Queen's Proclamation of 1858 very clearly stated that the British Government, in future, would not annex the Indian states. The proclamation said, "We shall respect the Rights, Dignity and Honour of the Native Princes as our own." The Indian rulers were given the right of adoption.

British Paramountcy in India

While giving the rulers of Indian states, it was made very clear to them that they cannot claim equality with the British crown. No Indian ruler could claim to negotiate with the British Government on equal footing. It is to be noted that the British Government stressed the subordinate position of Indian states although they were guaranteed their perpetual existence. British residents were appointed in Indian states to keep a watch on them and to protect British interests. An Indian ruler could neither accept any foreign title nor could confer any title on anybody without the consent of the British Government. The Government of India had complete control over the issue of all licenses for arms and ammunition.

The Indian rulers of the states had the solace that their states were safe from merger in the British Empire. The British policy paid dividends and more than 550 Indian princes became loyal to the British Government.

POLICY OF DIVIDE AND RULE

The British rulers had fully realised after the Revolt of 1857, in which the Hindus and the Muslims had fought shoulder to shoulder, that they could rule India, only after following systematically the policy of 'Divide and Rule'. So far, they had followed this policy in inciting one ruler against the other and accordingly siding with the party that could prove to be most useful to them. Now they decided to expand the scope of this policy in the following manner:

First, they divided their conquered territories into two categories. One consisted of provinces which were directly under the British administration. The other consisted of subjects of princely states which were under their indirect control.

Second, the British rulers made all possible efforts to create a rift between the Hindus and the Muslims.

Third, they created a wedge between the zamindars and the non-zamindars.

Fourth, they created a clash of interest between the educated Indians under the British system of education and the illiterate masses, as well as Indians educated under the indigenous system of education.

Fifth, they began to recruit sepoys in large numbers from certain areas like the Punjab and very few from Uttar Pradesh and Bihar etc. Earlier, a large number of sepoys belonged to Oudh.

HOSTILITIES OF THE BRITISH RULER TOWARDS THE EDUCATED INDIANS

In the first half of the 18th century, the Britishers began to take interest in the education of the Indians on modern lines, as recommended by Lord Macaulay. On his recommendation, Lord William Bentinck, the Governor-General of India, announced his policy through a Resolution of 1835. It clearly stated that the great object of the British Government was to be the promotion of European literature and science among the natives of India, and all funds appropriated for the purpose of education would be best employed on English education alone. This policy received support from several prominent Indians. For the implementation of this policy vigorously, a detailed scheme of education was formulated in 1854. Universities of Calcutta, Bombay and Madras were established in 1857. Higher education among Indians spread rapidly thereafter. Educated Indians in general did not participate in the Revolt of 1857. But gradually the educated class began to analyse the imperialistic nature of the British rule. The British rulers, therefore, began to look upon them with suspicion. They began to take measures to stop their entry in the I.C.S. and higher posts in various administrative departments including army. They commonly referred to them as 'Babus'. In spite of this policy, quite a large number of educated Indians remained loyal to the British and actively participated in suppressing freedom movements.

ATTITUDE OF THE BRITISH TOWARDS THE ZAMINDARS

The Zamindars were the favourite class of the foreign rulers. All possible efforts were made to make friendship with the Zamindars and to use them against national sentiments. After the Revolt of 1857, the lands of most of the Zamindars were restored to them. Their sons were given preference for employment in civil and army jobs. They were honoured with various titles like Rai Saheb and Rai Bahadur.

ATTITUDE TOWARDS SOCIAL REFORM

There was a great change in the attitude of the British towards social reforms in India. The events of 1857 led them to believe that their support to social reform, like the abolition of the practice of 'Sati' and widow remarriage, had been a major cause of the dissatisfaction of a large section of Indians. The British rulers, therefore, by and large, abandoned their policy of social reforms in India. The proclamation of Queen Victoria in 1858 made it clear that the British Government would pay due regard to the customs of the people of India and would not interfere in them. This policy evoked mixed reactions. Those radicals who wanted action in the abolition of social evils were dismayed and the conservatives were delighted. Jawaharlal Nehru, in his *Discovery of India* has put it as, "Because of this natural alliance of the British power with the reactionaries in India (orthodox people in India), it became the guardian and upholder of many an evil custom and practice, which it otherwise condemned."

BACKWARDNESS OF SOCIAL SERVICES

Social services like education, public health and sanitation, water supply and means of transport in rural areas remained almost neglected in India. In England, these services were given attention mostly at par with economic services. One of the chief reasons of this neglect in the rural areas was the mounting expenditure on the maintenance of armies and waging wars by the British rulers for expanding their empire in the different parts of the world. India had enough resources for this purpose. It is estaimated that in 1886 more than 40% of the revenues of the state were spent on the army. Civil administration accounted for more than 35 per cent. Less than 5 per cent of the revenue was spent on social services including education, medicine and public health.

LABOUR LEGISLATION

The Indian worker was one of the most exploited in the world. It was underfed, and housed like animals. Factories were without air, light and water. Wages were very low. Working hours were very long.

There were two types of workers. One who worked in factories and the other who worked on the plantations.

Factory Labour Legislation

The factories were mostly under the control of the Indians and the tea plantations under the British capitalists. The manufacturers in England were afraid that cheap labour would enable manufacturers to overtake them. At the same time, the public opinion in India was to protect the labour, especially the child labour.

The First Indian Factory Act passed in 1881 contained the following provisions.
(a) Children between the ages seven and twelve would not work for more than nine hours a day
(b) Children would get four holidays in a month
(c) Children would not handle dangerous and unsafe machines.

The second Factory Act passed in 1891 provided for the following:
(i) Eleven working hours per day for women workers
(ii) Seven working hours per day for children.

Working hours for workers were remained untouched.

Labour Plantation Legislation

As the tea gardens were controlled by the British capitalists, the British rulers provided them every help which resulted in the exploitation of the plantation workers to the extent that they lived like slaves. The climate of Assam, where the tea gardens were located, was very unhealthy. Labour, therefore, was not easily available. The government passed several acts in 1863, 1865, 1870, 1873 and 1883 which were very favourable to the the owners of tea gardens. It was stipulated in the laws, that once a labourer had signed a contract to work on the plantation, he could not refuse to do so. It was a miserable way of exploiting labour for serving British private interests by taking support of law.

PRESS IN INDIA

The history of the press in India would reveal two important facts. First, from its very inception, it has seen several ups and downs as regards its freedom. Second, it has played an important role in cultural, educational, economic, national, political, religious and social awakening.

The early history of freedom of press may broadly be divided into four periods.
(i)   Between 1780 and 1834; Period of Restriction
(ii) Between 1835 and 1857; Liberation of the Press

(iii) Between 1858 and 1881; Period of Restriction
(iv) Between 1882 and 1905; Liberation of the Press

The first period was marked by restriction on the press. Hicky, the pioneer of journalism in India who started *The Bengal Gazette* as a weekly in 1780 for his criticism of the policies of Warren Hastings, was arrested and imprisoned, and the journal had to be stopped in 1782. Subsequently, the editors of the *Indian World*, the *Telegraph* and the *Calcutta Gazette* had to face the displeasure and censorship of the rulers. Several restrictions were placed on the freedom of the press.

In 1835, Sir Charles Metcalfe, the acting Governor-General of India, liberated the press from several restrictions.

Alarmed by the Revolt of 1857, the press again came under strict censorship. The most important step taken against the press was the passing of the Vernacular Press Act of 1878. This Act put severe restriction on the freedom of the Indian newspapers published in Indian languages.

There was a great public reaction to restrictions on the press. Lord Ripon, usually known for his reform and liberal views repeated the Act in 1882.

The Indian press enjoyed considerable freedom for the next twenty five years. After 1905, when the Swadeshi Movement and the Boycott movements were started, the government put curbs on the press in 1908 and 1910.

Most of the political leaders who played a major role in the freedom struggle had started newspapers and magazines to arouse public opinion for the freedom movement.

POLICY OF RACIAL DISCRIMINATION

The English refused to accept the Indians as their equals in spite of Queen's Proclamation of 1858. The English were full of arrogance and racialism. Indians were treated at par with dogs as regards their entry in select hotels, restaurants and clubs. It was not unusual to find the notice "Dogs and Indians not allowed." Social discrimination was quite discernible when even waiting rooms at railways stations were reserved for the Europeans. Places in railway compartments, parks, swimming pools, etc. were reserved for the English. Racial discrimination was inherent in the very concept of colonialism and imperialism. Generation after generation, year after year, India as a nation and Indians as individuals, were subject to insult, humiliation and contemptuous treatment. It was believed by the English that their race had the 'God-given' right to govern Indians and keep them in subjection.

EXERCISES

A. Very Short Answer Type Questions

1. List any two important changes made in the central administration after 1858.
2. List any two important changes made in the field of provincial administration in India.
3. Give any two changes made in the Civil Services after 1858.
4. Mention any two reasons for the very limited entry of the Indians in the Civil services.
5. Mention the changed policy of the British towards social reform in India.
6. What was the attitude of the British rulers towards educated Indians?
7. List any two forms of social discrimination adopted by the British in India.

B. Short Answer Type Questions

1. "Divide and Rule" policy of the British was followed to consolidate their hold on India". Support your answer with two examples.

2. What were the reasons for the change of the British attitude towards princely states and zamindars after 1858?
3. Why was the army reorganised after the Revolt of 1857? What steps did the British take in this regard?
4. State the different phases of the freedom of the press since the beginning of the British rule in India up to the beginning of the 20th century.
5. Describe the condition of the plantation labour in India.

C. Essay Type or Long Answer Type Questions

1. Explain the important changes made in the administration of India after 1858.
2. Why was the administrative reorganisation inevitable after the Revolt of 1857?
3. Describe the role of the press in national awakening. Why were the British rulers keen to impose restriction on the press?
4. State the working of local self government after 1858.

CHAPTER 11

India and Her Neighbours (India's Foreign Policy)

Background

India in the east is separated from Burma (Myanmar) by a series of mountain ranges. In the north it is adjoined by Sikkim, Bhutan, Nepal, Tibet and China. In the north west, Afghanistan is India's neighbour. The Gulf of Mannar and the Palk Strait separate India from Ceylon (Sri Lanka). This is the picture of British India's neighbours before the formation of Bangladesh and Pakistan and the control of China over Tibet.

Focus of the Foreign Policy of the British Government

India was a prized possession of the British. The British domination in India gradually extended its natural geographical boundaries from the trading factories on the sea-coasts to the ice capped Himalayan hills. The British, therefore, were out to exert a preponderant position in all the adjoining countries, namely Nepal, Burma, Sikkim, Bhutan, Tibet and Afghanistan. They would not allow any other imperialist power to intrude not only into India, but also into her neighbouring countries. Thus, the guiding principles of the British rulers in India were:

(i) To maintain their political and economic stronghold in India and not to allow any other power to make commercial profits at their cost.
(ii) To expand their sphere of influence in the neighbouring countries of India and to check the influence of other European or foreign powers.
(iii) To expand their empire by capturing India's neighbouring countries.

INDIA'S RELATIONS WITH NEPAL

Background

Nepal is in north of India with an area of 1,41,000 sq. km. (55,000 sq. miles) and a population of about 22 million. Its capital is Kathmandu. The highest mountain in the World, Everest stands just within its frontiers. The Gurkhas, known for their bravery and toughness as soldiers, came from Nepal to join the British army in India. Nepal has the unique distinction of being the only Hindu kingdom in the world.

War with Nepal (1814-16)

The Gurkhas had grown in strength by slow degrees and embarked upon a programme of expansion. They established their control over the hilly region, from the frontier of Bhutan in the east to Sutlej in the west. The Gurkhas occupied the districts of Butwal (north of Basti District) and Sheoraj (East of Butwal). These districts were under the British influence. The British reoccupied these areas. This led to more border clashes and war in 1814.

Nepal was invaded by four armies from four different directions. The three British armies had to suffer heavy losses partly because of the bravery of the Gurkhas, and partly on account of lack of knowledge of the topography of the area. The fourth army, however, was successful and the famous Gurkha General, Amar Singh, was defeated. The Gurkhas had to surrender.

Treaty of Saguali (1816)

This treaty between the Gurkhas and the British proved very useful to the latter. Following were the outcomes of this treaty.

(i) The provinces of Garhwal and Kumaon came under the British rule (ii) The British got several hill stations such as Simla, Mussoori, Almora, Ranikhet, Nainital, Dehradun and Landour (iii) The Gurkhas withdrew from Sikkim (iv) The Gurkhas abandoned their claim to the Tarai areas (v) The Gurkhas accepted to keep a British Resident at Kathmandu.

Importance of the Treaty:

(i) The treaty of 1816 established an abiding friendship between India and Nepal (ii) The recruitment of the Gurkhas in the British army added strength to the British empire (iii) The British gained facilities for trade in Central Asia (iv) The British got a large territory from Nepal (v) The British got several important hill stations. (vi) Sikkim came under the complete control of the British (vii) Nepal served as a buffer state between India and China.

RELATIONS WITH BURMA (MYANMAR)

Burma has an area of 678,000 sq. km. (262,000 sq. miles) which is more than five times as large as England. It was once a part of India under the domination of England. Before 1824, it was an independent state. The British fought three wars in 1824-26, 1852 and 1885 respectively after which the entire territory of Burma came under the British and became a province of India with a special status. After the passing of India Act of 1935, it was separated from India in 1937. It became an independent nation on January 4, 1948. The population of Burma is nearly 47 million.

Burma's tropical forests produce valuable wood such as teak. Rice is the principal crop. The country is rich in minerals, including precious stones and oil.

During the Second World War, Burma was occupied by the Japanese, but after the defeat of Japan, it again became a part of the British empire.

Causes of Anglo-Burmese Wars and Conquest of Burma

Following were the important causes:

(1) Imperial design of the British to expand its empire (2) Checking the influence of the European powers in Burma (3) Procuring profitable commercial opportunities for the British traders by taking advantage of the forest wealth of Burma and also using Burma as a market for their goods (4) Checking the imperialistic desire of the Burmese rulers to expand their kingdom, as by conquering the neighbouring territories it already reached the border of British India.

Three Wars:

Three Wars took place between the English and the Burmese. The First Burmese War was fought between 1824-26, the Second in 1852 and the third in 1885 after which Burma became a part of the British empire in India.

Main events

In 1824, The First Burmese War broke out. After some initial difficulties, the British forces drove the Burmese out of Assam, Cachar, Manipur and Arakan. Rangoon was occupied and the British forces reached very near Alva, the capital of Burma.

Peace was restored according to the *Treaty of Yandabo*.

According to this treaty the Burmese Government agreed (i) to pay one crore of rupees as war compensation (ii) to part with its coastal provinces of Arakan and Tenasserim (iii) to abandon all claims to Assam, Cachar, and Jaintia (iv) to recognise Manipur as an independent state (v) to negotiate a commercial treaty with Britain (vi) and to accept a British resident at Alva, the Capital of Burma.

The Second Burmese War took place in 1852, primarily on account of the imperialist and expansionist policy of Lord Dalhousie. Of course, the excuse was that the Burmese ruler did not honour his commercial commitment. This time, the War was shorter than in 1824-26. The British annexed Pegu, the only remaining coastal province of Burma. The Burmese fought guerilla war for about three years but without any success.

After the annexation of Pegu, relations between Burma and the British remained cordial for about two decades. The Third Burmese War was fought in 1885 on account of two reasons. One, the Burmese king wanted to establish commercial relations with France — an action not liked by the British. Second, the Burmese ruler imposed a heavy fine on a trading company associated with the British. The British forces attacked Burma and within two weeks of fighting, Burma was captured and annexed to India.

India had to bear a very heavy economic burden on account of these wars. The entire expenditure incurred on the 40,000 soldiers, who fought the three Burmese Wars, was borne by India, without any benefit to its people.

RELATIONS WITH AFGHANISTAN

General Background

Afghanistan is an independent nation in Central Asia to the north and north-west of India (now north and north-west of Pakistan). It is a land of barren mountains. Although the counrty is a little larger than France, it has only about 20 million inhabitants, almost all of whom are Muslims. The Pathans among the inhabitants are the most prominent. Dried fruits and lamb skins are the chief exports. Its capital, Kabul, stands on the river of the same name.

Factors Governing India's Relations with Afghanistan

Afghanistan had a crucial importance for the British on account of the following considerations:
1. It could serve as an advanced post outside India's frontiers for checking Russia's military threat.
2. On account of its geographical location, it could conveniently become a buffer between the two hostile powers — the British and the Russian.
3. It was placed in such a strategic position that it could serve commercial interests of the British in Central Asia.
4. The British wanted to weaken and end Russian influence in Afghanistan.
5. The British wanted to keep Afghanistan a weak and divided country so that they could exercise their influence on it.

Three Afghan Wars

The First Afghan War (1839-42):

'Forward Policy' of the British and its Failure:

Lord Auckland (1836-42), the Governor General of India proposed a resolution on the basis of Subsidiary Alliance to Dost Muhammad, the ruler of Afghanistan, which the latter rejected as it interfered with the freedom of Afghanistan. Dost Muhammad's request for compelling Ranjit Singh to return Peshawar to

Afghanistan was rejected. He thereafter began to establish friendly relations with Russia. In these circumstances, Auckland entered into a Triple Alliance in 1838. The three parties of the alliance were: Maharaja Ranjit Singh, the British and Shah Shuja, who had been dethroned from Afghanistan by Dost Muhammad, and was living at Ludhiana in Punjab, on British pension. In the beginning, the British army was able to capture Kandhar, Ghazni and Kabul. Dost Mohammad was defeated and Shah Shuja was put on the throne of Afghanistan. The people of Afghanistan were full of hatred for Shah Shuja who was considered as a traitor. The Afghans rose in rebellion. The British forces had to retreat. Out of about 16,000 soldiers of the British army, only one could save his life. It may also be noted that Ranjit Singh's forces did not go beyond Peshawar. Therefore, the whole burden of carrying on the war fell on the British. Dost Muhammad again became the ruler of Afghanistan.

Result of the First Afghan War:

(i) It was a complete failure for the British (ii) India had to incur an expenditure of Rupees one and a half crore on account of British interests. (iii) The army lost about 20,000 soldiers.

Policy of Non-Interference/Masterly Inactivity:

During the period 1842 to 1877, the British followed a policy of non-interference in the internal affairs of Afghanistan. After Dost Muhammad's death in 1863, in the war of succession among his sixteen sons, the British adopted the policy of neutrality. Not only this, the British gave aid to the ruler of Afghanistan in disciplining his internal opponents who were posing problems for the internal security of Afghanistan.

The Second Afghan War (1878-1879):

Forward Policy:

There was a change of government in England. The new government in England wanted a forward policy towards Afghanistan. There was intense Anglo-Russian rivalry. To force new terms on Sher Ali (son of Dost Mohammad), the ruler of Afghanistan, an attack was launched in 1878. This is known as the Second Afghan War. This time the British were successful. Sher Ali fled to Turkestan and a *Treaty of Gandamak* was signed in 1879 with Yakub Khan, the son of Sher Ali. The Treaty of Gandamak was as follows:

(i) Yakub Khan was recognised the ruler (Amir) of Afghanistan
(ii) The Amir was to conduct the foreign policy under British advice
(iii) A British Resident was stationed at Kabul
(iv) Yakub was to get a subsidy of rupees six lakhs annually
(v) The districts of Kurrum, Pishin and Sibi of Afghanitan were to be ceded to the British
(vi) The British troops were to be withdrawn from Afghanistan.

The Third Afghan War (1919):

The relations between Afghanistan and the British remained comparatively cordial during the period between 1879 and 1917. Russia's defeat at the hands of Japan in 1905, as well as the Anglo-Russian Alliance of 1907, eased the pressure on the Afghan frontiers. Russia accepted Afghanistan outside the Russian sphere of influence and England also agreed not to change the political status of Afghanistan. The First World War and the Russian Revolution of 1917 again created bitterness in the Anglo-Russian relationship which also affected Anglo-Afghan relationship. The Russian Revolution inspired Afghans to be completely free from the British. The Afghan policy of the British to interfere in Afghan affairs annoyed the Afghans. The Afghan ruler raised a revolt against the British. This is called the Third Afghan War. The *Treaty of Rawalpindi,* 1919 ended the War. Afghanistan became completely free in her foreign affairs also.

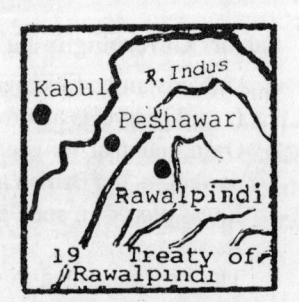

Map 22: **Treaty of Rawalpindi**

Failure of the British Policy in Afghanistan:

Following were the chief reasons of the failure of the British to conquer and influence Afghanistan:
(1) The people of Afghanistan, by nature, were freedom loving. They could be defeated or subdued, but not kept under control for a long period.
(2) Afghanistan being a mountainous country, it was not possible to conquer it with ease and once it was conquered, it was not possible to hold it long.
(3) The geographical location of Afghanistan is such a strategic one, that it could get assistance from countries like Persia and Russia.
Therefore, the British failed to conquer it.

RELATIONS WITH TIBET

Background

The whole of Tibet covering an area of 1,222,000 sq. km., is a part of the Himalayas. It is the highest country in the world. For centuries, it remained virtually cut off from the outside world. Its population is about 18 lakhs. Lhasa is its capital. The people of Tibet are the followers of Buddhism with Lamas as priests. In 1950, the People's Republic of China claimed the country as a province and a few years later, its spiritual leader, the Dalai Lama, came to India and settled down here.

Policy Considerations

The British policy of Tibet was guided by four factors. (i) Safety of the north frontiers of the British empire in India (ii) Weak hold of China over Tibet (iii) Lure of trade and (iv) Mineral resources of Tibet.

All these factors necessitated some sort of political influence over Tibet.

Events:

The conflict with Tibet started in 1887, when the Tibetans invaded Sikkim, which was a protected state under the British. The attack, however, was repulsed. The British tried to establish commercial relations with Tibet but it showed no interest. The British felt that Tibet had been gradually coming under Russian influence. In 1904 Lord Curzon sent an expedition to Tibet and a treaty was signed.

This *Treaty of Lhasa* (1904) contained the following.

(i) A war indemnity of Rs. 25 lakhs was imposed on Tibet (ii) The Chumbi Valley in Tibet was to be vacated by the British (iii) Russia was assured that there would be no interference in the affairs of Tibet by the British (iv) The Tibetans assured that they would not allow any foreign power to set their foot in Tibet.

RELATIONS WITH SIKKIM

Background

Sikkim became an integral part of India in 1975. It has an area of 7,300 sq km, with a population of about 4 lakhs. Gangtok is its capital. Sikkim lies in the heart of the towering Himalayas. Kanchenjunga, situated on Sikkim's western border with Nepal, dominates the land.

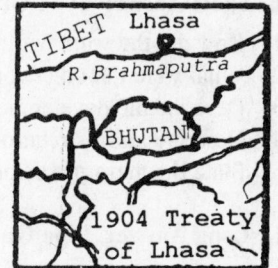

Map 23: **Treaty of Lhasa**

In the earlier times, the kingdom of Sikkim served as a buffer between India and China. It controlled the trade routes between India and Tibet. In 1835, the Raja of Sikkim was persuaded to cede Darjeeling to the British for an annual payment of Rs. 3,000, which subsequently was raised to

Rs. 3,000. In 1849, a military action was taken against Sikkim as two British travellers were arrested by Sikkim authorities. Some hilly areas of Sikkim were annexed to the British empire. In 1860, after a military action, Sikkim became a British protectorate.

RELATIONS WITH BHUTAN

Background

Bhutan is a small kingdom of 47,000 sq. km. in the south-east of the Himalayas between India and Tibet with a population of about 1.6 million. Its capital is Thimphu. At present India has a special responsibility regarding Bhutan's defence, external relations and communications. In recent years, India has extended considerable help to Bhutan in the development of roads, telephone system and construction of airport.

Invasion of Bhutan and a Treaty in 1865

In the beginning there were friendly relations between Bhutan and the British. The British in Bengal used to trade with Tibet through Bhutan. Bhutanese began to plunder the border areas of Bengal which were under the British. In 1885, a short military action was taken against Bhutan. Bhutan signed a treaty which contained the following:

(i) The hilly passes (Duras) adjoining Bengal and Assam were surrendered by Bhutan for a sum of Rs. 50,000 (ii) The British shouldered the responsibility of Bhutan's defence and foreign relations (iii) Bhutan was opened to British trade (iv) The British agreed not to interfere in the internal matters of Bhutan.

EXERCISES

A. Very Short Answer Type Questions

1. Give two evidences to show that the First World War and the Russian Revolution of Oct. 1917 created a new situation in Anglo-Afghan relations.
2. Write two main terms of Indo-Burma settlement in 1865.
3. Give any two reasons of the failure of Afghan policy of the British.
4. Mention the names of any four neighbouring countries of India in the 19th century.
5. Mention any two neighbouring countries of India that did not exist in the 19th century.
6. What were the causes of conflict between Sikkim and India?

B. Short Answer Type Questions

1. How did the wars with Nepal prove advantageous to the British?
2. What were the chief considerations that guided the British rulers in India towards India's neighbours?
3. Describe the developments relating to the annexation of Burma.
4. Describe India's relations with Bhutan. Why were the British interested in acquiring 'duars'?
5. State the main provisions of the Treaty of Saguali.

C. Long Answer Type Questions

1. Explain the British policy towards Nepal. What were its chief gains for the British?
2. What were the main considerations that guided the policy towards Tibet? What were its effects?

CHAPTER 12

The Economic Impact of the British Rule on India

OVERVIEW OF THE ECONOMIC CONDITION OF THE PEOPLE

The pitiable state of the people of India during the British rule can be imagined from the observations made by William Digby, a noted British writer, who criticized Curzon's self-complacence and proved the charge of growing poverty under the British rule. "Even in the favoured division of Gujarat, the cultivator gets only a six or nine month's supply from his field and the numerous deaths are caused by bad or insufficient clothing, food and housing... In Gurgaon District, the standard of living is perilously low, herbs and berries are consumed for want of better food... In Banda, they are half starved... In Rai Bareili, hunger is very much a matter of habit... The Commissioner of Allahabad writes that there is very little difference between the poor classes and semi-starvation; but what is the remedy?" The picture given by Digby, based on official records and reports of collectors of different parts of the country, makes a history of tears. This is because the British economic policy of exploitation and extortion systematically drained India of its capital resources, disrupted the traditional economy of India, ruined the artisans and craftsmen, neglected the country's industrial development, enhanced the land revenue year to year, forced the peasants to carry a heavy burden of perennial debt, caused the death of three crore people during frequent famines between 1854 and 1901, and reduced the population of the major part of India to abject poverty.

Economic Drain

Dadabhai Naoroji (1825-1917), a pioneer in political and economic awakening of the Indian masses, was the first to bring to the notice of the people that India was being made 'economically destitute' on account of constant draining of her revenues to alien coffers. His book, *Poverty and Un-British Rule in India,* became a classic. Ranade deplored that industry and commerce were passing out of the hands of India. Gokhale condemned 'the exploitation of our resources by the indigo, tea, coffee and other planters.' R.C. Dutt, a distinguished member of the I.C.S., and later a President of the Indian Congress, showed through his two great works, that the major cause of India's poverty was that a good part of country's national wealth was exported to England as 'Home Charges'. Home Charges included (i) Pensions and gratuity of thousands of Britishers who came to India on very fat salaries (ii) Money spent on foreign wars in Afghanisthan, Tibet, Persia, etc (not concerned with Indians) (iii) Interest on Public Debt of India incurred for internal wars in India and suppression of the Mutiny of 1857 (iv) Dividends paid to the East India company's shareholders as stipulated by the Act of 1833 (v) Marine charges for British ships anchored in India's seas (vi) The working expenses, the interest on capital spent and profits guaranteed to private companies concerning railways and public works and (vii) establishment of Secretary of State for India. R.C. Dutt has shown that most of these charges were neither just nor necessary and could have been avoided if the British really felt a genuine interest in the material welfare of India. R.C. Dutt pointed out that the annual remittance of 17 million sterlings in 1901-02 for Home Charges represented nearly one-half of India's net revenues annually sent out to England without any visual return.

The Mughal rulers and other rulers also spent huge amounts of money on their wild pursuits but, the money remained in India. It did not go out. During the British rule, India became a plundered nation in the hands of 'ruthless plunderers'- i.e. the British. It was a constant plunder that continued unabated for about two centuries. The Indians were reduced to the position of 'hewers of wood and drawers of water.'

DISRUPTION OF TRADITIONAL ECONOMY OF INDIA

In the words of Dr. Tara Chand, a noted historian, "Imperial Britain treated dependent India as a satellite, whose main function was to sweat and labour for the master, to subserve its economy and to enhance the glory and prestige of the empire." Indian economy became a handmaid of British economy. The basic pattern of the self-sufficient rural economy almost disappeared. The peasant, the artisan, and the trader, all lost their traditional economic structure. The Britishers exploited Indian resources and carried away India's wealth. The self-sufficiency of Indian economy, which was like a milch cow now became barren, all devoid of its glorious past. The blossoming economy of India, which attracted foreigners, became its own enemy. During the very years when England was developing into a leading capitalist country, India was heading towards an economic doom.

RUIN OF ARTISANS AND CRAFTSMEN

Background

The Industrial Revolution in England led to its rapid economic development and colonial and imperial domination over a vast territory of the world. But it proved to be a curse for the artisans and craftsmen of India, who had made a mark in the production of goods of fine quality. Their ruin became one of the major factors of the poverty of India. It is an irony of fate that the very mastercraftsmen whose products attracted worldwide attention and tempted the European traders to trade with India, could not cope up with the competition from machine-made goods. The glory of their artistic production dimmed and misery darkened their life. The East India Company came to India 'as a hawker and pedlar', not for the good of India but for the goods of India. Down to the beginning of the 19th century, the Indian tapestries and textiles, carpets, mosaics and muslins, adorned the public and private mansions of Rome and Europe. At one time, Indian steel was used for making cutlery in England. But then all was gone. The British commercial policy strangled the Indian handicrafts and ruined the artisans.

Causes

Among the important causes, following may be mentioned:

1. Highhandedness of the British Rulers:

After the battles of Plassey and Buxar, the English turned trade into plunder. They committed all sorts of atrocities on the craftsmen. They even went to the extent of cutting off their thumbs if they refused to work for the Company.

2. Lack of Patronage of Indian Rulers:

As state after state fell into the British hands, the rulers were no longer in a position to extend patronage to the artistic and rare products of the Indian handicraft industry.

3. Policy of Free Trade in India and its Reverse in England:

With a view to encourage the sale of British made goods in India, all restrictions on their import in India were revoked. On the contrary, Indian goods were subjected to various duties when exported to England.

4. Cheaper Goods:

Cost of production of goods with the help of new machines was considerably low in England, with the result that handmade goods of Indian craftsmen could no longer compete with them.

5. Speedy Means of Transport:

The railways enabled British manufactures to reach the remotest villages of the country and uproot them and their products.

6. Neglect of Industrial Development in India:

The tragedy of the artisans and craftsmen in India was heightened by the neglect of modern industries in India. Thus, the ruined artisans and craftsmen had little opportunities to find alternative employment.

7. Loss of Raw Materials:

As the Industrial Revolution in England progressed, there was scramble for India's material. Thus the artisans also lost raw materials along with patronage.

On the one hand, the Indian artisans were deprived of the home as well as European markets, on the other hand, the English manufacturers, industrialists and traders enjoyed the monopoly of supplying civil and military requirements of the Government of India. The Indian articles were completely beaten.

IMPOVERISHED PEASANTRY

The peasantry was impoverished day by day and totally crushed under the triple burden of the government on account of high land revenue, zamindar's exacting demands and the unscrupulous methods adopted by the moneylenders. The hardships that the peasants suffered, are discussed in the following paragraphs:

1. Defective Land Revenue Policy

Land revenue policy was guided by one dominant demand—to obtain the maximum revenue, firstly, to meet the cost of the wars and secondly to meet the demands of the top-heavy administrative setup with very highly paid British employers whose salaries, gratuities and pensions required massive chunks of money. The revenue came mostly from the peasants. Thus the peasantry was fleeced and impoverished to meet the heavy expenditure. Several land revenue experiments were tried. But all these—whether it was the Permanent Settlement of Bengal, or temporary zamindari system, or the Ryoatwari system — made the peasants pay through the nose. Every year the rate of revenue was increased. The Secretary of State for India rightly observed that the revenue each year exceeded the limit of the previous year and "there is no doubt that excessive enhancement of revenue inflicted severe blows to the farmers."

2. Oppressive Methods for Realisation of Land Revenue from the Peasants

Not only the quantum of land revenue was excessive, but the methods involved in its realisation were very oppressive. The hard hearted revenue officials forced their peasants even to sell their personal property to pay off the revenue.

3. Indebtedness of the Peasants

The land revenue demands went on increasing, year after year, but the produce went on declining on account of the backwardness of agriculture. The peasants got little economic return from the land. The government on its part, spent very little on the improvement of agriculture. On the failure of the peasants to pay land revenue, either the government put up their land on sale to realise the revenue, or the peasants themselves sold part of their land or they borrowed money from the moneylender to pay the revenue. In all these cases, the peasants suffered. The moneylender adopted various undesirable methods to dupe the illiterate but needy peasants. Methods adopted were: false accounting, forging signatures, making the peasants pay far larger amounts than the actual amounts borrowed. Thus, the peasants were perpetually in debt. Sometimes the situations became so serious that the peasants had to sell their lands. The process of law was also so complicated that the peasants had to suffer. Between 1911 and 1937, the total rural debt is estimated to have increased six times i.e. from Rs. 300 crore to Rs. 1800 crore. The moneylender had become a major and an important cause of peasants' poverty. The condition of the peasants, in the second half of the 19th century, was equally bad. An English traveller, Wilfred Blunt, who visited India during the rule of Lord Ripon (1880-84) observed in his book, *India Under Ripon,* that "there was at that time hardly a village in British India which was not deeply and heavily in debt."

4. Unremunerative Price for Agricultural Produce

For meeting their immediate needs, the poor peasants were forced to sell their produce just after the harvest, at whatever price they could get. Thus, they were left at the mercy of the traders and the moneylenders who purchased their produce by dictating their own easy terms.

5. Commercialisation of Agriculture

Areas were set apart, where crops were grown for export to foreign countries, primarily to England. Some of the areas were: Wheat lands of Punjab, cotton lands of Gujarat, Khandesh and Berar and jute and rice areas of Bengal. In this export process, the grain merchant, the moneylender and the government joined hands to fleece the peasants who grew crops.

RUIN OF OLD ZAMINDARS AND RISE OF NEW LANDLORDISM

Comparison Between Old Zamindars and New Zamindars

	Old Zamindars	*New Zamindars*
1.	They lived in the villages.	They lived in towns and cities. They visited the villages occasionally.
2.	They lived among the farmers/cultivators/peasants/tenants.	They lived away from the farmers.
3.	They shared the joys and sorrows of the farmers.	They came like the honeybees to collect money and store it in their beehives.
4.	They were receptive to the daily needs of the farmers.	They were interested only in collecting as much revenue as possible.
5.	Their life styles were comparatively not so luxurious as they were not so rich.	They lived a life of luxury.
6.	They had relatively a soft heart for the farmers. They could appreciate the genuine difficulties of the farmers and at times were helpful to them.	They were rather very harsh and even cruel on the farmers and were not moved by the their pitiable conditions. They considered it their birthright to collect revenue by inflicting cruelties on the farmers, if so needed.
7.	They continued to remain loyal to the British rulers.	They were usually very loyal to the British rulers and would try to find occasions to please them.

Emergence of New Zamindars

Before the British rule, the village Zamindars were assigned the duty of collecting land revenue. Warren Hastings, the Governor-General of India, introduced the system of auction for land revenue. The merchants and other wealthy persons, residing in the town, began to offer very high bids for the collection of land revenue. The village Zamindars failed to compete with the new bidders. The new bidders used all sorts of harsh methods to collect land revenue from the cultivators. By the year 1815, more than half of the Zamindars of Bengal belonged to the new category that had emerged on account of the new bidding system of collection of land revenue from the cultivators. Other methods of land settlement followed in North Madras, U.P. and other areas, were equally harsh on the old Zamindars. Gradually, more and more land began to be passed into the hands of new Zamindars. The traditional rights of ownership of land of the tenants were also taken away from them at numerous places, primarily because of the tenant's inability to pay the land revenue in time. The land was transferred into the hands of the moneylenders, the merchants and also the rich peasants. This new category of land owners began to lease out the land for cultivation and raising crops to land hungry tenants, who had no other means of livelihood, on exorbitant rent.

STAGNATION AND DETERIORATION OF INDIAN AGRICULTURE

Important factors leading to the stagnation and deterioration of agriculture were (i) Little investment in land (ii) Overburden on agriculture and sub-division and fragmentation of land holdings (iii) Lack of irrigation facilities and gamble in monsoon (iv) Low productivity; Lack of improved seeds, manures, and cattle etc. (v) Old implements of agriculture (vi) Absentee landlords (vii) Neglect of research in agriculture (viii) Neglect of agricultural education (ix) Indebtedness of the agriculturists (x) Higher rates of revenue on land (xi) Government's overall indifference. For these reasons agricultural production fell by 14% between 1901 and 1939.

Little Investment in Agriculture

The British rulers, on account of their interest in trade and profits from manufactured goods, paid little attention to make investment in agriculture. As such, agriculture received a stepmotherly treatment. It is estimated that by 1905, while the Government of India spent over 360 crores of rupees on the railways, which were needed by the British for advancing their commercial interests, it spent less than 50 crores of rupees on irrigation works, which would have benefited millions of Indian agriculturists. R.C. Dutt very rightly pointed out about the investment policy of the British in India, "when we turn from railways to the subject of irrigation works, we turn from unwise extravagance to unwise niggardliness."

Uneconomic Land Holdings

With the decline of handicrafts and cottage industries during the British rule, more and more people began to work and live on agriculture. Thus holdings fragmented and became very small. It became very difficult for the cultivator to sustain on them.

Agriculture, a Gamble in Monsoons

Agriculture depended primarily on rain water. Failure of rain often led to less production which consequently led to famines. Little attention was paid to provide adequate irrigation facilities.

Low Productivity

Agricultural produce per acre was very low on account of several reasons like non-availability of proper seeds, and implements etc. Cowdung was used by the cultivators of land for warming their hearths rather than as manure. There was no provision for any training in agriculture. Research centres were altogether missing.

Old and Outdated Agriculture Implements

Not to talk of the use of modern implements and technology which were used all over the world at that time, even ordinary agriculture implements in India were centuries old. It is surprising to note that even in 1951, there were just nine lakh iron ploughs in use while wooden ploughs numbered 32 lakhs. The production of wooden ploughs must have been very high in the 19th century and also in the first half of the 20th century.

Absentee Landlords

Landlords, both old and the new (a class created by the British rulers), took very little interest in the improvement of agriculture. Their chief concern was to collect as much land revenue as possible. They did not invest any capital in the improvement of agriculture. They squeezed their tenants and took all sorts of 'begar' (forced work) for their work.

Neglect of Research in Agriculture

There were no centres to conduct research on the use of chemical manures, to try new varieties of seeds and new methods of sowing, croping, harvesting and storing of agricultural produce.

Overall Indifference of the Rulers

In general, the British rulers paid little heed to the various issues involved in the development of agriculture. They were not sensitive to the needs of the peasants.

All the above factors led to the ruin of the agrarian economy of India. The moneylenders, the zamindars and the merchants were able to make deep inroads into the villages.

DEVELOPMENT OF MODERN INDUSTRIES

Background

While in England, the development of modern industries began in the eighteenth century with the invention of steam engine by James Watt (1736-1819), it began in India, in the beginning of the 20th century, although the first cotton mill was started in India in 1853. By 1914, India had nearly 260 cotton mills, employing nearly two lakh persons. There was a rapid expansion after independence. At present, textile industry employs about 200 lakh persons. Similarly, there was very slow development of modern industries in other fields. The following table provides a broad picture of development of industries in selected areas.

TABLE
Brief History of Devleopment of Modern Industries in India
(Upto the first World War)

Year	Development of Industries
1853	Starting of the first cotton textile mill in Bombay by Cowasjee Nanabhoy.
1855	First jute mill in Rishra (Bengal).
1879	56 cotton textile mills in India employing nearly 43,000 persons.
1882	20 jute mills, most of them in Bengal, employing about 20,000 persons.
1901	36 jute mills employing nearly 615,000 persons.
1905	206 cotton mills, employing nearly 2 lakh persons.
1906	Coal mining industry employing nearly 1 lakh persons.
1914	264 cotton mills in India.

Chief Characteristics

1. Slow and stunted growth of modern industries.
2. Development of large-scale, machine-based industries and not machine-making industries.
3. Modern industries usually owned or controlled by British capital.
4. In several cases even Indian-owned industries controlled by foreign-owned or controlled managing agencies.
5. High profits made by foreign capitalists who invested capital in industries.
6. Easy credit facilities to foreigners and very few for Indians.
7. Predominance of foreign banks. In 1914 foreign banks held over 70 per cent of all bank deposits in India. By 1937, their share had decreased to 57 per cent.
8. Low railway freight rates for British goods and higher for domestic products.
9. Almost complete absence of heavy or capital goods industries; no big plants to produce iron and steel or to manufacture machinery.
10. Lack of basic industries such as steel, metallurgy, machine, chemicals and oil.
11. Little development of electric power.
12. Growth of plantation industries such as indigo, tea and coffee—almost under European ownership—almost all items of export on a large scale.
13. Paltry development of industries in India as compared with other countries.
14. Employment in modern industries to only about 23 lakh people out of India's total population of 3570 lakhs.
15. Very negligible opportunities of employment to those artisans and craftsmen who were displaced from their traditional industries. According to the estimates of the Indian Planning Commission, the number of persons engaged in processing and manufacturing industries, fell from 10.3 million in 1901 to 8.8 million in 1951, even though the population increased by nearly 40 per cent.
16. Development of modern industries without government help and often in opposition to British policy.
17. Indian politics, agriculture, trade and industry etc. determined by British interests.
18. Lopsided development of modern industries in India. Large parts of the country remained totally undeveloped.
19. Birth of two new social classes in Indian society—the industrial capitalist class and the modern working class.

Important Causes of Slow Growth or Backwardness of Industries

1. Discriminatory policy of the British rulers.
2. Competition from machine-made goods manufactured abroad.
3. Export of raw materials from India for providing raw materials to British industries.
4. Lack of capital in India to invest in industries as a result of drain of capital from India and its export to England.
5. Lack of credit facilities.
6. Neglect of technical and vocational education in India.
7. Heavy import duties on Indian goods in England.
8. Restrictions on the sale of Indian goods in England.
9. Higher freight charges on Indian goods by the railways in India, as compared with lower freight charges on foreign goods transport to various parts of India.
10. Policy of free trade followed in India and lack of protection to Indian industry against unfair competition of foreign goods.

11. Providing guarantee of profits to the British capitalists to invest in Indian industries and the denial of such a guarantee to Indian capitalists.
12. Atrocities and cruelties of the British rulers on Indian artisans—cutting off their thumbs for quality production, compelling them to manufacture goods at very low rates.

DE-INDUSTRIALISATION OF INDIA

Meaning

De-industrialisation of India implied that while traditional Indian small-scale and cottage-industries, which were an important source of the import of wealth from outside, decayed and declined, their place was not filled up by the development of modern industries.

Secondly, whatever Indian industries were developed, they, by and large, were with British capital, under British control and for British profit.

Thirdly, the number of workers which the modern industries employed was much below the number of artisans and craftsmen they displaced. In the balance, therefore, India was getting de-industrialised.

Consequences of De-Industrialisation of India

1. The working force in the industries went on decreasing. It is estimated that just 3.3 per cent of the people were employed in industries for the period 1911 to 1921. This percentage fell down to 1 per cent by 1947.
2. The working force in agriculture constantly increased. The population dependent on agriculture increased from nearly 61 per cent in 1891 to 73 per cent in 1921.
3. There was a heavy drain of India's wealth to England.

Non-Existing Industries in India During the British Rule

The following industries were almost non-existent in India:-

(i) Production of petroleum (ii) Steel castings (iii) Cotton textile machinery (vi) Jute mill machinery (v) Sugar mill machinery (vi) Machine tools (vii) Cement machinery (viii) Railway wagons (ix) Motor cycles/scooters (x) Earth moving equipment (xi) Agricultural tractors (xii) Automobile tyres (xiii) Medicines like pencillin etc.

POVERTY AND FAMINES

Poverty

Background:

Even a cursory glance of the pages of history under the British rule shows that despite her rich mineral wealth, plenty of raw material, abundant labour power and fertile soil, the people of India had to live under the haunting spectre of poverty and starvation. Poverty of India was man-made and not nature-made. India presented the paradox of 'poor people living in a rich country.'

Some Facts About Poverty:

The national income per capita in India at the end of the 19th century was as low as £9.50 in contrast to that of Canada (143), Australia (154), France (156), U.K. (195), Germany (225) and U.S.A (240).

During the period 1925-34, India and China had the lowest per capita income in the world.

The average life expectancy of an Indian during the 1930's was only 32 years i.e. just half of people living in West-European and North-American countries.

In the 19th century, about 400 lakh people of India habitually lived on insufficient food.

In the 20th century, the quantity of food available to an Indian declined by about 29 per cent in the 30 years between 1911 and 1941.

Important Causes of Poverty of the People of India:

These may be summed up as (i) Decay of indigenous industries (ii) Failure of modern industries to replace indigenous industries (iii) Drain of wealth to Britain (iv) Backward agrarian structure (v) Exploitation of the poor peasants by landlords, merchants, moneylenders, princes, zamindars and officials.

Famine

India has been frequently subjected to horrors and devastations of famine. Natural causes like failure of rains, droughts, floods, and locusts have no doubt been largely responsible for these. But factors like British indifference and lack of sympathy, heavy taxation, unjust revenue policy and general poverty, aggravated the suffering and wiped out crores of lives from the country by the cruel blow of starvations, resulting in more than 2 crore deaths. This was one of the darkest features of this period.

The 1860-61 famine, covering the north-western provinces, was followed by a Famine Commission, which only pointed out the causes and did not say anything about the relief. The Orissa famine of 1866-67 during the Governor-Generalship of Lawrence, affecting the whole east coast—from Calcutta to Madras, was followed by a Famine Commission which made the government responsible for it. The great famine of 1876-78, during the Governor-Generalship of Lytton, affected vast areas in the Bombay and Madras Presidencies, Hyderabad, Mysore, Oudh and North-Western Provinces. It was, as usual, followed by a Famine Commission after which, a relief code was made to tell how to administer relief work. The famine of 1896-97 affected the North-Western Provinces, Oudh, Bihar and other parts. In 1898-1900 there was a terrible famine, "the greatest in extent and intensity which India had experienced in 200 years", during the time of Curzon. As usual it was followed by a Famine Commission.

Root Causes of Starvation and Deaths:

1) The most important cause was lack of industry and manufacture. So 80 to 90 per cent of population had only agriculture to depend upon. It was against British commercial interest to encourage industry.

2) The heavy land revenue further filled their cup of misery. As a result, the cultivator in most parts of India, could not get even two square meals a day.

3) The government continued to export food grains, mostly rice and wheat, even when the country remained in the grip of terrible famines. The export of food grains rose from £ 3.8 million in 1858 to £ 9.3 million in 1914.

The Government remained indifferent to plan or take preventive measures to reduce the massive impact of famines, and to provide adequate and prompt relief at the time of famines, in spite of the regular appointment of Famine Commission after each major famine, to find out the cause and to suggest remedies. The Government did not relent pursuing vigorously, its commercial policy of discouraging or stifling Indian industrial enterprises, of increasing revenue taxation every year and of increasing the export of rice and wheat from India. The policy of export of food grains was so obstinately pursued, that the government turned down the proposal of Sir George Campbell, the Lt. Governor of Bengal, to stop the export of rice from Bengal, part of which was in the grip of famine in 1876. Lord Northbrook, the Governor-General, was very much shocked by the proposal that a Lt. Governor should make. The export of rice continued to feed the people of Britain while starvation, accompaned by death, continued to knock the doors of poor peasants of India.

Details regarding the famine are tabulated below

Table Showing the Important Years of Major Famines and Their Impact in Different Regions

Year/Years of Famine	Areas Affected by Famines	Loss of Life (People)
1860-61	Agra, Oudh (Western U.P.) and parts of Punjab	over 2 lakhs
1866-67	Orissa, Bengal, Bihar and Madras	20 lakhs (Orissa alone 10 lakhs)
1868-70	Western U.P., Bombay the Punjab, Marwar Bikaner, Ajmer (last three in Rajputana)	14 lakhs (Rajputana lost one-third to one-fourth of its population)
1876-78	Madras, Mysore, Hyderabad, Bombay Western U.P., Punjab	10 lakhs (Bombay lost nearly 8 lakhs)
1896-97	Country-wide famine	45 lakhs
1898-1900	Country-wide famine	30 lakhs
1943	West Bengal	30 lakhs

In free India, there might be a few stray cases where people have died of starvation but no famine-like situation ever occurred.

EXERCISES

A. Very Short Answer Type Questions

1. Mention any four measures taken by the British which ruined the agriculturists of India.
2. List any four reasons which led to the ruin of indigenous industries of India.
3. State two classes which rose as a result of industrialisation.
4. Explain the term 'landlordism'.
5. Give the meaning of indigenous industries.
6. List any four causes of famines in India during the British rule.
7. Name any four industries that did not come up during the British rule in India.
8. Give the meaning of free trade imposed by the British in India.

B. Short Answer Type Questions

1. Explain the statement "India is a rich country inhabited by the poor".
2. Give the meaning of 'economic drain'. What were its causes?
3. How did the New Zamindars differ from the Old Zamindars?
4. Explain the term 'De-industrialisation of India'. What were its causes?
5. Describe the impact of the British rule on Indian agriculture.
6. What methods were adopted by the British to drain away wealth from India? Explain any two.

C. Essay Type/Long Answer Type Questions

1. What were the causes of the slow progress of industrialisation in India during the British rule?
2. State the chief characteristics of industrialisation of India.
3. What was the impact of the British policies on Indian agriculture and industry?
4. Explain the factors that led to widespread poverty and famines in India.

D. Map Work

Locate the main areas that often faced famines in India.

CHAPTER 13

Social and Religious Reforms after 1858; Growth of New India

PERIOD OF REFLECTION ON SOCIAL AND RELIGIOUS ISSUES

The second half of the 19th century was marked by strenuous attempts to rediscover, reassess and regenerate Indian society by eschewing orthodoxy and rejecting Western materialism. The social and religious reformers emphasized that the truths revealed by sages and the theologians of the ancient ages, should be seen in their right perspectives. The main streams of new movements may be summed up as purging society of superstitions, reaping the fruits of science, believing in the idea of one God, and working for the spiritualization of society, brotherhood of mankind and restoration of the ancient glory of the society. There were movements in almost every part of India. The leaders of the movements made missionary tours over different regions of the country for promoting a rational outlook. Raja Rammohan Roy, Keshuv Chandra Sen, Mahadev Govind Ranade, Swami Dayanand, Ramkrishna Paramhansa and Swami Vivekanand were the outstanding reformers among the Hindus. Among the Muslims, Sir Syed Ahmed Khan was the chief reformer. These reformers were convinced that social and religious reforms were essential for the all round development of the country. Among the important factors which led to the reformatory movements were: the growth of nationalist sentiments, emergence of new economic forces, undue criticism of the Indian society by the foreign rulers and missionaries, impact of Western ideas and culture, spread of modern education and an enviornment of open debate on social and religious issues.

Among the several socio-religious movements started to reform the Indian society and religion, the following were the most popular at that time:

1. The Brahma Samaj (Already discussed)
2. The Arya Samaj
3. The Ramakrishna Mission
4. The Theosophical Society
5. The Aligarh School
6. The Akali Movement.

Keshuv Chandra Sen (1838-1884)

Keshuv Chandra Sen was greatly concerned with the fallen state of India and its helpless subjection. He said, "What we see around us today is a fallen nation—a nation whose primitive greatness lies buried in ruins." He took note of the plight of the people of the whole of Asia, which was suffering under the onslaught of European imperialism. He observed, "The scriptures and prophets, the language and literature of the East, nay, her customs and manners and her very industries have undergone a cruel slaughter."

Keshuv Chandra Sen is regarded as a "stormy petrel" of renaissance in India. He travelled widely and spoke emotionally. He vigorously preached the principles of the Brahma Samaj. Under him, by 1865, Brahma Samaj became an All-India reformatory organisation with its centres all over India. He arranged several inter-caste marriages. He was instrumental in the birth of a dozen journals. It was on his initiative that a large number of educational institutions like the Calcutta College, the Native Ladies Normal School and Evening School for Adults were established. He worked for the removal of untouchability, promotion of female education, self-employment with vocational training, widow remarriage and above all promotion of moral, spiritual and humane values.

Swami Dayanand (1825-1883)

Swami Dayanand worked throughout his life for a reformed Hindu society, free from superstition and caste distinctions. In the Vedas, he sought a solution of the problems of human misery and final salvation. He founded the Arya Samaj Movement. Swami Dayanand's original name was Mulshankar. He was born in a brahman family, at Jankara, in Morni state of Kathiwar. From his early life, he sought answers to many riddles of life, death, salvation, reality and truth. At the age of 19, he left home, and for fifteen years, he wandered almost all over India in search of truth. At last he met Swami Virjanand Saraswati, one of the learned and noblest of the Hindu saints, and for two and a half years, he sat at the feet of his guru and learnt from him. To his guru, he pledged, that he would devote his life to the dissemination of truth and waged relentless war against falsehood.

Swami Dayanand spent his entire life in preaching, teaching, writing books and organising Arya Samaj throughout India. The force of his logic, the power of his oration, the depth of his scholarship, the dazzle of his intellect, the compassion of his heart, the sincerity of his purpose, the overpowering spirituality of his multi-dimensional personality and his profound mastery over language swayed the masses and evoked spontaneous reverence from them. It is, therefore, natural that a band of devoted workers gathered around him.

Swami Dayanand was a prolific writer whose works are spread over thousands of pages. He wrote commentaries on the Vedas. His *Satyarth Prakash* (Light of Truth) is his great monumental work. In this book, he describes the historical, doctrinal and ethical aspects of the Vedic life. He also makes a comparative study of various religions and tries to establish the supremacy of the Vedic thought.

Dayanand was an uncompromising lover of truth and for this he invited the wrath of the orthodox people and was secretly poisoned to death.

Swami Dayanand as a Social Reformer:

He condemned child marriage, enforced widow remarriage, discarded caste system and denounced prostitution and polygamy. He mocked at the false claims of astrologers. He believed in equality and humanitarian service.

As a Promoter of Education:

He put great emphasis on compulsory primary education, adult education and education of girls and women. It is not without significance, that a large number of educational institutions are named after him.

As a Moralist:

Swami Dayanand advocated clean life. He laid emphasis on Brahamacharya—celibacy.

Swami Dayanand as a Religious Reformer:

(1) He wanted to regenerate Hinduism on the basis of Vedic philosophy. His slogan was 'Back to the Vedas'. He believed in the divinity of the Vedas (2) He believed in the concept of one God (3) He believed in the doctrine of transmigration of soul or rebirth (4) He believed in the doctrine of Karma i.e. as you sow, so shall you reap (5) He presented the noblest aspects of Hinduism and created among them, a sense of pride (6) He opposed idol worship.

The Arya Samaj:

For propagating Vedic philosophy and its implications on daily life, Swami Dayanand founded the Arya Samaj Movement, which has produced several eminent nationalists, freedom fighters, educators, philanthrophists and social reformers.

The first Arya Samaj was founded by Swami Dayanand at Bombay in 1875 and then in 1877 at Lahore. Since then, a network of Arya Samaj's has come up, not ony in India but also in several countries of the world.

The Arya Samaj founded by Swami Dayanand is an integral part of Hinduism. It supports social equality, widow remarriage, and education of women. It condemns untouchability and child marriage. It emphasizes the teaching of the Vedas.It believes in one God—God that is Omnipotent, Light behind all lights, Force behind all forces. It provides an ethical and spiritual code. It also attempts to prevent the conversion of Hindus to other religions. It also takes up the 'Shuddhi' work i.e. reconversion of Non-Hindus to Hindus.

The Arya Samaj has established a network of educational institutions in the country which are known as Dayanand Anglo-Vedic (D.A.V) schools and colleges. The objective is to provide a happy blending of the modern scientific approach of the West and the spiritual philosphy of the East i.e. Vedic thought. Several followers of Swami Dayanand who wanted to maintain the original spirit of his philosophy, have founded many 'Gurukul's' (Residential institutions). 'Gurukul Kangri' at Hardwar, is the most important educational institution set up on the pattern of ancient Ashrams.

Paramhansa Ramakrishna (1836-1886)

The unlettered Gadadhar (original name of Sri Ramakrishna), became the embodiment of spiritual enlightenment. He is regarded as the personification of the highest and the best in Indian culture and tradition. He was originally a priest in a temple at Dakshineshwar, near Calcutta. On account of his holy life, simplicity of character, his skill in explaining complicated religious matters in a simple language and his catholic outlook, he became a great source of inspiration for the seekers of truth and for those who wanted to realise divinity. In his search for religious truth, he lived with the learned persons and saints of different faiths. He was not content with experiencing only the Hindu modes of approach to God or the Divine. He searched for God through other faiths. He practised the teachings of Islam, Christianity and Buddhism and through each of them, he reached the goal which these faiths promise to their followers.

Sri Ramakrishna's teachings may be summed up as under:
1. The various religions are varying paths to the same goal i.e. God realisation or salvation.
2. Service of man is service of God, for man was the embodiment of God.

Swami Vivekanand (1863-1902)

Swami Vivekanand (originally Narendra Datta), an ardent disciple of Sri Ramakrishna, took the vow of eternal *Sanyasa* (renunciation) after the death of his guru in 1866. Strength and service, celebacy and spiritualism, uplift of the poor and universal brotherhood were his watch words for humanity as a whole.

Vivekanand made a mark of his learning, oratory, scholarship and wisdom at the Parliament of Religions held at Chicago (USA) in 1893. In his address, beginning with the words 'sisters and brothers of America', he made a clarion call to the world: "Help and not Fight", "Assimilate and not Destroy", "Harmony and Peace and not Dissension".

Swami Vivekanand's call to the nation was: "O Indians ! Forget not that the lower classes, the ignorant, the poor, the illiterate, the cobbler and the sweeper are Thy 'flesh and blood".

Vivekanand condemned the caste system and narrow religious outlook. He bitingly remarked, "Our religion is in the kitchen. Our God is in the cooking pot and our religion is 'Don't touch me, I am holy'. If this goes on for another century, everyone of us will be in a lunatic asylum."

To the educated Indians, he said, "So long as millions live in hunger and ignorance, I hold everyman a traitor."

Some of his important teachings are:
1. Religion means self-realization.
2. Ethics and morality should be the real basis of life.
3. Love and renunciation should permeate the universe.
4. The best image for worshipping God is man, for God resides in every human being.
5. Service to mankind is the highest service to religion.
6. 'Karmayoga' - action without attachment - is needed for the attainment of self-control and self-realization.
7. The teachings of the Upanishads will lead to providing suitable solutions to our social and other problems.
8. 'Intellectuality' is not the highest good. 'Morality' and 'spirituality' are the things for which we should strive.
9. The character of a man is judged by how he carries out his most common actions.
10. Work for work's sake. Worship for worship's sake. Do good because it is good to do good. Ask no more.
11. Arise, awake and stop not till the goal is reached.

Ramakrishna Mission:

Swami Vivekanand started the Ramakrishna Mission in 1896, in the memory of his guru Ramakrishna Parmahansa. The Mission has been engaged in humanitarian work throughout the country and abroad. It has numerous branches all over the country. Its activities are designed to provide an important role in the cultural, educational and social reconstruction of society. It lays great stress on ethical, moral and spiritual values. It has drawn into its fold, several learned 'Sanayasis' who are engaged on full time voluntary basis in the activities of the Missions. It has a well-disciplined and dedicated monastic order. The Mission has set up a large number of educational institutions, libraries, orphanages, dispensaries etc. besides spiritual centres.

The Theosophical Society

The society was founded in 1875 at New York in America by a Russian lady, Madam Blavatsky (1831-91), and an American, Colonel H.S. Olcott. Later on, they came to India and established the Head Office of the society at Adyar in Madras. The society reached the climax of its glory under the leadership of Mrs. Annie Besant.

The term 'Theosophical' implies a system of philosophy which aims at attaining spiritual happiness through deep knowledge of self. The society wanted to blend together, the best principles of Hinduism and Zoroastrianism (religion of the Parsis). The society believes in one God and condemns the social as well as racial discrimination based on caste and colour. The society accepts the doctrine of the transmigration of soul. It preaches the universal brotherhood of man. The movement, led by Westerners, glorified Indian philosophical thought.

Annie Besant (1847-1933):

Annie Besant was one of the very few Westerners who came to India, settled here and adopted it as their home. She was an Irish lady who came to India in 1883 at the age of forty-six and worked for the regeneration of India in cultural, educational, social and political fields. She became a great lover of Hinduism and claimed that she was a Hindu in her former birth. She wore the Hindu costume and adopted Hindu ways of life. A free thinker, captivating orator and imdefatigable organiser, she remained the President of the Theosophical society of India from 1907 till her death. On account of her role in national awakening, she became the President of the Indian National Congress in 1918. She had a deep insight to understand the needs of the masses of India and prepared a national scheme of education based on the fundamental principal of Indian

Social and Religious Reforms After 1858; Growth of New India   121

culture. Furthermore, she urged, that the students should be made conscious and proud of the glory of the country. She edited several journals for the task of national awakening. She lectured in different parts of India. She established the Central Hindu High School of Banaras. She established Women's Indian Association, which later on bloomed as All India Women's Conference - an organisation for the uplift of women. She stood for equality of women. She condemned the practice of early marriage and other customs that hindered the progress of women. She wrote a number of books on Hindu philosophy and translated the *Bhagwad Gita* into English.

Reforms among the Parsis

In 1851, a group of educated Parsis organised the Rehnumai Mazdaysan Sabha, also called the Religious Reforms Association, for the regeneration of their society and religion. The focus of the movement was also on improving the status of women, abolishing the *'Purdah'*, raising the age of marriage and promoting female education. The Association also started a newspaper *Rast Goftar* (Truth Teller) for the propagation of its ideals. Among its important leaders were Naoroji Furdonzi, Dadabhai Naoroji and K.R. Cama. In due course, the Parsis became one of the most modern sections of the Indian society and played an important role in national awakening.

Naoroji Furdonzi was a brilliant writer in Gujarati and English. He was a pioneer of girl's education. K.R. Cama Institute of Oriental Research is a tribute to his service in the field of learning. He motivated people in favour of change and reform through his lectures in Gujarati and English. The famous revolutionary, Madam Bhikaji Cama was his daughter-in-law.

Dadabhai Naoroji (1825-1917):

Affectionately known as the 'Grand Old Man of India', Dadabhai Naoroji was one of the foremost reformers and leaders of the national movement in India. Even during his professorship at the Elphinistone College Bombay, till 1855, he devoted himself whole heartedly to all kinds of reforms—social, educational, political and religious. He championed the cause of female education. He was instrumental in establishing several girl's schools in Bombay. He advocated remarriage of Hindu widows. He founded many prominent institutions and organisations like the students literary and scientific society, the Bombay Association, the Framjee Cowasjee Institute, the Parsi Gurnasium, the widow Remarriage Association and the Victoria and Albert Museum.

He left for England in 1855, to manage a famous Parsi business firm. There, he inspired the formation of the East India Association in London. During 1892-95, he was the first Indian to be elected to the British Paliament on the Liberal party ticket.There was hardly any important Indian question which he did not bring to the notice of British Parliament.

Dadabhai became the President of the Indian National Congress three times, in 1886, 1894 and 1906. He advocated the concept of moral foundations of political power.

Dadabhai was a pioneer, not only in the political awakening of the Indian masses, but also was the first to bring to the notice of the people of the world that India was being made economically destitute on account of constant 'draining' of her revenues to foreign coffers.

Reform Movements Among Sikhs

The Namdhari Movements:

Bhai Ram Singh, an ex-soldier of the Khalsa army, founded this movement in 1857, at Bhaini, 16 miles from Ludhiana, in the Punjab. The movement was the outcome of the degeneration set in the path of morality and religion after the death of Maharaja Ranjit Singh. The Sikh society was being marked by intrigues and violence. Several social evils like Sati, sale of daughters and dowry had crept into the Sikh society. Satguru

Ram Singh asked his followers to give up drinking, drugs, polygamy, sale of daughters, worship of Pirs and graves, use of foreign goods and such practices as female infanticide. Against the dowry system, he initiated the system of the cheapest marriages in the world. The Namdharis are vegetarians and cow protectors. The disputes among the Namdharis were settled by their guru. They adopted Swadeshi element. They were supposed to do meditation and charitable acts. Common kitchen was another important characteristic of this sect.

The British rulers looked upon the Namdharis with suspicion. Heavy atrocities were committed on them. In 1872, more than sixty Namdharis were tied at the mouth of guns and blown off. It shocked the entire India. Even the conscience of some sections of people in England was stirred up. Guru Ram Das was exiled to Burma. The Namdharis were not deterred and they took an active part in Swadeshi and national movements.

The Singh Sabha Movement:

The movement started in the year 1874 at Amritsar was mainly confined to the opening of Khalsa Schools and Colleges in the Punjab.

The Akali Movement:

The Akali Movement, started in 1921, gave a great momentum to religious reforms. The primary objective of the Akali Movement was to purify the management of the Sikh shrines (Gurudwaras) which had come under the hands of the corrupt priests (mahants). The Akalis led a powerful, non-violent satyagraha to liberate the Gurudwaras. The Government of India was compelled to pass the Sikh Gurudwaras Act in 1922 which was amended in 1925. Hundreds of Akalis lost their lives in this struggle.

(Master) Tara Singh (1855-1967):

Tara Singh, commonly called Master Tara Singh, on account of his teaching career, was one of the most prominent leaders of the Akali movement. He took an active part in all the 'morchas' (struggles) of the Akali movement. He took a leading part during the twenties in the boycott of the Simon Commission. He completely identified himself with the 1930 Civil Disobedience Movement launched by Gandhiji. He was elected President of the Shiromani Gurdwara Prabandak Committee (S.G.P.C.) while in jail. He remained the President of the Akali Dal for a number of years. He broke with the Congress during the Second World War for he wanted to safeguard the interests of the Sikh community against the Muslim League's demand for Pakistan, inclusive of the Punjab. He continued his struggle for the protection of Punjabi language and for the formation of Punjabi Suba. In 1966, Punjab was reorganised and trifurcated into Punjab, Haryana and Himachal Pradesh.

Reform Movements among the Muslims

Syed Ahmad Khan (1817-1898) and the Aligarh School:

Syed Ahmad Khan was the most important religious and social reformer among the Muslims. He was firmly convinced that the Muslims could progress only by reconciling the Islamic thought with modern scientific thought. He urged the people to develop a critical and rational outlook. He considered Quran to be the sole authority on Islam. He was keen for the progress and advancement of the Muslim society. He urged upon Muslims to give up medieval customs. He advocated the removal of *'Purdah'* and pleaded for the spread of education among Muslim women, for raising their status. He also condemned the practice of polygamy and early divorce among the Muslims.

Promotion of science and modern education among Muslims remained the first task throughout his life. In 1864, he set up an organisation called 'Scientific Society'. The Society published Urdu translations of English books on science and other subjects. In 1875, he founded the Muhammedan Anglo Oriental College (M.A.O. College) at Aligarh for spreading western science and culture. Later on, this college grew into the famous Aligarh Muslim University.

Social and Religious Reforms After 1858; Growth of New India 123

In the earlier stages of his life, he was a believer in Hindu-Muslim unity but later on, he encouraged separatism.

Syed Ahmad Khan served in the judicial department of the East India Company for about 38 years i.e. from 1832 to 1870. He was appointed a member of Viceroy's Legislative Council for four years from 1878 to 1882.

Aligarh School:

Syed Ahmad Khan drew around him a band of dedicated followers which collectively came to be known as 'Aligarh School'. Among the important ones were Chirag Ali, Altaf Hussain Hali (an Urdu Poet), Nazir Ahmad, Maulana Shibi Nomani and Khuda Baksh. It is generally believed that most of the leaders of the Aligarh School were guided by the idea of separatism and they helped the British rulers in weakening the national movement.

(Sir) Muhammad Iqbal (1873-1938):

Dr. Muhammad Iqbal was a notable poet, a religious philosopher and a political ideologist. In his earlier poetry, he extolled patriotism, but later he encouraged Muslim separatism. The British rulers in India honoured him with a knighthood in 1922.

In his famous poem *'Tarangh-i-Hind'*, he eulogised India- *'Sare Jahan Se achcha'*.

On his return from Europe, Iqbal induced his Muslim brethren to imbibe in themselves, the dynamism of the West and the moral value of Islam. He suggested some reforms in Islamic thought. Unlike an orthodox believer, he would not like a man to resign passively.

Reform Movements in Maharashtra

Mention in an earlier chapter has been made of the Parmhans Mandali and the Prarthna Sabha which aimed at fighting caste system and idolatory.

Jotiba Phule (1827-1890):

Jotiba Phule was a great social and religious reformer of Maharashtra. He came from a family of flower-supplier to the House of the Peshwas. Thus, the family came to be known as 'Phule'. Jotiba was greatly inspired by Shivaji. He rejected caste distinctions and the supremacy of the Brahmans over Non-Brahmans. Jotiba and his wife devoted their lives for the uplift of the depressed classes and the women. In 1851, they started a girl's school at Poona and soon several schools came up. Jotiba established a good library for the low caste, a night school for adults and orphanage for the widows. He encouraged the adoption of children of the widows. In 1873, he founded the Satyashodak Samaj (Truth Seeking Society). He took a keen interest in bettering the living conditions of the mill workers. Jotiba Phule wanted priests to be kept out of the marriage ceremony. He condemned the practice of child marriage, infanticide and shaving of the heads of the widows. Jotiba Phule set forth his views in his book *Gulam-geri* (1872). On account of his qualities and character, his followers proclaimed him a 'Mahatama' - a great soul.

Mahadev Govind Ranade (1842-1901):

M.G. Ranade was a fervant patriot, champion of social amelioration, religious reformer, leader of thought, guide of men, noted historian, distinguished judge and eminent economist. In fact, Ranade dedicated his whole life for the regeneration of the teeming millions in all respects. He was one of the seventy-two members joining the first session of the Indian National Congress at Bombay. On account of his great intellect, he was called the 'Socrates of Maharashtra'.

Ranade's whole life was a ceaseless campaign for social reform. He became an active member of the Prarthna Samaj—a counterpart of the Brahma Samaj of Bengal. The Samaj worked for inter-caste dining, inter-caste marriages and remarriage of widows. According to Ranade, politics and social reforms were interwined. As a reformer, he wanted to convince the people, that the desired social reforms were in consonance with the Vedas and the Smritis.

Reform Movements in South India

The Veda Samaj and K.Shridharalu Naidu:

The Veda Samaj was founded at Madras in 1864. K. Shridharalu Naidu was the moving spirit behind the Veda Samaj. The movement was inspired by the Brahma Samaj. He translated a number of books of the Brahma Samaj in Tamil and Telegu. The Veda Samaj advocated discarding of caste distinctions. It worked for the promotion of widow remarriage and girls education. Its branches were established in some cities of Madras, Karnataka and Andhra.

Kandukuri Veeresalingam:

Born in 1848, in an orthodox Brahman family of Andhra, he dedicated himself to the cause of social reform. In 1876, he started a Telegu journal which was devoted to social reform. In 1878, he founded the Rajahmundri Social Reform Association. He promoted the cause of girl's education and widow remarriage.

Narayan Guru(1854-1928):

Narayan Guru's greatest contribution was his work for the emancipation of the oppressed sections of the society in Kerala. He was born in 1854, in an Ezhava family of untouchables. He started establishing temples without images. The first temple founded by him contained the following words, "Here is the place where all people live in fraternity, without caste distinctions." In 1903, he set up the Sri Narayan Dharam Paripalna Yogam—an organisation which attacked the priestly class and worked for the uplift of the Ezhavas. He attained the highest states of spiritual awareness by practising austerities. He believed in persuation and not hatred.

IMPORTANT IDEAS THAT LED TO RELIGIOUS AND SOCIAL REFORMS

The two most important ideas that influenced reform movements in religion were (i) Rationalism or reason (ii) humanism or human welfare.

The reformers laid great emphasis on applying the scientific principle of reason to religious beliefs. They tried to free religion from blind faith, irrational dogmas, unnecessary rituals and superstitions. Swami Vivekanand pointed out that the same methods of investigation which we apply to the sciences, should be applied to religious beliefs. Truth in religious scriptures must be evaluated by its conformity to logic and reason.

All religions stress that welfare of all human beings should be attended to. The religious and social reformers of the 19th century brought to light this aspect of the religion, which by and large, was neglected by the priestly class which tended to be the sole champions of religious thought. The reformers pointed out that they were not preaching something that was not in conformity with religious scriptures, and that they were rediscovering and re-emphasising something that was ignored by the priestly class.

SIGNIFICANT ASPECTS OF RELIGIOUS AND SOCIAL REFORMS

Certain social and religious beliefs and practices of some communities have kept some sections of the people, including women, condemned to a lower status and position, deprived of equal rights and privileges. These groups are fettered with disabilities, treated unjustly, looked down upon with disdain and sometimes made victims of cruelties and atrocities. Some religious orthodoxy held up one's freedom to think and act rationally and to choose one's own way of worshipping. The reformers tried to snap the fetters of such handicaps and to uplift the condition of the deprived sections. Some religious and social aspects that came into the focus of the reformers are set out below:-

Social and Religious Reforms After 1858; Growth of New India 125

(a) Religious Aspects

(i) Exploitation by the priests (ii) Prohibiting entry of low castes into temples (iii) Endless rituals involving heavy expenditure (iv) Religious superstitions hampering progress (v) Simple acts like sea voyages or crossing seas declared sinful (vi) Polytheism and idolatory to dominate the pattern of worship.

(b) Social Aspects

(i) Rigidity of caste system (ii) Untouchability (iii) Child marriage (iv) Female infanticide (killing of daughters at birth) (v) Low status of women (vi) Neglect of female education (vii) *Parda* system (viii) Dowry system (ix) Excess work load on women (x) General cruelty on women (xi) Easy divorce of wife among the Muslims (xii) *Sati* System (xiii) Degradation of widows through social restrictions (xiv) Restriction of widow marriage.

COMMON FEATURES OF THE RELIGIOUS AND SOCIAL REFORM MOVEMENTS

1. These reforms were the outcome of the reaction against the autocratic authority of the priestly class.
2. The reformers in most of the cases were influenced by the scientific approach of the Westerners to various issues.
3. The upper classes were oppressing the depressed classes.
4. The influence of Western education exercised a liberalising effect on the thinking of the educated classes.
5. The movements were generally confined to urban areas.
6. The reform movement first of all emerged in Bengal.
7. Each reform movement, by and large, remained confined to one or two regions only. Thus the Brahma Samaj was popular in Bengal, Prarthna Samaj in Maharashtra and the Arya Samaj in the Punjab.
8. There was hardly any movement on an all India level.
9. It is somewhat surprising that the provinces of Bihar, Uttar Pradesh, Madhya Pradesh and Rajputana did not produce any outstanding religious and social reformer in the eighteenth and nineteenth centuries.
10. All reform movements on the whole propagated equality and condemned caste system.
11. Almost all reformers worked for the uplift of women.

CONTRIBUTION OF REFORM MOVEMENTS

1. The reform movements pointed out the necessity of thinking rationally and scientifically.
2. They drew attention to various religious evils.
3. They brought to focus, the need to improve the condition of women.
4. They led to the opening of educational institutions which imparted Western education.
5. They led to the revival of ancient Indian Culture.

METHODS ADOPTED BY RELIGIOUS AND SOCIAL REFORMERS

The reforms were propagated and disseminated through the following ways:

(1) Organising lectures, debates and discussions (2) Interpreting the scriptures (3) Distributing pamphlets and writing books (4) Undertaking social work (5) Setting up institutions and organisations (6) Peaceful protest (7) Legislations.

LIMITATIONS OF THESE MOVEMENTS

(1) These socio-religious reforms remained confined mostly to the lower-middle class.

(2) Most of the reformers had the tendency to look forward as well as to look backward to the past glory.
(3) Some movements encouraged casteism and regionalism.

STRIKING BALANCE BETWEEN RELIGION AND SOCIAL REFORMS

Following points deserve mention in this context:
1. Encouraging Welfare Schemes such as opening of hospitals, orphanages and educational institutions.
2. Encouraging modern scientific education.
3. Encouraging the followers to make efforts themselves to improve their lot rather than depending upon destiny.
4. Highlighting India's past achievements in the material and spiritual fields to build self-confidence.
5. Emphasising a rational outlook.

EXERCISES

A. Very Short Answer Type Questions

1. Name any four social evils from which the Indian society suffered in the 19th century.
2. Name any four religious evils from which the Hindu society suffered.
3. Name any four disabilities from which women suffered.
4. List any four principles of Arya Samaj.
5. Mention any two reformers of Maharashtra of the 19th century.
6. Mention any two reformers who worked for the promotion of female education.
7. What were the chief aims of the Akali movement?
8. List any three limitations of the religious and social movements in the 19th century.

B. Short Answer Type Questions

1. Trace the development of religious and social reforms in South India.
2. State the common features of the religious and social reform movements of the 19th century.
3. What steps did Sir Syed Ahmad Khan take to make Indian Muslims more progressive?
4. Evaluate the role of rationalist thought in religious reforms.
5. Why did religious and social reform movements go hand in hand?
6. Describe the reform movements among the Parsis.
7. Describe the important factors that led to reforms in India in the 19th century.

C. Long Answer Type Questions

1. Against what social evils were the reform movements organised in the 19th century? To what extent were they successful in elevating the position of women?
2. Examine the role of Swami Dayanand in carrying out socio-religious reforms in India.
3. What were the teachings of Swami Vivekanand? Why is he often referred to as 'Karam Yogi'- a man of action?

CHAPTER 14

The Growth of New India

THE NATIONALIST MOVEMENT (1858-1905) NATIONAL AWAKENING

Introduction

The national awakening, witnessed in the great upheaval of the Sepoy Revolt of 1857 was the beginning before the whole country plunged into a long struggle for freedom, which India gained in 1947. This national awakening had the following characteristics. One, it was, in some significant way, motivated by the Sepoy Revolt of 1857, though it was of a different nature. It was not led by the Sepoys or the Indian rulers but was basically started by intellectuals. Second, it was a movement in which, all people and sections of society living in different parts of the country became united against the common enemy. Third, the national struggle for the freedom of India was not confined to Indians living in India but also abroad. Fourth, it was mostly non-violent. Fifth, after 1920 or so, it was dominated by Gandhiji. Sixth, it was the outcome of a large number of factors.

Reasons for National Awakening

Indian nationalism arose out of the conditions created by the British rulers. With the exception of a few vested interests, the entire people of India had lost faith in the British rulers. The following paragraphs, will throw light on the multitude of factors that gave rise to national awakening.

1. Nature of Foreign Rule:

The very intrinsic nature of the foreign rule with its expansionist, exploitative, imperialistic and oppressive designs created hatred for it. The British never treated India as their country. They came to India as foreigners, ruled India as foreigners, lived in India as foreigners and also left as foreigners. They considered it their 'divine right' to plunder India and take away its enormous wealth to Britain.

There is no doubt that the foreign character of the British domination in itself produced a nationalist reaction, since foreign regime invariably generates patriotic feeling in the hearts of a subject nation.

2. Consequence of Foreign Domination:

A foreign domination, always, directly or indirectly proves very harmful to the country under its control. There is invariably clash of interests between the foreign rulers and the natives. Experience shows that the welfare of the ruled class suffers. There is hardly any area of life of the ruled people that is not adversely affected by the selfish policies of the foreign rulers. The British rule became a stumbling block to India's overall development i.e. cultural, economic, educational, intellectual, political, social and spiritual. In fact, every action or policy of the British, even for the good of the Indian people was looked down upon with suspicion.

3. Ruin of Indian Economy:

Mention has already been made regarding the exploitative economic policies of the British which resulted in enormous economic drain from India to Britain, appalling poverty of the masses and recurrence of famines claiming crores of lives (human and animals), and destruction of crops. There was hardly a section of population which did not suffer from the economic oppression of the foreign rule.

A large number of cultivators became landless as they were required to pay very high land revenue. Their lands became less productive for want of facilities like improved seeds, irrigation facilities etc. They had to mortgage their lands and homes etc.

The Indian artisans and craftsmen lost their means of livelihood and were left on the brink of starvation.

The Indian traders suffered on account of unfair competition from British traders.

The Indian industrialists were at a great disadvantage compared with foreign industrialists who received all types of financial and other help in setting up industries.

The old Zamindars were deprived of their lands and their place was taken up by new Zamindars who were also being plundered by unscrupulous government officials.

The educated Indians felt there were very few chances to get into higher jobs as they were discriminated against Britishers.

The workers, especially plantation workers were ill-paid and ill-treated. They led a very miserable life.

Thus, there developed a hatred for foreign domination.

4. Widespread Famines:

There were widespread famines during the second half of the 19th century when crores of people lost their lives on account of famines. The famines were followed by epidemics. The hardships faced by the Indian people convinced them that the British rule in India was the major cause of their starvation, misery and death.

5. Role of Literature:

The literature that was produced during the period, accelerated the spread of national consciousness among the masses of India. Novels, plays, poems and stories written in various Indian languages greatly helped in national awakening. The novel *Anand Math* and the composition *Vande Matram* of Bankim Chandra, the famous Bengali writer, became a great source of inspiration to the people. For the first time, it was sung at the annual session of the Indian Congress in 1896. Vast literature produced by Bhartendu Harish Chandra in Hindi, Vishnu Shastri Cheplunkar in Marathi, Subramanya Bharati in Tamil, Rabindranath Tagore in Bengali and Altaf Hussain Ali in Urdu, helped in stirring the hearts of the Indian people and stamped their minds with the ideals of freedom.

The appalling condition of the masses, as depicted in the well documented and scholarly writings of Dadabhai and R.C. Dutt, touched the conscience of the intellectuals and made them aware of the exploitative nature of the British economic policies.

6. Role of the Press:

The contemporary press, newspapers and magazines, served a powerful media for mass awakening, infusing political ideas and patriotic sentiments. The government tried but failed to subdue or purchase the press. It was very vocal in its criticism of the policies pursued by the British in India. The editors wrote fearlessly and exposed freely the evils of foreign rule. Editors like Lala Lajpat Rai of the *Bande Matram* and *The People* and Bal Gangadhar Tilak of *Kesari* and *Maratha*, suffered deportation. Five editors of *Yugantar* were put behind the bars. By the year 1905, India had over 700 newspapers and an equal number of periodicals. The nationalist press had to pay a very heavy price for its nationalist views.

7. Recovery of India's Past Glory:

The study of India's past by the British and Indian scholars, including indologists and archaeologists like

Max Muller, John Marshall, Dayaram Sawhney, Wheeler and R.G. Bhandarkar helped profoundly, to bring to light, the richness of the ancient heritage of India. Masses began to feel proud of India's advances in arts, astronomy and sciences of ancient India. They began to take pride in the Indus Valley Civilization. They were thrilled to know that when the great Vedic Civilization flourished, England was inhabited by semi-barbaric tribes. They started reacting sharply to the western criticism of India's culture and civilization. They began to discard their sense of inferiority.

Several leaders brought to light the political and cultural achievements of Indian rulers like Ashoka, Chandragupta Vikramaditya and Akbar.

8. National Awakening by Religious and Social Leaders:

The writings and speeches of leaders like Swami Dayanand, Ramakrishna Paramhans, Vivekanand and others infused a new spirit of faith and courage. Besides reminding the people of the glory and greatness of India's past, they declared that there was no substitute for self-government. Swami Vivekanand, in his own way, exhorted the people of India to be strong and brave. It is said about him, "The queen of his adoration was motherland". He asked the educated people of India to be sensitive to the weak and the illiterate. He called for ceaseless efforts to rise and bring glory to the motherland. The founders of the Theosophical Society of India and Mrs. Annie Besant made their own contribution to the cause of national awakening.

9. Influence of Western Thought:

A large number of educated Indians who came into contact with western thought, were greatly influenced by the democratic, nationalist, rational and political outlook. Philosophers like John Stuart Mill (1806-1873) became their political guides. Nationalist leaders like Mazzini (1805-1872) and Garibaldi (1807-1882) of Italy became their political heroes.

10. Spread of Education:

The British rulers had hoped that the educated Indians would become the ardent supporters of the British rule in India. However, the effects were contrary. Spread of education became an important factor in the promotion of national consciousness among the Indians in a number of ways. First, modern education gave the educated Indians access to the liberal ideas of the West. They became acquainted with the ideals of democracy and human freedom and received inspiration from the nationalist movements and freedom struggles taking place in countries outside India. Second, the educated people were in a better position to make others aware of the evils of the foreign rule. Third, the growing middle class of western educated young people got disillusioned with the recruitment and racial policies of the British. Fourth, Universities of Bombay, Calcutta, Madras, Punjab and Allahabad were to produce graduates, quite a large number of whom were aspirants to high posts in civil services. They, however, found that the policy of discrimination followed by the British was a great barrier in their career. They, therefore, felt the need for an organised united action for national resurgence. In course of time, the best among them became the leaders of national movements. Fifth, English, as the medium of higher education created a certain community and unity of outlook and interests among the educated Indians. It became the medium of communication and exchange of ideas among educated Indians belonging to different regions.

11. Administrative and Economic Unification of the Country:

The British introduced a uniform system of administration throughout the country. It was based on a hierarchy of administrators right from Governor-General/Viceroy to the village patwari. The entire territory was divided into convenient units of administration called provinces which were subdivided into smaller administrative units. Laws were duly codified. Uniform legal procedures and precedents were followed. There developed a strong centralised administrator which kept provinces under strict discipline.

Setting up industries and trade helped to bring about an economic unification. Economic self-sufficiency of the village was replaced by its dependence on market forces.

12. Development of Means of Transport and Communication:

All major parts of the country were inter-connected with railways, postal services and other communication. Hence it became easier to spread the nationalist sentiments easily, to every nook and corner of the country.

13. Maltreatment and Racial Discrimination of the Indians:

The British always assumed an air of racial superiority and openly insulted even the English educated Indians. An Indian could rarely expect justice in a case involving a British citizen. The criminal procedure code of 1873 had put such restrictions that Indian judges in general were not permitted to decide cases in which Europeans were involved. Ilbert Bill (1882), which provided for bringing the Indian and European magistrates on the same footing, generated a lot of opposition from the British Community and ultimately it had to be modified. Indians could not travel in certain railway compartments, or entertainment clubs and restaurants. All this created a feeling of hatred for the British rule.

14. Heavy War Costs:

The British continued to wage a number of wars with other countries like Nepal, Tibet and Afghanistan and the cost of these wars was met out of the taxes collected from the Indians.

15. Callousness of the British:

The period from 1876 to 1884 has been called the seed time of Indian nationalism. It was the period of passing the notorius Vernacular Press Act, which put restrictions on the press to curb Indian sentiments. The Second Afghan War brought untold suffering to the army people. There was the Ilbert Bill controversy. Lakhs of Indians died in the famine that took place during the period. Lord Lytton held his famous Delhi Durbar and the people wondered at his callousness.

National Awakening Associations Before the Formation of the Indian National Congress

After the events of 1857, several associations came up for promoting national awakening among the people of India. Among the important ones were the following.
1. East Indian Association, London (1866)
2. Poona Sarvjanik Sabha (1870)
3. Indian Association, Calcutta (1876)
4. Madras Mahajan Sabha (1884)
5. Bombay Presidency Association (1885)

East Indian Association, London (1886):

Dadabhai Naoroji (1825-1917), popularly known as 'Grand Old Man of India', organised this association in London, primarily for two objectives, namely (i) to organise discussion on the plight of the Indian people and (ii) to influence British public opinion to promote the welfare of the Indians. Later on, he organised branches of this association in prominent cities of India (An account of the work and achievements of Dadabhai is given in an earlier chapter).

Poona Sarvjanik Sabha (1870):

It was launched by Justice Ranade (1842-1901). It organised Swadeshi movement and also stimulated political activity.

The Growth of New India

Indian Association, Calcutta (1876):

This Association, formed by S.N. Banerjee (1848-1925) became the forerunner of the Indian National Congress. Its aims were two-fold (1) To create strong public opinion in the country on political questions (2) To unify the people of India on a common political programme. With a view to attracting a large number of people under its fold, it fixed a low membership fee for the poor sections of the society. It opened several branches in and outside Bengal. In Bengal, it established its branches in the countryside also.

Madras Mahajan Sabha (1884):

It also aimed at political awakening. Its important leaders were M. Viraraghavachari, G. Subramaniya Iyer and Ananda Charbu.

Bombay Presidency Association (1885):

It was organised by Pheroze Shah Mehta, K.T. Telang, Badruddin Tyabiji and others for promoting public interest. It took an active part in organising the Indian National Congress in 1885.

INDIAN NATIONAL CONGRESS

Architect of India's Freedom:

Notwithstanding the controversy involved regarding the origin and its nature of work when it was founded, there is no doubt that the Indian National Congress, during the course of time, played the most prominent role in the freedom struggle of India. It gathered together under its banner lakhs of people who made invaluable sacrifices and underwent even inhuman suffering and sorrow to keep alive the flame of freedom. It is rather paradoxical that the organisation founded by a British national, A.O. Hume, a retired Civil Servant, blessed by Lord Dufferin, the then British Viceroy of India and first presided over in 1885 by W.C. Bannerjee, a British loyal barrister of Calcutta, spear-headed the struggle against the British. Later on Dufferin turned into the bitterest critic of the Congress.

Congress as a 'Safety Valve':

Hume did not want the repetition of the events of 1857. He wanted Indian feelings and problems to be expressed through the public platform. He desired that leading politicians and social workers should discuss contemporary issues concerning India, and present the solutions to the British officials. He desired to unify the discordant elements of the Indian society so that the interests of the people of India were well looked after. He wanted a gradual regeneration of the Indian nation. He was very keen to establish cordial relations between the officials and the non-officials. He stressed that the British rule must be based on enlightened principles and all this could be achieved by setting up a forum which found its birth in the formation of the Indian National Congress.

The 'Safety Valve' theory offers a partial explanation of the aims and objectives of the Indian National Congress. The early Congress leaders hoped to use Hume as a 'Lightening Conductor'. He himself possessed a sincere love for India. Hume published a pamphlet entitled *An Old Man's Hope* in which he made an appeal to the people of England in these words, "Ah Men! Well fed and happy! Do you at all realise the dull misery of these countless myriads? Toil, Toil, Toil; Hunger, Hunger, Hunger; Sickmen, Suffering, Sorrow; these alas, alas, alas are the key notes of their short and sad existence."

Initial Aims of the Indian National Congress:

These may be mentioned as under:
1. Promotion of friendly relations among nationalist political workers of different parts of the country.
2. Development and consolidation of the feelings of national unity, irrespective of caste, region or province.

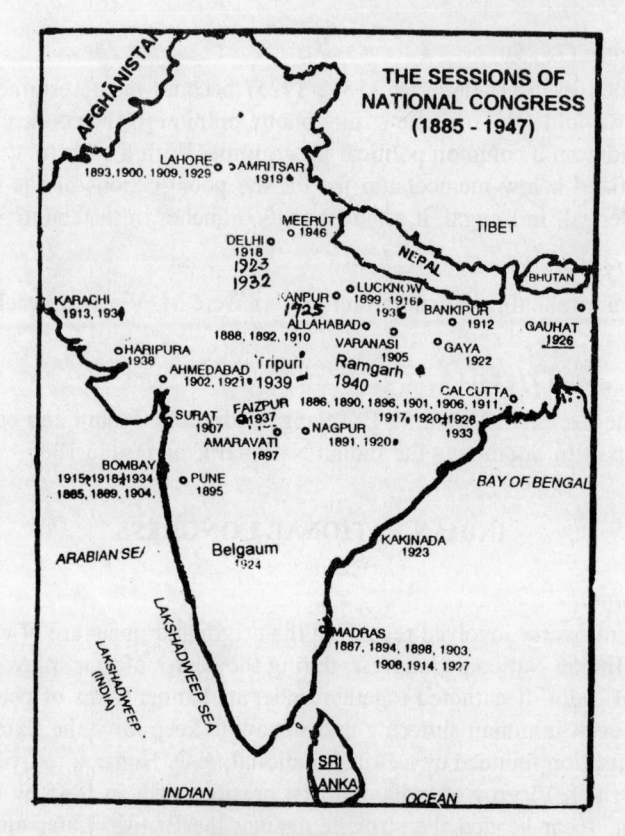

Map 24: Congress Sessions 1885-1947

3. Formulation of popular demands of the people and their presentation before the government.
4. Organisation of public opinion in the country.

Factors Leading to the Emergence of the Indian National Congress:

Several local organisations in different parts of the country took up reforms in a piecemeal manner without having a larger national perspective and without co-ordination with the efforts of other associations. A need for a well-knit organisation that could embrace in its fold, several sections of population belonging to different religions and regions was acutely felt. This need led to the founding of the Indian National Congress. The Indian National Congress attracted in the beginning, only the educated classes, but in due course, it became a mass organisation under whose umbrella all sections of the population fought for the freedom of the country.

Congress as the Representative of the Cross Section of India's Population:

The composition of delegates of the first session of the Congres held at Bombay indicates that it included people from different walks of life, regions and communities. The first session held in 1885 attended by 72 delegates was held at Bombay, the second at Calcutta attended by 434 delegates, the third at Madras which drew 607 delegates, the fourth at Allahabad with 1248 delegates. The places of Congress Sessions held during the period between 1885 and 1947 are shown on the map.

The first session was attended by editors, lawyers, retired civil servants, scholars, writers etc.

Some of the important leaders who attended the first session included Dadabhai Naoroji, Badr-ud-din Tyabji, Subramania Iyer, Dinsha Wacha, Ranade, Pherozeshah Mehta, etc.

The Growth of New India

The history of the Congress became almost the history of the struggle for independence. The programme and activities passed through phases.

PHASES OF THE WORK OF THE CONGRESS AT A GLANCE

Phase	Period	Main Objective	Prominent Leaders	Nature of the Programme
1.	1885-1905	Gradual introduction of reforms	Dadabhai Naoroji, Surendranath Banerjee, Gopal Krishna Gokhale, Badru-ud-Din Tyabji (Moderate leaders)	1. Organisation of public opinion through meetings etc. 2. Passing resolutions. 3. Sending Petitions. 4. Constitutional means.
2.	1905-1918	Seeking Salvation of motherland	1. Bal Gangadhar Tilak 2. Lala Lajpat Rai 3. Bepin Chandra Pal (Extremists/militant leaders)	1. Swadeshi Movement 2. Boycott and hartal 3. Non-cooperation 4. Fiery speeches through public platform and press.
3.	1919-1927	Greater control in the working of the government.	Gandhiji's leadership	1. Technique of Satyagraha. 2. Use of Khadi 3. Slogan of Hindu-Muslim Unity 4. Mass agitation 5. Non-Cooperation Movement
4.	1928-1947	Goal of Poorna Swaraj (Complete Independence)	1. Gandhiji 2. Jawaharlal Nehru 3. Subhas Chandra Bose 4. Sardar Vallabh Bhai Patel 5. Maulana Abul Kalam Azad	1. Demonstrations, hartals 2. Participation in Government. 3. Congress Ministries in several provinces. 4. Civil Disobedience Movement 5. Satyagrahas, Fasts 6. Quit India Movement 7. Negotiations for Independence.

THE MODERATES OR THE MODERATE NATIONALISTS

Who were Moderate Leaders?

The early national movement was guided by leaders who were called Moderates or Moderate nationalists on account of their cautious, cooperative and peaceful approach to national issues. They included leaders like Dadabhai Naoroji, Surendranath Banerjee, Badruddin Tyabji, Pherozeshah Mehta, Gopalkrishna Gokhale and others.

Main Objectives of the Moderates

The Moderates had three main objectives before them (i) To build up a strong public opinion in India by arousing the consciousness of the people towards administrative, economic and political reforms (ii) To unite the people on one political platform irrespective of caste, religion and region (iii) To persuade the British government and British public opinion to introduce reforms.

Major demands of the Moderates

The moderates worked for the gradual introduction of reforms in the working of the administration of India. They asked for more powers for the Indians to the Legislative Councils and election of members. They also demanded major changes in the economic policies of the government for facilitating the growth of industries in India. Other major demands included providing more opportunities for Indians to compete for higher posts in administration, freedom of speech and expression etc.

Political Methods adopted by the Moderates

The Moderates had faith in the British rule and believed that the British rule could be reformed from within. They had no plan to drive away the British rulers from India. Thus, their whole approach was one of 'conciliation and not confrontation'. Their agitation was confined to hold meetings, pass resolutions for fulfilling their demands, and send petitions and prayers to the government. It was believed that the authorities would accept their demands/requests gradually and step by step.

British Government's Attitude towards the Indian National Congress

During the first two years of its inception (1885-87), the British response was well-disposed towards its activities. The Viceroy, Lord Dufferin, had entertained the Congress leaders at a garden party, at Calcutta in 1886. The Governor of Madras had also organised a similar party in 1887. The growing demands of the leaders for a representative and responsible government alarmed the authorities. In 1888, the Congress started a paid agency in London, for political propaganda, for the welfare of the people of India. This all the more irritated the British rulers. Pro-government papers also began to criticise the Moderate leaders. On the demands of the Moderate leaders for a representative government in India, Lord Dufferin criticised the activities of the Moderate leaders in 1886 with these words, "Congressmen were seeking to sit in the Chariot of sun... How can any reasonable man imagine that the British Government would allow this microscopic minority to control the administration of that majestic and multi-form empire."

In 1897, the Secretary of state for India, George Hamilton, referring to the Congress demands, said in the House of Commons, "The liberties of the British constitution did not apply to criminal lunatics."

The British officials branded the Congress leaders as "disloyal babus", "Seditious Brahmans" and "violent villains". The Congress was described as a "factory of sedition." Lord Curzon, the Viceroy of India, declared in 1900, "The Congress is tottering to its fall and one of my great ambitions, while in India, is to assist it in a peaceful demise."

The British rulers began to describe it as the organisation of the Hindus and followed the policy of "Divide and Rule". They tried to drive a wedge between the Hindu and Muslims.

Review of the Work Done by the Moderates

(1) Moderates and Constitutional Reform:

The Moderates had complete faith in the solemn pledges given by the British Government to the people of India from time to time. Surendranath Banerjee regarded the Queen's Proclamation of 1858 as "The Magna Carta of rights and liberties". For constitutional reforms, the Moderates believed in constitutional and orderly agitation. Badruddin, the Congress President in 1887 said, "Be moderate in your demands, just in your criticism, correct in your facts and logical in your conclusions."

As a result of the pressure brought by the Indian National Congress, under the influence of the Moderates, the government passed the *Indian Council's Act of 1892*. The Act enlarged the function of the Legislative Councils. They were authorised to discuss the annual financial statement under certain conditions. The members of the councils were given the right to ask questions from the government on matters of public interest. The number of members was increased.

The 1892 Act fell short of expectations. Dadabhai Naoroji, in his presidential address of the Indian National Congress in 1893 at Lahore, terms the provisions of the Act as 'arbitrary'. About elections to the Councils, R.C. Dutt observed, "Half a dozen members elected under somewhat complicated rules can scarcely express the views of the people of a province with a population of 30 to 40 million or more."

Budget could now be discussed but there was to be no voting. The Congress leaders termed the Act as a 'hoax'. They raised the slogan associated with the war of American Independence, "No taxation without representation." By the beginning of the 20th century the demand for self-government within the British empire was made from the Congress platform by Gokhale in 1905 and Dadabhai Naoroji in 1906.

(2) The Moderates and the Administrative Reforms:

The Moderates criticised the administrative set-up on these accounts. It was very costly. It was full of red tapism. Indians were excluded from higher posts. I.C.S. examination was held outside India. The demand for Indianisation of the higher grades of administrative services was put forward on economic, moral and political grounds. Economically, there were two factors (i) Higher salaries paid to the Europeans (ii) Payment of pension to Europeans, retired and returned to Britain, at a very high rate causing economic drain. Morally, it developed inferiority complex even among the most talented Indians that they were unfit to carry on the work of administration involving responsible duties. Politically, the European Civil Servants ignored the needs of the Indians.

In 1897, Gopal Krishna Gokhale gave a very convincing evidence before the Royal Commission, which proved that there was need for the Indianisation of administrative services. In the Civil Department, there were only 55 Indians out of 1276 officers; only one military officer out of 856 and in military only 25 officers out of 1303 in the same income bracket. In the police, there were just 3 Indians as District Superindents out of 230.

(3) Moderates and Economic Reforms:

Perhaps the most notable part of the Moderates' political work was their systematic and factual criticism of the economic policy of the British rulers through press and publications. They highlighted the evil consequences of the exploitative economic policies of the British rulers pursued in all the three important areas of trade, industry and finance. They vehemently opposed British economic imperialism which led to the subordination of the Indian economy to the British economy. Naoroji's book *Un-British Rule in India,* R.C.Dutt's book *The Economic History of India in the Victorian Age,* Digby's work *Prosperous India* and Lajpat Rai's *Unhappy India* provided a graphic picture of heavy taxation, costly wars, discriminatory tariff policy, neglect of industries, enormous export of India's raw materials, recurring famines, growing national debt, occurrence of epidemics, rising death rate, heavy foreign capital investment and the unending huge drain of India's wealth to England. About the drain of wealth, Dadabhai caustically remarked, "The English stand sentinel at the front door of India... and carry away by the back door, the very treasure they stand sentinel to protect."

The Moderates organised a powerful agitation against almost all important official economic policies. They popularised the idea of *Swadeshi* or the use of Indian goods and launched a movement for the boycott of British goods. In 1896, students in various parts of Maharashtra publicly burnt foreign clothes. They launched an agitation for the reduction of heavy land revenue payments. They demanded that the government should provide cheap credit facilities to the peasants through agricultural banks. They urged upon the government to make available irrigation facilities on a large scale. They pleaded for improving the conditions of work of the plantation labourers. They asked for a radical change in the existing pattern of taxation and expenditure which put a huge burden on the poor. They made representations against the abolition of salt tax which hit hard, the poor and the lower middle classes.

(4) Moderates and the Defence of the Civil Rights:

From the very beginning, the Moderates put up a strong defence for the civil rights i.e. freedom of speech, the Press and association. In 1897, the arrest of B.G. Tilak and several other leaders and editors evoked a country-wide protest. About the arrest of Tilak it was said, "There is scarcely a home in this vast country where Tilak is not now the subject of melancholy talk and where his imprisonment is not considered as a domestic calamity."

(5) Moderates and Diverse Issues of Public Interest:

The Moderates demanded separation of the judicial powers from executive powers so that people may get protection from the arbitrary actions of the bureaucracy and the police. They criticized the high cost of the judicial process as well as delays involved in it. They strongly criticized the oppressive and tyrannical behaviour of the police and other government officials towards the common people. They laid a good deal of stress to undertake welfare activities for the people. They urged the government to take speedy action for the promotion of primary education. They pleaded for greater facilities for technical education. They demanded extension of health and medical facilities. They protested aganist the aggressive policy of waging wars against India's neighbours. They spoke up in defence of Indian workers, who, on account of poverty, had been compelled to migrate to foreign countries such as Malaya, Mauritius, the West Indies, British Guiana and South Africa.

Contribution of the Moderates to the National Movement

The Moderates, the founders of the Indians National Congress, played a significant role in national awakening. They were the path finders and the torch bearers. They were aware of their limitations and accordingly initiated a moderate action. Perhaps time was not ripe for a revolutionary approach. Without minimising the important significant role that the extremists played in the freedom struggle, it must be admitted that it took four decades after 1907, the year when the extremists came into prominence, to achieve independence. Even the extremists could not achieve substantial results. The last phase of struggle for freedom was led not by an extremist but by a leader who believed in the power of satyagraha. There is no doubt that the moderates, the extremists, the militants, the revolutionaries and the Gandhivadis, all contributed to the nationalist movement.

The achievements of the Moderates included the following:
1. They founded the Indian National Congress.
2. They evolved a common economic and political programme.
3. The programme and activities of the Moderates were based on the hard realities of the country and not on any kind of sectarian or religious sentiments.
4. They did pioneering work in exposing the exploitative nature of British Imperialism in India.
5. The Moderates made the people of India conscious of their right to freedom.
6. The Moderates paved the way for close interaction in national matters.
7. The Moderates helped in popularising the basic concepts of democracy, civil liberties, freedom of the press etc.
8. The Moderates initiated the process of importing political training of the educated Indians.
9. The Moderates built up a strong public opinion on economic and social issues.
10. They worked for promoting national unity irrespective of caste, religion or region.

Limitations/Weaknesses of the Nationalist Movement Under Moderate Leadership

The nationalist movement under the Moderates suffered from arm-chair discussions, resolutions and appeals and ineffective methods.

The movement in the first phase was confined to a limited section of society. Only educated people took part in its activities. It was confined to 'paper work' which consisted of passing prayers and petitions to the government. The programmes were not action oriented with the result that the masses had no contribution to make.

Summing up. Taking into consideration the pros and cons of the issues, it can be concluded very safely that the movement was successful to a considerable extent to achieve the goals it set forth before it. It worked quite effectively under the parameters of its aims and objectives.

The Growth of New India

Prominent Moderate Leaders

Allan Octavian Hume (1829-1912):

He was a retired British official of the Indian Civil Service who was one of the prominent founders of the Indian National Congress in 1885. He had great love for the Indians primarily because his life had been saved by his Indian friends during the Revolt of 1857. He wanted cordial relations between the officials and non-officials. He firmly believed that the British rule must be based on enlightened principles. After his retirement, he devoted the rest of his life to the cause of Indian welfare. On March 1, 1883, he exhorted in a letter to the Calcutta University graduates, to work for the uplift of their motherland, "Even if fifty among you cannot be found with sufficient power and sacrifice and love and pride in your country... there is no hope for India." He addressed the following lines to the people of India.

> "Sons of Ind, Why sit ye idle?
>   Wait ye for some Deva's aid?
> Buckle to, be up and doing!
>   Nations by themselves are made!"

Badruddin Tyabji (1844-1906):

He was a great lawyer, just judge, acknowledged public leader, social reformer, a persuasive public speaker and a redoubtable champion of Indian interests. He presided over the third session of the Indian National Congress in 1887. He was a member of the Bombay Legislative Council for five years from 1882 to 1886. Through Anjuman-i-Islam of Bombay, he tried to educate the Muslim community in India. He tried to weaken the hold of purdah. He declared that it was the height of injustice to the whole of Indian community to declare that even the best of Indian magistrates and judges were not fit to try against the Europeans.

Pherozeshah Mehta (1845-1915):

Pherozeshah Mehta, who claimed himself to be an Indian first and Parsi afterwards, played an important part in the activities and programmes of the Indian National Congress from the day of its foundation in 1885 to 1915, the year of his death. He presided over the Calcutta session of the Congress in 1890. For his services to Bombay, he was known as the "Lion of Bombay". He was considered as Moderate. While having faith in the sense of justice of the Englishmen he once said, "England must raise India to her own level or India will drag her down to hers."

Surendranath Banerjee (1848-1925):

He was the first to be selected in the ICS, but he was disallowed to join it on account of some discrepancy in his age. He was a great national leader and at the same time professor, editor, educationist and social reformer. On account of his undaunted spirit, his agitations and struggles for the redressal of the grievances of the oppressed under the British rule in his early career, he was known as 'Surrender Not'. He presided over two sessions of the Indian National Congress—in 1895 and 1902. He was one of the founders of the Indian National Congress. He was a political moderate and advocated constitutional agitation for self-government. He was the leader in the first phase of the agitation against the Partition of Bengal. Surendranath Banerjee was a great Parliamentarian. He was a member of the Bengal Council from 1893 to 1901 and a member of the Imperial Legislative Council from 1913 to 1918.

This was his view regarding non-coopeation:

"There are occasions where we must not cooperate and follow it up as a protest. But, I altogether repudiate persistent policy of non-cooperation, especially when the government is prepared to move along progressive lines."

Gopal Krishna Gokhale (1866-1915):

Gandhiji called Gokhale his "Political Guru". Lokmanya Tilak described Gokhale as "the diamond of India, the jewel of Maharashtra and the prince of workers." He has been described by many as a "constructive statesman of the first rank, harbinger together of the East and the West and prophet of the new era of inter-racial goodwill and cooperation. At the age of 20, Gokhale became a professor, at 22 a member of the Bombay Legislative Council, at 36 a member of the Supreme Council and at 39, the President of the Indian National Congress. Gokhale was a moderate. He firmly believed that the situation required "not the policeman's baton or the soldier's bayonet but the statesman's insight, wisdom and courage." From 1905 to 1915, he virtually dominated the Congress, thwarting the bid of Extremists to control it. He played the role of a 'reconciler'.

He criticized the Salt Tax on the ground that the poor were hit by it. He disapproved the policy of the Government of India, of excluding Indians from higher posts. He denounced the Partition of Bengal. He persuaded Gandhiji to come to India from South Africa. He worked for the poor peasants. He was in favour of constitutional methods for the realisation of the goal. He had no faith in revolutionary methods.

EXERCISES

A. Very Short Answer Type Questions

1. Name any two political associations which were predecessors to the Indian National Congress.
2. Mention any two characteristics of the Moderates.
3. Mention any two fields in which they criticized the British rulers.
4. Mention any two methods followed by the Moderates.
5. Mention any four names that fall under the category of Moderate leaders.
6. List any phases of the work of the Indian National Congress.
7. Why did A.O. Hume form the Indian National Congress?

B. Short Answer Type Questions

1. Describe the contribution of Dadabhai-Naoroji to Indian national movement.
2. Why was the Indian National Congress founded? State its objectives.
3. Describe the salient features of the various phases of the work of the Indian National Congress.
4. Describe the contribution of Surendra Nath Banerjee and Gopal Krishna Gokhale to the Indian National Movement.
5. Why did the British rulers change their attitude towards Indian National Congress?
6. Why were the leaders of the Congress during its early phase called the Moderates?

C. Essay Type/Long Answer Type Questions

1. Assess the contribution of the Moderates to the Indian National Movement (1885-1905).
2. Examine the factors responsible for the growth of national consciousness in India.
3. Explain any four factors which led to the growth of national awakening.

D. Map Work

On an outline map of India, locate any five cities where Annual Sessions of the Indian National Congress were held.

CHAPTER 15

The Nationalist Movement (1905-1918)

BACKGROUND OF THE RISE OF MILITANT OR EXTREMIST NATIONALIST MOVEMENT

The period during the years 1905 to 1918 is usually referred to as the period of militant/extremist nationalism, for during this period, the earlier approach of 'reconciliation' followed by the Moderates was replaced by the new approach of 'confrontation' with the British rulers. The Moderates believed that there was great scope of progress for the Indians under the British rule which they termed as 'benevolent control'. The leaders of the new movement were firmly convinced that India could not make any progress under the 'exploitative, ruthless and oppressive' regime of the British imperialists. They found that the British Government was not receptive to the appeals, petitions and resolutions sent by the Moderates to it. They thought that the peaceful methods adopted by the Moderates had no worthwhile impact. The Militants, therefore, adopted aggressive methods to achieve their objective of self-rule in India i.e. rule of the Indians in India and not that of the British.

As the 19th century was about to close, the political environment in India was already charged on account of persecutions of the leaders, famines, plagues and high expectations of the Indians and British indifference, injustice and arrogance. Then, there emerged Lord Curzon, the new Viceroy of India (1899-1905), who had behaved from his early days as the 'most superior person'. The key-note of his administrative approach was, "The British bureaucracy knows what is for the good of the Indian people." The movement of adopting aggressive postures emerged after the partition of Bengal in 1905.

Rise of Militant Nationalism: Internal and External Causes

The internal causes included (i) Recognition of the true nature of the British rule (ii) Growth of self-respect and confidence among the Indians (iii) Growth of education among the Indians (iv) Increasing unemployment in India (v) Partition of Bengal (vi) Repressive measures of the British rulers.

External causes included (i) Publicity of India's condition abroad (ii) Independence movements abroad (iii) Reforms in foreign lands (iv) Victory of Japan over Russia.

Recognition of the True Nature of the British Rule:

The true nature of the British rule was exposed by the poverty it spread, the man-made famines it created, the racial arrogance it displayed, the drain of India's wealth it led to, the exports of India's raw materials it encouraged and the policy of employment it followed in respect of the educated Indians. Although these were in visible evidence for a long time but certain circumstances brought to light their evil effects. The India Council's Act of 1882 was a complete disappointment. In 1896, plague took a very heavy toll of lives. The 1898 law put restrictions on freedom of speech. In 1899, the Calcutta Corporation Act completely officialised the Calcutta Corporation. The disastrous famines which ravaged India from 1896 to 1900 and took over 90 lakhs of lives, symbolized the evil economic consequences of the foreign rule.

The Indian Official Secrets Act of 1904 restricted the freedom of the Press.

The Indian Universities Act 1904 reduced the autonomy of the universities and such changes were made in the Syndicates, Senates and Faculties of the Universities which led to the prominence of the Europeans. The most severe blow came in the partition of Bengal in 1905.

The speeches of George Hamilton, Secretary of State for India and Lord Curzon, clearly reflected the true nature of the British rule. On August 5, 1897, Hamilton termed the Indians as 'criminal lunatics'. Lord Curzon called the Indians 'cheats.'

The extremists exposed the nature of the British rule through press and platform.

Growth of Self-Respect and Self-Confidence:

Leaders of the new movement tried to develop self-respect and self-confidence among the Indians. Sri Aurobindo asserted, "The fate of the country is in ourselves. It is not in any outward force. It is in hearts, in our courage." Lala Lajpat told the masses, "They would have to strike the blow for freedom. The harder the contest, the more glorious is the triumph." B.C. Pal reminded the people "self-help and self-sacrifice" was the real force in the field of nationalism. Swami Vivekanand, though not a political leader, asked the people to have confidence in them. He declared, "If there is a sin in the world it is weakness; avoid all weakness, weakness is death... And here is the test of truth—anything that makes you weak physically, intellectually and spiritually, reject as poison, there is no life in it, it cannot be true". It is of interest to note that he felt the need of arousing political consciousness among the masses. "The only hope of India is from the masses," he said.

Growth of Education Among the Indians:

In the 1900s, The University and collegiate education in India presented a motely picture. On the one hand, there had been considerable expansion of higher education, on the other hand, the efficiency of the new colleges was not very high. The Western education had created a solid class of intellectuals who became conscious of the Western ideals of democracy, nationalism and radicalism.

Discriminating Policy of Employment and Increasing Unemployment:

The development of higher education was very lopsided. Professional education in general, and industrial and technical education in particular remained neglected. There were fewer avenues of self employment for the educated and thus they faced unemployment. Added to this was the lack of avenues in services, and when employed, they received very low salaries as compared with their counterpart Europeans. Thus, the economic plight of the educated made them look critically at the British rule. The anti-India policy of Lord Curzon led to all the more bitterness and discontentment. The view of Lord Curzon was, "The highest ranks of all civil employment must, as a general rule, be held by Englishmen."

Inspiration from International Events:

The nationalist leaders drew great inspiration from the following international events:
(i) A backward Japan, an Asian country, coming up as a first rate industrial power.
(ii) The defeat of Russia-considered to be a giant nation-by a small nation like Japan.
(iii) The victory of the Ethiopians, an African power, over Italy, an European power.
(iv) Revolutionary movements in China, Egypt, Ireland, Russia and Turkey.
(v) Liberal ideas of Gladston (1809-1898), a British Prime Minister.
(vi) Second Socialist International Meet at Paris, emphasising the building up of a new culture.
(vii) The philosophy of the Fabian Society in England with its stress on liberalism.

All the above factors led to the development of this popular feeling among the people of India, "What one Asiatic has done others can do. If Japan can drub Russia, India can drub England with equal ease. Let us drive the British into the sea and take our place side by side with Japan, among the great powers of the world."

THE PARTITION OF BENGAL-1905

The need for Partition

The Presidency of Fort William originally comprised Bengal, Bihar, Orissa and Assam. It had long been considered too large to be adminstered by a Lt. Governor. In 1874, Assam was made a separate province under a Chief Commissioner with three districts of Bengal attached to it. Even then, the Presidencey remained too large. Several schemes were considered thereafter to divide the Presideney into two provinces. When Curzon came, he took the final decision and partitioned the Presidency. One of them called 'Bengal' comprised the western districts of Bengal proper, Bihar and Orissa. The other called the 'Eastern Bengal and Assam' comprised the eastern districts of Bengal proper and Assam. The Bengali speaking Hindus became a minority and Muslims a majority in the newly carved Eastern Bengal and Assam Province. The official justification of partition is stated above. But Curzon made the partition in such a way as to serve his political purpose which he explained to his superiors in London, "Bengal united is a power", he wrote, "that power was to be broken by partition". Lord Minto, who succeeded Lord Curzon, fully approved of it as he said, "Crippling of Bengali political power is, in my opinion, one of the strongest arguments in favour of partition." There was also the motive of placating the Muhammadans and creating a solid Muhammadan bloc against the Hindus in respect of political views. It was clear to all that partition was a measure deliberately adopted to kindle rivalry and animosity between the Hindus and Muslims, and the Hindu-Muslim riots of 1907 in East Bengal proved it.

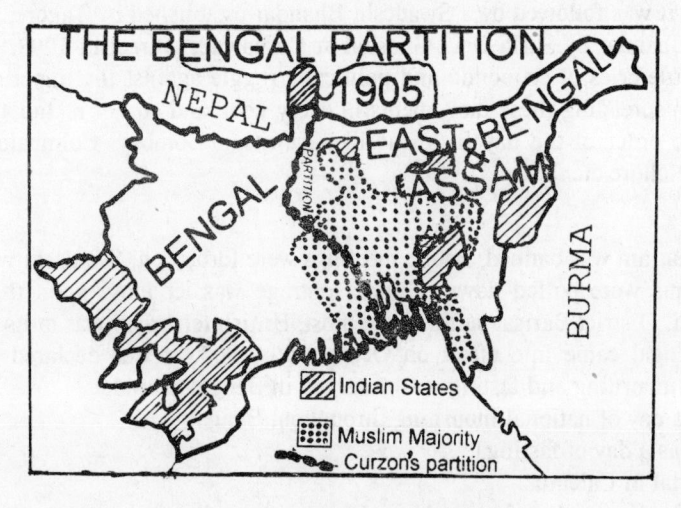

Map 25: **Partition of Bengal 1905**

The agitation against Partition

The Partition of Bengal was conceived and settled in secret by Lord Curzon. On July 20, 1905, Lord Curzon issued an order dividing the province of Bengal into two parts in utter disregard of public opinion in the entire Bengal. The Indian National Congress and the different sections of the population—zamindars, merchants, lawyers, students and even women—rose up in spontaneous opposition to the partition and appealed for the immediate cancellation of the order. But Curzon did not care and cynically and arrogantly, disregarded the popular feelings. Lord Curzon had fired a very big gun but the recoil was tremendous. The Anti-Partition Movement was initiated on August 7, 1905, when a massive demonstration was organised in the Town Hall. Surendranath Banerjee, a moderate leader took up the leadership. He wrote in *Bengalee*, a paper edited by him, "We are on the threshold of an agitation, which for its intensity and its universality will be unrivalled in the annals of this province." Never was a prophesy more literally fulfilled. The streets rang with the cries of Bande Mataram, the immortal hymn to Motherland, composed by Bankim Chandra. More than two thousand public meetings attended by both Hindus and Muslims were held in different parts. The Indian Press and large sections of Anglo-Indian Press of many provinces joined in the protest. Extremist leaders like Aurobindo Ghosh and Bepin Chandra Pal actively supported and promoted the agitation.

Boycott and Swadeshi Movement:

The whole Bengal rose as one to resist the wrong inflicted by partition. But no weapon could match the armed might of the British. So, people adopted the most practical means of throwing a direct challenge to the British authority by boycotting British goods.

Swadeshi meant self-dependence which in its turn engendered self confidence in one's own self and in one's own country. When all the people set out to fight for a common cause by the Boycott and *Swadeshi* movements, it was bound to develop a national consciousness among the people. The students of Calcutta, who had already taken the vow of Boycott and *Swadeshi,* played a very crucial role. Shops selling foreign cloth were picketed; burning of foreign cloth was organised at many places. The Swadeshi Movement had an immense success. In the economic field it meant fostering of indigenous industries, so it happened. Many textile mills, soap and match factories, national banks, etc were opened. It also encouraged national education.

Swadeshi was not a new thing in Bengal. It owes its origin to the year 1891 when a Swadeshi Emporium was set up at Calcutta. It was followed by a Swadeshi Bhandar established by Tagore, at 82 Harrison Road in 1897, and the Lakhir Bhandar by Sarla Devi Ghoshal at Cornawallis Street in 1903. But now Swadeshi and Boycott became the battle-cries of economic and political struggle against the imperialist injustice. Students played an active part in spreading these movements in every nook and corner of India. Swadeshi and boycott movements became the order of the day in towns like Amritsar, Bombay, Coimbatore, Dehradun, Lahore, Madras, Madurai and Nellore etc.

Ruthless Repression:

Singing of Bande Matram was banned, Public meetings were forbidden, Swadeshi workers were prosecuted and imprisoned, students were pulled down. Gurkha outrage was let loose upon the Hindus. Government servants were dismissed. District Barisal suffered the most. British terrorism was at its height.

The Partition of Bengal came into effect on October 16, 1905. It was declared by the people as anti-partition day. A day of mourning and fasting was observed in Bengal as under:

(a) It was declared a day of national mourning throughout Bengal.

(b) It was observed as a day of fasting.

(c) There was a hartal in Calcutta.

(d) People went to the Ganges barefoot in the early morning and took their bath.

(e) Rabindranath Tagore composed a national song for this occasion. It was "Amar Sonar Bangla,' my golden Bengal. The song was sung by huge crowds parading the streets. (The song in 1971 became the National Anthem of Bangladesh).

(f) There were cries of Bande Mataram.

(g) The ceremony of Raksha Bandhan was observed.

All India Impact of the Movement

Within a very short period, the partition of Bengal attracted the attention of the nationalist leaders of other provinces. The issue was no more of one or two Bengals, but whether the British rule should continue. The following ideals became the four pillars of the nationalist movement:

(i) Attainment of Swaraj (Self-Government)

The Nationalist Movement (1905-1918)

(ii) Promotion of national education
(iii) Boycott of foreign goods
(iv) Promotion of Swadeshi (Indian made goods).

Four nationalist militant/extremist leaders namely Bal-Pal-Lal (Bal Gangadhar Tilak, Bepin Chandra Pal and Lala Lajpat Rai) and Aurobindo Ghose emerged, who spread the nationalist movement all over India.

Lala Lajpat Rai thundered about the methods of the Extremists, "We desire to turn our faces away from the Government Houses and turn them to the huts of the people. We want to stop our mouths so far as an appeal to the Government is concerned and open mouth with a new appeal to the masses of our people. This is the psychology, this is the ethics, this is the psychological significance of the boycott movement."

In his whirlwind tour of the country, Tilak declared, "Swaraj is my birth right; and I will have it."

In 1907, Lajpat Rai and Sardar Ajit Singh were arrested in the Punjab and deported to Burma.

The same year, Bepin Chandra Pal was arrested and kept in various jails. Sri Aurobindo Ghose was also arrested for having published certain articles in *Bande Mataram*. His arrest, trial and acquittal made him one of the foremost leaders of the new movement.

In 1908, Tilak was arrested, imprisoned for six years, and kept in Burma in virtual solitary confinement in a prison cell.

National Education Movement

One of the most significant developments of this period was the birth of the concept of national education. The movement of national education was born immediately after the partition of Bengal and was basically the outcome of the Swadeshi and Boycott movements. The Swadeshi movement, although economic in origin and application, its spirit affected every walk of life. A demand for *Swadeshi* education soon began to be put forward and was immediately strengthened by repeated conflicts with the official policies and the utter failure of Indians to make the officials to realise the Indian point of view in education. The National Council of Education was set up in 1906. The Bengal College with Sri Aurobindo Ghosh was formally inaugurated after two months of the founding of the National Council of Education. The movement for the national education spread to various parts of India.

Summing up

As already stated, the partition of Bengal had an all India impact on national awakening. It accelerated the national movement. The Moderates in the Congress lost ground to the Extremists. It led to the birth of two important movements namely, the Swadeshi and the Boycott, which in turn led to the national education movement. The partition of Bengal also became responsible for the emergence of militancy and growth of revolutionary terrorism in India.

The agitation brought into prominence the great value of passive resistance as a more effective weapon than petition-making, so far the only method of political agitation known to the country and approved by the Congress. But the partition agitation did much more than this. It awakened into action, the dormant poltical consciousness of the people, and gave a definite shape to the spirit of nationalism which had been gathering for some time. "Bengal left the beaten track followed by the Congress, conceived new ideals, adopted new methods for their achievement, shed all tears, braved all sufferings and fearlessly faced death." Gokhale was convinced that Bengal's heroic fight made a deep impress upon Indian politics. "For the first time since British rule all sections of the Indian community began to act together in offering resistance to a common wrong". Lala Lajpat Rai echoed the same sentiment, "If the people of India will just learn that lesson from Bengal, I think that the struggle is not hopeless".

Cancelling the Order of Partition

In 1910 Lord Hardinge suceeded Lord Minto. At Calcutta, he realized the political unrest and terrorism that prevailed due to the partition. He became much anxious for a policy of conciliation in view of the impending visit of the King and Queen to India within a year's time. He declared, "We feel bound to admit that the Bengalis are labouring under a sense of real injustice which we believe to remove without further delay." In the Delhi Durbar of 1911 attended by the King and Queen, amouncements were made to cancel the order of partition of Bengal and also to shift the British capital from Calcutta to Delhi. To Lord Hardinge goes the chief credit of undoing the great wrong and uniting the Bengali speaking region. Bihar, Orissa and Chotanagpur were made into one province under a Lieutenant Governor, Assam reverted to a Chief Commissionership. The rest constituted the Province of Bengal under a Governor.

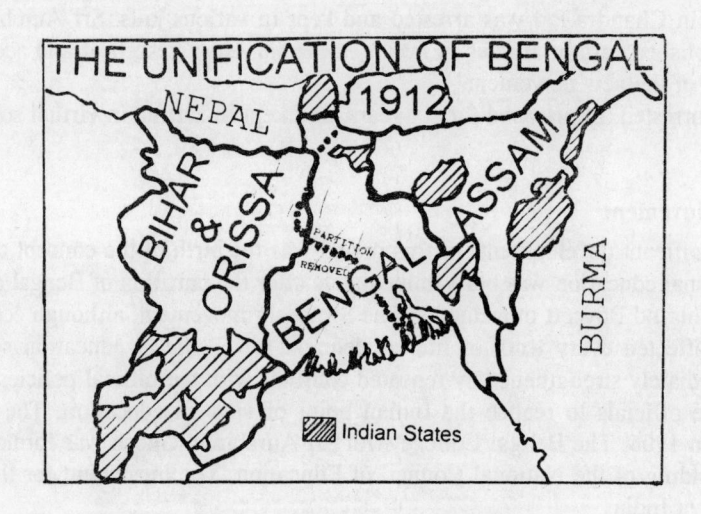

Map 26: **Partition Annulled 1912**

PROMINENT EXTREMIST LEADERS

Bepin Chandra Pal (1852-1932)

Popularly known as 'the father of revolutionary thought in India,' he along with Lala Lajpat Rai and Balgangadhar Tilak, became the 'Lal, Bal, Pal' trio usually associated with Extremists. He carried the message of the *Swadeshi,* the *Boycott* and the *Swaraj* to every nook and corner of India. His paper *New India* became the mouth piece of resurgent Indian nationalism. His eloquence had no parallel in those days. He was considered as the 'arch-seditionist' in India by the British for which he was jailed. He once wrote, "Indian money is taken away by Feringis (the British), while the people starve for want of money. The Indians should not be afraid of jail and must be ready to go to any jail at any moment shouting only *Vande Mataram"*. While in London, B.C. Pal lectured widely condemning the policy of violence and terror let loose by the British in India. He also published a fortnightly called *Swaraj* while in England. About the freedom movement he said, "Freedom is man's birth right. It is inherent in the very making of man, Prince or peasant, Brahman or Pariah, man or woman, Hindu or Mohamedan, Buddhist or Christian, rich or poor, ignorant or learned, we are eternally free... Our faith is in God and because we have this faith, we believe in the success of our Movement- namely that of Swaraj."

The Nationalist Movement (1905-1918)

DIFFERENCES BETWEEN THE MODERATES AND THE EXTREMISTS

S.No.	Moderates	Extremists
1.	The Moderates in general, were loyal to the British. They believed that the British rule, with some reforms could be beneficial to India.	○ Swaraj was the ultimate goal.
2.	The aim of the moderates was very limited. They wanted some representation in the running of government. They also emphasised the need of reforms in the administrative and economic structure.	○ The Extremists believed that constitutional methods would lead them nowhere.
3.	The moderates believed in adopting constitutional methods for the fulfilment of their objectives.	○ The British rule was considered as a curse.
4.	They believed in sending petitions, prayers and resolutions to the Government for consideration and implementation.	○ They believed that national problems could be solved by agitation.
5.	They believed in conciliation.	○ They believed in confrontation.
6.	They were alergic to Swadeshi and Boycott.	○ They considered Swadeshi and Boycott as important weapons.
7.	They had faith in the goodwill and sympathy of the English people.	○ They did not believe in such notions.
8.	The Moderates believed that the people of India were not yet fit for self government.	○ The Extremists believed that the Indians were fully competent to handle their own affairs.
9.	The Moderates hoped that they could get their requests acceded to, without any substantial sufferings and sacrifices.	○ They were convinced that without hardships and sufferings, salvation of India was not possible.
10.	The Moderates wanted to follow the path of least resistance.	○ The Extremists were prepared to follow the path of active resistance.
11.	The Moderates confined their activities to the small section of intelligentia and assigned a passive role to the masses.	○ They had immense faith in the masses and made them active partners in the national struggle.

Bal Gangadhar Tilak (1856-1920)

Tilak, remembered as Lokmanya (Loved and respected by the people), was the first leader to use the slogan, "Swaraj (freedom) is my birth right and I shall have it." He waged a fierce struggle against the British with his three P's ie. Pen, Press and Platform as against three P's of "Pray, Please and Protest." He founded two papers *Kesari* and *Maharata* for developing patriotic feelings for the motherland. He is called a militant nationalist. He was imprisoned several times for his stirring speeches and writings. He was a great terror and nightmare to the British Government. Apart from Indian jails, Tilak was put in Mandalay jail (Burma) from 1908 to 1914. At a public meeting in Calcutta, Tilak declared, "It is impossible to expect that our petitions will be heard unless backed by firm resolution backed by solid force. Look to the examples of Ireland, Japan and Russia and follow their methods." Tilak was often called 'The father of Indian unrest'. He believed that power in India must be with the People of India. Tilak used the following methods to awaken people:-

1. He started newspapers for arousing nationalist feeling among the masses.
2. He organised the Ganpati festival with a view to infuse among youngmen, both religious and patriotic fervour.
3. He started the Shivaji movement in 1895 with a view to inspire the youth of India to follow the example of Shivaji.
4. He organised meetings and gave fiery speeches.

5. He wrote *Geeta Rahasya* while in jail and propounded the philosophy of action.
6. He started Home Rule Movement.
7. He made Indian philosophy the guide for remaking of India.

(Lala) Lajpat Rai (1865-1928)

Popularly known as 'Punjab Kesari' or 'Sher-i-Punjab' (Lion of Punjab) for his fearlessness and strength, he owed his patriotic feelings for the motherland to the influence of Arya Samaj. He was an eminent journalist, a prolific writer, a fiery speaker, successful lawyer and a staunch fighter against the British rule. He was arrested several times for his anti-British activities. He spent seven years in Japan, U.K. and U.S.A. in lecturing and mobilising public opinion in favour of India. His work for awakening patriotic sentiment among the people may be summaried as:

1. He started two nationalist papers namely *Bande Mataram* in Urdu and *People* in English.
2. He wrote short biographies of Mazzini, Garibaldi, Shivaji, Sri Krishna and Swami Dayanand etc. to develop the sentiments of patriotism, fearlessness and spiritual consciousness.
3. He wrote books on cultural, economic, educational and political issues to awaken the people regarding the wrongs done by the British to the people of India. Among his important publications are: *The Arya Samaj, Young India, The Political Future of India, England's Debt to India, Unhappy India* and *Problem of National Education in India*.
4. He participated in several movements. He was one of the trio—Lal-Bal-Pal—all associated with Extremists in the Congress.
5. He founded the Home Rule League in America.
6. He proposed the boycott of Simon Commission in 1928, suffered a 'lathi' blow while agitating against it which proved fatal. At a public meeting the same day he said, "Every blow that was hurled at us was a nail in the coffin of the British empire."

(Sri) Aurobindo Ghose (1872-1950)

A scholar turned revolutionary, nationalist turned saint, Aurobindo Ghose exercised a profound influence on political and spiritual matters. Aurobindo's participation in the freedom struggle lasted for six years only i.e. from 1905 to 1910. But during this short period, he proved one of those radical leaders of the early 20th Century who trasformed Indian nationalism into a mighty mass movement. He condemned the moderates' policy of petition and prayer. Through *Bande Mataram*, he aroused the consciousness of the educated masses of India. He described foreign rule as "Unnatural and fatal to a nation." In his *Essays on Gita*, he defined killing of national enemies as 'Dharmayuddha'. He remarked, "The Gita is the best answer to those who shrink from battle as a sin." To quote him, "The work of national emancipation is a great and holy *'Yajna'* of which boycott, Swadeshi, national education and every other activity, great and small, are only major or minor parts." Sri Aurobindo was arrested n 1907 for the articles that he wrote. He was acquitted as charges against him could not be proved. He was again arrested for the revolutionary activities in 1908 and released in 1909. During one year in jail, he devoted much of his time to 'Yoga', meditation and study of religious books which transformed his life. The remaining 40 years (1910-50), he spent on philosophical and spiritual pursuits in his Ashram at Pondicherry.

GROWTH OF REVOLUTIONARY TERRORISM

Background

A section of the youth of India began to feel that the Indian leadership had failed to show any tangible results from their programmes. They realised that the passive resistance to the British rule was of no avail.

The Nationalist Movement (1905-1918)

They even lost their faith in movements like the Swadeshi and the Boycott. They were convinced that the British would have to be 'physically expelled' from India.

The background for such violent action had already been prepared in 1897 when the Chapekar brothers assassinated two unpopular British officers at Poona. In 1904, V.D. Savarkar had organised the 'Abhinav Bharat', a secret society.

But it was not till the great upheaval in Bengal caused by the partition that these societies developed into a well-knit organisation that gradually spread all over India. The Youngmen in Bengal at first hoped that they would be able to annul the partition by the Swadeshi and Boycott movement. But all their agitation resulted in sheer frustration due to the ruthless suppression of the British Government.

Gradually, it dawned upon a section of youngmen of Bengal, Maharashtra, Punjab and other parts of the country that these means were insufficient to achieve the desired end. More violent means were necessary to gain their objective. But it was not possible to organise an open armed rebellion against the mighty British power. As such they fell back upon the secret societies. Since, now they were going to play for high stakes, putting their life on it, their objective was higher, not just to rub out the line of partition from the map, but to wipe out the Britishers from India. The secret societies of this type were the outcome of the new nationalism. It was a further step of the same spirit in an extreme form. Apart from intense patriotism and spirit of sacrifice, they felt the call of a higher life as expounded by Swami Vivekanand. A firm faith in the immortal soul led them to shed the fear of death and bodily pain. Nationalism for them was a religious attitude which made them realise God in the nation and Sacrifice everything at the altar of their Motherland.

These youngmen willingly left their homes, and all that was dear and near to them, to carry on a life-long struggle for freedom, for they could not tolerate the dishonour of their motherland lying trampled under the boots of foreigners. Fear of death and physical torture more terrible than death, did not deter them, obstacles and dangers like Himalayan barriers could not stop or deflect them from their goal. Deserted by friends and relatives, ignored and distanced by their countrymen for fear of police, without food to eat, without means to live, moving from shelter to shelter, they carried on the fight from day to day, month to month, year to year, knowing fully well that chances of success were slender but death was sure. They died in order that others may live. One may call them emotional, unrealistic and misguided. But their countrymen, barring a few, never doubted their patriotism which is proved by the homage they paid to them. The country was in tears when Khudiram and others were shot dead or hanged. The news of their death was an event of great mourning in every house, as if some very near and dear one was lost for ever.

Methods and Techniques Employed by the Revolutionaries

The Revolutionaries took recourse to these methods to terrorise the British rulers (i) Organising secret societies (ii) Distribution of revolutionary literature (iii) Organising secret mobs (iv) Taking oaths and pledges for the freedom of the country and to adopt all sorts of techniques for the achievement of their objectives relating to motherland's freedom (v) Gita studies to infuse a spirit of bravery and doing one's duty (vi) Physical training (vii) Weapon training (viii) Making of weapons including bombs (ix) Killing of oppressive British officers (x) Killing of police informers (xi) Looting government treasuries (xii) Looting rich persons for the manufacture and purchase of weapons etc. (xiii) Establishing revolutionary societies abroad (xiv) Creating sedition among the Indian soldiers of the British army stationed outside India. Revolutionary nationalists were mostly active in Bengal, Maharashtra and the Punjab.

Revolutionary Activities in Different Parts of the Country

Bengal:

In Benga , volutionary literature in the form of poems, prose writings and press played a leading role in promoting revolutionary ideas. It is of interest to note that the Government ordered a wholesale seizure of

Dhotis as they had a poem printed on them, begining with the line "I shall go to the gallows with a smile."

Papers like *Yugantar, Bande Matram* and *Sandhya* were in the forefront. The *Yugantar* wrote on April 22, 1906, "The Thirty crores of people inhabiting India must raise their sixty crores of hands to stop this course of oppression. Force must be stopped with force."

Two famous books *Bhawani Mandir* and *Mukti Kon Pathe* preached the use of force and winning over the soldiers for attending freedom. The writer of the popular poems titled *Pantha* was sent to jail for 18 months.

Barindra Ghosh, the brother of Aurobindo Ghosh was the main motivating force behind the murders of the British officers. He said, "We are determined and are still so, to take the life of the Lt. Governor of Bengal," for his oppressiveness. In 1908, Khudi Ram, a young boy, was hanged for his murderous attack on a British officer. Perhaps he was the first martyr in the revolutionary activities. Schools were closed for two to three days as a tribute to his memory. Youngmen began to wear 'Dhotis' with the name of Khudi Ram woven into their borders.

Khudiram

The revolutionary upsurge in Bengal remained unabated till 1911, when partition of Bengal was annulled.

Maharashtra:

The Marathi press in general, was revolutionary in tone. Papers like *Arunodya, Hind Swarajya, Kal, Kesari, Rashtramukh, Vihari* and *Vishvavritta* were very vocal against the policy of oppression and suppression followed by the British. The editors of these papers were arrested and sentenced. Among the revolutionaries, the names of Savarkar brothers come to the forefront. They founded the Abhinav Bharat Society. V.D. Savarkar, who went to England, sent a parcel containing two Browning automatic pistols with ammunition to Bombay, concealed in the fake bottom of a box forming part of the luggage of one Chaturbhuj Amin, who was working as a cook in the India House, London. The pistols were to be used by members of the Abhinav Society to murder Jackson, District Magistrate of Nasik and other British officers who were very oppressive. This resulted in the Nasik Corspiracy Case in which Jackson was murdered. Three out of 40 youngmen involved, were hanged and the rest were imprisoned.

There was a lot of revolutionary political activity at Poona, Nasik, Kolhapur and Bombay. The statue of Queen Victoria was mutilated at Bombay and similar acts were done at other places. In Maharashtra, several religious festivals, like Shivaji and Ganpati festivals, became the springboards of revolutionary activities.

Punjab:

The revolutionary group in Punjab, led by Ajit Singh, consisted of Sufi Amba Prasad, Lal Chand Falak, Kishen Singh, Zia-ul-Huq, Ghulam Kadir and others. Ajit Singh used to distribute revolutionary literature through the Bharat Mata Society of Lahore. He addressed several meetings which began with the song "Pagri Sambhal Oh ! Jatta" (O peasant ! take care of the turban, i.e. self respect). He was arrested and deported to Burma in 1907. Several Arya Samaj leaders who took part in revolutionary activities were arrested and prosecuted.

Delhi:

On December 23, 1912, when Lord Hardinge, the Viceroy of India, was taken in a procession on the back of an elephant in Delhi, a bomb exploded which injured the Viceroy and killed his bodyguard. Rash Behari Bose, who threw the bomb was able to escape. He went to Japan and played an important role in organising the Indian National Army. This incident is also known as Delhi Conspiracy Case. Thirteen persons including Master Amir Chand, Bhai Balmukand, Balraj Bhalla, Basant Kumar, Avadh Behari and Dina Nath were arrested and four of them were hanged. Avadh Behari had an interesting inspiring conversation with an

Englishman before he was hanged. When the Englishman asked him about his last wish Avadh Behari's reply was, "The end of the British rule."

Prominent Revolutionary Leaders

Vinayak Damodar Savarkar (1883-1966):

The revolutionary activities of V.D. Savarkar began with the formation of a secret society, 'Mitra Mela', for the freedom of the country, while he was just 16 years of age. The society later on took the shape of Abhinav Bharat Society (New India Society). He drew inspiration from Tilak and Chaphekar brothers who killed the oppressive British officer Rand, of Nasik. In 1909, he published a pamphlet which contained several inflamatory verses. In one of the poems he said, "Take up the sword and destroy the Government because it is foreign and aggressive." The title of another poem was: "Who obtained independence without a battle?" Savarkar went to London where he lectured on the events of 1857 which he called "India's First War of Independence." Under his influence, Madan Lal Dhingra shot dead Sir Curzon Willie in 1909. Sir Willie used to watch the activities of the Indian students in England. Savarkar qualified for the Bar but was not allowed to practice as he refused to give an undertaking that he would not participate in the freedom struggle. He was arrested in England and sent to prison. He was to be deported to India. While being sent by ship to India, Savarkar created history by escaping through the port hole of the ship and swam in the sea to reach Marsellies, on the French soil. But he was captured and brought to India where the court sentenced him for two consecutive life transportations (50 years transportation) on charges of treason. For 10 years (1911-21) he was in Andaman Jail. For 3 years (1921-24) he was in Yervada, Nasik and Ratnagiri jails in Maharashtra. For 13 years (1924-37) he was not allowed to leave Ratnagiri district where he carried out social reforms. After the removal of restrictions, he was elected the President of the Hindu Mahasabha. Among his several books of poems, philosophy and history, *Hindutva* and *India's First War of Independence* deserve special mention.

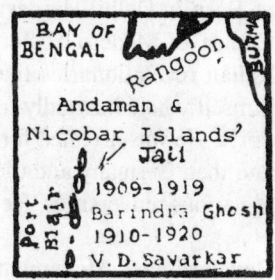

Map 26: **Andaman & Nicobar Island's Jail**

Madame Bhikaji Cama (1861-1936):

The first prominent revolutionary lady, Madame Bhikaji Cama, coming from a Parsi business family, operated the revolutionary activities for the freedom of India, from Paris for over 30 years. In 1907, she unfurled the flag of India's freedom (flag which was the precursor of the present flag) at the Socialist Congress at Stuttgurt. She came into contact in London, with eminent Indian revolutionaries like Savarkar, Shyamji Krishna Verma and Birendranath Chattopadhya. She addressed meetings at Hyde Park (in London) regularly on the theme of India's freedom. From 1909 onwards, she made Paris her centre of activities. She believed in the violent methods for the cause of liberty. She smuggled revolutionary literature and explosives to India through Pondicherry. She arranged training for Indian revolutionaries in bomb making.

Madanlal Dhingra (1887-1909):

A young lad of 22, who had gone to London for an engineering course, went to the gallows as an Indian revolutionary. While in England, he came into contact with revolutionaries like V.D. Savarkar and Shyamji Krishna Varma and his mind began to remain disturbed on account of the atrocities committed on the Indians by the British. In 1909, he shot dead an English officer, Sir Curzon Wylie, in England, for his spying activities on Indian revolutionaries. At his trial in a court in England, he told the judge. "The only lesson required in India at present is to learn how to die and the only way to teach it is by dying ourselves. Therefore, I die."

Hardayal (1884-1939):

Born in Delhi, Hardayal went to England in 1905 as a state scholar for studies at Oxford for his Honours Course in Modern History and Ph.D. from the London University. In London, he came into contact with Indian revolutionaries like. V.D. Savarkar and Madame Cama. He threw away his scholarship and devoted himself whole heartedly to the cause of India's freedom. In 1913, he went to America and founded the Ghadar Party. He was arrested for his fiery speeches and revolutionary activities. He jumped bail to reach switzerland and then Germany and then to Sweden. In 1927, he returned to America and served as a Professor of Sanskrit at various universities. He died under mysterious circumstances.

Revolutionary Movement Outside India

The revolutionary movement for the freedom of India did not remain confined to India. In England, the prominent leaders were V.D. Savarkar and Shyamji Krishna Verma. It was spread to France by Madame Cama, to America by Hardayal and to Japan by Rash Behari Bose. They helped the movement in a number of ways like, inciting Indian patriots to kill British officers who had committed atrocities on the Indians and had gone back to Enland, moulding public opinion in foreign lands, organising societies, sending revolutinary literature and weapons to revolutionaries in India.

Berlin, Cairo, Geneva, London, New York, Paris and San Francisco were the important centres of the activities of the revolutionaries.

Achievement and Impact of the Militant/Revolutionary/Extremist Leaders

They helped in developing self-confidence and self-reliance among several sections of the population, especially the educated, the middle class and the youth. They introduced new methods of political struggle. However, in general, the common people, the peasants and workers were still outside the main stream of national struggle.

THE INDIAN NATIONAL CONGRESS (1905-1914)

The Indian National Congress suffered great setback during the period 1905 to 1914 on account of two factors (1) Split in the Congress at Surat Session (2) Half-hearted Morley-Minto Reforms of 1909.

Surat Session 1907 and the Split in the Congress

A serious controversy had been raging for some time between the Moderate and the Extremist leaders of the Congress: In the first five years of the 20th Century, the Congress sessions had been presided over by the Moderate leaders of the Congress. The partition of Bengal and the policies followed by the Moderates were not in tune with the prevailing mood. The four-fold programme of Swadeshi, Boycott, Swaraj and national education chalked out by the Extremists sent alarm bells to the Moderates and they feared that the Calcutta Session of the Congress in 1906 might be dominated by the Extremists. The Moderates, therefore, requested Dadabhai Naoroji who was in England, to come to India and preside over the Lahore session. Naoroji's presence saved the Congress from split and the Moderate leaders accepted the four-fold programme under pressure from the Extremists. There were frequent meetings between the Moderate leaders and the Viceroy. The Congress Session at Surat on December 27, 1907, witnessed an open and ugly confrontation between the Moderates and the Extremists. After this, the Government took repressive measures against the Extremist leaders. In 1907, Lala Lajpat Rai and Ajit Singh were deported from the Punjab to Burma. In 1908, Tilak was arrested and sentenced to six year's imprisonment. Aurobindo Ghose was prosecuted. The Moderates, who

The Nationalist Movement (1905-1918)

still controlled the Congress and dominated the Congress Session at Madras in 1908, did not condemn the arrest of the Extremist leaders. For the next eight years, India's nationalist movement remained a house divided against itself.

Morley-Minto Reforms

In 1909, The Government introduced some constitutional reforms in India, with a view to please the Moderate leaders and strengthen their position in the Congress. These reforms are named after Lord Minto, the Viceroy of India, and Lord Morley, the Secretary of the State for India, who piloted the bill through the British Parliament.

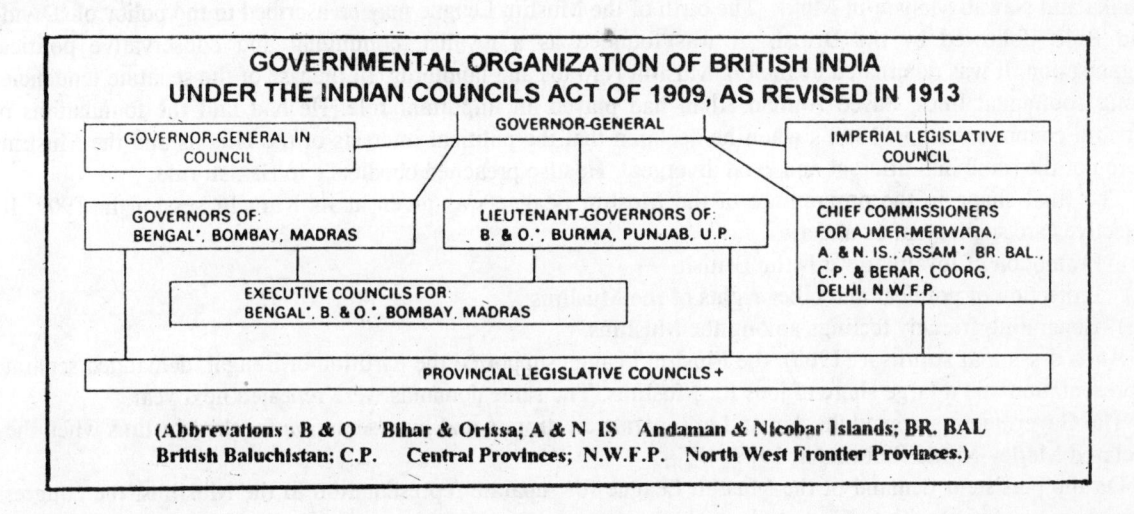

GOVERNMENTAL ORGANIZATION OF BRITISH INDIA UNDER THE INDIAN COUNCILS ACT OF 1909, AS REVISED IN 1913

GOVERNOR-GENERAL
- GOVERNOR-GENERAL IN COUNCIL
- IMPERIAL LEGISLATIVE COUNCIL
- GOVERNORS OF: BENGAL*, BOMBAY, MADRAS
- LIEUTENANT-GOVERNORS OF: B. & O.*, BURMA, PUNJAB, U.P.
- CHIEF COMMISSIONERS FOR AJMER-MERWARA, A. & N. IS., ASSAM*, BR. BAL., C.P. & BERAR, COORG, DELHI, N.W.F.P.
- EXECUTIVE COUNCILS FOR: BENGAL*, B. & O.*, BOMBAY, MADRAS
- PROVINCIAL LEGISLATIVE COUNCILS +

(Abbrevations : B & O   Bihar & Orissa; A & N IS   Andaman & Nicobar Islands; BR. BAL   British Baluchistan; C.P.   Central Provinces; N.W.F.P.   North West Frontier Provinces.)

Chart 3: **Act of 1909**

Main Provision of the Reforms:

(1) It increased the number of the elected members in the Imperial Council (2) The number of members of the Provincial Councils also increased substantially (3) The Act provided for separate electorates for separate representation to different communities, classes and interests (4) Muslims were given separate representation (5) Disqualifications were imposed on political offenders and they could not offer themselves for elections.

Effects of the Reforms:

The reforms fell short of popular expectations. The Extremists termed the Moderates as 'old fossil's' and the reforms as "ingenious fraud". The reforms sowed the seeds of conflict between the Hindus and the Muslims by providing *Separate Electorate*. It is usually held, that the provision of excessive weightage, separate electorate and preferential voting rights for the Muslims, infected a poisonous element in the political life of India which ultimately resulted in the partition of the country. The non-official members were usually 'yes men'. The number of delegates at the Congress sessions began to dwindle. The Congress received a temporary setback. The leaders of the Muslim League felt very happy at the reforms.

Provision of separate electorate for Muslims was an important strategy of the policy of 'Divide and Rule' of the British. Special care was taken to see that "class was set against class, community against community".

THE ALL INDIA MUSLIM LEAGUE

Introduction

The birth of the Muslim League in 1906, and its subsequent role in the political field, proved very harmful to the unity and integrity of India. It led to the birth of two-nation theory which became responsible for the partition of India; first into two countries i.e. India and Pakistan and then into three, with the division of Pakistan and the creation of Bangladesh.

Objectives of the Muslim League

The Muslim League was founded in 1906 under the leadership of the Agha Khan, the Nawab Salimullah of Dhaka and Nawab Mohsin-ul-Mulik. The birth of the Muslim League may be ascribed to the policy of 'Divide and Rule' followed by the British. It was founded as a loyalist, communal and conservative political organisation. It was dominated by the big Muslim Nawabs and landlords. In the rise of the separate tendencies along communal lines, Sayed Ahmad Khan had played an important role. He had laid the foundations of Muslim communalism in 1880's when he declared that the political interests of the Hindus and the Muslims were not the same but different and even divergent. He also preached obedience to British rule.

The final shape to the programme of the Muslim League was given at its Karachi session in 1907. Its objectives are spelled out as under:

(i) Promotion of loyalty towards the British.
(ii) Protection of political and other rights of the Muslims.
(iii) Generating friendly feelings among the Muslims.

At its session at Amritsar (1908), the Muslim League supported the partition of Bengal, demanded separate representation and a large share of jobs for Muslims. The same demands were repeated next year.

The Government accepted the demand of separate electrorate and representation for the Muslims when they declared Morley-Minto Reforms in 1909.

On the persistent demand of the Muslim League for separate representation to the Muslims, the congress signed an agreement with the League known as *Lucknow Pact (1916)*, accepting separate electorate.

In 1930, the Muslim League raised the demand for Pakistan and in 1934, at the League session at Lahore, M.A. Jinnah put forward the 'Two Nation Theory' i.e. Hindus and Muslims form two separate nations. As usual, the British rulers followed the policy of 'Divide and Rule' and supported this theory and ultimately despite Gandhiji's opposition, the Congress accepted the proposal of the creation of an independent separate state of Pakistan in 1947.

NATIONAL MOVEMENT AND THE FIRST WORLD WAR

Background

The First World War (1914-18) was fought between two imperialist groups of hostile nations. On the one side there were Britain, France, Russia and Japan (later joined by Italy and U.S.A.), known as "Allies" and on the other, there were Germany, Austria, Hungary and Turkey, called the "Axis" Powers. The "Allies" won the war. India, because of its being a colony of the Britain had to bear the brunt of the war.

The First World War affected the National movement in a number of ways. Broadly speaking, some changes in the national movement took place during the war itself and some immediately after the war was over.

Impact on National Movement During the War

During the war, the national movement witnessed the growth of the following organisations and

The Nationalist Movement (1905-1918)

movements:
1. Growth of the revolutionary movement in India and the *Ghadar* (rebellion) party outside India.
2. The Home Rule Leagues.
3. Temporary re-approachment between the Congress and the Musilm League and the Lucknow Pact (1916).
4. Unity between the Moderates and the Extremists.

Map 28: **Lucknow Pact**

Lucknow Pact:

Turkey, which was regarded as the 'Sword of Islam' was fighting for its survival against the onslaught of Britain and its allies. The Muslims felt greatly disturbed inspite of the British assurances. There was thus, a great change in their policy towards the British rulers and the Indian National Congress. Tilak, who had been imprisoned for six years in 1908, was released from jail in 1914. He, along with Mohammad Ali Jinnah played a leading role in bringing the Congress and the League nearer each other. Tilak declared, "When we have to fight against a third party, it is a very important thing that we stand on this platform united—united in race, united in religion—as regards all different shades of poltical creed." Jinnah, the League president at Lucknow declared, "Hindu-Muslim reapproachment as the first sign of the birth of a United India." This resulted in the Lucknow Pact (1916). The Pact provided for separate electorate and representation to Muslims in the Councils and Assemblies.

Lucknow Congress Session (1916):

The growing nationalist feeling in the country led to the unification of the Moderates and the Extremists.The Moderates, after the death of Gokhale in 1915, became leaderless and at the same time there was some change in the attitude of Tilak who was released in 1914 after serving six years imprisonment in Burma. To reconciliate the moderate nationalists, he declared, "I may state once and for all, that we are trying in India, as the Irish Home Rulers have been all along doing in Ireland, for a reform of the system of administration and not for the overthrow of Government; and I have no hesitation in saying that the acts of violence which have been committed in different parts of India are not only repugnant to me, but have, in my opinion, only unfortunately retarded to a great extent, the pace of our political progress." At the Lucknow Session, both the groups decided to work together.

Announcement of Reforms by the Government:

The reapproachment between the Congress and the Muslim League and between the two groups of the Congress, changed the attitude of the British Government. Hitherto, it had relied heavily on repression to subdue the nationalist leaders. Now, in order to appease the nationalist opinion, the British Government announced in August 1917, that its policy in India was "the gradual development of self-governing institutions with a view to the progressive realisation of responsible Government of India, as an integral part of the British Empire."

Home Rule Leagues:

Background:

Some of the nationalist leaders began to realise, that neither the policy of absolute conciliation followed by the Moderates, nor the policy of absolute confrontation with the British rulers was yielding the desired results. They, therefore thought of some alternative progamme that could serve as a via-media between the two diametrically opposite programmes. At the same time, they had before them, the experience of some other countries like Ireland, which though under the British empire had devised such a system, in which they had an important say in running the affairs of the Government.

Meaning of the Home Rule Leagues:

The following statement of Mrs. Annie Besant (1847-1933), one of the chief organisers of the movement, clearly explains the concept of the Home Rule. She said in 1914, "India asks only that she shall be recognised as a nation, shall be given self-government and shall form an integral part of the Empire, composed of self-governing communities. She asks no more than this."

Tilak another protagonist of the Home Rule, considered to be an Extremist, who was released from jail in 1914, appreciated the change in the situation and set out to unify the two streams of congressmen by modifying his stand.

In simple words, Home Rule movement was a movement which was designed to compel the government to provide Indians with sufficient powers to govern themselves. It was far more than merely representation of Indians in the councils and Provincial Assemblies. It was, however, less than independence for India.

An All India Movement:

Two Home Rules having identical programmes were started in 1915-16, one by Annie Besant which activated the entire country, and the other by Tilak which was confined to Maharashtra. Annie Besant, an English lady but admirer of India's culture and a freedom fighter of India, moved in major cities of India, delivering inspiring speeches and enthusing the people of India for Home Rule. Home Rule branches were established almost in every big city. Public mobilisation took place as never before. The movement soon attracted the anger of the Government. Tilak's entry was banned in Punjab and Mrs. Besant was disallowed to enter central Province and Bombay. Finally in June 1917, she was arrested. Popular pressure and protest forced the Government to release her in September 1917. Annie Besant became the most popular figure of Indian politics in the year 1916-17. She presided over the Congress Session in 1917. Students participated enthusiastically in the Home Rule movement.

Impact of the Home Rule Movement:

The voice of the Home Rule Movement became the voice of India. It transformed the national movement into the people's movement. It influenced several British M.P's. On 20th August, 1917, Montague declared in the House of Common, that India would be increasingly associated in every branch of administration and there would be a gradual development of self-governing institutions for the progressive realisation of responsible government in India. Accordingly, some steps were taken in this direction after the close of the War.

The Ghadar Party:

Meaning, Aims and Objectives of the Ghadar Party:

There appears to be no exact equivalent word for '*Ghadar*'. Usually it implies 'rebellion'. The Ghadar Party for the liberation of India was formed by the Indians who had gone overseas. Most of the members of the party were Punjabi Sikh peasants and ex-soldiers, who had faced the brunt of economic and racial discrimination. They had gone to other countries for livelihood. The leaders of the party were however, educated Hindus and Muslims. Important leaders of the party were Lala Hardayal, Mohammad Barkatullah, Bhagwan Singh, Jawala Singh, Kartar Singh, Ram Chandra, V.G. Pingle and Sohan Singh Bhakna. The party was founded in 1913 at Stockton in America, with Sohan Singh Bhakna as the President and Hardyal as Secretary.

Methods and Techniques:

The Ghadar Party was pledged to wage revolutionary war against the British rule in India. The party carried on its propaganda through an Urdu Weekly *Ghadar* which carried the caption '*Angrezi Raj ka Dushman*' (An enemy of British rule). It used to make appeals to people for joining its activities. Its advertisement frequented under the caption 'wanted.. heroic soldiers for Ghadar Party' with the following

The Nationalist Movement (1905-1918)

duties and service conditions:

Remuneration	-	Death
Reward	-	Martyrdom
Pension	-	Freedom
Field of Work	-	Hindustan

In a few months, the party became the supreme organisation of immigrant Indians residing in Canada, Indo-China, Japan, Philippines, Malaya, Singapore, Mexico and the U.S.A.

Funds worth millions of dollars were collected to lit the torch of national revolution.

Rash Behari Bose, Sachindra Sanyal, Ganesh Pingle and Baghi Kartar Singh prepared a master plan for the armed revolt. February 21, 1915 was fixed the date and vigorous preparations were made for that purpose. Messages were sent to leaders in India, especially in the Punjab. Unfortunately, the British authorities came to know of these plans and took immediate action. The rebellious regiments were disbanded and their leaders were either imprisoned or hanged. Seven hundred men of the 5th Light Infantry at Singapore revolted but the revolt was crushed. Several soldiers were publicly executed and many transported for life.

Almost all leaders of the Ghadar Party in Punjab were arrested. They were tried in the Lahore Conspiracy Case. Out of 291 members, 42 were acquitted and others transported for life/sentenced to death/imprisoned for varying terms. Among the prominent leaders were Baghi Kartar Singh, Bhai Parmanand, and Ganesh Pingle.

Prominent Leaders of the Ghadar Party:

Maulana Barkatullah (1859-1927). One of the important members of the Ghadar Party, he went to Germany and joined the Indian Independence Committee in Berlin. He was a member of Mahendra Pratap's Mission to Kabul and became the Prime Minister of the Provisional Free Indian Government.

Rashbehari Bose (1886-1945). After an attempt on the life of Viceroy Hardinge, he went underground. During the First World War, he planned the arms revolt and the date of the uprising was fixed on the 19th of February 1915. Unfortunately, a traitor leaked out the news to the Government and the plan failed.

Mahendra Pratap (1886-1979). As soon as the First World War broke out, an Indian Independence Committee, 1915-18 (Berlin Committee) was formed in Germany. The Berlin Committee, on the one hand established contact with the Ghadar Party and on the other hand they sent their members to the Middle-East. At the request of the Berlin Committee in 1915, Mahendra Pratap went to Kabul as a leader of an Indian Mission and set up a Provisional Free Government in Kabul and became its president. He remained in exile for a number of years and was allowed to return to India when an Interim Government was set up in India in 1946.

Immediate Effects on National Movement after the End of War

There was a radical change in the attitude of Indians towards Europeans. They began to give up the feeling that the Europeans were superior to them morally and technically. The Indian soldiers, who had fought valiently and won victories for the British, filled the Indians with a sense of pride.

The Russian Revolution of 1917 also had a profound influence on the minds of the Indians. They felt that if Russians could over throw an imperialist regime, the Indians could also do so.

In July 1918, the British Government announced the Montague-Chelmsford Reforms, which of course failed to satisfy the nationalists.

EXERCISES

A. Very Short Answer Type Questions

1. Give any two reasons for the growth of extremism in India in the early 20th Century.
2. Give any two points of difference between the Moderates and the Extremists.

3. Mention any two movements launched by the Extremists.
4. Give any two reasons for the split of Congress at the Surat Session.
5. List any two reasons for the unification of the two groups of the Congress at the Lucknow Session.
6. Mention any two reasons for the founding of the Muslim League.
7. Mention any two methods adopted by the Ghadhar party.
8. Mention any one provision of the Lucknow Pact.
9. Give the meaning of the following terms: Swadeshi, National Education, Boycott, Swaraj, Communalism, Separate Electorate.

B. Short Answer Type Questions

1. How did the partition of Bengal affect the national movement?
2. State the main provisions of the Morley-Minto Reforms.
3. Explain the Swadeshi Movement.
4. Trace the causes that led to the Boycott Movement.
5. Explain the Home Rule Movement in India.
6. Explain the main points of differences as regards the aims and methods followed by the Moderates and the Extremists.
7. Give the contribution of any one Moderate, any one Extremist and any one Revolutionary to the cause of India's struggle for freedom.

C. Essay type/Long-Answer Type Questions

1. Explain the impact of the First War on India's national movement.
2. Describe the growth of Revolutionary Movement in India from 1905 to 1918.
3. Examine critically the factors that led to the growth of communalism in India in the early years of the 20th Century. Discuss in this regard the British policy of 'Divide and Rule.'

CHAPTER 16

The National Movement (1919-1928)

IMPACT OF THE FIRST WORLD WAR

Factors Giving Impetus to the National Movement after the First World War

Nationalism in India received a new vigour as well as turn after the First World War. Important factors which led to the resurgance of nationalism are briefly discussed below.

1. India's Heavy Contribution to War and Expectation:

(a) India had made a valuable contribution to the success of the war. More than 10 lakh soldiers from India fought at different war-fronts outside India. India made an enormous contribution to the War Fund and the Red Cross.

Gandhiji had also said, "... it was our duty to help them win by standing by them in their hour of need".

Unfortunately the hopes of Indian's were belied after the war, on account of the indifferent attitude of the British rulers.

(b) Appreciation of India's Role:

The British greatly appreciated India's war efforts. She was admitted to The Imperial War Conference and The Imperial War Cabinet.

(c) War for Freedom:

The British Prime Minister regarded Indians as equal custodians of 'Common interests and fortunes'. Montague, the Secretary of State for India referred to the "common loyalty" of Britain and India to the ideal of freedom. President Wilson of America uttered these memorable words that war was meant to make "the world fit for free men to live." Naturally all these sentiments had kindled hopes for India's freedom after war.

2. Adverse Economic Impact on India:

The prices during the war shot up. A large number of industries during war had come up but after the war, no protection to Indian industries was given. Indian industrialists on their part did not share their mounting profits with the labour. This led to labour unrest and trade unionism, and this affected production. In the villages, the poor people and the peasants were groaning under mounting taxes. With the decline in economic activity after the war, the urban youth were facing acute unemployment. It all resulted in frustration. Thus, people thought national government was the only solution.

3. Inspiration from the Russian Revolution:

The success of the people of Russia in overthrowing the cruel rule of the Czarists in 1917, influenced greatly the nationalist movement in India. The natural question was, if the Russians could overthrow their own despotic rule, why Indians could not free themselves from the foreign oppressive rule! The Russian Revolution infused courage, confidence and faith in Indians for achieving their objective of self-government.

4. Ill-Treatment of the Defeated Nations:

The imperialist powers did not show any regard to the sentiments of the people of those countries which were defeated in the war. The victorious nations of the Paris Peace Conference, redivided among themselves the colonies of Germany and Turkey in Africa. This action on the part of the Allies created suspicion of their motives among the people of countries under foreign domination. India also was affected.

5. Anger of Indian Muslims:

Turkey, a source of inspiration for the Muslims, was dismembered by the Allies after the war. The Sultan of Turkey became a virtual prisoner in the hands of the imperialist powers. The Indian Muslims considered the British Government responsible for the sad plight of Turkey.

6. Role of Indian Soldiers:

Indian soldiers, who had played a significant role in winning victories for the Allies in Asia, Africa and Europe, on their return to India, imparted some of their confidence to the rural people of India.

7. Favourable International Environment for Nationalism:

Disillusionment on the policies followed by the victorious powers in the war led to the resurgence of nationalism all over Asia and Africa. Nationalism also surged forward in Ireland and several Arab countries.

8. Half-hearted Montague-Chelmsford Reforms (1919):

The reforms envisaged in the August (1919) Declaration 'after the end of the War' did not at all inspire the Indians and they began to distrust the British all the more. The prophetic words of Mrs. Annie Besant, which she said in 1914, turned out to be true after the end of the war, "India claims the right, as a Nation, to justice among the people of the Empire. India asked for this before the war. India asks for this during the war. India will ask for it after the war, not as a reward but as a right. On that there must be no mistake."

EMERGENCE OF GANDHIJI ON THE POLITICAL SCENE OF INDIA

The passing away of the three great leaders namely Gokhale in 1915, Naoroji in 1917 and Tilak in 1920, created great void in the nationalist movement in India. The need for a dynamic leader to guide the masses to participate effectively in the struggle for freedom was acutely felt. The void was filled up by Mohan Das Karamchand Gandhi. Gandhiji had already made his mark in taking up the people's cause in South Africa during his stay there. From 1904 to July 1914 he had launched *'Satyagraha'* a number of times. It was through his peaceful, tireless efforts that Indians began to be treated as human beings in South Africa.

Back to India in 1915

After the conclusion of the *satyagraha* struggle in South Africa, Gandhiji arrived at London on 6th August 1914 as desired by Gokhale to return home via London. It was just two days after the outbreak of the Great War. He pleaded with the Indians in London to help Britain thinking that he could convert the British by love. From London he returned to India in January 1915.

Gandhiji's Early Activities in India

In India, the first phase of his public life began with the establishment of an Ashram on the banks of Sabarmati in 1915. His political career began in 1916, when he joined the Indian National Congress. The way he tested the

Map 29: **Champaran Gandhiji's Visit**

The National Movement (1919-1928)

power and technique of *Satyagraha* in Indian situations and politics and displayed the qualities of his leadership and fearlessness is described below in stopping the Indenture System and campaigning for Indigo cultivators at Champaran, labourers of a mill at Ahmedabad and peasants of Kheda.

In India, the first thing that disturbed and pained him was the refusal of the government to introduce a Bill for the immediate abolition of the Indenture system of recruiting Indian labourers for the British colonies. He was fully aware of the evils of the system that brought degradation, torture and suffering to the Indian labourers. Gandhiji toured the country with an open challenge to start an all-India agitation by launching a *Satyagraha*. Immediately the Government announced that the Indenture system would be stopped.

This triumph was followed by another of great significance. In 1917, he proceeded to Champaran in Bihar, to relieve the cultivators from the oppression of the Indigo planters, the Britishers. For over 100 years, in Bihar and Bengal where Indigo could be grown, the helpless cultivators were forced to cultivate indigo on their best land, at their own cost, neglecting their own food crops, and to sell them to the European planters for their Indigo factories at less than half the market price. They were treated like slaves. If they refused, they were dragged and flogged or locked up in the factory godowns and sometimes killed; their houses were burnt; and all these various acts of oppression occurred before the eyes of the police, judges and magistrates. Gandhiji defied the ban on his entry. When he was tried in the court, he pleaded guilty, but added that he disregarded the order of quitting the place "not for want of respect for lawful authority, but in obedience to the higher law of our being, the voice of conscience." As people all around got ready to join the struggle in response to Gandhiji's courageous act for a noble cause, the Government withdrew the case against Gandhiji and made him a member of a committee to inquire into the grievances of the indigo cultivators. The result was the Champaran Agrarian Bill of 1917, the first triumph in India of *Satyagraha* or Civil Disobedience.

Satyagraha was again used by Gandhiji in an industrial dispute in Ahmedabad in 1918. He lead the strike of the labourers for increase of pay.

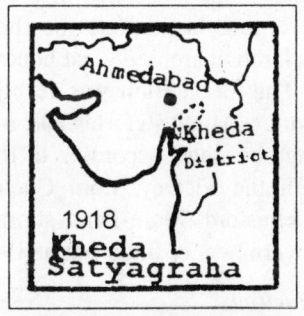

Map 30: **Kheda District**

After two weeks, when the strikers were losing the zeal, Gandhiji warned that he would not touch any food till a settlement was reached. So after 21 days strike, a favourable settlement was reached.

Immediately after the strike was over, Gandhiji plunged into a *Satyagraha* campaign in the Kheda (or Kaira) district of Gujarat, where, under rules, the peasants should have got the exemption from the payment of land-revenue as the yield of their crops fell below 25% due to famine and plague. But the Government officials refused to accept the demand of the peasants. Gandhiji advised the cultivators to resort to *Satyagraha*. Gandhiji was joined here by Vallabhbhai Patel. The cultivators stood firm. Fear of officials passed away. They faced attachment of property and threat of forfeiture of their land. The Government had to yield. With the triumph of Champaran and Kheda began the third phase of the struggle as the people perceived, that their freedom depended on *Satyagraha* which demanded infinite capacity for suffering and sacrifice.

1919-22

Movements and Reforms

In 1919, while Europe was signing a Peace Treaty in the Hall of Mirrors at Versailles at the end of World War I, India was bleeding under the brutal onslaught of British repressive savagery. The year 1919 constitutes an important landmark in the history of British India. It will ever remain memorable for four outstanding events: First, the Government of India Act on the basis of the Montague-Chelmsford Report; second, The Rowlatt Bill; third, the emergence of Mahatma Gandhi and the start of agitation against the Rowlatt Bill; fourth, the ruthless opression and the reign of terror in the Punjab, culminating in Jallianwalla Bagh Massacre and barbarous enforcement of martial law in the Punjab.

The two—the India Act and the Rowlatt Bill—picturesquely show the British as a great diplomatic upholder of the twin policy of conciliation and coercion. The Act contained, for the first time, some provisions of concession towards self-government. It looked so simple and innocuous like the '1' of 1919. But Rowlatt Bill was a crooked idea like the crooked shape of the first '9' of 1919. Naturally, the Rowlatt Bill greatly agitated the public and Mahatma Gandhi gave a lead for non-violent *hartals* and *satyagrahas*—simple and innocuous like the second '1' of 1919. But the government with vengeance, let loose, massive power of massacre and bloodshed; it was so heinous and crooked like the second '9' of 1919.

Montague-Chelmsford Reforms/Government of India Act (1919)

Why reforms!

With a view to enlisting the cooperation of the Indians in the war efforts, the British Government had been telling them that after the end of the war, they would be given adequate powers. In 1917, Montague, the Secretary of State for India, declared in the House of Commons (British Parliament) that the Indians would be increasingly associated in every branch of administration and there would be gradual development of self-governing institutions for the "progressive realisation of responsible government in India." The above declaration aroused great hopes among the people of India.

This declaration was revolutionary, in the sense that it promised 'responsible government', which the Morley-Minto Reforms had ruled out. However, this was merely a statement of a distant goal to be reached stage by stage, according to the discretion of the British rulers. Montague discussed his scheme of reforms with the Viceroy, Lord Chelmsford. The scheme of these discussions was embodied in the Montague-Chelmsford (Mont-Ford, shortened term) Report which was published in July 1918. Based on this report, Government of India Act of 1919 was passed in December 1919 and came into operation on January 1, 1921.

Reactions:

The publication of the Report in 1918 had different reactions in different quarters. Three different forms of opinion emerged in the Indian National Congress. The Moderates regarded the proposals progressive; the exteme left considered them radically wrong, beyond the possibility of modifications; and the intermediate groups looked upon the report as unsatisfactory but pleaded for some modifications and not total rejection.

The Chief Provisions of the Government of India Act, 1919:

Central Legislature:

(1) It consisted of the Governor-General and two chambers—the Council of State and the Legislative Assembly (2) The Council of State consisted of 60 members—26 nominated by the Governor-General and 34 elected (3) The Legislative Assembly (4) The Governor-General retained his powers of legislating through ordinances. Thus the Executive remained outside the control of the Legislature (5) Separate electorates remained as a permanent feature of Indian political structure, though Montague-Chelmsford Report considered the system of separate electorate 'as a very serious hindrance for the development of the self-governing principle.' So there were several types of separate electorates for Muslims, Sikhs, Zamindars, Anglo-Indians etc.

System of Dyarchy or Dual Government in the Provinces:

Under this system subjects, like finance, law and order, police, justice etc. were called as 'reserved' subjects and they remained under the direct control of the Governor of the Province. Other subjects like local self government, education, public health etc. were put under the control of Ministers who were responsible to the legislature. The Governor, however, had the authority to overrule the Ministers on any ground. The legislature had no control over the Governor.

The National Movement (1919-1928)

```
GOVERNMENTAL ORGANIZATION OF BRITISH INDIA
UNDER THE GOVERNMENT OF INDIA ACT OF 1919
```

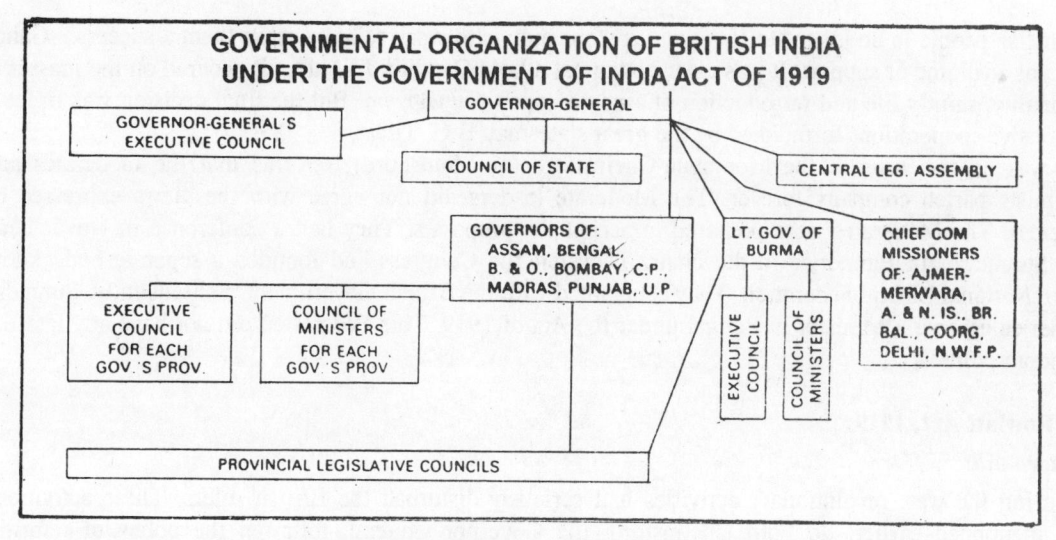

Chart 4: **Government of India Act of 1919**

The Provincial Legislature consisted of a single House called the Provincial Legislative Council. The number of Members in the Provincial Councils varied in accordance with the population of the province.

Criticism:

(i) The franchise was extremely limited. In 1920, out of a total population of about 25 crore in India, there were 9 lakh voters for the Lower House and 17000 for the Upper House (ii) Property qualifications to be eligible to vote were pitched very high (iii) Women could neither vote nor stand for election (iv) The constituencies were grouped on communal basis (v) The Governor could overrule the decision of the Ministers (vi) The Viceroy could overrule his council. It meant that both the executives—the Governor General and the Governor—were not responsible to the legislatures (vii) Dyarchy or the double executive betrays a lack of confidence in the capacity of Indians and that is why only these subjects were transferred to their care as were politically unimportant. Under Dyarchy a minister had to serve two masters- the Governor and the legislature (viii) It took away administrative efficiency as ministers had responsibility without power and legislature had power without responsibility (ix) Subjects vitally related to another were divided into 'reserve' and 'transferred'. Minister of Agriculture did not have 'Irrigation' which was a reserved subject.

Merits:

(1) For the first time Indians were appointed Ministers as the leaders of elected majorities. This was responsible government although to a very limited extent (2) For the first time in the history of British Rule, it provided for transfer of power, however limited it might be (3) It gave training in the art of government (4) It also gave an opportunity to the people for influencing the action of the Government.

Reaction to the Government of India Act, 1919:

The reaction to the Act was more or less the same as noted in connection with the publication of Montague-Chelmsford Report published in 1918. The Moderates though not wholly satisfied stood for whole-hearted cooperation for making it work. In the Congress, differences were on the point of cooperation with the government in working out the reforms embodied in the Act. C.R. Das was in favour of rejecting the reforms. Tilak was in favour of 'responsive cooperation.' Gandhiji said that the Reform Act was an earnest intention of the British people to do justice to India and so "our duty is to work so as to make them a success." Gandhiji's view got a volume of support. It was clear how great a hold Gandhiji had already secured on the masses by his personality, saintly life and introduction of a new weapon-*Satyagraha*. But the final decision was in favour of 'responsive cooperation' formulated by the great statesman B.G. Tilak.

It was on the issue of the Montague-Chelmsford (or Mont-Ford) Reforms that the moderates and the extremists parted company forever. The Moderate leaders did not agree with the views expressed by the Congress. The Moderates were prepared to accept the proposals. They had a conference in November 1918 with Surendranath Bannerjee in the chair. They left the Congress and founded a separate body known as Indian National Liberal Federation. They cooperated with the British Government. Subsequently, Surendranath Bannerjee became a Minister in Bengal under the Act of 1919. This Federation did not have any later impact on Indian politics.

The Rowlatt Act, 1919

Background:

During the war, revolutionary activities had seriously disturbed the British rulers. These activities have been mentioned earlier. So Lord Chelmsford, the Governor General, followed the policy of reform-cum-repression followed by his two predecessors, Minto and Hardinge, as they were convinced about the effectiveness of the twin policy in India. So, on December 10, 1917 while he was busy formulating the constitutional reforms, he appointed a committee of five members, including two Indians, to find out the extent of the criminal conspiracies connected with revolutionary activities and to suggest new laws for their suppression. A British judge, Sir Sydney Rowlatt was the President. Two Bills based on the Committees recommendations were framed without any loss of time and placed before the Governor General's Legislative Council in February 1919. These contained drastic provisions denying protection of law to Indians. All the non-official Indian members of the Council unitedly opposed the measure and four of them resigned by way of protest. Indeed, such a unique opposition of Indians to a Government measure was never witnessed since the Partition of Bengal. The Government just dropped one of the Bills but passed the other as The Anarchial and Revolutionary Crimes Act, 1919, usually known as Rowlatt Act.'

The Provisions of the Act:

The Rowlatt Act implied (i) Arrest of a person without warrant (ii) Summary trial (iii) No provision of appeal (iv) No open trial (v) Restriction on movement of individuals (vi) Security for good conduct (vii) Any evidence could be accepted even if not according to the Laws of Evidence.

Reactions:

The Act came like a sudden blow to the people of India who had been promised the extension of democracy. It was a cruel joke to deprive Indians of all liberties and rights and to stop them seeking protection under law. Only suspicion was sufficient to cage them for life or hang them. A widespread public agitation was bound to engulf the country.

Agitation Against Rowlatt Bills/Act:

Gandhiji appealed to the Viceroy to withhold his consent to these obvious measures. When his appeal was ignored he took the lead and started *Satyagraha*, as a challenge to the Government. A campaign was organised and as a first step, Gandhiji made an all-India appeal to observe *hartal* for a day. The date originally fixed as March 30, was changed to April 6. The *hartal* was a unique success. But there were clashes between the police and the people.

As there was great popular exitement in both Delhi and Amritsar, Gandhiji was called there. But the police forcibly removed him from the train and sent him to Bombay and then set him free. A vast crowd was roused

The National Movement (1919-1928)

to a pitch of mad frenzy by the news of Gandhiji's arrest and people committed acts of violence in Ahmedabad. Gandhiji did not mince matters. He addressed the people of Ahmedabad, "*Satyagraha* admits of no violence, no pillage, and still in the name of Satyagraha we burn down buildings, loot money, stop trains, cut off telegraph lines, kill people," For such misdeeds, he wished himself to be arrested or hanged. It suddenly dawned upon him that it was a Himalayan miscalcuation to call upon people to launch *Satyagraha* without preparing them. He suspended the *Satyagraha*.

Agitation and Repression:

Even before Gandhiji suspended his *Satyagraha* campaign on 18th April, events had been moving fast in the Punjab where the Lt. Governor, Sir Michael O'Dwyer, had already terrorised the whole of the Punjab by his ruthless suppression. He interned hundreds of educated men, gagged the vernacular press and used all sorts of tyrannical methods, as considerable part of the Punjab was aflame after the peaceful *hartal* of April 6. In Lahore processions of students and crowds attending meetings were fired upon. In Gujranwala, on April 14, the trouble started over the killing of a calf and hanging it on a railway bridge. Two railway bridges were burnt. In Kasur, the crowd got out of control on April 12, burnt the post office and did other acts. A train was attacked and two European soldiers were beaten to death.

In Amritsar two *hartals*, on March 30 and April 6, passed off peacefully. But on April 9, Sir Michael O'Dwyer deported two prominent local leaders Dr. Satyapal and Dr. Kitchlew. *Hartal* was immediately declared. A large crowd of demonstrators marched peacefully but indiscriminate firing was opened on them. After that, things seemed settled on the 11th. But things took a bad turn with the arrival of Brigadier General Dyer on the evening of the same day. He immediately established Martial Law, though it was not officially proclaimed before April 15. He began his regime on 12th by indiscriminate arrests and issue of a proclamation banning all meetings.

The Jallianwala Bagh Massacre:

However, the proclamation of banning meetings and gatherings was not read in many parts of Amritsar. This omission, deliberate or accidental, was very unfortunate, as the people had already announced a public meeting at Jallianwala Bagh on the 13th, the Baisakhi Day, at 4.30 pm. Dyer fully knew of this omission, but he took no steps to warn the people not to enter the Bagh or to put troops at the entrance to stop the people from entering. But soon after the meeting had begun, Dyer arrived on the spot with armoured cars and troops with rifles. The Bagh had only one small exit on one side and all the three sides were enclosed by buildings. About 10,000 people had gathered there. Dyer, plugged all possible exists and stationed himself and his troops on a rising ground at the only entrance, and then, without issuing any warning ordered 'Fire' at about 100 yards 'range'. "The panic-stricken multitude broke at once,

Map 31: **Amritsar Jallianwala Bagh 1919**

but for ten consecutive minutes, he kept up a merciless fussilade–in all 1650 rounds–on that seething mass of humanity, caught like rats in a trap, vainly rushing for the few narrow exits or lying flat on the ground to escape the rain of bullets, which he personally directed to the point where the crowd was thickest."

The Jallianwalla Bagh massacre was a calcuated piece of inhumanity and unparalleled for its ferocity in the history of British administrators. And all this happened before the Martial Law was declared. Martial Law was proclaimed at Amritsar on the 15th April and in five districts of the Punjab, between 15th and 24th April.

And what happend to the dead and wounded? The wounded lay in their agony and the dead lay putrefying in the heat of Amritsar and the vultures came to tear the flesh of innocent victims of this dreadful holocaust. It was because on the very day (13th April), a curfew order to shoot at sight after 8 pm was issued and, therefore, the anxious and weeping relatives of the wounded and dead remained terrified behind their closed doors and could not come out to take charge of the dead or wounded. Dyer, when questioned by the Hunter Commission frankly said that it was not his job to look after the wounded; it was for them to go to the hospital if they liked. He even admitted that he would not have hesitated from still greater killing if the narrowness of the entry of the Bagh had not compelled him to leave his machine guns behind. He also admitted that he could have dispersed the crowd without firing but that would have lowered his dignity. Such a brute arrogance clearly indicates that some of the rulers of the British colonies and some of their officers considered the coloured Indians worse than slaves, not worthy of being treated as human beings.

The Martial Law:

The regime of Martial Law was a veritable reign of terror. General Dyer cut off the water supply and the electric supply of the city. His fertile brain invented the 'crawling order'. Everyone passing through some streets was ordered to crawl with belly to the ground. And while the men and women, old and young were crawling, they were kicked by the soldiers with their boots. Public platforms for whippings were erected at various places. When people became senseless after some stripes, water was poured into their mouths and after they gained consciousness, flogging was resumed. Some officers removed the veils of women, used abusive language and spat on them. Under the Martial Law, many were sentenced to death, many were transported for life and many were imprisoned.

The Punjab was treated by the military even worse than an enemy territory. The Lieutenant Governor, Sir Michael O'Dwyer, conceived the idea of sending aeroplanes to throw bombs upon the rioters even when there were no rioters. Bombs were freely used even when there was no gathering with arms. R.A.F. bombed and machine-gunned from the aeroplanes wherever they found people moving about or talking or working in the fields.

Enquiry Committee:

An Enquiry Committee appointed by the Congress condemned the Punjab Government and the Government of India. The Viceroy appointed an enquiry committee (Hunter Committee) with five British and three Indian members including Lord Hunter as Chairman of the Committee. The British and the Indian members differed in their views on Dyer's conduct and justification of Martial Law.

The Englishmen regarded Dyer as the saviour of the British Empire. The Government of India and a section of the British people—men and women, women more than men—both in India and in Britain, endorsed Dyer's action. A few Englishmen condemned Dyer's action. Some said, "Every Englishman should be ashamed"; some said, "Worst of all, we bombed unarmed crowds from aeroplanes. Our atrocities stand on a level with the outrage committed by Germany in Belgium, France and Poland".

It may be mentioned that Tilak was the leading figure in the Congress which was completely dominated by the Nationalists after the Moderates left it in 1918. But in September 1918, Tilak left for England for the work of the Congress and for Home Rule League and, therefore, he could not accept the Presidentship of the Congress though he was elected to the office on the eve of his departure. While Tilak was busy in England, momentous events like Jallianwala Bagh Massacre and Martial Law occurred in India. In his absence, during this crisis, the political leadership gradually passed into the hands of Gandhiji.

Impact of Jallianwala Bagh Massacre:

(1) It became a turning point in the history of India as it made the national movement a mass movement (2) Gandhiji emerged as the most prominent leader of the national movement. He, who had been so tolerant all these years, now lost practically all hope in the bonafides of the British Government (3) It helped in strengthening Hindu-Muslim unity (4) Rabindranath Tagore was so shocked that he renounced his knighthood, which had been conferred upon him by the government, in protest and declared, "The time has come when badges of honour make our shame glaring in their incongruous context of humiliation, and, I, for

my part, wish to stand shorn of all distinctions, by the side of my countrymen, who for their so-called insignificance, are liable to suffer degradation, not fit for human beings" (5) It gave a great fillip to revolutionary tendencies. One of the injured at Jallianwala Bagh was a youngman of 20, named Udham Singh. He was imprisoned for five years after which he went to London for studying engineering. There in 1940, he shot dead Sir Michael O'Dwyer, the notorious ex-Governor of Punjab, responsible for Jallianwala Bagh massacre. He was hanged to death the same year. Udham Singh declared in the court, "I do not mind dying. I am dying for my country. What is the use of waiting until you get old."

Gandhiji was greatly shocked by the grim tragedy brought about by the *Satyagraha* campaign which he suspended on April 8, 1919. He called on the *Satyagrahis* to work for constructive programmes, viz., use of *Swadeshi* goods and unity between Hindus and Muslims. On the other hand, Pandit Madan Mohan Malaviya collected all the details of the tragic incidents and sought to place them before the Central Legislative Council, but this was disallowed by the Viceroy. The details collected by Pandit Malaviya sent such a thrill of horror over the whole country that the Viceroy immediately announced the appointment of a Committee of Enquiry, already mentioned earlier.

The anguished feelings of Indians for the brutal acts of Dyer were further outraged by the approval of his conduct by the Englishmen. In any case, the Punjab atrocities created a river of blood between India and Britain which could never be bridged. The relation between the two could never be what it was before 1919.

The Khilafat Movement (1919-20)

Background:

The British Government was bent upon crushing the National Movement by ruthless repression to terrorise the people and by creating divisions betwen the Hindus and the Muslims. It had been Gandhijis utmost concern to reinforce the Hindu-Muslim unity as strongly as possible to make the freedom struggle successful. Soon, such an opportunity arose.

The Muslims of India, like Muslims in other countries, respected and revered the Sultan of Turkey who was their Caliph, their supreme religious head. In the First World War, the Sultan joined Germany and fought against England and her allies. The natural sympathy of the Muslims was with the Sultan and they found it difficult to support the British in the war against the Sultan of Turkey. Suspecting some of the Muslim leaders as disloyal, the British Government put them in internment. Among them were Mohammad Ali and Abul Kalam Azad. The British Government also tried to win the sympathy and support of the Muslims during the war, so the British Prime Minister, in 1918, declared that they were not fighting to deprive Turkey of its territory and gave assurance of sympathetic treatment of Turkey at the end of the war. But all these hopes of the Muslims were doomed after the defeat of Turkey, when portions of Turkish Empire passed under the control of England, France and Greece and the Sultan was deprived of all real authority, even in the remaining dominions. The Muslims regarded this as a great betrayal going against their assurances - a *Khilafat*.

Agitations:

Early in 1920, the Indian Muslims started a vigorous agitation to bring pressure upon Britain to change her policy towards Turkey. This, known as the Khilafat Movement, received enormous strength and support from Gandhiji as he felt that the Muslim cause was just and he should help them to secure the fulfilment of the assurance given by the British Prime Minister. Gandhiji looked upon the Khilafat Movement as "an opportunity of uniting Hindus and Mohammedans as would not arise in a hundred years." Gandhiji issued a Manifesto on March 10 embodying the idea of Non-cooperation, to be pursued in the Khilafat Movement. This Manifesto provides the first definite idea of Gandhiji's Non-violent Non-cooperation: "Non-cooperation is the most effective when it is free from all violence. It becomes a duty when cooperation means degradation or humiliation." The Khilafat Committee under the guidance of Gandhiji launched the Khilafat Movement beginning on August 1, 1920 in the form of *hartal*. It is a coincidence that Tilak passed away on the same day the Non-Cooperation Movement was launched. The void was filled up by the leadership of Gandhiji. At the time of launching the Khilafat Movement on August 1, the Khilafat wrongs were the single issue. The Punjab atrocities and winning of *Swaraj* were gradually tagged into the main issue at a later date. Thus, Gandhiji's Non-Cooperation Movement was the direct outcome of the Khilafat Movement.

Impact of the Khilafat Movement:

The Movement engendered a strong sentiment of Hindu-Muslims Unity. Hindus and Muslim were marching together shoulder to shoulder.

The Non-Cooperation Movement (1920-22)

Main Objectives of the Movement:

The movement was launched with the view of making it known to the British rulers that they would not be able to run the adimnstration of India unless they received the cooperation of the Indian people. Broadly speaking, it had three objectives (i) Settlement of the Khilafat question to the satisfaction of the Indian Muslims (ii) Atonement for atrocities committed at Amritsar (iii) Establishment of Swaraj or Self-government.

Launching of the Movement and its Programme:

The movement was lauched by Gandhiji on August 1, 1920. The two movements, the Congress Non-Cooperation and the Khilafat Movement based on Non-cooperation, continued side by side, or as a single force. What a happy occasion for Hindu-Muslim Unity! The following seven-point programme was approved at the special session of the Congress in September 1920:

(1) Surrendering all honorary posts and titles.
(2) Refusal to attend any government function.
(3) Boycott of all government and government aided schools and starting National Schools.
(4) Gradual boycott of Law Courts.
(5) Refusal of Civilian and Military personnel to serve in Mesopotamia (to protect the oil tanks of Anglo-Persian Oil Company).
(6) Boycott of all Legislatures.
(7) Boycott of all foreign goods.

A great momentum:

The movement picked up fast in the country. There were frequent lathi charges, mass arrests and ban on processions and public meetings. Thousands of students left government schools and colleges.

Non-cooperation at Work:

Student processions and mammoth meetings became the order of the day. The boycotting students adopted a novel method of picketing for preventing others from entering the schools or colleges. A number of them lay flat, side by side, blocking the entrances. Many students resumed their studies in newly started national schools and colleges. The boycott of foreign cloth was the most sustained part of the movement. The boycott of legal profession was heralded by the magnificent self-sacrifice of Pandit Motilal Nehru and C.R. Das who earlier enjoyed princely income. Their example was followed by a large number of lawyers including C. Rajagopalachari, Rajendra Prasad, Sardar Patel. All the Congress candidates withdrew from election contest to the Council. Their seats were filled up by non-congressmen. The boycott of titles and honours, as well as

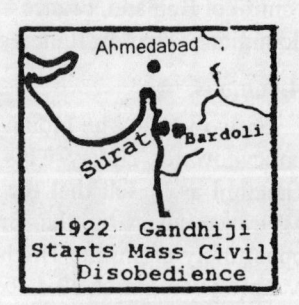

Map 32: **Bardoli 1922 starting Mass Civil Disobedience**

The National Movement (1919-1928)

Government offices was a hopeless failure, for a few resigned from their government jobs, including Subhas Chandra Bose who resigned from the I.C.S. C.R. Das in Calcutta organized large number of volunteers to sell *Khadi*. Within a few days prisons were filled with political prisoners. Camp-prisons were then opened, but they too were filled up in no time. Orders were given to release a large number of old prisoners, but no one would leave the prison. The prisoners were thereupon taken forcibly to the prison-gate and set free, so that the new flow of prisoners could be accommodated. The British jail had lost its terror and imprisonment became a badge of distinction. Outside prison, arrests were stopped, as there was no place in the prisons and sticks and batons were freely used against the demonstrators. Except Gandhiji, most of the important leaders of the Movement were behind the bars.

Nearly 40 thousand Congress workers were in jail in December 1921 when the Annual Congress Session was held in Ahmedabad. The Congress Session decided to organise not only individual civil disobedience but also mass civil disobedience. Gandhiji then gave an ultimatum to the Viceroy in a letter sent on February 1, 1922: "This lawless repression has made immediate adoption of Mass Civil Disobedience", unless the Viceroy declared a policy of non-interference with all non-violent activities for the redress of the Khilafat or the Punjab wrongs or for Swaraj. Finding no response from the Viceroy, Gandhiji started from Bardoli, his Mass Civil Disobedience Movement including non-payment of taxes. The whole of India watched with suspense. But the battle was lost before it had properly begun due to the violent actions committed by the people of Chauri Chaura on being provoked by the violent actions of the police on February 5.

Chauri Chaura Incident (February 5, 1922) and Suspension of the Movement:

The Congress had asked all satyagrahis to take a pledge to "remain non-violent in word and deed." The movement had spread among the masses. When the movement was at its height, violence occurred at Chauri Chaura, a village in the Gorakhpur District of U.P. when a procession of 3,000 peasants was fired upon by the police and atrocities committed on the processionists. In retaliation, the angry mob took to violence and burnt the police station causing death to 22 policemen.

Gandhiji was shocked. It was not his way. He became convinced that people were yet not ready for a non-violent movement. The working committee of the Congress hastily met at Bardoli and upheld Gandhiji's view of suspending the Civil Disobedience Movement on February 12. But the people were stunned and disappointed and considered the suspension a great blunder when the movement was at an exciting tempo. However, their faith in Gandhiji remained unshaken. This pent-up energy found an outlet in the Hindu-Muslim riots during the next few years. The Government took full advantage of the situation by arresting Gandhiji, a step not dared earlier for fear of popular outbreak. Gandhiji was sentenced to six years' simple imprisonment.

Map 33: **Chauri Chaura 1922 Movement Suspended**

After the suspension of the Movement and the imprisonment of Gandhiji, the Khilafat movement lost its momentum. A few months later, in October 1922, Mustafa Kamal Pasha established a Republic in Turkey and after two years abolished the office of Caliph. Thus, the Khilafat movement also came to an end and its leaders, except one, left the Congress. Abul Kalam Azad of the Khilafat Movement remained a true Congressman. The breach between the two was inevitable for the Congress was fighting for India's Independence while the other for a religious cause.

The Swarajists (1922-26)

Gandhijis imprisonment brought demoralisation among the rank and file of the Congress workers. There was a sort of political void. Some of the leaders of the Congress began to feel that it was time that a new policy, different from Non-Cooperation should be followed which would have a greater impact. Among the important leaders of this view were C.R. Das and Motilal Nehru. The group came to be known as the Swarajists or Pro-changers as they wanted to drift away from the current Congress policy. The Swarajists were of the view that they should contest elections and fight for their cause from within the Councils and Assemblies. This strategy of council entry was opposed by the staunch followers of Gandhiji like C. Rajagopalachari (popularly called Rajaji), Sardar Patel, Dr. Rajendra Prasad and Dr. Ansari. They were known as no-changers (who did not want any change from the non-coperation policy of the Congress). However, a special session of the Congress held at Delhi in September 1923, arrived at a compromise by adhering to the principle of Non-cooperation but allowing those Congressmen to contest elections who wanted to enter the legislatures.

Watchwords of the Swarajists:

Their strategy may be described as (i) End the boycott of the Legislative Councils (ii) Contest elections and enter the Councils (iii) Obstruct the working of the Councils according to official plans (iv) Expose the plans of the officials (v) Transform the Councils into arenas of political struggle (vi) Use Councils to arouse public enthusiasm.

The two groups i.e. the Swarajists and 'no changers' agreed to remain in the Congress but to work in their separate ways. The 'no changers' engaged themselves in constructive work.

Contesting Elections:

Under the Montague-Chelmsford Reforms (1919), elections to the Central Legislative Assembly were held and the Swarajists won 42 seats out of 101 elected seats. They agitated in the Assembly through powerful speeches and pleaded for self-government, civil liberation and industrial development. In due course, they felt that they were not effective in compelling the government to change their authoritative methods. They left the Assembly in 1926. C.R. had died in 1925 and a split also occurred among the Swarajists on account of their different views on communalism. Thus, the Swarajists faded away within a short period of four years.

Whether the Non-cooperation Movement (1920-21) was a Success or a Failure

The correct view would be that it was neither a complete success nor a complete failure. It is true that it failed to achieve any of the three objects. The boycott of Councils, law courts and educational institutions proved ineffective. The boycott of foreign goods and liquour had only a temporary success. In constructive programme, the spinning wheel was revived but it was not very popular and today it remains as a ritual.

But no one can deny the outstanding features of the movement (1) The general awakening of the masses (2) Loss of faith in the British administration (3) Increased faith in the Congress (4) The belief that India can win freedom only by its own efforts and sacrifice (5) Failure of repression to cow down the people (6) Overcoming fear of the British might and readiness to endure hardships and punishments inflicted by the government (7) Congress becoming for the first time, a real mass movement (8) Congress changed from a speech making platform to an organized force with its object closely resembling militant nationalism.

CONSTRUCTIVE PROGRAMME (1922-28)

With the withdrawal of the Non-cooperation Movement, two groups emerged in the Congress namely the 'Swarajists' and 'No Changers'. Reference has already been made to the programme of the Swarajists. The 'No Changers' led by Sardar Vallabh Patel, Dr. Ansari and Babu Rajendra Prasad opposed Council entry and laid stress on undertaking constructive work as laid down by Gandhiji.

The constructive programme which involved the masses included the following:
(i) Spinning (ii) abstenence from alcoholic drinks (iii) Strengthening Hindu Muslim Unity (iv) Removal of

untouchability (v) Grassroot work in the villages (vi) Grassroot work among the poor.

All these activities were meant to prepare the country for a new round of mass struggle.

THE SIMON COMMISSION (1927-28)

Framework of the Simon Commission:

Elections, in accordance with the Government of India Act had taken place. The Swarajists had joined the Councils and later on walked out of them. On all counts, public opinion was not satisfied with the reforms as envisaged in the 1919 Act. People were getting restive on the apathy of the government. The British Government, therefore, appointed a Commission under the Chairmanship of Sir J.A. Simon to inquire into the working of the Act of 1919 and to study what changes were needed for the establishment of responsible government in India.

Composition of the Commission and Hostility Towards it:

The Commission had all the seven members from the English Community. No Indian was included in it. This sent a wave of anger against the Commission throughout India. The Indian National Congress at its session passed a resolution "to boycott the Commission at every stage." The Commission was boycotted by the Hindu Mahasabha and the Muslim League. When the Commission landed at Bombay, it had to face a total *hartal* in the city. The cry of "Go back Simon" greeted its members from city to city. The government resorted to repressive measures and the police lathi-charged the demonstrators. At Lahore, a peaceful demonstration was subjected to repeated baton blows and Lala Lajpat Rai was severely beaten up by the blows and died after 18 days on account of serious injuries. At other places, Jawarharlal Nehru and Govind Ballabh Pant also received lathi blows.

Impact of the Simon Commission on Indian Political Condition:

The death of Lala Lajpat Rai due to *lathi* blows, helped to generate the climate of political revolution aimed at securing freedom for India. The death of Lala Lajpat Rai enraged the youth, and on December 17, 1928, three revolutionaries namely Bhagat Singh, Azad and Rajguru assassinated Saunders, the British police officer who had led the *lathi* charge. [The Simon Commission report was published in 1930 and the government took no notice of it.]

Nehru Report (1928)

Setting up a Committee:

The Simon Commission was boycotted because it did not include any Indian as its member. It was decided by the Indian leaders that they would themselves prepare a report on the reforms to be carried out in India for the establishment of a responsible government. An All-Party Conference was held in Delhi under the Chairmanship of Dr. M.A. Ansari. The Conference constituted a committee with Pandit Motilal Nehru as its Chairman. The committee included eminent legal experts like Sir Tej Bahadur Sapru, Sir Ali Imam etc. besides Subhas Chandra Bose and other leaders.

Important Recommendations:

Among the important recommendations of the report were,
- There should be full responsible government in India with Dominion status.
- There should be two Houses of Parliament i.e. Senate and House of Representatives.
- The Governor-General should act on the advise of the Executive Council.
- The statute should embody 19 fundamental rights like freedom of speech, expression and religion etc.

End Result of the Report:

The All-Party Convention in 1928, failed to accept the recommendations of the Nehru Report. Jinnah of the Muslim League, did his best to undermine the report. The Congress appreciated the report and insisted that the British Government should accept it before December 21, 1929, otherwise the Congress would declare '*Poorna Swaraj*' as their goal and launch a struggle to achieve it.

THE REVOLUTIONARIES OR THE REVOLUTIONARY TERRORIST MOVEMENT

Hindustani Republic Association and Hindustan Socialist Republic Association:

After the withdrawl of the Non-Cooperation Movement, a new political movement called the Revolutionary Terrorist Movement also emerged along with the Swarajist Movement and the Constructive Programme Movement. The revolutionary movement believed in armed revolution in the country for realising the objectives of free India. In fact, it was the revival of early revolutionary movement. Among the important revolutionaries were Ashfaqulla, B.K. Dutt, Bhagat Singh, Chandra Shekhar Azad, Ram Prasad Bismil and Surya Sen.

The Hindustani Republican Association was formed in October 1924 to organise an armed revolution.

Kakori Conspiracy Case:

On August 25, 1925, few revolutionaries stopped a train near Kakori railway station near Lucknow in Uttar Pradesh and looted the mail van. The revolutionaries were arrested. Four revolutionaries namely Ashfaqulla, Ram Prasad Bismal, Rajendra Lahiri and Thakur Roshan Singh were hanged and many others were given long sentences.

The Hindustan Socialist Republic Association:

The revolutionaries soon came under the influence of socialism. Chandra Shekhar Azad became the President of this association.

Murder of Saunders (December 1918):

A notable activity of H.S.R.A. was the murder of Saunders, the Superintendent of Police at Lahore, who had ordered the brutal lathicharge on the peaceful procession in which, Lala Lajpat Rai had received severe lathi blows that later resulted in his death. The death of Lala Lajpat Rai had greatly enraged the youth of the Punjab.

Bomb in the Central Legislative Assembly (April 8, 1928):

The most dramatic act of the revolutionaries was the throwing of a bomb in the Assembly. Bhagat Singh and B.K. Dutt threw two bombs in the Assembly. The aim was not to kill. The revolutionaries could have escaped easily but they deliberately chose to be arrested as they wanted to make use of the court as a forum for revolutionary propaganda. They started shouting, "Long Live Revolution", "Down with Imperialism" and "Workers of the World, Unite". They also distributed hand bills with the slogan that they have thrown the bomb "In order that the deaf might listen, the noise must be powerful." After their arrest, the revolutionarie gave a historical statement in the court of the Delhi Sessions Judge, "The revolutionaries believe tha deliverance of their country will come through revolution". Bhagat Singh and B.K. Dutt were given li sentences.

The Martyrdom of the Revolutionary Jatindranath Das (September 13, 1929):

The revolutionaries in jail were treated brutally. They went on a hunger strike for two months. Jatin Da died after 63 days of hunger strike. The unique sacrifice of Jatin Das roused the entire nation as never before

Bomb at the Viceroy (1929):

To protest against the death of Jatin Das, Chandra Shekhar Azad made an attempt on the life of the Viceroy of India. The bomb exploded near the Viceroy's special train near Delhi but the Viceroy remained unhurt.

Martyrdom of Several Revolutionaries:

The revolutionaries, including Chandra Shekhar, continued their activities. The government offered a reward of Rs. 10,000 to anyone who could seize him dead or alive. Chandra Shekhar was betrayed and was surrounded by the police as he entered Alfred Park in Allahabad in 1931. He was riddled with bullets and fell dead.

Surya Sen was arrested in February 1933 and soon hanged.

Bhagat Singh, Rajguru and Sukhdev were sentenced to death. Indian leaders pleaded with the Viceroy to condone their death sentences but to no avail. The three revolutionaries were hanged on March 31, 1931. The news of their hanging filled the entire country with great grief. By their heroic sacrifice, and those of several other revolutionaries, they inspired the people of India to work fearlessly and resolutely for the freedom of the country.

Bhagat Singh (1907-31):

Remembered as 'Shahid-i-Azam' Bhagat Singh who belonged to the family of freedom fighters, gave to Indian people, the patriotic cry of *'Inquilab Zindabad'* (Long live the Revolution) which was raised by crores of his countrymen. A product of the D.A.V. College Lahore, a born youth leader, stirred by the execution of Ghadarites in 1915, provoked by the Rowlatt Act, and the Jallianwala Bagh tragedy of 1919, Bhagat Singh became an ardent revolutionary. He and his friends killed Saunders, the notorious police superintendent of Lahore, who was responsible for the lathi charge on Lala Lajpat Rai. He was arrested after he threw a bomb in the Legislative Assembly in 1929. He along with other revolutionaries was tried and hanged in the Lahore Central Jail on March 23, 1931.

Chandra Shekhar Azad (1906-1931):

A great revolutionary, Azad was the son of a Brahman watchman. With almost no formal education, he possessed an undaunted spirit of adventure in the path of nationalism. He took a prominent part in several bomb blast cases including one on Viceroy, Lord Irwin in 1929. As already mentioned, he was betrayed and died in Alfred Park, Allahabad in 1931.

Surya Sen (1894-1934):

A legendary revolutionary of East Bengal, Surya Sen is associated with the capture of Chittagong on April 18, 1930. He organised a group of young revolutionaries into an organisation named the Indian Republic Army. He kept Chittagong 'independent' for four days. Thereafter, he extended his revolutionary activities in other parts of Bengal. Finally, he was arrested and hanged.

EXERCISES

A. Very Short Answer Type Questions

1. List any two main features of India Act, 1919.
2. Mention any two methods used to protest in the Non-Cooperation Movement.
3. Name any four revolutionary leaders who emerged after the withdrawal of the Non-Cooperation Movement.
4. List any four activities under the construction programme.

5. Name any two leaders who belonged to the group of 'Pro-changes'.
6. Name any two activities of the Swarajists.
7. What was the Kakori conspiracy case?
8. Mention any two features of the Nehru Report.

B. Short Answer Type Questions

1. Why was the Rowlatt Act passed? What was the reaction of the people to it?
2. Why did the Khilafat movement start? What was the role of the Indian National Congress in this movement?
3. What was the impact of the Jallianwala Bagh Massacre on Indian politics?
4. Why was the Simon Commission appointed? Why was it boycotted?
5. Write brief notes on the work of any two terrorist revolutionaries.
6. What was Chauri Chaura Incident? What was its effect on the national movement launched by Gandhiji?

C. Long Answer Type/Essay Type Questions

1. What were the factors which gave impetus to the National movement after the First World War?
2. What is the meaning of Dyarchy? Why did this system fail?
3. Examine the main features of the Act of 1919.
4. In what ways were the Non-Cooperation and Khilafat movements a departure from the earlier national movements of the moderate phase? Which of the world events influenced these two movements?

CHAPTER 17

The National Movement (1927-47)

HISTORIC LAHORE SESSION OF THE CONGRESS (1929) AND PURNA SWARAJ (COMPLETE INDEPENDENCE)

Background

There was an uneasiness in the mood of people of India in 1929. A change was bound to come. In the first place there was a revival of revolutionary activity as mentioned earlier. There was also a widespread labour unrest. The death of Jatin Das also gave a fillip to the youth movement and student organisations grew up all over India.

In England, in 1929, the Labour Party came into office, and on the suggestions of Sir John Simon, it authorized Lord Irwin, the Governor General, to make a statement in India regarding the acceptance of Simon's proposal. Lord Irwin's declaration contained the following important statement: "I am authorized, on behalf of his Majesty's Government, to state clearly, that in their judgement, it is implicit in the declaration of 1917 that the natural issue of India's Constitutional progress... is the attainment of Dominion Status." This is what the Nehru Report demanded. In India, the declaration of Lord Irwin was welcomed by all the political parties. But the British Press and both the Conservative and Liberal Parties opposed it in the British Parliament. As the Labour Party, the largest party, did not command absolute majority, nothing could be done. So when Gandhiji, Nehru and others met the Viceroy on December 23, and asked for a definte asurance that the Dominion Status would be granted to India, the Viceroy was unable to give that assurance.

The Congress Session of 1929

A Congress session was immediately held at Lahore on December 29, 1929 in a tense atmoshpere. The choice of Jawaharlal Nehru, an embodiment of youthful enthusiasm for independence, as President of the Session, lent a special glamour and courage to the vast assembled Congressmen. The resolution embodied with a spirit of defiance and determination read: "The Congress declares that the word *Swaraj* in Article I of the Congress Constitution shall mean Complete Independence... and hope that all Congressmen will henceforth devote their exclusive attention to the attainment of Complete Independence for India." The adoption of Independence as the goal of India was hailed with befitting solemnity. As the clock struck midnight between December 31, 1929 and January 1, 1930, Pandit Jawaharlal Nehru came out in a solemn procession to the banks of the Ravi and hoisted the tricolour flag of Indian independence.

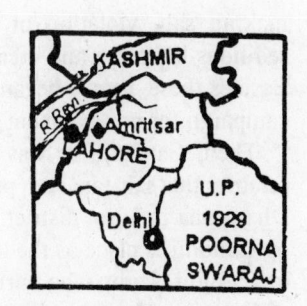

Map 34: **Purna Swaraj Lahore Session**

The new Working Committee of the Congress met on January 2, 1930 and decided the following line of action:

1. The members of the legislatures should resign.

2. The 26th of January should be observed all over India as the *Purna Swaraj* day (day of Complete Independence).

3. A declaration prepared by Gandhiji should be read out on the occasion.

The declaration contained the following important policy:- (1) "The British Government has ruined India economically, politically, culturally and spiritually... We hold it to be a crime against man and God to submit any longer to a rule that has caused this fourfold disaster to our country."

(2) We will withdraw, so far as we can, all voluntary association with the British Government.

(3) We will prepare for Civil Disobedience including non-payment of taxes.

(4) Every Indian was to make a declaration of Complete Independence and take a pledge of loyalty to the Indian National Congress and to the sacred fight for India's liberty.

January 26, 1930 was celebrated as the First Indendence Day all over the country with great enthusiam. The National Flag was unfurled and everyone took the pledge of loyalty to the Congress and to the Freedom Struggle. The Working Committee met again from February 14 -16, and authorised Gandhiji to start Civil Disobedience.

THE DANDI MARCH

The Beginning of the Civil Disobedience Movement

Gandhiji started the Civil Disobedience Movement on March 12, 1930, when he left the Sabarmati Ashram on foot with 78 male inmates of the Ashram to reach Dandi, a village on the sea coast of Gujarat, to disobey the Government and break the salt law by obtaining or making salt without paying the salt tax. The villagers flocked from all sides, sprinkled the roads with water, strewed leaves and sunk on their knees, as the peasant like frail figure, with a lathi in hand walking with his followers passed them. Over 300 village headmen gave up their job. The slow march on foot, from village to village, covering about 350 km, on an averege 12 to 14 km a day, was by itself an automatic propaganda rousing the entire countryside and the whole of India to a realistic sense of the coming struggle. On April 5, Gandhiji reached Dandi. On April 6, he picked up a handful of salt from the sea and defied the salt law as a symbol of India's refusal to live under British laws. It was a signal of countrywide repetition of the same. Where natural conditions did not permit for making salt, violation of other laws were resorted to, like openly reading seditious literature and breaking the Law of Sedition (using words to incite people to rebel against authority). Besides these, people began to cut down timber in Central Provinces and Bombay in defiance of forest laws. A campaign for non-payment of taxes and land revenue started in Gujarat, U.P., and in Bengal.

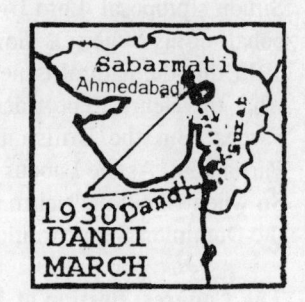

Map 35: **Dandi March**

Then, Gandhiji, as was his usual practice before starting any political agitation, wrote to the Viceroy to remove the salt-tax and prohibition on making salt privately, otherwise he would raid the salt depot of Dharasana in Surat district. But before Gandhiji set out for Dharasana, he was imprisoned. Abbas Tyabji took up Gandhiji's place as the leader of the Salt *Satyagraha* but he was also arrested. Then his place was taken up by Sarojini Naidu, who hurried to Dharasana and directed the raid. On May 21, 2500 volunteers from all parts of Gujarat took part in it. Raids continued day after day, but the most demonstrative raid took place on June 7 with 15,000 volunteers. Everywhere, the volunteers were mercilessly beaten. Mr. Weble Miller, a foreign correspondent of U.S.A. who was an eye witness wrote:

"Suddenly, at a word of command, scores of native police rushed upon the advancing marchers and rained blows on their heads with their steel-shod *lathis*. Not one of the marchers even raised an arm to fend off the blows.... From where I stood, I heard the sickening whacks of the clubs on unprotected skulls... In two or three minutes the ground was quilted with bodies. Great patches of blood widened on their white clothes. The survivors, without breaking ranks silently and doggedly marched on until struck down... When everyone of the first column was knocked down... Then another column formed with the leaders with them to retain their self-control."

This is a graphic picture of the wonderful spirit of self sacrifice and discipline which Gandhiji had instilled into the minds of his devoted followers. The 'Charismatic' influence exerted by Gandhiji could be witnessed everywhere. On April 10, 1930 he made an appeal to the women of India through his paper *Young India* to take up the work of picketing and spinning. The effect was miraculous. Thousands of women responded, even from orthodox and aristocratic families who had never before come out of their seclusion. They worked and offered themselves for arrests and imprisonment. It was a great accomplishment of the Civil Disobedience Movement towards the emancipation of the women of India. The awakening of women redoubled the activites of the men.

There were several examples of brave deeds. In the North-West Frontier Province, the home of the fierce warlike Pathans, the Red-Shirt volunteers, organised by Abdul Ghaffar Khan (better known as Frontier Gandhi) followed, in a non-violent manner, an intense anti-Government movement including non-payment of taxes. The police fired at them with machine-guns at Peshawar. Many were killed but the brave people refused to budge from their activities or to retaliate with violence. Two Garhwali platoons refused to fire on non-violent demonstrators, taking the risk of long-term imprisonment. Rani Gaidilieu, at the age of 13, raised the banner of revolt and suffered 15 years of imprisonment from 1932 to 1947 when Independent India released her.

Government Repression

The Government did not first take the campaign seriously. Many ridiculed the campaign. The *Statesman* wrote: "The Mahatma could go on boiling sea water till Dominion Status was attained." But before a month passed, the Government realised the gravity and struck hard in a ruthless manner. Repressive laws were made to declare the Congress unlawful and to gag the press. There were wholesale arrests packing the jail with about 75 thousand *Satyagrahis*. Most of the leaders, including Jawaharlal Nehru, were in prison. Finally, Gandhiji was arrested on May 4, 1930. The whole country seemed to be in jail. Laws and arrests were just minor parts of their device to terrorise the people. The brutal assaults made, and atrocities committed on unarmed non-violent men and women, make for horrendous reading. Firing, resulting in maiming and deaths of hundreds of people within minutes, looting of property, burning of houses and torturing people through various devices were the daily normal routine. An English lady, Miss Slades, saw how *Satyagrahis* at Dharasana Salt Depot were being treated by the police. She gave details in *Young India* about the injuries inflicted on the *Satyagrahis*: Lathi blows on stomachs, heads and joints, thrust of lathis on delicate parts, dragging wounded men by legs and arms, throwing the wounded into thorn hedges, riding horses over men as they lie or sit in the ground, thrusting pins into the bodies, using very foul language and 'other vile things, too many to relate'.

The Movement tunred out to be the greatest mass struggle so far. Almost all sections of people of the country—men and women, young and old, the workers and the professionals, the Moderates and the Swarajists, students and teachers—participated in varying degrees. Excepting a few Nationalist Muslim leaders, the Muslims keept themselves aloof from the Movement.

The First Round Table Conference (1930-31)

The Report of the Simon Commission was published in June 1930. The continuance of the Civil Disobedience Movement and the British brutal repression made the British Labour Government quite uneasy and worried. The First Round Table Conference presided over by Mr Ramsay Macdonald, the Labour Prime

Minsiter, and attended by 16 members from the British parties, six from British Indian states and 57 from British India discussed the Report of the Simon Commission and the proposals of constitutional reforms. The prominent leaders of the Muslim League and the Hindu Mahasabha were there but the Congress did not attend as the Civil Disobedience Movement was on. The conference adjourned on January 19, 1931 without any agreement on basic issues. It failed to serve any purpose in the absence of the Congress.

The Gandhi-Irwin Pact (January 1931)

While winding up the First Round Table Conference, the British Prime Minister declared that "Steps would be taken to enlist the cooperation of those sections of public opinion which had held aloof from the Conference." It was felt that the British Government would have to hold consultations with the Congress. Lord Irwin, the Viceroy of India appealed to the people of India to consider the statement made by the Prime Minister of Britain. He also released the Congress leaders from jail. Discussions between the Viceroy and Gandhiji continued for 15 days and Gandhi-Irwin Pact was signed on March 5, 1931.

Following were the provisions of the Pact:
(1) Civil Disobedience to be withdrawn.
(2) Political prisoners to be released.
(3) Repressive Ordinances to be withdrawn.
(4) Coastal people to be allowed to make a limited quantity of salt for personal use.
(5) All Government employees who had resigned in the wake of the Civil Disobedience Movement to be reinstated if the posts were vacant.
(6) Congress to reconsider proposal of giving responsibility for certain functions.

The Karachi Session of Congress and the Second Round Table Conference (1931)

The Karachi Session of the Congress paved the way for the Second Round Table Conference by ratifying the Gandhi-Irwin Pact. The Congress also decided to discontinue the Civil Disobedience Movement for the time being.

Government released all political prisoners as agreed to in the Gandhi-Irwin Pact.

Gandhiji went to England to attend the Second Round Table Conference (September 7-December1). The British Government declined to accept the nationalist demand for freedom on the basis of immediate grant of Dominion Status for India. Further, no agreement was reached between Indians regarding communal questions.

Revival of Civil Disobedience Movement (1932)

After the failure of talks, Gandhiji revived the Civil Disobedience Movement. The Government again resorted to repression and issued four ordinances to crush the movement. The Ordianances were (i) The Emergency Power Ordinance (ii) The Unlawful Instigation Ordinance (iii) Unlawful Association Ordinance (iv) Prevention of Molestation and Boycott Ordinance. Within a short time, the number of Ordinances reached 13, covering every activity of national life. The Congress was declared illegal. Swadeshi concerns were also declared illegal. All leading Congress leaders were put behind bars. Lathi Charges on peaceful demonstrations became the order of the day. All various devices to torture and terrorise the Indian masses, as described earlier, were used with all its ferocity. Even women were beaten, molested and dishonoured. Punitive and collective fines on villages and seizures of village land and property were ways to terrify the rural masses.

Prime Minister's Communal Award and Poona Pact (1932)

While the Civil Disobedience Movement was continuing in full swing, in spite of the fury of repression and the imprisonment of about 90 thousand men and women along with their leaders, the Prime Minister announced his 'Communal Award' on August 16, 1932, as he had been authorised earlier by the Second Round Table Conference to decide the matter of communal representation. The 'Communal Award' was a scheme granting separate electorates for different communities like Muslims, Sikhs, Anglo-Indians, etc. But the scheme also gifted separate electorates for the depressed classes to elect their representatives for the 75 reserved seats. This was done by dividing the Hindus into Depressed classes and Non-Depressed Classes to create disunity. It provoked Gandhiji who was then in Yervada prison in Poona. He undertook a fast on September 20. A settlement was arrived at only when or Ambedkar agreed to have a joint electorate but on condition that the reserved seats of the Depressed classes were doubled. This was known as the 'Poona Pact.'

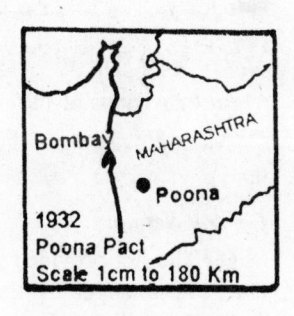

Map 36: **Poona Pact**

This settlement, hit hard the caste Hindus but it maintained the integrity of the Hindu Community. The Government modified the Constitution accordingly and Gandhiji broke his fast on April 26, after 7 days. In the same jail, once again he undertook a fast in support of his campaign for the untouchables (the Harijans). The Government released him on August 4 and he got intensely busy in Harijan Welfare work. In respect to the appeal made by Gandhiji, temples and public wells throughout India began to be thrown open to the Untouchables.

Third Round Table Conference (1932)

The British Government called the Third Round Table Conference which lasted from November 17 to December 24, 1934, to review the political situation and to take up constitutional reforms in India. The Congress did not participate in the Conference. There was less enthusiasm among the members as regards a satisfactory settlement better than what was the case a year before.

Withdrawal of the Civil Disobedience Movement (1934)

Two factors namely the Communal Award and the repressive measures adopted by the Government dampened the spirit of the leaders of the Congress and the Civil Disobedience Movement gradually waned. The Congress officially suspended the movement in May 1933 and started Individual Civil Disobedience Movement from August 1, 1933. Gandhiji's prestige suffered to some extent and he temporarily withdrew from active politics. Several important leaders of the Congress felt despair.

By the beginning of 1934, both the Individual and Mass Civil Disobedience was tailing off. The Individual Civil Disobedience was almost dead. Those who were released from the jail were too tired to face another conviction; so, slowly and silently it faded away, unnoticed, though in some places it dragged on up to May 1934.

THE GOVERNMENT OF INDIA ACT (1935)

Background

In August 1935, the long process of administrative and constitutional reforms ended with the passing of the Government of India Act, 1935. It took eight long years. The reforms were proposed in 1927, debated in the three Round Table Conferences, drafted and circulated in the form of a 'White Paper' (report about the Government's policy) and thoroughly discussed by a Joint Select Committee of the British Parliament. The final Act, 1935, emerged after intense debate in the British Parliament. The Indian National Congress was not consulted regarding the various provisions of the Act. It provided an all-India federation and provincial autonomy. The scheme of federation never materialised due to opposition of the Congress and the Indian princes.

Main Provisions of the Act

Main provisions of the Act may be broadly classified under two heads (i) Central Set-up (ii) Provincial Set-up.

Central Set up:

(1) The Act provided for an All India Federation—Federation of the Provinces, under the direct control of the Government called the British India, and the Princely States, that is, states under the Indian rulers (2) The Federal Legislature was to consist of two Houses ie. the Upper House and the Federal Assembly (3) The Upper House was to have 156 members from British India and not more than 164 from the Princely States (4) The Federal Assembly was to have 250 members from British India and 125 from the Princely States (5) The Governor-General was to have a Council of Ministers, not more than ten (6) The Governor-General was to have exclusive power in subjects relating to Defence, External Affairs etc. (7) The Governor-General was given wide discretionary powers.

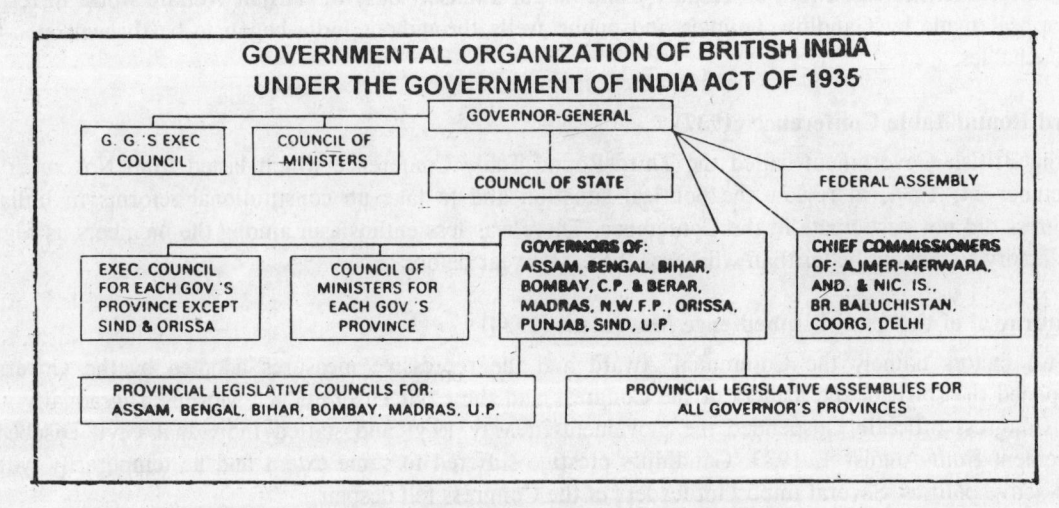

```
GOVERNMENTAL ORGANIZATION OF BRITISH INDIA
UNDER THE GOVERNMENT OF INDIA ACT OF 1935

                           GOVERNOR-GENERAL
  G. G.'S EXEC     COUNCIL OF
  COUNCIL          MINISTERS
                           COUNCIL OF STATE        FEDERAL ASSEMBLY

  EXEC. COUNCIL    COUNCIL OF      GOVERNORS OF:           CHIEF COMMISSIONERS
  FOR EACH GOV.'S  MINISTERS FOR   ASSAM, BENGAL, BIHAR,   OF: AJMER-MERWARA,
  PROVINCE EXCEPT  EACH GOV.'S     BOMBAY, C.P. & BERAR,   AND. & NIC. IS.,
  SIND & ORISSA    PROVINCE        MADRAS, N.W.F.P., ORISSA, BR. BALUCHISTAN,
                                   PUNJAB, SIND, U.P.      COORG, DELHI

  PROVINCIAL LEGISLATIVE COUNCILS FOR:        PROVINCIAL LEGISLATIVE ASSEMBLIES FOR
  ASSAM, BENGAL, BIHAR, BOMBAY, MADRAS, U.P.  ALL GOVERNOR'S PROVINCES
```

Chart 5: **Government of India Act of 1935**

Provincial Set-up:

(1) The system of Dyarchy introduced in the provinces under the 1919 Act was abolished (2) The total number of provinces was now to be 11 with the creation of two new provinces of Sind and Orissa (3) Burma was separated from India and was to be no more a part of India (4) Complete provincial autonomy was to be granted (5) The Ministers were to be responsible to the Legislature (6) The Governor was to have several discretionary powers.

Critical Review of the Reforms

(1) The Federal provisions did not come into operation (2) The Muslim League was not satisfied as it sought more powers for the provinces and fixed number of Ministerships for the Muslims (3) The Congress felt that the reforms did not go much further as provided in the 1919 Act (4) Only 14% of the total population of British India was given the right to vote (5) Defence and Foreign Affairs were outside the control of the

The National Movement (1927-47)

Central legislature (6) The Governor General and the Governors were given special powers to veto the Ministers (7) The Governor-General and the Governors were to be responsible to the British Government only (8) The Governors retained full control over the civil service and the police (9) Foreign rule was to continue as before. Only a few popularly elected ministers were to be added to the British administrative structure in India (10) The Federal part was never introduced (11) The position assigned to the Council of Ministers at the Centre was ornamental.

Criticism and comments against the provisions came from every side. Jawaharlal Nehru described the new set up as a "machine with strong brakes and no engine." Another called it a "grim joke which the joker (The British Government) may enjoy but not those Indians at whose expense the joke is cracked.' In the words of M.A. Jinnah, the scheme of 1935 is "thoroughly rotten, fundamentally bad and totally unacceptable."

The Provincial Autonomy came into operation from April 1937. On the assurance of the Provincial Governors, that they would not ordinarily interfere with the work of Ministers, the Congress decided to work the provincial part of the new constitution.

Formation of Congress Ministries

Congress Victory in Elections:

Elections to the provincial assemblies under the provisions of 1935 Act were held in 1937 and in spite of the fact that the Congress had criticised it, it contested the elections. It formed its own ministries in seven provinces namely Madras, Bombay, Bihar, Orissa, C.P., U.P. and North West Frontier. It formed coalition ministries in Assam and Sind. In the Punjab, the Unionist Party formed the ministry and in Bengal, the Muslim League and the Krashak Praja Party formed a coalition ministry.

The Congress did extremely well in the elections. The Muslim League failed to make its impact even in the Muslim constituencies.

Functioning of the Congress Ministries:

(1) Ministers set their own good examples:

Important features of the working of the Congress Ministers were as under: (i) They tried to cut all red tapism and bureaucratic delays and attended to people's problems without delay (ii) The Ministers worked on nominal salaries (Rs. 500 per month), allowances and perks etc. (iii) They tried to set up high standard of honest work done by Ministries and public morality.

(2) Work done by Ministries:

The Congress Ministries took the following measures for winning the cooperation of the people in the task of national reconstruction in different areas:

(i) Political prisoners were released.
(ii) Restrictions on the press were removed.
(iii) Trade union activities were allowed.
(iv) Powers of the police were curbed.
(v) Agrarian legislation was passed to provide for tenancy rights to cultivators, security of tenure, rent reduction, and protection to the peasant-debtors.
(vi) Introduction of prohibition in selected areas.
(vii) Several measures for the uplift of the Harijans were taken.
(viii) Greater attention was paid to primary, secondary and higher education.
(ix) Basic education was popularised.
(x) Technical education was encouraged.
(xi) Support was given to Khadi and other village industries.
(xii) Modern industries were encouraged.
(xiii) Communal riots were firmly handled.

The people regarded the Congress ruled provinces as "islands of self rule where they could breathe freely and stand upright with dignity."

Jinnah's attack on Congress Ministries:

The result of the elections widened the rift between the Congress and the League. At that time Jinnah openly declared, "Muslims can expect neither justice nor fairplay under the Congress Government." The majority of the Muslims accepted this view and began to support the Muslim League. Jinnah suddenly acquired a new personal authority. He now started to complain of the unfair treatment of the Muslims in the Congress provinces and circulated rumours of 'atrocities' which were never proved. When the Congress Ministers resigned in November 1939, Jinnah heaved a sigh of relief and asked the Muslim League to observe a day of deliverance. As the Congress was out of power throughout the war, the British Government had no alternative but to pamper the Muslim League so that the Muslim community may not weaken their war efforts. This also encouraged the Muslims and widened the rift between the League and the Congress.

Forward Bloc:

About this time there was a split in the Congress camp. The Rightists led by Rajaji and Vallabhbhai Patel were not yet prepared to organise the forces of national life for the overthrow of the British Government in India. The Leftists were led by Subhas Bose, who stood for a bold policy and thought that the time was ripe for an all-out national resistance against the foreign rule. The differences between the Rightists and Leftists came to a head over the election of the President of the next session of the Congress, to be held in Tripuri in the Central Provinces in March 1939. Never since 1920 was there any conflict of views regarding the choice of President, for it depended on the choice of the Congress leaders. Subhas Bose sought for re-elections for Presidentship but the rightists set up Dr. Pattabhai Sivaramaya as a rival candidate. Bose won the election but was forced out of office by the right-wingers who prevented him from securing a favourable Working Committee. Subhas Bose then formed a new group known as the Forward Bloc.

Beginning of the Second World War and the Resignation of Congress Ministries:

The Second World War broke out in 1939 and the British Government declared war against Germany on September 3, 1939. The Viceroy of India proclaimed that India too, was at war with Germany. While announcing this, he did not consult the Central Assembly and the representatives of the people. This was resented, by the Congress and it registered a strong protest against the policy of the British rulers. The Congress demanded that it would help the war efforts of the Government only if India was declared an independent country after the end of the war, and in this regard it wanted a firm declaration from the British Government. Negotiations between the Congress and the Government failed. Therefore the Congress Ministries resigned in October-November 1939. The resignation of the Congress Ministries as already stated was hailed by the Muslim League.

LIMITED INDIVIDUAL SATYAGRAHA (1940)

The All India Congress made several offers to cooperate with the British rulers subject to acceptance of their demand of complete freedom to India after the end of the war but the British rulers gave no assurance. On the contrary, they tried to put the Muslims and other minorities and also the Princes against the Congress. The Ramgarh Session of the Congress held in March 1940, presided over by Maulana Abul Kalam Azad reiterated, "Nothing short of complete independence can be accepted by the people of India." It also contemplated the Civil Disobedience campaign under the leadership of Gandhiji. But Gandhiji was now in favour of Individual *Satyagraha* and not mass *Satyagraha,* because he felt that Mass Civil Disobedience at a time when Britain was engaged in a life and death struggle would not be appropriate, but it was necessary to impress that India was not interested in the war. So, in Octber 17, 1940 Gandhiji started the individual/limited Satyagraha. Gandhiji, in a letter to the Viceroy of India, explained the aim of this movement in these words, "The Congress is as much opposed to Victory for Nazism as any Britisher can be... And since you and the Secretary of State for India have declared that the whole of India is voluntarily helping the war efforts, it becomes necessary to make clear that the vast majority of the people of India are not interested in it. They make no distinction between Nazism and the double autocracy that rules India".

Vinoba Bhave was the first leader to offer Satyagraha. Thousands were arrested. But it created little enthusiam. Gandhiji suspended it on December 17, 1940.

CRIPPS MISSION (1942)

Some important events changed entirely the nature and dimension of the war. Nazi Germany, after capturing Poland, Belgium, Holland, Norway etc, attacked the Soviet Union on June 22, 1941. In December 1941, Japan also joined war on the side of Germany and Italy and launched a surprise attack on the American fleet at Pearl Harbour. It soon overran the Philippines, Indo-China, Indonesia, Malaya and Burma. It also occupied Rangoon and thus the war was on India's doorstep. England itself was under severe attack. It was subjected to constant bombing by waves and waves of German planes. The I.N.A., under Subhas Chandra Bose, was rising to its full height. The situation was becoming very desparate for the British Government. Now they thought of securing the cooperation of Indians in their war efforts. Sir Stafford Cripps, a Cabinet Minister was sent to India with the following main proposals:

(i) India to have Dominion Status after the War.
(ii) An elected body to be set up after the war to frame a new constitution of India.
(iii) Any province of India to have the right to reject that constitution and to have its own constitution if so desired.
(iv) The princely states to be represented in proportion to their population.

The Cripps proposals were rejected by almost all sections of the society. The Congress also rejected these proposals for it was worse than the partition of India and conceding Pakistan by the backdoor. It would mean like tearing India into pieces, each piece representing religions, majority power, vested-interest lobby or autocratic princely rule. Muslims, though happy, rejected it as the proposal of Pakistan was not conceded in that particular form of demand. Other parties like the Sikhs, the Hindu Mahasabha also rejected it.

QUIT INDIA MOVEMENT (1942)

Background

The failure of Cripps Mission made a few things very clear to the Congress leaders. The Cripps Mission was not a genuine effort of Britain towards granting even Dominion Status, when India was demanding Complete Independence. It was perhaps the critical stage of the War and the American pressure that needed some 'show' to assuage the national sentiments. It was also transparently visible that the Muslim League was being pampered with assurances to foment communal discord and to widen the Hindu-Muslim divide with the aim to weaken the nationalist movement, and if ever India was to be left at its fate, it would be a truncated and chaotic India. Churchill, Prime Minister of Britain, had bluntly said "No, Sir" to a question asked in the Parliament, whether the famous Atlantic Charter, promising the rights of man—liberty, equality and fraternity to be enforced throughtout the world—will

Map 37: **Wardha 1942 Quit India Resolution**

be applicable also to India. British mind was very clear: How could they leave India, the largest and wealthiest colony of the empire conquered with so much arduous skill and cleverness and ruled with so much prestige and power and for so long?

There was also a change in the attitude of Gandhiji. He was hitherto definitely opposed to any mass movement during the World War, but now he again started thinking over it. This was his novel idea of asking the British to quit. At this time the advance of Japan towards India was viewed with great concern. Even then, he wrote in *Harijan*, "Whatever the consequences therefore, to India, her real safety, and Britain's too, lies in orderly and timely British withdrawl from India." (April, 26). Gandhiji once more assumed the leadership of the Congress which he had relinquihed during India's negotiations with Cripps.

The circumstances that prevailed then appear to exhaust the patience of Gandhiji and all the people. It will be clear from his ideas expressed in his paper *Harijan:* "The time has come during the war, not after it, for the British and the Indians to be reconciled to complete separation from each other... The presence of the British in India is an invitation to Japan to invade India. This withdrawl removes the bait... free India will be better able to cope with the invasion". (May 10). "Leave India in God's hands, in modern parlance, to anarchy, and that anarchy may lead to internecine warfare for a time... from these a true India will rise in place of the false one we see." (May 24). Gandhiji's changed attitude to Britain also brought about a change in his method about a mass movement, "I waited and waited until the country should develop the non-violent strength necessary to throw off the foreign yoke. But my attitude has now undergone a change. I feel I cannot afford to wait... That is why I have decided that even at certain risks, which are obviousy involved, I must ask the people to resist the slavery." All these go to show how circumstances change men, their ideas, strengthen their invincible determinations and transform helplessness into indomitable courage to fight the mightiest without arms, no matter what risks, what fate awaits them.

Quit India Resolution

On July 14, 1942 the Congress Working Committee met at Wardha and passed a resolution known as the 'Quit India' resolution. It renewed the demand that 'British rule in India must end immediately'. After the resolution was passed, Gandhiji said, "There is no room left in the proposal for withdrawl or negotiation. There is no question of one more chance. After all, it is an open rebellion."

The Working Committee referred its resolutions to the All India Congress Committee (A.I.C.C.) which met at Bombay on August 7, 1942. The A.I.C.C., after discussing the resolution on 7th and 8th, passed it with an overwhelming majority. It emphasized the demand for the withdrawl of the British power from India. It sanctioned the non-violent mass struggle under the leadership of Gandhiji. It also instructed, "A time may come when it may not be possible to issue instructions... When this happens, every man or woman who is participating in this movement must function for himself or herself, within the four corners of the general instructions issued." The Resolution declared, "The immediate ending of British rule in India is an urgent necessity, both for the sake of India and for the success of the United Nations... A free India will assure this success by throwing all her great resources in the struggle for freedom and against the aggression of Nazism, Fascism and Imperialism."

Do or Die Mantra:

Addressing the Congress delegates on the night of August 8, Gandhiji declared, "I, therefore, want freedom immediately, this very night, before dawn, if it can be had... Fraud and untruth today are stalking the world... You may take it from me that I am not going to be satisfied with anything short of complete freedom... Here is a *mantra,* a short one, that I give you. You may imprint it in your hearts and let every breath of yours give expression to it. The *mantra* is: "Do or Die". We shall either free India or die in the attempt; we shall not live to see the perpetuation of our slavery."

The National Movement (1927-47)

The Movement

No Government faced with an impending invasion from Japan would tolerate the growth of a rebellion inside the country. The Government was closely following the activities and the meetings of the Congress. The A.I.C.C. meeting terminated late at night on August 8. Before the next day dawned, Gandhiji, Azad and all other important leaders of the Congress were arrested. Within a week almost everyone who mattered in the Congress was in jail. All A.I.C.C. and all the Provincial Congress Committees were declared unlawful. The news of the arrest of Gandhiji and other Congress leaders was immediately followed by non-violent popular demonstrations like *hartals* and processions, but when the Government resorted to firing to disperse processions, it led to violence on the part of the people. The official version gives an idea of the nature of the disturbances.

"It was from August 11 that the situation began to deteriorate rapidly. Apart from the *hartals* and protest meetings, outbreaks of mob violence, arson, murder and sabotage took place, and in almost all cases they were directed either against communications of all kinds (including railways, posts and telegraphs), or against the police. Moreover, these outbreaks started almost simultaneously in widely separated areas, in the provinces of Madras, Bombay, Bihar and also in the Central and United Provinces. ...The position was at one time extremely serious in the whole of Bihar and in the eastern part of U.P...Assam, Orissa, the Punjab and the N.W.F.P. remained free from serious trouble... and there was comparatively little disorder in Sindh... 104 railway stations were attacked and damaged, 15 being burnt down... over 425 cases of sabotage to telephone and telegraph wires were recorded... 119 post offices were destroyed."

In several parts of Andhra, Bengal, Bihar, Maharashtra, Orissa and Tamil Nadu, the British authorities disappeared for a while. Revolutionaries set up parallel governments in some areas such as Ballia in Uttar Pradesh, Tamluk in Midnapore district of Bengal and Satara district of Bombay. The students, peasants and workers were in the forefront of the struggle. The bureaucracy and the upper class remained loyal to the government.

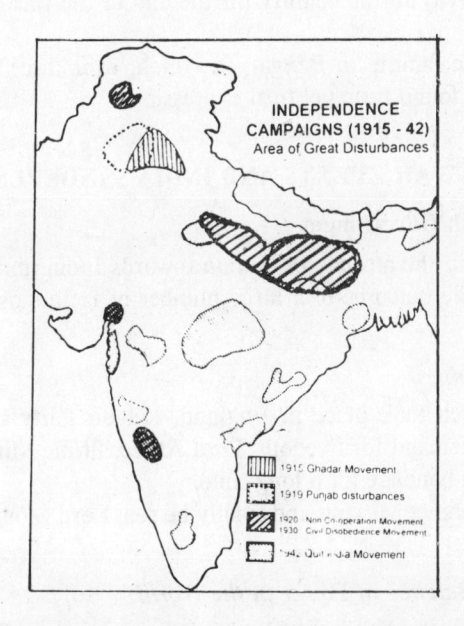

Map 38: **Independence Campaigns, Movements, Places of Disturbances**

The Repression

The repression of the Government knew no bounds. The police and military reigned supreme. The demonstrators were even bombed from the air. Churchill, the then British Prime Minister stated in the House of Commons (September 10, 1942), "The disturbances were crushed with all the weight of the government." K.C. Neogy, a member of the Central Assembly, listed the charges against the administration as "general pillage and arson and wanton damage to property by the police and the military, random shooting on innocent persons when hooligans had already left, assault or shooting of non-violent crowds, whipping and official indignities on all and sundry." The number of the people killed was officially estimated as 1,028, while the popular estimate was about 25 thousand. Jawaharlal Nehru commented, "Perhaps 10 thousand may be nearer the mark."

The movement gained momentum after the escape of Jayaprakash Narayan and his colleagues from Hazaribagh jail in October 1942, when efforts were made to co-ordinate the activities in all the states with the help of Aruna Asaf Ali, Achyut Patwardhan and Dr. Ram Manohar Lohia by remaining underground.

The violent acts in the 1942 movement were really due to the fact that whatever might have been its original character, the movement merged itself into the revolutionary movement which was always an active political force running on a parallel line with the non-violent policy of Gandhiji.

Impact of the Movement

Though the 1942 movement was practically crushed in less than a month and finally collapsed within two months, it would be a mistake to consider it a failure. The violent mass upsurge clearly signalled that freedom's battle in India had begun in right earnest. The readiness to suffer and sacrifice everything for the freedom of the motherland displayed by a very large number of people and responded by the vast country from the Himalayas to Kanyakumari, showed and proved, India's grim determination to free herself from the chains of British slavery. But out of these failures, success came in less than five years.

There was little political activity in the country till the end of the war as all the prominent leaders of the national movment were in jail.

In 1943, there was a terrible famine in Bengal, in which, over three million people died of starvation. However people's anger on this found little political expression.

POST-WAR EVENTS AND INDIA'S INDEPENDENCE

Changed Attitude of the British Government

There was a radical change in the attitude of Britian towards India immediately after the war came to an end. This attitude, which was the outcome of a large number of factors as given below, went a long way in granting independence to India.

1. Labour Government in Britain:

In the general elections which took place in England, Labour Party came to power. Labour Party was already sympathetic to India's demand for freedom. Lord Attlee, Prime Minister, came to the conclusion that England could not keep India in bondage for a long time.

To begin with, he sent the Cabinet Mission and finally he sent Lord Mountbatten to complete the process of transfer of power in India.

2. Change in the Equation of Balance of Power in the World:

After the war, the U.S.A. and the USSR emerged as the big powers. Britain's domineering posture was subdued. Both U.S.A. and USSR supported India's demand for freedom.

3. Shattered Economic and Military Power of Britain:

The economy of great Britain was almost exhausted. The Englishmen had too many problems to face at home. The military strength had also been reduced.

4. Loss of Confidence in Indian Forces:

The British Government had so far depended on Indian forces. The I.N.A. factor caused erosion in the loyalty of the Indian army. There were several revolts in the Royal Indian Navy and Air Force at Bombay, Calcutta and Karachi.

5. I.N.A. Trial:

After the end of the war, the British authorities decided to put on trial in the Red Fort at Delhi, Shah Nawaz Khan, Gurdial Singh Dhillon and Prem Sehgal, officers who joined the I.N.A. deserting the Indian Army. The people of India, who had welcomed them as national heroes, felt very indignant and angry when they were branded as 'traitors' by the British authorities. After their release, these leaders toured all over India and they were greeted with cries of 'Jai Hind'.

6. Labour Unrest all Over the Country:

There was hardly an industry in India in which there was no large scale labour unrest. Peasant movements also acquired a fresh thrust after 1945.

7. Freedom Struggle in Princely States:

There was popular upsurge in several princely states, such as Hyderabad, Travancore and Kashmir.

8. World Opinion in Favour of Freedom:

India's cause of freedom was advocated by a large number of distinguished persons in the world. The Indian point was put forward before the conference at San Francisco which met to finalise the charter of the United Nations.

9. Determination of the People of India:

The Quit India Movement of 1942 and the deeds of the INA had revealed the heroism and determination of the people of India.

The Cabinet Mission (May 16, 1946)

As earlier stated, the Labour Government in England was quite considerate to India's demands. They, therefore, sent a Cabinet Mission to India to find out ways and means by which Indians would decide their future. The Mission consisted of Lord Pethic Lawrence, the Secretary of State for India, Sir Stafford Cripps, President of the Board of Trade and A.V. Alexander, First Lord of the Admiralty. Prolonged discussions took place between the members of the Mission, the Muslim League and the leaders of the Congress already released at the end of the war. The Mission announced the following scheme with the approval of the British Government.

(1) Union of India embracing both British India and the Princely states.
(2) Immediate arrangements for drafting the future constitution of India.
(3) Rejection of Muslim League's demand for Pakistan.
(4) The Union of India to deal only with Foreign Affairs, Defence and Communication.
(5) The provinces to form regional groups and each group to determine the subjects to be taken in common.
(6) Group A to have Hindu majority provinces of Madras, Bombay, United Province, (U.P.) Central Province (C.P.) and Orissa. Group B to have Muslim majority provinces of Punjab, North West Frontier Province (N.W.F.P) and Sind. Group C to have again Muslim majority provinces comprising Bengal and Assam.

To Group A were added the Chief Commissionerships of Delhi, Ajmer, Marwara and Coorg and to Group B British Baluchistan.
(7) Each province left free to come out of the group after elections under the new constitution.
(8) The Constituent Assembly to have 398 members, 292 to be elected from Provinces, 4 from Chief Commissioner's Provinces, 93 from the Princely states and the rest to be nominated.
(9) An Interim Government to be formed at the Centre with 14 members.
(10) Communal representation to include Muslims and Sikhs.
(11) After the attainment of independence, the Indian Government free to decide whether to remain in the British Commonwealth or not.

Direct Action by the Muslim League:

Negotiations between the Congress and the Muslim League began for the formation of the Interim Government. Jinnah of the Muslim League insisted on parity between the Congress and the League. The Muslim League, thereupon called for a Direct Action Day, causing bloodshed in several parts of India.

Interim Government:

Lord Wavell, the Viceroy of India, invited Pandit Jawaharlal Nehru, the President of the Indian National Congress to form the Interim Government. Jawaharlal Nehru's Government took office on September 2, 1946. After initial hesitation, the Muslim League joined the Interim Government on October 13, 1946. The Interim Government remained in office till the partition of India in August, 1947. The Muslim League created all sorts of trouble in the smooth working of the Interim Government as it had set its eyes on the formation of Pakistan.

The Constituent Assembly:

Elections to the Constituent Assembly were held in July 1946. The Constituent Assembly met for the first time in New Delhi on December 9, 1946. The Muslim League did not participate in its deliberations.

The Mountbatten Plan (June 3, 1947)

The British Minister, Attlee, declared in February 1947 that the British Government would leave India before June 1948. He had observed, "The present state of uncertainty is fraught with danger and cannot be indefinitely prolonged. His Majesty's Government wishes to make it clear that it is their definite intention to effect the transfer of power to responsible Indian hands by June 1948."

In March 1947, Lord Mountbatten replaced Lord Wavell as Viceroy of India. His talks with the Indian leaders convinced him that partition of India was the only viable solution and he therefore put forward his plan on June 3, 1947, in which he suggested the partition of India. The scheme was accepted both by the Congress and the Muslim League.

It may be observed that the Congress leaders in the beginning were averse to the partition of India but gradually they began to reconcile with the situation and ultimately accepted the Mountbatten Plan.

The Plan provided for.
(1) Division of India into two Dominions i.e. India and Pakistan.
(2) Partition of Punjab and Bengal on the basis of a Boundary Commission headed by Sir Cyrill Radcliff.
(3) Referendums in N.W.F.P. and Baluchistan.

Indian Independence Act (July 18, 1947) and Achievement of Independence

On the basis of the Mountbatten Plan, a Bill was introduced in the British Parliament on July 5, 1947 which was passed in both the Houses and it became an Act on July 18 to become operative on August 15, 1947. The Act contained the following main provisions:
(1) India to be partiontioned and the two Dominions of India and Pakistan to be established.

(2) The British Government to have no control over the affairs of the Dominions.
(3) The Legislatures of the two Dominions to have full powers to make laws.
(4) All treaties and agreements entered upon by the Princely states to lapse.
(5) Both the Dominions to have the full powers and rights to leave the British commonwealth of Nations, if they so desired.

Following position emerged after the implementation of the Independence Act:

A. Territories of India:

The following provinces were included (1) East Punjab (2) United Provinces (3) Bihar (4) West Bengal (5) Orissa (6) Bombay (7) Madras (8) Central Provinces (9) Assam exclusive of Distt. Sylhat (10) Madras.

B. Territories of Pakistan:

The following provinces were included (1) West Punjab (2) N.W.F.P. (3) Sind (4) East Bengal (5) Sylhat District of Assam.

Princely States:

A vast majority of Princely states joined India, only a few adjoining states joined Pakistan.

On 15th August 1947, Lord Mountbatten became the Governor General of Indian Dominion, and Jinnah became the Governor General of the Pakistan Dominion. Pt. Nehru was appointed the Prime Minister of India and Liaquat Ali Khan of Pakistan. Neither the British Government nor the British Cabinet were to have any authority over Indian administration. The new system was brought into operation at midnight on August 14-15.

Immediate Problems Facing India

Immediate problems facing India on becoming independent were (1) Rehabilitation of the displaced persons (2) Integration of princely states (3) Strengthening relations with Pakistan (4) Framing constitution of India.

Rehabilitation of Displaced Persons:

Country was faced with the unprecedented influx of refugees (displaced persons) particulary in the Punjab which had been partiontioned along with Bengal. Large scale killings also took place in East Punjab as well as West Punjab. By November, about 8 million displaced persons had crossed the frontier— Muslims going westwards into Pakistan and Hindus and Sikhs migrating eastward into India. The displaced persons had to be provided with immediate relief, business opportunities and jobs. Their rehabilitation was a huge task. Displaced persons were also put up into relief camps. University examinations were suspended for sometime and students also were put on relief work. The Government of India and the people of India extended all possible help to them. Fortunately, the problem was solved in a very satisfactory way. The displaced persons showed courage, patience, and enterprise.

Integration of Princely States:

At the time of independence, there were 562 Princely states in India. The Indian Independence Act of 1947 left them free to join India or Pakistan. Sardar Patel popularly called the 'Iron Man of India' was the Minister of Home and State Affairs of India. Just after Independence, he was able to persuade all the big and small states to accede to the Indian Union with the exception of Junagadh, Hyderabad and Jammu & Kashmir. Junagadh, a predominantly Hindu state in Saurashtra, was ruled by a Muslim Nawab. The Nawab announced his intention to join Pakistan though this state did not have any frontier with Pakistan. India sent its forces and the Nawab fled to Pakistan and the state was merged with India after a referendum.

The Muslim Nizam of Hyderabad, a predominantly Hindu state, surrounded by India, was determined to stay independent. The Hindu population rose in revolt against Nizam's decision. The Nizam tried to suppress the agitation of the people for the merger with India. Having failed to persuade him, the Government of India took recourse to police action which resulted in the accession of the state to India.

The issue of Kashmir proved to be very complex and thorny. Tribesmen from Pakistan invaded Kashmir and began to march towards Srinagar. The Hindu ruler signed the Instrument of Accession on October 26, 1947. The Government of India tried to liberate the state from the invaders. Pakistani troops joined the invaders in the disguise of volunteers. After the 1957 elections, the representative government of Jammu & Kashmir voted for integration with India.

Relations with Pakistan:

Pakistan tried to take Kashmir forcibly in September 1947 and succeeded in cutting off some areas of the state. The dispute was referred to the UNO and there was a cease fire in January 1948.

Framing of the Constitution of India:

The work of framing the constitution was in progress when India became independent. The constitution Assembly had first met in December 1948. It completed its work on November 26, 1949. The constitution came into force on January 26, 1950 and India became a Sovereign Democratic Republic. First General Elections under the Constitution were held in 1951.

Merger of Areas Under the Domination of France and Portugal:

Apart from Princely states, there were small territories owned by the French and Portuguese imperialists. The French had five territories—Chandernagar, Pondicherry, Karaikel, Yanam and Mahe. By 1954, all these colonies became an integral part of India. Portugal had five colonies namely Goa, Daman, Diu, Dadra and Nagar Haveli. Dadra and Nagar Haveli were liberated on August 2, 1954. Goa was liberated on December 16, 1961 when an armed expedition defeated the Portuguese army in Goa. Daman and Diu were simultaneously liberated.

Prominent Leaders of the Freedom Struggle of the Last Phase

Mohan Das Karam Chand Gandhi (Karam Chand father of Mohan Das) (1869-1948)

Popularly known as *Bapuji* out of love and respect, *Mahatma,* on account of saintly virtues of simplicity, truth and non-violence and Father of the Nation for creating the nation, Gandhiji defied the might of the British empire through his weapon of Satyagraha. He started his political life in South Africa through several Satyagrahas.

Important events and movements with which he was associated have already found mention at the appropriate places. A recapitulatory listing follows:

(1) Champaran Satyagraha (II) (1917) (2) Ahmedabad Mill Strike (1918) (3) Satyagraha of peasants in Kaira district (1918) (4) Non-Cooperation Movement (1920) (5) President of the Indian National Congress (1924) (6) Civil Disobedience Movement (1929) (7) Dandi March (1930) (8) Gandhi Irwin Pact (1931) (9) Quit India Movement (1942) (10) Pilgrimage to Noakhali (West Bengal) to check Hindu Muslim riots (1946) (11) Fasts for purification and political issues (1924, 1932, 1933, 1934 and 1947).

Gandhiji made the national struggle a mass movement in which all sections of population including children, students and women participated.

Gandhiji's General Ideas and Philosophy Underlying Satyagraha:

The word *Satyagraha* is a compound of two words- *satya* (truth) and *agraha* (holding fast). It means 'holding on truth'- no matter what happens. It gives the ideas of 'Truth-force' that is, Truth is force, a power, a weapon. Th term was coined in South Africa and Gandhiji himself described it as 'Passive Resistance' but later he made a difference between the two ideas. "*Satyagraha* differs from Passive Resistance as the North

Pole from the South. The latter (Passive Resistance) has been conceived as a weapon of the weak, and does not exclude the use of physical force or violence for the purpose of gaining one's end; whereas the former (*Satyagraha*) has been conceived as a weapon of the strongest, and excludes the use of violence in any shape or form."

Non-violence which forms the very basis of *Satyagraha* is thus explained by Gandhiji—"When a person claims to be non-violent, he is expected not to be angry with one who has injured him. He will not wish him harm; he will wish him well."

About *Satyagraha* Gandhiji says, "*Satyagraha* is the law of love for all. It eshews violence absolutely... The idea behind it is not to destroy or harass the opponent, but to convert him or win him over by sympathy, patience and self-suffering."

Gandhiji referred to non-cooperation and civil resistance (meaning the same thing as Civil Disobedience) as the two offshoots of *Satyagraha*. In addition to these two, the *hartal* (temporary strike), picketing, non-violent raids or marches (as the Dandi March), and fasting are considered by some as different forms of *Satyagraha*.

Jawaharlal Nehru (1889 to 1964):

Usually called the architect of modern India, among the freedom fighters, he comes next only to Gandhiji. Born in a very rich family; Educated in England; Left practice and richly life for the sake of India's freedom; Started political career by participating in the Non-cooperation Movement in 1920; courted arrested several times in Satyagraha; Imprisoned many times; became General Secretary of Indian National Congress (1923-25); Presided over the Lahore Session of the Indian National Congress, December 29, 1929 when Poorna Swaraj Resolution was passed; Presided over the Congress Session in 1936; was chosen the second Satyagrahi in 1940; Moved the Quit India Resolution in 1942; Prime Minister in the Interim Government in 1946 and in the Independent India till his death. His memorable words from his historical speech 'Tryst with Destiny' on August 14, 1947, on the eve of India's independence were: "The service of India means the ending of poverty and ignorance and disease and inequality of opportunity." He was author of distinction; his popular books include *Jawaharlal Nehru: An Autobiography; Glimpses of World History; Letters from Father to His Daughter*.

Subhas Chandra Bose (1897-1945):

Popularly known as *Netaji* (leader), is associated with the slogans Jai Hind, *Delhi Chalo* (March to Delhi), *Khoon do, main tumhe Azadi doonga* (Give me blood and I will give you freedom); Resigned from the most coveted I.C.S. and Joined the freedom struggle; President of the Indian National Congress in 1938 and 1939. Secretly disappeared in 1941 from 'house arrest' in Calcutta; Went to Peshawar and then Kabul where he remained underground for 45 days, and reached Berlin, where he built an Indian army; Left Germany in 1943 and became the Supreme Commander of the Indian National Army (I.N.A); Raised in the I.N.A., a women's Battalion known as the Rani Jhansi Battalion led by Capt. Laxmi Bai. Subhas Chandra Bose is said to have been killed in an aircrash on August 18, 1945.

He established the Azad Hind Government; Became the President of the New Government; I.N.A crossed the Burma border and stepped on Indian soil in Manipur and captured Kohima. Heavy rains and nature went against the I.N.A.

Vallabhbhai Patel (1875-1950):

Popularly called the 'Iron Man of India' on account of his steadfastness and strength of mind; Given the title of 'Sardar' by Gandhiji for his powerful leadership in the Bardoli peasant upheaval (Satyagraha 1928) against the government's decision to increase land revenue; President of the Indian National Congress (1931); imprisoned several times; First Deputy Prime Minister of India; A great diplomat and as Minister of Home

Affairs and states, led to the peaceful merger of about 554 Princely states to India immediately after independence; Resorted to force only in the case of Hyderabad; Was very bold and honest, too blunt and stern if needed and swift in action.

Jaya Prakash Narayan (1902-1979):

A leading socialist leader and a revolutionary; Joined the freedom movement in 1921 under the leadership of Gandhiji; Participated in the Civil Disobedience Movement in 1934; Along with Acharya Narendra Dev, founded the Congress Socialist Party; Won a hero's fame as crusader for emancipation of motherland in the 1942 movement; Escaped from jail and organised from underground, the struggle for freedom; After independence joined Bhoodan Movement and Sarvodya Movement.

Abul Kalam Azad (1888-1958):

President of the Indian National Congress 1923 and from 1940 to 1946; One of the greatest scholars of Muslim Culture; Imprisoned several times on account of participation in the freedom struggle. In a trial court for his participation in the Non-cooperation Movement he said, "Superiority does not lie in race, nationality or colour; it is only action that counts, and the greatest man is who does his work best."

Acceptance of the Demand for Pakistan by the Indian National Congress

The Britisher's 'Divide and Rule policy', is primarily responsible for the growth of communalism. The rise of militant nationalism and the Non-cooperation Movement made the Britishers plan to raise the Muslims as a political entity against the Congress Party. They availed of the service of Sir Syed Ahmad Khan, who was in the beginning a devout nationalist but slowly he propounded the two-nation theory. The partition of Bengal by Curzon in 1905 was meant to weaken the strength of the Hindu Bengalees and to please the Muslim Bengalees. The Act of 1909 granted a separate electorate to the Muslims. The Congress adopted the policy of appeasing the Muslims and agreed to the separate electorate through the Lucknow Pact of 1916.

In June 1945, at the Shimla conference, the Governor General, Lord Wavell's, plan failed because the Muslim league did not accept it. The Cabinet Mission finding the irreconcilable differences between the two parties, announced on May 16, 1946, its own proposal and declared the formation of Interim Government and the Constituent Assembly.

The Muslim League did not accept the proposal but on the invitation of Lord Wavell, Nehru formed the Interim Government on 24th August 1946.

The Muslim League now took a course of action which had no parallel in the recorded history of the British period. It declared 16th August to be observed as 'Direct Action Day' for holding meetings all over the country to achieve Pakistan by getting rid of British slavery and future Hindu domination. In Calcutta, the orgy of murder and arson continued for four days. It was followed by similar happenings in Noakhali and Tipperah (East Bengal). In Bihar retaliation started.

The 'Direct Action' begun in Lahore followed the pattern of Calcutta and spread to Multan, Rawalpindi, Amritsar and N.W.F.P. Some 60 lakh Hindu and Sikh refugees streamed out of the West Punjab and demanded the partition of the Punjab and Bengal.

On February 20, Attlee made the historic announcement of transferring power not later than June 1948. Lord Mountbatten was sent to replace Lord Wavell for transferring the responsibility for the government in a manner best suited for the future happiness of India. Now, rethinking started. The Muslim League also joined the Interim Government. The bitter experience of six months of working in the Interim Government of joint Congress and the Muslim League taught the Congress that the only way of deliverance from anarchy and bloodshed caused by the breakdown of administration, is to create Pakistan.

It is fair to remember that the Congress had unanimously passed resolutions, though indirectly, conceding Pakistan in 1942, 1945, and March 1947. No Congress leader liked the idea but some had to accept it as an evil necessity. Patel's experience of working with the League members in the Executive Council had convinced him of the impossibility of working with the Muslim Leauge as he said, "whether we like it or not, there were two nations in India." Dr. Rajendra Prassad felt that by accepting Pakistan, it would be possible to govern the remaining position, in a better way. Pandit Nehru felt, "A large India would have constant troubles, constant disintegrating pulls. And also the fact that we saw no other way of getting our freedom in the near future. And so we accepted it and said—let us build up a strong India." Gandhiji was fully against Partition. When opposition to the acceptance of Partition was running very high in the A.I.C.C. meeting on June 14, 1947, Gandhiji spoke urging the acceptance of the partition. He concluded by saying that he was steadfastly opposed to the idea but sometimes certain decisions, however unpalatable, had to be taken.

Lord Mountbatten, after getting approval of the Government of Britain on June 4 announced that the transfer of power to India as well as Pakistan would be effected not in June 1948 but probably about August 15, 1947. The announcement resulted in the immediate improvement in the communal relations.

EXERCISES

A. Very Short Answer Type Questions

1. What was the resolution passed at the Lahore Session of the Congress in 1929?
2. Who was the President of the Indian National Congress at the Lahore Session?
3. Name the parties of the Poona Act (1932).
4. With which important place, the Civil Disobedience Movement of 1930 is associated?
5. List any two effects of the 1930 Civil Disobedience Movement.
6. Who were 'Red Shirts'?
7. Who is called the 'Sarhadi Gandhi'?
8. Mention any two provisions of the Gandhi-Irwin Pact.
9. List any two slogans associated with Subhas Chandra Bose.
10. State the role of the INA in the national struggle.

B. Short Answer Type Quetions

1. Give the meaning of Poorna Swaraj. Why was it adopted as the national goal?
2. What was the difference between the policy of the Swarajists and the 'Changers'?
3. Why was the Dandi March undertaken? What was its impact?
4. Explain the significance of the 1929 Session of the Congress.
5. Why were the Round Table Conferences held?
6. Why was the Civil Disobedience Movement withdrawn in 1934?
7. Why was the 'Quit India' Movement launched? What was its impact?
8. State the main features of the Mountbatten Plan.
9. Explain the significance of 'Do or Die' slogan of 1942.
10. Why did the attitude of the British Government Change after the Second World War?
11. What was the impact of the Second World War on the national movement?
12. Explain the contribution of any two prominent leaders to the national movement.

C. Long-Answer Type or Essay Type Questions

1. Why was the 1935 Act passed? State its main provisions. What was its impact?
2. Explain the chief characteristics and events associated with the National Movement during the War.
3. Why was the Indian Independence Act 1947 passed? State its chief provisions.
4. Why did the British finally decide to quit India? Illustrate your answer with examples.

CHAPTER 18

Growth of Other Movements and Ideas

MOVEMENTS OF PEASANTS AND WORKERS: ORIGIN OF THE MOVEMENT

The origin of the Movements of peasants and workers may be traced to the Champaran Satyagraha of 1917, launched by Gandhiji. The satyahgraha, which was aimed at improving the conditions of the peasants working on the Indigo Estates of the British planters, resulted in the passing of *The Champaran Agrarian Bill* (1917).

In 1918, Gandhiji, with the help of Sardar Patel organised satyagraha for the betterment of the working conditions of the textile mills at Ahmedabad.

Again in 1918, Gandhiji led the movement for the remission of tax on the peasantry of Kheda in Gujarat.

Impact of the First World War on the Peasants and Workers' Struggle

Movements among peasants and workers grew rapidly after the First World War. The prosperous capitalist class was not prepared to share their increased profits with the workers who suffered from rising prices. The Russian Revolution also encouraged the workers to assert themselves and demand their due. The war-ravaged imperial government increased taxes on the peasantry. The feudal oppression upon the workers became more acute in rural India. The workers and peasants were led to an organised action in 1920s.

All India Trade Union Congress

The first session of the All India Trade Union Congress was held at Bombay on October 30, 1920 and was presided over by Lala Lajpat Rai.

The Civil Disobedience Movements

The movements of 1920-22 and 1930-34 led to nationwide awakening of the peasants and workers in India.

Railway Workers Strike (1927-1928)

The railway workers' strikes were held at Kharagpur and at other places against the retrenchment policy. There was the All India Railway general strike in September 1927.

Bardoli Satyagraha (1928)

The peasants of Bardoli Tehsil of Gujarat protested against increase in land revenue. The movement was peacefully led by Sardar Vallabhbhai Patel. The government accepted the peasants' demands.

Bombay Textile Workers Strike (1928)

It was a longdrawn strike. The membership of the communist led Girni Kamgar Union increased to almost one lakh.

The Kisan Sabha (1929)

In Bihar, Kisan Sabha was founded by Swami Sahajananda in 1929. The peasants' movement grew up in Andhra Pradesh in areas where Zamindari predominated. The Congress Socialists became active in the field after 1934. The All India Kisan Sabha was born on April 11, 1936. Swami Sahajanand presided over the session. Among others it was attended by Jaya Prakash Narayan, Dr. Ram Manohar Lohia, Prof. V.G. Ranga and Sohan Singh Josh.

Jute Workers' Strike (1937-38)

The Jute Workers' strike in Bengal lasted for 74 days. More than two lakh workers participated in the strike. Leaders like Subhas Chandra Bose and Jawarharlal Nehru lent support to the strike which was called to reinstate retrenched workers.

General Strike in Calcutta (1916)

It is estimated that in 1946, 1629 strikes took place in Bengal, participated by about 20 lakh workers.

GROWTH OF SOCIALIST IDEAS

Origin

It was Robert Owen (1771-1858), a Welsh social reformer and a factory owner, who is said to have first used the word 'socialism' somewhere about 1830. It implied in the beginning, the idea of a levelling up between the rich and the poor and a more or less equal distribution of property. In each of the three leading industrial countries in Europe—England, France and Germany- socialism developed somewhat differently in accordance with the strength and character of the working class in each country.

Socialism has been viewed differently by different thinkers.

Nehru's concept of socialism

Urging the Indian National Congress to accept socialism as its goal, Nehru, in his presidential address to the Lucknow Congress in 1936, explained the nature, meaning and importance of socialism in these words, "I am convinced that the only key to the solution of the world's problems and of India's problems lies in socialism... in the scientific, economic sense... the ending of vested interests in land and industry, as well as the feudal and autocratic Indian states system. That means the ending of private property, except in a restricted sense, and the replacement of the present profit system by a higher ideal of cooperative service. In short, it means a new civilisation, radically different from the present capitalist order."

Socialism and Revolutionaries (1928)

Sardar Bhagat had great faith in socialism. He wrote, "The peasants have to liberate themselves not only from foreign yoke but also from the yoke of landlords and capitalists." According to him socialism means the abolition of capitalism and class domination. In 1924, the revolutionaries founded the Hindustan Republican Association but under the influence of socialist ideas, in 1928 changed its name as Hindustan Socialist Republican Association (HSRA). Chandra Shekhar Azad became the chairman of this organisation.

Socialism and the Economic Depression (1929)

In 1929, the capitalist countries like Germany, U.K. and U.S.A. witnessed a great economic depression which led to a steep decline in production and increase in large scale unemployment. The depression brought the capitalist system into disrepute. On the other hand, Russia under the influence of socialism remained not only unaffected by the economic depression but also continued to have a robust economy. Obviously, leaders of the nationalist movement learnt a lesson from such contrasting situations, and drew towards socialism.

Socialism and the Congress (1930's)

A major development of the 1930's was the increasing acceptance of radical economic policies by the Congress. Within the Congress, the socialist tendency found reflection in the election of Jawaharlal Nehru (who had been greatly influenced by socialism) as president of Congress in 1929, 1936 and 1937 and also of Subhas Chandra Bose (another prominent Congress leader under the influence of socialism) in 1938 and 1939. Nehru, in his presidential address at the Lucknow Session of the Congress in 1936 urged the Congress to accept socialism as its goal and to bring itself closer to the working class and the peasantry.

The Congress Socialist Party (1934)

There was a group of Congress leaders who felt that the Congress did not have a strong base in the working classes and peasants. This led to the formation of the Congress Socialist Party in 1933, in Nasik jail. Acharya Narendra Dev became its president in 1934. Among the other prominent members were Jaya Prakash Narayan, Ram Manohar Lohia and Achyut Patwardhan. The first conference held at Patna in 1934 made the following demands (1) Right to work (2) Nationalisation of key industries (3) Redistribution of land (4) End of landlordism and Princedoms (5) Liquidation of public debt (6) State monopoly of foreign trade.

The word socialism became so popular with the leaders that it found its place in the Preamble of Indian Constitition. India became a Sovereign Socialist Secular Democratic Republic. The words Socialist and Secular were added later on in 1976.

Congress and International Developments

Indian National Congress, from the very beginning began to take a keen interest in the international affairs and generally supported the efforts made in various parts against colonialism and imperialism. It objected to the deployment of Indian troops in foreign lands for imperial purposes. The British rulers and the Indian soldiers in Abyssina, second Afghan war (1879-81), Egypt, Eastern and Central Africa (1897-98), the Boer War (1902-04) and Tibet (1903-04).

In 1927, Jawaharlal Nehru, on behalf of the Indian National Congress attended the Congress of oppressed Nationalities at Brussels organised by political exiles and revolutionaries from the countries of Asia, Africa and Latin America. The Congress in its Madras session (1927) warned the government that the Indian people would not support the government in its imperialist designs. In the 1930's it condemned Fascism which was gaining ground in Germany, Italy and Japan, and provided moral support to the people of Czechoslovakia, Spain and Ethiopia. In 1937, when Japan attacked China, the National Congress called upon the people of India not to use Japanese made goods as a mark of their protest. It also sent a Medical Mission to China.

Jawarharlal Nehru was a great internationlist. He played an important role in mobilising public opinion to shape the independence of Indonesia by overthrowing the Dutch imperialists. The Congress always perceived India as a part of the world community.

MOVEMENT OF STATES' PEOPLE

Broadly speaking there were two types of units in India under the British. One was called British India which consisted of 11 Provinces and a few Chief Commission's territories. The other was called Princely states consisting of 562 states. The provinces were under the direct control of the British Government whereas

Growth of Other Movements and Ideas 195

the states were under the direct charge of the Indian rulers but under the overall charge of the British rulers. The Indian National Congress was confined to British India.

The British rulers often used the Princely states to prevent the growth of national unity. Most of the rulers of the Princely states were indifferent and insensitive to the needs of the people. They lived a life of luxury whereas their subjects led a very miserable life. The rulers in general were very autocratic, feudalist and extortionists. There was little freedom of speech.

In 1927, the All India States People's Conference was founded to coordinate political activities in the states. The state Peoples' movement awakened national consciousness among the people of the states.

The Indian National Congress supported the states Peoples' struggle and called upon the rulers of these states to introduce a democratic representative government.

Under the initiative of Jawarharlal Nehru, All India States Peoples' Conference adopted in October 1937, a resolution supporting the mass movement in the Princely state of Mysore. Within a few months, the movement for an elected government took the shape of a mass movement.

In 1938, the Congress at the Haripura Session declared very unequivocally that the Congress ideal of *Poorna Swaraj* included the independence of Princely states also.

In 1939, Jawaharlal Nehru became the President of the All India States Peoples' conference.

In Orissa, a militant struggle with bows and arrows started in several Princely states namely Dhenkanal, Talcher, Nilgiri and Ranpur. The Congress Socialist leader Nabakrishna Chowdhry (later on Congress Chief Minister of Orissa) and his wife Malati Devi led the Dhenkanal struggle.

The Congress Government was formed in the Princely states of Travancore and Cochin in 1937 and 1938 respectively. Within a short time, the main driving force was in the hands of the socialists and the communists. A.K. Gopalan was the most prominent communist leader who fought against the despotic Dewan, Sir C.P. Ramaswami Aiyar. In Hyderabad, the Arya Samaj launched a powerful movement. Jaipur, Kashmir and Rajkot were the other states where popular struggles were waged.

GROWTH OF COMMUNALISM

In brief, communalism in India was the outcome of the British policy of 'Divide and Rule'. India had to pay a very heavy price on account of communalism. India is the only country in the world which became independent, only after its division into two independent countries was accepted.

The seeds of communalism, resulting in the partition of the country on communal basis, were sown by a Muslim social reformer, Syed Ahmed Khan (1817-1898), whose views claiming a separate status for Muslims in India were supported by the British as evident in the British policy of 'Divide and Rule'. The All India Muslim League came into being in 1906. The British rulers made the full use of this and announced that they would protect the "Special interests" of the Muslims.

The Hindu Mahasabha which championed the cause of Hindus came into existence in 1915, to counteract the activities of the Muslim League. Nevertheless, it could not influence the Hindus by its communalism.

The nationalist leaders from the very beginning of the national movement had firmly opposed the communal tendencies. Yet, it failed to counteract the communal challenge posed by the Muslim League. In the end, Muslim League's communalism won and the country was partitioned on the basis of two-nation theory.

The Muslim League did not support the nationalist movement. In fact, it opposed the Civil Disobedience Movement at its Allahabad session held in December 1930. The Communal Award announced by the British government in 1932 provided for separate Muslim and Non-Muslim electorates.

The failure of the Muslim League to form its Ministry in any of the eleven provinces after the 1937 elections convinced it to adopt such a strategy which would make them the sole representatives of the Muslims. In the elections it could barely get 51 seats out of 482 seats in all provinces. Muslim League was yet a feeble force, Muslims of Punjab voted for the Unionist Party. The Muslims in Bengal followed the Krishak Party of Fazul Huq. The U.P. Muslims preferred the Nationalist Agricultural Party of Nawab of Chhatari. The Independent Muslim Party of Abdulla Harun won Muslim votes in Sind. The N.W.F.P. was fully swayed by Khan Abdul Ghaffar Khan, whose followers were affiliated to the Congress. In other provinces, the Congress party won handsomely. In these circumstances, M.A. Jinnah raised the cry of 'Islam in Danger'. The League raised a lot of hue and cry that the Congress Ministries were not protecting the Muslim interests. He began to work upon a scheme which would provide a separate homeland for the Muslims of India. The demand for Pakistan was made in 1940 at the Lahore Session of the Muslim League. Gradually, they refused to consider anything less than Pakistan. Jinnah began to insist that the League was the only representative body of the Indian Muslims. Jinnah's demand before the British Government was 'Divide and Quit'. Although there were hundreds of Muslim stalwarts in the Congress, but their voice was not given its due place. It was rather very unfortunate that the Muslim communalism under Jinnah could break up India into two parts-India and Pakistan- before freedom could be achieved.

THE INDIAN NATIONAL ARMY (I.N.A.)

While in India, the Congress carried on the struggle for the freedom of the country, the Indian National Army, under the leadership of Subhas Chandra Bose, was marching from outside towards the eastern frontier of India. Subhash Chandra Bose formed the Azad Hind Fauj or Indian National Army (I.N.A.) in 1943 at Singapore, to conduct a military campaign for the liberation of India. He received valuable help from Rash Behari Bose, an old revolutionary, who was spending his days in exile in foreign lands. Necessary spade work was done by General Mohan Singh who had been a captain in the British Indian Army. A large number of Indian residents in South-East Asia and the Indian soldiers and officers who had been captured by the Japanese forces in Malaya, Singapore and Burma joined the I.N.A. It may be mentioned that out of about 65,000 Indian Prisoners of War, about 20,000 joined I.N.A. Subhas Chandra Bose set up a Provisional Government of free India at Singapore. The soldiers of the I.N.A. fought strenuous battles on several fronts in South East Asia and demonstrated remarkable courage. Intensive military training was given to civilians who had joined the I.N.A. The I.N.A. was divided into four Brigades named after Gandhi, Nehru, Azad and Subhas. Captain Lakshmi Sahgal was incharge of the Rani Jhansi Regiment. It was a regiment of Housewives in Singapore.

The Japanese were satisfied of the military skill and efficiency of the I.N.A. Instructions were issued that the main body of the Subhas Brigade would proceed to Kohima. And as soon as Imphal, the capital of Manipur should fall, they should rapidly cross the Brahmaputra and enter Bengal. As such, leaving some men at Haka and Falam, the rest marched towards Kohima, the capital of Naga Hills. Kohima had already been captured by the Japanese forces accompained by some soldiers of I.N.A. who hoisted the tricolour flag on the hill top. A few days later, the Japanese forces and the Subhas Brigade had to withdraw. At a different site, three auxiliary units of the I.N.A were attached to the Japanese forces attacking Imphal, the capital of Manipur. The Indian soliders planted the national tricolour flag for the first time on the liberated Indian soil on 19th March 1944. There was tremendous enthusiasm to have set foot on the free Indian soil. But the monsoon started before the fall of Imphal and it became impossible to supply ration and ammunition to the forces besieging Imphal. Thus the Japanese and the INA had

Map 39: **INA Hoisting Flag**

to withdraw on account of torrential rains, short supplies, lack of air support and the losses inflicted by American bombers. With the defeat of Japan, I.N.A. also had to surrender. Subhash Bose and his companion

Habib-ul-Rehman, took the plane from Formosa on August 18, 1945, which is said to have caught fire and crashed on way to Tokyo.

The trial of some of the captured army officers of the I.N.A., Such as Shah Nawaz, Prem Sehghal and G.S. Dhillon evoked patriotic feelings among all sections of the Indian people. Such was the popularity of the I.N.A., that the slogan *"Lal Quile Se Aye Aawaz, Dhillon Sehghal Shah Nawaz"* rent the sky all over the country. Leading lawyers of India appeared for the officers of the I.N.A and tore the prosecution case into shreds. Several documents presented before the court revealed startling instances of chivalry of the warriors of freedom. Nehruji himself donned the lawyers gown to defend the officers. The British court gave death punishment to these officers, but when it caused nationwide protest and resentment, the government thought it wise to release them.

On July 6, 1944, Netaji in a broadcast on Azad Hind Radio addressed to Gandhiji had said, "India's last war of Independence has begun. In this holy war of India's liberation, we ask for your blessings and good wishes."

EXERCISES

A. Very short Answer Type Questions

1. Name any two peasants and workers movements for their rights.
2. When did the Indian National Congress include the independence of the Princely states in its agenda of freedom?
3. Name any two important socialist leaders.
4. State the organisation that played an important role in launching freedom movement in Princely states.
5. Name any two organisations that spread communal tendencies in India.
6. Name any two important leaders of the I.N.A. against whom prosecution was launched in India.
7. List any two causes of the failure of the I.N.A.
8. What was the difference between British provinces and Princely states.

B. Short Answer Type Questions

1. What was the general condition of the people under Princely states?
2. In what ways did the idea of socialism influence the national movement in India?
3. Explain the course of growth of socialist ideas in India.
4. Why was the I.N.A. formed? Assess its role in India's freedom.
5. What were the main objectives of the states peoples' movement? Why did it become an integral part of India?

CHAPTER 19

Selected Passages from the Speeches of Famous Leaders

INTRODUCTION

The following passages are included for a two-fold purpose. Firstly, it is to enable the students to make their answers to questions more effective by quoting the relevant passage or lines from the passages. Secondly, to prepare them for making their communication and speeches more impressive and inspirational.

PASSAGES

1) "The loyal heart is a stronger weapon than any, that the hand of the tyrant will ever forge. It is therefore necessary that some reasonable scope should be now given to their just and legitimate aspirations. Such timely concessions given with grace and without asking, will carry with them a force of gratitude, which cannot be attained by yielding to pressure and with a bad grace. All unnecessary obstacles should be removed. Something needs be done, by which those natives who have talents and attainments, may be able to enter the various services, with only as much trouble as Englishmen are put to. The problem is clear, and there is no use shirking it".

– *Dadabhai Naoroji* (1825-1929). Speech on May 2, 1867 at the East India Association.

2) "The impoverishment of an Indian Province under British administration is a more serious calamity than any defeat or disaster which had been known in the history of British Rule in India".

– *R.C. Dutt* (1849-1909) Letter to Lord Curzon in 1900.

3) "I hold strongly British rule has produced disastrous results. On this point,. I claim some right to speak, for I have been studying this phase of the question for nearly twenty years now... The only solution that is possible—a solution demanded alike by our interests and by your interests, as also by your national honour—is the steady introduction of self-government in India".

– *Gopal Krishna Gokhale* (1866-1915). Speech in England on 'Indian Affairs' under the auspices of the New Reforms Club.

4) "It is difficult to realize unless one goes thoroughly into it. It has been my belief for the past twenty-five years, that every little product of the Indian handloom purchased by us, puts a little money into the hands of some poor countrymen of ours. I therefore look upon it as a religious duty to purchase an article of indigenous make whenever we can get it, and even at a sacrifice if we can afford to make it, in preference to an article of foreign make.

– *Madan Mohan Malaviya* (1861-1946). Presidential address at the Second United Provinces Conference at Lucknow in December 1908.

Selected Passages from the Speeches of Famous Leaders

5) "I want to say from this platform that every blow that was hurled at us this afternoon was a nail in the coffin of the British Empire. We have to avenge ourselves of this cowardly attack, not by violently attacking them but by gaining our freedom. I wish to warn the Government that if a violent revolution takes place in this country, the responsibility for bringing it about will fall on such officers as misbehaved themselves this afternoon. Our creed still stands and we are pledged to a struggle of peaceful non-violence. But if the Government officers continue to behave like this, I would not wonder if the young men were to go out of our hands and do whatever they choose with the object of gaining the freedom of their country. I do not know whether I shall be alive to see that day. But whether alive or dead, if that day is forced on them by the Government, my spirit from behind will bless them for their struggle."

– *Lala Lajpat Rai* (1865-1928) speech on October 1928 at a public meeting held to condemn the brutality of the British on peaceful demonstrations.

6) "I again say that the demand for Swaraj involves no sedition. It has nothing to do with the invisible sovereign government. The essence of Swaraj is that we should manage our domestic affairs according to our wishes...and it is with this purpose in view that I have chosen this subject for today's discourse."

"We want our rights. We want a particular kind of rule that will secure our happiness. I believe that we shall get it. We have to exert ourselves in the right direction and set ourselves to the task in the full faith that the work is our own. I am perfectly sure that by the grace of God, even if you do not get the fruit of your labour in your lifetime, the next generation will not fail to reap the benefits."

– *Lokmanya Bal Gangadhar Tilak* (1856-1920) Speech at Belgaum on May 1, 1916.

7) "India demands Home Rule for two reasons: One essential and vital, the other less important but weighty. First, because Freedom is the birthright of every Nation, secondly, because her most important interests are now made subservient to the interests of the British Empire without her consent, and her resources are not utilised for her greatest needs. It is enough only to mention the money spent on her Army, not for local defence but for Imperial purposes, as compared with that spent on primary education."

– *Annie Besant* (1847-1933) Presidential address at the annual session of the Indian National Congress in 1917.

8) "Here is a *mantra*, a short one, that I give you. You may imprint it on your hearts and let every breath of yours give expression to it. The *mantra* is: 'Do or Die.' We shall either free India or die in the attempt: we shall not live to see the perpetuation of our slavery... and will die, if need be, to attain that goal. Take a pledge with God and your own conscience as witness, that you will no longer rest till freedom is achieved and will be prepared to lay down your lives in the attempt to achieve it. He who loses his life will gain it, he who will seek to save it shall lose it. Freedom is not for the coward or the faint-hearted."

– *Mahatma Gandhi (Mohandas Karam Chand Gandhi)* (1869-1948). Speech on August 8, 1942 at Bombay at the All India Congress Committee meeting.

9) "Soldiers of India's Army of Liberation! Today is the proudest day of my life. Today it has pleased Providence to give me the unique privilege and honour of announcing to the whole world that India's Army of Liberation has come into being. This army has now been drawn up in military formation on the battlefield of Singapore-which was once the bulwark of the British Empire."

"Comrades! Soldiers! Let your battle-cry be- "To Delhi, To Delhi!" How many of us will individually survive this war of freedom, I do not know. But I do know this, that we shall ultimately win and our task will not end until our surviving heroes hold the victory parade on another graveyard of the British empire-the Lal Kila or Real Fortress of ancient Delhi."

– *Netaji Subhas Chandra Bose.* Speech at Singapore on July 5, 1943.

10) "Long years ago we made a tryst with destiny, and now the time comes when we shall redeem our pledge, not wholly or in full measure, but very substantially. At the stroke of the midnight hour, when the world sleeps, India will awake to life and freedom. A moment comes, which comes but rarely in history, when we step out from the old to the new, when an age ends, and when the soul of a nation, long suppressed, finds utterance. It is fitting that at this solemn moment we take the pledge of dedication to the service of India and her people and to the still larger cause of humanity."

– *(Pandit) Jawaharlal Nehru.* (1889-1964). Speech at Midnight 14-15 August 1947.

EXERCISES

1. What were the reasonable demands of the Indian people from the British as put forward by Dadabhai Naroji?
2. In what ways the British Government was responsible for the impoverishment of the Indians? Explain the concept 'Wealth Drain' from India.
3. What were the disastrous results of the British rule over India? What was the solution suggested by Gopal Krishna Gokhale?
4. Why did Madan Mohan Malviya advocate the promotion of cottage and small scale industries in India?
5. Why was the Simon Commission boycotted in India? What was the reaction of Lala Lajpat Rai on the lathi charge made by the police on the demonstrators?
6. Why did Lokmanya Tilak put forward the demand for Swaraj? What was his concept of Swaraj?
7. Explain the meaning of Home Rule Movement? Name two Indian leaders who put forward this demand.
8. What was the 'mantra' enunciated by Gandhiji? Why did he raise this slogan? What was the reaction of the Government?
9. What was the name of the army formed by Subhas Chandra Bose? Why did he form this army?
10. What was the tryst that we made? What were the aspirations of the Indian people? How can these aspirations be fulfilled?

＃ PART TWO
Contemporary World

CHAPTER 20

Introduction

DIVISION OF HISTORY INTO PERIODS

History is usually divided into periods as each period is supposed to have its specific cultural, economic, political, religious and social characteristics and these differ from other periods. Here, it is important to remember that it is the overall or the sum total of differences that determines the specificity of a period.

Such divisions of a massive mass of historical knowledge of happenings and a vast ocean of facts into periods or meaningful units help in the study or writing of history. It becomes easy to grasp, to intelligibly link up the various facts like a chain and to have an insight into the spirit of the time—we see how the prevailing thoughts and beliefs pervade the whole gamut of political, economic, social and cultural activities of the time and how changes—though vaguely perceptible and slow at first—creep in and grow into a formidable force to shatter the whole fabric of the period already worn out and to usher a new beginning. As one goes through the period, one feels the unity of time and action due to the common basis or theme used for making the divisions.

Generally, history is divided into the traditional three periods—the ancient, the medieval and the modern. But there are other ways to divide history into periods or units. Following are some of the main criteria to divide the history of a region, country or world into different periods.

1. Dynasty as the Basis

History may be divided into dynasties such as the Mauryan dynasty and the Gupta dynasty in Indian history or the Tudor period and the Stuart period in the history of England. The rulers of the same dynasty become the dominant theme to integrate the period. It is worth noticing how rulers having the common background differ, sometimes to a marked degree, regarding temperament and administrative ability, interest and initiative, prestige and power, care and concern for the people, foresight and planning, courage to face challenges, and zeal to think out and implement new radical ideas.

2. Political Development as the Basis

In India, the British period of history with altogether a new political set up, distinctly marks off from the Mughal period of Indian history. Also take the case of the Pre-period and the Post-period of the French and American Revolution. In both, the Post-period is very different from the Pre-period due to an avalanche of political and social changes.

3. Religious and Racial Development

Indian history may be divided into a Hindu period and a Muslim period due to the dominance of religion in the administration and lives of the people.

4. Development in Certain Specific Aspects

The movements like Renaissance, Reformation and Industrial Revolutions can themselves make a period of their own due to the great transformation in economic and cultural conditions of living.

5. Regional Basis

History of North India and history of South India are examples of studying history regionwise.

6. Pre-Historical and Historical Periods

This is another example of making division.

7. Basis of Stages of Development of Society

The three divisions of Indian history — Ancient age closing by 8th century, the Medieval age closing by the middle of the 18th century, and the Modern age — are on this basis. However, these three divisions differ from country to country due to the stage of development. In the history of the Western Europe, the ancient period came to a close by the early centuries of the Christian era and the medieval period by the 16th century with the decline of feudalism.

MODERN HISTORY

Modern History of the world is said to have begun in the fifteenth-seventeenth centuries or about the 16th century. Of course, this concept of modern history is not applicable to all the regions and the countries of the world. Even in one country, the period of the beginning of the modern history may differ from region to region when we take into consideration all the characteristics of the modern age. There was a great time lag between the occurrence of changes in the economic and social life of one country from the other. In general, following characteristics mark the onset of the modern period.

(1) Renaissance and spread of new knowledge and science.
(2) Industrial Revolution in England and other European countries resulting in new forms of production and classes.
(3) Reformation and consequent changes in religious outlook and relationship between the church and the government of a state.
(4) Disintegration of feudalism and its replacement by a new system.
(5) Predominance of industrial economy over rural economy.
(6) Emergence of new classes called the *bourgeois* i.e. owners of industry and controllers of trade and the *proletariat* or the working class.
(7) Emergance of socialist ideas.
(8) Formation of nation-states.
(9) Growth of nationalism.
(10) Colonisation and exploitation of the colonised countries.
(11) Emergence of democratic ideas.
(12) Rise of a new wave of imperialism.
(13) A new balance of military strength and formation of secret alliances and finally, division of Europe into opposing blocks as a prelude to the First World War.

For some countries the onset of the modern period was the harbinger of an era of economic prosperity while for others, like India it was marked by the worst form of colonial exploitation. Thus, it is very clear that the concept of modern period is different for different countries.

Modern period, in the case of several countries begins with their independence and in that case it may coincide with the contemporary period of some other countries. The modern period, therefore, in such cases, merges with the contemporary period and vice versa. This fact is generally not taken note of by the Western scholars and also by many Indian scholars.

Introduction

MEANING OF CONTEMPORARY HISTORY

What is 'contemporary history'? There are different views and interpretations about what contemporary history connotes. The word 'contemporary' means 'belonging to the same time', 'living at that time', 'the present time', or 'the recent time'. But the history of the 'same time', 'the present time' or 'the recent time' may mean different things to different people. Literally, it might mean 'the history of what is already happening at the moment of writing', or 'a record of events through which the historian has lived'. Again, in terms of years, this interpretation may mean a very short period or a very long period of history. Historians rightly emphasize that like other periods of history, the 'contemporary history' should be well defined in terms of years as a specified period of history with specific characteristics for the common benefit of students, scholars and historians. Some historians consider recent modern history to be contemporary history. One historian specifies the period from 1945 to the present day as it covers the 'crucial years'. Another historian would start the contemporary history from 1917, the year of the Socialist Revolution of Russia, which radically changed the fate of mankind by freeing it from the exploiting classes. But most historians now think that the twentieth century could be considered as a specific period to be referred to as contemporary history. This period of modern history has a well-defined character. It awakened the present world "to a sense of world community in which all were inescapably involved". Anything that would happen at one place must affect the whole world directly or indirectly. This century witnessed two great world wars, recorded scintifice inventions of great dimensions, brought in terrible suffering and miseries as well as great prosperity and hope, and ushered in great change and transformation in the quality of living as well as great problems — the greatest being that of survival. All these are different in quality and content from the preceding periods and mark this century as a distinctive slice of time that is close and near to us, that is well-known to us, that affects our life one way or the other and that has changed our mode of seeing, thinking and feeling. In short, we live in this century, in this contemporary world, in this contemporary history.

Barraclough, another historian believes that the actual problems of the 20th century did take visible shape in the last decade of the 19th century. As such we should begin contemporary history from this decade. This book and the present prescribed courses of study follow this view of starting the contemporary history from 1890.

Distinction Between Contemporary and Modern History

It must be admitted that it is not possible to draw a hard and fast line of demarcation between the modern period and the contemporary period. We cannot pinpoint a specific date or even a specific decade where one period of history ends and the other begins. However, there are very broad characteristics which enable us to draw some distinction between the contemporary history and the modern history.

Characteristic	*Modern History*	*Contemporary History*
1. **Part or complete period**	Modern history forms a complete and full part of history of a period.	Contemporary history is only a part of modern history.
2. **Beginning of the period**	The modern period started about the 16th century	For some historians, contemporary history starts with the First World War (1914).
3. **Duration of the period**	The modern period of history embraces about four centuries.	The contemporary history covers a few decades or at the most one century.
4. **Relation with events**	We have distant relation with the events and heroes of the modern period.	We are more familiar and sometimes have several opportunities to come in contact with great personalities.
5. **Objectivity**	Usually we are not influenced by our likes and dislikes.	Personal prejudices may blur our vision.

Characteristic Features of Contemporary History

The contemporary history has some special characteristics which distinguish it as a specific period in history. Some of the most important characteristics of contemporary history are given below:

1. A. More integrated World:

The World has become more integrated and it is sometimes referred to as a global village. There are several factors for making the world more integrated. First, the problems of mankind have become common. Second, there has been a rapid development of communication, bringing people closer to one another. Third, the fear that the atomic and nuclear power may destroy the entire world has compelled the people of all countries to come nearer to each other. Four, various countries are being involved in solving global problems through united efforts.

2. An Open-Ended History:

The contemporary history does not provide us a larger perspective of "knowing what happened in the end" as we are living among the contemporary events of history and will never know the consequences of the present economic and political changes.

A historian dealing with the events of an earlier period say, the Battles of Panipat or the 1857 Revolt, knows how these events ended and what was their long term impact on the history of India. But with the same certainty one cannot write about the end of the Indo-Pak relations.

The nature of problems does not remain the same. It changes with the times. All these factors make contemporary history open-ended, for it cannot take any directions. There are other hurdles also. Non-availability of certain important historical documents which are kept confidential for some period hinders in having a comprehensive perspective of contemporary events.

3. Collapse of Imperialism and Colonialism:

The period has witnessed the ending of European hegemony or leadership over the world and the rise of what is commonly know as the Third World — The people of Africa, Asia and Latin America. They are a third force in world affairs. In general, they became independent one after another in 1947 and thereafter.

4. Emergence of Communism:

After the 1917 October Revolution in Russia, a wave of communistic ideas swept several parts of the world. Slogans like "Workers of the world unite" became very popular. The USSR and China became the strongholds of communist philosophy. However, the year 1991 saw the decline of the communist philosophy with the disintegration of the USSR into several independent nations.

5. Philosophy of Social Justice:

Earlier, most of the economic and social activities were geared to the welfare of a few sections of society but now the masses have begun to receive more attention.

6. Emergence of Democratic States:

With the end of imperialism, all countries which were under foreign domination became free and accepted democratic forms of government.

7. Explosion of Expectations:

The people of newly freed countries began to have high expectations of better standard of living and more particpation in the day-to-day affairs of the state. In several countries when their hopes were belied, there were internal conflicts and armed struggles also.

8. Desire for Peace and International Understanding:

There has been a great desire among the people of the world to see a peaceful world. Accordingly, towards the close of the Second World War, 50 nations of the world met at San Francisco to adopt a charter that formed the Untied Nations Organisation (UNO). Now its membership has reached about 190.

9. Growing Economic Gap:

The process of industrialisation in the countries of the world has been very uneven resulting in a wide economic gap between the developed, developing and least developed countries.

10. Tremendous Changes:

Contemporary history is characterised by revolutionary changes in every aspect of cultural, economic, political and social life.

11. Change in the Functions of the State:

The nature and functions of the state have radically changed. Now state is no longer merely concerned with the maintenance of law and order and protection from foreign danger. Its functions embrace directly or indirectly all walks of life.

12. Secularisation of Life:

Various aspects of life like art and literature, philosophy, politics and society have been secularised. People have begun to look at issues not from sectarian point of view but from a liberal point of view. Notwithstanding the growing stress on secularism in some parts of the world, religious fundamentalism is also raising its ugly head.

13. Class Struggles in the Capitalist Countries:

The contemporary history has been greatly affected by an upsurge among the workers. The fiercest class struggles took place in several capitalist countries. In defence of their economic and social gains, workers organised mass demonstrations which sometimes led to bloodshed also. As a result of workers' struggles, wages of workers increased and their working conditions also improved.

14. Explosion of Knowledge:

Contemporary history is characterised by radical changes in every walk of life on account of explosion of knowledge in science and technology.

15. Terrible Twentieth Century:

Winston Churchill, Britain's Prime Minister, the architect of Britain's victory in the Second World War, described the twentieth century as the "terrible century" for, no other century has had such mass destruction and misery as this century.

16. Emergence of Super Powers:

The period saw the emergence of the United States of America and the Union of Soviet Socialist Republics as political 'Super Powers'. However, in the 1990's, USSR lost its identity on account of its breakup into several states. Japan has emerged as a super power in the economic field in recent years.

Problems Faced by the Contemporary Historians

Contemporary historians are usually reluctant to write contemporary history on account of a number of causes. First, there is the non-availability of important official documents relating to important policies pursued by the government. Several official documents are considered as 'confidential'. They are normally not available for a few decades.

Second, important persons who are deeply involved in policy decisions and implementation usually do not publish their diaries or memoirs in their life time.

Third, it is very difficult to present an objective view of events when one is actively involved in the events and developments. One is likely to be carried away by one's emotions and philosophical thought.

Fourth, records of personal discussions between leaders of various countries are not made public lest they may lead to bitter international relations.

Fifth, historical perspective i.e. 'knowing what happened in the end' is usually missing. History is often open-ended i.e. provisional.

A Survey of Historical Background of Contemporary World

It may be borne in mind that there was no abrupt change in the situation in the twentieth century, as the forces that were to shape the events had already begun to emerge in the 19th century.

Before the beginning of the 20th century, imperialism and colonialism were the most dominating forces operating in the world. Powerful industrialised nations were exploiting their colonised nations which created a situation of confrontation among the imperialist nations. The colonised countries were also on the warpath with the rulers for their independence.

A wave of narrow nationalism was sweeping Europe. Germany had begun to be very ambitious.

Importance of its Study

It is vital that we should actively involve ourselves in creating the future on the basis of the sound knowledge of contemporary history. Contemporary history enables us to assess the values and achievements of our own age in the light of the recent past. Contemporary history serves us as the 'key' to the understanding of the present.

EXERCISES

A. Very Short Answer Type

1. List any two important features of contemporary history.
2. Mention any two important features of modern history.
3. State any two events/developments which serve as background to the contemporary history.
4. Write any two advantages of the study of contemporary history.

B. Short-Answer Type

1. Contemporary history is called 'open-ended'. Explain.
2. Differentiate between contemporary history and modern history.
3. "The world has become more integrated in the contemporary times". Elucidate.
4. Why is the 20th century called a 'terrible century'?
5. Why is history divided into distinct periods? What are the criteria generally used by historians to divide history into different periods.
6. Why is the 20th century treated as the contemporary history?

C. Essay Type or Long Answer

1. Why are the contemporary historians reluctant to write contemporary history? What are the difficulties and problems faced by them in this regard?
2. Explain the important features of contemporary history.

CHAPTER 21

The World upto the First World War

IMPERIALISM

Age of Imperialism

The period after 1870 and before the outbreak of the First World War (1914-18) has come to be termed as the 'Age of Imperialism'. Imperialism comes from a Latin Word ' Imperium' meaning—power. So, imperialism implies the desire and policy of nations to rule over the weak and backward nations. It includes political domination, economic exploitation and racial empowerment. The imperialist countries think that their culture and civilisation are superior to others and that they have the 'divine right' to spread their influence over the backward. The imperialist countries exploit the economic and non-economic resources of their colonies. Fortunately, imperialism now no longer holds good. All countries of the world are free from foreign domination.

Developments upto 1914

Among the important developments in Europe towards the end of the nineteenth century and upto the year 1914, mention may be made of industrialisation of Europe, need for more markets, voyages of discovery, growth of imperialism, increase in military power, conquest of other nations and their exploitation and spread of Christianity in other lands.

Methods Adopted by Imperialists

These include (1) Open aggression and annexation (2) Getting leasehold places and territories (4)Investment in undeveloped countries (5) Establishment of colonies (6) Carving out spheres of influence or spheres of interest (7) Establishment of protectorates (indirect political control) (8) Financial control.

Causes of Rapid Imperialistic Expansion

These are (i)geographical discoveries and exploration (ii) Economic causes (iii) political causes (iv) religious causes (v) philosophical causes.

Europe's Hegemony or Leadership

The new phase of imperialism began in the 1870's and it continued upto 1914. During this period, Europe had brought under its control almost all Africa and Asia and several areas in other parts of the world. Europe dominated the world both politically and economically. About 45 per cent of the world trade and 60 per cent of the world market for manufactured goods was controlled by Britain, Germany and France.

The British empire was the largest in the world, in terms of both area and the number of people under the British rule.

Britain, a country of about 45 million people at that time controlled colonies with about 400 million population. France, with a population of about 39 million ruled over an empire of over 50 million people.

The following chart presents the picture of European Hegemony.

Chart Showing Countries under European Rule

Britain	France	Germany	Italy	Portugal	Spain	Holland	Russia	Japan
Africa	**Africa**	**Africa**	**Africa**	**Africa**	**Africa**	Indonesia or East Indies (Java, Sumatra, Bali, Borneo etc)	2. Smarkand	Formosa after defeating China in 1895
1. Egypt	1. Algeria	1. German East Africa	1. Libya	1. Angola	Ril De Oro	**Latin America**	3. Botchao	2. Defeated Russia and seized Korea
2. Sudan	2. Tunisia	2. South-West Africa	2. Somali Land	2. Mozambique	**Latin America**	1. Dutch Guyana (Surinam)	4. Kho Kand (All in Central Asia)	
3. Rhodesia	3. Morocco	3. Cameroon		3. Portuguese Guinea	1. Venezuela	1. Tashkand	1. Captured	
4. Uganda	4. The Sahara	4. Togoland		**Latin America**	2. Colombia			
5. British East Africa	5. Dahomey			1. Brazil	3. Ecuador			
6. Sierra leone	6. Madagascar				4. Peru			
7. Gold cost, (Ghana)	7. French Congo				5. Bolivia			
8. Nigeria,	8. French Guinea				6. Paraguay			
9. South Africa	9. Senegal				7. Uruguay			
Asia	**Asia**				8. Chile			
1. India	1. Indo-China (Vietnam, Cambodia Thailand, Laos)				9. Argentina			
2. Malaysia	2. Some Possesions in India				10. Mexico			
3. Sri Lanka	**Latin America**				11. Guatemala			
4. Burma	1. French Guiana				12. El Salvador			
	2. Guadeloupe				13. Honduras			
	3. Martinique				14. Nicaragua			
					15. Costa Rica			
					16. Cuba			
					17. Puerto Rico			
					Note : Most of these colonies regained their independence by 1795			
					Asia			

CHIEF CHARACTERISTICS OF POLITICAL SITUATION IN EUROPE

Intense Rivalry Among European Imperialist Powers

The competing claims among the European imperialist powers over colonies in Africa and Asia was accompanied by conflicts and rivalries. Efforts, however, were made by these powers to resolve conflicting claims through mutual agreements on the basis of 'give and take' i.e. something given in exchange for receiving something. In spite of all these negotiations, fear and distrust among the imperialist powers led to the growth of militarization. Several countries resorted to conscription i.e. making military training compulsory for everyone. Still, every country claimed that it was increasing its military strength for its defence and not for offence.

Uneven Progress in the Countries of Europe

While referring to industrial progress in Europe, it is sometimes overlooked that out of 25 big and small states of Europe, only Britain, Germany and France were the most industrialised countries. Other countries were still in a pre-industrial stage even though some of these had acquired colonies. Russia, the most populous country was primarily an agricultural country.

Rise of Socialism in Europe

Karl Marx (1818-1883) and Friedrich Engels (1820-1895), both from Germany, played a prominent role in giving a scientific shape to the ideals of socialism and in organising the socialist movement in several countries of Europe. In 1864, the International Working Men's Association, popularly known as the First International, was formed. In 1889, the Second International was formed and it took the decision to organise on May 1, a great international demonstration by workers in all the lands. Since then, May Day is being observed throughout the world as a Day of Solidarity of the Workers. The Second International formed in 1889 took up the issues of the colonies, militarization and war. In 1907 the 'Second International' in its Congress held at Stuttgart in Germany unanimously passed a resolution condemning the imperialist powers for the subjugation of colonial people and to do everything possible to educate them for independence. Dadabhai Naoroji, one of the pillars of India's freedom movement, attended the conference. At the conference, Madame Cama, an Indian revolutionary, unfurled India's flag of freedom which she had designed. Vladimir Ilyich Vlyanoy Lenin (1870 - 1924) of Russia was another prominent leader to make a major contribution to the conference. The socialist movement challenged the existing order in Europe.

RISE OF THE UNITED STATES OF AMERICA

Introduction

The United States of America is economically and politically one of the most powerful countries in the world. It is the fourth largest country. Its size is about three times that of India but its population is less than one-third of India.

After the discovery of America by Columbus in 1492, several European powers had established their colonies in various parts of America. After the American War of Independence in 1783, Great Britain acknowledged the independence of the United States of America then comprising thirteen colonies.

At that time, its western frontier was up to Mississipi River. During the 19th century, the U.S.A. expanded its territory up to the Pacifc Coast. In 1803, it purchased a large territory between Mississipi and the Rocky Mountains called Louisiana (the present central region) from France for 15 million dollars. In 1819, Spain ceded Florida and in 1846 Britain ceded the Oregon Country (the present north-west region) to the U.S.A. In

1848, its victory in the war with Mexico gave it the western territory up to the Pacific Ocean. In 1867, Alaska was purchased from Russia. In 1898, Hawaii was annexed.

With such vast expansion, the Union increased to 50 states.

U.S.A. Towards the End of the 19th Country

Within about three decades after the end of the Civil War, the U.S.A. emerged, industrially as well as politically, one of the foremost powers in the world.

Industrially, its significant achievements by the end of 19th century were (1) In almost every branch of industry the U.S.A. led every other country in the world (2) It was producing about one third of the total production of iron and steel in the world (3) The rail-roads in the country exceeded the combined rail-roads in Europe (4) Its production and consumption of oil and natural gas was more than the rest of the world put together (5) It created a huge market in the country itself.

The U.S.A. as a New Capilatist Power

The U.S.A. emerged as a new capilalist power by the 1890's. The remarks of a US Senator indicate the ambitions of the people of the U.S.A. "Today we are raising more than we can consume. Therefore we must find new markets for our produce, new occupation for our capital, new work for our labour. And this could be done through a policy of expansion by controlling other countries".

Dollar Diplomacy and Dollar Imperialism of the U.S.A.

The United States was able to exert a powerful influence over the economic and even political conditions of Central and South America as well as other parts of the world by means of her vast investments. This kind of diplomacy known as 'Dollar diplomacy' is almost as effective as a foreign army of occupation. It was said of this diplomacy, "If money talks, the American dollar shouts." The U.S.A. had the soaring ambition to develop what came to be called 'Dollar Imperialism'. It succeeded in realising its ambition of becoming a super power during the course of time.

Preventing European Interference in America's-North and South:

In 1823, when Spain tried to recover its revolting colonies in South America by suppressing the revolts of colonised people, President Munroe declared the famous doctrine that Europe should not interfere in American problems and in turn the U.S.A. would not interfere in European problems. In a word, this doctrine, known as Munroe Doctrine, proclaimed the principle of 'America for the Americans'. Later, the U.S.A. interpreted the doctrine elastically to suite its own varying interests including its interference in the affairs of other countries and extending its own empire.

Right to Interfere in other Countries' Affairs:

In 1904, Roosevelt declared, that the U.S.A. had the right not only to oppose European intervention in the American Continent, but also to intervene in the affairs of her neighbours and others to maintain peace and order in the world.

Foreign Policy Since the Civil War:

After the end of the Civil War in 1865, the U.S.A. became free to enter into world-politics by abandoning its old ideal of aloofness. It became ambitious to become a world power. The following examples will prove it.

(a) It enforced the Munroe Doctrine against France which was ruling Mexico after a prolonged war. It ordered the French to quit America and the French had to withdraw its troops from Mexico.

(b) U.S.A. challenged the British position on the Caribbean Sea. It intervened in the Britain-Venezuela quarrel over their boundaries and settled the issue by forcing an arbitration under its chairmanship.

American Imperialism:

The Munroe Doctrine of 'non-interference of others in American matters' changed into the U.S.A.'s interference in matters of the world. It slowly took the shape of American Imperialism. Examples:

(a) In 1895, feelings in the U.S.A. were greatly stirred when the Spanish army used very ruthless and savage means to suppress the rebellion of Cubans to become free. The U.S.A. asked Spain to grant independence to Cuba. This provoked Spain to declare war on the U.S.A. Spain being defeated, ceded to the U.S.A. the Island of Porto Rico in the West Indies and Guam and the Phillipine Islands in the Pacific, receiving monetary compensation for giving the Philippine Islands This marked the definite beginning of American Imperialism. For the first time in its history, the U.S.A. acquired colonies outside its own Union. (b) In 1898, the Hawaii Island was annexed as it became indispensable as a coaling station and a naval base in the Pacific (c) In 1899, by an agreement with Germany and Britain, the U.S.A. acquired the largest share of land in Samoa Islands in the Pacific (d) Cuba, for whose independence the U.S.A. had fought Spain, became an American protectorate (e) Nicaragua in Central America also became a U.S.A. protectorate.

The USA as a World Power

By the opening of the 20th century the U.S.A. started playing the role of a world power. The new attitude found its powerful champion in Theodore Roosevelt who remained President from 1901 to 1908. Examples :

(a) Roosevelt was bent upon asserting the position of the U.S.A. as a world power. He showed his uncompromising attitude in a boundary dispute between Alaska and Russia and settled it by securing most of its demands (b) He showed his strong attiude in controlling the Panama Canal. Britain, a joint sharer with the U.S.A. to construct and control the Panama Canal, later agreed to hand over the whole power to U.S.A. As Columbia objected to this, Panama being its province, the U.S.A. helped Panama to revolt and to gain independence from Columbia. The U.S.A. then purchased the Canal zone and constructed the Panama Canal in 10 years which shortened the route between the Pacific and the Atlantic by thousands of kilometres (c) In Russo-Japanese War of 1904, the U.S.A. succeeded in persuading Russia to recognise Japan's control of Korea and Southern Manchuria. In this settlement, the U.S.A. also acquired diplomatic gains against Japan. When Japan, for this, developed an ill feeling against the U.S.A., Roosevelt sent an American fleet to the Pacific to impress Japan with the might of the U.S.A. (d) It took part in the Algerian Conference of 1906 to settle the Moroccan question, though it was purely an European matter and against the Munroe Doctrine of America's non-interference in European matters.

All this could happen because the U.S.A. was being recognized as a world power by acquiring colonies and coaling stations in the Pacific, ensuring a monopoly of canal routes, setting up protectorates, becoming a great industrial and capital power, helping countries with dollars, strengthening its military power, presiding over arbitration matters, creating revolts and threatening nations.

Socialist Ideas in the U.S.A.

In the 1880's emerged several social groups and there were waves of strikes and demonstrations. On May 1, 1886, on the call given by the American Federation of labour (AFL), strikes and demonstrations all over the U.S.A. took place to press for the demand of eight hour working day. In 1901, the Socialist Party of America was formed.

DEVELOPMENTS IN ASIA

Background

With one-third of world's area (44, 250 thousand kilometres), Asia ranks as the largest continent. About 58 per cent of world's population lives here. There are 45 countries excluding USSR. Two largest countries are China and India.

India

In the first part of this book, a detailed account of the British conquest of India has been given. As the 20th century progressed, there was increasing agitation for independence. India nationalist movement was one of the first nationalist movements to emerge in colonies. India achieved independence on August 15, 1947 but another nation of Pakistan was created out of it.

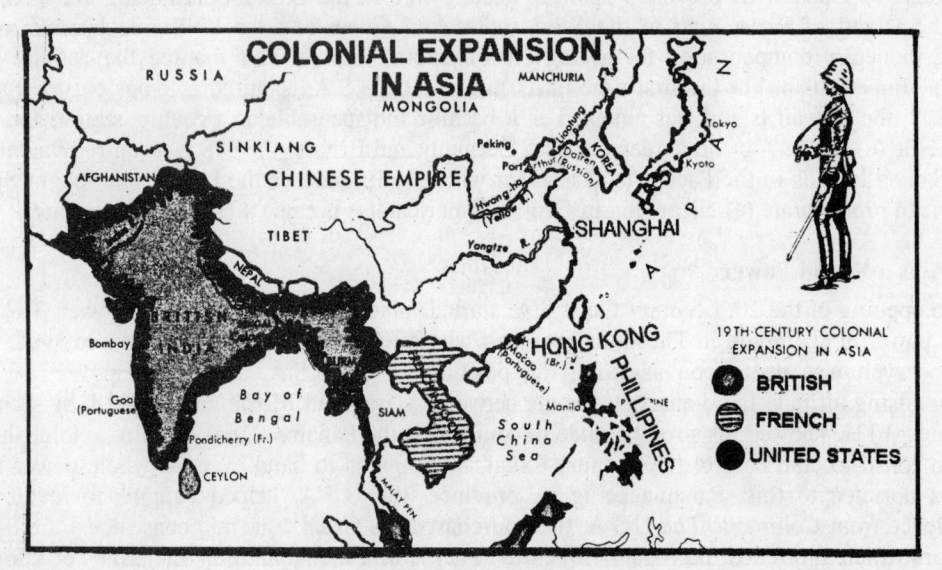

Map 1: **Colonial Expansion in Asia**

China

China, one of the oldest civilisations in the world and at present, the most populated country, fell a prey to European imperialists although there was no annexation of any part of the mainland by any foreign power.

Opium Trade:

In the eighteenth century, the European powers especially England, France Germany, and Russia were making huge profits by exporting opium to China as the Chinese were very much addicted to opium. The Chinese government, anxious to save their own people from the devastating effect of the drug, repeatedly prohibited its import and in 1800 declared the opium trade as illegal, but to no purpose. In the smuggling of opium into China the British merchants took the lead. This later led to two 'Opium Wars' resulting in the defeat of China in both the conflicts. The victory of England in the First Opium War (1840-42) led to the Treaty of Nanking which gave England the port of Hong Kong and threw open five other, Chinese ports to European trade. The Second Opium War (1856-58), in which England was joined by France, resulted in the Treaties of Tientsin (1858). Defeated China agreed to open eleven more ports to foreign trade, to allow foreigners to trade in her empire, to protect Christian missionaries and to pay a large war indemnity to England and France. Thus, China was opened up. The Europeans extended their economic tentacles and within thirty years, all the European nations joined in the scramble and entered into Chinese trade, though the lion share was secured by the Britishers.

Political Agression and Japan's Victory:

To the economic exploitation was added politcal aggression. Though the integrity of China was respected,

The World upto the First World War

its outlying dependencies began to be snatched away from her. In the north, Russia secured the province of Maritime Manchuria. In the south, France secured more territory from China in Indo-China. But England would not be left behind. England declared war upon Burma and annexed it as well as Sikkim. Russia and other foreign powers were planning to have a foothold in Korea. Japan could not allow Korea, a neighbouring country, to slip into the hands of foreign powers. Hence, it forced a war upon China in 1894 and completely defeated China in 1895. Under a treaty, Japan acquired Formosa and Korea.

'Open door' doctrine of the U.S.A.:

The U.S.A. made a protest against the international scramble for concessions in China. The U.S.A. had not joined the international scramble but its interest was in future trade with China. The U.S.A. feared that the European powers might take a monopolistic advantage by shutting out outside trade within the territories under their influence. It declared that China should remain open for all. This was known as the 'open door' doctrine which helped China not to break up under imperialistic greed of foreigners.

Boxer Movement:

The protest against foreign encroachment and exploitation also came from within China. It took the shape of a violent anti-foreign movement led by a secret society called the Righteous Fraternity of Fist-Fighters, better known as the Boxers. The Boxers resented everything foreign. The movement reached its climax in 1900, supported by the government, when several Christian missionaries were murdered and the German minister in Peking was shot down in the street. An international force was sent to China and it crushed the Boxer rebellion. Chins had to pay a huge war indemnity.

Anglo-Japanese Alliance:

The third development which prevented the breakup of China was the Anglo-Japanese Alliance. The fear of ever-increasing ambition of Russia in the Far-East became intensified by Russia's attempt to take over Manchuria. This alarmed both England and Japan and they made an alliance to support one another for maintaining and preserving the independence and territorial integrity of China and Korea. This strengthened the position of Japan which defeated Russia in 1904 and checked its advance in the Far-East.

The Reform Movement and the Rebellion:

The reform movement in China began after its defeat in the Sino-Japanese War in 1895. It realised the necessity of remodelling its institutions on western lines. But after one hundred days of reform activites in 1898, the movement had to be stopped due to the Boxer rising which was both anti-reform and anti-foreign in its policy. But the failure of the Boxer rising and the consequential entry of the foreign troops in Peking convinced China that reform was the only alternative to the breaking up of the empire. Thus, China began westernizing by encouraging education on western lines and following western models. But such reforms were not radical enough to satisfy the Young China Party. Soon the young revolutionary party tried to overthrow the Manchu dynasty which was foreign, corrupt and incompetent. Sun-Yat-Sen, a doctor of medicine graduated from Hong Kong skilfully turned the anti-Manchu agitation into a republican movement. The Imperial Government offered sweeping concessions including the grant of Parliamentary form of Government. But the followers of Sun-Yat-sen would agree to no compromise with the Manchu autocracy and in 1911, took up arms against the Manchus, captured Nanking and made it the capital of their provisional republic with Sun-Yat-Sen as President. It was in February 1912 when the crowning success of the revolution was achieved after the boy emperor, the last of the Manchus, abdicated the throne and the whole of China was made a Republic. Dr Sun soon resigned his Presidency in favour of Yuan-Shi-Kai, an able general and shrewd politician, with the hope that the Republic would be consolidated under the influence of a younger man of strength and determination. This hope was belied as Yuan sought the help of foreign powers to strengthen his postion and in 1915, started propaganda for the restoration of monarchy. His plan was opposed by the warlords as well as Dr Sun. Dr Sun formed the Kuomintang, that is, the National Party, and gave a call for a 'Second Revolution.' The party was banned and Dr Sun was exiled. However, with the death of Yuan in 1916, the crisis was averted. But soon China came under the rule of warlords who fought with one another for supremacy and the weak central Government existed only in name. After the First World War the revolutionary movement acquired a new strength.

Japan

Background:

Japan, called the 'land of rising sun' is a group of several islands in the north-western Pacific. It was the only country in Asia which rose as an imperialistic power towards the second half of the 19th century. Two factors that led to its rise were—a stable government and the discipline of the people.

End of Isolation of Japan:

The U.S.A. was successful in entering the treaty of Kanagawa with Japan in 1854. Americans were allowed to carry on limited trade under Japanese regulation. With this, the isolation of Japan was broken. This paved the way for the exploitation of Japan by several foreign powers. In 1863, there occurred a clash between Japan and the combined forces of the British, French, Dutch and American. Japan was defeated and foreign powers extracted extra-territorial rights and other concessions from Japan.

Meiji Era (1868-1912) and Japan:

In 1868, Japan ended the rule of good-for-nothing military generals and restored monarchy by putting a 15 year old monarch on the throne. The young monarch adopted Meiji (enlightened peace) as the name of his reign of 45 years till 1912. The Japanese decided that their country could survive only by building it on a western model. The Japanese imitated the British navy, the French army and later the German army and the public schools of the U.S.A. Within three decades, Japan became an industrial power. Its all round progress became an envy of big nations.

Japanese Imperialism:

With a strong economy, efficient military, disciplined people and enterprising rulers, Japan pursued colonial ambitions on the pattern of European imperialism. Following were the important imperialist pursuits of Japan.

Sino-Japanese War (1894-95):

Without any justifiable reason, Japan declared war on China, defeated it and then entered into a peace treaty in 1895. It resulted in (a) Japan's gaining Formosa and other Chinese territories and (b) China's agreeing to pay a huge war indemnity to throw open several ports to Japan and to provide special trade concessions to Japan.

Anglo-Japanese Alliance (1902):

England and Japan agreed to preserve the independence of China and Korea.

Russo-Japanese War (1904-05):

The commercial and territorial ambitions of both caused war in which Russia was defeated and by the resulting treaty Japan gained great prestige and emerged as a world power.

Other Imperialist Adventures:

Japan annexed Korea in 1910 and made southern Manchuria its sphere of influence leaving the north to Russia.

Indonesia

Background:

Indonesia is a Republic made up of a large group of about 3000 islands off south-East Asia. The cultural background of most of the islands has strong Hindu and Buddhist elements. Conversion to Islam occurred between the 13th and 15th centuries.

Dutch Imperialim in Indonesia:

The Portuguese imperialists were the first to establish their power in Indonesia. But they were thrown over by the Dutch of Holland (Netherlands) who had formed the Dutch East Company—a trading company in 1602. Thereafter began the ruthless exploitation of Indonesia. From Indonesia, the Dutch secured huge supplies of spices. The Dutch government took over the administration from the company in 1799. In the 19th century, national awakening began to emerge. Indonesia became independent on December 29, 1949.

Indo-China

Background:

Indo-China lies in south-east Asia. The French, who came into this country in the 17th and 18th century, ultimately made Indo-China a group of protectorates ruled by a Governor-General appointed by the French Government. The national movement in Vietnam was led by the communists under the leadership of Ho Chi Minh (1892-1969). North Vietnam declared complete independence in 1945. In 1976, the whole of Vietnam was unified.

South-West Asia:

Most of the south-west Asia remained under the Ottoman empire of the Ottoman Turks till the empire declined in the 19th century, The countries started breaking away from the Turkish rule. The great powers of Europe, particularly Great Britain and France, wanted to secure a stake in Persia and the Middle Asian lands but could not conveniently step in. Most of the land being a desert, it did not encourage imperialistic greed and rivalry till 1914 when oil was discovered in parts of these territories. During world war I, some European countries had gained much economic and political influence in this area. In the war, the Ottoman (Turkish) empire joined with Germany but the Arabs supported the European allies with the hope of winning freedom from Ottoman Turks. In 1917, Britain issued the Balfour Declaration to establish the national home of Jews in Palestine while fighting to capture Palestine. After the war, the League of Nations divided most of the Arab lands into mandated territories (that is to be protected and ruled by other nations). France took control of Lebanon and Syria, and Biritain of Iraq, Jordan and Palestine.

DEVELOPMENTS IN AFRICA

The Beginning of European Control

During the 1400's, the Portuguese began to explore the west coast of Africa. Portugal's control of Angola began in 1482 with the discovery of the estuary of the river Congo. They soon began to ship Africans to Europe as slaves. Later, Denmark, Holland and England established 'slave stations' on the west coast. During the 1600's, the Dutch took over many of Portugals west coast trading ports. They also settled in Cape Colony in 1651. Between 1850 and 1900 the interior regions of Africa were explored, charted and claimed by a number of European countries. The British wanted to control the continent from the south to the north and the French from west to the east.

Partition of Africa

France:

The first important European penetration was made by French who occupied Algeria in 1830. In 1881, the French occupied the neighbouring Tunis with the approval of England and Germany. In return, England occupied the island of Cyprus with the approval of France. In 1905, France established a protectorate over Morocco. Italy and Spain backed France in this move. In return Italy was backed to occupy Tripoli and Spain for a slice of Morocco. At the beginning of the First World War in 1914, France controlled large areas in western and central Africa besides Algeria, Tunis and Morocco. Though blocked by British occupation from Egypt to south Africa, France still could reach east to occupy French Somaliland and the large island of Madagascar.

Britain:

The Turkish sultan, Ismail Pasha had gone deeply into debt as he could not pay back the huge money borrowed from European banks for the Suez Canal and modernization of Egypt. In 1875, he sold his stock in the Canal Company to the British government. Having gained interest in the canal, Britain sent a military expedition to suppress some disorder in Egypt and took the country as a British protectorate. The British defeated the Sudanese and then joined with Egypt and both ruled the country, though Britain remained the dominant power. Cecil Rhodes extended the British territory by adding Rhodesia, named after him, and Bechuanaland. In addition to these, Britain acquired Nigeria, the Gold Coast, Uganda, Kenya, Nyasaland and British Somaliland.

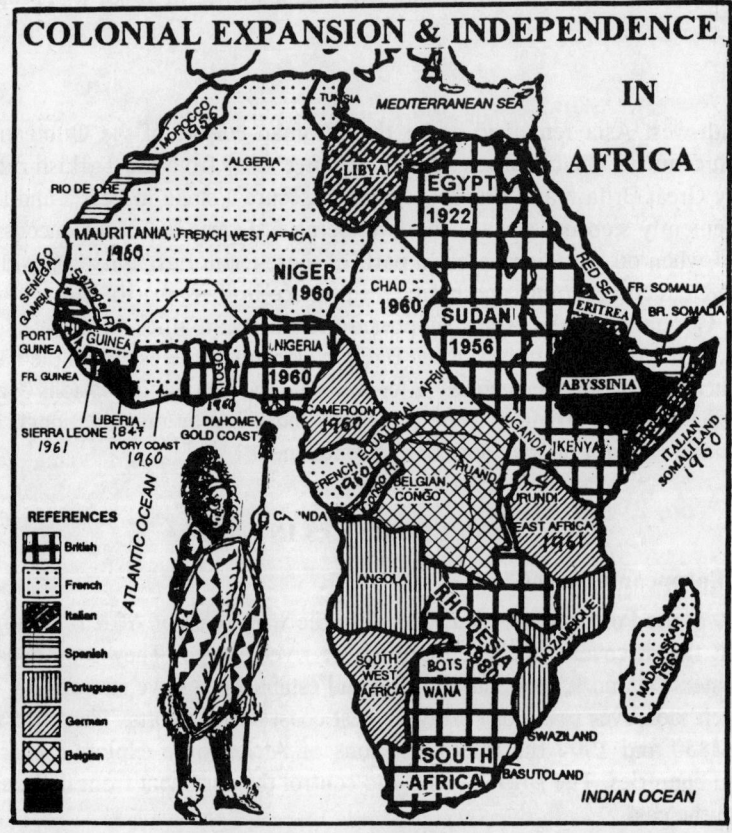

Map 2: **Colonial Expansion and Independence in Africa**

The World upto the First World War 219

South Africa:

Boers (meaning farmers) was the name given to the Dutch settlers who first established themselves in South Africa. The British settlers came late and tried to drive away the Boers whose strong resentment climaxed into the Boer War in which the Boers were defeated. Under a treaty (1902), the two provinces of Transwal and Orange Free State were annexed to the British empire. In 1909, under the Act of Union all the four provinces of South Africa joined to form the Union of South Africa.

Italy and Germany:

Germany and Itlay were late comers. Germany obtained the colonies of German East Africa, Togoland, Cameroon and German South-West Africa. Italy obtained fairly easily the Italian Somaliland and Eritrea in eastern Africa, but when Italy invaded Abyssinia in 1896, it was defeated by the native forces.

Belgium & Portugal:

Belgium acquired the Congo Free State. Portugal possessed Portuguese East Africa and Angola. By 1914, except Abyssinia and Liberia, the great continent had been divided among the European powers.

DEVELOPMENTS IN LATIN AMERICA

Latin America is a large region that consists of South America, Central America and Mexico, that is, all the territories South of the U.S.A. in the new world. Columbus reached Latin America in 1492. This created great excitement and people from Spain and Portugal started settling down in this new continent. By the mid-

Map 3: **Colonial Expansion Latin America**

1500's, groups of Spanish conquerers defeated the great civilsations—the Maya of Southern Mexico, the Aztec of Central Mexico and the Incas of the west coast of South America—and established the Spanish colony from Mexico to Chile on the west of Latin America. The Portuguese colonised Brazil, the eastern part of the region. Since the majority of Latin Americans speak Spainsh and Portuguese, each of which developed from Latin, the region is called Latin America.

Independence of Latin Countries

The political and economic injustices suffered by the colonists for 300 years became intolerable and a keen desire grew for independence. The two greatest heroes in the fight for independence in Spainsh South America were the Venezuelan General Simon Bolivar and the Argentine General Jose de San Martin. Mexico won independence in 1821. The Central Americans won their independence in 1822 without bloodshed. In 1824, Bolivar's army won a victory to free the colonies of the northern South America. San Martin's forces freed Argentina, Chile and Peru. Brazil won the freedom from Portugal without firing a shot in 1822.

IMPERIALIST RIVALRIES AND CONFLICTS

Chief Causes

Imperialism created discord, conflicts and rivalries among the competing imperialist countries namely England, France, Italy, Spain, Portugal and Germany. It also created conflicting groups in the colonised countries by following the policy of 'Divide and Rule.' In grabbing the new lands for marketing their manufactured goods and for getting cheap materials for their industries, the imperialist powers became enemies of each other. To outwit each other they resorted to secret as well as open alliances. Thus, the so-called civilized world of Europe became uncivilized and responsible for so much bloodshed. Apart from local battles, the imperialists waged two bloody world wars and that too in the name of democracy, humanism, equality and liberty. Imperilist rivalries and conflicts led to the First World War.

A Brief Description

A brief review of imperialist rivalries and conflicts among different imperialist powers in different regions and countries is given below.

1. Scramble for Power in Africa:

Scramble for power among the European countries led to the partition of Africa in several small countries which remained very backward for a number of centuries. Important conflicts were (1) The Boer war was fought between the British and the Dutch. The Dutch settlers were defeated (2) There was war tension for several years between Britain and France on the control over Sudan (3) The French questioned Britain's right to occupy Egypt. An agreement was reached between the two and the French had a free hand in Morocco.

2. Rivalries and Conflicts in India:

The sea-route discovered by the Portuguese sailor Vasco Da Gama (1469-1524) on May 17, 1498 was a turning point in India's history and it paved the way for European imperialism. The Portuguese conquered Goa in 1510 and Diu and Daman in 1534. However, their domination in India was limited to few areas only. The French dreamt to establish their empire in India. But they failed to meet the challenge of the British. There were fierce struggles leading to several bloody battles between the two powers.

3. Russian and British Rivalries in the Middle-East:

For British imperialists, the middle east was tremendously important as a zone of defence for protecting

British India from European rivals, above all from Russia. Taking advantage of England's preoccupation in the Boer War in South Africa, Russia quietly resumed spreading her influence in Central Asia, Persia, Afghanistan and Tibet.

4. Imperialist Conflicts in Arab Countries:

The position of Sultan of Turkey, who was also the Caliph of Islam, became so weak that he began to be called 'the Sick Man of Europe.' Before the First World War, Britain taking the advantage of the weak position of Turkey, wanted to bring the Arabs under its control. It, therefore, came into clash with Turkey. The imperialist powers made all efforts to keep the Arabs divided. The British and the French came into clash.

5. Imperialist Clash:

Conflicts over trading rights occurred among the Dutch in China. Japan and Russia also witnessed a clash of interests in China over commercial and territorial matters.

6. Imperial conflicts in the Balkan:

Discussed in the next chapter.

EXERCISES

A. Very Short Answer Type

1. Name one country each in Asia and Africa affected by imperialism.
2. Name the two main imperialist powers that came into clash in India.
3. List any two chief characteristics of imperialism in Europe.
4. Name any two factors that led to imperialism.
5. List any two forms of imperialism.
6. Name the imperialist countries that had several territories in its possession in Latin America.
7. State the meaning of 'Open Door Policy' in China.
8. What was the main item of trade in China that led to imperialist lust.

B. Short Answer Type

1. Explain hegemony of Europe.
2. Explain the term 'Latin America' and list the name of any ten countries in Latin America.
3. How did socialism originate in Europe?
4. How did U.S.A. become an imperialist power?
5. Explain the term 'Dollar Diplomacy'.
6. Why was war fought between Japan and China? What was its impact?
7. Explain 'Boxer Rising' in China.
8. State the contribution of Dr.Sun-Yat-Sen to national awakening in China.
9. How did Japan become a major political power towards the second half of the 19th century?
10. What were the causes of Russo-Japanese War? State its effect.
11. Explain the significance of 3CS of European powers in respect to Africa.
12. State the measures taken by the U.S.A. to strengthen its position in Latin America.
13. Explain in brief important events related with rivalries and conflicts of the imperialist powers in China.

CHAPTER 22

The First World War (1914-1918)

19TH CENTURY BUILT UP HOPES FOR A BETTER 20TH CENTURY

The Great War, known as the World War I, made a mockery of the peace and abundance prophesied by the statesmen and scientists of the 19th century. Truly, in many senses the 19th century had been a 'wonderful century'. By 1900, conditions for the working men were greatly improved. Many countries achieved universal suffrage and education reached to lower classes. Science had made tremendous gains along with industry and technology. Inventions, one after another in every field, were making impossible things possible. The conquest of medicine over diseases had become miraculous in gifting mankind health and longevity. Many persons thought civilization and happiness had attained a new height.

Efforts for Peace

But the fall was not far away. Signs were undoubtedly pointing towards a holocaust in spite of the fact that efforts to keep the peace were on. As fear of war grew, people began to talk more and more and write against war. Many books were published which pleaded the causes of peace. *The Great Illusion,* by Angell, pointed out that no one really wins wars. In 1898, *The Future of War* by Ivan Block pointed out that a modern war would bring starvation and bankruptcy all over the world. Two international peace conferences held at Hague in 1899 and 1907 and the creation of the Court of Arbitrations in 1899 helped to reduce the tension of war and settle quarrels. At the same time many international organisations were bringing about better understanding among the people of the world. The industrialisation necessitated economic interdependence and cooperation among nations. Alfred Nobel established the Nobel Prize in 1896.

But the imperialistic ambitions, rivalries and opposing alliances, rabid nationalism, militarization, the race for armies and armaments, the growing fear, suspicion, antagonism, clashes and conflicts and the Balkan issue brought the world on the brink of war.

REASON FOR CALLING THE WAR AS WORLD WAR

The war was called as the World War on account of several reasons. First, it engulfed almost all the countries in the world directly or indirectly. Second, it was fought on an unprecedented scale. Third, the War had its impact on the material and non-material resources of the entire world. Fourth, it was fought in the world on the land, on the sea, under the sea and in the air.

Warring Countries : The Allies and the Central Powers

The First World War was fought between two rival groups called the Allies and the Central Powers. The Allies comprised England, France, Italy, Russia, America and Japan. The Central Powers comprised Germany, Austria-Hungary, Turkey and Bulgaria.

The First World War (1914-1918)

The U.S.A. entered the war in April 1917 on the side of the Allies. In all twenty-nine countries of the world directly participated in the War. Out of about 65 million soldiers mobilised in the War, 42 million were mobilised by the Allies and about 23 millioin by the Central Powers.

The whole of Europe except Scandinavia, Holland, Switzerland and Spain joined the War.

CAUSES OF THE WAR

The Crisis that Arose in the Balkans:

It is helpful to have the background of the Balkan issue before understanding the Balkan crisis.

Background:

The Balkan peninsula is in the south-east Europe comprising Serbia, Albania, Bulgaria, Greece, Motenegro, Thrace and areas of Bosnia and Herzegovina. The various races residing in the Balkans are Serbs, Albanians, Slovens, Macedonians and Croats. From the 15th until the 19th centuries most of the Balkan Peninsula was part of the Ottoman (Turkish) empire. On account of the mixture of races, languages and cultures, the Balkans had been a politically unsettled region, troubled by frequent rebellions and wars. Most of the Balkan states were trying to free themselves from the oppressive control of the Ottoman empire.

In 1877, Bulgaria revolted against Turkey but was ruthlessly crushed. All Europe protested at the slaughter and bloodshed of the Bulgarians. In 1878, Russia, showing sympathy in rescuing the Slavs, waged war on the Turks and defeated them. Russia's help was with the motive of getting an access to the Mediterranean Sea through Dardanelles and Bosporus straits. After its success, Russia got the Treaty of San Stefano signed which made Serbia, Rumania, Montenegro and Bulgaria independent states but made Bulgaria "Greater Bulgaria" by adding some part of the Ottoman Empire. The Treaty displeased many. England did not want Russia to get access to the Mediterranean and Austria, Greece and Serbia, each wanted to have the extra territory that was added to Bulgaria.

Thus, in response to such discontent, the General European Conference was held in 1878 under the Presidentship of German Chancellor Bismark for arriving at a settlement. A new treaty, the Treaty of Berlin, was signed to undo the four months old Treaty of Stefano. As a result, Bulgaria was much reduced in size and about one third of its territory was returned to Turkey. Austria made some territorial gain. In addition Austria was made the protector of Ottoman provinces of Bosnia and Herzegovina. Turkey still retained some European territory comprising Albania, Macedonia and Thrace. German Chancellor helped Turkey, as Turkey's support was necessary in building a German railroad from Berlin to Baghdad to tap the natural resources of Mesopotamia and to obtain some trade with the Far East.

As most of the Balkan states were freed from the Turkish regime, the Slavs residing in these countries were determined to free other Slavs. Serbia had a large Slavic population. It dreamt of creating a greater Serbia and started Pan-Slavism, a nationalistic movement to unify the Slavic people. This ambition was chiefly aimed against Turkey and Austria, both of which governed many Slavic people. Bosnia and Herzegovina, under the protection of Austria-Hungary, had a large Slav population and so Serbia's ambition was to annex the two regions. But in 1908, Austria annexed the provinces as part of a secret arrangement with Russia, and in return Russian warships were to be allowed to use the Dardanelles and Bosporus. Britain, however, objected to the Russian claim and did not allow Russia to use the two straits. Austria's seizure of the two provinces, which were under Austria's guardianship, angered the Serbs as their own plan to absorb these two in the plan for a Greater Serbia collapsed. In 1912, encouraged by the Russians, the First Balkan War broke out when Bulgaria, Greece, Montenegro and Serbia attacked European Turkey intending to drive it from Europe and to free Albania, Macedonia and Thrace. The Balkan countries won. Turkey had to give up all her territories in Europe except Constantinople.

The Balkan nations soon fell quarrelling among themselves. Serbia and Greece demanded Macedonia which Bulgaria claimed to be hers. Macedonia is between Greece in the south and Serbia and Bulgaria in the north. As a result, Bulgaria started the Second Balkan War in 1913 by making a surprise attack on Serbia and Greece. Within a month, the War was over with the defeat of Bulgaria, as Turkey and Rumania also attacked Bulgaria in support of Serbia and Greece. A new peace treaty was made and, at the instance of Austria, the artificial state of Albania was created just between the sea and Serbia, thus preventing Serbia from getting any outlet to the sea. The results of the Balkan war were serious. It resulted in bitter enmity between Serbia and Austria. The Serbian blood was already at boiling point as Serbia had been robbed of its birthright when Austria annexed Bosnia and Herzegovina, provinces akin to Serbia in blood and language. But Austria was determined to prevent Serbian expansion. Again, Austria bottled up Serbia by preventing its expansion up to the sea coast. But in spite of Austrian opposition, Serbia managed to double her territory and to heighten her prestige and to intensify her impassioned patriotic agitation for a Pan-Slav empire. Austria was also concerting measures to isolate and crush Serbia.

The Balkan issue was indeed quite dangerous and sensitive, but by itself it could not have engulfed the globe with the fire and smoke of a war. But, there were other contributory causes building up for long with latent potentiality of massive dimension to completely destroy one another, whoever came in the way. It will be seen how almost every powerful nation became every other nation's enemy if it came in its way. The last chapter describes how the fire of rivalry was spreading. Enemies became friends, friends enemies if it suited them to achieve their purpose. Selfishness, chicanery, hypocrisy, cruelty, dishonesty, lust and greed ruled the roost.

Old Imperialism:

European expansion and its imperialistic lust are as old as the 15th century when Europe turned her eyes upon the non-European world. In the course of 16th and 17th century, Spain, Portugal, Holland, England and France laid the foundation of their colonial empire. Much of the history of Europe during this period is taken up with the rivalries of European nations for colonial and commercial expansion. But, in the early part of the 19th century, the colonial rivalry, tension and fever seemed to have lost much of its excitement. This was because the colonial empires built with so much blood and sweat were crumbling down on all sides. There was not a single empire that did not suffer colonial losses. Great Britain was the only exception, but it too had felt the pangs of losing the 13 colonies in America, which later through annexations and War built up what we know as U.S.A. The Spanish colonies in Latin America also revolted and became free between 1800 and 1822. The Portugal's Brazil became free in 1822. These colonial disasters and disappointments convinced the European statesmen that empire building was hardly worth the trouble and it was a sheer waste to spend money on this development. For, one day or the other, these colonies were going to slip away from their grip.

Disraeli, the Prime Minister of Britain, depicted the prevailing mood of discouragement and loss when he said, "These wretched colonies will be independent in a few days and are like a mill-stone round our neck."

The New Imperialism:

But, as the 19th Century progressed, several forces coincidentally gathered together and created a new impetus for colonial grabbings and expansion. It was a new upsurge, a new adventure, a set of new conditions and causes, a revival of old rivalries and feverish activities to possess territories in Africa and Asia. It was called the *New Imperialism* or revival of imperialism that once arose in the 15th century and faded out at the begining of the 19th century. It was largely the result of the new economic conditions produced by the Industiral Revolution. So, both the economic and political aspects of this New Imperialism are described below.

(a) Economic Imperialism (Capturing and monopolising markets):

The Industrial Revolution and technological advancement had created a new kind of imperialism — the economic imperialism. The world's most powerful nations had become great industrial nations. The factories started producing such abundance of manufactured goods in such a short time that their surplus supplies needed immediate marketing in an easy way. Besides, these powerful countries needed raw materials to feed their factories, markets for selling their surplus products and food to feed their growing population. Banks and other investors sought profitable enterprises in which to invest surplus capital earned through industrialized capitalistic system. It is worth noting that Europe being in a temperate zone, did not have enough food to feed its people nor any raw material like cotton to feed its textile factories. It lacked in different types of mineral resources. Its chief food crops were rye, potatoes and turnip and chief mineral resources were coal and iron. The best markets to suit its purpose were far away in Africa, Asia and Latin America which grew enough food and raw material and were so undeveloped that it could be possible to monpolise these markets for selling their goods at desired monopolistic prices and to invest capital for developing these countries at huge profis. Science and technology had given Europe big steam ships and navigation instruments to reach these markets easily carrying heavy load of goods and men and also new types of weapons to use in unfavourable eventualities interfering with their commercial enterprises. However, this new type of imperialism started a race for capturing and monopolising markets for their own goods and preventing goods of other countries to enter the market. Such a race for markets naturally engendered powerful rivals. The story of the rivalries was described in the previous chapter.

(b) Political Imperialism:

However, the economic imperialism is bound to turn into political imperialism. Economic imperialism, is monopolistic capture and domination over the markets. For this, political rights become a necessity, so that other competitors could be resisted or kept at bay. This is only possible through complete administrative control. The only way is to conquer a country and colonise it so that economic exploitation to any degree could be possible. This was the case with the industrially powerful nations who came to trade with the far away countries, India being one of the cases. Every strong nation wanted to grab as much foreign territory as was possible, for larger the empire larger the power and prestige. This race for territorial possession created clashes of interests and started wars, as was the case in India to decide whether France or Britain would be the future rulers. France had a hand of winning cards but Robert Clive won the game.

Nationalism:

Nationalism was another great cause that drifted the nations towards war. Nationalism inflamed the racial pride of the people, stimulated them to exalt their country above all others and made them arrogant, intolerant and aggressive in their attitude to their neighbours. It was the excess of nationalism that embittered the relations and intensified the rivalries among nations like Germany and Great Britain. It was the outraged nationalism of the French that wanted to take revenge against Germany for taking away their rich region of Alsace-Lorraine. The unsatisfied national aspirations of Balkan people made the Balkan peninsula a tinder box. Nationalism also consolidated a strong feeling that each racial group under a different racial domination must have an independent autonomous government or must join with others of the same nationality.

Nationalism led to the unification of Italy and Germany. But this was not always possible. Austria-Hungary was made up of many different races. For reasons of nationalism, Serbia carried on the Pan-Slavic agitation. Narrow nationalism based on the belief of "My country, right or wrong" was a threat to world peace.

Rivalries Drag down to Destruction:

Imperialism creates rivalries among nations and nationalism incites and intensifies rivalries. Rivalries flare up enmity and hostility. These in turn inflame a spirit of revenge and aggression to attack and destroy the enemy blocking the way to imperial ambition and land grabbing, or in case of being attacked, to get prepared for defence. This gives rise to militarization and alliances — a race to become stronger as much and as fast as possible and to strengthen friendly ties with those who would join in case of launching an attack or come to rescue when attacked. The previous chapter has referred to the various rivalries between nations caused by scramble for territories in Africa, India, Middle East, Arab countries, China and the Balkans. Among other important cases of conflicts and rivalries mention may be made of the following :

1) Franco-German rivalry due to France's loss of Alsace and Lorraine grabbed by Germany after the Franco-German War of 1870-71.
2) Anglo-German rivalry due to Britain's naval supremacy being challenged by Germany.
3) Russo-Austrian rivalry due to their interest in the Balkan issue.

Militarism:

Militarism was a strong factor for war. European statesman often held, "If you wish for peace, prepare for war". The best way to prevent a war was to remain prepared to meet the challenge of a war. Germany, France and Russia adopted a new programme of arms expansion. Great Britain increased its already large naval expenditure. As a corollary, Germany, in fear of an anticipated attack from France, initiated a system of military alliance. This, in its turn, provoked counter alliances.

Sale Promotion of Ammunition:

The ammunition makers, in order to promote their sales of war material, aided in building up a war spirit. Recent investigations have shown how the Vicker-Armstrong of England, Schneiders and Krupps of Germany worked together to influence politicians to promote the sale of their commodities.

Alliances among Nations:

The cause of peace suffered further because the European powers had aligned themselves into two opposing groups. Such alliances made governments bolder.

Following were the important alliances:

(1) Dual Alliance (1879):

Germany and Austria - Hungary joined hands by making a secret alliance known as the Dual Alliance with the objective of helping each other against a possible Russian attack.

(2) Triple Alliance (1883):

Italy was disgruntled on the creation of French Protectorate of Tunis in Africa as it had a large Italian population. Italy joined the Dual Alliance of 1879 and it became the Triple Alliance.

(3) Secret Franco-Russian Agreement (1894):

Russia wanted to check Austria in the Balkans and France wanted to recover its territories that it had lost to Germany in the Franco-German War (1870-71). So both entered into a secret agreement with the main aim of helping each other in case a big neighbour attacked them.

(4) Entente Cordlate — Friendly Understanding (1904):

The common fear of Germany made the traditional rivals friendly. They decided to settle their mutual imperialist claims amicably.

(5) Triple Entente (1907):

The Anglo-French Alliance was enlarged by associating Russia with it. Japan became a close associate of the Triple Alliance.

Fear Psychosis:

Under the influence of imperialsim, nationalism, militarism and military alliances, nations were gripped with fear. They did not trust each other. Secret agents and spies moved secretly to secure information about

The First World War (1914-1918)

other nation's military strength and degree of preparedness. This was the case between 1900 and 1914. This fear and uncertainty spurred to action for more preparedness, more militarism, further enlargement of armies and stock of armaments, inventing more destructive bombs and deadly instruments of war.

The Unification of Germany and Italy:

The unification of Germany and that of Italy brought in two new states, young and dashing, in the European family of nations. It changed the whole complexion of international relations in Europe. By 1900, much of the world had been divided into colonies. Germany and Italy remained dissatisfied with their share. They emerged as strong nations after 1870 and thus, both had been late in entering the race for colonies. Germany demanded a place in the sun, as it industrially expanded very rapidly and left many industrial nations behind. The colonies that Germany and Italy obtained in Africa were not so potentially rich as those possessed by Britain, France and others. As one of the greatest industrial nations in Europe, Germany needed additional markets and raw materials. And so, jealousies and rivalries started becoming intenser as Germany's ambition was to become a great power.

Lack of International Organisation:

There was no effective international organisation to reconcile conflicting interests of nations. The Hague Conference of 1882 and 1907 which tried to do some work of reconciliation failed to show any results.

Immediate Cause of the War:

The immediate cause of the War was that on June 28, 1914 a Serb murdered prince Archduke Francis Ferdinand, the nephew of the emperor of Austria and heir to the throne, and also his wife Sophia. The town where the murder took place was in Bosnia which had been annexed by Austria. The murderer Gavrilo Princip, a 24 year old Serb was said to have hatched a plot to have an independent kingdom of all Serbs. The organizer of the assassination of the Prince was a member of a secret society called the "Black Hand" or "Union of Death" — a society formed for uniting all Serbs into a single Serbian state. A storm of anger over the murder rose in Austria and Germany. The Emperor of Austria wrote to the German Emperor, "The crime

Map 4: Europe in 1914

against my nephew is the direct consequence of the agitation carried on by Russians and Pan-Slavists, whose sole aim is to weaken the Triple Alliance and shatter my Empire." With the approval of the German Emperor, Austria served an ultimatum on Serbia making eleven demands on it and for its reply fixed a time-limit of forty-eight hours for compliance. Serbia's reply did not satisfy Austria. On July 28, 1914, Austria declared war on Serbia and on July 29 bombarded Belgrade, capital of Serbia.

Summing Up:

The gun-powder of the War was already ready and it needed a spark to ignite it which was provided by the murder of the Prince.

In fact, the War was a culmination of several developments. The event was the occasion, not the real cause, for the War. Tension had developed so much in intensity that only a slight incident was needed to measure swords with opponents.

COURSE OF THE WAR

June 28, 1914 and June 28, 1919 are the two significant dates in the history of the world. June 28, 1914 was the day when the prince of Austria was murdered. Thus, this date may be taken as the beginning of hostilities. On June 28, 1919, the Peace Treaty was signed by Germany and the day may be treated as the end of the War, though the actual war ended on November 11, 1918, when Germany signed the armistice. Germany began the War with soaring hopes, vim and vigour but lay in the dust when the War ended.

It may be remembered that all the 29 nations did not enter the War on the same day and also did not participate till the end. For instance the U.S.A. entered the War in April 1917 and Russia withdrew itself from it in February 1917 — much before the end of the War. Following, in brief, is the course of entry of some of the most important nations of the world.

ENTRY BY VARIOUS NATIONS IN THE WAR

Chart showing the date of entry of each country into the War and the reason

Country	Date of Entry	Most significant Reason
1. Austria (attacks Serbia)	July 28, 1914	Murder of Austrian prince.
2. Serbia	July 28, 1914	Attacked by Austria.
3. Germany (declares war on Russia)	August 1, 1914	Anticipating attack from Russia.
4. Russia	August 1, 1914	Germany's declaration of War against it.
5. France	August 3, 1914	Germany declares war on France.
6. Belgium	August 4, 1914	Germany enters Belgium to attack France.
7. Britain	August, 4, 1914	Germany's refusal to withdraw from Belgium.
8. Montenegro	August 7, 1914	Joins Serbia, a fellow Slav country.
9. Ottoman Empire Turkey	October 20, 1914	Bombards Russia to help the Central Powers.
10. Japan	August 23, 1914	German Emperor makes some insolent references to Japan.
11. Italy	May 23, 1915	The Allies promise to help Italy to get Trentino and Trieste.
12. Bulgaria	September 1915	After the rout of Russia, Bulgaria joins Central Powers and invades Serbia on being given rosy promises
13. Portugal	March 9, 1916	Being an old ally of Britain declares war on Germany.
14. Rumania	August 27, 1916	Declares War on Austria, takes Britain's side.
15. United States	April 6, 1917	(Discussed below.)
16. Greece	July 2, 1917	Compelled to join the war by Allies.

The First World War (1914-1918)

Late Entry of the US

Originally when the war broke out, President Wilson (1913-21) of the United States proclaimed that his country would remain neutral. But, gradually the U.S.A. had to change its stand. Germany also promised that it would not attack US ships. But when Germany started submarine warfare against British war ships as well as merchant and other ships, the U.S.A., on Jaunary 31, 1917, suddenly withdrew its promise and threatened to prevent the entry of all ships in the seas around Britain, France, and Italy. Germany did not heed to the threat and destroyed a merchant ship in which nearly 100 Americans were killed. This raised a storm of protest in the United States. The U.S.A. became apprehensive of Germany's attack on it with the help of Japan and Mexico. U.S.A. was also running a risk as U.S.A. bank's huge investments in the allied countries were at stake.

The U.S.A., therefore, declared War on Germany on April 6, 1917 and on Austria in December 1917. A few months later Siam, Liberia, China, Brazil, Gautemala, Costa Rica, Nicaragua, Haiti and Honduras followed the U.S.A.

The entry of the U.S.A. was a turning point in the War. The balance was clearly tilted in favour of the Allies. The U.S.A. poured its huge resources on the side of the Allies.

President Wilson's 14-Point Programme:

Thomas Woodrow Wilson, American Democratic President (1913-21), who kept his country out of World War I until 1917, propounded in January 1918, his famous 'Fourteen Points' for a just peace to bring about the Armistice. In fact, in these 14 points he also laid down the War aims of the Allies.

1. No secret diplomacy, but open covenants of peace.
2. Absolute freedom of the seas in peace and war.
3. Elimination of economic barriers to international trade.
4. Reduction of national armaments.
5. Impartial adjustment of all colonial claims.
6. Evacuation of Russian territory with full opportunity for Russia to determine her own future development.
7. Evacuation and restoration of Belgium.
8. Evacuation of French territory and restoration of Alsace and Lorraine to France.
9. Readjustment of Italian frontiers.
10. Self-determination for the peoples of Austria-Hungary.
11. Self-determination of Serbia, Montenegro and Rumania.
12. Self-determination for Turkey.
13. Independence for Poland.
14. Establishment of the League of Nations.

On October 4, 1918, Germany and Austria appealed to President Wilson for an Armistice on the basis of the Fourteen Points. Towards the end of October, the Allies agreed to enter into a Peace Treaty.

Main Events of the War

1914
June 28   Archduke Ferdinand was assasinated.
July 28   Austria-Hungary declared War on Serbia.
            Next week followed other declarations of War.
Aug. 4   Germany invaded Belgium. Austria-Hungary invaded Russia.
Sept. 6-9   The Allies stopped the Germans in France in the First Battle of Marne.

1915
May 23   Italy declared War on Austria-Hungary.

1916
Feb. 21   The Germans opened the Battle of Verdun
May 31   The British fleet fought the German fleet in the Battle at Jutland.
1917
Feb. 1   Germany resumed submarine warfare.
April 6   The U.S.A. declared war on Germany.
June 24   American troops landed in France.
Dec. 15   Russia signed an armistice with Germany ending the fight on the eastern front.
1918
Jan. 8   US President Wilson announces his 14 points as the basis of peace.
March 3   Russia signed the treaty of Brest-Litovsk.
Sept. 26   The Allies began their final offensive on the Western Front.
Nov. 11   Germany signed an armistice ending World War I.

1914

The Allies were stronger than the Central Powers as they had superior reserves of manpower and greater national resources. But the Central Powers had many other advantages : their complete unity of command given by Germany only, their geographically central position in Europe to act quickly and efficiently both on the east and the west, Germany having the best trained army in Europe, and German national zeal built up by a superior race propaganda. On August 3, the German troops entered Belgium and swiftly crushed it and with a lightning speed reached within 15 miles of Paris brushing aside the British resistance on the way. At the Marne River, the concentrated French forces checked the German advance. It is said that the 'Battle of Marne saved Europe and the World'. Germans retreated some miles and dug trenches. Thus the trench warfare continued for four long years. Both the sides dug trenches, line after line, along the war front, some 600 miles from Switzerland to the North Sea. It wa a *War of Attrition* - a question of which side would exhaust itself first. For soldiers it was a nightmare in the trenches, living for years in the dug holes with filth, mud, lice, rats and death. The monotony was broken only when they climbed up and rushed towards the enemy trenches. Their hand-to-hand bayonet fighting was followed by intense artillery bombardment. The deafening sound of bursts of shells and shots of bullets would suddenly come to a halt piling heaps of dead bodies and drenching the ground with blood. And again, the silence would be broken with a counter attack. From 1914 to 1917, the bitter fighting on the Western Front raged back and forth, but niether side made significant advances; the War of attrition continued.

War on the Eastern Front:

On the eastern front, the armies of Germany and Austria defeated the Russians in the Battle of Tannenberg. In Africa and Asia, the English gained success in Mesopotamia and Palestine.

1915:

Germany started the use of poison gas to achieve the breakthrough. In the beginning, Russia achieved some success but it was short-lived; later on, it suffered heavy losses and the forces of the Central Powers entered many territories of the Russian empire. Bulgaria, which joined the German camp, crushed Serbia very badly. The British navy captured several German colonies in Africa and Asia.

1916:

The English used tanks for the first time. The Germans began to use submarines.

With a view to face the submarine, the English tightened the blockade of the German coast. Both Germany and England suffered heavy losses in the Battle of Dagger Bank and the Battle of Jutland.

In 1916, Rumania declared War on Germany and Austria but was defeated and lost its capital.

The First World War (1914-1918)

1917 and the Entry of U.S.A.:

Mention has already been made of the reasons that led the U.S.A. to enter War on the side of the Allies.

Egypt joined the Allies and declared War on Turkey. The forces of Turkey had to face terrible setbacks and England captured Baghdad and Jerusalem.

Withdrawal of Russia from the War:

Russia had suffered heavy losses. The number of Russian soldiers taken prisoners was nearly one million. The plight of the Russian people was very miserable. The Russian Government itself was very corrupt and so were the army generals. The real brunt of the War was borne by the Russian peasants, drafted in millions in the army, ill-clothed and ill-trained and always under-equipped. In 1917, the Russain Revolution took place and the autocratic, oppressive and corrupt rule of Tsar Nicholas II, ruler of Russia, was overthrown and a communist Republic was established. Russia had no alternative but to surrender and withdraw from war and signed the humiliating Treaty of Brest Litovsk with Germany on March 18, 1918.

THE END OF THE WAR IN 1918

Germany launched a severe attack on France but was badly beaten in the Second Battle of Marne. The U.S.A. sent huge forces to the aid of the Allies and by the end of September, Germany had lost all French territory. The Allies hit back against Germany's submarine attacks. The tide turned against the Central Powers. On September 30, 1918, Bulgaria surrendered unconditionally. A month later, Turkey and Austria followed the footsteps of Bulgaria. Rebellions broke out in Germany on the failure of the Government. The German Emperor William Kaiser abdicated the throne and fled to Holland. The Chancellor of Germany begged for peace, and at dawn on November 11, a German delegation signed armistice terms with Marshal Ferdinand Foch, the Supreme Commander of the Allied Forces. At 11 A.M. on November 11, 1918, all guns were silenced and the terrible War came to an end.

Use of New War Weapons and Strategy

(1) Technology Provided Deadly Weapons:

Science, invention and manufacture combined to make weapons more effective and frightful than ever before in history. Battles were fought in the air and under the sea as well as on land and sea. Britain uesd big battleships and Germany countered it with submarine attacks. By 1917, both sides developed fighters and bomber squadrons. The British introduced tanks and later Germans adopted them. Instruments were yet not developed to accurately hit the war targets, therefore, bombs were just dropped by hand in the general war target areas, hoping to have scored a successful hit, and some bombs did suprise and kill the city dwellers in their apartments. Sea and land mines, torpedo boats, hand grenades, flame throwers, machine guns, poisonous gases, and many other devises for mass killing were invented or improved by technological advances.

(2) Use of Propaganda:

Powerful propaganda on a large scale, through radio or by dropping leaflets over enemy territory, was used to convince the people at home of successes, boost the morale of their own army and to instigate the people of the enemy against their government.

(3) War of Attrition:

It is to wear out the enemy by mobilising more and more soldiers and using enormous amount of bombs, shells and bullets.

(4) Blockade:

It is to prevent the supply of food and war materials and weapons from reaching the enemy by blocking the sea or land passage so that the enemy may starve as well as get weakened due to the lack of war material.

The Paris Peace Conference and Treaties (1919)

Armistice was signed betwen Germany and the Allies on November 11, 1918. The Peace Conference was held in January 1919, a few miles away from Paris in Versailles (pronounced V*e*r-sa*i* : the *e* as in s*e*nd and *i* as in *i*ce). It outlined the terms of peace. The Conference was attended by 70 delegates representing 32 nations but was not attened by any of the defeated nations. The Big Four, namely, Lloyd George, the British Premier, Clemenceau, the French Premier nicknamed Tiger, Woodrow Wilson, President of the United States and Orlando, Premier of Italy were the chief stars of the Conference. The following five treaties were drafted :

(1) The Treaty of Versailles with Germany on June 28, 1919.
(2) The Treaty of St. Germain with Austria on September 10, 1919.
(3) The Treaty of Nevilly with Bulgaria on November 27, 1919.
(4) The Treaty of Triannon with Hungary on June 4, 1920.
(5) The Treaty of Serves with Turkey on August 20, 1920.

Main Provisions and Impact of the Treaties:

Germany was Reduced and its African Colonies were Stripped Off:

Alsace and Lorraine, once taken away from France, were restored to France and other small territories were given to Belgium and Denmark. Last slices of West Russia went to Poland. The parts of Memel and Danzig were taken away. Germany's coal mines in the Saar were to be supervised by the League of Nations for 15 years and their output of coal was to go to France. The west bank of the Rhine was to be demilitarised and occupied by Allied forces until the terms of the treaty were carried out. Germany was to pay a huge amount as war indemnity and was to begin paying at once, but the total amount would be fixed later after assessing the total war losses.

Germany's standing army was reduced to one lakh. No one explained how Germany would pay such indemnity when its coal and other means of making money were snatched away.

Map 5: **Europe in 1919**

The First World War (1914-1918)

The Former Huge Empire of Austria-Hungary Ceased to Exist:

The empire was broken up. Austria and Hungary were separated as two independent states of greatly reduced sizes. Large slices of the old empire went to Czechoslovakia, Rumania, Poland, and Yugoslavia. The population of Hungary suffered extreme hardship as the newly reduced territory was not big enough to hold the Hungarians. The new boundaries left three million Hungarians living outside Hungary, and no arrangements were made to determine the fate of these border regions.

Czechoslovakia Benefited Most in the Break up of Austria-Hungary:

The treaty generously drew its borders. Slovaks joined with Czechs in forming the new country.

Poland also Became Independent:

The new Poland gained territory at the expense of Austria, Germany, Russia and Lithuania. Still not satisfied, Poland invaded Russia during the Russian Civil War. It also occupied Vilna, the capital of Lithuania.

Yugoslavia:

Its creation was the result of a long agitation for independence by the South Slavs. The new country was a mixture of Serbs, Croats, Slovenes and others. Its territory included Serbia, Montenegro, and parts of Austria and Hungary. To give Yugoslavia an outlet on the Adriatic sea, the port of Fiume was placed within its borders.

Rumania:

The country was richly rewarded for her slight services to the Allies. Its size was doubled.

Bulgaria:

It lost Macedonia to Yugoslavia and part of Thrace to Greece.

Italy did not Receive what it Expected:

Austria lost to Italy the Trentine and Trieste and two islands off the Dalmatian coast. Yet, the Italians were not satisfied for they had been promised the coast at Dalmatia (which went to Yugoslavia) and a share in Germany's African empire. The Italians wanted the part of Fiume but the Allies steadfastly refused to take this part from Yugoslavia. Later, Yugoslavia gave Fiume to Italy in exchange of a piece of territory.

Turkey:

Greece was given Smyrna (a sea port of Turkey) and other parts of the Turkish empire.

Russia:

A part of Western Russia went to Poland and Bessarabia to Rumania.

Japan Gained but was Less than Satisfied:

Japan got Shantung on the condition that it would be returned to China after sometime. It was returned in 1923.

CAUSES OF THE SUCCESS OF THE ALLIES AND THE FAILURE OF THE CENTRAL POWERS

First; Germany's sea power could not match the sea power of the Allies. In the beginning, the German submarines inflicted heavy losses on the British navy but these losses were made up by vigorous ship building activities in the U.S.A. and Britain. Secondly, the entry of U.S.A. with its rich resources in money and materials changed the entire course of the War.

Thirdly, England, by virtue of its having a vast empire in the World, was able to mobilise its resources.

Fourthly, after some setbacks in the beginning of the War, the Allies were able to develop a unified command under very capable generals.

Fifthly, the general condition of the people of the Central Powers was very miserable. With setbacks, the people's morale sank very low. Riots broke out at several places. Even the German army could not remain free without military revolts.

CONSEQUENCES OF WORLD WAR I

The War proved economically, industrially, politically and even morally disastrous not only for the vanquished nations but also for the victorious one's. Some of the glaring consequences of War are given below in brief.

Unprecedented Loss of Life:

Of the 65 million people mobilised in the War about 9 million lost their lives and about 22 million were wounded out of which more than seven million were totally disabled.

Most of them killed were between the age of 18 and 35. Russia was the heaviest loser of more than two million, Germany nearly two million, France and her colonies nearly one and a quarter million and the British Empire nearly one million. The U.S.A. lost about one million lives. The rest belonged to other nations who participated in the War.

Economic Burden:

The total cost of the war is estimated to have reached a grand total of $ 18,000,000,000. The average daily cost amounted to $ 12 crore 60 lac from the declaration of War to the signing of the Armistice.

Crippling Economies:

Industries were strangled immediately after the War. Business in Europe, in the years following the War, was reduced to about one-fourth its earlier turnover. Labour was dissatisfied. Strikes became common throughout the world. Resources were exhausted, infra-structure and machines were destroyed, and thus future production of wealth sharply declined.

To all, the victor as well as the vanquished, the War was economically ruinous.

Miserable Condition of the Common Man:

There were miserable conditions all around. There was starvation. There was disease. Prices became very high. There was shortage of essential commodities. Unemployment became rampant. Savings of the people were wiped out overnight.

Inflation Spiral:

The inflation of some countries touched such a height and became so devastating that paper money was hardly worth the paper on which it was printed.

Heavy Borrowing:

Several countries were reduced to bankruptcy. Many governments had to borrow heavily. The Allied powers borrowed around ten billion dollars from the U.S.A. As a result the U.S.A. was able to control the European markets and dollar became the medium of exchange.

End of Monarchies:

The autocratic rule of four emperors of Austria, Germany, Russia and Turkey adopted democratic institutions. The ruthless and despotic rule of the Tsars in Russia was toppled and a republican form of government was set up. Likewise, Turkey became a republic.

Rise of Dictatorship:

In some countries, autocratic governments were replaced by dictatorships after some years. These dictatorships were even less democratic than most of the hereditary monarchies.

Intensification of Nationalism:

Nationalism was intensified. Overlapping territorial claims and racial hatreds became more intense.

Emergance of New States:

Many nations disappeared in their existing forms and several new nations came into existence. The map of the world was redrawn as boundaries of different countries had to be changed.

Humiliation of the Defeated Powers:

The Central Powers suffered unconceivable humiliation at the hands of the victors who under treaties forced them to part much of their territories, military power and equipment and to pay huge war damages.

New Nations were Formed:

The Dual Monarchy of Austria-Hungary came to an ignominious end as Austria and Hungary became two separate small countries, the parts carried out from the once large empire helped to create the independent republics of Czechoslovakia and Yugoslavia.

Russia also was divided into several states. The Ottoman Empire was broken up. Egypt and the Arab State of Hedjaz were given independence but were placed under British Protectorate. Likewise, Palestine became independent and was placed under British control. The British who got Mesopotamia, renamed it as Iraq and appointed an Arab king to rule under its control. Thus Turkish empire (Ottoman empire) was dismantled.

This humiliating treatment of the defeated nations sowed the seeds of the Second World War.

Supremacy of the Allies:

The victorious nations obviously gained at the cost of the defeated nations. Britain, though exhausted by the War, became stronger with the enlargement of its territories in Africa and Asia. Its sphere of influence increased. France was able to recover its lost territories of Alsace and Lorraine that were conquered by Germans in 1871. The U.S.A. also became stronger. It became the "real victor". American industries had a roaring business. It was able to increase power through "dollar diplomacy". Its investments in Europe received a great boost. Italy, although not very happy with its spoils of War, also got several areas which were formerly under Austria.

Japan became more powerful at the expense of Germany, China and Russia.

Birth of the League of Nations:

The Treaties of Paris in 1919-20 provided for the establishment of the League of the Nations, an international organisation to settle mutual disputes and to check wars among nations. (Disussed separately in detail)

Barbarism Exposed:

In the imperialist power politics, the values enshrined in the Renaissance Movement, French Revolution, American Declaration of Independence and President Wilson's Fourteen Points were thrown to winds in World War I. It also exposed the hypocrisy of the so called civilised European nations. Never had the world seen such mad ruthless barbarism, cruelty, degradation and inhumanity as witnessed during this War. All canons of morality were disregarded. Perhaps, the man of the beginning of the 20th century became more uncivilized than the man of the Stone Age before the dawn of history.

Birth of Fascism:

The decisions arrived at the Paris Conference were so harsh towards Germany, that it gave rise to fascist tendencies under the Nazism of Hitler. Italy, though sided with the Allies, was unhappy that it led to Mussolini's fascism.

Sowing of Seeds of World War II:

The Treaty of Versailles sowed the seeds of World War II on account of the following reasons.
(1) It violated the 14 points of President Wilson.
(2) The Central Powers were not represented in the Peace Conference at Versailles.
(3) Humiliating conditions were imposed on the defeated nations and especially on Germany.

But the most tragic consequence of the War can never be measured in terms of the number killed and maimed or in dollars and cents. The real loss lies in the sorrow of women who lost husbands, sons and fathers, in the suffering of children who were subjected to semi-starvation, in the destruction of homes and cities and, most of all, in weakening and humiliating our precious civilization and in losing faith in men and in ourselves.

EXERCISES

A. Very Short Answer Type

1. Why is the War which broke out in 1914 called the World War?
2. Explain how economic imperialism was one of the main reasons of the First World War.
3. In what way can Germany be held responsible for World War I?
4. Explain the term 'war of attrition'.
5. What is blockade?
6. Why did the U.S.A. join the war late?
7. Name the powers that constituted 'Allies'?

B. Short-Answer Type

1. Explain how the issue of the Balkans contributed to the World War I.
2. Discuss the major events of World War I.
3. State the various issues which brought Europe to the brink of War in the years preceding World War I.
4. What factors led the U.S.A. to join War?
5. List the 14 points of Wilson.
6. State any three factors which made the World War I inevitable.
7. Explain any three new war strategies used in World War I.

C. Essay Type/Long Answer Type

1. Discuss the economic and political consequences of the World War I.
2. Why were alliances formed before the World War I? State any three alliances.
3. Give the main provisions of the Paris Peace Treaty and state how it sowed the seeds of the Second World War.
4. Describe the underlying conflicts among European nations which led to the First World War.
5. "The Treaty of Paris (Versailles) contained the seeds of the Second War". Justify the statement with suitable examples.

D. Map Work

1. On an outline map of the World mark the places where any six battles were fought in the First World War.
2. On an outline map of the World, mark six important countries that fought the First World War.
3. On an outline map of the world, show the new countries that emerged after the War.

CHAPTER 23

Russian Revolution

CONDITION IN TSARIST RUSSIA

There were four Revolutions in Russia during the twentieth Century. The first revolution took place in 1905. The second in February 1917, the Third in October 1917 and the last in December 1991. Russia, in the year 1991, saw almost the reverse of the 1917 October Revolution. Revolutionary changes in the economic, political and social life took place. Communism received a great setback.

In place of a rigid way of thinking, an openness emerged in 1991. The Union of Soviet Socialist Republics, that came into being in 1922, witnessed its disintegration. Its place was taken by the commonwealth of Independent States.

REVOLUTION IN RUSSIA (1905)

Background

In the 19th Century, the nobility of Russia lived in a world marked by luxury and extravagance while the Russian people lived in a different world of misery and poverty. Russian economy was basically an economy of agriculture which was extremely backward. The political system was very autocratic under the Tsar (Czar) i.e. emperor or king. Nicholas II (1894-1917) was the ruling Tsar. He was weak in both body and mind. He was under the influence of his minister Vyscheslav Plehve and a priest, Rasputin, "The Holy Devil". Plehve was against all reforms and believed in autocratic institutions. Rasputin was filthy, immoral and repulsive. He dominated the Tsarina (wife of the Tsar) and through her, directed the Government of Russia. Immorality, corruption and degeneracy gripped the Russian administration. People yearned for a change.

Another factor that was responsible for the Revolution of 1905 was the emergence of socialist ideas. The ground for socialist philosophy had already been prepared by Karl Marx (1818-83). Leon Trotsky (1879-1940) was the leader who inspired the revolution. The next most important leader of the Russian Social Democratic Party formed by various socialist groups was Vladimir Illyich Ulyanov Lenin (1870-1924), popularly known as Lenin. In 1903, the party was divided into two groups called the Bolsheviks (the majority) and the Mensheviks (the minority). The Bolsheviks believed in the establishment of socialism. They proposed their immediate tasks as the establishment of a republic by ending the autocratic rule of the Tsar, abolition of inequalities in land, end of feudal oppression of the peasants and eight hour working day for the workers. Lenin became the leader of this group. Mensheviks on the other hand, were moderates in their approach.

The 18-month Russo-Japanese War (1904-5) ending in the defeat of Russia gave further evidence of the incompetence of the Russian ruler.

From above, it is quite clear that all these created great discontent. The Russians wanted a change. The people turned against the ruler and a revolution broke out in January 1905. The revolutionaries paraded the streets and raised the slogans "Stop the War", "Down with Autocracy". On January 22, 1905, in a peaceful procession of workers going to the King's palace at St. Petersburg for requesting the Tsar Nicholas II to summon a constitution assembly, hundreds of workers lost their lives in police firing. This day was known as "Bloody Sunday". The coming months witnessed a wave of strikes. There were mutinies, both in the navy and the army.

The strikes and unrest forced the Tsar to announce the conversion of the despotic monarchy into a constitutional monarchy. A parliament named 'Duma' was formed after elections. The 'Duma' was called thrice but no work could be transacted on account of the autocratic nature of the Tsar who was not at all serious to give any power to the people.

An armed rising on December 10, 1905 was ruthlessly suppressed. The Tsar abolished the Duma and imprisoned and exiled those members who dared to oppose him.

Impact

The 1905 Revolution, although failed, but it aroused the people to fight for their rights, and paved the way for the 1917 Revolution. This Revolution proved a dress rehearsal for the Revolution of 1917.

THE RUSSIAN REVOLUTION (1917)

An Overview

One of the most significant events in the history of the world is the Russian Revolution of 1917. It completely changed the economic and political scenario of a major part of the world.

Causes

The 1917 Revolution took place on account of a number of causes : political, economic, social, revolutionary philosophy and reverses in wars :

1. Political Causes:

The political causes included:
(1) Absence of constitutional means to express grievances (ii) Rotten monarchy (iii) Political corruption.

2. Economic Causes:

Russia under the Tsars was economically very backward. Agricutural and industrial production was very poor. There was merciless exploitation of the masses. Agriculture was very backward with very low agricultural production. In 1910, agricultural production in Russia was the lowest in Europe. The average yield of grain per acre was one third of the yield in Germany.

The nobles did not give any incentive to the peasants to improve the techniques of agricultural production. Land revenue charged was very heavy. The system of land distribution was imbalanced and unjust. The Tsar family, the nobles and the clergy who constituted less than 10 per cent of the population owned 60 per cent of the land.

Russia's industrial production fell far short of the industrial production of Britain, France and the U.S.A. Foreign capital dominated Russia. About half of the deposits in all Russian banks came from foreign countries. Factory workers were greatly exploited. The means of transport and communications were very meagre.

Social Causes:

The bulk of the population which consisted of peasants and workers had little social status and they were frowned upon by the ruling class, the nobles and the clergy. The Russian nobles treated the common folk as beasts. For petty offences, flogging, slitting of the nose and torture were common. There was little place for human dignity. People in general were mentally and physically poor, being illiterate and malnourished.

Growth of Socialist and Communist Ideas:

The philosophy of Karl Marx (1818-1883) and Engels (1820-1895) gradually influenced the minds of the exploited people. People were convinced that they had the right to revolt against their oppressive rulers and overthrow their government.

Russian writers like Turgenev (1818-1883), Dostoevsky (1821-1881) and Tolstoy (1828-1910) infused revolutionary ideas into the minds of the young.

In the early decades of the 20th century, Trotsky and Lenin emerged as the two great leaders of the revolutionary movement in Russia.

Russo-Japanese War (1904-05) and the World War I (1914-18):

We have already mentioned about the humiliation of Russia in the war of 1904-05. The World War I proved all the more disastrous for Russia. Tsarist Russia joined the World War in 1914 as a member of the Triple Entente (Agreement with Britain, France and Russia). Though temporarily successful, Russia could not bear the full brunt of the German War machines. Just to help Serbia, Russia, with an ill-equipped and ill-trained army, and poor means of transport and communication invaded Germany and Austria. The Russians got some early success but in the important Battles of Tannenburt (August 26-29) and Masurian Lakes (August 26-31, 1914), the German forces played havoc on Russian armies. By September 1915, the whole of Poland and major part of Lithuania were occupied by the Central Powers. The losses of Russia went on mounting. Out of nearly 12 million soldiers who had been mobilized, two millon were killed, about 5 million were wounded and about 2.5 million were either missing or had been taken prisoners.

The War further worsened the already poor state of the economy of Russia. The country was on the brink of starvation. The capital city of Petrograd with its 2 million population was the worst sufferer. (Peter I, the Great, founded the city in 1703 and in 1712 the capital was transferred here from Moscow. It was renamed Petrograd, a Russian version, in 1914 and finally Leningrad in 1924. The capital was transferred back to Moscow in 1918).

There were long queues for bread which was in short supply. There grew great unrest in the country which led to strikes. Russia was left with only one alternative and that was to surrender, and Russia surrendered.

In 1917, in the bloody Bolshevik Revolution, the Tsar was overthrown and Russia sued for peace with Austria and Germany. It signed the humiliating Treaty of Brest Litovsk on March 18, 1917 and surrendered Eastern Poland, the Ukraine, Lithuania, Estonia and Latvia. From the events in Russia, it is clear that the failure of the Tsar of Russia in the World War I hastened the Russian Revolution for which ground had already been prepared.

Course of Events

Usually the course is divided into two events i.e. February Revolution and October Revolution which is treated as one of the most important events in the history of the world.

February 27, 1917 (March 12, 1917) Revolution:

The date in the brackets is from the Russain Calendar, the dates of which are about 11 to 13 days later than those of the International Calendar.

The developments in Russia reached a climax in 1917. The Revolution started in an unexpected manner. On February 25 (March 11), it being the International Women's Day, the housewives demonstrated on the streets of Petrograd, protesting against shortage of food. There were long queues on the baker's shops. Strikes were widespread and all of a sudden the crowds attacked some shops. There was disorder and the police resorted to repressive measures but the disturbances continued.

The demand for ending the war and the end of the rule of Tsar grew and on February 27 (March 12), several regiments of the army joined the striking workers. Political workers were freed. Tsarist ministers and generals were arrested. By evening, the workers and the soldiers acquired full control of Petrograd. The Tsar ordered the suppression of the revolt and dissolution of the Duma. On March 2 (March 15) the Duma decided to take power in its own hands and the Tsar was forced to abdicate. His autocratic rule came to an end.

On March 2 (March 15), a Provisional Government was set up under the premier Prince Kerensky, who was a Moderate and his followers were called Mensheviks. In the meanwhile, the Russian army was defeated at various fronts.

All the five members of the Bolsheviks, who had opposed the War when it broke out, were arrested and exiled. Kerensky introduced some reforms but he was not in favour of ending the war. During the seven months of its existence, the Provisional Government went through frequent changes and lost touch with the people's aspirations. Kerensky failed to assess the mood of the masses and to read the writing on the wall. Another revolution was around the corner. So the inevitable happened.

Bolshevik Party, under Trotsky and Lenin, was able to win the goodwill and support of the army. On October 20, 1917, the Petrograd Soviet set up the Military Revolutionary Committee (M.R.C.) with Trotsky as its chairman. On October 24, Lenin also arrived at Petrograd. On the morning of October 25 (November 7), Kerensky, finding that the MRC had become very powerful, escaped from Petrograd. On the night of October 25, under orders, the MRC (including Lenin and Trotsksy) occupied several public buildings including post offices, bridges, railway stations and banks.

But on that day, in the evening around 6 PM, the troops of the MRC besieged the Winter Palace where the Government was holding its office. The troops of the MRC known as Red Guards threatened to bombard the palace if ministers did not surrender within half an hour. However, the troops waited till 8 PM during which some ministers and their guards managed to move away from the Palace. Around 2.00 PM, in the night between October 25 and October 26, all the ministers present there were arrested. "Within one night, almost without bloodshed, the Bolsheviks had become masters of the capital". The surprised population awakened in the morning to read posters, "The Provisional Government has been overthrown. Government authority has passed into the hands of the Revolutionary Military Committee which leads the proletariat and the garrison of Petrograd."

The uprising had begun on October 25, 1917 (November 7) and therefore it is called October 25 Revolution. The Revolutionary Government was headed by Lenin.

Work of the Revolutionary Government:

The first act of the new government was the adoption of the Decree of Peace and to withdraw from the World War I. The second was to issue Decree on Land. This Decree abolished private property in land and declared it to be the property of the entire nation. Following were the other laws passed by the new government.

October 29, 1917, Power to close down hostile newspapers.
October 29, Eight hour working day in industrial concerns.
November 10, Abolition of class distinctions and uniform social status.
December 18, Equal status for women, civil marriages.
January 21, 1918, Cancellation of all domestic and foreign loans.
February 5, 1918, Church separate from the state.

Civil War (1918-21):

Civil War lasted for about three years. Reforms were opposed by clergymen, landlords, big traders and the supporters of the Tsar. It resulted in the civil war between the upper and lower classes. Lenin suppressed all opposition by an iron hand, and violent means. Atrocities were committed on all those who opposed reforms.

Russian Revolution

There was a Reign of Terror The Tsar and other members of his family were shot dead in July 1918. After Germany's surrender, Russia repudiated the Treaty of Brest-Litovsk. The efforts of the foreign powers like Britain, France and U.S.A. to check the Revolution failed.

Prominent Leaders of the Revolution

Lenin:

Vladimer Ilyich Ulyanov Lenin (1870-1924), the architect of the Bolshevik Revolution in Russia, became a socialist at the age of 17 after his brother was hanged for plotting against the life of Tsar Alexander III (1881-1894). Expelled from the University of Kazan for his revolutionary views, he lived in exile in Siberia during 1897-1900 and spent most of the period during 1900-17 in East Europe working for the cause of the Social Democratic Party of Russia. He led the Bolsheviks to power in 1917 and introduced revolutionary reforms in Russia and ruthlessly crushed the opposition.

Extract from his broadast at 10 A.M. on October 25, 1917 to the citizens of Russia.

"The Provisional Government has been deposed. The cause for which the people have fought, namely, the immediate offer of a democratic peace, the abolition of landed proprietorship, worker's control over production, and the establishment of Soviet power...this cause has been secured."

Trotsky, Leon (1879-1940):

Worked closely with Lenin to bring about the Russian Revolution of 1917 — Became the Chairman of the Petrograd Soviet in 1917, Commissioner of Foreign Affairs (1917-18) and Commissioner of the army and the navy (1918-25) — Carried on negotiations with Germany for bringing Russia out of war at any cost — A leading Bolshevik orator and a highly distinguished writer — Believed in the establishment of world communism — Had a struggle with Stalin after the death of Lenin—Exiled and murdered in 1940.

Significance of the Revolution

A Landmark Event:

The Russian Revolution was an epoch-making event that had far-reaching consequences not only in the history of Russia but also in the world.

(A) Significance for Russia:

Onset of a New Socio-Economic System:

The social set-up was formed on the basis of "Everyone according to one's ability and everyone according to one's work." Discipline in individual and social life was emphasised. A new set of values emerged.

State Control:

The state became all powerful and the individuality of individuals was reduced to nothing. Land, factories, industries, mines and all other sources of production were nationalised.

Supremacy of the Proletariates:

Land was taken away forcibly from the landlords and given to workers. Workers got the management of factories.

End of Autocratic Rule of the Monarch:

The monarchy was abolished.

Emergence of Russia as a Super Power:

Within a few years of the revolution, Russia made spectacular progress and surprised the world by her new schemes of economic, educational, social and scientific development.

Universal Compulsory Education:

Russia made rapid strides in making education easily available to the mass of illiterate people.

Application of Marxian Ideology:

The philosophy advocated by Marx found its actual application in Russia under the leadership of Lenin, Trotsky, and Stalin.

Suppression of Religious Freedom:

Following the Marxian philosphy that 'religion is the opium of the people', in January 1918, by a Decree of Church, the Revolutionary Government of Russia separated the church from the state and all church property was confiscated. All church schools were suppressed. Clergymen lost their right to vote. Several clergymen were exiled and executed.

By about 1933, about 70,000 churches were closed down.

An Era of Planning:

With the introduction of a planned economy under Stalin in 1928, Russia achieved a remarkable progress in the economic field. Its nagging economy became a vibrant economy.

Totalitarian Communist Dictatorship:

Press was ruthlessly suppressed. Newspapers were to express news and views in favour of communist dictatorship. All agencies were to serve the ends of the communist government. Scholars having liberal ideas were purged. All sorts of cruelties were inflicted upon those who showed any difference of opinion with the Communist leaders. Lenin wiped out thousands to achieve his objective of establishing his regime. A bloody civil war took place in Russia.

End of Russian Imperialism:

After the Russian Revolution, several countries which groaned under the Russian bondage were set free. Poland, Finland and Georgia etc. became free without any struggle.

(B) Significance for the World:

Other Revolutions Inspired by Russia:

The Russian Revolution led to the successful revolutions staged by workers in countries like Albania, Bulgaria, Czechoslovakia, Hungary, Poland, Rumania and Yugoslavia in Europe, Mongolia, Korea and Vietnam in Asia. Communist regime was also set up in China in due course.

Rise of Nationalism and Awakening in Afro-Asian Countries:

The success of the Russian Revolution created awakening on a gigantic scale in Afro-Asian Countries.

A New Wave of Equality:

The popularity of socialism was very helpful in the redefinition of democratic values. Democracy was redefined to mean not only political equality of the people but also social and economic equality.

Arousal of a New Consciousness:

The events in Russia created an urge/desire amongst the exploited millions to get rid of oppression and injustice inflicted upon them by the capitalist classes.

Promotion of Internationalism:

Communist parties on the lines of the Communist Party of Russia began to be organised in different parts of the World. The Soviet Union gave support to other countries to achieve their independence.

Emergence of Two Power Blocks:

As Russia became one of the big powers in the world, two power blocks came into being. One block was led by the Soviet Union and the other by the U.S.A. The USSR and its satellites formed the communist block whereas the U.S.A. and its allies constituted the capitalist block.

Rise in Violence:

The standards set by the Russian revolutionaries became examplary standards. Among these also included repression and violence to achieve the desired results. Thus violence turned out to be a creed for subsequent revolutionaries.

Birth of a New Elite Class:

A new class of intellectuals who were arm-chair academicians arose and looked at every aspect of life from a socialist angle. In several cases they acquired typical manners and modes of dress.

EXERCISE

A. Very Short Answer Type

1. What was the effect of Russo-Japanese War on Russia?
2. List any two causes of the defeat of Russia in World War I.
3. Why did Russia join the World War I?
4. Name any two leaders of the Russian Revolution.
5. What is the meaning of 'Bloody Sunday'?
6. Who was Rasputin?
7. What was the nature of the February-March Revolution in Russia in 1917?
8. Explain the meaning of Bolshevik.

B. Short-Answer Type

1. Describe the course of the 20th October Revolution.
2. Give the contribution of Lenin and Trotsky to the Russian Revolution.
3. What was the impact of the Russian Revolution on world affairs?
4. How did the autocratic rule of the Tsar lead to the Russian Revolution?
5. In what way did Russia's participation in World War I contribute to the success of the Russian Revolution?
6. What were the consequences of the Russian Revolution of October 1917 on the world?

C. Essay Type or Long Answer Type

1. Discuss the main causes of the Russian Revolution.
2. Why was the Russian Revolution an event of great significance?
3. "The Russian Revolution changed the course of history". Discuss this statement.

CHAPTER 24

Peace Settlement after the War and the League of Nations

PEACE SETTLEMENT AFTER THE WAR AND THE LEAGUE OF NATIONS

With the signing of the Armistice by Germany at 11 AM on November 11, 1918, First World War came to an end. The terms and conditions relating to war with the defeated Central Powers still remained to be settled. Accordingly, the Peace Conference was held at Versailles, a suburb of Paris on January 18, 1919, nine weeks after signing the Armistice with Germany. In all, 32 states sent their 70 delegates to the Conference. The vanquished Central Powers were not invited to discuss the terms and conditions. The Big Four, namely, President Wilson of the U.S.A., Premier Lloyd George of Britain, Premier Clemenceau of France and Premier Vittorio Orland of Italy dominated in the drafting of the Peace Treaties to be signed by the defeated nations. The Prime Minister of Japan and several other countries and a few Princes of Princely states from India also attended the Conference. The drafts of five different treaties with Germany, Austria, Bulgaria, Hungary and Turkey were separately prepared for different dates.

Name and Date of the Five Treaties

S.No	Name of the Treaty	Country with which Treaty made	Date of Treaty
1.	Treaty of Versailles	Germany	June 28, 1919
2.	Treaty of St. Germain	Austria	September 10, 1919
3.	Treaty of Nevilly	Bulgaria	November 27, 1919
4.	Treaty of Trianon	Hungary	June 4, 1920
5.	Treaty of Sevres	Turkey	August 10, 1920

1. Treaty of Versailles (1919)

Germany signed the treaty unconditionally on June 28, 1919 at Versailles. It contained 440 articles and 20 annexes, running into more than 400 pages.

Main Provisions:

Provisions may broadly be divided under four heads :

1. War Guilt and Reparations:

Germany was held fully responsible for the War as stated in that treaty. "The Allied and Associated Governments affirm and Germany accepts the responsibility of Germany and its Allies for causing all the loss and damage to which the Allied and Associated Governments and their nationals have been subjected as a consequence of the War imposed upon them by the aggression of Germany and its Allies."

Accordingly, following conditions were imposed upon Germany (i) Payment of 6000 million dollars as War indemnity (ii) Payment to Belgium of all the amounts it was forced to borrow on account of War (iii) To hand over its 50 per cent of ships and 25 per cent of its steam trawlers and fishing boats (iv) Supply of large quantities of coal to France, Italy and Luxemburg (v) Supply of various kinds of other materials to the Allies.

2. Surrender of Territory:

Germany had to surrender these territories (a) Alsace and Lorraine to France (b) Eupen, Malmedy and Moresnet to Belgium (c) Northern Schlesweign to Denmark (d) Colonies of German New Guinea, German Islands, South of the Equator and German Tanganyika to Britain (e) Posen and West Prussia to go to new Polish republic.

3. Heavy Military Restrictions on Germany:

These restrictions were (i) Size of the German army not to exceed 100,000 (ii) Army not to have any military aircraft, tanks etc. (iii) Germany not to have any submarine (iv) Abolition of conscription (v) Demilitarisation of some areas (vi) Fortification of strategic places to be removed.

4. Demand for the Trial of Emperor Kaiser William II:

Kaiser had fled to Holland, a neutral country and Holland refused to hand over Kaiser for trial.

2. Treaty of St. Germain with Austria (May 1919)

Provision of the Treaty:

1. The Austria - Hungary Empire was broken. It was converted into two small states.
2. Several areas of the old empire were included into the new states of Czechoslovakia, Poland and Yugoslavia.
3. Austrian army's strength was not to be more than 30,000.
4. Austria was to pay a huge war indemnity. The size of the old empire was reduced to one-fourth.

3. Treaty of Nevilly with Bulgaria (November 27, 1919)

1. The size of Bulgaria was reduced. A major portion of the areas which it had won during the Balkan wars (1912-13) was given to other states.
2. Yugoslavia received the major part of Macedonia.
3. Rumania got Dobruja.
4. Greece secured Western Thrace.
5. The size of the army of Bulgaria was reduced to 30,000.
6. An indemnity of half million dollars was to be paid.

4. Treaty of Trianon with Hungary (June 4, 1920)

1. Hungary was separated from Austria and emerged as a new state with much less area.
2. Its area was reduced to 36,000 sq. miles as against its earlier area of 125,000 sq. miles.
3. Rumania got Transylvania while Yugoslovakia secured Croatia from Austria. Both shared the Banal.
4. The army of Hungary was reduced to 35,000 soldiers.
5. Hungary was to have only a few patrol boats.
6. Hungary was to pay war indemnity.

5. The Treaty of Sevres with Turkey (August 10, 1920)

1. The Arab state of Hejaz became independent.
2. Armenia was to be a free Christian republic.

3. Palestine, Mesopotamia (Iraq) and the Transjordan were separated from the Turkish empire and placed under Britain as mandatories.
4. Syria was detached from Turkey and made mandatory under France.
5. Greece was to secure Symrna and the nearby territories.
6. The Dardanellis and the Bosphorus were to be internationalised.

AN ESTIMATE OF PEACE SETTLEMENT

Justification of the Treaty

Justifying the treaty, Lloyd George, British Prime Minister observed, "I do not think anyone can claim the terms imposed constitute injustice to Germany unless he believes justice in War was on the side of Germany. The terms of the treaty in some respects were terrible. But terrible were the deeds which justified them and still more terrible would have been the consequence had Germany triumphed. The world is reckoning and rolling under the blow that followed. If the blow had succeeded, the liberty of Europe would have banished." There seems to be a great truth in this statement when we look at the extraordinary ambitions of Germany to become a world power by all means, fair and foul. It received the treatment it amply deserved.

Following arguments are given in favour of the Peace Treaties :

1. Areas forcibly occupied by Germany were got vacated from it. For instance, Belgium did not belong to it and was occupied during the War.
2. New states like Czechoslovakia, Finland, Latvia and Poland were created on the basis of the nationality of the peple residing in these areas.
3. The leading statesmen of the world realized that there was an urgent need to set up an international machinery to settle disputes between states and create an environment of peace and international understanding in the world. This led to the formation of the League of Nations.

Arguments Against the Treaty

First, the defeated nations were not given adequate opportunity to express their views in framing the terms of the Peace Treaty.

Secondly, Germany was declared unilaterly guilty of War while France, Russia and Serbia were also responsible for War. Thirdly, the Prime Minister of France, from the very beginning, was vindictive towards Germany. The result was that "Germany was economically crippled, politically segregated, militarily humbled, nationally humiliated, physically exhausted."

Fourthly, while deciding the terms of the treaty, President Wilson's 14 points were disregarded. The colonies that had hoped to gain independence after the War, felt cheated.

Fifthly, disarmament was imposed on the Central Powers alone.

Sixthly, it was totally improper and unjust to divide Germany into two parts for giving passage to Poland to the sea and opening the Port of Denzing to all countries.

Seventhly, small states were created by carving out areas from Austria and Germany and these states were not strong enough to protect their freedom. Obviously they became satellites to big powers. In this way a new form of imperialism came into existence.

Eighthly, the imposition of heavy war indemnities on the defeated nations put a heavy strain on the people of these countries.

Effects of World War I and the Treaty of Paris

A. Political Consequences on Europe; Paved the Way for the Second World War:

Great changes took place on the political map and the political philosophy of Europe. The defeated countries—Austria, Hungary, Germany, Bulgaria and Turkey—found their large territories and the population therein reduced in size.

Several suppressed nationalities became independent as the territories they were occupying inside themselves got separated from the empires and they were made independent. These were Poland, Estonia, Latvia, Lithuania, Finland, Yugoslavia, and Albania.

Absolute monarchy made way for republican forms of governments in various countries.

The Russian empire was torn into pieces and the territory was redistributed.

The defeat of Russia became the most immediate cause for starting the October Revolution which completely changed the political and economic thinking of the people of Europe. Turkey also witnessed a revolution that freed its people from the Ottoman rule.

The Paris Treaty was so humiliating to Germany that it became very angry, agressive and revengeful. It gave birth to Nazism in Germany. Likewise, Fascism in Italy took its birth. The result was that when Hilter came into power, he refused to honour the Peace Treaty of Paris and in full disregard of disarmament clause, started the expansion of the empire and the increase and strengthening of his military power. Gradually, he began to conquer one after the other, several territories in Europe.

The colonies possessed by the Central Powers were snatched away from them and the Allies put them under their control directly and indirectly. The Central Powers felt disgraced and humiliated.

The victorious European powers were not under any obligation to reduce their armies while the vanquished powers were compelled to do so. As the time passed, the defeated nations began to increase their armed strength. Thus, a race for armaments again created a psychology of War.

Political Consequences of the First World War on Africa and Asia:

The defeat of the Central Powers encourged the imperialism of the Allies in Africa and Asia as several countries were gifted mandatory powers by the League of Nations to control certain countries which became free after the world war. Egypt and the Arab state of Hedjaz was taken away from Turkey and placed under British supervision. Syria was put under French control. Palestine became independent and was placed under British protectorate. The British, who secured Mesopotamia, renamed it as Iraq and appointed an Arab king to rule under their influence.

The British empire was enlarged in Africa and Asia.

Japan became more powerful at the expense of China, Germany and Russia.

The strength of both the victor and the defeated nations was reduced to a considerable extent and their weakness gave impetus to the nationalist movements in the colonies.

India had hoped that Britain would grant it self-rule but it did not respond favourably. The people of India, therefore, intensified their nationalist efforts.

The unjust treatment meted out to Turkey by the Allies made the nationalist Indian Muslims indignant against the British and the Khilafat movement took place, in which the Congress Party played an important role.

THE LEAGUE OF NATIONS

Why?

Realising the horrifying consequences of the War, the philosophers, the politicians, statesmen and other thinkers felt the necessity of an international agency that could settle the mutual disputes of the nations, maintain the world peace and prevent the occurrence of wars. The ground for the setting up of such an organisation had already been prepared by President Wilson of America, when he, in 1917, formulated his famous Fourteen Point Programme. The Peace Conference at Paris in 1918 had inserted a clause on the establishment of an international association of states for replacing war as a means of settling international disputes.

Birth of the League of Nations

The League of Nations was formed on January 10, 1920 (the day on which the Treaty of Versailles came into operation). Originally it had 24 members. The first Assembly was convened on November 15, 1920, when the number of members had risen to 42. Subsequently, the number increased to 60. Ironically, the U.S.A. whose President Wilson had mooted the idea of this organisation did not join as there was a change in the political set up of the U.S.A. Wilson belonged to the Democratic Party. But now the Republican Party won a majority in the Senate which had to ratify the Peace Treaties.

The Central Powers were admitted late into the League, Hungary in 1922 and Germany in 1926.

Soviet Russia was not given admission till 1934.

In 1933, Germany and Japan were in a different mood. They wanted war. So they gave notice of quitting the League and this became effective from 1935.

Geneva in Switzerland, a neutral state became the headquarters of the League.

Objectives of the League of Nations

1. Promotion of international cooperation.
2. Achievement of international peace and security.
3. Acceptance of obligations not to resort to war.
4. Establishment of open, just and honourable relations between nations.
5. Development of the understandings of international law as the actual rule of conduct among governments.
6. Maintenance of justice and a scrupulous respect for all treaty obligations in the dealings of organized peoples with one another.

Measures to be Taken for the Realization of these Objectives:

1. Settling all disputes among nations by arbitration.
2. Reducing national armaments to the lowest point consistent with national safety.
3. Non-resorting to secret diplomacy.
4. Safeguarding the interests of racial and religious minorities.
5. Securing justice for backward and subject people by the system of mandates.
6. Maintenance of territorial limits and sovereignty of other nations by not resorting to conquests.
7. Non-interference in the internal affairs of other states.
8. Mutual disputes to be placed before the League.
9. Boycotting commercially and socially a country that declares war on any other country.
10. Honouring all mutual agreements.

Nature of the League

It was not a federation of states or a Super State or a World Government. It was an international association of states, each retaining its sovereignty. It had no sovereignty and could not take action against any nation. It was a forum of exercising moral pressure on the defaulting states. It had no military force to impose its resolutions. There were no citizens or subjects directly under its control.

Composition and Structure of the League of Nations

The League had five main organs (1) The Assembly (2) The Council (3) The Permanent International

Court of Justice (4) The International Labour Organization (ILO) (5) The Secretariat. In addition, there were several Advisory Committiees.

The Assembly:

The Assembly was the chief organisation consisting of all members. Each state could send three delegates but was entitled to one vote only. The Assembly functioned like a legislature. Its session was held once a year but special sessions could be held in emergency. It could discuss any matter falling within its sphere. The Assembly performed these main functions (i) Discussing disputes referred to it by the concerned member states (ii) Appointing judges of the International Court of Justice and the Secreatary General of the League (iii) Electing non-permanent members of the Assembly (iv) Admitting new states to the League (v) Amending the League Constitution, if necessary (vi) Framing the annual budget.

The Council:

Initially, the Council had its members, four permanent and ten non-permanent. The permanent members were (1) England (2) France (3) Japan (4) Italy. The number of permanent members rose to five when Germany was admitted in 1926 and to six in 1934 with the admission of the Soviet Russia. The meetings of the Council were held thrice a year but emergency sessions could be held at anytime. The Council was the executive organ of the League. Hence, it performed all the functions falling under the objectives of the League. The Council appointed several commissions and committees to assist it in the discharge of its functions.

The International Court of Justice:

It had elven judges elected for a nine-year term. It settled disputes among the member states in accordance with the international laws and agreements. It also gave advice to the League on various matters.

International Labour Organisation (ILO):

Its headquarters were at Geneva. Its important function was to bring about inmprovement in the labour conditions by shortening the hours of work, increasing wages, protecting workers from sickness and injury and rendering assistance during their unemployment period. It had a governing body consisting of 24 members— 12 representatives of governments, six representatives of labour organisations and six employee's representatives with a term of three years.

The Permanent Secretariat:

The secretariat looked after the routine day-to-day work of the League. Its important functions were (i) Registering and publishing treaties (ii) Collecting data on international problems (iii) Preparing agenda for the meetings of the Assembly and the Council (iv) Communicating decisions to member states.

Achievements of the League

During the course of its existance for 19 years (1920-1939), though formally it was dissolved in April 1946, the League was quite successful in settling political disputes between nations and in promoting international cooperation in non-political fields like economic, humanitarian and social fields. The Leauge was able to settle the following disputes (i) Between Finland and Sweden over the sovereignty of the Aaland Islands in the Balkans (ii) Between Poland and Lithuania over the city of Vilna (iii) Between England and France over the Nationality Decrees in Tunis and Morocco (iv) Greece and Italy regarding the murder of four Italians in Greece (v) Greece and Bulgaria on the violation of frontiers (vi) Turkey and Iraq (vii) Bolivia and Peru.

Humanitarian Work:

Among the non-political fields, the achievements of the League of Nations were (i) Establishment of a Permanent Health Organisation for protecting public health by international cooperation (ii) Exercising control over the manufacture and distribution of narcotic drugs through Permanent Central Opium Board (iii) Suppressing immoral traffic in women and children (iv) Studying, collecting and disseminating scientific facts regarding problems of children through its Child Welfare Committee (v) Doing relief work through the International Office for Refugees (vi) Repatriation of five lakh war prisoners to their homelands (vii) Setting up a Permanent Committee for pulling down the remnants of slavery (viii) Signing a covention for suppressing the production and distribution of obscene literature (ix) Setting up the Minorities Commission for securing equal political and civil rights.

Economic Work:

For economic reconstruction of war-torn nations, the League undertook the following activities (i) Convening International Financial Conference for controlling inflation (ii) Holding World Economic Conference for bringing about the free flow of capital, labour and goods in all countries, promoting international cooperation and not competition in the industrial field (iii) Organising International Monetary Conference to discuss problems relating to economic crisis of the 1930s.

Failure of the League

Following were the important failures—Failure (i) to check Japan's aggression on China when in 1931 it seized Manchuria (ii) to check the aggression of Italy over Ethiopia in 1934-35 (iii) to check destruction of the Republic of Spain through internal sabotage by Germany and Italy in 1936 (iv) to remain just a helpless spectator when Hitler of Germany broke treaties, annexed Austria and dismembered Czechoslovakia in 1938 and seized Albania in 1939 (v) to check Stalin of the Soviet Union while invading Finland in 1939.

The League collapsed in 1939 when Germany invaded Poland.

Causes of the Failure of the League:

The League failed on account of the following reasons:

First, the League had no enforcement machinery to make its decisions binding on its members. The League was toothless and too weak to punish anybody. Second, it did not become a representative body of the world. All the countries did not join it. Third, the rule of unanimity on major issues proved a stumbling block in its functioning effectively.

Fourth, the League was handicapped without the U.S.A. It was a crew without a captain.

Fifth, the big powers dominated the working of the League. By and large, they proved to be hypocrites.

Sixth, the League was tied to the unjust and vindictive peace treaties entered into after the First World War.

Seventh, the statesmen who dominated the League lacked practical wisdom. Their approach remained somewhat utopian.

Eighth, small as well as big nations had no confidence in the League. The small nations had no trust in it becuase it could not protect them. The mighty nations had no respect for it because it was weak. Germany, Italy, Japan and Russia openly violated the League principles and it could do nothing.

In view of the utopian ideas of the leaders who dominated the League, it began to be called by some as 'Geneva Council of Fools'. For the open high handedness of the big powers, some called it as a 'League of Robbers'.

EXERCISES

A. Very Short Answer Type

1. List any four Treaties entered into after the First World War.
2. List any two provisions of the Treaty of Versailles.

3. What was the main objective of the Paris Peace Conference?
4. List any three aims of the League of Nations.
5. Why did the U.S.A. not join the League of Nations?
6. List any two achievements of the League in the economic field.
7. Mention any two achievements of the League in the humanitarian field.

B. Short Answer Type

1. What were the political consequences of the Peace Treaty on Europe?
2. How did the Peace Conference affect Africa?
3. In what way did the political scenario in Asia change after the World War I?
4. Explain the political achievements of the League of Nations.
5. Mention any five objectives of the League of Nations.
6. Describe the functioning of the League of Nations.

C. Essay Type or Long Answer Type

1. What were the limitations of the Paris Peace Conference?
2. State the reasons which led to the failure of the League of Nations.
3. Descrie the main clauses of the Treaty of Versailles? What were the unjust features of this Treaty?
4. "The Treaty of Versailles contained the seeds of the Second World War". Justify the statement with suitable examples.

CHAPTER 25

Between Two World Wars: Europe, USSR, U.S.A. and Latin America

OVERVIEW OF EUROPEAN SITUATION

The immediate post-war years were a period of unrest—economic, political and social. The most important of these was the economic dislocation of almost every country of Europe and it became the source of all other unrest. Political leaders and statesmen had different views and theories to grapple with issues. This added to the confusion and led to conflicts, sometimes with much bloodshed.

One of the immediate results of World War I was the general discredit of monarchies. In Europe, a dozen republics were established. These included Austria, Czechoslovakia, Estonia, Finland, Lithuania, Turkey and Ukraine.

The dispute over territory was a constant threat to the world.

Trend towards dictatorship, even in republics, was also evident.

The worst form of dictatorship emerged in Germany, Italy, Japan and Russia.

Turkey, though, having a democratic form of Government, was under the rule of a dictator who tolerated no interference with his administration and planning. Of course, he did not resort to imperialism and militarism.

The period was marked by the revolutionary economic policies of Russia which attracted the attention of the entire world.

Europe witnessed the Great Depression which engulfed every industrial country except Russia.

Fascism and Nazism dominated for some years but died on account of the defeat of their protagonists in World War II.

FASCISM IN ITALY

Meaning of Fascism

The term 'Fascism' is derived from the Latin word 'Fasces' meaning a bundle or group. In ancient Rome, a bundle of rods with an axe was the symbol of authority. The Roman Emperors after their victory used to enter the capital with a bundle of royal rods in their hands as a symbol of their imperial authority. Thus, fascism implies the rule of the 'rod'. It also implies the authority of one individual.

Mussolini of Italy, who is associated with fascism, organised in the beginning groups of young persons or gangs called the '*fasces*', to create terror among the people who were considered enemies of the nation.

Fascism may be defined as a political philosophy, movement or regime that glorifies a nation or a race above the individual and stands for a centralised autocratic rule headed by a dictatorial leader.

Fascism rests on four pillars of charismatic leadership, single party rule under a dictator, terror and economic control.

Mussolini believed in the efficacy of these slogans and their accompanying action : "Believe, Obey, Fight" and "The More Force, The More Honour."

Principles and Practices of Fascism

The following statements of Mussolini throw considerable light on the various dimensions of fascism.
"Everything in the state, nothing out of the state and nothing against the state."
"Peace is absurd. Fascism does not believe in it."
"Fascism is based on the revolutions."
"Fascism is based on the work and objectives of the state."
"State is complete but the individuals and institutions are incomplete."
"All parties must end, must fall." "Italy must expand or perish."
"Fascism knows no idols or worships".
"Italian people, rush to arms and show your tenacity, your courage, your valour."

Emergence of Italy as a Fascist State

The prevailing economic, social and political conditions were very favourable to the rise of fascism in Italy. The six important factors were :

Economic Crisis:

Italy was faced with a great economic crisis on account of the huge expenditure incurred on the War. The national debt increased manifold. The cost of living went up nearly five times. Prices shot up. Production was falling. Trade and industry were in ruins. There was an acute shortage of foodgrains. Inflation was shooting up.

There was great dismay and frustration after the Treaty of Paris. Although a victor and constituent of the Allies, Italy did not gain substantially from the spoils of War. It led to great discontentment in Italy. Italy had lost half a million people in the War.

Incompetence of the Rulers:

Constitutional monarchy was unable to solve the pressing problems of the country. It could not assert itself in the Peace Conference. The ruler failed to find suitable solutions to the increasing economic hardships of the people.

Disruptive Activities of the Socialists:

On account of the revolutionary ideas of the socialists, unrest had spread in the country. This led to chaos, indiscipline, lawlessness and anarchy in the society. The Communists by their inflamatory speeches instigated the workers and the peasants. Lock-outs and strikes became the order of the day which further worsened the economy of the country.

Chaotic Political Scenario:

There were very sharp mutual differences among a host of political parties. There were several small factions even among the main parties. Italy witnessed six coalition governments between 1919 and 1922. No political party or political leadership was strong enough to provide a stable government.

Need for a Charismatic Leader:

The situation demanded a bold leadership and the same was supplied by the fascist leader Mussolini. Thus, it was the urgent need of a strong and unified force that formed the background for the rise of fascism in Italy.

Mussolini, Benito (1883-1945)

A teacher turned politician, had to flee from Italy for his revolutionary ideas. He lived in exile for a number of years. On his return to Italy, he organised the National Fascist Party in November 1921. The Fascist Party declared that it would solve all problems of the country. Mussolini first seized power in a coup d'etat (prounced 'Koo-day-ta) in 1922 as the leader of the party. He exercised control by such methods as murder, exile and imprisonment. His policy was overwhelmingly supported by his black shirted military squads (the fascist workers wore black shirts). He established a totalitarian dictatorship. Mussolini was a great organizer and a silver tongued orator who could easily make a straight appeal to the hearts of the patriotic and the nationalist Italians and captured their hearts. Under his leadership, the Fascist Party with the eye catching black uniforms, parades and grand rallies attracted thousands of youngmen to its fold. Mussolini, at 39 became the youngest Prime Minister of Italy in 1922. In due course, he assumed the powers of a dictator and he became a 'Superman' of Italy. Mussolini also carried out several reforms besides his imperialist exploits. Like most of the dictators, Mussolini's end was very tragic. Italy, under him, lost the World War II. His own people executed him.

Italy under Mussolini : Seizure of Power by the Fascists:

In October 1922, the fascists under Mussolini held a grand Fascist Congress at Naples to display its strength. Nearly 40,000 fascists paraded on the streets in military uniforms.

At the Conference Mussolini declared, "Either the government will be given to us or we shall seize it by marching at Rome." On October 24, 1922, the fascists organized a march on Rome and captured it. The Government surrendered. Thus the Fascist Revolution became a spectacular success as the Fascists seized power without bloodshed. But the aftermath of Revolution was marked by suppression, murder and exile. Fascist dictatorship under Mussolini came into existence.

Totalitarian Control:

Mussolini ruthlessly suppressed all Non-fascist groups. He banned all other political parties and butchered people who came in his way. He relied heavily on violence. He brought to an end, the system of fair and free elections. The press was enslaved. Educational institutions were brought under fascist control.

From top to bottom the fascist structure dominated.

Achievements of Italy under Mussolini:

First, Mussolini established peace and order. He provided a stable government.

Second, He infused a new and dynamic spirit in Italy. He made Italians proud of their land.

Third, Mussolini was able to attract almost all sections of people — army, politicians, retired bureaucrats, scholars, farmers, traders, workers, landlords and capitalists. And all these groups found in Mussolini, a new hope, in the post-war period.

Fourth, Mussolini brought order and discipline in the industrial field. The "Charter of Labour" issued by him provided great relief to workers. Industries were freed from the strike epidemic.

Fifth, Mussolini took several measures to increase production. Marshes were drained. Canals were dug. Reclamation projects were launched. Hydroelectric schemes were undertaken. Railways and other means trasportation were improved. A fair degree of self sufficiency was achieved.

Sixth, as a realistic administrator, Mussolini patched up with the Pope. A conflict that had been going on for nearly 60 years came to an end.

Seventh, for the spread of education, several schools, colleges and libraries were opened. Of course, all efforts were made to include such contents as promoted the ideals and values of fascism. Military training was made compulsory.

Eighth, special measures were made to strengthen military force. Areoplanes and naval ships were built.

Aggressive Foreign Policy that Ends in Disaster:

Mussolini's slogan before the nation was "Italy must expand or perish." For a while, his imperialist policy gave Italy an important position of prestige in the international field. Mussolini was hardly in power for a year when he captured the Greek Island of Corfu to get war indemnity from Yugoslavia. He bullied Bulgaria, Austria and Hungary. In 1936, he annexed Ethiopia. He left the League of Nations in 1937. He captured Albania in 1939. Mussolini made common cause with Hitler, another war monger. He joined the Rome-Berlin-Tokyo axis. The Second World War (1939-45) brought disaster to Italy. In 1941, Italy lost its territories in Africa. Mussolini failed to cope up with the financial burden of the war. Th Anglo-American force heavily bombarded Sicily in 1943 and landed in the island. If Mussolini's, rise to power was sudden and meteoric, his end too was sad and tragic. He was shot dead by his own countrymen and his corpse was dishonoured.

Support for Fascism

The ruling class supported fascism on account of the following reasons.

First, it was believed by the ruling class that fascism could save them from socialist revolution. They were afraid of the impending bloodshed.

Second, the popularity of left wing parties created a fear psychology among the ruling class including industrialists, landlords, and senior army officials.

Third, fascists encourged expansion and War which were opposed by the socialists.

Fourth, socialism clashed with nationalism. The ruling class feared the domination of Russia.

Fifth, fascism seemed to promise a glorious future for Italy.

NAZISM IN GERMANY

Early Revolutions and their Failure

There was a great discontent in Germany over the 'dictated peace' and harsh and humiliating provisions of the Peace Treaty entered into after the World War I. Several authoritarian groups had emerged in war which denounced democracy, advocated the repudiation of the Versailles Peace Treaty, extolled war and organised conspiracies to overthow the democratically elected government and to replace them by dictatorship. Two attempts were made to revolutionalise but both failed. The Communist Party's attempt did not succeed in 1923. The same year in November 1923, the Nationalist Socialist Party also called the Nazi Party, formed in April 1920, organised the *'Putsch'* - a sudden revolutionary outburst in Munich in a beer hall. The coup failed and Hitler fled from the scene. However, after two days, he was arrested, tried and put behind bars for about a year.

Rise of Nazism

Fascism and Nazism rose and fell almost on the same pattern. In the earlier pages, significant reasons were given that led to the rise of fascism. Here, only a brief mention is made of the circumstances that gave rise to Nazism. Among the most important ones were (i) Disintegration of the German empire (ii) Loss of huge territories (iii) Loss of Colonies (iv) Vindictive Treaty of Versailles (v) Heavy war indemnity (vi) Great economic distress (vii) Multiplicity of parties (viii) Instability of the government—21 Ministries in 14 years (1919-1933) (ix) Charismatic personality of Hitler.

Leaders of both, Fascism and Nazism met the tragic fate. After defeat in World War II, Mussolini was shot dead by one of his countrymen while Hitler committed suicide.

Hitler, Adolf (1889-1945)

A destitute for a while, when he lost his parents before the age of 18, with no aristocratic, diplomatic or administrative traditions, Hitler, with his oratorical thunder and hypnotic words rose to become the outstanding

Nazi leader, chancellor and dictator of Germany. He stirred his fanatical followers to do what he wished. He himself believed in the supreme power of the spoken word, for, he wrote, "Every great movement on the globe owes its rise to the great speakers and not to the great writers."

The acute economic and social problems which faced Germany after the war helped him to gain support. He was imprisoned after his failure to seize power in Munich in 1923. During his imprisonment he wrote *Mein Kampf* (My Struggle), which became the Bible of Nazism. The book became the best seller for several years. He became the Chancellor of Germany (the most powerful post in Germany) in 1933. Very soon he suppressed all opposition, started to persecute Jews and followed an aggressive policy of uniting all German speaking people in one '*Reich*' or one nation. The annexation of Austria in 1938 and the partition of Czechoslovakia in 1939 led to the start of World War II. After doing very well for sometime, he was defeated. He commited suicide in Berlin a few years before the final surrender by Germany in 1944.

Chief Philosophic Chracteristics of Nazism

Following were the principles of Nazi philosophy.
1. Supremacy of the state. People exist for the state and not the state for the people.
2. A single line integrated authority. One nation. One religon. One leader. No discordant note between command and action.
3. Rejection of the parliamentary system of government.
4. No faith in ideals of equality and freedom.
5. Superiority of the German race.
6. Jews considered as a parasite race.
7. Rooting out liberalism, communism and socialism.
8. Belief in the survival of the fittest.
9. Belief in the Aryan creative power.

Chief Measures for the Realization of the Aims

1. Glorification of War.
2. Suppression of all opposition with an iron hand.
3. Violent propaganda.
4. Persecution of the Jews.
5. Formation of alliances with like-minded powers i.e. Italy.
6. Denouncing the Treaty of Versailles.
7. Complete militarization.
8. Complete efficiency in administration and in economic fields.
9. Getting support from commercial and agricultural classes.
10. Disregarding the League of Nations.
11. Making Germany a police state.
12. Control over media—the radio and newspapers etc.

Reforms Introduced Under the Nazi Rule

While ruling with an iron hand, Hitler also introduced several reforms. He organised the economy of Germany with the main objective of making it self-sufficient. He encouraged agricultural and industrial production. Factories were set up to provide work to the unemployed. He provided job to every jobless and removed the problem of unemployment. Workers were given several facilities but not the right to strike. Trade was encouraged. To maintain favourable trade balance, imports and exports were controlled.

The Nazis undertook numerous public works projects. Government offices, art galleries, and stadiums were built. House building programmes were launched.

Education was given to the young people to infuse in them a staunch spirit of 'My country right or wrong'. Nazi philosophy became the core of the curriculum.

Several reforms were undertaken to strengthen militarism. War material like aeroplanes and ships were produced on a large scale. The Nazi slogan was, "Guns first, butter afterwards."

It is of interest to find that most of the significant events in Germany took place in the month of March : March, 33 — Hilter assuming dictatorship; March, 35 — rearmament of Germany; March, 36 — Occupation of Rhine; March, 38 — annexation of Austria; March, 39 - Occupation of Czechoslovakia.

Downfall of Germany

Policy of Aggression and Repudiation of the Treaty of Versailles:

The foreign policy of Hitler was guided by the following considerations (i) Hitler's contention that German race was superior to other races and it had the right to rule over others (ii) Hitler's desire to bring back the lost glory of Germany (iii) To take revenge of the humiliation of German people on their defeat in World War I (iv) To undo the unjust and dictated Treaty of Versailles, which took away a considerable part of its territories and colonies and imposed heavy war indemnity. Hitler, therefore, adopted the following measures to restore Germany its lost pride.

First, Germany militarised itself and increased its naval power along with the army and the air force.

Second, in October 1933, Germany withdrew from the League of Nations.

Third, in March 1936, German troops occupied the Rhineland which had been demilitarised by the terms of the Paris Treaty.

Fourth, Germany signed a Naval Treaty with England which was contrary to restrictions put on it.

Fifth, Germany with the connivance of Italy marched its troops into Austria in 1938 and captured it.

Sixth, Czechoslovakia was seized in 1939.

Seventh, Germany demanded the return of the corridor and the city of Danzing. Failure of Poland to do so led to the Second World War in 1939.

Hitler, by following the path of aggression and overestimating his strength, dug his own grave and that of Germany also. Hitler, the Messiah of Nazism became Germany's destroyer.

ROME-BERLIN-TOKYO AXIS (1936-37)

The agreement signed by Italy, Germany and Japan for mutual cooperation is known as the Rome-Berlin-Tokyo Axis — each capital city signifying the representative nature of its country. The agreement was motivated by the ambitions of the three countries. These were Germany's desire to establish her supremacy over Europe, Italy's ambition to conquer the Balkans, the Arab countries and large parts of Africa, and Japan's objective of becoming supreme in Asia and the Pacific.

THE SOVIET-GERMAN AGREEMENT (1939)

When Hitler annexed Sudetenland, Czechoslovakia and Austria in 1938, both France and England kept quiet and left Russia in a lurch. Russia tried to conclude a treaty with France, England and Poland but there was no response. Russia was afraid of the aggressive policy of Germany. Although both Germany and Russia were arch enemies, they signed a Non-Aggression Treaty on August 23, 1939 but the treaty was very short-lived.

COMMUNISM AND NAZISM-A COMPARISON

Communism was the outcome of the philosophy of Marx and had its Bible in the famous book *Das Capital*. Communism is still an important creed not only in Russia but also in several countries of the world. On the other hand, Nazism was based on the belief in the superiority of the German race and therefore Germany was the fittest to rule the world and the idea was confined to Germany alone. In fact, it died with the death of Hitler, its orginator. In Nazism private property and private enterprise and state property and state enterprise could flourish side by side but in communism, only state property and state run enterprise could flourish. Both believed in dictatorship. Nazism believed in colonisation of the world, but it was not so with communism. Communism believed in revolution to finish capitalism in each country but not in war to conquer the whole world, but Nazism encouraged war. Both Communism and Nazism had scant regard for indivudal's rights as they would weaken the state and interfere with the dictator's rule as he wished. Recently, communism has undergone several changes, but its emphasis on the dominating role of the state in the economic field still persists.

FASCISM AND NAZISM — A COMPARISON

The story of the rise and fall of both, Fascism and Nazism, is the same. Similar was the fate of its founders. The only difference was that while Nazism believed that the Germans should rule the world due to the superiority of the German race over others, Fascism had no such belief about the Italian race. Both were the product of dissatisfaction they felt over the Peace Treaty in two different ways. Germay was defeated and was subjected to very harsh and humiliating terms as it was the leader of the Central Powers. Italy was a victor but was not satisfied with the distribution of the spoils of war among the Allied Powers, as it got much less than what it expected while other victors had what they wished.

UNION OF SOVIET SOCIALIST REPUBLICS (USSR)

Consolidating Gains of October 1917 Revolution

Soviet Russia or the USSR was able to consolidate the gains of the Bolshevik Revolution and register tremendous progess in agricultural, industrial, scientific, military and other fields after some set back during 1918-21. The era of spectacular advancements began under the leadership of Lenin, the father of the Bolshevik Revolution. Thereafter, under Stalin (1924-53), the USSR became a power in the beginning and a Super Power after 1945 by its own right. As a Super Power, its place was equated with the only other Super Power, namely the U.S.A. The Communist Party of the USSR engaged itself in nation-building activities with an unprecedented enthusiasm after liquidating all its enemies. The Communist Party became synonymous with the Government of the USSR and vice verse. The USSR economy became so vibrant that when almost all industrialised countries were adversely affected by the Depression of 1930's, it remained as strong as ever.

Lenin's Concept of 'War Communsim' and its Result (1918-21)

Lenin, the architect of the October Revolution, wished to bring about rapid changes, as if on war footing, in the socio-economic life of Russia by establishing a Communist Society based on the philosophy of Karl Marx. He was convinced that the reconstruction of the war-torn Russian society was possible only through communism, by following its principles as fast as possible and through harsh compulsion in a dictatorial manner. He, therefore, adopted a policy which came to be known as 'War Communism'. It was to change and raise the Russian economy by changing the ownership of property and to work on war footing. The important features of this policy were (i) Distribution of land among the peasants as stateland by taking it from the landlords (ii) Confiscation of private property (iii) Nationalisation of banks, factories, industries, mines and railways etc. (iv) Cancellation of all debts of the Tsar regime (v) Cofiscation of the property of the Church (vi) Rendering labour work compulsory for all (vii) Fixation of prices of agricultural produce (viii) Opening of cooperative stores in place of private commercial establishments.

The period of War Communism lasted from the summer of 1918 to the spring of 1921 when production of large scale industry dropped to 12 per cent of its pre-war level. Net output of coal fell to zero in 1921. Agricultural production declined by a third. The rationing and the distribution system broke down. Five million people starved to death and nearly forty million persons suffered from malnutrition. The results of War Communism were very frightful.

There were three most important reasons for the failure of War Communism. First, it coincided with the Civil War. Second, it was prepared and implemented hurriedly. Third, it suffered from lack of experience and technical skill.

New Economic Policy-NEP (1921-24)

Realising the complete failure of War Communism, Lenin abolished it and a new policy was introduced. He was forced to reconcile between state socialism and capitalism. The new policy included the following characteristics (i) Imposition of a tax on peasants which could be paid in cash or kind (ii) Nationalisation of big industries and factories (iii) Small industries and factories to remain under private ownership (iv) Foreign capital allowed (v) Opening of government stores side by side private retail stores (vi) Partial freedom to trade unions. New Economic Policy proved very useful for the health of Russian economy.

USSR under Stalin

Joseph Stalin (1879-1953) guided the destiny of Russia for 29 years from 1924-1953. His name is associated with these concepts : Dictatorship of the Proletariat, Stalin's Cult of Personality, Five Year Plans and the Great Purge.

Son of a shoemaker, Stalin became one of the most prominent personalities of the World.

After the death of Lenin, a major power struggle took place between Stalin and Trotsky. In the power struggle, Stalin emerged victorious in 1927 and Trotsky was expelled from the party, exiled and assassinated in 1940, in Mexico.

In the beginning, Stalin raised the slogan of 'Dictatorship of the Proletariat'. However, this culminated in the 'Stalin's Cult of Personality' consolidating all power in the hands of Stalin. It was the dictatorship of an individual overshadowing the state and the party.

Like Trotsky, Stalin liquidated all his opponents and individuals in the Communist Party who had even slightly different views about his way of administration. And this was done in a very cruel manner.

It is estimated that as many as 80,000 party members were killed, including six of the 13 members of the Politbureau (the highest policy making body of the Communist Party) and 98 of 138 members of the Central Committee. In the army, the killed included three of five marshals, 14 of 16 army commanders and the like. The list is endless. Thousands were imprisoned and exiled. This is known as the 'Great Purge'. Russia had never witnessed such terror and violence as in the Stalinist regime.

Five Year Plans (1928-37)

Undoubtedly, Stalin is called the "Father of Five-Year Plans" in the World. The prime objectives of these plans were to reconstruct the nation, to increase production, to increase industries and to attain self-sufficiency in the economic field by increasing production.

The First Five Year Plan was launched in 1929 and the Second in 1934.

During the planning period, all private enterprises were taken over by the state. Private ownership and control of land, private industries and trade became non-existent. The individual small holdings of the peasants were brought together and collective farms called *Kolkhozes* were set up. The peasants worked collectively on farms. "Many million peasants are believed to have perished during the period of collectivization." There was a strong opposition to collectivization and force had to be used to break the opposition. The USSR witnessed a severe famine in 1932 which caused millions of deaths.

Heavy industries were set up for the production of tractors and agricultural machinery. Huge steel plants were established. Several river valley projects were launched and completed. Electricity was produced on a large scale. The production of coal, iron and petrol doubled.

During the Second Five Year Plan (1934-38), the production of consumer goods was stepped up. Russia became self sufficient in food grains by the end of the Second Plan.

The Five-Year Plans were very successful in raising the economy and providing a stable economic base. That made it the only country to escape the adverse effects of the Great Depression of the 1930's.

Russia's position was second in the world in the production of raw materials and third in the production of steel in the world.

The volume of agricultural and industrial production increased tremendously, the problem of unemployment was solved and hunger and poverty were removed by the end of the Second Plan. The peasants and workers enjoyed a decent living.

All this was achieved by hard work and initial sacrifices. Every possible effort was made to harness the human and non-human resources efficiently and scientifically.

Educational Development

It goes to the credit of Russia that by 1935 i.e. less than 20 years after the Revolution, 80 per cent of the people became literate. Education was made compulsory up to the age of 17.

Suppression of Religious Freedom

Following the Marxian doctrine that religion is the opium of the people, no religious freedom was allowed. By 1933, nearly 70,000 churches were closed down and several clergymen were exiled and executed. Churches were converted into recreational centres.

Constitutional Reforms

With the proclamation of the new constitution in 1924, all the Soviet Republics were brought under one union— the Union of Soviet Socialist Republics (USSR). In 1936, when another constitution came into force, there were 11 republics constituting the USSR which later increased to 16. According to the constitution, they were free to cede from the Union. Generally speaking, each nationality of a republic was free to promote its own culture and language. However, the political control was very rigid.

Russia's Relations with other Countries (1917-39)

The foreign powers became hostile to the Russian Revolution when they found that it had its own designs which were completely opposed to their policies. They, therefore, tried to put all sorts of obstacles in the way of Russia. Russia tried to establish friendly relations with important countries. In 1921, a treaty was signed with Afghanistan, Iran and Turkey.

Russia signed a commercial treaty with England. It also signed the Treaty of Rapallo with Germany and got loan from it. Both the countries resumed full diplomatic relations.

Germany recognised USSR in 1922 and Britain, France and Italy in 1924. Several other countries also followed suit. The U.S.A. recognised Russia in 1933.

Russia joined the League of Nations in 1934 and became the permanent member of its council.
In 1939, Russia signed a Non-Aggression Pact with Germany.
By the time of the beginning of the Second World War, Russia had gained international influence.

The Communist International (Comintern) or The Third International

The Communist International (Comintern, for short) was the outcome of the Russian Revolution. It was formed in March 1919 for bringing together the communist parties of several countries. The 1919 Comintern was attended by the representatives of the communist parties of 30 countries. By the mid-1930s, their number rose to 60. The Communist Party of China had also emerged as a powerful party. The communist parties played a prominent role in organsing the workers against the exploitation of the capitalists. The Comintern, with its headquarters at Moscow, was dominated by the Soviet Communist Party. Moscow used to guide the activities of the communist parties of other countries.

The capitalist countries feared the effect of communism on the minds of the people. The dictators—Hitler and Mussolini—hated that Russia would have a global domination through communism.

THE GREAT DEPRESSION OF THE 1930s (1929-32)

The Depression of the early 1930s was one of the most important events between the two wars. It is called 'Great' as it adversely affected almost all the great countries of the world except the USSR. Its consequences were extremely devastating. The Great Depression which began in the U.S.A. affected almost every country in the world. Its effects on European countries were extremely grave.

The period 1929-30 has been described as the "beginning of a nightmare" which continued till 1932 when a period of recovery began.

Economic Consequences of the Depression

The Depression was marked by the deterioration of the economic conditions of the capitalist countries. There was a great fall in the industrial and agricultural production. Workers were laid off the factories and thousands of factories closed. The industrial production in 1933 was only half of the 1929 production. More than 8 crores of people became unemployed in the world. The ghost of poverty haunted the poor people.

France:

Industrial and agricultural production in France fell almost by one-third.

Germany:

Germany's industrial production declined by almost 40 per cent. Two-thirds of workers were partially employed or unemployed.

Great Britain:

Great Britain was threatened with bankruptcy. Prices slumped to a point where production was not profitable. Factories had to be closed. Unemployment increased. Britain started retrenchment and cutting down government expenditure.

Political Consequences

The political consequences of the economic crisis in Europe were disastrous for democracy. In most of the countries, authoritarian, semifascist and fascist regimes were established. In Germany, Nazism emerged with all its force. The Communist parties gained strength in France. The nationalist movements in the colonies grew in strength. The international position of Britain became weak. Ruhr Valley was taken over by Germany.

Social Consequences

In France, workers and petty employees were virtually outcast from the French society which was dominated by business classes and corrupt politicians. In Britain, hostility developed against the Jews as they were considered as foreigners syphoning off British economy.

The Causes

During the war the industries were overhauled to produce war materials instead of consumption goods. The end of war ended such production and made it difficult to resume the production of consumption goods. The war had destroyed many factories and industries. The huge need of war exhausted almost all crucial resources. Massive capital was invested to cope up with the war. Production so slimmed that it could not match with the normal demands. Inflation and high prices became the rule. Unemployment shot up for lack of factories and jobs and capital for investment. Such factors gathered to cause depression in the country's economy.

THE UNITED STATES OF AMERICA (U.S.A.)

U.S.A. in Immediate Post-War Period

The U.S.A., with its tremendous power, had played a prominent role in the victory of the Allied Powers in the First World War. The prestige of the U.S.A. skyrocketed as a result of this decisive victory. It became the real beneficiary of the war. The U.S.A. never became any war theatre of battles and therefore its territory was saved from the awful destruction of war. The U.S.A. capitalists and industrialists made huge profits by investing their capital in the foregin countries.

U.S.A. and the Great Depression

Up to 1929, there was great industrial expansion. America had emerged as the main creditor nation in the World. Industrial expansion had been greatly facilitated by major advances in technology. On October 24, 1929 began the Great Depression which proved devastating to American economy. With the fall in the prices of shares began the crash. It created panic and people began to sell their shares speedily, which led to a further fall. The stock market collapsed. This was followed by the failure of banks which led to the non-availability of credit which affected industrial growth. The credit-starved industries closed which led to unemployment. Unemployemt led to poverty. The closure of banks affected agricultural credit also. The prices of agricultural produce also fell.

New Deal:

In the 1933 American elections, Democratic Government under President Roosevelt came into power. He formulated a policy to combat economic depression in the U.S.A. and this policy is known as the 'New Deal'. The measures adopted under the New Deal proved very effective. Roosevelt explained the main objectives of the New Deal in these words, "What we seek is balance in our economic system, balance between agriculture and industry and balance between the wage earner, the employer and the customer." He further said to the American people, "I pledge you, I pledge myself of a New Deal for the American People."

Important featues of the new programme were :

(a) 3 R's of Relief, Recovery and Reform:

Relief meant assitance to the poverty stricken millions without food and shelter. Recovery implied taking the country out of depression. Reform implied that the shortcomings and the ills of the society had to be removed for taking the country forward.

(b) Creation of Organisations for Implementing the Programmes Under 3 R's:

Important organisations were (i) Civilian Conservation Core (CCC) (ii) Federal Emergency Relief Administration (FERA) (iii) Tennesse Valley Authority (TVA) (iv) National Recovery Administration (NRA) and (v) Agricultural Adjustment Administration (AAA).

The CCC was formed to give relief work to young men in reclamation projects, national parks and forests.

The FERA was provided with five hundred million dollars to be given to the state and local governments for the relief of the unemployed.

The AAA provided compensation to farmers who curtailed production of wheat, cotton, corn, rice, etc. thereby to raise prices.

The TVA was established for the promotion of the construction of dams, powerplants, navigation projects, flood control project, soil conservation and reforestation programmes and electric power and fertiliser production. NRA looked after diverse problems.

National Industrial Recovery Act (NIRA) was passed to reform the conditions of work of the workers by raising wages and lowering their working hours. Restrictions were imposed on employing child labour.

Federal Reserve Bank was set up to provide loans to industries and banking institutions.

Several steps for the improvement of soil fertility, prevention of erosion and economic use of farms were taken.

For stabilising agricultural production, a system of crop loans, crop insurance and crop control was introduced.

Speculation was discouraged. Gold coin and gold certificates were withdrawn from circulation and gold exports forbidden.

The Social Security Act introduced old age pension schemes and unemployment insurance. For improving foreign trade, mutual agreements regarding tariffs were conducted.

Results of the New Deal:

Barring a few limitations, the New Deal strengthened the American economy. It restored confidence in the government. It laid a firm foundation for industrial prosperity and led to increased production. President Roosevelt became so popular that he was reelected in 1936, 1940 and 1944.

Social Consequences:

Miserable Condition of the Black People of America : The Black People were the worst sufferers of the Economic Depression. It has been estimated that in 1932, about one-third of the Blacks were unemployed. Over 2 lakh Blacks had served as soldiers in Europe during World War I. On their return, they found themselves without jobs. White racists demanded that no jobs should be given to 'niggers' unless every White was employed."

Political Consequences:

Radical political movements advocating socialism emerged. A strong trade union movement began to grow. The Communist Party of the U.S.A. also grew in strength.

Foreign Policy of the U.S.A.

Important events of the foreign policy of the U.S.A. were as under : First, the U.S.A. did not join the League of Nations. Second, the U.S.A. was greatly concerned over the growing strength of Japan and its desire to control China. So, in 1922, a treaty was signed with Britain, France, Italy and Japan which aimed at ensuring an 'Open Door' in China so that it was not possible for any country to establish its exclusive control over China.

Third, like other Western Countries, U.S.A. did not involve itself to check aggressive acts of Japan in occuping Manchuria in 1931, Germany's acts of capturing Rhine in 1936 and Italy's aggression in Ethiopia, etc.

Fourth, the U.S.A. did not recognise the Government of the USSR for 16 years.

Fifth, the US economic domination over Latin America was further strengthened and its direct military intervention continued until 1933 when Roosevelt became American President.

FRANCE

Problems before France

France had to face several problems during post-war period. Its important problems were (1) Government stability (2) Reconstruction of France (3) Economic recovery (4) Security and defence of France (5) Problem of Alsace-Lorraine.

Government Stability and Constitutional Problem:

Between 1871 and 1940, 110 times a new ministry was formed one after the other due to the multiplicity of political parties, as no single party could obtain an absolute majority. The defective constitutional and political system of France was a great hindrance in framing and implementing sound policies and providing an effective and efficient administration.

Reconstruction of France:

Poincare, the Prime Minister of France (1922-24) played an important role in undertaking massive reconstruction work. He took such fiscal measures as helped to increase the value of French currency.

Recovery of Economy:

French efforts did not work much to recover the economy.

Security and defence of France:

In 1920, France concluded a treaty with Poland on the eastern side. It signed separate treaties with Czechoslovakia (1924), Rumania (1926) and Yugoslavia (1927).

Locarno Pacts (1925)

With a view to strengthening friendship among nations, under the initiative of the representatives of Belgium, Czechoslovakia, England, France, Germany, and others, a conference was held at Locarno in Switzerland in 1925. The Conference led to several friendly pacts among the nations.

The principles of the League of Nations were strengthened. The principle of collective security emerged. Locarno Pacts seemed to be a beginning towards relaxing tension in Europe but such hopes proved to be a mirage. The breach of agreements began in 1930.

BRITAIN

Problems

Like any other European country, England was also faced with the following problems.

Economic Problems:

These emerged as a result of the First World War and the Great Depression (i) In 1921, there were two million umemployed people (ii) Britain's foreign trade was more than halved (iii) Industrial output was nearly 68 per cent of the pre-war level (iv) Country's debt grew more than 12-fold in the war years (v) The value of

British currency fell substantially (vi) A large number of factories closed down.

The financial condition of the country became very grave for these reasons.

Up to 1933, almost all measures taken to reconstruct the economy failed. Britain began to recover from the economic crisis after 1933.

Unstable Governments:

Different types of governments were formed during the period 1919 to 1924. There were four Prime-Ministers—Lloyd George, Bonar Law, Baldwin and Ramsay Macdonald representing a variety of political parties.

In the 1929 elections, the Conservative Party under Ramsay Macdonald (1929-31) took over the government. It was the period of economic depression.

Baldwin failed to check the deteriorating state of the economy. After the 1936 elections, Macdonald succeeded in forming a National Government. His policies gave a few positive results.

Constitutional Reforms:

The Act of 1918 had granted the right of vote to all women over the age of 30, while men over the age of 21 had the right to vote. The Act of 1928 gave the right to vote to all men and women over the age of 21. Thus, England became a true democratic nation in 1928.

Foreign Affairs:

India

The National Movement in India gained momentum. Some steps were taken to pacify the Indians. Among the important events were : The Rowlatt Act (1919), the Simon Commission (1927-29), Three Round Table Conferences (1930 to 34), and the Government of India Act (1935). However, all these steps did not pacify the nationalists nor could curb the tempo of the freedom struggle.

Ireland:

Ireland was granted independence in 1922 but without Ulster. The nationalists continued their struggle under the leadership of De Valera. Ultimately, in 1937, Ulster was given to Ireland and De Valera became the Prime Minister (1937-41).

Australia, Canada, New Zealand and South Africa:

In 1931, the British Government accepted the freedom of the Dominions of these four countries.

OTHER COUNTRIES

Germany

England and Germany concluded an Anglo-German Naval Agreement in 1933. According to this agreement, England allowed Germany to increase her military strength more than that of England.

Russia

In 1930, England concluded a trade treaty with Russia.

Hungary

Two basic problems confronted the country. One was the necessity of economic reconstruction and the other was its defence and security. The country was essentially an agricultural one and most of the land was controlled by rich landlords. Nothing substantial could be achieved in this direction before the World War II. In 1927 Hungary signed treaties of friendship with Italy and Germany.

Turkey

Turkey, after its defeat, had to enter into a humiliating Treaty of Serves in 1920. Its empire was broken. In 1923, Mustafa Kemal Ataturk (1880-1938) revolutionized Turkey by introducing several reforms designed to bring it into line with the Western-style, customs and practices. He tried to free Turkey from the orthodoxy of the Muslim priestly class. The veil for women was forbidden and women were raised to a position of dignity. School attendance was made compulsory up to the age of 16. An open attack was made on illiteracy. But Kamal Ataturk, unlike the Ottoman regime, did not nurse any ambition of foreign conquests or imperialism.

LATIN AMERICA

The Great Depression of 1929 also had an adverse effect on the economy of the Latin states.

The U.S.A. helped the Latin American countries during the economic depression by giving loans of billion dollars to overcome this crisis. There was a great change in the American policy. Discarding its old policy of interference, the U.S.A. began to rely on what was called the 'Dollar Diplomacy' i.e. policy of making investment in these countries and controlling their economy rather than on direct military intervention or annexation.

All the states of Latin America made social and democratic progress. Some of them like Brazil, Chile, Argentinga and Mexico made rapid and spectacular development in their countries.

Several steps were taken to check feudalism. Elementary education was expanded. Females were given the right to vote. System of secret ballot was introduced. Steps were taken to ensure social justice. Efforts were made to end the domination of foreign capital. Land was distributed among the peasants. Industries were encouraged.

President Roosevelt of the U.S.A. (1933-1944) adopted the policy of "Good Neighbour" towards Latin America. As a good neighbour, it withdrew American troops from Nicaragua and Panama, but not from the Panama Canal zone which remained with the U.S.A.

Nevertheless, the U.S.A. launched multinational corporations in Latin America.

Between 1930 and 1940, fascist groups and parties began to infiltrate in the Latin American countries. Other Fascist countries like Italy and Japan etc. also encouraged emigration to the countries of Latin America. The Fascist danger was averted by the US Policy of "Good Neighbour."

Brazil

In 1934, a new constitution based on fascist principles was formed. In 1937, President Getullio Vargas set up his dictatorship which continued for eight years.

Chile

In January 1939, a devastating earthquake occurred. During 1938-48, left democratic governments were formed.

Cuba

In August 1933, as a result of revolution, President Machado had to leave the country. For the next 15 years, Cuba had several Presidents but power was exercised by Col. Batisa who was virtually a dictator.

Dominican Republic

After several ups and downs, the country came under the dictatorship of Army General Trujillo in 1930. He remained President for eight years (1930-1938).

Mexico

In 1927, there was an abortive revolt during the Presidentship of Plutarco (1924-28).

Nicaragua

In the 1930s, a popular revolt took place under the leadership of Augusto Cesar Sandino against the puppet government installed here with the help of the US troops. In 1933, US withdrew its troops.

FORMATION OF POWER BLOCKS

Italy-Japan-Germany

All the three countries followed fascist dictatorial and militarist designs. They believed in the expansionist policies. By and large all the three were against the Allied Powers i.e. England, France and U.S.A., on account of one or the other reason. Germany was bitter on the harsh terms of the peace conference imposed on it. Italy, though, one of the Allies, was not given its due share in the spoils of War. Japan was not happy with the Washington Conference (1920-21) decisions which had put restrictions on the expansion of its naval power. So, the common interests made them enter into Rome-Berlin-Tokyo Axis in 1937.

England-France and the U.S.A.

Although there were certain irritants among these countries, but by and large they followed democratic pattern and believed in international peace as against the fascist and militarist outlook of Germany, Italy and Japan.

AGGRESSION AND POLICY OF APPEASEMENT

Meaning

Aggression implies an unprovoked attack by one country over another to bully and dominate the other. It usually results in the encroachment of other country's territorial integrity. Appeasement on the other hand means avoiding or buying off aggression by granting concessions and sacrificing principles.

Acts of Aggression by Fascist Powers

It has already been mentioned that three fascist powers namely Italy, Germany and Japan had emerged in the 1930's. As these powers believed in expansionist policies, they began to dominate other countries on one pretext or the other. They attacked several countries and occupied large parts of their territories. They violated the principles of the League of Nations. Other big powers like France, England and the U.S.A. remained silent spectators. They began to tolerate the acts of aggression done by Italy, Germany and Japan. They tried to adopt the methods of conciliation and also to buy peace. Their intention was to save the world from a greater danger, that of war. They thought that by this policy it would be possible to keep the bullying powers within limits. But their appeasement policy failed and instead encouraged the fascist powers to commit more and more acts of aggression that ultimately led to the Second World War.

Italy, under Mussolini, attacked Ethiopia in 1935-36 and occupied it. The League of Nations condemned it and passed economic sanctions but it had no effect on Italy. The Western powers made no efforts to check the aggression of Italy. Italy also rendered great assistance to the rebels who started civil war in Spain. England and France helplessly followed the policy of non-intervention.

Japan started the policy of expansion after the First World War. In 1931, it attacked China and captured Manchuria, China's north-eastern province. The U.S.A., England and France did nothing to check Japan.

While denouncing dictatorship and the policy of aggression by Italy and Germany, it is usually forgotten that England, France and other victors, like dictators, imposed dictatorial terms on the helpless vanquished countries and sowed the seeds of vengeance and retaliation at the Peace Treaty of 1919, which later erupted like a volcano 20 years later in the World War II.

Map 6: **Annexations by Germany and Italy**

The fact remains that almost all the imperialist powers followed motivated policies to grind their own axe. They resorted to war when Germany attacked Poland but they forgot very conveniently that they had also usurped the sovereignty of dozens of nations, including India, and their conscience did not prick at their naked aggression on the numerous helpless nations of Africa and Asia under their control.

Munich Pact

A new state of Czechoslovakia had been created in Europe after the Treaty of Versailles in 1919. The new state included Sudetenland which had a large German population. Sudetenland was an important industrial centre also and bordered Germany. The German population was illtreated by the Czechs and it wanted merger with Germany. Hitler, who was for German supremacy, demanded this province from Czechoslovakia in 1938 and gave it an ultimatum that non-compliance would mean attack on it. The fear of war became imminent. With a view to averting it, the British Prime Minister Chamberlain, the Prime Minister of France, Daladier, the fascist leader Mussolini of Italy and Hitler, the Nazi leader of Germany met in a conference at Munich in Germany in September 1938 and made the following decisions to appease Germany (i) Germany's claim over Sudetenland was accepted (ii) Germany gave up the demand for other territories (iii) England, France, and Italy took the responsibility of the security of Czechoslovakia.

It is of interest to note that Czechoslovakia, which was to be greatly affected by the agreement, was not invited to attend the conference. Likewise, Russia that had entered into an alliance with Czechoslovakia was not invited to this conference.

The Munich Pact was very short-lived. In March 1939, Germany marched its troops in Czechoslovakia and occupied it.

SPANISH CIVIL WAR (1936-39)

Spain

A republican government was formed in Spain in 1936. It consisted of various political parties like the Communists, the Socialists, the Leftists and Anti-fascists and was known as the Popular Front. This government was opposed by fascist groups called 'Falange'. A section of the army under General Franco (1892-1975) also supported the fascist movement. With the help of Hitler of Germany and Mussolini of Italy, Franco was able to capture power in Spain in 1939 and became dictator and chief of the state until his death in 1975. Italy and Germany helped the rebels openly by supplying arms and troops. General Franco's government was recognised by England and France and later by the U.S.A.

EXERCISES

A. Very Short Answer Type

1. List any two features of European situation after the First World War.
2. Mention any two features of Nazism.
3. Mention any two features of Fascism.
4. Give reasons for the formation of Rome-Berlin-Tokyo axis.
5. What is meant by the 'policy of appeasement'?
6. State the problems of the Blacks in the US.A. during the inter-war period.
7. Differentiate between communism and fascism.
8. State the policy of War Commuism. Why did it fail?
9. Explain the New Economic Policy of Lenin.
10. Explain the Communist International.

B. Short-Answer Type

1. In spite of unprecedented growth in economy, why did the U.S.A. face economic depression in 1919? How did it meet with the situation?
2. Why did the ruling class support the fascist movement in Italy against the socialist movement?
3. What were the circumstances that gave rise to Nazism in Germany? What was the internal as well as the foreign policy of Hitler?
4. Why did fascism develop in Italy? State the contribution of Mussolini to Italy.
5. Why did the U.S.A. change its policy towards Latin America? State the changes that occurred in this policy.
6. What were the major developments in the Soviet Union in the inter-war period?
7. Explain the causes and effects of the Great Depression.
8. Why did Russia start Five Year Plans? What were their consequences?
9. State the foreign policy of England during inter-war period.

C. Essay Type/Long Answer Type

1. Why was the Munich Pact signed? What were its main provisions? Why was it generally condemned as an act of appeasement?
2. Describe the acts of aggression committed by Germany, Italy and Japan before the Second World War. Why were these acts not checked by other countries?
3. Explain the policy of appeasement followed by France and England. Give examples.

CHAPTER 26

Developments in Asia and Africa

ASIA

The inter-war period saw the growth of the national movement in every part of Asia. Everywhere, the pattern of the movement was almost identical. The important factors that led to the growth of national movement are (i) Economic exploitation of the conquered nations by the conquering nations (ii) Social humiliation and racial discrimination (iii) Spread of Western education and culture (iv) Contribution of great national leaders (v) Role of the media (vi) President Wilson's 14-Point Programme emphasising democratic values and freedom (vii) Success of the Russian Revolution providing hope and confidence among the Colonial people to fight against injustice (viii) Weakening of the power of the imperialists on account of loss of men and materials in the War.

India

A detailed account of the developments in India has already been furnished in the first part of this book. Here it is only intended to summarise the developments (i) Failure of Montague-Chelmsford Reforms (1918-19) (ii) Dissatisfaction among the Indians over the failure of these reforms, the repressive measures adopted by the British rulers under the Rowlatt Act (1919) (iii) Jallianwallah Bagh Tragedy (1919) (iv) Non-Cooperation and Khilafat Movement (1920-21) (v) Withdrawal of the movements after the Chauri Chaura incident (1922) (vi) Formation of the Hindustani Republican Association by the revolutionaries (1924) (vii) Boycott of the Simon Commission (1928) (viii) Lahore Session of the Congress and demand for Poorna Swaraj (1929) (ix) Civil Disobedience Movement and Dandi March (1930) (x) Three Round Tables Conferences in London and their failure (1930-33) (xi) Government of India Act (1935) (xii) Elections under the Act and the formation of Congress Ministries in 9 provinces out of 11 (xiii) Participation of India in the Second World War against the wishes of the Indian people and resignation of Congress Ministries (1939).

China

In one of the earlier chapters, the history of China was traced up to the point when after the death of Yuan in 1916, China was brought perilously near to the brink of disintegration. This was due to the military governors of the north who ruthlessly exploited the territories under their control and created chaos and confusion by constantly fighting with one another for supremacy. The unfortunate common people were left to face famine and starvation. At this time, a new force in the form of a revised Kuomintang, came from the south and established a government at Canton and elected Sun-Yat-Sen as the President of this new Chinese Republic.

Beginning of National Movements:

It was the Chinese students who were the first to voice the protest against the award of Shantung to Japan by the Peace Conference of Paris in 1919. The students' violent agitation set all China ablaze. The movement was a striking demonstration of Chinese national spirit. The widespread movement reached its climax on May 4, 1919 when people from all walks of life, particularly merchants and peasants, joined it and faced ruthless suppression.

Civil War:

The Communist Party of China formed in 1921 joined the Sun's National Party, but remained a separate group, and in 1925, at the death of Sun Yat-Sen, ended the alliance. Sun, though dead, remained a source of inspiration to the party. Sun's place was taken by his disciple, Chiang-Kai-Shek, a brilliant military officer. With Nanking as his capital, he began to rule with the declaration that out of the Three Principles of Sun, he had achieved 'Nationalism' and now he would take up the other two principles—'Democracy' and 'Livelihood'. In 1926, Chiang led his army northward, and two years later he captured the government of Peking and united all of China in 1928. Chiang built factories, railroads and highways and started a vigorous educational programme. This nationalist government was recognised by the Western powers.

Rift Between Communists and Kuomintang:

The communists found an able and experienced leader in Mao Tsetung who became the Chairman of the Chinese Soviet Government. Against Chiang's anti-communist drive, the communists were driven into hiding in the mountainous regions of Southern Kiangsi under Soviet governments armed forces. There, in Sovietised areas, land was distributed among peasants, irrigation works were undertaken and wages of labourers were raised. These efforts popularised communism. The Nationalist government, realising the danger in the growth of Communism, carried out five attacks to drive out the Communists from Kiangsi. The Communists, being defeated, started on their memorable long march of more than six thousand miles to join the Communist forces on the north-west. Thousands perished on the way and reached the province of Yenan and consolidated their position for future fighting with the National Party.

Sino-Japanese War:

In the meantime Japan conquered Manchuria. Mao sent an appeal to the Kuomintang to end the civil war and present a united front to the common enemy, Japan. Chiang, after some reluctance, agreed to the proposal and the Kuomintang forces had to do the major part of the fighting against Japan, but the communist army rendered valuable help by carrying on effective guerilla warfare. The League of Nations made several efforts to force Japan to withdraw from China but it failed. Meanwhile, the World War II began. In 1941, with Japan's attack on Pearl Harbour, the Sino-Japanese War merged in the global conflict.

Japan

Japanese Imperialism:

Military had been a great force in the political life of Japan. On account of its military strength, Japan had inflicted a crushing defeat over China in 1915 and got special rights in Manchuria and inner Mongolia from China. In the First World War, Japan had sided with the Allies and its position became very strong after the War.

Washington Conference (1921-22):

Japan was not happy with the Five Power Naval Treaty signed after the Washington Conference. It put limits on the naval powers of the signatories i.e., England, the U.S.A., France, Italy and Japan. The five powers agreed not to build anymore ships for a period of 10 years. However, this did not prevent Japan from increasing its military strength. (Japanese acts of aggression are taken up in the latter part of this chapter.)

Militarism in Japan:

From the early 1930s, Japanese military became very aggressive. A large number of secret societies had been formed in Japan which advocated national chauvinism, the superiority of Japanese culture and preservation of its purity from foreign influence. These societies considered ideas of socialism, democracy and peace, foreign to Japan. 'Emperor Worship' was the creed for them. Their slogan was "To die for the emperor is to live forever." Thus, the political system which emerged in Japan has been called 'military fascism' and was almost in affinity with the Fascist government of Italy and the Nazi government of Germany.

Important causes which gave rise to militarism in Japan may be summed up as (1) Physical qualities like sturdiness (2) Moral qualities like self-confidence, and discipline (3) Patriotism (4) Nationalism (5) A vibrant economy which motivated them to make inroads in foreign markets and adopt strong postures (6) Successes in aggression with the weak parliamentary government (8) Great desire to become a strong military power (9) Protection of Japanese capitalists who had made heavy investments at various places outside Japan (10) Weak political parties.

Rapid Industrial Development but Labour Unrest:

After the First World War, Japan made a remarkable progress in the industrial field. There was a great expansion of iron and steel and heavy industries. In fact this speedy development became the main reason of its expansionist designs and consequently rise of militarism.

The Japanese agricultural production was not self-sufficient. Most of the farmers had very small pieces of land and a large number of them worked as tenants. Therefore, the living conditions of the peasantry were very miserable.

The 1920s saw agricultural worker's as well as industrial worker's strike. High price of rice led to the looting of the shops of rice traders and the houses of the rich. These are generally referred to as 'rice mutinies'. Trade unions were formed and several communist groups emerged to voice their feelings for the working class and the peasants but they were suppressed ruthlessly.

OTHER COUNTRIES IN ASIA

Burma (Myanmar)

The Communist Party of Burma raised the demand for the independence of Burma in 1930. It may be recalled that Burma had been occupied by the British in the year 1885. As the national movement grew, Burma was separated from India in 1937. Japan captured it during the War but the British reganied it after the War.

Indo-China

France had been exploiting Indo-China since its occupation in 1886. The movement for independence gained momentum in 1930 under the guidance of Dr. Ho Chi Minh (1890-1969) and the Communist Party organised by him. However, the movement was crushed. It was occupied by Japan during the Second World War.

Indonesia

The Communist Party formed in 1920 organised a revolt in 1920 but it was crushed by the Dutch rulers. Dr. Sukarno (1901-1970) organised the nationalist movement in Indonesia by bringing together various parties. It was occupied by Japan in 1942.

Korea

After the First World War, the movement for the independence of Korea from the colonial rule of Japan became powerful. The movement received a boost from the success of the Russian Revolution. In 1918, the nationalists of Korea drafted a Declaration of Independence which was read out in public meetings. There was a country-wide uprising which was suppressed by the Japanese army. After 1931, following the capture of Manchuria by Japan, the movement again became strong.

Iran

In 1919, Britain, which had great interest in the oil of Iran, signed an agreement with the Government of Iran which led to British control over the army and also its economy. This led to several uprisings in different parts of Iran which were suppressed. In 1921, the pro-British Government of Iran was overthrown. The new government discarded the 1919 agreement. In 1925, the Shah of Iran was deposed and the Iranian Constituent Assembly called the '*Majlis*' made Reza Khan, an army officer, as the Shah (Emperor) of Iran. The dynasty of Reza Khan came to be known as the Pahlavi dynasty. The Shah's rule was tyrannical and the common people of Iran suffered.

Palestine

After the World War I, Palestine became a British Protectorate. The Jews, who had been driven away from Palestine by foreign rulers, had been living scattered in different parts of the world. They launched a strong movement for going back to their 'Holy Land', called Zionism. Founder of Christianity, Jesus Christ and his Apostles were all Jews. The Jews had rendered a great help to the British Government during the First World War. Appreciating their services, the British Foreign Secretary Arthur James Balfour announced in November 1917, that the British had decided to give support for carving out a Jewish national home in Palestine. The population of the Jews grew by leaps and bounds in Palestine. Jews from different parts of the World began to migrate to Palestine. This led to a great resentment among the Arab population of Palestine. In 1929, anti-Jewish riots became widespread. In 1930, the British Government suspended immigration permits.

Philippines

It became an American colony in 1898. A peasant uprising which took place in 1930 was suppressed. Several political movements took place for the freedom of the country. In 1935, Philippines was granted autonomy with the promise of complete independence in 1945.

Syria and Lebanon

These countries had become French Protectorate. The people of these countries rose in revolt against the French rule. In 1925, there were serious revolts which were crushed. In 1936, The Popular Front came into power in France and its French Government promised independence within three years.

AFRICA

Background

In an earlier chapter, it was noted how the powerful imperialist countries of Europe conquered Africa in the 19th century and partitioned it among themselves. By 1912, the whole continent of Africa, except Ethiopia and Liberia came under European imperialists. Big slices of Africa were under the control of Britain, France, Italy and Germany and the smaller ones to Belgium, Portugal and Spain. The imperialists ruthlessly bullied and exploited the Africans. The Africans were made slaves and semislaves in their own country and denied freedom and justice.

It is of interest to note that even at the end of Second World War in 1945, in the whole of Africa, there were only four independent states out of a total of 50. These were (i) Egypt (ii) Ethiopia (iii) Liberia and (iv) The White governed South Africa.

Brief History of Freedom Struggle

The year 1919 is an important year in the freedom movement of Africa as during 1919 the first Pan-African Congress at Paris was convened by W.E.B. Du Bois during the Peace Conference after the end of the First World War. The Congress passed two important resolutions, one demanding equal political rights for the Black People in the US and the other parts of the world and the second, the right of self-determination for the African people. The Pan-African Congress Sessions held in 1921, 1923 and 1927 in different capital cities of Europe brought together black intellectuals from Africa, the U.S.A. and the Caribbeans.

Important Causes of National Awakening in Africa

Important causes may be listed as (1) Ruthless exploitation by the imperialist powers (2) Impact of Western education and spread of liberal ideas (3) President Wilson's principle of self-discipline as reflected in his 14-Point Programme (4) Influence of Western Culture (5) Anti-imperialist propaganda by Soviet Russia (6) Japan's victories over Western countries providing encouragement to African and Asian people (7) Dynamic and inspiring role of African leaders (8) Role of the Negritude movement (9) Organisation of political conferences laying stress on independence and condemning colonial policies (10) Formation of several Leagues and associations for the promotion of Black culture.

Egypt

Egypt had been occupied in 1882 by Britain and had become Britain's protectorate. During the First World War, Britain introduced forced conscription and compelled them to provide grain and livestock at exceptionally low prices. The British patronised Christian missionaries. After the end of the War, Egyptian leaders were not invited to the Peace Conference whereas some Princes of India and Arab Sheikhs were invited. All these factors created great resentment against the British rule. A Wafd Party (the Nationalist Party) was formed by Saad Zaghlul Pasha, a lawyer, to fight for the cause of Egyptian freedom. Saad Zaghlul Pasha took the initiative and led a delegation to Paris to plead for the national cause. The British rulers treated this act as sheer impertinence and arrested the members of the delegates and sent them to Malta. The arrest of Zaghlul Pasha and others provoked revolt in Egypt. In 1922, Britain tried to appease the Egyptians and proclaimed Egypt as "an independent sovereign state" but with certain conditions. The defence was to be in the hands of Britain. Sudan, which was rich in cotton was to be under British control. In 1923, the British promulgated a new constitution in Egypt. The Wafd Party won a majority in the Egyptian Parliament and Zaghlul, who had returned from exile became the Premier. The Egyptians continued their struggle for complete independence and ultimately Egypt got independence in 1956.

South Africa

In an earlier chapter, we detailed the circumstances leading to the Dutch supremacy in South Africa and the Boer Wars with their consequences. It may be recalled that although the whites comprising the Boers of the Dutch origin and the English of the British origin constituted about 20 per cent of the population, they ruled South Africa. The government was completely in their hands. The government followed the policy of discrimination known as 'Apartheid' or policy of segregation. The White settlers treated the Africans with contempt. The Africans could reside in specified areas only. The people of South Africa had to wage a fierce struggle. The year 1994 saw the end of the White supremacy when Nelson Mandela of the African National

Congress, an organisation fighting for the cause of the African people, became the President of South Africa.

The Universal Negro Improvement Association, set up by Marcus Garvey in 1914 organised another Pan African Movement to encourage Black Americans to emigrate to Africa. The movement also aimed at developing a sense of pride among the Black people everywhere in the world.

In the 1920s and 1930s, a cultural movement called as the *Negritude* movement emerged for promoting a sense of identity and pride among the Black people and rejecting the white and colonial domination. Its basis was "a belief in a common cultural heritage among all African and African-descended peoples." It also glorified beauty of African art and music. Among the prominent leaders of the movement were three eminent poets namely Aime Cesaire of Martinique (a French colony in the Caribbean), Leopold Sedar Senghor of Senegal (Leopold later became the President of Senegal) and Langston Hughes of the U.S.A. Claude Mckay, another poet of Jamaican origin, inspired Black people to revolt against their common hardships and assert themselves to preserve their dignity.

African leaders like Wilmost Blyden raised the Slogan "Africa for the Africans."

In short Negritude movement aimed at :

(i) Promotion of sense of identity and pride among the African people.
(ii) Rejection of Colonial and White domination.
(iii) Stress on Black culture.
(iv) Appreciation of their common cultural heritage.
(v) Development of sense of belonging among the Blacks.

EXERCISES

Very Short Answer Type

1. List any four factors that led to the growth of national movements in Asia.
2. State any two features of student's movement in China.
3. What is the significance of the year 1919 in the freedom struggle of Africa?
4. State the role of W.E.B. Du Bois in the freedom struggle of Africa.

Short Answer Type

1. State the salient features of rift between Communists and Kuomintang.
2. Write a note on Japanese imperialism.
3. Give the important causes which gave rise to militarism in Japan.
4. What were the main issues involved in Palestine? State the role of the British Government.
5. Explain the policy of 'Apartheid' followed in South Africa. What was the role of Nelson Mandela in ending this policy.
6. Explain the 'Negritude' movement.

CHAPTER 27

The Second World War

INTRODUCTION

Nature of the Second World War

The Second World War, fought after an interval of 20 years and nine months from the First World War, was more devastating in nature. It was also longer than the First War. France, England and the U.S.A. were the main winning parties in both the wars. Germany was the worst loser on both the occasions. Russia had to enter into a humiliating treaty with Germany in 1917 during the course of the First World War, but in the Second World War, after initial losses it inflicted heavy casualties on Germany. Japan in the First World War, was with the Allied powers and had gained, but in the Second World War, it sided with Germany and was a loser. The role of Italy was also reversed. In the First War, it was with the Allies and in the second it was with the Axis Powers of Germany and Japan. In the First War, Austria-Hungary and Germany and their partners were called Central Powers and in the Second War, they were popularly known as Axis Powers. In the second War, England was, for a short period, on the brink of extinction but with courage and fortitude it not only saved itself, but also came out with a glorious triumph. Immediately after the end of the Second World War, the process of granting independence to the colonies began rapidly. In short, the Second World War was wider in scope than the First War. It was also different in nature. While the First War was a trench warfare, the Second war was an aerial war. Besides, more deadly weapons were used in the Second War.

Warring Parties

Several big and small countries were entangled in the War. On the one side were the Axis or central powers comprising, Germany, Italy, Japan etc. Their supporting powers were Finland, Hungary, Rumania, Albania and Bulgaria. On the other side were the Allies consisting of England, France and the U.S.A. Italy joined the Allies after its defeat. Russia in the beginning helped Germany but later joined the Allies. China also later on joined the Allies. The Allies were supported by 26 countries. Among these were: Belgium, Denmark, Estonia, Greece, Latvia, Lithuania, Norway and Holland. Neutral countries were: Ireland, Portugal, Spain, Sweden and Switzerland.

CAUSES OF THE SECOND WORLD WAR

The Second War was caused on account of following causes (1) Harsh, unjust and vindictive Treaty of Versailles (2) Aggressive Nationalism (3) Imperialist interests (4) Race for armaments (5) Problem of minorities (6) Relative aloofness of U.S.A. (7) Conflict of ideologies (8) Failure of the League of Nations (9) Policy of appeasement (10) Germany's overestimate of its own power and underestimate of others (11) Saving civilization (12) Immediate cause.

Treaty of Versailles

It has been rightly said, "The Treaty of Versailles contained the seeds of the Second World War." The Treaty of Versailles totally disregarded President Wilson's 14-points that included "There shall be no annexations, no contributions, no punitive damages." It was based on the slogan raised by the British Prime Minister Lloyd George during his election campaign, "Make Germany Pay. Hang the Kaiser (ruler of Germany)." Like him, the Prime Minister of France, Clemenceau, was filled with hatred of Germany. These were the two more prominent leaders who played a leading role in drafting the Peace Treaty after the end of the war. The overall passion of hatred for Germany made the Allies blind in their hour of victory when they should have exhibited a sense of magnanimity and moderation accompanied by fairness and justice. The peace makers were so vindictive that they went to the absurdity of "demanding that Germany hand over to France and Belgium 140,000 cows and 130,000 sheep within three months after the signing of the document."

It was very clear why the Treaty made Germany, Italy and Japan very unhappy and angry. (a) Germany had been deprived of several territories which include Alsace-Lorraine which it had seized from France in 1871. Newly created State of Poland was provided with access to the sea by giving her about 65 km. of 'corridor' which separated one part of Germany from the other and Danzig was made a free city under the political control of the League of Nations and economic control of Poland. Belgium, Denmark and Lithuania also gained territories from Germany. The Saar coalmines in the area were transferred to France as compensation. Germany was disallowed to join with Austria. The Rhineland was to be permanently demilitarised and occupied by the allied troops for fifteen years. The strength of the German army was fixed at 100,000. Germany was not allowed to have any air force and submarines. The number of ships was also limited. Germany was required to pay £ 66000 million as war reparations. The colonies of Germany were divided among the victorious powers. Most of German East Africa-Tanganyika went to Britain. Some portions went to Portugal and Belgium. Congo, Cameroon and Togoland were divided between Britain and France. Ruanda-Urundi was given to Belgium and South-West Africa to South Africa. The Pacific Islands under German control were divided among Australia, New Zealand and Japan. Three million German speaking people were included in the newly created State of Czechoslovakia (b) Italy had joined the First World War on the side of the Allies with high hopes. It felt dissatisfied with the Treaty of Versailles. The frontiers of Italy were not redrawn on the basis of nationality (c) Japan was not fully satisfied with the gains that it obtained from the peace Treaty of Versailles. The war enabled Japan to consolidate its gains of the Russo-Japanese war (1904-05). Japan wanted full control over Shantung but was denied the same. Thus, Japan felt that it did not get enough. What it secured at the peace conference was not equal to its efforts made in winning the war. Another factor that made Japan unhappy was the contempt with which the White races treated their coloured races. Japan felt humiliated when at the Washington Conference in 1920, in which several big nations participated, it was asked to limit its naval power as compared with the U.S.A. and Britain. In view of these, it is clear that the seeds of the Second World War had been sown by the peace Treaty of Paris, conducted at the end of the First World War.

Aggressive Nationalism

Concepts like 'Japan for Japanese', 'Italy for Italians,' 'Germany for Germans' and 'My country right or wrong' which emphasise nationalism in a fanatic manner must necessarily lead to tensions. Germany even went to the extent of boasting that German race was the most superior race on earth and had the right to rule the world. No doubt 'Nationalism is needed to develop love for ones country and to rise above regionalism for the unity and integrity of a nation, but when it crosses all limits it assumes alarming proportions'.

Imperialist Interests

The imperialism of all the European countries had poisoned the international situation for a long time.

Germany was accused of 'war guilt' in the First War. The European powers that dominated the world for about 200 years forgot that they could also be accused of 'war guilt.' They had ruthlessly exploited their colonies whom they had captured by force. In fact, war is inherent in the system of imperialism which develops a rat race for expansion. Germany, France, England, Japan etc. all were responsible for the Second World War for their lust and greed for territories.

Race for Armaments

Almost all countries engaged themselves in racing for armaments. The Peace Treaty of 1919 had forced the defeated nations to accept disarmament. They were forbidden to produce any war materials. But the victorious nations themselves were not prepared to pursue the policy of disarmament. Hitler declared, "Rearmament was the only road to power and national achievement." France set up its 'Maginot Line' and Germany its 'Fried Line.' As already mentioned, in the Washington Conference, Japan was asked to cut its naval power disproportionately as compared with the U.K. and other countries. Naturally, Japan began to expand its naval power secretly.

Problem of Minorities

After the First World War, a number of new nations had been created but no clear cut principle of nationality was followed. Several countries like Poland, Austria and Czechoslovakia were formed by joining territories having different cultures, languages etc. Since nationalism dominated, the interests of the minority groups were usually disregarded. The Spanish Civil War took place on the issue of minorities among other issues. Germany came to the help of the minorities.

Relative Aloofness of the U.S.A.

The U.S.A. did not join the League of the Nations and this deprived the world of its sobering influence. Even in the Peace Treaty, the U.S.A. did not assert itself. The European political scene remained dominated by powers having conflicting interests.

Conflict of Ideologies

The post-First World War World witnessed a conflict of ideologies. Democratic forms of government, totalitarianism, communism, Fascism and Nazism were based on different ideologies. In several countries of Europe and elsewhere, republican governments failed and gave way to dictatorship. The dictators were wedded to the principles of war and might and wanted to impose the same on other countries.

Failure of League of Nations

The League of Nations which was dominated by big imperialist powers could not act fairly, justly and uprightly. It failed in its primary duty of preventing the race for armaments and restraining nations from committing acts of aggression.

Policy of Appeasement

England and France made no attempt to enforce even the minimum of the Peace Treaty. Each country pursued its own line of approach. It has been observed about the policy of appeasement, "the statesmen of the major world powers ignored and evaded their responsibility and resorted to the policy of appeasement. But appeasement did not satisfy the aggression and tension between which the powers increased steadily and it resulted in the Second World War."

The Second World War

Germany's Over Estimate of its Own Power and Underestimate of Other Powers

Hitler was very proud of his own strength and had firm faith in the capacity of Germany over other nations. After signing the Soviet-German Non-Aggression Pact on August 23,1939, Hitler said to his commanders, "Our opponents are little worms. I saw them in Munich."

Saving Civilization

There appeared to be no end to the expansionist designs of Hitler and Mussolini. Their intention was to enslave the entire Europe and spread Fascist doctrines by ending democratic values. Western civilization was in danger and the various European powers, especially England and France, decided to take a firm stand to save democratic values cherished by Britain, France and U.S.A. from being crushed under the boots of Nazi soldiers.

Immediate Cause

After signing a pact of friendship and non-aggression with Russia on August 24, 1939, Germany put forth 16 points of demand before Poland on August 29, 1939 and broadcast the same on August 31. Poland was asked to reply within a day. However Germany, without waiting for Poland's reply, started showering bombs on Poland at about 4.45 A.M. on September 1,1939. On september 3, Britain and France, who had an alliance with Poland, declared war on Germany. Thus the Second World War began.

MAIN EVENTS OF THE WAR IN EUROPE AND NORTHERN AFRICA

1939
Sept. 1   Germany invaded Poland starting World War II.
Sep. 3   Britain and France declared War on Germany.

1940
April 9   Germany invaded Denmark and Norway.
May 10   Germany invaded Belgium and the Netherlands.
June 10   Italy declared war on France and Great Britain.
July 10   Battle of Britain began.

1941
April 6   Germany invaded Greece and Yugoslavia.
June 22   Germany invaded the Soviet Union.
Sept. 8   German troops completely blockaded Leningrad which lasted until Jan. 1944.

1942
Aug. 25   Hitler ordered the capture of Stalingrad.
Nov. 8   Hitler troops landed in Algeria and Morocco.

1943
Feb. 2   The last German troops surrendered at Stalingrad.
May 13   Axis forces surrendered in northern Africa.
Sep. 3   Italy secretly surrendered to the Allies.

1944
June 6   Allied troops landed in Normandy in the D-Day invasion of northern France.
De. 16   The Germans struck back at troops in the battle of the Bulge.

1945
April 30   Hitler took his life in Berlin.
May 7   Germany surrendered unconditionally ending World War II.

MAIN EVENTS OF THE WAR IN THE PACIFIC

1941
Dec. 7 — Japan bombed US military bases at Pearl Harbour at Hawaii.
Dec. 8 — The US, Great Britain and Canada declared war on Japan.
1942
Feb. 15 — Singapore fell to the Japanese.
April 9 — US troops on Bataan surrendered.
April 18 — US bombed Tokyo.
June 6 — The Allies defeated Japan in the battle of Midway.
1944
Oct. 20 — The Allies began landing in the Philippines.
1945
Aug 6 — An atomic bomb was dropped on Hiroshima.
Aug 8 — The USSR declared war on Japan.
Aug 9 — An atomic bomb was dropped on Nagasaki.
Sept. 2 — Japan signed surrender on the US battleship Missouri which lay anchored in Tokyo Bay.

CHIEF EVENTS OF THE WAR

Defeat of Poland and 'Phoney' War

At 5.30 on the morning of September 1,1939, without a declaration of war, Nazi troops crossed the Polish frontier. On September 3, Britain and France declared war on Germany. The Nazi technique was a *blitzkrieg*. *Blitzkrieg* (pronounced : blits crig) means sudden intensive attack, with a massive force, with great rapidity like lightening. Such an attack devastates everything that comes before it. The German mechanised divisions rolled through towns and villages crashing through barricades and destroying everything in their paths. Simultaneously, the planes of *Lutwaffe* (German air force) bombed civilians and military alike. The Poles, who met the enemy with an outmoded harsh cavalry, were overwhelmed. Meanwhile, Russian forces, on September 17, advanced into Poland from the east. Poland did not receive direct help from its Allies, England and France, who found there was very little to send and it was already too late to help. Within a month, by the end of September, Germany and Russia conquered the country and divided Poland between themselves. The world was amazed at the speed with which Germany accomplished the conquest. France might have caused a diversion by attacking Germany from the west, but the French army did not move. The Allies believed that Germany could be defeated by naval blockade and defensive action along the Maginot (pronounced : mazhino) Line, the entrenched fortifications built by France. After September 1939 up to the end of March 1940, almost no fighting took place except a few minor naval clashes. This period was known as the time of 'phoney war,' that is no real war. It does not, however, look appropriate to call it a 'phoney war' which demolished a nation like Poland, killing thousands of men, women and children.

Hitler Seized Denmark and Norway

This attack was planned for two reasons. Sweden was a major supplier of iron-ore to Germany, most needed at the time to manufacture war weapons. As such the occupation of Denmark and Norway was a must to ensure safe transport without any obstruction on the way. Secondly, there were many Nazi sympathisers in Denmark and Norway. In Norway, they were headed by a Fascist, Vidkun Quisling, whose name became synonymous with a traitor, as he helped Germany to win his own country. Hitler's paratroops (disguised in uniforms of other nations) landed in these two countries and prepared an easy way for the German attack.

The Second World War

Denmark surrendered without much resistance. Norway proved more stubborn but with the inside help of Quisling, Norway was conquered.

Hitler Moved into Belgium and Holland

The conquest of Norway and Denmark gave Hitler air and sea bases close to England and facility to import food, iron and other resources easily. On May 10, 1940 The Nazi armies launched a *blitzkrieg* on the western front. Merciless bombing brought the surrender of Holland on May 14. Between Holland in the north and France in the south is Belgium. The French and British Soldiers quickly moved north into Belgium to stop the German army from conquering Belgium. Another German division with great rapidity passed through the gap left due to the movement of the British and French soldiers to the north, and trapped them from both west and north. On May 28, Belgium surrendered to Hitler.

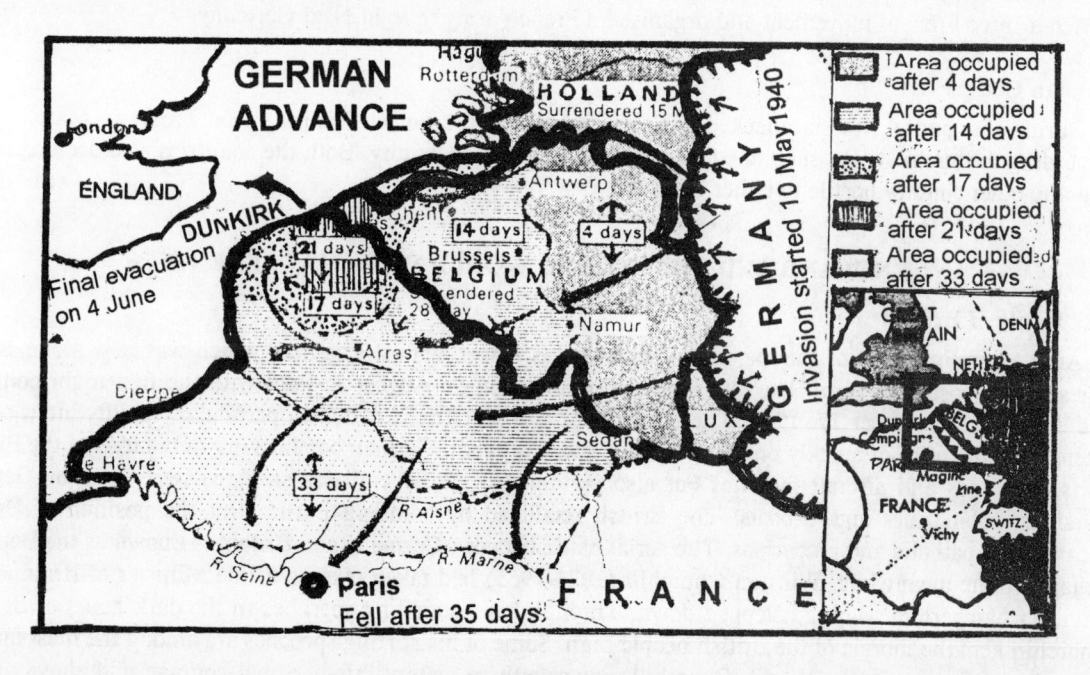

Map 7: **German Advance**

Dunkirk Miracle

The British and French forces then had no choice but to retreat to the English channel coast of France at Dunkirk. Here capture and destruction of the trapped soldiers seemed inevitable. However, in one of the most amazing events of the war, a sort of miracle, 600 civilian crafts—yachts, barges, motorboats and various types of private boats—from England crossed the English Channel to Dunkirk under the cover of night and joined the 200 British naval ships. With the air protection of British Royal Air Force, the hastily assembled fleet evacuated more than 335,000 soldiers to England. They left behind all their heavy equipment. Churchill called this rescue 'a miracle of deliverance.' It saved the Allies from ruin.

Vichy France

After the Dunkirk miracle, situation in France became very alarming. Germany's invasion of France in the first week of June was so dreadful that the French Government left Paris on June 9, 1940. On June 10, the victorious German troops entered Paris whose deserted streets were a picture of deadly silence. The capture of Paris was a big feather in Germany's cap—Two French Premiers had to resign on account of their diplomatic failure. Now it was the turn of the new premier, Henri Phillipe Petain, a French hero of World War I. He was expected to put up a fight; instead, he appealed for peace and an agreement was signed between Germany and France. Nearly half of France was occupied by Germany. Petain's Government became a puppet government and it moved to Vichy—an important place in France. This part of France which was under Petain was known as Vichy France.

Free French

Some military officers were not in favour of surrender. Colonel Charles De Gaulle (1890-1970) who later on became the General and then President of France (1959-69), managed to escape to England. There he started a 'Free French' movement and organised a French army to fight Nazi Germany.

Russian Conquests

During this period, Russia attacked Finland and signed the Soviet-Finnish Peace Treaty in March 1940. According to this treaty Russia gained a naval base and some territory. Both the countries also decided not to join any other country hostile to either of them.

ENGLAND AND THE SECOND WORLD WAR: MAIN EVENTS

The Battle of Britain

After trampling most of Europe, Hitler directed his power against England, which was now alone, all its allies having lost their wars. The invasion of Britain began on August 8, 1940 with the first night bombing and ended on September 17, 1940. The bombing of British cities, London in particular, rapidly increased in intensity in the hope of quickly breaking Britain's will to resist. German bombers not only targeted the British ports, air fields and aircraft factories but also civilian places. Several British ships were sunk by German warships, submarines and U-boats. The British retaliated by bombing Berlin. But the position of Britain became very pathetic and precarious. The aerial battle between Germany and Britain is known as the Battle of Britain. In the meanwhile, Winston Churchill (1874-1965) had taken over as Prime Minister of Britain from Neville Chamberlain who had stepped down. Through his resounding speeches in the dark hours of Britain, Churchill kept the morale of the British people high. Some of his stirring speeches are among the most famous examples of oratory in the World. Churchill's own faith in victory, his personal courage and above all the magic of his words inspired the British people to achieve a glorious victory. Offering his countrymen nothing but "blood, toil and sweat," in one of his speeches Churchill said, "Even though many old and famous states have fallen, we shall go on to the end. We shall defend our island whatever the cost may be, we shall fight on the beaches, we shall fight on the landing grounds, we shall fight in the fields and in the streets, we shall fight in the hills, we shall never surrender." He further said, "You ask what is our policy? I will say: It is to Wage War against a monstrous tyranny, never surpassed in the dark, lamentable catalogue of human crime. You ask, "What is our aim? I can answer in one word. *Victory-Victory* at all costs, *Victory*." Indeed his magnetic appeal cast a magic spell on his countrymen. The battle in the air was by no means one-sided. With the help of radar, a newly invented device, and a splendid fighter plane named Spitfire, the R.A.F. gradually gained surperiority over German bombers. At the end of three months, the British had destroyed about twice the number of planes that they themselves had lost. Hitler was then forced to abandon his plan of conquering Britain. With a united action full of patience, tact and courage, Britain was able to save its airfields from any serious damage and to increase the production in its aircraft industries with the result that it could make up its losses in the Battle of Britain.

ITALY'S ENTRY IN THE WAR

Encouraged by the success of Germany in Europe, Italy also joined War on the side of Germany. On September 27 1940, Italy, Germany and Japan signed a Tripartite Agreement. This agreement provided for each country to give full support to the others in the case of any attack by any other power. Germany and Italy accepted Japan's claims to East and South-East Asia which also meant Japanese conquest of China as well as Manchuria. Germany also made some other European countries like Hungary, Rumania and Slovakia join the Tripartite Agreement. These countries thus became the allies of Germany, Italy and Japan. With the help of German troops, Italy was able to subjugate Greece and Yugoslavia. By June 1941, Germany and Italy had captured almost all of Europe except Britain and Soviet Union. In the beginning, Italy achieved great success in its war campaign in Africa. Germany also sent its forces in Africa to help Italy. It captured Libya, Somaliland and Egypt. During 1942, the Fascist powers of Italy and Germany reached the height of their power but in 1943, they faced defeat on every war front. British General Montgomery gave a crushing defeat to German troops under General Rommel in the battle of El Alamin. All hopes of Italy to exercise control in Africa were dashed to the ground.

HITLER'S BETRAYAL AND ATTACK ON RUSSIA

The two warring great dictators of the world namely Hitler of Germany and Stalin of Russia had entered into a friendly agreement on August 24, 1939 and the agreement came as a great surprise to most of the statesmen of the world. It had happened just a few days before the outbreak of the Second World War. In spite of the agreement, Hitler considered Russia as an enemy. Hitler was a sworn enemy of communism. He also had an eye on the fertile Ukraine region.

Operation Barbossa

Germany started planning of the invasion of Soviet Union in early 1940 and gave it the name of 'Operation Barbossa'. Hitler had a very low opinion of the Red Army of the Soviet Union. He called it " no more than a joke." Hitler was over confident that as Germany had conquered Poland, France, Yugoslavia and Greece, it would be easy to conquer Russia. He believed that his generals were invincible. The maximum period for the success of Operation Barbossa was seventeen weeks. Hitler's calculation failed. The invasion or the Operation led to the destruction of not only the Nazi regime but also of Hitler himself.

Hitler's Attack on Russia

Hitler and Stalin already had a friendly agreement signed on August 24, 1939. In spite of the agreement, Hitler considered Russia as an enemy. A number of reasons led to the German attack on Russia. There was no point to attempt another invasion of Britain which was now very well fortified and Germany was inferior to Britain in naval power. Hitler still believed that his greatest enemy was communist Russia, the communist ideology of which was spreading all over the world and was going to weaken the dictatorial forces. The earlier agreement was just a strategic military gesture to keep Russia inactive while he attacked the west. Now he believed that west would remain inactive while he attacked Russia. He wanted to possess the fertile fields of Ukraine and the oil of the Caucasus.

Finland, Rumania, Hungary, and Slovakia joined Germany in the War. As soon as Hitler attacked Russia, Churchill offered Russia, an alliance with Great Britain. This really surprised many in Britain as well in U.S.A. since Churchill had always been a foe of communism. How strange it looked that Hitler's war made friends of two powers which were enemies of peace time, but then everybody realised that Hitler should be defeated at all costs. At first German methods of warfare seemed as successful in Russia as they had been in

Map 8: **Russian Front**

Poland. The Red Army of Russia was driven back. Germany took Kiev and it was 60 km from Moscow. It seemed Leningrad would fall. But neither Moscow nor Leningrad fell.

By the end of October 1941, the winter set in. However, Hitler, like Napoleon, had underestimated the severity of the Russian winter. Snow soon blocked the roads and German supply lines bogged down. German soldiers, inadequately clothed for the Russian winter suffered miserably and the army came to a standstill waiting for the spring of 1942. Russians on the other hand being accustomed to their own climate, slowly prepared for a counter offensive. The Russians reoccupied many cities and relieved the pressure on Moscow.

Battle of Stalingrad

Throughout 1942, War was fought almost exclusively between the German and Soviet troops. In July 1942, the German troops launched an offensive on Stalingrad and by the middle of September they reached the outskirts of that city. 'The greatest single trial of strength' began. Till the middle of November bitter fighting went on the streets of Stalingrad for every inch of the land. Had the Germans taken the city, they would have stopped all traffic and communication. But Stalingrad did not fall, notwithstanding enormous damage inflicted upon it. By the end of November 1942 it was clear that German offensive had failed. With the coming winter, the Russians began their counterattack. Advancing north and south of Stalingrad, they surrounded and cut off 22 German divisions. On January 31, 1943, about 140 thousand men surrendered. The failure at Stalingrad was Germany's first major defeat. It was both an Allied and Russian victory.

In the middle of 1943, Germans again launched another military operation against Soviet-Union. After suffering a crushing defeat they retreated in January 1944.

JAPAN'S ENTRY IN THE WAR

Japan wanted to have hold in the Far-East. It aimed at conquering Indo-China, Siam, Burma, Malaya and Dutch East Indies. Its eyes were particularly fixed on oil, tin, rubber and bauxite of these countries. It was delighted to learn of Hitler's attack on Russia. It wanted to take full advantage of the difficulties of Britain and France. The peace-loving Japanese Premier Konoe was compelled to resign and General Togo, a man as war-minded as Hitler and Mussolini appeared on the scene. Japan had already entered into Rome-Berlin-Tokyo Axis. Thus Japan joined war on the side of Italy and Germany.

On December 7, 1941, Japan suddenly attacked the American fleet in the Pearl Harbour (Hawaii) with 423 planes. The attack disabled eight US battleships and left about 250 Americans dead. This was an unprovoked attack, as the Japanese envoys were then having 'peace talks' with the U.S.A. in Washington. The very next day i.e., on December 8, 1941, the U.S.A. declared War on Japan. Japan also destroyed two big English warships named ' 'Prince of Wales' and 'Repulse'. The successful Pearl Harbour attack encouraged Japan to pursue its imperialist pursuits. Japan succeeded in conquering Shanghai, Hong Kong, Malaya, Singapore, Philippines, Java, Borneo, Sumatra, Bali etc. After conquering Burma, Japan started bombing on the north-eastern frontiers of India. The surrender of Hong Kong and Singapore in 1942 brought the prestige of Britain to the lowest ebb in the world.

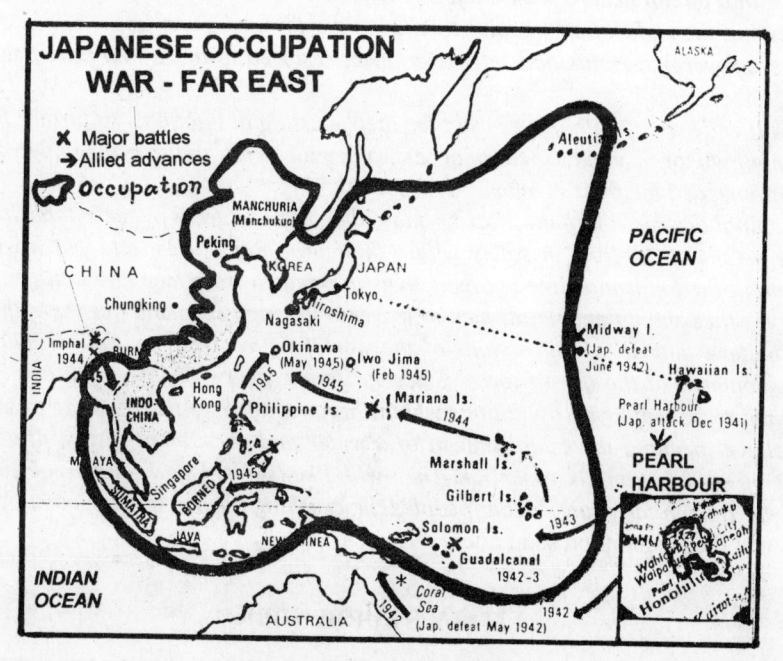

Map 9: **Japanese Occupation**

ENTRY OF THE U.S.A. IN THE WAR

The U.S.A. remained aloof from the war for about two years. The spectacular victories of Germany in 1940 created a strong sense of awakening on the War issue. For the first time the US Congress introduced compulsory training and plans were drawn to strengthen the US navy. The U.S.A. began to provide assistance to Britain with War material on a large scale to face Germany. The multi-billion dollar Lend-Lease Act of March 1941 passed by the U.S.A. enabled it to provide Britain a continuous supply of War materials. In November 1941, the US 'Lend-Lease' system War extended to the U.S.A. Simultaneously the U.S.A. industries began to produce enormous quantities of armaments, aircrafts and ships. The US had 3,00,000 aircrafts and 85,000 tanks and it came to be regarded as the "Arsenal of Victory." After Japanese attack at

Pearl Harbour, the US Naval base, on December 7, the U.S.A. declared War on Japan on December 8, 1941. Germany and Italy declared War on the U.S.A. and the U.S.A. declared War on them.

ATLANTIC CHARTER

The Atlantic Charter issued in August 1941 by the British Prime Minister Churchill and the US President Roosevelt is usually treated as a statement of War aims. This very charter encouraged the Indian leaders to demand independence. In view of its great importance, its full text is given below.

The President of United States of America and the Prime Minister, Mr. Churchill, representing His Majesty's Government in the United Kingdom, being met together, deem it right to make known certain common principles in the national policies of their respective countries on which they base their hopes for a better future for the world.

First, Their countries seek no aggrandizement, territorial or otherwise; Second, They desire to see no territorial changes that do not accord with the freely expressed wishes of the peoples concerned;

Third, They respect the right of all peoples to choose the form of government under which they will live; and they wish to see sovereign rights and self-government restored to those who have been forcibly deprived of them;

Fourth, They will endeavour, with due respect for their existing obligations, to further the enjoyment by all States, great or small, victor or vanquished, of access, on equal terms, to the trade and to the raw materials of the world which are needed for their economic prosperity;

Sixth, After the final destruction of the Nazi tyranny, they hope to see a peace established which will afford to all nations the means of dwelling in safety within their own boundaries, and which will afford assurance that all the men in all the lands may live out their lives in freedom from fear and want;

Seventh, Such a peace should enable all men to traverse the high seas and oceans without hindrance;

Eighth, They believe that all of the nations of the world, for realistic as well as spiritual reasons, must come to the abandonment of the use of force. Since no future peace can be maintained if land, sea or air armaments continue to be employed by nations which threaten, or may threaten, aggression outside of their frontiers, they believe, pending the establishment of a wider and permanent system of general security, that the disarmament of such nations is essential. They will likewise aid and encourage all other practicable measures which will lighten for peace-loving peoples the crushing burden of armaments.

Russia also joined the Declaration soon after.

ITALY'S SURRENDER

Italy was badly defeated in Africa in March, 1943. Thereafter, the Allied troops devoted their attention to Italy itself. They found an opportunity in July-August 1943 during the Battle of Kursk, when Germany was engaged in a fierce struggle with Russia. They invaded Sicily. By this time, there was widespread discontent in Italy. The dissatisfaction had also spread in the armed forces which had suffered defeat everywhere. There were frequent strikes in Italy. On July 25, 1943, Mussolini was dismissed and a new government under General Badoglio was formed. Mussolini was put under detention. The new government of southern Italy made peace with the Allies on September 30, 1943 and declared War on Germany.

There were thousands of German troops in Italy. On September 10, 1943, they occupied northern Italy, including Rome. Mussolini was rescued by them from detention and he set up his government in northern Italy under the protection of German troops.

By June 1944, Allies had also captured several Italian cities including Rome. In the meantime the anti-Fascist Italian forces intensified their anti-Mussolini activities.

On April 28, 1945, Mussolini was captured and executed. The German troops in Italy surrendered. Thus came the total surrender of Italy.

TEHERAN SUMMIT (1943)

Churchill, Stalin and Roosevelt held the Teheran Summit to discuss several issues relating to the War, strategies to be followed by them. The summit decided to open the Second Front by landing Anglo-American troops in France in May, 1944. The Soviet Union agreed to join the War against Japan after the defeat of Germany.

SURRENDER OF GERMANY

Second Front in Europe and the D-Day

Since joining the War, Russia had been appealing to Britain and the U.S.A. to open a second front in Europe, the first front being in Russia itself. The idea of opening the second front was to divert the attention of Germany. However, Britain and the U.S.A. had sent their forces in Africa. Russia had been left alone to fight Germany. After the German defeat at Stalingrad there was greater coordination among the three powers namely Russia, Britain and the U.S.A. On June 6, 1944, first batch of the Allied troops landed at Normandy on the north-coast of France. General D.D. Eisenhower (1890-1969), who later became the President of the U.S.A. (1953-61), led the troops. By the end of July, the number of troops had risen to 1,600,000. The Allied armies liberated Luxemburg and Belgium by September 1944. In December 1944, the Allies launched the last major offensive against Germany.

The Yalta Conference (1945)

Three top leaders of the Allies namely Churchill, Stalin and Roosevelt held a conference at Yalta in Russia from 4–11 February 1945 while The Second World War was still going on. Following were the major decisions taken by the conference.
1. Unconditional surrender was declared as the chief aim of the conference.
2. After the surrender, Germany was to be divided into four zones, each one under Britain, France, the Soviet Union and the U.S.A.
3. Frontiers of Poland were demarcated.
4. By a 'Declaration of Europe' the three countries of France, Britain and U.S.A. pledged to assist the countries of Europe in establishing democratic institutions.
5. It was decided to set up the United Nations and to work out the details at San Francisco in April, 1945.

Soviet Victories

The Soviet troops, by early 1945 had defeated Finland, an ally of Germany. Thereafter Russia liberated Poland, Rumania, Bulgaria, Hungary and Czechoslovakia. The Fascist troops were also driven out of Greece, Yugoslavia and Albania.

Surrender of Germany

The collapse of Germany became evident by early January 1945. Germany had been defeated on both the fronts, Eastern as well as Western. In March the troops of Britain and the U.S.A. had started their offence in the west and by mid-April had occupied large parts of Germany. In the east, the Soviet troops moved into Germany in April and by April 25, encircled Berlin. On April 30, 1945, Hitler and his wife Eva Braun committed suicide. Germany's other two powerful persons namely Goebbels and Himmler also followed suit.

Hitler's successor Admiral Doentiz unconditionally surrendered before the representatives of the U.S.A., France, Britain and Soviet Union on May 7, 1945. May 8, 1945 was celebrated as the V-E Day (Victory in Europe Day)

Potsdam Conference (1945)

After the German surrender, a conference was held at Potsdam in Germany. Clement Italy, Prime Minister of Britain, Stalin of the Soviet Union and Henry S. Truman, President of the U.S.A., attended this conference. Following decisions were taken at this conference :

First, to end militarism and Nazism in Germany; Second, to ban Fascist organisations; Third, to compose War indemnities on Germany; Fourth, to divide Germany into four occupation zones as decided in the Yalta conference; Fifth, to try Nazi criminals; Sixth, to transfer northern part of East Prussia to Russia and southern part to Poland.

SURRENDER OF JAPAN

Cairo Declaration (1943)

The Cairo Declaration was signed by the representatives of Britain, the United States and China in December, 1943. It called for:
(i) The unconditional surrender of Japan
(ii) Return of all areas conquered by Japan after 1894.

First use of Atomic Bomb in World History

Even after the surrender of Germany, War continued for sometime in Asia and the Pacific. According to the Potsdam Declaration, Japan was asked to "surrender or to face prompt and utter destruction." As if in fulfillment of the threat, on August 6, an American bomber dropped a single bomb on Hiroshima, a city with a population of about 35 thousand. This one bomb entirely destroyed an area of 4 square miles. It killed 78 thousand people. On August 9, a second bomb was dropped with similar results, this time on the port city of Nagasaki.

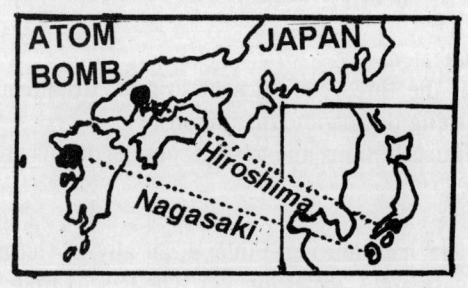

Map 10: **Atom Bomb**

The US official documents described what happened after the atomic bomb was dropped on the city of Hiroshima:

"Following the flash there was a blast of heat and wind. The large majority of people within 3,000 feet of ground were immediately killed. Within a radius of about 7,000 feet almost every Japanese house collapsed... Persons in the open were burned on exposed surfaces, and within 3,000-5,000 feet many were burned to death. In many instances clothing burst into spontaneous flame and had to be beaten out. Thousands of people were pinned beneath collapsed buildings... ." The development of the atomic bomb was a great break through in scientific knowledge. It had ushered in the horror of atomic warfare. The bombs killed over 320,000 people in these two cities. Meanwhile on August 8, Russia had declared War on Japan. By the end of August, the Japanese forces in Manchuria had surrendered to the Russian army. In the South-East Asia, it surrendered to the English army and in China it surrendered to the armies of Chiang Kai-Shek and the Chinese communists. On September 2, 1945, Japan unconditionally surrendered and on the same day, the Japanese signed the surrender terms with General Douglas Mac-Arthur of the U.S.A. on the battleship *Missouri* in the Tokyo Bay.

Thus the Second World War which began on September 1, 1939 came to a close on September 2, 1945 - after six years and one day.

CONSEQUENCES AND RESULTS OF SECOND WORLD WAR

No country was free from the adverse effects of War directly or indirectly. It has been rightly observed "No conflict in human history has been as destructive to life and property as this War turned out to be." The main effects of the War are given below.

Great Holocaust

It resulted in thorough destruction and suffering. Though estimates vary about the impact of War on the loss of human life, yet, it is admitted that on all counts the holocaust was unprecedented.

In his publication *Contemporary Europe Since 1870* published in 1958, Carlton Hayes describes the loss in these words, "To the American people alone, the immediate and direct cost was nearly 400,000 deaths, and a financial expenditure of something like 350 billion dollars. The direct expenditure of other countries has been estimated at a trillion (1,000 billion) dollars while loss of property must run to another trillion and of human lives atleast 22 million dead and 34 million wounded. The indirect and long range cost to the world is simply incalculable." About 20 million civilians fell victim to war. Millions of people on all fronts were uprooted from their homes. Several countries in which battles were actually fought were torn to pieces. Hundreds of factories, public works and buildings were razed to the ground.

Use of Atom Bomb and Air Raids etc.

For the first time in history, so many deadly weapons were used in the War not only against the fighting armies but also upon the innocent citizens who had no responsibility for the War at all. The two bombs used by the US on the two cities of Japan as stated earlier killed in two days 320,000 men, women and children. Several statesmen of the world have regarded this act by the US as an "abominable" act. Perhaps this act even surpassed the brutalities of the Nazis. But then it may also be true that without this act, Japan might have been able to inflict several times more losses than this. About 1,500,000 civilians were killed in air raids during the Second World War. Although Germany was the first country to resort to air raids on the civilians on a massive scale, the Allies also were not left behind. On 13-14 February 1945 British air raids on Dresden, a German city took 135,000 lives.

Broken Germany

Like the First World War, in this war also, Germany became the worst hit. It was partitioned into two parts. The eastern part was taken over by Russia and the western part came under the domination of England, France and America. Like the country, its capital Berlin was also divided into two parts. The eastern part came under the control of Russia and the western part under the Allies. A wall separated the two parts of Berlin. It was on August 31, 1990, that East and the West German representatives signed a political unification treaty. Thus, the united Germany again emerged after more than four decades.

Map 11: **Post-War Europe**

During the War, Germany's industries were more or less crippled. Its military strength was drastically reduced. Prominent German leaders were tried as war criminals and sentenced or executed.

Japan's Loss of Sovereignty

Japan lost its sovereignty. It was put under the control of the Far Eastern Commission with General Douglas Mac Arthur as the Supreme Commander for the Allied Forces. Old imperial constitution came to an end. Japan agreed to surrender all territories acquired by it during the War. The country was demilitarized.

Several Japanese leaders were tried and executed.

The formal occupation of Japan ended in 1951 when Japan signed the San Francisco Treaty with 49 nations.

England

In spite of its victory, England's status in the international field was lowered. The strain of war was very heavy. Its empire was shattered and within a few years after the War, it had to lose its control over its colonies.

France

France was War-ravaged and it lost its former status in the international field. France became the battle scene of important conflicts. It came under German occupation which was subsequently vacated. Its empire received a great blow.

Greece

The Greek King and his government flew to Cairo after Germany's invasion. It also witnessed Civil War.

Italy

Italy's empire was broken. Italy had to surrender Libya, Eretria and Italian Somaliland. It lost some of its territories to France and Yugoslavia. It also ceded a few islands to Greece.

Poland

Poland was the worst sufferer. It suffered at the hands of Russians as well as Germans. Nearly 20 per cent of its population was wiped out.

Russia

Notwithstanding Russia's loss of about ten per cent of its population, it became stronger after the War. It became a 'Super Power' in the world. Russia extracted as many concessions as possible from the Allies. It extended its empire by annexing half of Poland, Estonia, Latvia, Lithuania, eastern side of Czechoslovakia, some parts of Finland and Germany. Stalin emerged as one of the few most outstanding leaders in the world.

U.S.A.

The United States had played a decisive role in winning the War. It became the creditor of several nations including England. No major problem of the world could be solved without the involvement of the U.S.A. After the Second World War, the U.S.A. began to take more interest in world affairs and its voice began to be heard and accepted.

Rise of Communism

Since Soviet Russia became a Super Power, it fully exploited its position to spread communism in several parts of the world.

Momentum to National Movements

In a sense, the Second World War came as a blessing in disguise to the people under the foreign yoke of British, Dutch, French and other countries. In the case of India, independence came within two years after the end of the War. The era of independence began in the case of almost all countries.

Resistance Movements

The War years saw the emergence of several antifascist movements in the countries invaded by the Axis Powers. Several uprisings took place in countries like Czechoslovakia, Poland, France and Yugoslovakia.

Persecution of Jews

It is estimated that about six million of Jews which constituted 75 per cent of the total population of Europe were murdered by the Nazis.

Moral Degradation

With the sole aim of winning the War, by hook or by crook, almost all leading statesmen of the world, and especially of the warring nations lost their conscience. Spine-chilling atrocities were committed on combatants, non-combatants and innocent women and children.

Economic Hardships

There was a great shortage of essential commodities of life. Prices rose very high. Traders and hoarders began to charge exorbitant rates. The phenomenon of 'black market' emerged.

POST-WAR RECONSTRUCTION

All the countries that were involved in the Second World War directly or indirectly suffered heavily. They launched plans for the reconstruction of their shattered economies. Truman, the President of the U.S.A. proclaimed his doctrine of giving aid in May 1947. Subsequently, a European Recovery Plan, also known as Marshal Plan, in the name of Secretary of State, General George Marshall, came into operation in June 1948. Under this plan, the U.S.A. sent food stuffs, machinery and raw materials worth 13 million dollars to European countries.

Several agencies of the UN also took up the rehabilitation and relief work.

THE UNITED NATIONS

What is the United Nations?

The United Nations is an international organization, established in 1945, at present having 185 members. It has the following main objectives :
1. To maintain international peace and security.
2. To develop friendly relations among nations.
3. To work together to help raise people's living standards and to encourage respect for each other's rights and freedoms.
4. To be a centre for helping nations achieve these goals.

Principles of the UN

The principles of the UN are embodied in its Charter. Its constitution contains 111 Articles. Important principles are :
1. Sovereignty and equality of all members.
2. Settlement of disputes by peaceful means.
3. Avoidance of threat and violence in solving international disputes.
4. No interference by the UN in the affairs of a country.
5. No help to a country against whom UN takes action.
6. All members to perform international matters according to UN charter.

Why Establishment of the UN

Following were the important considerations which prompted the nations to establish the UN :-
(a) Destructive nature of the Second World War.
(b) Establishment of peace in the world.
(c) Removal of distrust and suspicion among nations.
(d) Saving mankind from the use of destructive weapons.
(e) Fear of the Third War.
(f) Raising standard of living by curtailing military expenditure and using the same for welfare work.
(g) Failure of the League of Nations to achieve its objectives.

Background of the Establishment of the UN

The *Charter* (Constitution) of the UN was signed on June 26, 1945 at San Francisco by the representatives of 50 nations who had assembled for a clear mission—to create an organization that would end forever the scourge of War.

Laying the groundwork for the new organization had begun four years earlier when in 1941, President Franklin Delano Roosevelt of the United States and the Prime Minister Winston Churchill of the United Kingdom proposed a set of principles for international collaboration in maintaining peace and security. The document signed during a meeting came to be known as the Atlantic Charter. The Charter was signed by representatives of 50 states. The document came into force on October 24, 1945.

Map 12: **UNO**

Principal Organs of the UN

General Assembly:

The General Assembly is the UN's main deliberative body. All Member states are represented in it, and each has one vote. The Assembly has the right to discuss and make recommendations on all matters within the scope of the UN Charter. It does not have power to compel action by any government, although its recommendations carry the weight of world opinion. The Assembly also sets policies and determines programmes for the UN Secretariat, sets goals and directs activities for development, approves the budget of peace-keeping operations, and calls for world conferences on major issues. The Assembly considers reports from other organs, admits new members, approves the UN budget, and appoints the UN Secretary-General upon recommendation of the Security Council.

Because of the great number of questions that the assembly debates at each session, it allocates most questions to its six main committees. These are: First Committee (Disarmament and International Security), Second Committee (Economic and Financial), Third Committee (Social, Humanitarian and Cultural), Fourth Committee (Special Political and Decolonization), Fifth Committee (Administrative and Budgetary) and Sixth Committee (Legal).

Security Council:

The UN Charter gives primary responsibility for the maintenance of international peace and security to the Security Council. The Council can be convened at any time when peace is threatened, and it may deploy peace-keepers to prevent the outbreak of conflict. Member states may bring any dispute before the Security Council and are obliged to carry out its decisions.

The Council has 15 members. Five of these—China, France, the Russian Federation, the United Kingdom and the United States—are permanent members, which have the right to veto any council decision. The other ten are elected by the assembly for two-year terms.

When a threat to international peace is brought before the Council, it usually asks the parties to try to reach agreement by peaceful means. The Council may undertake mediation or set forth principles for a settlement. It may request the Secretary-General to investigate and report on the situation. If fighting breaks out, the Council tries to secure a cease-fire. It may, with the consent of the parties involved, send peace-keeping missions to troubled areas to reduce tension and keep opposing forces apart. The Council has the power to enforce its decisions by imposing economic sanctions and ordering collective military action.

Economic and Social Council (ECOSOC):

ECOSOC, with 54 member states, coordinates the economic and social work of the United Nations system. It oversees nine functional commissions, five regional commissions and five standing committees, as well as keeps relations with NGOs. ECOSOC's functional commissions are on crime prevention and criminal justice, human rights, narcotic drugs, social development, science and technology for development, sustainable development, the status of women, population and development and statistics. The regional commissions are: Economic Commission for Africa, Economic Commission for Europe, Economic Commission for Latin America and the Caribbean, Economic and Social Commission for Asia and the Pacific, and Economic and Social Commission for Western Asia. The standing committees are on human settlements, programme and coordination, and non-governmental organizations.

A range of the UN's economic and social programmes, funds and agencies report to ECOSOC, including the United Nations Conference on Trade and Development (UNCTAD); UN Children's Fund (UNICEF); UN Development Fund (UNDF); UN Population Fund (UNPF); the World Food Programme (WFP); and specialized agencies such as the Food and Agricultural Organization (FAO); World Health Organization (WHO); International Labour Organization (ILO); UN Educational, Scientific and Cultural Organization (UNESCO); and the UN Industrial Development Organization (UNIDO). The Bretton Woods Institutions (World Bank and the International Monetary Fund) and the World Trade Organisation (WTO) also participate in ECOSOC sessions.

International Court of Justice (ICJ):

The International Court of Justice, also known as the World Court, is seated in The Hague, Netherlands. It is the principal judicial organ of the UN and is available to all member states. The court's 15 judges are elected by the General Assembly and the Security Council. Only countries may be parties in cases brought before the court. A country does not have to take part in a proceeding if it does not wish to, unless required by special treaty provisions. However, if the country accepts to take part, it is obliged to comply with the court's decision. The General Assembly, Security Council and other organs of the UN can ask the court for advisory opinions on legal questions.

Trusteeship Council:

This UN organ, made up of the five permanent members of the Security Council, was established to ensure that governments responsible for administering Trust Territories, take adequate steps to prepare the territories for self-government or independence. The task of the trusteeship system was completed, since all trust territories had attained self-government or independence as separate states or by joining neighbouring independent countries. The Trusteeship Council, which amended its rules of procedure, now meets only when needed.

United Nations Secretariat:

The UN Secretariat, based in New York, Geneva, Vienna and Nairobi, carries out the diverse day-to-day work of the organization, services UN organs, and implements the programmes and policies laid down by them. A major feature of the Secretariat's work is servicing the intergovernmental bodies, particularly the

The Second World War

General Assembly and its committees, the Security Council, and ECOSOC and its subsidiary bodies. The Secretariat deals with the full range of issues addressed by the United Nations.

Achievements of the U.N.

There is no doubt that the UN has been playing an important role not only in promoting peace and international understanding but also changing the entire structure of mankind for a happier world. Thanks to the efforts of the UN, peace and security are no longer seen only in terms of military confrontation and conflict. The common interests of mankind are also seen to be affected by social and economic considerations such as illiteracy, poverty and hunger problems which are often at the very heart of national, regional and international tensions. Economic and social developments are intrinsic part of maintaining peace. A lasting peace requires international action to eradicate poverty and promote a better life for all.

Prevention of War and Cases of Reconciliation:

Following are the important cases.

1946 Settling dispute between Syria and Lebanon. Settling conflict between Soviet Union and Iran. Checking aggression in Indonesia.
Finding amicable settlement of the dispute between Greece and its neighbours.
1947 Korean dispute referred to UN.
1948 Lifting Berlin Blockade by USSR. Ceasefire between India and Pakistan on Jammu and Kashmir Issue.
1948-49 Checking the intensity of the dispute between the Arabs and Jews.
1950 Military action in Korea.
1956 Solving Suez Canal problem when England, France and Israel invaded Egypt.
1960 Compelling USSR to withdraw its forces when it attacked Hungary.
Solving Congo Crisis.
1964 United Nations Peace-keeping Force.
1967 Ceasefire in Egypt when fighting broke out between Egypt, Jordan and Syria on the one hand and Israel on the other.
1973 Fighting between Egypt and Israel and Ceasefire.
1974 Ceasefire in Cyprus by negotiations between Greece and Turkey.
1979 U.N. intervention during intervention in Cambodia by Vietnam.
1980 Intervention of U.N, during Military intervention in Afghanistan by USSR.
Dispute between Iran and Iraq.
1987 Intervention in five Latin American states to settle their disputes.
1988-89 After negotiating for about eight years, the USSR withdrew its forces from Afghanistan. Withdrawal of troops by Vietnam.
1990-91 Attack by Iraq on Kuwait in August 1990. Withdrawal of Iraqi forces by the end of February 1991.
Peace Settlement between Palestine and Israel.
1991 Independence of Namibia through UN efforts.
1991 Cambodian Agreement signed. Rehabilitation of refugees.
United Nations Observer Mission to monitor all agreements.
1992 Agreement between North Korea and South Korea. Agreement arrived at between the Salvadorian Government and FMLN-a liberation front.

Disarmament:

Following are the important steps taken in this field.
1959 The Antarctic Treaty providing for the demilitarization of Antartica.

1963 Partial Test Ban Treaty Banning Nuclear Weapons Tests in Atmosphere, in Outer Space and Under Water.
1967 Outer Space Treaty on Principles Governing the Activities of States in the Exploration and Use of Outer Space.
Treaty for the Prohibition of Nuclear Weapons in Latin America and the Caribbean.
1968 Non-Proliferation Treaty to prevent the spread of nuclear weapons.
1971 Seabed Treaty - Destruction of Nuclear Weapons on Seabed.
1972 Convention on the Prohibition of the Development of Biological and Toxic Weapons.
1977 Convention on the Prohibition of Military use having adverse environmental influence.
1985 The South Pacific Nuclear Free Zone Treaty.
1991 Strategic Arms Reduction Treaty.

Among the recent important Summits seeking global agreement on concrete actions that must be taken to ensure advancement, mention may be made of the following.
- World Summit on Children, New York, 1990.
- UN Conference on Environment and Development, Rio de Janeiro, 1992.
- World Conference on Human Rights, Vienna, 1993.
- International Conference on Population and Development, Cairo, 1994.
- World Summit for Social Development, Copenhagen, 1995.
- World Conference on Women, Beijing, 1995.
- United Nations Conference on Human Settlements, (Habitat II), Istanbul 1996.

EXERCISES

A. Very Short Answer Type

1. Name any chief warring countries in the Second World War.
2. Mention any two main causes of the Second World War.
3. Name any three countries of the Axis Powers.
4. List any three countries of the Allied Powers.
5. What was the immediate cause of the Second World War?
6. What is the meaning of 'Phoney War'?
7. Explain 'Dunkirk Miracle'.
8. What do you mean by 'Vichy France'?
9. Why did Russia join War?
10. Why did the U.S.A. join War?
11. Explain 'Operation Barbossa'.
12. State the significance of the Battle of Stalingrad.
13. What is the significance of the Atlantic Charter?
14. Name the chief organs of the U.N.O.

B. Short Answer Type

1. Explain the policy of appeasement. What was its impact?
2. Elucidate the Battle of Britain.
3. "Russian invasion dug the grave of Hitler". Explain.
4. What is the meaning of the Second Front? What was its impact?
5. Why did the U.S.A. join the Second World War? What was its impact on the consequences of War?
6. What led to the establishment of the U.N.O.?

The Second World War

7. Explain Anti-Fascist Resistance Movements during the Second World War.
8. How did the Second World War end in Europe?
9. Describe the events that led to the Second World War.

C. Essay Type or Long Answer

1. Discuss the main causes of the Second World War.
2. "Though invasion of Poland was the immediate cause of the outbreak of the World War II, the real causes were deeper". Explain.
3. "The Second World War was inevitable". Discuss.
4. Explain the main achievements of the U.N.O.
5. "Second World War was the most destructive war in the world." Explain.
6. "The Treaty of Versailles contained the seeds of the Second World War." Justify the statement with suitable examples.
7. What were the main objectives for the establishment of United Nations? How far has it been successful in achieving them?

D. Map Work

1. On an outline map of the World mark the Axis Powers and the Allied Powers.

CHAPTER 28

After the Second World War - Since 1945

The European hegemony collapsed gradually. The imperial domination of the world ended. The nationalist and anti-imperialist movements became very powerful.

After the Second World War, the U.S.A. and the Soviet Union (USSR) emerged as the two greatest powers in the world. Other powers, once so great, Germany, Italy and Japan, had been defeated and almost crushed for years to come. There were now two powerful blocks. One was led by the U.S.A. which included countries of Western Europe, North America and the Pacific. These countries called themselves as the 'Free World'. The other block led by the Soviet Union comprised countries of Eastern Europe and later China and North Korea.

A new term known as the 'Third World Countries' became very popular. The Third World Countries are those countries which remained under the domination of the imperialist countries at one time or the other and thereafter gained their independence. These countries did not join either of the two blocks i.e. the Russian or the U.S.A. Most of these countries were in Africa and Latin America.

ECONOMIC AND TECHNOLOGICAL CHANGES

Socio-Economic Changes

With the increasing popularity of the socialist and communist movements, many important changes have taken place. Economic systems based on the philosophy of communism and socialism were established in many countries after the War. A few years after independence, India adopted the policy of 'mixed economy' which included some characteristics of both capitalism and socialism. The word 'Socialist' became so popular in India that in 1976, it was incorporated into the Preamble of the Indian Constitution. Under the influence of new philosophies, most of the advanced capitalist countries began to pay more attention to labour welfare and welfare of the common man.

The period after World War II has been a period of tensions and conflicts among nations. Many military pacts came into being. This state of the World came to be known as the 'Cold War'. Fortunately in recent years, the world has seen lessening of tensions in the world.

Technological Changes

Besides the political and socio-economic changes, there have been marked technological changes since the World War II. These technological advances have transformed the economies of several countries, especially of the already advanced countries. Besides the U.S.A., Japan and Germany have made rapid advances in their economies. In general, technological advances resulting in advances in economies have divided the world into three broad categories i.e. the developed countries, the developing countries and the least developed countries.

DISINTEGRATION OF THE COLONIAL IMPERIAL SYSTEM

The World War II weakened the imperialist countries of Europe, including Britain, France etc. It destroyed Fascism of Germany, Italy and Japan. The economic, military and political power of these countries was shattered.

Imperial countries were no longer in a position to keep their colonies under them. They were faced with the post-war problems of reconstruction. In the changed political scenario, imperialism was no longer considered as a mark of 'superior civilization'. It began to be increasingly associated with brute force, inhuman injustice and immoral exploitation.

One of the dominant ideas of the Post-War period was concerning the grant of independence to people subject to colonial rule. Atlantic Charter emphasised the peace aims of the Allies and declared that all people had the right to choose their own form of government.

The UN Universal Declaration of Human Rights, proclaimed on December 10, 1948, further strengthened the national movement for freedom in the colonial countries.

The process of the disintegration of the Colonial Imperial System started in 1947 with the independence of India. It took several decades after the Second World War to end the Colonial Imperial System in the World.

New Colonialism and Old Colonialism

'Old Colonialism' meant political domination or political control by one country over the other. Primarily it was done through wars and conquests. On the other hand 'New Colonialism' implies economic control and domination but political independence. 'New Colonialism' consists in advancing loans to other countries, spreading their business in other countries through different means, giving military assistance and setting up military bases. Sometimes under 'New Colonialism', industrially advanced countries or even developing countries may set up semi-official business enterprise to control economic activities.

Russia increased its domination over other countries through the Communist Party of Russia. The Communist movement in different countries was guided by the Communist Party of Russia.

The U.S.A., on the other hand, strengthened its hold on Spain, Portugal and several other countries in Africa and Asia by rendering military help to them. It also entered into military pacts with them. Where needed, it provided economic aid to the war-torn countries for their post-war economic and industrial reconstruction.

In short, new colonialism is based on indirect control or domination over independent countries as against direct political rule and control through conquest.

EMERGENCE OF THE U.S.A. AS A WORLD POWER

Overview

After the end of the Second World War, the U.S.A. emerged as the pre-eminent economic and military power in the world. Several parts of the world came under the purview of US interests. Its influence was so great that there emerged a trend in the U.S.A. to describe the 20th Century as the 'American Century'.

The Post-War period has been marked by an unprecedented economic growth and prosperity. GNP of U.S.A. rose from about $ 100 billion in 1940 to about $ 5000 billion in 1997. i.e. a rise of 50 times while the population rose from 132 million to nearly 263.5 million i.e. nearly double. Its GNP per capita in 1997 was estimated at about 26000 US $ as against 330 US $ of India, 90 US $ of Muzambique and 80 US $ of Rwanda.

The growth of what is usually described as 'consumer culture' or 'consumerism' is reflected in the emergence of the affluence of the American people. There occurred an unprecedented growth in the production as well as consumption of a large variety of consumer goods. The motor car became a symbol of this American culture. There was a growing 'interfusion' of economic and military production.

Factors for Making U.S.A. A Super Power

America's economic prosperity led to its becoming a Super Power in the world. Among the major factors that contributed to the power and prestige of the U.S.A. after the Second World War are (1) Historical background (2) Far away from war theatre (3) Leading role in the victory of the Allies (4) Assistance to several countries in their post-war reconstruction programmes (5) Support for human rights (6) Leadership of the anti-communist group.

Undoubtedly, the U.S.A. became one of the two Super Powers in the World after the Second World War, but it had, behind it, a great background of a century and half during the course of which it could acquire titanic strength. In the First War, U.S.A.'s entry changed the entire course of the War. Its strength largely contributed to the victory of the Allies. In the depression of the 1930's, the New Deal proved very effective in easing the situation.

In the Second World War, the U.S.A. remained neutral in the beginning but helped the UK and France in the acquisition of military equipment. Its entry in the War changed the fortunes of the Allies. During the War it displayed a giants strength everywhere in the world. It gave help generally to the countries in their programmes of reconstruction and got much more by way of huge profits. U.S.A. itself never became a war theatre though it fought in other lands.

The Atlantic Charter of 1941, that emphasised the freedom aspect, enhanced its prestige in the eyes of the colonised countries. The U.S.A. became the self-appointed saviour of democracy and spent millions of dollars to save several countries from communism. In May 1947, the US President Harry Truman proclaimed his doctrine of giving massive economic and military aid to the communist threatened countries.

DEVELOPMENT OF THE USSR AS A WORLD POWER

The significant role played by the USSR in the defeat of Nazi Germany in the Second World War won for her the admiration of the world. The people of the USSR had fought the war with the utmost patriotic fervour. They regarded it as the 'Great Patriotic War'. They made all possible sacrifices to win the War. It goes to the credit of the Soviet leaders and the Soviet people that in spite of the loss of 20 million people in the Second World War, destruction of nearly 70,000 villages and about 1700 cities, demolition of thousands of industrial establishments and vast tracts of land laid waste, Soviet Russia emerged as a Super Power immediately after a few years of the post war period. Perhaps the ruthless dictatorship of Stalin (1879-1953) during 1924-53 proved very beneficial in successfully completing the Five Year Plans. The process of formulation and implementation continued after the Second World War also. The Fourth Plan covered the period 1946-51 and the Fifth 1951-56 during which Soviet Russia made spectacular progress. Immediately after the Second World War, Soviet Russia launched a massive programme of reconstruction. Before the beginning of the 1950's, the industrial production had been restored to the pre-war level. Agriculture was mechanised by having collective farms. Agricultural production also reached the pre-war level during this period. In terms of GNP, Soviet Union became the second most powerful economy in the world.

In 1954, USSR announced that it possessed the Hydrogen Bomb. In 1957, it astonished the entire world by launching the first 'Sputnik'. It continued to make rapid advances in science and technology.

In 1947, Stalin revived the pre-war Communist International (Comintern) under a new name of Cominform at Warsaw. As a Super Power, Soviet Russia became a leader of the Red Empire of Satellite Communist States, covering about one-third area of the world. In 1950, Russia signed a 30-year Mutual Aid Treaty with Communist China.

The loss of England and France in terms of power and prestige in global politics was a positive gain for the Soviet Union. It not only took their place but also went ahead to become equal to the U.S.A. Like the U.S.A., the Soviet Union too had global responsibilities.

After the Second World War — Since 1945 301

(Note : We have used the terms USSR, Soviet Union interchangeably with Russia although Russia was one of the 16 Republics constituting the Soviet Union. Russia covers three-fourth of the whole country's area as well as population.)

U.S.A. AND WESTERN SPONSORED MILITARY ALLIANCES

Mutual Recrimination

There were ideological sharp differences between the philosophical thought and practices followed by the US and Western Europe on the one hand and on the other followed by Russia and its allies of the Eastern Europe. Both regarded each other as sworn enemies. The alliance between Russia and the other powers of France, England and the U.S.A. towards the closing years of the Second World War was purely temporary and therefore it did not last long on account of fundamental differences regarding socio-economic and political policies. The U.S.A. as the champion of democracy, capitalism and liberalism assumed a posture which was diametrically opposed to that of the USSR, the champion of communism, red imperialism and totalitarian dictatorship. The two countries presented an antithesis. It was natural that their satellite countries divided into two power blocks—one led by the U.S.A. the other by Russia.

Military Alliances

Mutual recrimination among the protagonists of democracy and communism led to the formation of the following military alliances.

North Atlantic Treaty Organisation NATO (1949):

The NATO came into being on April 4, 1949 as a defence mechanism against the expansion of Russian communism. The immediate reason was the rejection of the proposal of the U.S.A., France and England to introduce a uniform currency in all the four zones of Germany by Russia. The Foreign Ministers of the U.S.A., England, France, Canada, Belgium, Portugal, Denmark, Norway, Luxemburg, Iceland, Italy and the Netherlands met at Washington under the leadership of the U.S.A. and signed a treaty. Greece and Turkey became its members in 1952 and the Federal Republic of Germany in 1955. The U.S.A. declared to meet the lion's share of the NATO's contribution to the development of military force to fight armed communist attack. Soviet Russia condemned the NATO as an alliance for aggressive activities by the Anglo-American block in Europe. A military committee of the Chiefs of Staff of the member countries was set up to monitor military affairs.

Following were the major provisions of the treaty.
(1) Mutual financial help to be provided to each other.
(2) Mutual disputes to be solved through mutual talks.
(3) An armed attack against any member or members to be considered as an attack against all of them.
(4) Every member to organise its military strength with the help of the U.S.A.

Anzus (1951) or Pacific Defence Alliance:

With a view to check the influence of Russia and China, Australia, New Zealand and the U.S.A. organized this alliance.

South East Asia Treaty Organisation SEATO (1954):

For checking the communist expansion in South East Asia, this treaty was organised by Australia, Britain, France, New Zealand, Pakistan, Philippines, Thailand and the U.S.A. The U.S.A. promised to provide military help to the signatories of the treaty. Bangkok in Thailand was made its headquarters. India did not join this treaty as it felt that it would convert the area of peace into an area of potential war.

Central Treaty Organisation CENTO (1955 or Baghdad Pact):

Initially it was signed by Turkey and Iraq but later on England, Iran, Pakistan and the U.S.A. also signed it and it came to be known as CENTO. Iraq later left this group. It was entered into to offer collective defence against any Russian attack and to check the Russian advance towards the south. A nuclear research centre at Baghbad was set up.

The Warsaw Pact (1955):

In order to strengthen its position and to guard against the military alliance formed under the leadership of the U.S.A., the USSR took the lead in forming a powerful alliance on the pattern of the NATO. The pact was formed with Albania, Bulgaria, Czechoslovakia, East Germany, Poland and Rumania. The Warsaw Pact countries brought the Soviet Satellites (these countries) closer to each other for fighting against a common enemy under Russian leadership.

The overall result of these alliances was the emergence of Cold War.

On July 1, 1991, the Warsaw Pact was dissolved.

COLD WAR

Meaning

Cold War is the term used to describe the intense rivalry that developed after World War II in 1945 between USSR and its Communist allies (known as Eastern Block) and U.S.A. and its democratic allies. The power struggle was called the Cold War because it did not actually lead to fighting or 'hot war'. It was a state of affairs where countries lacked mutual trust and understanding. It was a period of tension and frictions, suspense and suspicion, fear and hostility between the rival groups or blocks.

Ideological Differences

The crux of the problem lay in the ideologies of the two blocks—the communists and the capitalists. The communists regarded the capitalist democracy as an exploitative and aggressive system and the Western democratic leaders looked upon communism as the harbinger of an autocratic and dictatorial system which crushed individual liberty. Thus, these two diagonally opposite principles of the two systems, Capitalist and Communist, created distrust, fear and uncertainty.

After the war ended, the USSR cut off nearly all contacts with the democratic countries of the West. The West adopted a containment policy to hold back Communist expansions. In 1948, when Western Allies announced to unify Germany in the West, the USSR blocked the German city of Berlin. This is how it happened.

Blockade in Germany:

After the Potsdam Conference in 1945, Germany was divided into four occupation Zones, one each under Britain, France, the United States and the Soviet Union. In 1946, the city of Berlin was also divided into two parts as Western and Eastern. In 1948, the Russians stopped all traffic by rail and road between Berlin and the West. The supplies to Western Berlin were cut off. The Western Allies conducted a massive airlift of supplies to the starving Western Berlin. Nearly 3,00,000 plane-loads of food supplies, fuel and medicines etc were airlifted. The Soviet Union ended the Blockade after 11 months in May 1949. In 1961, to stop Germans escaping from Berlin to the West Germany, the Russians built walls across Berlin as well as along the whole Eastern bloc frontier. In 1996, the western powers including USA merged their zones in Germany.

After the Second World War — Since 1945

Map 13: **Berlin - Blockade**

Civil War in Greece:

Another occasion when the two blocks opposed each other was when a Civil War broke out in Greece. The British troops which had been sent to Greece wanted to restore the rule of the King. This, however was opposed by the communists of Greece. The British Government felt that it was not in a position to support the royalist and informed the U.S.A. accordingly. The U.S.A. decided to bear the burden of the War and to help the Government of Greece. In due course, it came to be known that the communists in Greece were receiving training and arms from Yugoslavia, Albania and Bulgaria which were the camp followers of the USSR. Suspicion and mistrust was widened among the nations.

Establishment of Communist Government:

Within a short period of four years (1946-50) communist governments were established in Albania, Bulgaria, Czechoslovakia, Hungary and Rumania. Thus, Russian control was firmly established in the whole of Eastern Europe. In 1949, Communist rule was established in China. These events sent alarm bells to the U.S.A. Again, distrust and suspicion raised their heads.

President Truman's Proclamation:

In May 1947, the US President, Harry Truman, proclaimed his doctrine of giving massive economic and military aid to the countries threatened by communism. Truman proclaimed that communism posed a threat to the 'Free World' of which the U.S.A. being the head, would not allow it to succeed. The U.S.A. began to see every revolution in the world as being the creation of the expansionist policy of the USSR. This, again, was a cause of deepening the hostility between the two blocks.

Conduct of an Atomic Bomb Test:

In 1949, when the USSR conducted an atomic bomb test, the U.S.A. was shocked. A suspicion arose among the top US leaders that some of the American scientists associated with the production of the atom bombs in the U.S.A. had leaked out the secrets. The 'Spy Scare' further worsened the climate of fear and hostility towards the Soviet Union.

There was no end of events distancing the two blocks. In 1949, Allies formed NATO, USSR formed COMECON. In the same year, the communist victory in China strengthened the communist powers. The first testing of atomic bomb added fear and mistrust on both the sides. In 1952, U.S.A. tested the Hydrogen bomb. Just the next year, USSR tested its own hydrogen bomb, as it did not want to be left behind.

Tension between the two was heightened by the Hungarian uprising of 1956, building of the Berlin wall in 1961, the Cuban missile crisis of 1962 and the Soviet invasion of Czechoslovakia in 1968. From the 1960's, the US involvement in the Vietnam War threatened to turn the Cold War into a general war.

In the 1970's, USSR and China quarrelled, France withdrew its troops from NATO, China was admitted to the UN in 1971, and Arms Limitation Agreement was reached between the U.S.A. and the USSR in 1972. The tension was decreasing but the Cold War revived with the Soviet invasion of Afghanistan in 1979.

In 1988-89, USSR withdrew its troops from Afghanistan. Gorbachev allowed more democracy and freedom of expression. The tension of the Cold War was getting eased. Communist rule came to an end in a number of Eastern European countries. Germany was reunified in 1990. In 1991 the Soviet Union broke up. Many believed that such events marked the end of the Cold War.

Consequences of the Cold War

The Cold War led to four important consequences as given below :

Military alliances:

Mention has already been made of the five alliances namely (i) NATO (1949) (ii) Angus (1951) (iii) SEATO (1954) (iv) CENTO and (v) Warsaw Pact (1955).

Race for Rearmament:

A fear was lurking in the minds of every nation that war may break out any moment and the race for manufacturing and piling up deadly weapons was in full swing. Russian atomic explosion took place in 1949. After 1953 both the Super Powers came to possess different types of bombs like hydrogen bomb, long range bombers, rockets etc.

Division of World into Two Military Camps:

A large number of countries got divided into two hostile groups. One was led by the U.S.A. and the other by the USSR.

Conflicts Among Nations; Local Wars but no Global War:

The following conflicts took place as a result of the Cold War.

(i) Korea:

Korea had been captured in 1910 by Japan but after the Second World War, with the defeat of Japan, Korea was divided into two parts. A communist regime known as the Democratic People's Republic of Korea came into being in North Korea and in South Korea, a Right Wing Republic of Korea was formed. Russian troops left Korea in 1948 and the US troops in 1949.

Neither government accepted the division of Korea and each part claimed reunification of the country as its objective. In June 1950, war broke out between the two. The United Nations Security Council held North Korea responsible for the War. North Korea almost overran South Korea. However, with the assistance of the US forces, South Korea was saved and the US forces pushed back the North Korean troops. At this time the Communist China moved its troops and the US troops were forced back. There developed a possibility of the third War but it was averted due to the efforts of neutral countries like India and an armistice was signed in July 1953 which restored the position that existed before the War.

(ii) Iran:

In 1951, Iran's Parliament nationalised the Anglo-Iranian Oil Company, a British controlled company, and Mohammed Mussadeq, who was considered pro-Russia, was appointed the Prime Minister of Iran. The Central Intelligence Agency (CIA) of the U.S.A. helped a coup which led to the overthrow of Mussadeq and the Shah of Iran, Mohammad Reza Pahlavi established his despotic rule with the support of the U.S.A. The rule of Reza Pahlavi ended in 1979 by the Islamic revolution in Iran.

(iii) The Vietnam War:

After the defeat of Japan in the Second World War, the Vietnamese led by Ho Chi Minh set up the Republic of Vietnam in 1946. The Nationalist forces in Vietnam were led by the Communist Party. The Vietnamese forces received help from the Soviet Union and China. The French who had been ousted by Japan tried to restore their rule. In this, France was aided by Britain and the U.S.A.

In July 1954, an agreement was signed in Geneva according to which the French rule in Vietnam was ended. Vietnam was divided into South Vietnam and North Vietnam. The U.S.A. started building the South Vietnamese army and to crush the South Vietnamese guerillas. The U.S.A. sent its own troops to fight. It also sent massive amount of war equipment. Not only this, it very heavily bombarded the Vietnamese territory. This action of the U.S.A. evoked strong protest not only in the U.S.A. itself but also in the world at large. The U.S.A. and Vietnam had to suffer a heavy loss of troops. Besides, Vietnam was ravaged. The US troops had to leave in early 1975 and this ended the conflict. On April 30, 1975 Vietnam emerged as a united country.

Crisis in Cuba:

Conflict in Cuba is considered as one of the most serious crisis in the history of the Post-Second War. In 1959, a leftist revolution took place in Cuba and Fidel Castro assumed the power of a dictator. Thousands of refugees from Cuba took shelter in U.S.A. The new government of Cuba had friendly relations with the USSR. The United States became hostile to Cuba and broke off diplomatic and economic relations with it in January 1961. It planned a Cuban refugee invasion on Cuba and accordingly landed a few thousand refugees in the Bay of Pigs in Cuba on April 17, 1961 with the hope that the disgrunled Cubans would rise in revolt against Fidel Castro but the move proved abortive. The US President Kennedy declared, "We do not want to abandon Cuba to the communists." The U.S.A. was condemned by the world. The USSR began to render massive aid to Cuba and also installed missile sites in Cuba from which nuclear missiles could be hurled at targets over a distance of 1,400 miles. On October 22, 1962, President John Kennedy of the U.S.A., in a television broadcast gave a stern warning to the USSR about the serious consequences if the missiles were not withdrawn. Premier Nikita Khrushiev of the USSR sent a message to President Kennedy that the USSR would remove its missiles from Cuba if the US agreed not to invade Cuba. An agreement on this issue was reached and the world was saved from nuclear warfare.

Conflict in Egypt:

After the Second World War nationalism grew in Egypt. Monarchy was overthrown. In 1954, Britain was asked to withdraw its troops from the Suez Canal area. At this juncture, Egypt began to build up its military strength with the help of the USSR. On July 26, 1956, the Suez Canal was nationalised. The troops of Israel, Britain and France bombarded Egypt. The U.S.A. denounced it strongly in the U.N.O. The USSR issued an ultimatum to the invaders to withdraw from Egypt and threatened to use missiles to defend it. An agreement was arrived at and the ceasefire ended. Thereafter Russian influence increased in the region.

DISARMAMENT AND BAN ON NUCLEAR WEAPONS

Background

The history of disarmament dates back to the year 1899 when at the Hague Conference of the nations of the world, some countries addressed the question of amassing armaments to the detriment of peace and welfare of mankind. The League of Nations formed after the First World War tried in vain to persuade the members of the countries to come to an agreement on disarmament. The Second World War, however, put a temporary stop to any kind of disarmament. On the other hand for the first time nuclear weapons were used in Hiroshima and Nagasaki in Japan in 1945, killing several thousand innocent people. Since its inception in 1945, the UN has been asking member states to pursue disarmament programme which envisages limiting of armed forces, eliminating all nuclear and chemical weapons and freezing military expenditures. Way back in 1954, India was the first UN member to call for complete elimination of nuclear weapons. However, it could not muster enough support from UN members.

Recent Developments

In 1963, the U.S.A., the UK and the USSR signed the Partial Nuclear Test Ban Treaty (PNTBT) calling for a ban on nuclear tests in outer space or in the deep oceans and sea beds. Although having nuclear capability, France and China could not be brought into the treaty.

In 1980, the draft of the Nuclear Non-Proliferation Treaty (NPT) was endorsed by more than 100 countries. Major goals of the NPT were three (1) To prevent the spread of nuclear weapons (2) To use nuclear technology for peaceful purposes and (3) To start negotiations to end the arms race.

Since then a number of talks such as Strategic Arms Limitations Talks, SALT I and SALT II and the talks on Strategic Arms Reduction Pact and Mutually Assured Destruction (MAD) have been held by the U.S.A. and the USSR to limit nuclear stockpiles in their respective countries.

In September 1996, the CTBT was signed by 158 members of the UN in a conference of the General Assembly, held at Geneva. The treaty seeks to achieve a total ban on future testing, except in laboratory conditions using computer simulation.

Milestones in the Gradual Ending of the Cold War

Year	Event
1955	Geneva Summit of four heads of States of England, France, U.S.A. and USSR. US President Eisenhower's declaration, "The time has come when we should drop all the curtains, whether of guns or laws."
1956	Russian Prime Minister Khruschev's declaration of peaceful co-existence.
1961	Start of the Non-Alignment Movement. Albania's withdrawal from the Warsaw Pact.
1963	Nuclear Test Ban Treaty by Britain, U.S.A. and USSR.
1966	France's withdrawal from NATO.
1971	China's admission in the U.N.O.
1969-72	Strategic Arms Limitation Talks (SALT) between the U.S.A. and USSR and agreement on limiting certain categories of missiles.
1973	Pakistan's withdrawal from SEATO.
1974	France's withdrawal from SEATO.
1985	Gorbachev's policy of liberalism.
1990	Unification of Germany.
1991	Disintegration of the USSR into 15 independent states.

EXERCISES

A. Very Short Answer Type

1. List any two political changes in the world after the Second World War.
2. Write any two economic changes in the world that took place after the Second World War.
3. List any two factors that led to the disintegration of the imperial system.
4. Differentiate between New Colonialism and Old Colonialism.
5. Explain the term 'American Century'.
6. Explain the term 'Consumer Culture'.
7. What was 'Sit on' movement?

After the Second World War — Since 1945

8. What is MAD? What was its effect on Cold War?
9. Explain the concept 'brinkmanship.'

B. Short Answer Type

1. Explain the factors that were responsible for the rise of the U.S.A. after the Second World War.
2. What is 'Truman Doctrine'? What was its impact?
3. What is the meaning of the Civil Rights Movement in the context of the U.S.A.? What was its impact?
4. What were the factors which made the USSR a Super Power?
5. What led to the formation of military alliances after the Second World War? What was their impact?
6. Explain any two main conflicts that took place after the Second World War.
7. "The race for armaments led to the intensification of the Cold War after the Second World War." Support your answer with suitable examples.

C. Essay Type/Long Answer

1. What is the meaning of Cold War? How did it develop? What led to its end?
2. Elucidate the major factors that brought about the collapse of imperialism in the Post Second World War period.

CHAPTER 29

Developments in Asia, Africa and Latin America (after 1945)

ASIA

National Liberation Movements

The economic, military and political powers of Germany, Italy, Britain and France were shattered during the Second World War. The USSR and the U.S.A. had emerged as the greatest powers in the world and these countries had to face gigantic problems of reconstruction in their own countries. In the changed climate in the world, imperialism was greatly hated. Various international forums like the United Nations and the Non-Alignment Movements were used by the independent countries to support the cause of national awakening for freedom from the foreign domination. There also developed a sense of solidarity among the leaders of the freedom movement in different countries. A country after gaining independence, actively aided the national movement in other countries. The forums of the Commonwealth were also used for promoting the cause of independence.

Twelve countries of Asia got freedom between 1945 to 1959.

Dates of Independence of Asian Countries

	Country	Date	From
1.	Indonesia	Aug. 17, 1945	Holland
2.	Philippines	1946	U.S.A.
3.	Pakistan	Aug. 14, 1947	Britain
4.	India	Aug. 15, 1947	Britain
5.	Mynmar (Burma)	Jan. 4, 1948	Britain
6.	Sri Lanka (Ceylon)	Feb. 4, 1948	Britain
7.	Israel	May 15, 1948	New State (Carved out of Palestine)
8.	South Korea	Aug. 15, 1948	First from Japan, then from U.S.A.
9.	North Korea	Sept. 9 1948	First from Japan, then from USSR
10.	Vietnam	1954	France
11.	Malaya	1957	Britain
12.	Singapore	1959	Britain

India

A detailed account of the nationalist movement in India has already been given in the first part of this book Important events of the movement have been given in an earlier chapter up to 1939 when India was forced to participate in the Second World War against the wishes of the Congress Ministries. Here are the milestones tracing the course of developments in India after 1939 :-

(i) Muslim League Session at Lahore and declaration of 'Pakistan' as their goal (1940) (ii) Cripps Mission

Developments in Asia, Africa and Latin America (after 1945)

and its rejection by the Congress (1942) (iii) The Quit India Movement and arrest of Congress leaders, (1942) (iv) Formation of the INA outside India to wage war for the liberation of India (1943) (v) Cabinet Mission, (1946) (vi) Elections to the Constituent Assembly and formation of Interim Government under Jawaharlal Nehru as the first Prime Minister of India (vii) Direct Action by the Muslim League for the creation of Pakistan (1946) (viii) Communal Riots (1946-47) (ix) Declaration of the British Prime Minister, Clement Altee to leave India (February 1947) (x) Mountbatten's Plan (June 1947) (xi) Acceptance of the Plan by the Congress and the League; Independence Act (1947).

China

Civil War in China, which had been going on for a long time, had stopped China to fight Japan. After the defeat of Japan it was again resumed in 1946. Chiang Kai-Shek's government was in power and was deadly opposed by the communists. Chiang Kai-Shek (1887-1975) was helped by the U.S.A. in the struggle against the communists of China, led by Mao Tse Tung (1893-1976) and Chou-En-Lai (1898-1976). Chiang Kai-Shek was forced to flee to Taiwan (Formosa) which had been freed after the defeat of Japan. For a long time, the overthrow of the communist rule in China and the restoration of the rule of Chiang Kai-Shek remained the major aim of the foreign policy of the U.S.A. The U.S.A. with its allies kept China out of the UN.

Friendly relations between China and the USSR ended in early 1960's as China criticized the Soviet policy of peaceful co-existence with the West and betraying the aims of Communism.

In 1962, China betrayed India's friendship of *Hindi-Chini Bhai Bhai* and committed aggression on India by seizing thousands of square miles of Indian territory across the McMohan Line.

Soviets refused to support China in its border war. In 1966, Mao gave his support to the radicals in the Communist Party. This started conflict between the radicals and moderates within the party. In 1971, U.S.A. favoured UN membership both for the Republic of China and Taiwan, but only the former was voted for membership. In 1984, the party began economic reforms that led to less government control. In 1989, students demonstrated in favour of more democracy in Beijing's Tiananmen Square. The army killed hundreds of student protesters.

Other Countries of Asia

Burma:

In 1937, Burma had separated from India and it became a British colony. It was occupied by Japan during the Second World War. In 1944, the Burmese formed the Anti-Fascist People's Freedom League to fight against the Japanese and to win freedom. After the defeat of Japan in the Second World War, the British again established their rule over Burma.

Indo-China:

Three countries—Vietnam, Cambodia and Laos—combined together and formed Indo-China.

(a) Vietnam:

During the Second World War, Japan occupied it from France. Ho Chi Minh (1892-1969) played a leading role in the independence of Vietnam. In 1939, he had organised the Vietnam Independence League. After the defeat of Japan in the Second World War, Ho Chi seized Hanoi and declared the independence of Vietnam and set up the republic in 1946. France again tried to recapture it in 1954 but failed and Vietnam became free. Before leaving, France divided Vietnam into two parts North Vietnam and South Vietnam. Ho Chi Minh tried to unite the two and it led to a Civil War. North Vietnam was under the influence of the communists. The U.S.A. came to the help of South Vietnam. A full fledged war between North Vietnam and South Vietnam started. The U.S.A. sent more than 400,000 soldiers and modern equipment to help the government of South

Vietnam and brought about a lot of destruction on North Vietnam. The U.S.A. had lost about 75,000 soldiers in the War. This evoked a lot of protest, both in the U.S.A. and outside. On account of public pressure, the U.S.A. had to withdraw from Vietnam in 1973. The Vietnam War ended on April 30, 1975 when South Vietnam surrendered to the communists of the North. The communists unified the two Vietnams in 1976. In 1978, Vietnam invaded Cambodia. In 1989, Vietnam claimed to have withdrawn all its troops from Cambodia.

(b) Cambodia:

In the Second World War, Cambodia was captured by Japan from France but after the War, France again occupied it. Cambodia became independent on November 9, 1953. The Geneva Conference (1954) recognised it. Different groups in Cambodia had always been at daggers with each other. In 1977, disputes led to fighting between Cambodia and Vietnam. The Vietnamese troops and Cambodian Communists won control of most of Cambodia in 1979. By the mid-1980's, thousands of Cambodians had fled to Thailand. In 1980's the Cambodian government relaxed control of the economy with the result that Cambodians were allowed to have their own business and small farms. In 1991, a UN sponsored treaty was signed to end the War, under which UN took over the administration of Cambodia. The 1993 election of the members of Legislature replaced the UN administration.

(c) Laos:

Here also, the Japanese replaced the French and recognised its independence in 1954 but France continued to interfere in its affairs. However, French interference came to an end in 1974 and monarchial form of government was set up there. In 1975, the King gave up his throne and the country became a Communist State.

Indonesia:

Dr. Ahmed Sukarno (1901-1970) was the most prominent leader of the nationalist movement in Indonesia. On December 29, 1949, the Federal Republic of the United States of Indonesia was established with Sukarno as President.

Indonesia was conquered during the Second World War in 1942 by Japan from the Dutch. Subsequently, with the defeat of Japan, in 1945, the Dutch again tried to re-establish their supremacy over Indonesia. Unlike the British who gracefully withdrew from India in August 1947, the Dutch had to withdraw when the United Nations intervened and under the Hague Agreement it granted independence to Indonesia, which, in 1949 became a republic. On March 27, 1968, General Suharto was installed as the country's second President. He was reelected unopposed in 1973, 1978, 1983, and 1988. In 1985, Suharto introduced a law to require all political organizations to adopt as their principle *Panchshila,* the state philosophy to encourage political consensus and religious tolerance.

Israel:

Israel, a Republic in the Middle East (West Asia), came into being on May 15, 1948. It is a Jewish state surrounded on three sides by Arab countries. It occupies an old portion of the ancient Palestine. Israel came as a result of the partition of Palestine between the Jews and the Arabs in accordance with a resolution of the UN in November 1947. Neighbouring Arab states invaded Israel but Israel was successful not only in checking this invasion but also increasing its territory by one-third. The U.S.A. has always taken a keen interest in the welfare of Israel. In 1967, there was a 'Six Day War' between Israel and Egypt. Israel captured Gaza strip and some other places. In March 1979, a peace treaty was signed and Israel vacated the occupied territories. In August 1993, Israel approved autonomy to Palestine in some areas.

Palestine:

Arabs of Palestine had been fighting for a separate land for themselves for more than four decades. The

Palestine Liberation Front (PLO) set up in 1964 under Yassar Arafat had been pleading the case of the Arabs. In 1974, when PLO had set up its headquarters in exile, in Algiers, the UN had granted it permanent observer status. About 80 nations including India had recognised the new nation.

On May 13, 1994, a historical accord was signed between Israel and Palestine under which Arafat established a self-government in Palestine.

Japan:

Japan's recovery after the Second World War has been very spectacular. It smashed the Western superiority. Out of the ashes of the Second World War arose a new buoyant and pulsating Japan. Japan became unrivalled in the production of several fast selling commodities in recent years. In the production of machinery also it has made enormous progress. In the manufacturing of small cars it became very famous. In a very short period Japan's economy became very vibrant.

Japan's relations with both, the communist powers of China and the USSR, remained very sour till 1970.

From the very beginning, the U.S.A. had wanted to strengthen the hands of Japan on account of its apathy towards China, it being a communist country. In 1951, Japan signed a peace treaty with 49 states at San Francisco Conference. In March 1954, it signed the Mutual Defence Assistance Agreement with the U.S.A. The USSR and its communist satellite countries refused to sign any treaty with Japan. Sino-Japanese relations improved only after a rift arose between China and Russia in 1971.

AFRICA

National Awakening and Developments in Africa

As already mentioned, the Second World War proved to be a blessing in disguise to the colonised countries. The nationalist movements became strong in varying degrees in all the countries under foreign rule. During the period 1952 to 1994, all the countries of Africa numbering 51 became independent. The pattern of the movement of national struggle for freedom was the same in the countries of Africa and Asia. In South Africa, the white rule came to an end as late as the year 1994.

In 1994 also, an independent state of Palestine was created.

In 1996, Hongkong was handed over to China by Britain. Thus, every part of the World became free.

The period of revolt movement commenced in Africa when Kwame Nkrumah (1909-72), who later on became the Prime Minister of Ghana (1957-60) and its President (1960-66), returned to Africa from Britain in December 1947 to work as Secretary of United Gold Coast Convention Party (UGCC). In 1960, he and his party followed the Gandhian technique of passive resistance. March 6, 1957 was the date of Independence of Ghana which was formed by the Union of Gold Coast and the British Territory of Western Togoland. Nkrumah greatly inspired the people of other parts of Africa to rebel. Jomo (burning spear) Kenyatta was another great leader who roused Africans to assert their independence.

The South-West African People's Organization (SWAPO) formed in 1960, which led Namibia's struggle for independence, was a full member of the Non-Aligned Movement and it used this forum for promoting the cause of independence of all African countries.

The Organization of the African Unity (OAU), formed in May 1963 at Addis Abba by the heads of 32 African States aimed at the unity and solidarity among African states, elimination of colonialism and defence of the independence of members. It played a crucial role in national awakening among the other African states.

There were many factors that helped the freedom movements in various countries. The declaration during the war, that it was being fought to make countries free and democracy safe, the sympathy and advocacy of statesmen and leaders of leading countries, the force of public opinion, the freedom struggles within the countries, inspiration from India's way of gaining freedom and the growth of solidarity among the countries—all these produced a cumulative force, a global stir, an upsurge of sympathy and support and voices questioning the moral right to keep people bound with chains of imperialism.

Dates of Independence of African Countries

1.	Algeria	5-7-1961
2.	Angola	11-11-1975
3.	Benin	1960
4.	Botswana	30-9-1966
5.	Burkinafaso	5-8-1960
6.	Burundi	1-7-1962
7.	Cameroon	1-1-1960
8.	Cape Verde	5-7-1975
9.	Central African Republic	13-8-1960
10.	Chad	11-8-1960
11.	Comoros	6-7-1975
12.	Congo	31-8-1960
13.	Djibouti	27-6-1977
14.	Egypt	23-7-1952
15.	Equatorial Guinea	12-10-1968
16.	Ethiopia	(Always free except from 1936-41)
17.	Gabon	17-8-1960
18.	Gambia	18-2-1965
19.	Ghana	6-3-1957
20.	Guinea	2-10-1958
21.	Guinea Bissau	24-9-1974
22.	Ivory Coast	7-8-1960
23.	Kenya	12-12-1963
24.	Lesotho	4-10-1966
25.	Libya	1951
26.	Madagascar	26-6-1960
27.	Malawi	6-7-1964
28.	Mali	1960
29.	Mauritania	28-11-1960
30.	Mauritius	12-3-1968
31.	Morocco	2-3-1956
32.	Mozambique	25-6-1975
33.	Namibia	21-3-1990
34.	Niger	3-8-1960
35.	Nigeria	1-10-1960
36.	Rwanda	1-7-1962
37.	Senegal	20-8-1960
38.	Seychelles	28-6-1976
39.	Sierra Leone	27-4-1961
40.	Somalia	1-7-1960
41.	Sudan	1-1-1956

Developments in Asia, Africa and Latin America (after 1945)   313

42.	Swaziland	6-9-1968
43.	Tanzania	9-12-1961
44.	Togo	27-4-1960
45.	Tunisia	20-3-1956
46.	Uganda	9-10-1962
47.	Zaire	30-6-1960
48.	Zambia	24-10-1964
49.	Zanzibar	1964
50.	Zimbabwe	18-4-1980
51.	South Africa	10-5-1994

Course of Achievement of Freedom

After the Second World War, Ghana was one of the first countries in Africa to achieve independence in 1957 from the French and South Africa was the last country to end the White rule, in 1994. The year 1960 is called the 'Africa Year' as during this year, as many as 17 African countries won freedom. Out of these 17, 13 belonged to the French. Namibia got its freedom from South Africa in 1990. The movement of freedom was so strong in March 1960 that the British Prime Minister Harold Macmillan had to observe, "whether we like it or not the growth of national consciousness is a political fact and our national policies must take account of it."

Algeria

Algeria came under French occupation in 1830. In 1960, when France gave freedom to 13 of its colonies in Africa, Algeria still remained under it. After the Second World War, freedom movement took a violent turn. In 1954, the National Liberation Front (NLF) declared its armed struggle. In 1958, the NLF declared a Provisional Government. The French army in Algeria had over 800,000 soldiers who resorted to large scale tortures and atrocities. The Provisional Government of the Front was recognized by several countries. In the meanwhile, General de Gaulle, in power in France, favoured a settlement in Algeria. In the referendum held in France in 1962 on the question of Algeria's independence, the French people voted overwhelmingly in favour of independence. In a similar referendum in 1962, 99 per cent of Algerians voted for complete freedom. France then recognized the independence of Algeria on July 3, 1962. In the War of Independence, 15 lakh Algerians lost their lives at the hands of the French troops.

Namibia

Formerly known as South-West Africa, it became a colony of Germany in 1884. After the defeat of Germany in the First World War, South Africa was given a mandate by the League of Nations to administer it. Later on, South Africa annexed this territory and set up a puppet government. The UN in 1946 did not allow this arrangement but South Africa went on defying it. In 1960, the South West African People's Organization (SWAPO) was formed with the objective of liberating it from South Africa. In 1978, the UN passed a resolution asking South Africa to vacate Namibia. South Africa did not abide by this resolution. Various countries imposed economic sanctions against South Africa to pressurise it to give freedom to Namibia. Elections were held in Namibia in 1889 in which SWAPO won majority. A new constitution was framed and in April 1990, Namibia got freedom.

South Africa

The most vicious system of racialism was being followed in South Africa. Reference has already been made to the policy of 'apartheid' followed in South Africa and the rule of the White minority over the Black majority. South Africa defied the UN and the world public opinion for several decades after the Second World War. In 1990, attitude of the White's somewhat softened towards the 80 per cent Blacks who had been agitating for a long time. The government lifted the ban on the ANC and 71 year old Nelson Mandela was released from jail after 27 years of imprisonment. In 1993, a new constitution came into being and in April 1994, Mandela's ANC under Mandela won elections and on May 10, 1994, he was sworn in as the first Black President. With this, the 'apartheid' ended.

Other Countries

Belgian Congo (Zaire):

In Belgian Congo, the freedom movement was led by Patrice Lumumba, the outstanding leader of the National Congolese Movement. A great revolt took place in 1960 and the Congolese were granted independence. However, with the help of the Belgian imperialists, Katanga, one of the provinces of Belgian Congo seceded from Belgian Congo and declared its independence. When a civil war broke out, UN had to intervene. Ultimately in 1965, Joseph Mobutu, who headed the army of Congo, captured power and became the President of Belgian Congo and renamed it as Zaire.

Ghana:

Ghana (Gold Coast during the British rule) was the first African country to gain its freedom in 1957 under the leadership of Kwame Nkrumah. He also played an important role in uniting the African people for freedom. In 1949, he founded the Convention People's Party which in 1956 elections won more than 70 per cent seats.

Kenya:

Kenya became free in 1963 under the leadership of Jomo Kenyatta. National Movement in Kenya started in the 1920's. It was strengthened by Kenya African Union which was set up in 1943 by Kenyatta. In 1952, Mau Mau rebellion, mainly a peasant revolt, took place. It was suppressed by the use of brute force by the British. In this rebellion about 15,000 Kenyans were killed. In 1953, Kenyatta was arrested on the charge of leading the rebellion. The action of the British was condemned worldwide. Kenyatta was freed in 1961. On December 12, 1963, Kenya won its freedom and Kenyatta became its first President.

Zimbabwe:

Earlier known as Southern Rhodesia, it was a British colony but the white minority settlers under the leadership of Ian Smith captured power in 1965. The white minority government followed the pattern of South Africa. A powerful guerrilla movement aided by the neighbouring African states and the Non-Aligned Movement grew in Rhodesia. The white minority submitted to this pressure and elections were held in 1980. The nationalist parties swept the polls. Robert Mugabe headed the new government formed by the Blacks.

Portuguese Colonies:

The Portuguese had four colonies namely Angola, Cape Verde Islands, Guinea-Bissan and Mozambique in South Africa. The Government of Portugal was not ready to grant independence to its colonies. However in 1974, the government was overthrown by the army with the support of the people of Portugal. The new government supported by the communists, the socialists and the revolutionaries was not in favour to continue under foreign domination and in 1975, all the four colonies, mentioned above, gained their independence.

NATIONAL AWAKENING IN LATIN AMERICA

Of the 20 Latin American states, 18 had become independent by about 1820. Only two states, namely Guyana (formerly called British Guiana) and Surinam (formerly known as Dutch Guiana), had remained under the domination of the British and the Dutch respectively. They gained independence in 1966 and 1975.

Most of the Latin states even after the Second World War registered a slow progress. They faced the problems of disease, hunger, illiteracy and poverty. The United States of America had given financial aid worth crores of dollars to these states. In general, the political situation in most of the Latin states remained very fluid and unstable, changing like the clouds in the sky after the Second World War.

Guyana

Guyana (formerly British Guiana) became a British Colony in 1814 and an independent Sovereign State within the Commonwealth of Nations on May 26, 1966. Dr. Cheddi Jagan and Forbes Burnham played an important role in the freedom struggle. In the 1953 elections, the People's Progressive Party, led by the two leaders mentioned above, won 18 of the 25 seats. Dr. Cheddi Jagan became the Prime Minister and he started carrying out a radical social and economic programme. However, after four months, his government was dismissed and the constitution suspended. Jagan and Burnham were arrested. British troops landed in Guyana. All this was done in the name of checking communism. After this, the British were able to cause split in the PPP by fermenting ethnic conflicts. In the 1957 elections, Dr. Jagan's party won and intensified the demand for independence. Again in the 1961 elections, Jagan's party was victorious but the government did not receive financial help. The British again created ethnic disturbances and violence. It may be noted that there are sizeable number of people of Indian origin and the African origin. In 1966, Guyana became independent. Ethnic conflicts continued in Guyana for several years.

Surinam

Formerly called Dutch Guiana, it became independent in 1975. A Military Council came to power in 1982. In 1987, civilian rule was restored. Political turmoil has continued for long with its adverse effects on the economy. The country is faced with ethnic strains on account of multifarious groups of Negroes, East Indians, Indonesians, Chinese, and Lebanese etc.

Cuba

Developments in Cuba have already been dealt with while discussing the Issues of Cold War.

Brazil

Called the 'Coffee Province' of the world for the production of coffee, Brazil, the largest state of Latin America, became independent in 1832 from the Portuguese rule. Monarchy was overthrown in 1889 and a republic declared. The armed forces took control in 1964 but a civilian government was restored in 1995. In the 1970's Brazil was the 10th largest economy in the world. Four key—sectors—steel, automotives, petrochemicals and utilities—have played a decisive role in industrial development and in the expansion of the economy.

1980s saw the beginning of bad days, resulting from heavy foreign borrowings, rising interest rates, income maldistribution, skyrocketing oil prices and an international recession.

In 1992, Brazil's foreign debt was the highest in the developing world, its inflation rate was close to 250 per cent, the highest in Latin America.

Argentina

Argentina, the second largest state of Latin America became independent in 1816. Argentina was the first Latin state to win independence. President Peron, who remained in power from 1946 to 1955, was both "God and Devil" for the people of this country. He worked for the welfare of the masses but his methods were autocratic. He reduced the importance of the constitution and abolished the Supreme Court. He had to leave his country on account of the dissatisfaction in the army and navy. Argentina returned to civil rule in 1983. Russian influence went on increasing. It remained an anti-American country for several decades.

PROBLEMS FACED BY THE COUNTRIES OF ASIA, AFRICA AND LATIN AMERICA

Most of the countries of Asia and Africa were under foreign domination and after the Second World War, movements for their independence became strong. Some of them had to face a lot of brutal actions of the imperialist powers.

The second problem faced by them was the problem of reconstruction of their political and socio-economic systems.

After the Second World War, the two Super Powers of the USSR and the U.S.A. had formed their own blocks and were exercising pressures on the countries of Asia, Africa and Latin America to join a particular block.

A large number of these countries desired to keep themselves aloof from the influence of Cold War. They, therefore, organised the Non-Aligned Movement to promote peace and international understanding.

ROLE OF THE COUNTRIES IN THE WORLD AFFAIRS

After the Second World War more than 60 nations of Asia, Africa and Latin America got their independence. Besides, Japan and China also emerged as great nations. It was, therefore, natural that the international scenario radically changed after the Second World War. These countries set up different forums for their own development, mutual development and also to exercise their influence in world affairs.

Almost all of them have become members of the UN and its agencies to actively involve themselves in global matters.

Following are the important initiatives and organisations which indicate their participation in international affairs.

1. First Asian Relations Conference (1947).
2. Second Asian Relations Conference (1948).
3. The Colombo Plan (1960) — an international organization of 26 newly independent Asian countries for post-war development.
4. The Commonwealth having 53 members representing a third of the nations of the world.
5. Organisation of the African Unity (OAU) established in 1963 with 53 member states.
6. Principles of Panchsheel enunciated in 1954.
7. Non-Alignment Movement — Bandung Conference and Declaration of Principles adopted in 1955. At present it has 114 member countries.
8. South Asian Association for Regional Cooperation (SAARC) comprising India, Maldives, Pakistan, Bangladesh, Sri Lanka, Bhutan and Nepal (1985).

Since 1989, it has been the practice to designate SAARC years to focus on specific themes of common concern to member states. Plans of action, both at the regional and national levels, were implemented in the following years.

1989	SAARC Year for Combating Drug Abuse and Drug Trafficking
1990	SAARC Year of Girl-Child
1991	SAARC Year of Shelter
1992	SAARC Year of Environment
1993	SAARC Year of Disabled Persons

1994	SAARC Year of the Youth
1995	SAARC Year of Poverty Eradication
1996	SAARC Year of Literacy

In addition, 1991-2000 A.D. was declared as the SAARC decade of the 'Girl-Child'.

9. League of Arab States created in 1945 to strengthen relations among its 22 member states.
10. Organisation of Petroleum Exporting Countries established in 1960 which aims at controlling production and prices of crude oil. It has 14 members.
11. Group of 77 is an economic group formed in 1964 to protect and defend the economic and trade interests in the developing countries of Asia, Africa and Latin America.

Panchsheel

Meaning:

Panchsheel or the Five Principles which were enunciated by Pt. Jawaharlal Nehru, the first Prime Minister of India, were incorporated in the preamble to an agreement arrived at between India and China on June 28, 1954 at New Delhi. The agreement was signed by Nehru, the Prime Minister of India and Chau-En-Lai (1898-1976), the Prime Minister of China.

The Five Principles were :
(1) Mutual respect for territorial integrity and sovereignty.
(2) Non-aggression.
(3) Non-interference in each other's internal affairs.
(4) Equality and mutual benefit.
(5) Peaceful co-existence.

Why Panchsheel:

After the Second World War, there developed an environment of Cold War among big powers of the world. It was feared that mutual conflicts among the nations of the world and especially among the two powers blocks, might disturb the world peace and that there was an urgent need to take some positive steps to ease the situation.

Secondly, the newly freed countries had embarked upon the process of building up a viable political and socio-economic system on the basis of the ideals and values they had cherished before their independence.

Historical Background of Panchsheel:

More than 2000 years ago, Gautam Buddha laid emphasis on five principles. Ashoka the Great got them engraved on the Edicts, spread over different parts of the world. These were tolerance (*Bahu-Sruta*), harmony (*Samavya*), sharing with all (*Samvibhaga*), purity of relationships (*Dharam Sambandha*), and gentleness (*Mardavam*). The United Nations Charter had also provided for settling mutual disputes through mutual consultation.

Disregard of Panchsheel by China:

It was very unfortunate that China, a signatory to the agreement, violated these principles in 1959 when it attacked Tibet and unleashed a reign of terror. Dalai Lama, the spiritual head of Tibet fled to India and established Government in exile at Dharamshala in Himachal Pradesh. The greatest shock to India came in October 1962 when China committed aggression on India in flagrant violation of the Panchsheel. The sweet slogan of *'Hindi Chini Bhai Bhai'* coined by the Indian people at the time of the agreement in 1954 received a great jolt.

Non-Aligned Movement (NAM)

Background :

A large number of countries of Asia and Africa became independent immediately after the Second World War. On attaining independence they started the process of reconstruction of their socio-economic system according to their own ideals. They wanted peace not only in their own lands but also in the world at large. A large number of the emerging nations in the Third World, the newly independent countries, were now no longer 'Petititioners in Western Courts'. Now, they wanted to stand on their own legs and to cooperate with others. They, therefore, decided not to be a member of any power block in the world. They were determined to retain their own freedom of judgement and decision in any given situation. While cooperating with others, they were determined to chalk out their course of action independently. They thought that a long spell of peace and reconstruction was more imperative for them rather than the call of imperious policies or Cold War. The idea was to keep out of Power Blocks and military alliances.

On the formation of the military pacts and alliances of the great powers, Jawaharlal Nehru, in his speech in the Lok Sabha on February 25, 1955, said, "I am not asking these countries to disband their armies or their forces. The only effect of these facts and alliances, it appears to me, is to hold a kind of threat."

Several outstanding leaders had emerged in Asia in the 1950's who wanted to keep themselves 'non-aligned' to power block's and to be free from the Cold War confrontation.

Origin of the Non-Aligned Movement:

Jawaharlal Nehru, Prime Minister of India (1947-64), Sukarno, President of Indonesia (1945-67), Chou-En-Lai, Prime Minister of China (1949-76) and Gamel Abdel Nasser, President, of Egypt (1956-1970) played an important role in starting the Non-Aligned Movement. On their initiative a conference of Asian and African countries was held at Bandung in 1955. Twenty-nine Asian and African countries attended the Conference which represented nearly half the population of the world.

The Bandung Conference was an important milestone in the history of the Non-Aligned Movement. It was also the first biggest conference of the countries of Asia and Africa. The conference stressed the need for promoting economic cooperation among the countries and ushering an era of international peace in the world.

In 1956, preparatory work for convening the first summit was done at Belgrade (Yugoslavia).

In 1960, the UN adopted the historical Declaration on Granting Independence to Colonial countries and peoples. This session was attended by five leaders of the non-aligned nations — Jawaharlal Nehru of India, Sukarno of Indonesia, Nasser of Egypt, Tito of Yugoslavia and Nkrumah of Ghana.

Belgrade Conference and Belgrade Declaration (1961):

The first conference of Heads of state or Government of Non-Aligned Countries was held at Belgrade, from September 1-6, 1961. It was attended by 25 countries. The Conference adopted a declaration which stated that "the principles of peaceful coexistence are the only alternative to the 'Cold War' and to a possible general catastrophe" and that lasting peace would be achieved only in "a world where the domination of colonialism, imperialism and neo-colonialism, in all their manifestations, is radically eliminated."

Meaning of Non-Aligned Nations:

Non-Aligned nations are those which do not belong to any power blocks of the world and object to lining up for war purposes with any military blocks, or military alliances and the like. It means they belong to neither this side nor that except the side that professes peace. The basic principle of the declaration as explained by Nehru is, "We propose as far as possible to keep away from power blocks or groups aligned against each other, which have led in the past towards war and which may again lead to disaster on an even vaster scale. We propose to keep on the closest terms of friendship with all countries. We shall be friends of America and intend cooperating with them. We intend also to cooperate fully with the Soviet Union."

Main Objectives of the NAM:

1. Maintenance of peace in the world.
2. Non-alignment with power blocks.
3. Promotion of disarmament.
4. Encouragement to the concept of one world based on cooperation and sharing.
5. Condemnation of racial discrimination.
6. Peaceful coexistence between nations.
7. Respect for the territorial integrity and sovereignty of nations.
8. Promotion of basic human rights.
9. Abstaining from defence/military pacts.
10. Promotion of a New Economic Order.

Achievements:

The concept of Non-Aligned Nations has become so popular that its number of 25 in 1961 rose to 114 in 1997. It has enabled the countries to follow their own policies without any pressure. It has helped in ending the Cold War. It has assisted in bringing nations together to discuss their common problems and find solutions. It has rendered a great help to the dependent nations to achieve their independence. The Non-Aligned movement has played an important role in reducing tensions and moving towards peace based on equality.

Summit Meetings of Non-Aligned Movement:

The Summit meetings of the Non-Aligned Movement have been held at Belgrade (Yugoslavia), 1961; Cairo (Egypt), 1964; Lusaka (Zambia), 1970; Algiers (Algeria), 1973; Colombo (Sri Lanka), 1976; Havana (Cuba), 1979; New Delhi (India), 1983; Hazare (Zimbabwe), 1986; Belgrade (Yugoslavia), 1989; Jakarta (Indonesia), 1992; and Cartagena (Colombia), 1995.

EXERCISES

A. Very Short Answer Type

1. Write down the history of freedom movement in Algeria.
2. List any three problems which the countries of Asia, Africa and Latin America had to face after the Second World War.
3. State the meaning of apartheid.
4. Name any four cities where 'Non-Aligned countries' conferences were held.
5. Mention the five principles of Panchsheel.
6. List any four organizations that played an important role in Asia and Africa.
7. State the main events that took place in Latin America after the Second World War.
8. Mention any four African countries that got independence in 1960.
9. Explain the role of the Palestine Liberation Organisation (PLO).

B. Short Answer Type

1. Describe the main stages in the struggle for freedom in Vietnam since 1945.
2. State the developments in China.
3. List the main stages in the freedom movement of India with special reference to the Post-Second World War.
4. Describe the circumstances under which Israel became an independent state.

5. What were the factors that helped in the freedom movement in Africa?
6. Describe how Namibia achieved its independence.
7. What was the position of the Black People in South Africa? How did it improve?

C. Essay Type/Long Answer

1. What were the main objectives of the Non-Aligned Movement when it was started? What is its role in the present unipolar world?
2. Describe the circumstances leading to Japan's emergence as an important power.
3. Why was the Non-Aligned Movement started? What are its objectives? To what extent it has been possible to achieve these objectives?

CHAPTER 30

Developments in Europe, the USSR and the U.S.A.

DEVELOPMENTS IN EUROPE

After the Second World War, radical changes took place in the political and socio-economic systems of Europe. Sharp differences in these systems were clearly visible between Western European countries and the Eastern European countries which included Soviet Russia, Poland, German Democratic Republic, Hungary, Czechoslovakia, Romania, Bulgaria, Yugoslavia, Albania etc.

Political Changes : Political Map and System

During the Second World War, the Central Powers/Axis Powers comprising Germany, Italy and Japan etc. had occupied a large part of Europe and a large part of Soviet Union. But during the last phase of the Second World War almost all the above mentioned countries were liberated from the German occupation.

After the Second World War, victorious countries i.e. Britain, France, U.S.A. and USSR divided Germany among themselves. In 1949, Britain, France and the U.S.A. which had occupied West Germany, named it as the Federal Republic of Germany and made Bonn as its capital. Russia named its occupied area as German Democratic Republic and made Berlin as its capital. In 1990, Germany was again unified. The boundaries of the Italian empire also underwent great changes. Russian empire expanded largely.

On account of the heavy losses suffered by the warring powers, victorious as well as vanquished, their influence declined in the colonies and gradually they were forced to withdraw from there. Their weakening military power paved the way to the freedom of large countries of Asia and Africa.

The sharp weakening of power of countries like Britain, Germany and France led to the emergence of two Super Powers of the USSR and the U.S.A.

Most of the Western European countries are in the American block. All of them have joined NATO military group organised by the U.S.A.

After the Second World War, a large part of Western Europe lay in ruins. A Council of Europe was formed in 1949 to take up a common programme for reconstruction and speedy recovery. The Council brought together all European democracies.

Almost all Western European countries follow either parliamentary or presidential type of democratic governments.

In 1964, eleven countries namely Belgium, Denmark, France, West Germany, Italy, the Netherlands, Spain, Denmark, Sweden, Switzerland and the UK established European Space Research Organization (ESRO) to promote collaboration among European States in space research and technology exclusively for peace purposes.

The countries of Eastern Europe established Communist governments and acted as satellites of the Soviet Union. To couteract the influence of NATO, SEATO etc, the Soviet Union organized a military pact known as WARSAW. This intensified the Cold War.

Economic Conditions

The war ravaged economy of the Western European countries was greatly helped by the Marshall Plan, also known as the European Recovery Plan initiated in 1948 by President Truman of the U.S.A. Earlier, in 1947, President Truman had proclaimed his doctrine of giving massive economic and military aid to European countries to withstand the danger from communist countries.

Another important factor which contributed immensely to the economic recovery of the Western European countries was the formation of the European Economic Community (EEC), commonly known as European Common Market in 1957. At present, 15 Countries of Europe, ie. France, Britain, Ireland, Denmark, Greece, Spain, Portugal, Austria, Finland, Sweden, Belgium, Netherlands, Luxemburg, Italy and Germany are its members. EEC has become the World's largest and most prosperous trading area. More recently it has come to be known as European Community (EC). The Eastern European countries followed a state controlled economic system up to the year 1991. Thereafter it provided a small dose of liberal economy.

Social Development

Countries of Western Europe are highly developed. People enjoy all the facilities of life and their standard of living is reasonably high. Their population is within their control. They enjoy freedom of speech and other freedoms. They are liberal in outlook.

As compared with the Western European countries, the people of Eastern Europe are relatively not so liberal and for long they did not enjoy freedom of press, freedom of speech and freedom of religion etc.

Sweeping Changes in Eastern Europe since 1989

Since the 1917 October Revolution in Russia, Communism had dominated Eastern Europe but its supremacy greatly declined in 1989, as the election held that year unseated most of the top communist leaders. Consequently, the Eastern European countries including Poland, Albania, Bulgaria, Romania, Hungary, Czechoslovakia, Yugoslavia, that were under the influence of Communist USSR also were affected. All these countries discarded communism and adopted the democratic form of government and liberal economic system—to a considerable extent free from rigid state control. In December 1991, Supreme Soviet was dissolved and Gorbachev stepped down. With this, the 74-year old monopoly of the Soviet Communist Party over the state came to an end.

DEVELOPMENTS IN THE USSR

The USSR remained one of the two Super Powers in the World upto the year 1990 i.e. till its dismemberment. Thereafter, its place, to some extent, was taken by Russia or Russian Federation as it is also called. The Communist Party of the Soviet Union (CPSU) guided the affairs of the state. It engaged itself in nation-building activities so much so that Soviet Union, in some respects, even went ahead of the USA, the other Super Power.

During the Second World War, the USSR and the U.S.A. helped and cooperated with each other in their common aim of defeating the Axis Powers but thereafter they followed diametrically opposed policies as were so required by their socio-economic systems. The USSR followed a communist philosophy and rigid state control and the U.S.A., on the other hand, followed a capitalist and democratic system. This led to Cold War which fortunately came to an end in 1990-91.

Main Developments Between 1945 and 1990 in the USSR

Following are the important phases of development in the Soviet Union.

The first era may be called the Stalin era (1945-1953) dominated by Stalin who made Russia a great industrial power by his Five Year Plans and followed the policy of ruthless suppression at home and aggressive imperialism abroad.

The Second era was of internal power struggle (1953-1957) when power was shared by five great leaders. They were (1) Premier Georgi Malenkov (2) Laurenti Beria (3) Nikita Khrushchev (4) Molotov and (5) Bulganin.

The third era (1957-1964) was dominated by Nikita Khrushchev who followed a Five-Point Policy (1) Peaceful co-existence (2) Non-aggression (3) Non-intervention in the internal affairs of other states (4) Mutual respect for territorial integrity and sovereignty (5) Equality and mutual benefit.

Khrushchev lifted the 'Iron Curtain' from the Soviet Union and established friendly relations with other countries, de-Stalinised Russia, made communism liberal and watered down its brutal methods.

Khrushchev was succeeded by Kosygin as Premier (1964-80). Kosygin resigned on health grounds and Brezhnev succeeded him. Kosygin and Brezhnev were also liberal as compared with Stalin.

Perestroika (Re-structuring) of Gorbachev

Gorbachev, who presided over the destinity of the USSR for about six years (1985-91) became a recipient of the Nobel Peace Prize in 1990 for his services to the cause of world peace. His period marked the end of the 'old-guard' leadership in Russia. Gorbachev introduced reforms known as *'Perestroika'* (Restructuring) and *'Glasnost'* (openness).

Gorbachev felt that there was a "greater need for efficiency, competence and professionalism in work". The all-powerful state, according to him, had increasingly antagonised the workers. Every third enterprise in the Soviet Union was operating at a loss. *Perestroika* meant disappearance of "arrogant, ignorant, puffed up incompetent individuals." It advocated liberal policies. *'Glasnost'* implied openness, democratization, tolerance of opponents, free elections, arms reduction, relaxation of tensions. Gorbachev asserted, "a country cannot achieve security by creating a threat to others." He advocated peaceful existence.

The USSR and the Commonwealth of Independent States (CIS)

The Union of Soviet Socialist Republics was officially set up in 1922. It comprisoned 15 Republic States including Russia. The Soviet Union extended partly in Europe and partly in Asia. Only 25 per cent of the area was in Europe but the population living in Europe was about 75 per cent. Eleven Republics out of 15 joined CIS which came into being on December 22, 1992 after the dismemberment of the USSR in 1991. Georgia, Estonia, Latvia and Lithuania did not join CIS. All the Republics Constituting CIS are independent. CIS is a form of federation formed for the purpose of common welfare and security etc. It is a very well-knit organization.

About the 15 Republics of the USSR (Pre 1991)

State	Area in sq km.	Population in million	Capital	Economic resources
Russia	17 million	147.0	Moscow	Oil, gold, gas, precious metals
Ukraine	5.5 million	51.6	Kiev	Iron and steel, coal, agricultural machines, chemicals, food processing, grains.
Kazakhstan	2.8 million	17	Alma-ata	Grains, coal and oil.
Belarus	0.2 million	10.3	Minsk	Agriculture, Peat.
Uzbekistan	0.4 million	23.0	Tashkent	Cotton, some oil and gas.

Tajikistan	0.14 million	6.1	Dushanbe	Coal, zinc, lead, cotton and wheat.
Kyrgyzstan	0.19 million	4.4	Frunze	Industries based on agriculture.
Turkmenistan	0.48 million	4.1	Ashkhabad	Cotton, oil and gas.
Azerbaijan	0.08 million	7.6	Baku	Oil, iron, cotton, citrus fruits and agriculture.
Armenia	0.03 million	4.0	Yerevan	Cotton, fruits, rice, tobacco, copper, zinc and lead.
Moldova	0.03 million	4.5	Kishinev	Agriculture and wine.
Georgia	0.07 million	5.6	Tbilisi	Wine, vegetables and fruits.
Estonia	0.04 million	1.5	Tallinn	Food processing, ship building, electronic engineering.
Latvia	0.06 million	2.6	Riga	Farm products, chemicals, machines, paper, furniture.
Lithuania	0.06 million	3.7	Vilnius	Ships, farm products, linen, textiles, paper.

(*Note* : The last four states did not join C.I.S.)

Russia/Russian Federation since 1991

Russia, a constituent of the erstwhile USSR, an independent country since 1991, after the break-up of the USSR, has now taken its place in the international field. However, it is not considered as a 'Super Power' like its predecessor. It includes 75 per cent of the former USSR (Soviet Union) and has 50 per cent of the total population. Seventy per cent of USSR's total agricultural and industrial output came from Russia. It has taken over USSR's seat on the UN Security Council.

On September 5, 1991, the Soviet Parliament voted to dismantle the Soviet Union and make it a loose Federation of Republics. On December 9, leaders of Russia, Ukraine and Byelorussia (all former Republics of the Soviet Union) signed an agreement to form a Commonwealth of Independent States (CIS). The CIS is not a state now but a community of 11 independent states which proclaimed itself the successor of the former USSR in international affairs. On December 21, the Soviet Union came to its formal end. On January 17, 1992, Russia decided to have two names—Russia and Russian Federation.

Boris Yeltsin, the architect of Russia and CIS, was the first Russian leader to be chosen by popular vote in 1989. He was elected Russian President twice in 1991 and 1996.

The year 1991 was a great landmark in the history of the world's economic and socio-political system. A new era of liberalism and democracy began in Russia. Moscow and St-Petersburg are the two important cities of Russia.

In 1993, Russia's first multi-party parliamentary elections were held. A drive to privatize thousands of large and medium-sized state-owned enterprises was launched. In 1994, Russia and the United States agreed not to target nuclear weapons on each other and signed a peace treaty with Ukraine to eliminate the World's third largest nuclear arsenal. In 1994, Russia also joined NATO's partnership for peace plan of military cooperation with former communist states.

DEVELOPMENTS IN THE U.S.A.

The U.S.A. has never been hit by any war after the Civil War (1861-63). Not a single bomb struck it during the two World Wars. Whereas the Second World War ruined the economy, industry and even major cities of all other powerful nations, the U.S.A. remained intact. It, therefore, became possible for it to devote its resources to the building up of a vibrant economy and providing a decent standard of living to the majority of its population. By virtue of its enormous wealth, it has been the biggest contributor to render help to the war-ravaged European countries. Naturally it has exercised tremendous influence on Latin America, Asia, Africa and Europe.

The U.S.A. has always claimed that it is the saviour of democratic values in the world.

On account of its antipathy to communism, it remained hostile to the USSR and its Satellite countries and for this phobia, it unnecessarily interfered in the affairs of some countries like Cuba, Korea and Vietnam.

For checking the influence of communism it organised several military alliances of democratic countries.

The U.S.A. follows a capitalist system of economy and a democratic presidential form of government.

Internal and External Policies of the U.S.A.

The 'Containment of Communism' has been the major aim of the foreign policy of the U.S.A. It became an important contributory factor in the Cold War. It also led to anti-communist and anti-radical hysteria in the U.S.A. The 'paranoic obsession' with 'godless communism' dominated the internal policy of the U.S.A. for a number of years after the Second World War. Loyalty of thousands of government officials, teachers working in schools, colleges and universities, film writers and producers was investigated into and those whose ideas were found 'un-American' were dismissed from service.

Civil Rights Movement

A powerful civil rights movement arose in the 1950's which achieved significant success in the U.S.A. *Martin Luther King (1929-1968)*, an American Clergyman, who was deeply influenced by Gandhiji, was the most powerful leader of civil rights. He launched a non-violent movement against segregation of the Black People from the White People. The movement started from a boycott of buses, spread to other areas. In restaurants, a movement known as 'Sit-in' was started. 'Sit-in' implied going to restaurants where segregation was practised and sitting there on being refused to be served. A powerful movement was also started for voting rights for the Blacks. The people who participated in the movement had to face severe hardships. *"We shall overcome"*, was the theme of the song sung by these fighters of civil rights. Martin Luther King gave memorable and stirring speeches. His famous speech '*I have a dream*' was delivered in 1963 at a huge mass rally, organised near the Lincoln Memorial in Washington. "I have a dream that one day men will rise and come to see that they are made to live together as brothers. I still have a dream this morning that one day every Negro in this country, every coloured people in the world will be judged on the basis of the content of his character rather than the colour of his skin."

In 1968, Martin Luther King was assassinated. The Indian Government appreciated his role and posthumously awarded him the Jawaharlal Nehru Award for International Understanding.

American Presidents after Second World War

President Franklin Delano Roosevelt (1882-1945):

He was elected Democratic President in 1933, 1936, 1940 and 1944. Before World War II he carried through very successfully a programme called the 'New Deal' to combat economic depression of 1930s. He opened the second War Front during the Second World War for crushing the Axis Powers.

Harry S. Truman (1874-1972):

US President (1945-53). He took initiative in holding the San Francisco conference in June 1945 for establishing the UNO; took the decision of dropping atomic bomb at Hiroshima and Nagasaki; introduced a New Fair Deal for giving a better standard of living to the Americans.

Truman is known for the 'Truman Doctrine' or 'policy of containment' formulated in 1945. Truman declared, "It must be the policy of the United States to support such people who are resisting subjugation by armed minorities or outside pressure." The purposes of Truman Doctrine were to protect independent nations from communist aggression, to pressure the balance of power, check Russia's influence in the Middle East and Balkan region.

Dwight Eisenhower (1890-1969):

American President (1952-60). A great General who led the Allies to victory in the Second World War. Twice President of the U.S.A. Stood for equality and against racial discrimination. Alarmed at the launching of Sputnik by the USSR, embarked upon the production of sophisticated missiles on a mass scale.

US's Initiative to Check Iraq's Aggression on Kuwait

On August 2, 1990 Iraq's armed forces invaded its neighbour Kuwait and occupied it swiftly—just in the span of six hours. This invasion was without any rhyme or reason and Iraq declared Kuwait one of its provinces. The invasion came as a shock to Kuwait, the U.S.A. and the entire world. This has never happened in any part of the world since the end of the Second World War. No sovereign country has been annexed before by a powerful neighbour. Iraq's invasion on Kuwait was condemned almost by the entire world. The UN imposed mandatory sanctions and forbade all states to conduct any business with Iraq. The U.S.A., the UK, Arab League, France, Canada, Australia, West Germany, the Netherlands and Belgium etc. sent their forces to expel the armed forces of Iraq. However, the major responsibility was taken by President Bush of the U.S.A. On August 8, 1990, President Bush stated the objectives of the American policy as follows :-

1. Immediate, unconditional and complete withdrawal of Iraq from Kuwait.
2. Restoration of the legitimate government in Kuwait.
3. Protection of lives of Americans.

On December 1, 1990, Iraq was given an ultimatum to leave Kuwait in six weeks by January 15, 1991 or face war. Iraq rejected the ultimatum. The war broke out on January 17, 1991. The U.S.A. started 'Operation Desert'. On February 25, 1991, the US forces entered Iraq. On February 26, Kuwait was fully liberated. Iraq surrendered and the Gulf War ended after three months in April 1991. The US army convoy entered Iraq and set up relief camps. The decision of the U.S.A. to actively fight Iraq was appreciated by the entire world.

CORDIAL RELATIONS BETWEEN THE U.S.A. AND USSR

In 1985, US President Ronald Reagan and Soviet leader Mikhail Gorbachev met in Geneva to discuss international issues. This was the first Super-Power Summit during the last six years. Reagan and Gorbachev again met to sort out issues. In 1988, a five day Kremlin Summit was held between the above mentioned two leaders. In 1989, Bush and Gorbachev met for their first summit. In 1991, Bush and Gorbachev signed the historic START in Moscow. President Bush announced sweeping reduction in US tactical nuclear weapons and asked the Soviet Union to do so. The USSR also followed suit. One year moratorium was put on nuclear tests. On Feburary 1, 1992 President Bush and President Yeltsin declared the end of enmity in a meeting at Washington. (See also Cold War in an earlier Chapter)

GRADUAL END OF THE COLD WAR

Although it cannot be claimed that the world scenario is entirely free from Cold War but it must be admitted that it has lessened substantially. There has been a great realization in the minds of the statesmen of the world that the policy of confrontation in international affairs is very harmful for the welfare of mankind. Four most important factors that have led to this approach are (i) Role of the UNO (ii) Role of the Non-Alignment Movement (iii) Liberal policies initiated by Gorbachev and the disintegration of the USSR into 15 independent Republics in 1991 (iv) Disarmament and Nuclear Ban Treaties.

Developments in Europe, the USSR and the USA

The popular movement against war, the reports of the scientists of total devastation in the event of a nuclear war, the MAD doctrine and several regional and international movements pressing for disarmament have eased the tension and created an atmosphere of detente. Mutually Assured Destruction (abbreviated as MAD) is a doctrine that believes that "peace is best maintained by threatening to obliterate an entire enemy society in retaliation for a nuclear attack," (Time). The logic is, "If we are killed, you will also not live; we sink or sail together." As such, when both the sides have a large number of nuclear weapons, none would dare to start a war, for it would mean sure death even of the attacker. This helps as a deterant. It will discourage countries from making war.

Detente : Detente (pronounced 'daytant') means ease of tension, particularly between communist and non-communist blocks. Brezhnev pursued a policy of friendly relations with the West. This easing of the tension between East and West became known as detente. In 1972, the Soviet Union and the United States signed two agreements to reduce nuclear arms. The collapse of detente began in 1980 when Soviet troops invaded Afghanistan. Under Gorbachev, the Soviet Unions relations with the West improved. In 1987, Gorbachev and Reagan signed a treaty to dismantle all their ground-launched medium-range nuclear missiles. In 1988-89 Soviet troops were withdrawn from Afghanistan. Again a period of detente began.

EXERCISES

A. Very Short Answer Type

1. What has been the main difference between the political and socio-economic system of the U.S.A. and the USSR?
2. Write any four events in the development of scientific research in the USSR.
3. Explain the terms 'Perestroika' and 'Glasnost'.
4. State the type of help rendered by the U.S.A. to the Western countries of Europe after the Second World War.
5. Name any four countries of Eastern Europe.
6. How was the USSR able to exercise its supremacy in Eastern Europe?

B. Short Answer Type

1. State the main political changes that took place in Europe after the Second World War.
2. Describe the changes that took place in East Europe after 1990.
3. In what ways Khruschev Era was different from the Stalin Era in the USSR?
4. Explain the difference between the set-up of the USSR and CIS.
5. Trace the circumstances leading to the break-up of the USSR.
6. Explain the foreign policy of the U.S.A.
7. Describe the movement of Civil Rights in the U.S.A.
8. How did cordial relations between the U.S.A. and USSR develop?
9. Who was Martin Luther King? With which movement was he associated? What was his dream?

CHAPTER 31

Developments in World Economy, Society & Polity: Changes in the Indian Economy

MAIN FEATURES OF CHANGES IN DIFFERENT ECONOMIC SYSTEMS

Human beings have unlimited wants. Some of these wants are satisfied by production and distribution of goods and services. This requires economic decisions by each country on four basic problems regarding production and distribution (1) What goods and services to be produced and how much? (2) How to be produced? (3) Where to be produced (to locate the units of produdction)? and (4) For whom to be produced? The different economic systems try to solve these problems in their own different ways.

Capitalism

It is the economic system prevalent in many countries. It is a private-enterprise system. It is called capitalism because individuals can own land and such capital as factories, buildings, electricity and railways. It allows people to carry on their economic activities largely free from government control. It flourishes in such a condition where means of production and a huge sum of money get concentrated into the hands of a small number of people. They freely take decisions of 'What,' 'How,' 'Where' and 'Whom' of production and distribution. Since the main aim under capitalism is to maximise the profits, the capitalism is open to new processes of production and new raw materials.

In the second half of the last century, certain qualitative changes took place as free enterprise was gradually replaced by monopoly. Monopoly was the agreement and arrangement among a handful of capitalists to control and regulate the production and sale of commodites. During the last three decades of the 19th century, technological changes took place. During the monopoly phase, the role of banks, due to the increasing concentration of deposits, dominated important economic decisions. Another change was the export of capital, that is, foreign investment in erstwhile colonies for their development. A Neo-Colonialism took shape. The once colonial rulers now exerted their economic dominance over the colonies that got liberated, by investing their surplus capital as loan for development in return for primary products.

The multinational corporations (MNCs) appear as one of the distinctive features of the capitalist system of the present day world. They now control one-third of production of the entire capitalist world and four-fifths of the exchange of the technological know-how. Developing countries do not have happy experience with the MNCs as in the developing countries the MNCs do not set up heavy industries or complete line of production and do not carry out Research and Development activities with the result that the new nations are deprived of new and latest technologies and have no alternative but to depend on obsolete and discarded technologoies imported from other countries.

Mixed Economies

Mixed economies involve more government control and planning than do capitalist economies. In a mixed economy, the government often owns and runs such important industries as railways, other transports, electricity and water. Most other industries may be privately owned. Some nations like India, Yugoslavia and many in the Third World with mixed economies are democracies. The economic system of such nations is often called democratic socialism.

Communism

In its traditional form, it is based on government ownership of nearly all productive resources and government control of all important economic activity. Government planners make all decisions about producing, pricing and distributing goods.

USSR adopted the communist system of economy but not at once. In 1921, Lenin established a New Economic Policy (NEP) to strengthen the country. Small industries and retail trade were allowed to operate under their own control. The peasants no longer had to give most of their products to the government. The government kept control of the most important segments of economy — banking, heavy industry, the transportation system and foreign trade. The economy recovered steadily under NEP. In December 1927 a decision was taken to end the NEP and take the path of planned economic development. It was realised that the strategy of industrialisation could not succeed so long as the agricultural structure was not changed. By 1937 entire agriculture came under government control. The socialized national income increased to 99.1%, only 0.9% was from private sector.

In socialist countries ownership of means of production is the foundation and economy is centrally planned to direct, regulate and control the economic activities, as was the goal of USSR. The communist party determined the direction of economy, approved five year plans and kept a watchful eye on performance of various economic bodies. Recently, the role of the Communist Party came in for criticism. Executive interference by the party which was exercising all powers did more harm than good. In early 1985, Gorbachev's leadership marked a radical break. A new economic strategy rested on three key concepts (1) acceleration of the pace of economic development (2) restructuring all aspects of economy—material base, technologies, investment, management, moral and psychological situation of the society etc and (3) openness (*glasnost*) of expression and frank debate. The Communist Party's role was very much reduced with the Government's voting in 1990 to permit the creation of non-communist political parties in the Soviet Union. The economic reforms did not succeed as expected. However, the political scence changed as the Soviet Union was dissolved on December 25, 1991.

GLOBALIZATION

Globalization means extending or spreading on a global scale, that is, all over the globe. For instance, information technology has so developed that information has become globalized. Multinational corporations have spread their business on a global scale. The concept of globalization also includes the transfer and movement of ideas, information, goods, services, technologies and human beings from one part of the globe to another with ease and speed without any interference, as if the globe has become one vast country.

As the globe is growing larger in terms of population, it is shrinking in terms of contacts and effects that people can have living across oceans and national boundaries. A decision taken in New York may lead to the clearing of equatorial forest and uprooting an entire tribe in Brazil. Pollution from British factories kills fish in Sweden. A Civil War at any place may threaten to involve Super Powers far away from the scene of fighting.

Another model of globalization is the business world and advanced economies based on network of alliances, consorts and specialized agencies to accomplish goals too large for any single nation to achieve. In the new economy, a car or a computer may be built in four different countries and assembled in the fith.

Markets too expand beyond national boundaries. Banking, insurance, securities all are racing to globalize in order to serve their global clients.

HOW TO SOLVE THE PROBLEMS OF DEVELOPMENT

Now at the end of the 20th century, the less developed countries have become of great concern for the whole world. Their political independence did not help them to industrialize rapidly or to modernize their social structure. They remain economically dependent on a world market dominated by the advanced capitalist countries in which they must sell their specialized primary products to be turned into manufactured goods that they would buy in return. Incomes and, as a result, living material standards will rise only through industrialization. The rapid industrialization would require rapid growth of the following conditions:

1. There should be adequate capital, either domestically generated or obtained as loan from advanced countries.
2. The agricultural production has to be increased to feed the growing population through introduction of more technology and scientific methods and help from the government.
3. The masses of rural unemployed and underemployed must be provided more production work.
4. The population increase must be controlled at all cost.
5. Illiteracy has to be eradicated, education and technical skill have to be disseminated on a wide scale.
6. Market for home produce has to be expanded and export of growing manufatured goods must find a place in the world market.

The developing countries have found out through their experience in the second half of the 20th century, that such objectives are not easy to achieve. They require coherent plans and programmes, will to change and compete, inexhaustible energy, hardwork and perseverance, proper and assertive leadership, full vigilance and drastic steps to check any trend towards corruption, a strong sense of national pride and prestige, smashing of vested interests and, above all, modernization of social attitudes and adopting new thinking and new ways of doing things. The problems of development, therefore are basically political problems.

But the new nations, in majority, have not yer proved their ability to overcome hunger, disease and illiteracy and to provide masses a tolerable level of material existence. But, it is hoped that time will force them as well as their leaders to face challenges and the international community will help them to succeed.

PATTERN OF SOCIAL CHANGES

Social change has a mix of tradition and modernity as well as of continuity and change. However, in various walks of life, far-reaching changes have taken place on account of the following factors.

Population Factor

Over population has resulted in the problems of unemployment, poverty, housing shortage, illiteracy, poor health and crowding of towns and cities as there is constant migration from rural to urban areas in search of job and attraction of better facilities.

Industrial Factor: Migration, Disintegration of Joint Family System etc

Industrialisation and agricultural revolution (Green revolution) along with transportation, communication, electrification and irrigation have changed the village scene to a large extent. The markets in the third world countries were flooded with foreign goods. It ruined traditional small-scale home industries. The workers in industrial towns live in dingy improvised accommodation huddled together. Some improved their social conditions by increasing their income and copying the ways of the city and sending their children to schools and taking all the advantages of living in a city. People became more mobile leaving their houses and settling at places of their jobs. Consequently, the joint family system started breaking up.

Cultural Factors

There has been a change in ideas, values, beliefs, rituals and religious practices. Caste has made inroads into politics, elections and government jobs. A caste group can elevate its position through education, better jobs and by emulating the ideas and practices of a superior caste group. In this process of change, the lower castes discard these traditional callings and practices which have kept them on lower positions for centuries. Conflicts between the upper and lower castes have occurred whenever the lower castes defied their traditional obligations towards the upper castes.

Legal Factors

The law has played an immense role in bringing about social changes in Indian society. The law has ensured radical changes in providing equal opportunity and status in many spheres to the deprived weaker and lower sections. Law has also helped to mitigate many social evils like untouchability. The constitution of India is the monumental base of the modern legal system of India. It incorporates the norm of equality, social justice, freedom and secularism. But law alone is not enough if not backed by public will, moral strength and sincere efforts of the authority. In 1950's legislations were formulated for bringing about land reforms but were implemented half-heartedly. Caste and untouchability are illegal, but are continuing in many states. Though there is provision for divorce against cruel husbands, but women are hardly helped to seek it and are left to harsher sufferings. An anti-dowry act exists with provision for severe punishment but it contiunes to grow openly without any restrictions.

Political Factors

Castes have been politicised. Elections are sometimes mobilised on the basis of castes, as number counts for success in elections. Many of the lowest castes, despite their social and educational backwardness, have risen through elections to occupy the ministerial seats. Their large numbers, unity and aggressive will led to the defeat of the upper castes which held them under subjugation for centuries. The people have awakened to the power and value of election and to react very strongly on crucial issues, as had been demonstrated in general elections. The Congress lost in 1967, came to power in 1971 and again lost in 1977, came to power in 1980 and again lost in 1989.

Economic Factors

The abolition of the traditional systems of land tenure, such as Zamindari and Jagirdari, a ceiling on land holdings, promotion of credit cooperative societies and other programmes of economic upliftment have brought in a new level of social transformation.

URBANIZATION

The term urbanization refers to the process by which a population becomes concentrated in cities or urban places.

India has the reputation of being a country of villages. In the beginning of the century, nine out of 10 persons lived in villages. The total urban population was nearly 26 million. By 1983, though the total population of India increased more than three times, the urban population rose eight times. In 1991, the urban population stood at 217 million out of the total population of 844 million. This counts for 25.7% of the total population. In 1901, the percentage was 10.84; in 1921, 11.18; in 1941, 13.86; in 1961, 17.97; in 1981, 23.34. Obviously, this upsurge in population growth in urban areas and cities has put great strain on the existing resources and services available in cities and people at times are devoid of basic amenities.

Causes:

The situation in villages is deteriorating. The growth of rural population and fragmentation of holdings have made small farmers surplus and they are pushed out to join the groups migrating to big cities in search of jobs. The exodus has quickened the establishment of big factories in the cities. Education centres, hospitals and civic facilities are added attractions. Besides, cities have their own growth of population.

Problems of Urbanisation:

The pressure of population on cities is increasing. The result can be seen in the surge of crowds, lack of houses, crowded public transport system, lack of civic facilities for the increased numbers, growth of slums, spread of dirty and unhygienic conditions, crimes and juvenile delinquency and shortage of essential things. Planning and restructuring of these cities has become necessary for originally the cities were not planned to accommodate so many people. Master plans of development have been drawn for Delhi, Calcutta, Bombay, Madras and all the metropolises. Another bad effect of urbanisation is pollution. Unplanned industries, transport and house-building have polluted the land, air and water in cities. Special efforts are made to save the environment from pollution through proper urban planning, civic amenities, reforestation, parks, open spaces and the like.

CHANGES IN OCCUPATIONAL STRUCTURE

The occupational structure of our population is very lop-sided. Two-thirds (about 66%) of our population still depends on primary occupation, mostly agricultural. In Japan, this primary sector has only 10%. Those in secondary occupation, that is, in the field of industry or manufacturing, constitute only 10% of the total working population. The rest 24%, that is, about one fourth of our population is in the tertiary or service sector. This occupational composition makes it clear that our total national income remains at a very low level because a very small proportion of our population is directly engaged in industry. But in the service sector their is a great change in the types and specializations of the personnel, as we have greatly qualified entrepreneurs, business magnets, scientists, technologists, computer specialists and doctors. The future has hopes of vast expansion in industries in India.

The growth of population in the last 50 years has had its impact on the occupational patterns. In developing countries, the number of dependents (non-working population) is in excess of working population. In the developed industrialised countries, persons entering the labour force get jobs but not in developing countries like India. In the developed countries, with the spread of education and vocational training, women are able to get employment in a variety of occupations in manufacturing industries and services, but in developing countries women are lagging behind. In India in recent years, with the spread of education and increasing awareness among women, the role of women is changing from that of a caretaker of the family to that of a bread winner.

SOCIAL DIVISION

Our Caste system provides the basis for social division. During the Vedic age, social grouping was the outcome of different specialised occupations. But the *Dharma Shastras* (law codes) of Manu and other law givers legalised the castes and saddled the *Shudras* with so many disabilities. By the time of Imperial Guptas, the castes and sub-castes were rigidly separated. The evil of untouchability has always been under constant attack by reformers throughout modern India. Mahatma Gandhi was the greatest champion of the victims of social evil. The Indian constitution and the subsequent legislative and administrative measures provide for the protection and promotion of the interests of the scheduled castes.

Article 46 of the Constitution provides : "The State shall promote with special care the educational and economic interests of the weaker sections of the people, and in particular, of scheduled castes and the scheduled tribes and shall protect them from social injustice and all forms of social exploitation. Article 17 abolished untouchability. There are reservations of 15% of vacancies for scheduled castes and 7.5% for scheduled tribes, besides relaxation of conditions of age and experience. Now, there is a real awakening among the scheduled castes. Many are educated, better off and elected members of Parliament, state assemblies and village panchayats. There is a quest for sharing the responsibility of the nation equally with other citizens. India is fully awakened to the belief that all men are born free but some are shackled and fettered; it is, therefore, the duty of every Indian to break those chains of their brothers and make them free to breathe in the fresh air of freedom.

ROLE AND POSITION OF WOMEN

Gender Differentiation and Different Roles

Mans's greater physical strength made him capable for hunting and warfare and woman's reproductive function confined her to the area of home. From this original division of labour in the early societies followed the social differences between men and women.

Child Bearing and Rearing Responsibility

One constant factor deciding the division of labour is that women are less mobile than men due to their incessant preoccupation with child bearing and rearing throughout the greater part of their youth.

World View

World over, even in advanced countries, women were, for a long time denied civil rights like property rights and political rights enjoyed by men. The first countries to grant women electoral equality with men were New Zealand (1893), Finland (1906), Norway (1913) and Denmark (1915). Equality of votes for women came in most leading countries during or after World War I: The Netherlands and the Soviet Union in 1917; Austria, Czechoslovakia, Poland and Sweden in 1918; Germany in 1919; the United States in 1920; and Great Britain in 1928; Spain in 1931 and France in 1944. Switzerland, one of the oldest democracies, did not give women the right to vote until 1971.

Early Indoctrination of Differences

In India and in all developing countries, the deep foundation of the inequality of the sexes is built through a socialisation process from the very beginning. Right from their earliest years, boys and girls are brought up to know that they are different from each other and they have different rights, privileges and roles. They are made to believe from their infancy that they too belong to two different worlds. The difference is strengthened in every way possible. In many families the birth of a son is preferred to that of a girl. A son is considered to be an asset due to many social reasons.

Status of Women after Marriage

She generally occupies a subordinate position, secluded in her home with fewer rights than her husband. Her status, role, rights and obligations are clearly defined in relation to her husband and husband's relatives within the framework of the community system. The husband is the decision maker and holds the authority being the bread winner. Even when the woman is the only bread winner, the husband enjoys rest but retains his authority in the house. In case she loses her husband, she leads a neglected, helpless and sometimes torturous and miserable life bound down with several social restrictions in a joint family. A widower can easily remarry but not a widow, except in very rare cases, though law allows it. A man with audacity may overstep moral norms, but a simple deviation of an innocent woman will never be excused. During the Vedic age women enjoyed general freedom and almost equal status. But during 200 BC - 1200 AD she lost many privileges and was bound with many restrictions. The Freedom Struggle, the teachings of Mahatma Gandhi, the phenomenal awakening of Indian womanhood, general education and the rise in the age of marriages — improved the status of women to a certain extent.

Scientific Studies of Male-Female Differences

With regard to the intellectual differences between the sexes, it has now been established that women are in no way inferior to men. The differences in their academic and professional achievements are due mainly to lack of adequate opportunities or to influence of traditional cultural patterns. There is also no psychological difference between the sexes.

The Constitution Provides Equal Rights and Status

In the Preamble of the Constitution, the people of India have resolved to secure to all its citizens equality of status and of opportunity. In the Directive Principles, there are articles which concern women directly. These include Art. 39(a) (right to an adequate means of livelihood for men and women equally); Art. 39 (b) (equal pay for equal work for both men and women).

Measures to Raise the Status of Women

Education:

The history of the movement for improving women's status all over the world shows emphasis on education as the most significant instrument for changing women's subjugated position in society.

Knowledge About their Own Rights:

Intensive effots should be made to make every woman know about her personal rights.

Small Family:

She should strictly follow the norm of a small family and at no cost should she allow the size of the family to grow.

Educating the Public:

Intensive efforts should be made to educate the public regarding the scientific findings about sex differences that intellectually and psychologically women are not inferior to men.

Employment:

Men now increasingly realise that under the economic crunch there is no way but to let women work outside the home to augment family income.

Women Themselves have to Exert:

Women also have to make their own efforts for raising their own social status, free from subjection and suppression.

Accelerating the Process of Social Change:

It is necessary to accelerate the process of change by deliberate and planned efforts. Responsibility for this acceleration has to be shared by the State, the Legislators, the Community, Mahila Mandals, and other organisations.

MINORITIES

Minority is a group of people who differ in race, religion, language, nationality, culture or in some other ways. The dominant group generally has greater political and economic power than the minority groups. In many cases, the dominant group discriminates against minority. An ethnic minority is identified chiefly by distinctive cultural practices, language, religion or way of life. Many minority groups develop when people leave their homeland and settle in another society. They move either voluntarily, as millions of non-English people from Europe settled in the US, or against their will, like millions of Black Africans were imported to cotton fields or plantations.

Relationship Between Groups

Sometimes, minority groups are given low social and economic positions due to their ethnic characteristics. Sometimes, the dominant group accepts the minority group into their society due to their having lived together long. Sometimes, the minority group achieves political and economic equality. The minority status sometimes brings a sense of isolation and common suffering which acts as a strong cultural glue to bind the members together. Some members of minority groups as happened in U.S.A., challenged segregation laws in court, refused to obey discriminatory laws, and in some cases, resorted to rioting and other forms of violence.

In South Africa, for many years, dominant Whites discriminated against Blacks. A government policy of *apartheid (separateness)* prohibited Blacks from participating in South African national government. All the laws of *apartheid* were abolished in 1991.

Many national minority groups live in the Commonwealth of Independent States after disintegration of the soviet union in 1991. Today ethnic tensions remain a threat to social stability in many of the countries. The racial, ethnic and religious minorities demand the right to be proudly different. Diversity is the new ideal. Everyone from Turks in Germany, Koreans and Filipinos in Japan or north Africans in France insist on preserving their cultural identity.

India

India is secular republic. There is religious freedom for all, without any interference of the state on religious matters. According to Article 29 (1) of the Constitution, any section of the citizens of India having a distinct language, script or culture of its own shall have the right to conserve the same. Thus, the Constitution gives protection to the linguistic and cultural minorities. Article 29 (2) states that no citizen shall be denied admission into any educational institute maintained by the state or receiving state aid only on grounds of religion, race, caste, language or any of them. Article 30 (1) states that all minorities based on religion or language shall have the right to establish and administer educational institutions of their choice. Art. 350A directs every state to provide adequate facitilies for instructions in the mother tongue at the primary stage. Art. 350B states that a special officer for linguistic minority shall be appointed by the President to investigate all matters related to the safeguards provided for linguistic minorities. Parliament enacted the National Commission for Minorities Act 1992 for monitoring the working of safeguards provided in the Constitution and in union and state laws.

POLITICAL GROWTH OF DEMOCRACY

Democracy began to develop in ancient Greece as early as 500 B.C. Athenian democracy was a direct democracy in which each male citizen served permanently in the Assembly. The Romans did not practise democracy as fully as Athenians though Roman political thinkers taught that political power came from the consent of the people. In the Middle Ages, the feudal court system protected the rights of the individual. The Renaissance and the Reformation brought cultural reawakening throughout Europe and strengthened the concept of democracy.

In 1215, the English nobles forced King John to approve the Magna Carta, a symbol of human liberty. English democracy developed slowly during the next 400 years. In 1642, Parliament, led by Oliver Cromwell, fought the followers of the king, beheaded Charles in 1649 and established commonwealth republic. In 1688, the English Revolution established the supremacy of Parliament, which in 1689 passed the Bill of Rights, assuring the people basic civil rights and liberties. In 1918, for the first time, all men were permitted to vote, but ten years had to pass before women of Britain could vote in 1928.

The writings of Montesquieu, Voltaire and Rousseau helped to bring about the French Revolution which promoted the ideas of liberty and equality. The American Revolution began more than 150 years later in 1775. The Declaration of Independence in 1776 established human rights as an idea and democratic objectives by which government must be guided. During 1800's, many countries followed the American and British examples of democracy. But some countries became dictatorships. In 1917, communist dictatorship halted Russia's progress towards democracy. In 1933, Hitler rose to power and brought a fascist dictatorship.

Most governments today claim to be democratic but many lack some essential freedoms. Many modern nations of Europe, the United States, Canada, Australia and New Zealand have a long tradition of democracy. India, Japan and some others have been democracies since the mid-1900's and several newly independent nations of Asia and Africa are trying to develop democratic institutions.

CHANGES IN THE ROLE AND FUNCTION OF STATE

Seventeenth Century Governments

Large states came into existence in Europe in the 17th century. The activites of the regimes were considerably limited. The government was supposed to protect the property and life of its citizens, keep law and order and defend the country from external dangers. The government was not considered duty bound to act in the fields of education, health and economy.

Eighteenth Century Governments

Industrial revolution took place in the 18th century. The *'laissez faire"* theory reigned supreme. It propagated the idea that governments and law should not interfere with business, finance or the working conditions of the wage earners. Adam Smith did not want the state to interfere in economic activities, excep' to raise resources through taxation. However, it is not true to say that the state really kept itself confined to the three functions. Britain, for example took several steps between 1760 and 1850 to facilitate the development f industrial capitalism.

Nineteenth Century

By the close of 19th century there were signs of change. The *laissez faire* greatly helped the development of industries but at the cost of workers whose conditions became miserable. People demanded that the State shall have to interfere in the economic life of the society and must remove the slums and the poverty. Karl Marx (1818-1883) was the most effective thinker at the close of the 19th century. He stressed upon an economic system which did not allow a man to exploit another man. In those days even liberal thinkers maintained that State should perform all those functions which tended to promote social welfare.

Twentieth Century - States as Instruments of Social Change

After the first World War, the activities of the state widened considerably. England, America, Canada and Australia championed the cause of peoples welfare. The idea of the Welfare State emerged. The concept of the Welfare State according to G.D.H. Cole is "Welfare state is a society in which a minimum standard of living and opportunity becomes the possession of every citizen." The modern nations have been trying to work as Welfare States as far as could be possible for them. In general they have been carrying out the following welfare functions in various degrees besides their normal routine :

1. Economic security. The advanced nations try to provide work for all the able bodied citizens and government subsidy during unemployment.
2. Free and compulsory education.
3. Provision for medical care.
4. Other developmental activities of several kinds.

India

The welfare activities of India have a socio-economic emphasis as portrayed in the peoples resolve in the Preamble of our Constitution to constitute India into a Sovereign, Socialist, Secular, Democratic, Republic and to secure for all the citizens Justice, Liberty, Equality and to promote among them all Fraternity assuring the dignity of the individual.

HUMAN RIGHTS

The idea that people have certain rights began thousand years ago. During the late 1600's, the idea was popularised by the writings of John Locke terming it as 'natural rights.' Locke's idea became part of three great documents : The English *Bill of Rights* (1689) after the Glorious Revolution in England which transferred the power to rule from the king to the parliament, the American *Declaration of Independence* (1776) which declared that 'all men are created equal' and the French *Declaration of the Rights of Men and Citizens* (1789) after the French Revolution which declared that 'Men are born and always continue, free and equal in respect of their rights.'

The international recognition of human rights came with the League of Nations. But whatever was achieved in the area of human rights was totally wiped out by the horrors of World War II. The ghastly happenings shook the conscience of the world. It led to the formation of the United Nations Organisation (UNO) whose Universal Declaration of Human Rights (1948) was adopted by the General Assembly on December 10, 1948, a date annually commemorated as Human Rights Day. This Declaration is very much respected and followed with a few exceptions here and there. The Human Rights were given firmer legal footing by two International covenants—one political the other economic—adopted in 1966.

India

Many of the rights enshrined in our Constitution have a close similarity with the Universal Declaration. For instance: Our Art. 15 (Prohibition of Discrimination), Art 29 (1) (Right to conserve language, script or culture) and Art. 45 (Provision of free and compulsory education) may be compared with the Declaration's articles 2, 18, 27, and 25 respectively. India is a staunch supporter of Human Rights. India continues to serve on the UN Commision of Human Rights. India stood by Namibia's freedom struggle, stood by Palestine against Israeli occupation and challenged South Africa's apartheid policy. Mahatma Gandhi was the first to raise his voice against racial discrimination in South Africa and challenged it through Satyagrahas.

EXERCISES

A. Very Short Answer Type
1. What is monopoly?
2. What is meant by 'globalization'?
3. Write briefly about 'urbanization'.
4. Name three human rights enshrined in our Constitution.
5. Define 'Minority.'
6. What is a 'Welfare State'?

B. Short Answer Type
1. What are the problems of development and how could these problems be solved?
2. Describe the various factors responsible for social changes in the 20th century.
3. Describe the growth of political democracy.
4. How does the society and economy interact? Give some examples to support your view.

C. Essay or Long Answer Type
1. Describe the main features of changes in the 20th century world economy with reference to capitalist and communist systems.
2. Write an essay on the role and position of women and measures that could help to raise their status.
3. Give a review of the course of industrialization after the First World War.
4. Describe the changes that occurred in the role and function of the state.

CHAPTER 32

Development in Science, Technology and Culture

REVOLUTIONARY DEVELOPMENT IN SCIENCE

Science and technology have revolutionised our world and our lives. Technology is a body of tools, machines, materials, techniques, processes and sources of power based on scientific inventions and principles and used to produce goods and services to satisfy our needs and make our lives and work easier. No sooner did science in the laboratory make important discoveries that technicians or technologists put them to work in everyday world.

Science in the Early 1900's

Revolutionary advances in physics marked the beginning. In 1901, Max Planck, a German physicist, advanced his quantum theory that radiant heat or energy is not given off continuously but travels irregularly in energy packages or 'quanta'. His discovery was extended to all the various forms of electromagnetic radiation. In 1905, another German physicist, Albert Einstein showed that light consisted of individual energy units which he called 'Photons'. The same year, Einstein published his special thoery of Relativity. Research into the structure of atom expanded rapidly. In 1911, the British physicist, Ernest Rutherford, gave an idea of atomic structure that each atom has a core, or nucleus which is positively charged. Scientists, after further experiments, went on to describe the atom as a kind of miniature solar system with the nucleus as the centre and negatively charged electrons whirling round it in different orbits. In 1938, two German scientists succeeded in splitting the atom of uranium. In the following year (1939) two Austrian physicists explained the process as fission and predicted it could release a large amount of energy.

Chemists used the knowledge of atoms to improve their ideas about chemical bondage. In biological science the importance of vitamins in diet was established. In 1928, Alexander Fleming discovered Penicillin, the first of many antibiotics. About 1910, an American biologist showed that genes are the units of heredity and genes are arranged in an exact order in the cell called *Chromosomes*.

Science in the Mid-1900's

The Italian born physicist, Enrico Fermi and his co-workers, on the basis of earlier discoveries, achieved the first controlled nuclear chain reaction in 1942 at the University of Chicago. This led to the use of nuclear energy in bombs due to the intensive research during World War II. Chemists expanded the periodic table through the creation of new radioactive elements. Medical science developed the polio vaccines and introduced organ and tissue transplants. Two biologists made a model of DNA, the substance that carries genetic information. The space age began in 1957.

Science also made important contribution to technology. Physicists invented the transistor which revolutionised the electronics industry. Portable transistors, radios, calculators and high-speed computers could be manufactured. The *laser* beams, the concentrated light beams, promised great advances in communication, electronics, medicine and weapons.

Science of Today

Scientific progress is faster today than ever before. From science and technology, research and development, wonderful ideas and products are flowing out and flooding the whole globe and making it a happier place to live in with a sense of relief, satisfaction and fulfilment. Technological processes and equipment are arriving with such sophistication and rapidity that it becomes difficult how to respond to the changing perspective. Coping with change has become the challenge of modern life.

Unimaginable advances in transport, comunication, space, science, biological sciences, medicine and surgery, information technology, new sources of energy and industrial production and in many other areas and all with such rapidity and within so small a time that this may be called a Scientific and Technological Revolution. This revolution is directly linked with great industrial advancement and massive output of products creating unprecedented heaps of wealth.

INDUSTRIAL PRODUCTION AND THE SECOND INDUSTRIAL REVOLUTION

This Scientific and Technological Revolution may also be called the Second Industrial Revolution after the first Industrial Revolution which continued steadily up to about 1860. The next hundred years saw many break-throughs in science and technology as described earlier. This Second Industrial Revolution is characterised by :

1. The rapid speed of scientific and technological advancement.
2. Close link among science, technology and industry.
3. Mass production and mass consumption.
4. Mechanical devices changing to electrical and then to electronic and automated devices in industry.
5. A search for alternative sources of energy.
6. The industrial plants becoming larger in size for large-scale production.
7. Faster movement of information, goods, services and people from one part of the world to the other.
8. All types of gadgets used in homes and in kitchens.
9. Speed is the key word of all activities.
10. Change in thinking, working, taste and life styles.

SPACE TRAVEL AND EXPLORATION

The space age began on October 4, 1957, when USSR launched Sputnik I, the first artificial satellite to circle the earth. The first manned space flight was made in 1961 when a Soviet cosmonaut Yuri A. Gagarin orbited the earth. US astronaut Neil A. Armstrong was the first man to step out of Apollo 11 on July 20, 1969 and put his left foot on a rocky lunar plain. A new era in space exploration dawned on April 12, 1981 when two US astronauts took off in the first space shuttle. A manned space lab took its first flight in a shuttle in 1983. In 1984, shuttle astronauts set a new record for working in space when they captured and repaired a faulty satellite.

Explorations of the planets have been carried out by unmanned probes. In 1976, American Viking soft landed on Mars. It did not reveal the existence of life in Mars. By 1986, all the known planets, apart from Neptune and Pluto, had been inspected at close range by spacecrafts. Now, both America and Russia are working towards permanently manned space stations.

Milestones of Space Travel

1957- Sputnik 1, world's first satellite launched from a Soviet rocket - Beginning of Space Age
1961- Soviet astronaut Yuri Gagarin, the first human to orbit the earth

1962- American astronaut John Glenn, the first American to orbit the earth
1963- Soviet astronaut Valentina Tereshkova, the first woman in space
1965- Soviet astronaut A.A. Leonov, the first person to walk in space for 10 minutes
1969- American astronauts Neil A. Armstrong and E.E. Aldrin, the first humans landed on moon
1975- First U.S.A. and USSR joint missions, docking of US Apollo with Soviet Souz
1981- First space shuttle flight of U.S.A.

Milestones of Space Probes

1970- First spacecraft to transmit data from Venus' surface after landing (USSR)
1971- Mars 3 carried capsule that made first soft landing on Mars (USSR)
1972- Pioneer 10 flew past Jupiter and sent back scientific data (U.S.A.)
1973- Pioneer-Saturn flew past closest to Jupiter and also flew past Saturn (U.S.A.)
1975- Venera 9, first unmanned spacecraft to photograph surface of Venus (USSR)
1977- Voyager 2 flew past Jupiter (July '79), Saturn (August '81), Uranus (January '86), Neptune (August '89); sent back photos (U.S.A.)
1978- Venera 12 sent back data on atmosphere of Venus and landed on it (USSR)
1990- Ulysses to examine polar regions of the sun in 1994 and 1995 (U.S.A.)

IMPACT OF DEVELOPMENTS IN BIOLOGICAL SCIENCES

In the 20th Century, in the biological sciences, important contributions were made in the understanding of genes, variations, structural details of cell, biology of virus and bacteria cell physiology. In 1970's and 1980's, scientists developed the ways to isolate individual genes and reintroduce into cells or into plants and animals. Such a technique called genetic engineering alters the genes (hereditary material) or combination of genes in an organism.

Genes are located within cells on tiny threadlike structures called chromosomes. Each chromosome contains a single molecule of a chemical substance called DNA (deoxyribonucleic acid). A molecule of DNA may contain thousands of genes. It stores within its chemical structure the information that determines the organism's hereditary property. To isolate a gene, scientists use a technique called gene splicing, in which a gene-sized fragment of DNA is isolated from the organism and joined to DNA molecule from another organism. This changes the hereditary character of an organism. Genetic engineering is used in medicine, industries and agriculture.

Impact

Diabetes can be cured by producing large quantities of insulin by splicing the insulin gene from human cells and then administering it to patients needing it. Sometimes a certain disease is cured by isolating genes from an individual and inserting them into a patient's cells outside the body and then returning these altered cells into the patients body.

In industry, genetic engineering is useful in controlling pollution. It can also improve the efficiency of food production. With the help of genetic engineering, dairy cows increase the amount of their milk and good varieties of crops can be grown and food production increased.

Despite its many benefits, genetic engineering has caused concern among the people. Some people oppose genetic engineering as it could manipulate the hereditary characteristics of human beings. Also there is a fear that, accidentally, some uncontrollable bacteria may be produced.

The Medical Revolution

Advances in many fields led to a revolution in the diagnosis and treatment of diseases during 1900's. Beginning with Fleming's discovery of penicillin in 1928, many kinds of antibiotics were developed to fight several diseases at once. Using genetic engineering, insulin was produced in 1982 and human growth hormone in 1985 to help children grow to normal height. In 1967, the first coronary bypass operation was performed. In the same year, Christiaan Barnard performed the first heart transplant.

Three developments to take inside image of the body have occurred since 1950's. In *Ultra Sonography*, used in 1958, the sound waves are bounced off the internal structures of the body. In *Computerized Tomography* (CT), developed in 1972, X-rays are passed through the body and the computers convert the data on the amount of X-rays absorbed by each tissue into a picture. The third development is the *Magnetic Resonance Imaging* (MRI), invented in 1973. It uses radio waves instead of X-rays to avoid several exposure to X-rays as in CT. Medical research has yet to find the underlying causes of the diseases of the heart and of cancer.

NEW SOURCES OF ENERGY

Energy is the fundamental need of modern society. In the 1970's some projections were made according to which there would be a devastating shortage of fossil fuels in the world in near future.

Nuclear Power

As such the future use of nuclear power was emphasised, but its expansion has not been as rapid as expected owing to the fears about safety and waste disposals, persistent problems and huge capital investment required. Despite all these problems and the consequences of the disaster at the Chernobyl nuclear power station in the Soviet Union in 1986, the supporters of nuclear power still claim that it is the cheapest, safest and most economic means available at present of generating electricity on a large scale. In searching for alternatives, Brazil is making fuel from sugarcane, China is converting waste into fuel, Ireland is harnessing geothermal heat to warm houses, while U.S.A. is trying to develop photovoltaic cells. Research into these forms of energy has often not been continuous.

Solar Engery

Photovoltaic cells directly convert sunlight into electricity. First used on an American Satellite in 1958, photovoltaic cells have become a major source for electric power in space. The cells require virtually no maintenance but they generate power at more than 10 times the cost of electricity from conventional sources. Another way of using solar energy is to absorb the sun's heat in something and pass it to heat water. Domestic solar heating will be cheaper than using the conventional electricity. But such devices need cloudless conditions to work effectively

Wind Power

The wind and waves are produced by the effect of sun's heat on the atmosphere; so the power from them may be regarded as solar energy received second-hand.

Power from Water

Wave power is a promising source of energy. Many designs have been tried to convert the up-and-down movement of the water into electric power.

The tides are another possible source of energy (lunar energy). In North France and in Britain tidal power plants are in use. The water is allowed to enter a river estuary as the tide rises and then it is passed through turbines as the tide falls.

Power from Plants

Rotting organic matter can produce inflammable gases (Biogas), notably methane. Rural areas have a great bulk of crop residue and animal wastes suitable for producing biogas. The foremost user of biogas is China. In 1970 experiments were made to extract ethanol (ethylalcohol) for mixing with petrol and then to use as motor fuel. Brazil is the leader in continuing the experiment with ethanol as a fuel.

Plant Oil Substituting Diesel Fuel

A number of plants produce oil that can be directly substituted for diesel oil. Brazil is using oil from a kind of palm as diesel fuel. USA is using sunflower seed oil and Phillipines is using coconut oil as a diesel fuel.

Urban Wastes

One tonne of urban refuse contains on an average the energy equivalent to 200 kg of coal. Munich, West Germany derives 10% of its electricity from garbage.

Geothermal Energy

Heat is stored inside the earth due to atomic reactions, molten rock that lie inside and gravitational collision. On an average, temperature increases around 25^0C with each kilometre of depth; but in many parts of the world there are 'hot spots' with temperature as high as 360^0C within two kilometres of the surface. In such areas, which include Italy, Ireland, New Zealand and U.S.A., heat can be tapped as an energy source. In Italy, continuous electrical power generation began from 1913 by using geothermal (earth's internal heat) steam.

TRANSPORTATION

The first electric trains and trams appeared in Europe and U.S.A. during 1880's. In the 1890's appeared diesel engines which replaced steam engines on many ships and on most trains. But the petrol engine brought about far-reaching changes in transportation. During 1890's, the first petrol-engined vehicles with car bodies were built. In 1903, two American bicycle makers, Orville and Wilbur Wright used a petrol engine to power a small aeroplane. The first commercial airlines began service in Europe in 1919. During the late 1930's, aeroplanes were built with jet engines.

Impact

The great advances in transportation during the 1900's have brought about enormous changes in people's lives. The commercial air travel has become almost a routine for those who can afford it. Goods that were once available in certain regions are now distributed worldwide. The development of motorcars has led to the growth of sprawling suburbs around big cities. Today, passenger transportation is an essential part of everyday life in industrial cities so that workers living far away can reach their factories in time. It has furthered the cause of education by transporting small children to and from school.

Problems of Modern Transportation

In U.S.A. and in many advanced countries more people are killed in car accidents every year than in all other transportation accidents combined. Most car accidents could be prevented if every driver obeyed all traffic laws and rules of safe driving. Second problem needing attention is the declining fuel reserves. At the current rate of use, the supply may be exhausted by the mid-2000's. To help reduce fuel consumption, car makers are producing smaller, lighter cars which travel farther per litre of petrol than larger models. Third problem relates to traffic congestion in urban areas and urban air pollution due to exhaust fumes. Strict pollution control standard, frequent checking of excess exhaust fumes in cars and manufacturing cars that give off clearer exhausts than earlier models may help to reduce pollution. A pool system for office goers and using public transport may reduce the congestion to some extent. Finally, the problem is of inadequate public transporation.

Transport-Milestones of Development (20th Century 2nd Half)

1. Rail Transport:
1960- First computer-controlled trains in Sweden.
1964- First monorail between Tokyo and Haneda.
1965- Japanese high speed electric train, maximum permitted speed 210 km/hr.
1979- Maglev passenger train with magnetic levitation (maglev) by which trains are suspended above the track, eliminating fiction.
1981- French Train Grande a Vitesse (TGV), World's fastest, 380 km/hr.

2. Road Transport:
1950- Power assisted steering.
1953- Plastic body.
1966- Electronic fuel.
1972- Tyre punctures automatically sealed by liquid compounds inside the tyre.
1977- Hydrogen gas as fuel.
1980- Four-wheel drive.

3. Water Transport:
1953- Air-cushion vehicle, compressed air raising the ship above water surface.
1954- First nuclear powered submarine.

4. Air Transport:
1954- Experimental flight of vertical take off.
1958- First commercial jetliner, Boeing 707.
1967- Computer guided systems.
1969- Anglo-French supersonic airliner Concorde.
1970- First wide-bodied 'Jumbo'.

REVOLUTION IN COMMUNICATION

The Beginning of the Electronic Age

Earlier, at the end of the 19th century, the only means of quick long-distance communication were the telegraph and telephone, both requiring wires to send messages. But the electronic age made possible the invention of radio, television and other wonders of modern communication for sendng signals through space. The idea of radio was born in 1895 when Marconi could send the first signals through space. In early 1900's, vaccum tube was invented to detect and amplify radio signals. After 1908, radio stations sprang up in many countries. Television working system was developed in 1926 and BBC transmitted the first TV broadcasts in

Development in Science, Technology and Culture

1936. In 1930's, recorders were developed to record sound on magnetic tape. Videotape recorders developed during the 1950's recorded pictures as well as sound on magnetic tape. Cassette videotape recorders developed during the 1970's.

Artificial earth satellites called *Communications Satellites* first relayed messages in 1960. The satellites could transmit radio, telephone and other communications. Before that time, TV signals could only be sent by cable. Satellites made it possible to relay TV signals across oceans. During the 1970's, many newspapers and books began to use computerized editing and typesetting systems instead of using typewriters. In the 1980's, several companies began marketing cellular mobile telephones. In the late 1980's, many businesses had begun to use a process called *facsmile,* or *fax* to speed communication.

Communication of the Future

Communication will involve many forms of light-wave energy and *laser* devices producing a narrow beam of intense light. Even today, *fibre optics* has made it possible to use light to send more messages faster than it could be done by electricity or radio waves.

INFORMATION TECHNOLOGY AND ITS IMPACT

Computer

It can store unbelievably large quantities of information. Stored informatioin is called *database*. A country's entire census might be contained in a single database. A computer can search a huge database quickly to find a specific piece of information. The information can also be changed quickly. The efficiency and speed with which computers store and retrieve information make them valuable in a wide range of professions. For example, Scientists can get results of experiments, librarians can get details of specific books or subjects, hospitals can get all information about a patient and the government can obtain information about election returns or census; all within seconds, once the respective data is stored in the computers. All kinds of businesses and banks store large quantities of information of all kinds about employees, customers, products, investments, products, current prices around the world or about account balances and credit cards. The automatic teller machine (ATM) of a bank connected with a computer terminal can inform about accounts and dispense cash when identification card and number are entered at anytime—day or night. The *word processing* is one of the most important uses of computers. A *word processing programme* helps to write articles, books and reports, to correct spelling errors, to rearrange the texts, to change the type and size of letters and to print on paper if a printer is attached.

Computers can produce pictures that look almost like photographs. Computers can handle *Computer-aided design* (CAD) to design aeroplanes, bridges, buildings, cars, electronic machinery and many other machines for the use of engineers and architects. In modern cars, enclosed computers control certain aspects of operations. Programmes are used in teaching called *computer - aided instruction* (CAI). Artificial intelligence systems called *expert systems* enable computers to 'think' about numerous possibilities — such as diseases that certain sysmptoms could indicate—and make a diagnosis or decision.

Computers can also be used to communicate information over long distances. A *computer network* consists of many computers in separate rooms, buildings, cities or countries, all connected together. Computer networks allow people to communicate by using *electronic mail* (in short E-mail). A piece of information or document typed into one computer is delivered to another computer in a few minutes. On the same principle, a computer having a question typed in it will receive back the reply through E-mail from any part of the country or world.

Cybernetics

It is the study of control and communication in machines and animals. Cybernetics or such a study helps to build machines that imitate human behaviour including decision making and analysis of data. The ideas of Cybernetics have made an impact in the fields of biochemistry, computer science and psychology.

Communication Satellite

It is launched by rockets or carried into space by space shuttles. Small booster engines guide the satellites into their orbits and keep them there. They are placed 35,900 km above the earth. When it circles the earth at exactly the same speed as the earths' rotation, it appears stationary. Broadcast from a satellite, orbiting at the same speed as that of the earth, covers about one-third of the earth. Thus, three or more satellites properly placed around the globe can transmit signals worldwide. The USA has more than 20 domestic satellites. Fifty countries including India now work satellite systems. Many of these satellites function as a network exchanging signals among themselves and helping those which do not have satellites. For example more than 140 countries use the services of the *Intelsat* system that reach more than 600 earth stations worldwide.

THE MASS MEDIA AND ITS IMPACT ON CULTURE

Everyone must need to know. Children know or learn from their parents at home and from their teachers and textbooks in schools. Adults must need to know what is happening in their country. It contributes to the success of living. The means of communication of information, news, ideas, comments, pictures and the like to all the people are the newspapers, the radio and the television. They are the mass media, means to reach the masses. These media of mass communication have a deep impact on the life and culture of the people. Whatever the people read, hear or see at the same time or the same day, they think over it, analyse and generally discuss among themselves, exhange their views and judge or think what is good and what is wrong about what is happening in their country or in the world. This helps them to think over the pros and cons about a subject, to feel what should be or should not be and to form judgement. This is the way the public opinion is formed. This exercise of thinking independently, analysing facts and judging for oneself contributes to the success of democracy. Radio and TV also provide entertainment and knowledge about many things besides news.

Newspapers

With the spread of literacy within the country, the demand for newspapers has grown. For educated people reading the newspaper is an essential morning routine. Even in villages the craze for news of the illiterate populace is satisfied by somebody reading the newspaper to them.

During the freedom struggle, the newspapers played a very important role in spreading national consciousness. Many freedom fighters started printing and distributing newspapers of their own for boosting the courage and spirit of their countrymen by reporting the truth about their conditions under the British rule and preparing and exhorting them to make the freedom struggle a success. Many were arrested and deported and their newspapers were banned.

Newspapers have certain advantages over the radio and TV as they cover more news and in much greater details than the other media. News stories cover the latest developments in such fields as government, politics, sports, science, business and the arts. The editorials offer critical comments on national problems, political events and the performance of the government. Sometimes, the government respecting the public opinion makes changes in its policy. Sometimes, the newspapers become the first to point out to the government about undersirable or corrupt practices being carried out under their nose in their own departments before any action is started.

Radio and TV

In India radio broadcasts first started in 1927. It was privately owned till the government took it over and in 1936 the radio broadcasts were operated by the All India Radio. The television service in India was started on an experimental basis in 1959 but it became a major mass medium from the early 1970's. Before the coming of the TV, the radio remained the most powerful medium for news, relay of matches particularly cricket, songs, dramas and other items of entertainment and cultural promotion. With the popularity of TV and wide coverage from relay centres, the craze for radio has decreased; but due to its small size and portability, children carry it to schools and adults to offices on occasion of cricket matches, budget speeches, election results, debates on no confidence motion and other crucial events. It remains quite handy on outings, long journeys or in gardens and kitchens for songs. The TV stations broadcast more entertainment programmes than any other kind. Entertainment programmes include games or quiz shows mostly on film songs, soap operas, serials, cartoons, fashion shows, cookery, children's shows, feature films and sports events. Educational programmes include documentaries about social issues, talks or discussions, Open University programmes, information on many subjects and live broadcasts of parliamentary sessions and special events. Television commercials appear between and during most of the programmes as advertisers provide substantial finance. Cable television is a television service that viewers pay for. Some cable systems carry more than 50 channels. Many cable channels are devoted to specific types of programming such as sports, songs, scientific discoveries and feature films. TV is informative, educative as well as entertaining and brings the whole family together; but parents do complain that children are devoting too much time to the TV and teachers complain that the students are paying very little attention to their studies.

Cinema

The first feature film in India was produced in 1912 and the first talkie (films with sound) in 1931. It gradually developed into a major art form. It continued to be the most popular form of entertainment until TV gradually cut into cinema audience. Many feature films helped in promoting sensitivity on social questions. To make the film earn maximum profit, the producers are pampering the inner subconscious or conscious urges of the audience by depicting more of violence and sex than of things that promote good taste according to social norms. But for those tired eyes which have seen only frustration and defeat in life, it is a beautiful feast.

COMMUNICATION IMPERIALISM AND NEW INFORMATION ORDER

The information technology has advanced so far that it has become possible for everyone to know what people of different countries are thinking, feeling, saying and doing, what new programmes and policies have been undertaken to achieve higher goals of welfare and progress, what problems are being created or solved and what is happening all over the world. It helps every country, particularly the developing one, to know the truth, correct wrong notions, learn good and useful things to adopt or follow and have a wholesome and encouraging impact on their social, economic and political progress. But the developing countries have a complaint that the developed countries exercise domination and control over the mass media. They disseminate such western cultural values that have a corrupting influence on their culture and they provide sometimes such information that is irrelevant, distorted or partially true. This domination may be termed 'Communication Imperialism.'

The developing countries demand that international exchange of information and ideas should be true and mutually beneficial. So the developing countries are trying to create a New International Order on the principle of free flow of good ideas through regional cooperation, Non-Aligned Movement, the UNO and UNESCO. In 1978, UNESCO adopted a Declaration concerning contribution of mass media to strengthen peace and international understanding and to promote Human Rights and counter Racialism, Apartheid and Incitement to War.

MEANS OF DESTRUCTION

The most destructive and spine-chilling weapons are nuclear-bombs and automatically guided missiles. The Second World War illustrated how two atom bombs could change the fate of nations. If the German nuclear scientists had also reached the stage of developing the nuclear weapons, the history of the world would have been different.

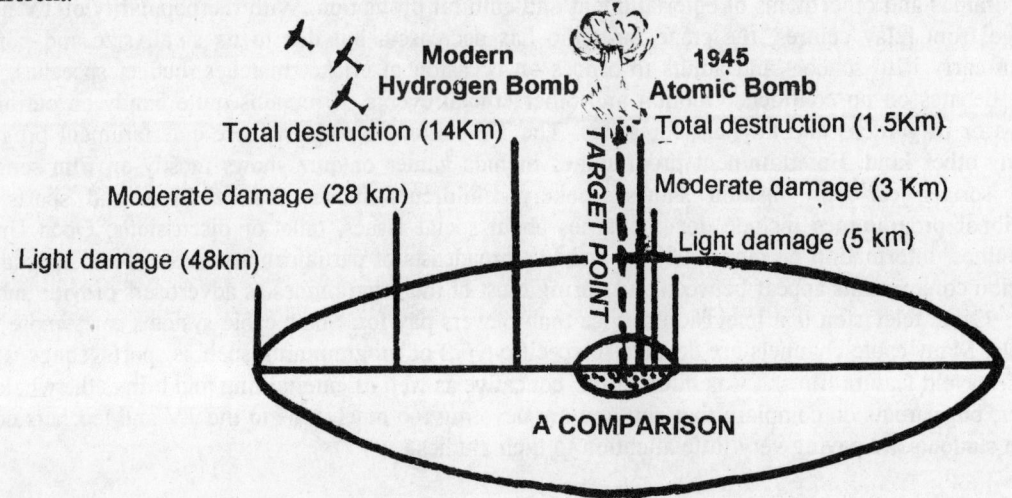

Modern Hydrogen Bomb
Total destruction (14 Km)
Moderate damage (28 km)
Light damage (48km)

1945 Atomic Bomb
Total destruction (1.5Km)
Moderate damage (3 Km)
Light damage (5 km)

TARGET POINT

A COMPARISON

Hydrogen Bomb, Atom Bomb : A Comparison

Nuclear Bombs

Each of the two bombs dropped on Hiroshima and Nagasaki had a destructive power of over 20 thousand tons of TNT. Both bombs killed a total of about 200 thousand people, and their radioactive effect remained deadly for many days. These two were the fission bombs releasing tremendous mass of destructive energy by fission or breaking the atoms of uranium-235, a fissionable element. The Hiroshima bomb weighing about 6 tons carried about 50 kg of uranium-235. Hydrogen bombs are thermonuclear bombs, or fission-fusion bombs based on the principle that the fission material in it produces enough heat to fuse or combine two atoms of hydrogen. The hydrogen bomb is several times more powerful and deadly than the fission bomb, that is, the atom bomb. Atleast five nations now possess hygrogen bombs : Russia, USA, Britain, France and China. The diagram above compares the areas of damage caused by the atom and hydrogen bombs.

Missiles or Rockets

The large thermonuclear bombs require large vehicles or some intercontinental delivery system, because even the largest fighter bombers cannot carry such big loads. The only successful missiles of this type used in the World War II were the V-1 and V-2 weapons developed and employed by the Germans. The V-1 weapons were pilotless, powered aircraft capable of flying at a speed of 350 miles per hour for distances of 150 miles and delivering a bomb of 2,200 pounds. They were first used against London on June 13, 1944. The V-2 was a true rocket with greater speed than V-1. The wingless V-2 rocket passed out of the atmospheric orbit and then came down to hit the target with a speed greater than that of sound. There was no effective defense about it. After the defeat of Germany, U.S.A. and Soviet Union entered Germany and captured the V-2 rockets along with the German scientists who developed them. On the basis of V-2, the two countries rapidly developed missiles or rockets to replace aircraft for delivery of huge nuclear bombs. The largest of the missile-delivery systems known as Intercontinental ballistic missiles (ICBMs) have sufficient range and accuracy to reach any spot on the globe. ICBMs in each of the two countries are kept safe in reinforced concrete below ground and no nuclear bomb can destroy it. Some of these have many warheads (explosive heads of weapons) and control systems for precise and accurate hitting of ten different enemy targets from a single rocket or carrier. U.S.A., Britain and Russia now have nuclear-powered submarines carrying the most modern newly developed missile, the Poseidon, which has the capacity of carrying ten automatically controlled warheads to hit accurately ten different targets one after the other. Possession of such nuclear bombs and rockets for carrying and delivering them has lessened the importance of other war weapons.

Other Post-World War II Missiles

Missiles below the standard of ICBM and the Poseidon class have been developed in bewildering numbers and types. There is a possibility that nuclear weapons can be used at a low or ground level instead of carrying them in rockets. Other technological advances have led to the introduction of miniaturization of nuclear weapons. It may be possible to develop portable nuclear weapons that could be fired by resting on the soldier's shoulders. Newer nuclear devices can be kept in projectiles as small and light as can be fired from a short gun for firing shells at a high angle.

Chemical Warfare

Gases and other toxic chemicals are extremely unpopular in world opinion and are difficult to use effectively. They were, therefore, never used in the two World Wars, though the two sides were ready with stockpiled chemical agents.

CONTEMPORARY WORLD LITERATURE

Literature, as an art, is the organisation of words to give pleasure; through them it elevates and transforms experience; through them it functions in society as a symbolic criticism of values.

Emergence of World Literature

The colonial subjects in Asia and Africa under their colonial rulers came in touch with foreign literature. They learnt how others in other countries thought and felt and expressed themselves in their literature. Europe became a world market of ideas. It influenced their own literary style. Thoughts and writings leapt out of their local boundaries and joined the main stream of world's thinking and writing. Thus emerged the concept of world literature.

The Spirit of Avant-garde

Avant-garde is a term used to describe people or their work in any field who break with tradition and conventional standards in their work. The term is used especially to describe movements in the arts. It is pronounced as *a*vong-ga*r*d : the first *a* is pronounced as *a* in *a*t and the second *a*, as *a* in *a*rt. The beginning of the 20th century witnessed a great flow of new inventions, new technologies, new ideas, new theories and new changes. 'Progress' became the key word and 'something new' became the ideal. The artists and writers realised that art and writing must constantly be revitalised.

This led to the movement called *art nouveau* (new art). It was also known as *avant-garde*. Paris became the centre of *avant-garde* where young artists and writers gathered to discover and practise the latest, the newest, in art and literature.

Trend of Realism in Literature

Literature usually reflects the contemporary scenario. The industrial advancement and material prosperity of Europe created untold misery for the factory workers and peasants. Wages were very low and the entire families worked 12 to 16 hours. Children, sometimes chained to machines worked like slaves. Women, hitched like horses to carts in coal mines, moved on their hands and knees to pull loads of coal to the surface. The writers looked around and wrote exactly what they saw. They portrayed the fears, hopes and trials of these miserable lot. The novel became the popular literary form. It would move the readers, sometimes to the point of tears.

In England, W.M. Thackeray and Charles Dickens, in France, Balzac and Zola, in Russia, Tolstoy and Dostoevski were shaking the roots of the upper class society through their realistic novels picturing the intolerable and revolting conditions of men and women.

English Literature

Literature between the Wars:

T.S. Eliot in poetry described the despair of the people in *The Waste Land* (1922). The popular novels were of D.H. Lawrence, Graham Greene and Alduous Huxley.

Literature after World War II:

George Orwell in his novel '1984' pictured a frightening society of the future and a number of younger writers of the 1950's, known as angry youngmen, expressed their discontent with English life and society. *The White Holel* (1981) of D.M. Thomas blended fiction with actual events; *Plenty* (1978), a drama of David Hare described about the decline in English society. Perhaps the three leading poets of today are Ted Hughes, Phillip Larkin and Donal Davie.

American Literature

After World War I, some writers used realism to expose social evils to achieve reforms. Sinclair Lewis, the first American Nobel Prize awardee, in his *Main Street* (1920) satirizes the hypocrisy of people. Nathanael West's *The Day of the Locust* (1939) and John Stenbeck's *The Grapes of Wrath* (1939) protests against the shallowness of the American Society. *The Sun also Rises* (1926) and *A Farewell to Arms* (1929), a tragic love story during World War I, established the fame of Ernest Hemingway. American poetry suffered a sad decline for 20 years after Walt Whitman who died in 1892. Robert Frost, with his famous poem *Stopping by Woods in a Snowy Evening* (1923) became a favourite poet. Among the most radical new poets were Ezra Pound and Amy Lowell.

After World War II, many American novels dealt with outcasts in poverty-stricken areas. Harper Lee's *To Kill a Mocking Bird* (1956) is a novel of racists. Black novelists and poets became a vigorous element in American Literature. The Women Liberation Movement inspired many books including Betty Friedans's *The Feminine Mystique* (1963).

Russian Literature

The Communist Revolution of 1917 began a new era in Russian literature. In the beginning the government tightened censorship, but after 1920 a certain amount of literary freedom was restored. During the World War II appeared the novel *Days and Nights* (1944) by Simonov dealing with individual suffering. With the publication of *One Day in the Life of Ivan Denisovich* (1962) by Alexander Solzhenitsyn describing labour camps under tyrannous regime of Stalin, strict censorship returned. Censorship prevented many works from being published. So, Boris Pasternak's novel *Doctor Zhivago* was published in Italy. He was awarded the 1958

Nobel Prize but was forced not to accept the award. Solzhenitsyn's *The Gulag Archipelago* (1973) was published in the west. He won the Nobel Prize in 1974. In mid-1980's, Soviet leader Mikhail Gorbachev introduced a policy of *glasnost* (openness) which began the publication of important works.

Latin American Literature

As Latin American countries were under the colonial rule of Spain and Portugal, their literature is in Spanish and Portuguese. In the first half of the 20th century an extraordinary band of women poets stood out with lyrical poetry. Among them Gabriela Mistral won the 1945 Nobel Prize. Mario de Andrade was a gifted poet of Brazilian literature. The literature of the third quarter of 20th century was characterised by dealing with the problems of man as the victim of evil forces of solitude and anguish. Borges' *Labyrinths* (1962) and Carpentier's *The Lost Steps* (1953) were models for the young writers of 1960's and 1970's.

Chinese Literature

The 1920's and 1930's influenced the mind of the people with Western European ideas and Russian Revolution. The most important Chinese writer of this period was Lu Hsun whose stories contributed to public awakening ridiculing the follies of the ultra-conservative society. This tradition of realism was carried by Mao Tun in his novel *Midnight* (1923). Mao Tse-tung, who came to power in 1949, ordered the communist writers to create works to be easily understood by peasants and workers, so countless literary works were produced to eulogise the proletariat and the Communist Party. During the Cultural Revolution (1966-76) all intellectuals were persecuted. After 1976, political themes dominated the writings. Some writers dared to criticize the government. Liu Binyan and Zhang Jie were among them. Now writers are prohibited to criticize the regime after the Chinese University Students demonstrated in Beijing's Tiananmen Square in 1989.

Japanese Literature

The Drifting Cloud (1889) by Shimei was the first modern Japanese novel. Natsume Soseki is considered one of the greatest novelists and his best known work is *Botchan* (1906), an autobiography of a teacher. During World War II, all serious writing ceased. The most powerful expression of revulsion at the War was *Fires on the Plain* (1951) by Ooka Shohei. *Black Rain* (1967) by Masuji is famous for depicting the dropping of the atomic bomb. The traditional forms of poems—tanka and haiku—were revitalised. Tanka (a short poem) consists of 5 lines of 5, 7, 5, 7, and 7 syllables and Haiku (still shorter poem) consists of 3 Lines of 5, 7, and 5 syllables. In Tanka, Akiko and Takuboku and in Haiku, Kyoshi made a name.

African Literature

African literature generally used as its medium, French, English or Portuguese.

French:

In French, the leading figure was Leopold Senghor who was elected the first president of the Republic of Senegal in 1960. In 1948, he brought out an anthology of poems on *Negritude. Negritude* is the awareness and development of African cultural values. The most important Negritude novelists are the Cameroonians.

English:

During 1950's and 1960's, there was an upsurge in poetry, novel and drama in Nigeria. Nigeria is ahead of other African countries in the development of literature. Wole Soyinka, a Nobel Prize awardee, published nine plays by 1970. Chinua Achebe is another internationally known writer of Nigeria. His important works include *Things Fall Apart* (1958) and *A Man of the People* (1970). Autobiographies are popular with South African writers. Hutchinson's *Road to Ghana* (1960) pictures the humiliations experienced by Negroes of South Africa.

Indian Literature

The distinguished Indian writers in each Indian language are legion. Here a glimpse of the Indian literary scene tries to capture tone, trend and texture of the Indian literature.

Tagore was the first Asian writer to win the Nobel Prize for Literature in 1913. He represented a happy combination of Indian tradition and European consciousness. He carried over the spirit of the 19th century with its deep religious convictions, its firm faith in the idealistic values of human life and its all pervading sense of beauty into the somewhat unsettled temper of the 20th century. Tagore gave a new type of lyric to Indian poetry, set the pace of modern short story and enriched every other genre of literature. The first important writer of novels at the close of 19th century was Bankim Chandra Chatterji. His *Anand Math* (1882) is well known, for it contains the song *Vandematram,* which became our National Anthem. Prem Chand, a novelist and short story writer in Urdu-Hindi carved a distinct place as he picturesquely narrated the peasants' misery and struggle. Tradition of the novel dealing with rural life was further strengthened by Bengali writers such as Bibhuti Bhushan Banerji and Tara Shankar Banerji. The tradition gained momentum in Oriya through Gopinath Mohanty's *Praja*, in Malyalam through Takuzhi Shivashankar Pillai's *Chemeen*, in Gujarati through Panna Lal Patel's *Makelajeet*, in Kannada through Shivram Karanth's *Chaman Doodi* and in Marathi through Bhal Chandra Nemade's *Kosla*. Sarat Chandra Chatterji is one of the most popular writers in Bengali. He awakened our social conscience from the slumber of centuries by his deeply sympathetic treatment of the unmerited suffering of the victims of social injustice. One of the writers dealing with moral conflict is U.K. Anantamurthy who wrote *Samskara* in Kannada.

After Independence, there was a Dalit Movement. One of the best known novels dealing with the life of depressed classes is Daya Pawar's *Achoot*. Among the famous short-story writers after Premchand are Yashpal and Jainendra in Hindi, Vaikom Mohammad Basheer in Malayalam, and Saadat Hasan Manto, Rajendra Singh Bedi and Krishna Chandra in Urdu.

In poetry special mention may be made of Mohammad Iqbal in Urdu, Jay Shankar Prasad and Nirala in Hindi, Keshavsut in Marathi and G. Shankar Kurup in Malayalam. Subramaniya Bharati was a distinguished Tamil nationalist poet. The new poetry progressed further after Independence. A new generation of talented poets came to the fore. Some of them are Kedarnath Singh (Hindi) Dilip Chitre and Arun Kolhatkar (Marathi) Ramakant Rath (Oriya) and Shakti Chattopadhya (Bengali).

In drama and theatre most significant contributions were made by Bengal, Maharashtra and Karnataka. The outstanding new dramatists include Vijay Tendulkar (Marathi), Girish Karnad (Kannada) and Badal Sarkar (Bengali).

THE ART OF THE 20TH CENTURY

Impressionism

The modernist movement in art may be said to have started with a group of French painters who rejected earlier art practices, styles, themes, and ideal prescriptions of what art should be. They were known as impressionists and included Claude Monet, Pierro Auguste Renoir and Edgar Degas. They did their major work between 1870 and 1910. They painted as they individually saw, perceived and felt and tried to express those personal feelings and impressions in their own individual styles. The imprint of their personality and individuality marked their paintings. Liberated from the traditional grip of the Medieval age, the people wanted to see something new and the artists wanted to paint something new. The modernists asserted their individuality and genius. These were the characteristics of the modern age.

Earlier, Edouard Manet, a French artist, had revolutionized painting in the mid-1800's. He emphasized the picture itself rather than its story-telling function. Like Manet, the impressionst rejected the idea that painting should tell a story. They based painting on the fact that nature changes continuously. Leaves move in the wind; light transforms the appearance of an object; reflections alter colour and form. Most of them took their easels out of their home to paint in the open air. They painted landscapes, seascapes, buildings and everyday scenes of city traffic.

Post Impressionism

It describes a group of artists that went beyond impressionism. The important members of the group included Paul Cezanne, Paul Gauguin and Vincent Van Gogh. Henri Rousseau, George Seurat and Henri de Toulouse-Lautrec. All were French except Van Gogh, who was Dutch. Unlike the impressionists, who emphasized changing light, Cezanne stressed form and mass. He found a new way of structuring his subject matter having a solid form and depth. Gauguin's pictures stressed flat colours, unshaded shapes and curved lines. He settled in the island of Tahiti in the South Seas where among the Polynesians he produced his most impressive pantings. Like Gauguin, Van Gogh wanted to express his inner feelings. He applied his oil colour directly from the tube without mixing them and used violent brush strokes. Rousseau painted dreamlike mysterious scenes like painting a sleeping figure besides a lion in a dreamlike landscape. Seurat created a painting style called pointillism. His paintings consist of tiny dots of pure colour.

Fauvism

In 1905, an exhibition of paintings in Paris included several paintings considered so radical with new experiments that they were isolated in a separate room and their painters wer dubbed "Les Fauves" (French for wild beasts). Fauvism, as this art came to be called, was characterized by brilliant colours. Henri Matisse led the movement. These artists tried to communicate a sense of comfort, joy and pleasure through rhythmic lines and bright colour.

Cubism

Cubism, grown up in France, began in 1907. The leading Cubists were Pablo Picasso of Spain and George Braque of France. They rejected story telling and avoided emphasizing light and perspective. They tried to reduce the figures in their basic geometrical shapes - triangles, cubes, rectangles and circles. Picasso became the most celebrated painter of this century. He died in 1973, leaving a rich legacy of his work including the famous painting "Guernica", the name of a town in Spain. The Nazis had bombed Guernica into heaps of rubble. 'Guernica' pictures terror, ruin and cruelty through Cubism as in the distorted angles of arms and legs, Expressionism as in the glances of part forms and Symbolism as in the shrieks of two open mouths of women, and the heads of a bull and a horse representing destruction and sacrifice. Some artists influenced by Cubism worked out a style of nonobjective painting. The period between the two world wars was one of artistic ferment in Europe. Within about a quarter century were born many art movements like Dadism, Futurism and Surrealism.

Futurism

The movement developed in Italy. The paintings of the artists glorified the mechanical energy of modern life and the speed and force of the industrial society.

Expressionism

It was an art movement developed in Germany. It distorted visual reality in order to express emotions freely. The work of some artists contained recognizable elements or figures greatly simplified or exaggerated. For example, a human figure was indicated by only a few daubs of colour. Russian-born Vasili Kandinski, who believed that colour and line alone could arouse emotions, created in 1910 the first non-objective painting—one that completely eliminated recognizable elements. Other expressionists retained recognizable forms.

Dadaism

It was perhaps the most shocking anti-art movement. Tristan Tzara, the founder of the movement in Switzerland, rejected and ridiculed all art theories. They portrayed everyday objects to mock the idea that art resembles junk, quite meaningless to life which itself is absurd.

Surrealism

Various movements rejected the trend towards non-objective art. Surrealism used realistic techniques to portray a world of subconscious fantasies. One group used the technique of placing two contradictory images, one recognizable and the other fantastic and dreamlike, having no logical connection with the other image. Another group called automatism, led by Max Ernst of Germany and Masson of France, believed that artists should free themselves from the conscious process of creation. They tried to let their brushes move freely, to let their subconscious minds create paintings.

Pop Art

It was a movement that began in U.S.A. during the late 1950's. The leading pop artists included Jasper Johns, Roy Lichtenstein and Andy Warhol. This movement developed as a reaction against abstract expressionism. The pop artists built their works around such common objects as road signs, soup can labels, newspaper photographs and drink bottles.

Op Art

It emerged as a European reaction to American Pop Art. Op art was derived from Optical art, an art which uses lines, stripes, circles, triangles, squares and other geometrical forms in such arrangements and with different colour combinations that the graphics provide an illusion of motion to the viewers. Rulers, compass and mechanical gadgets are used to create these figures or paintings to have an illusive effect on the retina.

Kinetic Art

The art pieces are arranged in such a way that they keep moving. The most famous among the Kinetic artists was the American sculptor, Alexander Calder. His metal sculptures hanging from the ceiling kept moving with the wind. He used oddly shaped light-weight metal pieces attached to thin wires hanging from the ceiling. Some artists like Frank Malina use electricity to move coloured lighted things rotating behind a painting on a transparent paper or screen fixed in a frame.

Modern Art in India

With the growth of western education, schools of art were established in Bombay, Calcutta and Madras. The syllabus and practice of painting, with new art materials like oil colour on canvas or water colour on paper, were modelled after the British Royal Academy pattern. These art schools, presided over by European artists, aimed at copying western paintings faithfully. In the last quarter of the 19th Century, Ravi Verma, connected with the princely family of Travancore, became famous in painting Indian mythological themes with all powers of European art. He learnt the art of painting from a traditional Indian artist as well as from an English painter, Theodore Jenson. He thoroughly mastered the Western technique of using oil colours, completely alien to Indian tradition. Though his paintings became very popular throughout the country, yet critics accused him of lacking individuality and failing to evoke Indian feeling out of the mythological subjects which had a European touch.

The controversy aroused by Ravi Varma's paintings helped to awaken a significant artistic movement in Bengal about the beginning of the 20th century. Several other circumstances like nationalist and patriotic awakening due to the freedom struggle and a search for the past rich artistic heritage could be responsible for this new movement in art. In 1896, E.B. Havell, an Englishman, joined as Principal of the Government School of Art in Calcutta. He was very much influenced by India's rich art heritage. At that time on one hand the discovery of the wall paintings in the caves of Ajanta and Ellora due to the efforts of Lord Curzon and on the other hand *Swadeshi* movement consequent to the partition of Bengal by Curzon made a great appeal to India's past glory.

The leader of the new movement of the Bengal school was Abanindranath Tagore, a talented colleague of Havell in the Art School. His style, a fusion of occidental and oriental models without any lack of Indian tradition, was the expression of his genius merged with the artistic feel, beauty and dream of the past. His draughtsmanship, mastery of lines and curves, dreamy and mystic treatment, lyrical quality, and a synthesis of many oriental trends including the Japanese, charaterised his work. Nandlal Bose was the most distinguished among the immediate disciples of Abanindranath. In his paintings, the bounding curves, sinuous plasticity, reflection of the Ajanta murals and emphasis on the dignity and majesty of form attract admiration.

The Kala Bhavan school of Art in Shantiniketan, under the fostering care of Rabindranath and guiding inspiration of Nandlal produced a number of talented artists, including Binode Bihari Mukherjee, Ramendranath Chakravarti and Ramkinker Baij. Ramkinker was a sculptor of immense drive. His sculptures had the warmth and suppleness of Indian forms.

Among the moderns, Jamini Ray is an outstanding personality. His style is distinctively his own, drawing his inspiration from the folk art at its best in the Kalighat paintings of the early 19th century. His figures, generally not crowded, use minimum of lines and bright colours on a plain base and point to the ever increasing possibilities of exploring the great potentialities of the Indian art. The new awakening in art may be realised from the surprising fact that the great poet Rabindranath Tagore emerged as a painter when he was nearing seventy. His paintings evolved out of calligraphic pictographs.

During the pre-Independence period, two great artists emerged who had thoroughly understood modern European art. One was Amrita Sher-Gil and the other, George Keyt. Amrita Sher-Gil was the daughter of a Sikh father and a Hungarian artist mother. She had a brief art education in Paris and was quite impressed by the rich colour of Basholi and South Indian Wall paintings. With a sensitive mind, moved by the sadness and sufferings of Punjabi peasants, she could depict genuine feelings with soft and superb artistry through compositions of bright colours and figures, mostly of women, having quaint physiognomy like that of Gauguin's women. Keyt was a Ceylonese of Dutch-Sinhalese descent and one of the founders of modern art in Sri Lanka. His style was his own version of Cubism with a flexible oriental stamp.

The modern painters of post-Independence are exploring new paths and trends and experimenting with new techniques and themes. The progressive Artists Group in Bombay founded in 1948 made F.N. Souza, K.H. Ara and S.A. Raza famous. Other popular artists of the time included H.A. Gade and M.F. Husain. In the next development, a group of young painters who made a mark include Shanti Dave, Jyoti Bhatt and G.R. Santosh from the School of Art of the Baroda University during the tenure of W.S. Bendre as the principal. The Madras School of Art under Debiprasad Roy Chowdhuri and K.C.S. Panikker became popular and influenced many artists. In this last quarter of the 20th Century, a large number of talented artists have distinguished themselves with the impress of their new original styles. Some of the names are Tyeb Mehta, K.G. Subramanyam, Satish Gujral, Ram Kumar, K.S. Kulkarni, Akbar Padamsee, Ganesh Pyne, A. Ramachandran, Jehangir Sabavala, Kishen Khanna and Arup Das. There have appeared fresh explorations and concepts as to the ways of handling colours and organizing forms with the growing revolt against what was considered the yesterday's 'best'.

EXERCISES

A. Very Short Answer Type

1. What is meant by the word 'science' and 'technology'?
2. Give the meaning of Communication Imperialism.
3. Explain the terms 'avant-garde' and 'art nouveau'.
4. What do you mean by 'realism' in literature?
5. Mention the names of outstanding Russian writers of the 20th Century.
6. What is meant by 'negritude'? Name any one writer connected with the 'negritude' movement.
7. Write a few lines on any two :- Cubism, Expressionism, Surrealism, the Bengal School.
8. Name two latest developments to take inside image of the body to diagonse diseases which cannot be known through simple X-ray plates.

B. Short Answer Type

1. What does the term 'Second Industrial Revolution' denote?
2. Briefly describe the progress made in Medical Science.
3. Write a note on Space travel and exploration.
4. What art forms are the distinct contribution of the 20th century?
5. Give a brief account of the works of two famous artists or writers — one from Europe and the other from India.

C. Essay or Long Answer Type

1. Describe the revolution brought in by communication and information technology.
2. What will happen if all the non-renewable sources of energy become scarce? What are the alternatives?
3. 'Nuclear Warfare would mean total devastation and destruction on earth'. Discuss the statement and state the chances of survival.
4. Describe the 20th century literature of any one country—England, America, India or Russia.
5. Describe the 20th century revolutionary developments of science and their impact on economy, polity and culture of different countries.

CHAPTER 33

The Future Outlook: Pointing Trends

One of the distinctive features of this period is that the world is becoming one. The technologies of transport and communication have shrunk the world. Distances have psychologically disappeared. Another new feature is the expanding tentacles of the multinational corporations all over the global business. Industrial wealth and capital have become great powers capable to dictate almost the entire globe. The world has come so close that a clap of cheer, or shock of disaster, or thunder of a threat, or cries of help will be heard or felt everywhere around the globe. An event at any one place will have spontaneous reaction or repercussion everywhere. Everything tends to have a global tremor, as if it is happening in your own house. Satellite technology and other media tools are cracking open national boundaries and cultures. The European single-markets seek to displace traditional national sentiments with super-nationalism. Today's economy requires more cross-national interdependence.

The world has come closer but not the human hearts. In some ways the world today seems full of divisions. No war has broken out directly between major world powers since World War II ended in 1945, but fighting has gone on in one part of the globe or another since then. In 1991, for example the U.S.A., Britain and other countries drove Iraq out of Kuwait, after Iraq had invaded and occupied Kuwait in 1990. Since the late 1980's, tensions between communist and non-communist nations have decreased and after the collapse of the Soviet Union in 1991, the fearsome uneasiness retreated, but the fear of a nuclear War hangs like the Sword of Damocles.

PROBLEMS AND ISSUES

Poverty — Gap between 'Haves' and 'Have Nots'

Poverty is a curse. Most of the vast population of the Third World are starving, hungry, unemployed, illiterate and helpless. They are fighting the battle of poverty without aid or arms. Their standard of living is even less than one tenth the standard of living of the people of industrially developed countries. Out of every thousand children born, 93 die before the end of a year, while in the developed countries all who are born live. Among the rural population 60% in Sub-Saharan Africa, 30% in Asia, and 60% in Latin America live in poverty. A billion in the world are illiterate. 500 million children do not go to school. Over 800 million people are non productively employed. One billion are "absolute poor" in the world. (See comparative list at the end of book.). The Third World continues to be mainly a producer and supplier of raw materials—agricultural and mineral, while the developed countries put these on the wheels of fortune of the giant industries, and amass heaps of wealth.

The economic gulf between the developed and developing countries—between 'haves' and 'have nots'—is growing year by year. About 25% (1/4th) of the world's people live in the industrial nations, but they consume about 75% (3/4th) of the world's resources annually; while 75% (3/4) of the world's people live in developing countries and they consume only 25% (1/4th) of the world's resources. According to the Secretary General of the Common Wealth Secretariat, "Three decades of international help devoted to development, may result by 1985 in a likely increase of $ 50 per capita in the annual incomes of the poorer groups compared with an increase of $ 3,900 per capita for those of the developed countries."

A globe, half basking in the sunlight of progress, prosperity and happiness and the other half drowned in darkness of despair and misery does not make mankind proud. The industrially advanced countries must bear a part of the guilt of conquering most of the countries of the Third World and keeping them helplessly bound under their colonial boots, crushing their economy, looting their wealth and sapping their creative spirit meant for adventure and success. Now, after gaining independence, the developing countries are trying to make the best use of their natural resources and to develop industries. It requires tremendous scientific development and capital, but the Third World has neither the scientific know-how nor the economic power.

This is the hour when the developed countries can extend an ungrudging help to provide solution to these massive problems of the people standing on the cross roads of destiny. This is the opportunity for the fortunate ones to seek atonement for the damage caused to these countries by blatant exploitation and misuse of power in the past. Otherwise, the gap will continue to grow—the rich will become richer, the poor poorer—and the dream of 'One World' of love and brotherhood will be lost for ever.

Population Explosion: Pressure on Economy

World Population Growth:

It took from the dawn of time to the year 1830 for the world to achieve a total population of one billion (1,000,000,000). By 1976, the population had become 4 billion. It is now projected to double to 8 billion by the year 2020. The projection figure is frightening. The number of people has increased at an annual rate of 1.7% since 1985. Yearly growth of population shows wide difference between the developed and developing countries. During the period 1990-95, it was estimated that the population increased by 0.2% in Europe, 1.1% in Australia, 1.2% in North America, 1.8% in Asia, 1.9% in South America and 3% in Africa.

India:

Now we turn to India. Here the population growth is alarming. In 1911, the growth was 0.55%, in 1951 it grew to 1.25% and in 1991 it was 2.12%. This is the case despite the efforts made to check the growth. If this trend continues, India's population will cross the hundred-crore mark by the turn of the century.

The cause is the slow decrease of average birth rate and the sharp fall of the average death rate due to growing medical and health services, control of epidemics and overall economic conditions of the Third World.

Effects:

The food production cannot keep pace with the population explosion. The world will soon have more people than it can support. It would mean starvation which will first hit the Third World; but the developed countries, depending on the agricultural produce of the Third World for food, will not remain untouched of the serious consequences. The overpopulation, besides creating food shortages, would create more dependents to feed and clothe. This will impede developmental work.

Population Control:

The only way is to reduce the birth rate and minimise the gap between the birth and death rates through family planning, knowledge of birth control devices, promotion of late marriages, compulsory education to widen the outlook of the people and policy of the government to take the message and services of family planning to the people. China's government has followed a strict policy of birth control limiting people to one child per family. No other child will be allowed to be born or born alive. India and many countries of the Third World may not be able to adopt a policy as strict as in communist China, but some deterrent measures along with public awakening have become a must to save the country from future hunger, poverty, misery and frustration. It has a global impact and, therefere, is a global concern.

Pollution : Polluting the Environment

Today, the threat of pollution has taken a very dangerous form. Air is polluted with smoke and gas rising from industrial units, power generating stations and automobiles due to the burning of coal and oil; water is poisoned with chemicals, industrial waste, sewage, garbage and oil thrown, dumped or spilled in oceans, lakes or rivers; soil is damaged with too much fertilizers and pesticides. Badly polluted air causes illness like respiratory diseases and even death, and kills animals and plants. Water pollution kills fish and other marine life like plants and animals, as oxygen from water is used up in the decaying process of wastes. Soil pollution damages the thin layer of fertile soil which is essential for growing food. Another kind of pollution, the most dangerous, is caused by radiation. Nuclear radiation comes from radioactive substances, including waste from nuclear weapon testing and from nuclear power plants.

Exposure to large amounts of radiation can cause cancer and harmful changes in the body. International agreements ban most testing of nuclear weapons in the atmosphere.

Three of the most serious consequences of air pollution are (1) The threat of planet warming (2) Acid precipitation and (3) Damaging the ozone layer.

(1) In 1984, the concentration of Carbon-di-oxide in the air rose to 343 parts for every million parts of air. The Co_2 acts as a greenhouse glass, allowing sun's radiation to pass through it but does not allow radiation to escape from the earth's surface. This raises the earth's temperature. In future, it may result in the rise of sea levels flooding low lying cities (2) Acid rain forms when moisture in the air combines with nitrogen oxide and sulphur dioxide released from motor vehicles, factories, etc and turns into sulphuric and nitric acids. These come down as rain and pollute lakes, harm crops and degrade forests (3) Earth's upper atmosphere contains a layer of the gas ozone which protects animals and plants by stopping sun's harmful ultraviolet rays. Certain pollutants damage this layer and create a hole in it. Scientists predict that further damage to the ozone layer will allow more of the sun's radiation to cause skin cancers and other health problems.

In recent years, environmental tragedies have made the people of the world to think seriously either to control the spread of pollution or to return to the pre-technological age. In 1984, a leak of poisonous gas from an American pesticide plant in Bhopal killed over 2,000 people. In 1986, an explosion and fire at a nuclear power plant at Chernobyl (USSR) released radioactive debris into the air killing 31 and injuring 200 seriously. In 1989, a tanker spilled 42 million litres of crude oil into the sea off Alaska, which six months later resulted in deaths of thousands of sea fish and seabirds. In 1991, the largest oil spill occurred during Persian Gulf War, when Kuwait released about 950 million litres of oil into the Gulf and Iraq set hundreds of oil-wells on fire severely polluting air over Kuwait.

All this is a world problem for the world to find a solution by concerted efforts of all; otherwise, we will be dragged towards a calamitous future. The wind and waves carry the pollutants across thousands of kilometers of land and occeans and cause damage and deaths in regions having no hand in creating the pollutants. So none will be spared.

Paucity of Resources in Future

Forest land is turning into deserts due to deforestation. Over 20% of the Earth's surface and homes of some 80 million people are under direct threat of desertification, according to UN estimate of 1977. In 1984-85, the famine that affected more than 20 African nations and 30 million people was primarily caused due to the disappearance of forests. Along with the disappearance of forests, the problem of conserving wild life, especially endangered species, comes to focus.

Minerals such as coal and oil are our main sources of energy at present. But since they are non-renewable resources, it is estimated that world's sources of oil may not last through the coming two centuries and the coal supplies may by exhausted before we reach 3000 A.D. World's consumption of coal, oil and other minerals is rapidly going up with the increasing population and rapid industrialisation.

It is interesting to know that the depletion of earth's resources is due to the high consumption level of these resources by the rich countries. It has been estimated that the consumption of energy in North America, having 6% of world's population, is about 33%, that is, on-third of world's total consumption of energy. Environmental degradation in any one part of the world threatens many species of migrating birds and animals of other parts. This is a global problem needing concerted efforts of all to conserve forests, animals and non-renewal resources and to develop and use new sources of energy.

Piles of Nuclear Weapons

We have already described the incomprehensible destructive power of the nuclear bombs that can totally destroy the whole world—every life, every building, every city. As a result of the mad race for creating more and more destructive weapons, there are over 50 thousand nuclear bombs in the world today with the destructive power equivalent to over 2½ million times of the bomb that destroyed Hiroshima.

Effects:

Imagine what would happen if, god forbid, a World War breaks out. A large nuclear weapon's explosion would produce these affects :

1. A one-mega ton explosion would form a fire blast wave and wind under great pressure. These will move 20 km within a minute destroying most buildings within 2 km and killing majority of the people within 5 km and some people within 10 km.

2. Thereafter, the thermal radiation of ultraviolet rays will cause skin burns and even deaths; the initial nuclear radiation will cause destruction of human cells and the residual nuclear radiation will result in mushroom-shaped cloud and radioactive fallout. Then nuclear winter sets in. It refers to worldwide environmental effects including reduced sunlight, less rain, lower temperature. It would stop the growth of all types of crops and cause death from starvation in the following year.

In a major nuclear war, all forms of life, which took millions of years to evolve, would cease to exist. There could be no defence against the nuclear attack. The accuracies of hitting the targets have developed so much that the bombs will miss neither the commanders nor the soldiers, neither the top leaders nor the paupers, neither palaces nor the arsenals. All know that if there will be a World War, it will be a nuclear war; and if there is a nuclear war on a large scale, nobody can hope to live. Yet, the possibility of a nuclear war is quite remote.

Deterrents:

The spine-chilling stock-pile of these weapons have acted as deterrents not allowing any World War after the Second World War, though hundreds of wars and armed conflicts took place in different parts of the world during this time. There came occasions when a World War looked a near thing, but it never broke out because everybody knew what a war would mean. Wisdom realises that man is born to live and not to kill; it inspires a positive impulse to create a world of harmony and peace and cautions against any self-destruction. Another thing is fear; it is the instinct of self preservation which keeps a safe distance knowing that a nuclear war is sure death. These act as deterrents and justify the piling of bombs and consider them as preservers of peace.

MAD:

On this basis that the nuclear arsenal is a deterrent, the doctrine of 'Mutually Assured Destruction' (abbreviated as MAD) has become current. "The doctrine holds that peace is best maintained by threatening to obliterate an entire enemy society in retaliation for a nuclear attack" (Time). The logic is, 'If we are killed, you will also not live; we sink or sail together'. When both sides have a large number of nuclear weapons it would lead to fear of a mutual holocaust.

Disarmament:

But how can one be certain that nuclear weapons could never come to use by any unfortunate accident or heat of madness of a dictator? Is there any guarantee that no finger will ever reach on the trigger of explosion? The only way, that the world can safely guarantee that there will be no nuclear war, is by total nuclear disarmament, by total elimination and destruction of the weapons. It does not stand to reason that the big powers who possess nuclear weapons justify their ownership on the basis of 'MAD' doctrine and exercise ban on others to achieve nuclear capacity. It should be total disarmament by one and all. The question of disarmament is closely connected with the question of development. It has been estimated that a mere five weeks of expenditure on armaments would be enough to provide sufficient drinking water to all, for there are millions of people in the Third World who have to walk over 6 km twice every day only to procure drinking water for their families and there are families who never had the fortune to sip clean water. Only a small part of the resources that are now spent on armaments would help end want and misery everywhere, provide two meals a day to 800 crores people who go hungry to their beds and accelerate the process of development in the world.

The Problem of Survival :

This brings the question of survival. Shall the nuclear weapons allow man to survive or not? Yes. Extinction is not the rule or law of nature, survival is. It has already been shown how the deadly weapons themselves will act as deterrents; for any aggression, if any, will be answered by retaliation with the result of Mutual Assured Destruction. But even accidents and madness have to be made out of bounds, so that nothing should be left on chance to trigger any nuclear explosion. And this is possible through understanding, thinking, cooperation and planning on a global basis, and through many other things that matter to life—the inner voice of conscience, the knowledge of right and wrong, the fear and common concern for all, the human bonds of love and kindness, the religion's eternal voice of compassion, father's and mother's hope for the future safety and happiness of their children, and the wonders of science and technology to devise ways to save the globe.

INTERDEPENDENCE AND INDIVISIBILITY OF THE WORLD

Every nation depends on other nations in some ways. The interdependence of the entire world and its people is called globalism. We have already indicated how the world is moving towards globalization. Nations trade with one another to earn money and to obtain manufactured goods or natural resources that they lack. Nations with similar interests and political beliefs come nearer and pledge to support one another in case of crisis or war. A sense of helplessness and the need for feeling secure bring the developing nations together. Certain policies, benefits, and objectives make nations to join hands like European Community, Non-aligned nations and SAARC. Developed countries provide developing nations with financial aid and technical know-how and assistance. Such aid strengthens ties and trade, sense of security and belonging.

Fear, faith, fortune, facilities and familiar problems form people into a fraternity to face a formidable future with fortitude. Interdependence is an inborn instinct. It is an imperative for survival. It brings people together and proves the indivisibility of the world. The deep desire of mankind, when free from blasts of circumstances and mutual jealousies, is to love, to join hands, to unite, to become One.

THE IMPERATIVE OF INTERNATIONATIONAL COOPERATION

The call for international efforts has become imperative to accelerate the process of development of the Third World and solve those problems that appear to darken the future perspective — the pathetic gap between the 'haves' and have nots,' the population explosion, the plantless planet of the future, the scarcity of coal and oil and the piling of nuclear weapons. And there is no problem that cannot be solved by a world based on international peace and cooperation. These problems are global, caused by global neglect. These have direct or indirect global impact, and will have to be solved by global cooperation.

A number of international organizations are already helping to promote cooperation among nations. The UN is the largest of such organizations. Nearly all independent countries are UN members. Many international organizations are designed to encourage progress or maintain peace among member nations. These include, at the regional level, European community, the European Free Trade Association, the Latin American Free Trade Association, Organization of African Unity, Non-Alignment Movement (NAM), South Asian Association for Regional Cooperation (SAARC) etc. On an International level, there are many agencies and organizations like International Development Association (IDA), International Finance Corporation (IFC), International Energy Agency (IEA), International Council of Scientific Unions (ICSU), World Bank, World Health Organization (WHO), International Air Transport Association (IATA), International Confederation of Free Trade Unions (ICFTU), International Court of Justice, etc.

The spirit of help and cooperation is inborn in mankind. We, as different nations, are islands in the ocean of isolation. The inner voice urges us all to join and make a continent of brotherhood, shedding our national egos. Love and help are sunshines of life. Let these international relations make us believe that we are all brothers born to make and share happiness.

A HISTORY OF HOPE

The history of mankind is a history of hope. History teaches that man need never despair; that he has infinite capabilities to tackle his problems. Throughout his long existence, he has been not only, a 'problem maker' but also a 'problem solver'. Problems will appear, they will be solved; others will take their place; they in turn will be solved. This is the way of human progress. His power to adapt himself to his environment or change the environment to suit his needs is one of his special traits. Guided by his enlightened conscience and the deep desire to make life meaningful, he will some day develop a society that provides peace, security and freedom for all and solves all problems through mutual love and cooperation. In times of terror man is prone to believe that the end of the world is at hand. But history reminds us that 'today is the tomorrow your worried about yesterday.' So we work with hope and live in hope — and history moves on.

EXERCISES

A. Very Short Answer Type

1. Name four major problems of the world connected with science and industrialization.
2. Explain global interdependence.
3. Give two reasons why some people think that the possibility of a World War is quite remote now.
4. Name three ways which have brought the world closer.
5. Explain briefly how industries pollute the environment.

B. Short Answer Type

1. 'The world is becoming One' — Explain the statement with examples.

The Future Outlook Pointing Trends

2. What is the state of poverty in the world'? How could the gap between the industrially developed and developing countries be plugged?
3. What methods can be adopted to ensure that rapid increase of population does not negate the economic gains of the Third World?
4. Explain what the term 'MAD' denotes and why disarmament is still the need of the hour.
5. What are the disadvantages of deforestation and how could these be checked?

C. Essay or Long Answer Type

1. How will the future look like? Discuss the various trends, factors and events that will shape up the future.
2. Describe in detail four major problems of the world and their solution.
3. Throw light on the important international and regional organizations and movements that could provide the necessary cooperation for a better, happy and secure world.

Marking Scheme and Sample Question Papers

FORM OF QUESTIONS AND MARKS (SUBJECT TO MINOR MODIFICATIONS)

S.No	Form of Question	Marks for Each Question	No. of Questions	Length of Each Question	Total Marks
1.	Very Short Answer	2	9	20 to 30 words	18
2.	Short Answer	5	8	up to 100 words	40
3.	Long Answer Essay Type	8	4	up to 250 words	32
4.	Map	5	2	—	10
	Total	—	23	—	100

SCHEME OF OPTIONS

1. There will be no overall option in the form 'Do any ten question or so.'
2. Internal choice may be given for all or some questions.

SAMPLE QUESTION PAPER I

Modern India   60 Marks

1. What were the two main effects of the Third Battle of Panipat? 2
2. State two reasons for the success of the English and the failure of the French in the struggle for power in India. 2
3. What steps did Maharaja Ranjit Singh take to prevent British encroachment on his kingdom? 2
4. What is meant by 'Wealth drain' from India? What was its effect on the economy of India? 5

   or

   What were the major controversies in respect of education in the early 19th centry? What part did Macaulay play in this controversy?

5. State the role played by Swami Dayanand in cultural and social awakening in India. 5

   or

   What were the causes of decay of Indian society in the 18th century?

6. Why did the British introduce the permanent settlement of Bengal? 2

   or

   State any two social reforms introduced by the British in the 19th century.

7. What was the system of subsidiary alliances? How did it help the British to consolidate their Position in India? 8

   or

   What were the chief causes of the Revolt of 1857? Did it have a popular character? Give reasons in support of your answer.

8. What were the changes in the British policy after 1857? What were the reasons of these changes? 5

or

What were the causes of frequent occurrence of famines in India in the 19th century? How was commercial policy of the British responsible for it?

9. Describe the methods followed by Gandhiji in the freedom struggle. State any two campaigns launched by him for the freedom struggle. 8

or

Explain the main differences between the moderates and the Extremists in their struggle for freedom.

10. Examine the factors responsible for the growth of national consciousness in India. 8

or

Explain the contribution of the revolutionaries, the Ghaddar party and the INA in the freedom struggle of India.

11. In what ways did the weakening of imperialism after the Second World War help in creating conditions for the independence of India? Support your answer with suitable examples. 8

or

Read the following passage carefully and answer the questions as given after it.

"I want to say from this platform that every blow that was hurled at us this afternoon was a nail in the coffin of the British empire. Our creed still stands and we are pledged to a struggle for peaceful non-violence. But if the Government officers continue to behave like this, I would not wonder if the youngmen were to go out of our hands and do whatever they choose with the object of gaining the freedom of their country. I do not know whether I shall be alive to see that day. But whether alive or dead, if that day is forced on them by the Government, my spirit from behind will bless them for their struggle".

(a) Name the leader who said these words. 1
(b) Why was the Simon Commission appointed? 2
(c) What was the reaction of the people of India on the appointment of the Simon Commission? 3
(d) What was the impact of the speech of the leader on the youth of the Punjab? 2

12. On an outline map of India, mark the extent of the British territories and also the princely states in India in 1947 before independence. 5

or

On an outline map of India locate ten places which became centres of the Revolt of 1857.

Contemporary World 40 Marks

13. "Contemporary history 'is open ended' Explain. 2
14. "Explain the meaning of Europe's hegemony and inter-imperialist rivalries. 5

or

What were the circumstances leading to the Russian Revolution in 1917? What were its effects on the national awakening in other countries.

15. Describe the causes that led to the First World War? What were its effects? 5

or

Explain the growth of fascism in Italy and nazism in Germany.

16. What was the aim of the League of Nations? Why was it set up? 2
17. What was the programme adopted at the Second International? 2
18. What is the meaning of the term 'Cold War'? What factors led to its end? 8

or

Trace the growth and development of the non-aligned Movement. What is the role that India has played in it?

19. Describe the main factors that led to the rapid collapse of imperialism after the Second World War? 5

or

Trace the circumstances that led to the unification of Germany.

20. What is meant by the Civil Rights Movement in the U.S.A.?   2

or

State the Darwin Theory of Evolution.

21. Illustrate by giving examples the main Features of the 19th century Indian Art.   2

or

Explain the term 'Expressionist painting'?

22. State the meaning of globalisation.   2

or

Differentiate between the socio-economic capitalist system from socio-economic socialism.

23. On the map of Africa identify any five countries which achieved independence in 1960.   5

or

On an outline map of the world show any three Allied countries and any two Axis countries during the Second World War.

SAMPLE QUESTION PAPER II

Modern India   60 Marks

1. Why did the Marathas fail to establish a strong empire in the 18th century?   2

or

In what way the lack of any definite law of succession among the Mughal rulers contributed to the fall of the Mughal dynasty?

2. State the consequences of the Battle of Plassey.   2

or

Explain the causes of the failure of Tipu Sultan to establish a strong empire.

3. Explain the system of 'Dual Government' in the context of the history of Bengal after the Battle of Buxar.

or

Describe the political developments which enabled the English and the French to interfere in the political affairs of India. What were the causes of the success of the British?   5

4. Explain the positive and negative effects of the British system of education in India.   8

or

Explain the main features of the Permanent Settlement of Bengal introduced by Lord Cornwallis. What was its effect on the Indian agrarian system?

5. "The Revolt of 1857 was the culmination of the unrest among the Indian people". Explain this statement. 8

or

How did the policy of the British led to the 'Wealth Drain' in India? What were its consequences?

6. Why was the partition of Bengal made? What were its consequences?   5

or

Describe the work done by the great reformers in the 19th century to raise the status of women.

7. Describe the changes introduced by the Act of 1858 in the administration of India by the British rulers. 5

or

What is meant by 'Safety Value' theory for the establishment of the Indian National Congress? Do you think this theory provided an adequate basis for national awakening? State in this regard the work done by any two nationalist leaders.

Marking Scheme and Sample Question Papers 367

8. State the contribution of Bal Gangadhar Tilak to the national movement. 2
9. Explain the meaning of 'separate electorates' introduced in India in 1909. 2
10. "Gandhiji resisted the might of the British empire with the might of the dumb millions of India." Explain this statement in the context of Gandhiji's contribution to the freedom struggle of India. 8

or

Explain the contribution of the revolutionaries, the Gadhar Movement and the I.N.A. in the struggle for freedom.

11. Read the following passage and answer the questions given below the passage.

"Long years ago we made a tryst with destiny, and now the time comes when we shall redeem our pledge, not wholly or in full measure but very substantially. At the stroke of the midnight hour, when the world sleeps, India will awake to life and freedom. A moment comes but rarely in history, when we step out from the old to the new, when an age ends, and when the soul of the nation suppressed, finds utterance. It is fitting that at this solemn moment we take the pledge of dedication to the service of India and her people and to the still larger cause of humanity".

   (a) Who is the author of this paragraph? 1
   (b) What was the tryst with destiny? 2
   (c) What were the three immediate problems before the nation after freedom? 3
   (d) How was the problem of political unity of the country solved? 2

or

What were the circumstances leading to the enactment of 1935 Act? State any three of its provisions. Why did the Congress Ministries formed after the elections held in accordance with the provisions of 1935 Act resign? 8

12. On an outline map of India, locate and show the following places: 5
   (1) Jallianwala Bagh, Amritsar (2) Lahore at River Ravi (3) Panipat (4) Champaran (5) Dandi (6) Bardoli (7) Sabarmati Ashram (8) Plassey (9) Buxar (10) Arcot.

or

On an outline map of India locate 10 places where annual sessions of the Indian National Congress were held.

Contemporary World   40 Marks

13. What were the consequences of the Sino-Japanese War of 1895? 2

or

State the effects of the Russo-Japanese War of 1904-05.

14. "Spread of colonialism and imperialism was the main cause of the First World War." Explain by citing examples. 5

or

What was the impact of the First World War on Russia? Why did it withdraw from the war?

15. Why was the League of Nations set up? Mention one main cause of its failure? 2
16. What was the impact of the Economic Depression on the industrial countries? 2

or

What steps did the U.S.A. take to meet the Economic Depression?

17. Why were military alliances formed among nations after the First World War? What was their impact on the political scenario of the world? 5

or

"The Treaty of Versailles contained the seeds of the Second World War." Explain this statement with suitable examples.

18. Describe the main stages of struggle for freedom in Vietnam and China. 5
19. What are the objectives of the U.N.? To what extent have these been achieved? 8
20. Mention any two problems of development. 2
21. Give the name of any one Indian artist and his contribution. 2
22. Write a note on space exploration. 2
23. Show on the map of Asia, five countries which became independent after the Second World War. 5

or

In the given outline map of Europe mark and name two new countries that emerged after the First World War and three countries that became independent after the First World War.

APPENDIX - 1

Changed Names of Cities, States and Countries

Old Name	New Name	Old Name	New Name
Abyssinia	Ethiopia	Leopoldville	Kinshasa
Angora	Ankara	Madagascar	Malagasy
Aurangabad	Sambhaji Nagar	Madras	Chennai
Banaras	Varanasi	Malaya	Malaysia
Baroda	Vadodara	Manchukuo	Manchuria
Batavia	Djakana	Mesopotamia	Iraq
Basutoland	Lesotho	New Hebrides	Vanuatu
Bechuanaiand	Botswana	Northern Rhodesia	Zambia
Bombay	Mumbai	Nyasaland	Malawi
British Guiana	Guyana	Ooty	Udhagamandalam
Burma	Myanmar	Panjim	Panaji
Calicut	Kozhikode	Peking	Beijing
Cape Canaveral	Cape Kennedy	Petrogard	Leningrad
Cawnpore	Kanpur	Persia	Iran
Central Provinces	Madhya Pradesh	Poona	Pune
Ceylon	Sri Lanka	Quilon	Kollam
Chnstina	Oslo	Rangoon	Yangon
Cochin	Kochi	Rhodesia	Zimbabwe
Congo	Zaire	Saigon	Ho Chi Minh City
Constantinople	Istanbul	Salisbury	Harare
Dacca	Dhaka	Sandwich Islands	Hawaiian Islands
Dahemey	Benin	Siam	Thailand
Dutch East Indies	Indonesia	Simla	Shimla
Dutch Guiana	Surinam	South West Africa	Namibia
East Timor	Loro Sae	Spanish Guinea	Equatorial Guinea
Egypt	United Arab Rep.	Stalingrad	Volgograd
Ethce Islands	Tuvalu	Tanganyika and Zanzibar	Tanzania
Gauhati	Guwahati	Tanjore	Thanjavur
Gold Coast	Ghana	Trichur	Thrissur
Holland	The Netherlands	Trivandrum	Thiruvananthapuram
Ivory Coast	Cote D'Ivoire	United Provinces	Uttar Pradesh
Jubbulpore	Jabalpur	Upper Volta	Bourkina Faso
Julundur	Jalandhar	Vizagapatam	Visakhapatnam

APPENDIX - II

United Nations Days and Years
A calendar for action

Decades

1985-1994	Transport and Communications Decade for Asia and the Pacific
1988-1997	World Decade for Cultural Development
1990-2000	International Decade for the Eradication of Colonialism
1990-2000	UN Decade of International Law
1990-2000	Third Disarmament Decade
1990-2000	Second Industrial Development Decade for Africa
1990-2000	International Decade for Natural Disaster Reduction
1991-2000	Second Transport and Communications Decade in Africa
1991-2000	Fourth United Nations Development Decade
1991-2000	UN Decade Against Drug Abuse
1995-2005	UN Decade for Human Rights Education

Years

1992	International Space Year
1993	International Year for the World's Indigenous Peoples
1994	International Year of the Family
	International Year of Sports and the Olympic Ideal
1995	50th Anniversary of the United Nations
	International Year for Tolerance
	Fourth World Conference on Women
	World Summit for Social Development
1996	International Year for the Eradication of Poverty
1999	International Year of the Elderly

Weeks and Days

8 March	International Women's Day
21 March	International Day for the Elimination of Racial Discrimination
22 March	World Day for Water
23 March	World Meteorological Day
7 April	World Health Day
3 May	World Press Freedom Day
15 May	International Day of Families
17 May	World Telecommunications Day
31 May	World No-Tobacco Day
4 June	International Day of Innocent Children Victims of Aggression
5 June	World Environment Day
26 June	International Day Against Drug Abuse and Illicit Trafficking
11 July	World Population Day
8 September	International Literacy Day

Appendix

3rd Tuesday in September	International Day of Peace
1 October	International Day for the Elderly
1st Monday in October	World Habitat Day Universal Children's Day
9 October	World Post Day
13 October	International Day for Natural Disaster Reduction
16 October	World Food Day
24 October	UN Day World Development Information Day
24-30 October	Week for Disarmament and Development
9-14 November	International Week of Science and Peace
20 November	Africa Industrialization Day
29 November	International Day of Solidarity with the Palestinian People
1 December	World AIDS Day
3 December	International Day of Disabled Persons
5 December	International Volunteer Day for Economic and Social Development
10 December	Human Rights Day

APPENDIX - III

Developmental Statistics (1996) of some countries compared

S.No.	Name of the Country	Population in Million	GNP Per capita US$	Life Expectancy	Adult literacy rate	Primary School Enrolment Ratio
1.	Afghanistan	20.1	280	45	32	31
2.	Bangladesh	120.4	220	57	38	78
3.	Bhutan	1.6	400	52	42	25
4.	Canada	29.5	19510	78	99	105
5.	China	1221.5	530	69	82	103
6.	Ethiopia	55.1	100	49	36	23
7.	France	58.1	23420	77	99	106
8.	Germany	81.6	25580	76	99	97
9.	India	935.7	320	62	52	102
10.	Japan	125.1	34630	80	99	102
11.	Kuwait	1.5	19440	75	89	65
12.	Israel	5.6	14530	77	92	104
13.	Iran	67.3	1033	69	69	105
14.	Iraq	20.4	1036	67	58	91
15.	Mexico	93.7	4180	71	90	112
16.	Myanmar	46.5	220	58	83	105
17.	Nepal	21.9	200	55	28	109
18.	Pakistan	140.5	430	63	38	44
19.	Russian Federation	147.0	2650	68	99	109
20.	Sri Lanka	18.4	640	73	90	106
21.	Sweden	8.8	23530	79	199	100
22.	Switzerland	7.2	37930	78	99	101
23.	United Kingdom	58.3	18340	77	99	112
24.	United States of America	263.3	25880	76	99	107